D1172845

DISCARDED

social psychology
and social relevance

– social psychology
and social relevance –

Alan C. Elms

UNIVERSITY OF CALIFORNIA, DAVIS

Little, Brown and Company   *Boston*

133625

3 0 1. 1
E + 8

COPYRIGHT © 1972, BY LITTLE, BROWN AND COMPANY (INC.)

ALL RIGHTS RESERVED. NO PART OF THIS BOOK MAY BE REPRODUCED IN ANY FORM OR BY ANY ELECTRONIC OR MECHANICAL MEANS INCLUDING INFORMATION STORAGE AND RETRIEVAL SYSTEMS WITHOUT PERMISSION IN WRITING FROM THE PUBLISHER, EXCEPT BY A REVIEWER WHO MAY QUOTE BRIEF PASSAGES IN A REVIEW.

LIBRARY OF CONGRESS CATALOG CARD NO. 73-186977

FIRST PRINTING

Published simultaneously in Canada by
Little, Brown and Company (Canada) Limited

PRINTED IN THE UNITED STATES OF AMERICA

credits

Portions of Chapter Three appeared in somewhat different form in *Psychology Today.* Copyright 1970 by CRM Publications, Inc.

Two figures have been redrawn from other sources: *Figure 6.1* from Dorwin Cartwright and Frank Harary, "Structural balance: A generalization of Heider's theory," *Psychological Review,* 63 (1956):285, Fig. 6. Copyright 1956 by the American Psychological Association, and reproduced by permission of the author and the publisher. *Figure 8.2* from Irving L. Janis, "Effects of fear arousal on attitude change," in Leonard Berkowitz (ed.), *Advances in Experimental Social Psychology,* vol. 3, 1967, p. 207, Fig. 7, by permission of the author and the publisher, Academic Press, Inc.

Poetry: *Page 1,* the three lines by Günter Grass are © 1968 by Harcourt Brace Jovanovich, Inc.; © 1967 by Hermann Luchterhand Verlag GmbH. From "Do Something" in *New Poems* by Günter Grass. Reprinted by permission of Harcourt Brace Jovanovich, Inc. *Page 310,* the four lines by Emily Dickinson are from "I Like a Look of Agony." Reprinted from *The Complete Poems of Emily Dickinson,* edited by Thomas H. Johnson, by permission of Little, Brown and Company.

for my mother and father,
Letona and Vernon Elms

acknowledgments

Many people helped in the preparation of this book. I am particularly grateful to those who read and commented upon substantial portions of the manuscript: C. Ray Carpenter, Irving L. Janis, Kalman Kaplan, Stanley Milgram, Robert M. Murphey, Robert Sommer, and Cheryl Brown Travis. My wife Roslyn was not only an enthusiastic reader but a source of continued sustenance, emotional and physical, throughout the book's development.

I also owe special thanks to those individuals described in Chapters Three and Four who participated in extensive interviews concerning their personal experiences and feelings. Descriptions of these research volunteers have been altered to protect their identities.

contents

*social psychology
and social relevance*

1
the immodest chapter

a particular relevance:
potential uses of social psychology

You see why the world of politics is in an indescribable
mess. Think of the opening of the baseball season. Think
of the ceremonial first pitch. Think what the baseball
season would be like if that sort of pitching went on right
through the summer. Then you have it — the present state
of affairs.

— Fred Hoyle, quoted in
The New York Times, February 4, 1968

There are laws of leverage.
But they hold it against the stone
that it will not budge.

— Günter Grass
"Do Something" *(New Poems)*

In this post-Berkeley era, college professors respond to any coincidence of views between themselves and their students with astonished delight. I teach social psychology and related subjects to several hundred undergraduates a year. Some of my students still judge any college course by what it will add to their market value at graduation. A smaller number seek mainly the egoistic gratifications of intellectual achievement. A few are so turned off toward anything other than the psychedelic vision and its real-world reminders that their occasional appearance in class itself partakes of mystery. The rest, perhaps a majority, are willing to interest themselves in social psychology on one condition: that I clearly show them its relevance.

1

Here is where astonishment and delight enter. During my own under-graduate years, I knew few students besides myself who looked for relevance in their courses. When I found it, I took it as a bonus, over and above the pleasures of the scholarly games to which my professors seemed devoted. But even as I continued to search, a large new audience of undergraduates were growing up to demand relevance as their due. Student demands have become an occupational hazard of college teaching, but this is one I can welcome.

Not all students who now use the word "relevance" have in mind what I had sought. Some look for personal relevance: immediate implications for their own personality development, solutions for their intimate psychological problems. They are more inclined to study personality theory or abnormal psychology; any personal relevance they find in social psychology is likely to be accidental. Others seek cultural relevance: references to drugs, rock music, astrology, and other aspects of the current youth culture. I sometimes fancy that I'm an amateur expert on Elvis Presley, whom the young still regard favorably as the grandfather of modern rock; but I suspect they can learn more about their culture by reading *Rolling Stone* than by insisting on class discussion of Dylan lyrics. Only when students want social relevance, meaningful contributions toward understanding and perhaps solving the serious problems they share with humanity in general, can social psychology put forth any special claims.

Social psychologists became concerned with social relevance long before I or my students arrived on the scene. For instance, the Society for the Psychological Study of Social Issues (SPSSI), whose announced aim is "to bring theory and practice into focus on human problems of the group, the community, and the nation as well as the increasingly important ones that have no national boundaries," was founded in 1936; it now has a membership of over 3,000 professionals in social psychology and closely related disciplines. As early as 1939, Robert Lynd's *Knowledge for What?* underlined the special obligation of all social scientists to conduct research that will help cope with the "acute problems" of American society. More recently, youthful insistence on such obligations, as well as the increasing seriousness of those now-chronic problems, have made psychologists even more conscious of the need for social relevance. SPSSI is thought by some psychologists to be too academic and too establishment-oriented to be very helpful, so another organization, Psychologists for Social Action, was founded in 1968 to pursue a more activist program. In 1969, the entire national convention of the American Psychological Association focused on the theme, "Psychology and the Problems of Society." More recent conventions have included dozens of panel discussions, informal interchanges, and formal speeches on similar themes. In 1971,

2

the *Journal of Applied Social Psychology* began publication, its primary concern announced as "applications of experimental behavioral science research to problems of society." Hardly a psychology textbook appears now without some obeisance to social concerns.

Unfortunately, all this increased attention to social relevance may generate as much disappointment as satisfaction. Those who look for relevance in the social sciences, concerned laymen as well as students, usually want immediate relevance — solutions today for today's problems. Social psychology has few such solutions to offer. Whatever importance the field may have lies less in its immediate than in its ultimate relevance, in its potential for yielding knowledge that will someday help provide lasting solutions to our chronically acute social problems.

I am confident that social psychology's ultimate social relevance will be great indeed. My estimation of the field's value may of course be biased; the private fantasies of any self-respecting man show the world crumbling without the services of his chosen career. He is often right: lacking garbage collectors, we would be as one with Nineveh and Tyre. But if we are to do better in the business of saving ourselves from ourselves, we particularly need a better understanding of people *as people.* That is what social psychology can give us: scientific knowledge of people not as sensory apparatuses, or as organisms, or as patients, or as parts of cultures or societies, but as people — living among other people, interacting with them, influencing them and being influenced in turn. Whenever people are the basic problem, social psychology should be able to lend a strong helping hand toward an eventual solution.

The field's strength has admittedly been slow to develop, but not for want of trying. People are hard to study, particularly in the context of their usual rather than their unusual behaviors. Further, social psychologists have not been at the job very long. The earliest social psychological experiment was done only seventy-five years ago (when a man named Triplett compared the performance of children winding fishing reels alone or in the presence of others); and Robert Zajonc (1966) estimates that over 90 per cent of all social psychological research has been carried out since 1945. Youth has ever been a convenient excuse for lack of wisdom; but I think we may reasonably expect much more from social psychology in the next twenty-five years than in the past twenty-five.

The argument I often hear from my students at this point is, "But we may not even be here in twenty-five years; ultimate relevance is really no relevance at all." Certainly we cannot wait to act until we have all the answers science can give us about human behavior; we shall often need to take stopgap measures and hope for the best. Man has been taking stopgap measures for several millennia, and at times they have worked. But somewhere we need to move beyond stopgaps. Wild guesses

3

are not relevant if they are wrong, and too many people — from the most staid government bureaucrats to the most radical political activists — are still operating mainly on the basis of wild guesses about human nature and human behavior. We can use a little ultimate relevance here and there, even if it is slow in coming.

Is the threat of force by one party really the best way to prevent further use of force by another party? Does man possess a natural impulse toward altruism, or must it be sown and nurtured with great care? What conditions promote social order without social stagnation? Social psychology is only beginning to deal with such questions meaningfully; but it does have some good, relatively objective methods for working toward eventual answers, and its progress toward such answers is worth the attention of those seriously concerned with the maintenance of our prevailing social systems. For those who wish to replace these systems, the questions may differ but good answers are no less useful. What sort of society must be created to prevent the generation of authoritarian personalities, of unquestioning obedience to orders, of unthinking social conformity? Why does age dampen ideological ardor, or does it? Is love the natural state of humanity, and if not, can it be made so? I grant that social psychologists have pursued such questions erratically if at all; that they have too seldom questioned the basic assumptions of the society that has nurtured them; that the science's solid fruits are so far only dimly visible in the foliage of trivia. But who except scientific researchers can answer questions like these with some degree of impartiality? And if they are not answered, how can society be properly changed? By the same brute force that has always been necessary to shift a society in the direction of the insurgents' own unsupported prejudices? Whether this nation finally turns to political radicalism for major social solutions or not, we are bound to repeat our historical errors endlessly if we continue to ignore the knowledge that empirical research can make available to us.

Social psychology often lacks both the brilliance and the entertainment value of our more prominent social critics. But it has a powerful approach of its own, in its willingness to subject even the most brilliant-sounding assumptions about man's social nature to empirical test. This general approach, rather than a single thinker's system, underlies the field's promise. Too many disciplines have been dominated by one man, so personally persuasive that his words have sounded like truth long after they should have been replaced with better ideas. Social psychology includes respected figures, but none command the scattered hundreds of researchers who try to explore human social behavior scientifically. Every researcher surely has his own ideological bent; but the prevailing orientation is eclectic and empirical. The questions the researchers attempt to answer

4

come from sources as diverse as society itself; the answers, when they come, should be useful to anyone concerned with making society work better.

This book does not review the research of all these hundreds of social psychologists. Instead it focuses upon one or two here, a dozen there, to show what social psychology can already tell us about certain important problems, and to suggest what the field may one day be able to tell us about others. As with social psychology in general, the book will seldom provide explicit answers about anything; but it should give frequent indication of the directions from which important answers will eventually come.

devils and definitions:
what social psychology is and isn't

We will not expect to be able again to exclaim, "What a piece of work is man; how infinite in capacity; in understanding how like a God," while believing that statement to be a full or complete account of the kind of creature man is. Our protest will go no further than to ask whether the rival account offered by mechanistic social psychologists is itself as full and complete as we have been assured that it is.

— Joseph Wood Krutch
The Measure of Man

During the 1964 presidential campaign, one of Barry Goldwater's favorite themes was the deterioration of American moral fiber through thirty years of liberal softheadedness. The liberal, according to one Goldwater speech, is soft on the criminal and on the schoolboy; the liberal is erasing punishment from our legal system and religion from our public life; the liberal "frowns on the policeman and fawns on the social psychologist."

From the careful conservatism of the late Joseph Wood Krutch to the reactionism of Goldwater and beyond, the image of social psychology as one of our modern devils has become peculiarly popular. Krutch and Goldwater are poles apart on what makes social psychology satanic — one sees it as a cold killer of the spirit, the other as a bleeding-heart seducer of personal and national responsibility — but they agree that it is dangerous. The very incompatibility of their views suggests that both men, as well as many others who have been as eager to accuse, have involved themselves in a case of mistaken identity or false arrest. Judging from his context, Goldwater seems to have had sociologists mainly in mind, or perhaps social scientists generally. He provided no indication that he

5

knew what a social psychologist's work involves. Most of Krutch's book (1954), up to the quoted protest, is a diatribe against B. F. Skinner, a strictly nonsocial experimental psychologist whose research has centered almost exclusively on learning processes in rats and pigeons — isolated rats and pigeons. Skinner (1948) has speculated about the design of an ideal society based on his pigeon research; but that does not make him a social psychologist. "Social psychology" just seems an easy phrase to use when you're dismayed with social change and suspicious that science is somehow involved.

What is social psychology? Unfortunately, social psychologists themselves have found it hard to define their field with any precision. Most social psychology textbooks begin with a definition so pretentious and comprehensive as to be meaningless — "the study of man in society," or whatever. Roger Brown (1965) has instead taken the interesting tack of defining social psychology as what's found on the contents page of a standard book of social psychological readings. But one book of readings, or one text, will differ so greatly from others that all you'll find through Brown's method is an author's or editor's personal biases. You might as well define social psychology as what's covered in *this* book. You'd still get a rather uncomprehensive picture, because I plan to cover only the parts of social psychology that I see as particularly interesting and significant — though I think my interests coincide with many of the field's most vital issues.

Even without definitive agreement, however, several common elements are usually included within social psychology's scope. Definitions typically refer both to the individual and to social behavior, not exclusively to either. The focus is usually upon psychological processes *within the individual* (such as his feelings, perceptions, attitudes), but processes that *influence or are influenced by other people*. This focus is, I think, the particular virtue of social psychology, because the further a social science gets from what is going on within the individual human being, the more tenuous any inferences about human behavior must be.

Experimental and physiological psychologists sometimes argue that the focus should be entirely on the individual organism, that social behavior need not be studied to be understood. They feel that in their controlled laboratory situations they are discovering, bit by bit, the pieces of psychological law which, when fully assembled, will explain all human behavior, social and otherwise. In this view, social psychologists simply add needless complications when they study social behavior directly. Some social psychologists have themselves accepted this position to such a degree that they limit their human subjects' social behavior in the laboratory to what might be expected of a rat, and refrain from using any of the subjects' exclusively human talents, such as the ability to talk

6

or to plan, for fear of contaminating the experiment or making it too complicated. Such research will not be discussed in this book. It may be of intellectual interest; but its contributions to social problem-solving are likely to be minimal.

✳ Solomon Asch (1952) has put the argument pungently:

> One cannot describe or deduce the facts of competition and cooperation, of leadership and submission if one does not observe them; language and law cannot be studied in a "generalized, human, normal, adult" mind purified of social experience. It would indeed be strange if we could produce a psychology of man without observing him in his natural medium — that of society.

Assembling bits and pieces about rats and "basic human behaviors" doesn't produce anything resembling complex social behavior, and it never will. Behavior is much affected by its context, social behavior particularly so. Even within the animal laboratory, such psychologists as D. O. Hebb (1949) have established that the bits and pieces don't necessarily add up to the behavior of a fairly complex lower animal, that unexpected relationships and unanticipated kinds of drives can be as important to behavior as the "basic" ones. If animal behavior cannot be so simply explained, then why human behavior?

Sociology is in certain ways almost the reverse of experimental psychology — paying hardly any attention to bits of individual behavior, and rather little to the individual human being as he influences or is influenced by social contact, but focusing instead on the abstract social systems that have developed through the formalization of these social contacts. Actually, one branch of sociology is itself known as social psychology; but, since the founding of both fields, the distinction between social individual and social system has largely divided this *sociological* social psychology from the *psychological* social psychology with which I'm concerned.

In 1908, the first two social psychology textbooks were published. One was by E. A. Ross, a sociologist; the other was by William McDougall, a psychologist. Both books are now thorough antiques. Ross spent a great deal of time endorsing ethnic stereotypes, and recommending that you build character in a boy by giving him a plot of land and a horse for which he can be responsible. McDougall argued, among other things, that war develops directly from the human instinct of pugnacity, whereas civilization rests mainly on the instinct of "acquisitiveness or cupidity." But though the specifics of their positions have long been discredited in both psychology and sociology, their general approaches foreshadowed the current distinctions between the two fields. Ross looked largely outside the individual, at society's influence in determining behavior.

7

McDougall looked within the individual, for sources of influence that themselves lead to the construction of society and motivate social behavior.

These differences are today embodied even in preferred methodologies. When a psychological social psychologist wants to study attitudes, he's likely to do so experimentally, or perhaps through intensive interviews with a few persons. The sociological social psychologist would be more likely to conduct a large-scale survey, or to study the way a particular attitudinal position spreads through a community. (I'm talking of likelihoods rather than absolute distinctions, which are hard to come by. Otto Klineberg [1965] put it this way: "What they [the other social sciences] *may* do, we social psychologists *must* do, namely, to keep the individual and the group simultaneously, constantly, and interdependently in mind.")

This contrast between the study of the individual and of the system largely holds true in distinguishing social psychology from the other social sciences as well — economics, political science, anthropology. Within each field, a few workers have adopted an essentially psychological orientation; and in this book, I'll discuss as social psychological research the work of people who focus upon the individual's social behavior, even if they are formally identified with another social science. But on the whole, these other disciplines concentrate on *structures,* with little direct interest in the individual human beings who compose or create the structures.

Other psychological disciplines do focus as fully upon the individual as social psychology does; and it's not always easy or useful to discriminate between them. Few psychologists try very hard to keep social psychology and personality research separate in their thinking, except when writing textbooks. The major professional journal in both fields, the *Journal of Personality and Social Psychology,* seems to operate on the assumption that there are no meaningful distinctions. Developmental psychology has preserved a somewhat separate identity mainly by stressing the study of children and adolescents (along with occasional old people), but its concerns are often shared by social psychology. Clinical psychology deals mostly with the mentally ill, whose capacity for social interaction is somehow impaired; but enough such people are wandering around without clinical attention, disrupting society or being further disrupted by it, to make their behavior sometimes part of the social psychologist's concern too.

No field exists within the social and behavioral sciences from which socially relevant information may not come. But many of our problems center upon those points where enduring aspects of man's individual nature lead him to behave well or badly in society. Such points constitute social psychology's principal domain.

enlarging the small print:
the author's intent

The progress of science is at the present time no longer hindered by the purely accidental fact that man attains to about seventy years, which was the case far too long. In former times people wished to master the entire extent of knowledge within this period, and all the methods of knowledge were valued according to this general desire. Small single questions and individual experiments were looked upon as unworthy of notice. . . . To solve everything at a single stroke, with one word — this was the secret desire.

— Friedrich Nietzsche
The Dawn

Social psychology has begun to involve itself with a number of the most urgent problems facing mankind. Most of these problems have disturbed the sleep and the working hours of philosophers and politicians for centuries. The field has seldom unearthed its own issues, either through dramatic new methodologies or by the discovery of behaviors in some ultraviolet zone of human existence. The problems are large, they have long been with us, and social psychology has taken them on because no one else has dealt with them successfully.

Yet few laymen know much about social psychology's successes or failures in tackling these large issues. Modern social psychologists have seldom been empire builders. Their books have usually been college texts or technical treatises, rather than extended arguments in terms understandable to the nonprofessional. The field has advanced largely on the basis of professional journal articles, reporting small-scale individual experiments. Much of this journal material has been published literally in small print, because journal space is at a premium. It has all been published figuratively in small print, because professional journals are never encountered outside the college library stacks or the psychologist's office.

Even if someone gave the American Psychological Association a grant to publish everything in twelve-point type, and placed the *Journal of Personality and Social Psychology* on the corner newsstand, there would be little public rush for understanding. The necessary use of technical terminology to communicate with other researchers as concisely and accurately as possible; the consistent employment of complex statistical analyses; and the quite appropriate practice of tying discussion closely to actual empirical data, rather than to the possible ultimate implications for mankind of a research area's further development, make most professional articles poor reading for the nonspecialist. Indeed, one careful

9

study (Garvey and Griffith, 1963) indicated that even among psychologists, hardly more than two hundred people are likely to read any one professional journal article upon its original publication, often many fewer than that. Some articles don't deserve many readers; but even the significant ones find a small audience.

The following chapters present several selected areas of social psychology in nontechnical terms, in hopes that they may gain a wider audience among concerned laymen, whether in or out of college. A selective approach is necessary because social psychology has long since become too large an area for comprehensive coverage in a single book, even at an introductory level. Only those areas that seemed to me to possess substantial current or potential social relevance are included. Research areas in which I have had some personal involvement are emphasized, not only because I find them more interesting but also because I suspect that the nonprofessional reader will find my descriptions of these areas more stimulating than second-hand discussions. Though other areas are also covered, they are mainly those in which I still hope someday to do useful work. Because of this personal involvement, I hold strong opinions about the value or wrongheadedness of particular lines of research in each area; and I have not hesitated to express these opinions, though I label them for what they are. Social psychology is still by no means a set of settled issues, and it would be both unfair and uninteresting to ignore the controversies that still enliven professional discussions beneath the passionless prose of journal articles.

In several ways, therefore, this is a distinctly personal book, rather than an impartial survey of social psychology. But "personal" does not mean that I ignore evidence with which I disagree, nor that I have shirked in my efforts to locate information which might confirm or contradict my speculations. Once I take up a topic, I will try as best I can to make sense of all the important evidence I can find, as well as occasional evidence that might appear trivial seen out of context. It won't always be possible to make sense of the data. One recurrent finding in social psychology is that human behavior is more complex, and therefore less likely to deliver the same empirical results twice, than anyone previously had reason to suspect. Perhaps the worst failing of scientific popularizers is to come up with definite conclusions when no grounds for definiteness exist. Sometimes I'll make guesses to supply the "sense," but when they're guesses I'll make that clear. Otherwise, I'll try to hew closely to the available empirical data.

The organization of the next nine chapters is somewhat arbitrary. Chapter Two examines the possibility that data on nonhuman primate social behavior may be relevant to human concerns. These data come largely from field studies rather than from experiments; the data in Chapter Three, on political extremists, are also mainly nonexperimental.

10

The remainder of the book is based almost entirely on experimental studies, reflecting the emphasis in social psychology as a whole. The early chapters are concerned mainly with social behaviors engaged in by individuals and small groups; later chapters move to a grander scale, as cities, nations, and ultimately the whole world become involved. The final chapter returns briefly to the individual in interaction with a few others: to the social psychologist himself, as he copes with his experimental subjects and tries to develop strategies for making his research both more immediately relevant and of greater ultimate value. His task will not be easy, as the remainder of this book attests; but it is at least as worthwhile a task as it is difficult.

2
social primatology

dumbbull monkeys:
the howlers of barro colorado

*These Creatures keep together 20 or 30 in a Company,
and ramble over the Woods; leaping from Tree to Tree
. . . chattering and making a terrible Noise; and a great
many grim Faces, and shewing antick Gestures.*

— Captain William Dampier
Voyages and Descriptions (1700)

One night when he was twenty-five, my father went out into the hills
of north central Arkansas with a giant dumbbull. A dumbbull may be
made from an ordinary tin can, but he had stretched a dried groundhog
skin over one end of an empty nail keg. A rosined string, with a knot at
one end to hold it in place, was threaded through the center of the skin
and out the open end of the keg. Sliding his fingers tightly along the
string, he could make the dumbbull roar like a wildcat or a bull elephant;
in clear weather, the noise would carry for a mile.

That first night, my father moved out along a ridge several miles from
town, pulling a scream from the dumbbull every few minutes. Horses
and mules began to snort all over the countryside. A family living at
the foot of the ridge ran half a mile to a neighbor's house, afraid the
monster was breaking into the stable to eat their cow. The next night
my father traveled in another direction. A farmer tried to sic his coon-
hounds on the monster, but at one fearsome roar from the dumbbull,
the dogs turned tail and ran under the house, while the farmer ran
inside and locked the doors. After that, people began to talk about

12

getting up a posse to hunt the crittur down, and word came from other counties about seeing strange beasts. When people got so scared they wouldn't go out at night to help sick neighbors, my father admitted that he and his dumbbull were the "monster." He stayed out of public view for a while, but most people took the hoax good-naturedly. They were happy it had been only a dumbbull.

The first time I heard a howler monkey clan roaring at the dawn on Barro Colorado Island, I remembered my father's dumbbull. The howler's full-throated vocalization is almost mythological in quality, the kind of echoing cry you'd expect from a banshee or a maddened minotaur. It makes the Panamanian rain forest sound like a real jungle. The howl has been recorded on small tape recorders, but it demands the sound system of a modern hard-rock group. If you've never heard a nail-keg dumbbull, try to imagine the noise of a pack of increasingly agitated beagles cornering a great barrel-chested lion, with an electronically synthesized Tarzan yodeling to the rescue.

The howler monkey is not barrel-chested but barrel-throated. An adult male weighs twenty pounds or less, but he has a built-in resonator, an unusual development of the hyoid bones of the throat. As the early evolutionist A. R. Wallace wrote (1878), "It is remarkable that this one group of monkeys should possess an organ not found in any other monkey or even in any other mammal, apparently for no other purpose than to be able to make a louder noise than the rest." It's more remarkable still, in that howlers have no obvious reason to make a louder noise than the rest; they usually live in an environment very like a Monkey Eden. This is particularly true of the howlers who have been most studied — the black howlers of Barro Colorado Island, in the Panama Canal Zone.

Barro Colorado has too much rain for paradise; when the rain comes, the howlers hunch their backs and bend their heads and roar at it, as if it were an animate evil. But when the rain stops, little else troubles them. Leaf and fruit eaters, they find it hard to starve in the midst of Panama's heavy vegetation. The high trees in which they live protect them from most potential enemies. The cecropia leaves that are a favorite food would serve better than fig leaves, were the howlers blessed with modesty; they are not. The adult male's scrotum shows a clear unmistakable white against his dark fur and the green foliage; the female, although she lacks the vivid sex skin of certain old-world primates, manages to make her needs known unashamedly by waggling her tongue in and out of her mouth, in a sort of remote French kiss. The usual ratio of adults (more than two females to each male), plus their unjealous promiscuity, guarantees a male for every female when she's in heat, and a female for every male when the urge moves him from lethargy.

13

As the waters of the Panama Canal rose around the mountain ridge that is now Barro Colorado Island, trapping the monkeys there for good, most large predators escaped, and almost none remain. The most serious threat to howlers, the human hunter, is banned from the island, which is a United States Government preserve. Botfly larvae swell the necks of infants, and older monkeys often wear botfly scars; yellow fever dropped hundreds of howlers during the late 1940's. But since then, the Barro Colorado howler population has exploded dramatically.

Curiosity, a serious threat to any paradise, seems minimal in howlers. They are imperturbable in the presence of sloths and anteaters, and usually look merely anxious, not inquisitive, about human observers. The effectance motivation described by Robert W. White (1963), which moves humans and perhaps certain apes to explore and manipulate their environment, hardly if ever moves the howler; when he is not eating, he mostly rests or sleeps. To his physical near-Eden, he has added (via evolution) an important element — not better means of need satisfaction, but the restriction of his own wants. Eden is not Eden when Adam desires what he cannot have.

But it is not their nearness to the angels which has made the howlers so attractive to social psychologists. Rather, it is the fact that they are social beings. Other creatures are social as well, from ants to springboks. But howlers and other primates seem to humans particularly social because — as they loll in the trees, snack frequently, grumble at each other occasionally, discipline the children when necessary — they look so human.

NATURALISTIC OBSERVATION OF HOWLERS

The howlers of Barro Colorado Island are especially attractive to the scientist because their natural social life is protected from the destruction that hunters have delivered to their mainland brothers. Since being made wards of the Smithsonian Institution earlier in this century, the Barro Colorado howlers have been protected, like the United States residents of the Canal Zone, from the whims of fortune and the attacks of the Panamanians. Barro Colorado Island is, in this way, a somewhat unnatural environment, but perhaps less so than the howlers' mainland habitat, with its recent (in the evolutionary time scale) addition of guns and traps and poisons.

This protected status does not exactly make Barro Colorado a paradise for human researchers. A boat dock, laboratory buildings, and sleeping quarters have been built on one little cove, and several trails have been cleared; but the rest of the 4,000 acres remains undisturbed tropical rain forest. In some areas the trees overhead are so thickly interlaced that little underbrush can grow, and travel away from the trails is easy. In other areas, the brush or the meaty serrated spears of *pita* are so

14

thick that passage even with a machete is nearly impossible. The howlers have the better idea of how to travel: at treetop level, they miss the occasional coral snake or boa constrictor, the scorpion or tarantula, and all the little bright-colored spike-backed spiders who hang their webs between the tree trunks.

Fortunately, the howlers move through the trees with much caution, so it's usually easy for an earthbound human observer, even as he dodges spiderwebs, to keep up with them. Their slowness, their noisiness, and their togetherness make it possible to study howler behavior under natural conditions more extensively than can be done with many other primates.

The first important effort to unite the study of comparative psychology with social psychology began on Barro Colorado Island in 1931. Animals have been much used for research by psychologists, but usually only in studying elementary responses — reflexes, simple learning, basic drive-reduction behavior. Until 1931, information about the social behavior of man's closest surviving relatives, the nonhuman primates, was either grossly unreliable, overly simplistic, or descriptive only of abnormal behavior in zoos. Some writers leapt to make generalizations about man and society from these atrociously inadequate data. Others showed their wisdom by keeping quiet.

Late that year a young psychologist, C. Ray Carpenter, went to Barro Colorado to study howlers. Rather than looking around haphazardly for what seemed momentarily interesting or supportive of a current theory (as in previous "scientific" primate observation), Carpenter spent hours a day observing a single group at a time. For several months he systematically surveyed the island's entire howler population. An indication of his thoroughness is that although an expert naturalist had estimated the Barro Colorado howler population as seventy animals in 1929, Carpenter was able to identify about four hundred howlers by the end of his survey in 1932, and added a hundred more during further study in 1933. Carpenter not only counted the animals (a harder task than it might seem, when you're classifying adult males and females, plus six categories of juveniles), but also made careful behavioral observations, largely through field glasses, and studied the howler's environment (Carpenter, 1934). He returned again briefly in 1935, then turned to studying other primate species. The howlers were left to themselves until the 1950's, when they were twice studied by other scientists; then Carpenter returned once more in the summer of 1959, with several associates and student assistants, including myself (Carpenter, 1965). Others have come since.

So the howler's social life has been studied scientifically over a longer period than any other primate's except man's. Observations of its behavior have raised complex questions that remain unsettled among behavioral scientists, but we can start with a few simple ones. How social is the howler? How does it show its socialness? And is the howler distinctive among primates for anything besides, possibly, its noisiness?

SOCIAL COHESIVENESS

First, howlers are definitely clannish. An adult male can occasionally be seen sitting alone on a high branch in the midst of the jungle, distant from any group, but such isolated animals are rare. Even their isolation may be temporary; one may sometimes be seen tagging after a group, as if he were trying to get in, or to get back in. Most howlers are born, live, and die within the same small group — provincials who are much disturbed by encounters with strangers or loners of their species. (At the most recent full census, Barro Colorado Island held forty-four groups, totaling over 800 howlers; but only a half dozen or so isolated animals were counted.)

The groups are stable, and seldom split. Splitting must sometimes occur, since the number of groups on the island has increased along with overall population growth; but the fission process has never been observed by humans. Groups do not appear to exchange members, unless those rare isolated males are in the slow process of transfer. In general, group composition changes only through birth and death. Varying group sizes have been observed, from 2 to 45; the mean is roughly 18 monkeys. Carpenter has calculated the average composition of a Barro Colorado howler group to be 3 adult males, 8 adult females, 3 dependent infants, and 4 juveniles. These proportions have remained roughly the same for over thirty years, longer than the probable life span of any howler, though mean group sizes have varied as a result of disease and environmental change (Chivers, 1969).

Talking about a howler "group" (or "clan," as Carpenter prefers) may imply both more and less than it should. A howler group isn't just a random collection of animals in a particular area. The group is usually relatively compact, every animal within a few yards of every other animal in the same tree or adjacent trees. When the group is moving, individuals may sometimes be strung out over several dozen yards; but like a progressing amoeba or a ball of silly putty, the group will contract again into a relatively tight knot of monkeys at feeding or rest time. If most of the group begins to move before one monkey finishes eating, the one will usually follow the group rather than eat.

On the other hand, the group is not overly organized. More often than not, adult males lead and bring up the end of a group progression through the jungle; males consistently initiate moves from one tree to another. But the adult males within a group seem to share this "responsi-

16

bility"; firm patterns of dominance and submission, or exclusive sexual relationships, or indeed *any* stable relationships (except between a mother and her immature offspring) have been hard to find. Further, the group is not in constant close social interaction, even of an unorganized nature. This is partly because howlers don't engage in very frequent action of any kind. Carpenter kindly refers to "low energy expenditures," but the plain fact is that in relation to many other species, howlers are lazy. In general they toil not, neither do they spin — except sometimes slowly, while hanging from their prehensile tails. The action in which they do engage is mostly self-oriented: they feed themselves, they scratch themselves, they sun themselves and take long naps, with little overt reference to other members of the group.

A group's typical day would involve a dawn awakening; a few howls at the sunrise, or at the howls of distant clans; scattered feeding and then perhaps a slow move to a new food tree; concentrated but leisurely feeding during mid-morning; a long midday siesta, during which the adults sleep or rest and the juveniles may play sporadically; possibly another move, probably another two or three hours of feeding in mid-afternoon, unless heavy rain interferes; then a period of settling down in a lodge tree for the night, with virtually complete inactivity from 7 or 8 P.M. until the next morning. The most remarkable aspect of all this behavior, for an animal who is distinctly a social being, is how little of it can really be called social. Much of it might best be described as *conjunctive:* the behavior of maintaining a fairly close proximity with other animals of the group, without directly orienting one's behavior toward them or acting in response to their behavior. Conjunctive behavior could be compared to a quiet human evening at home — the husband reading his newspaper in his easy chair, the wife sewing or knitting on the couch, and both getting a certain satisfaction from being in the same room, though they may hardly speak to each other for several hours. The howlers, however, don't even go off to bed with each other at evening's end. They may sleep in the same tree, but they sleep on separate branches.

POSITIVE SOCIAL ACTS

Occasionally, during all this passive and rather disinterested existence, the individual howler monkey may initiate or be on the receiving end of a specific social act. If it's in any way positive, the action will most likely come from his mother. If it's somehow negative, it's likely to come from another howler group, rather than from within his own clan.

I use the vague word "positive" because so little howler behavior can be called truly "cooperative." The howler mother gives her infant sufficient attention to keep him alive, and that's about it. She lets him hang

17

to the hair on her belly or back; as he grows older and begins to explore the tree-world, she'll retrieve him; when she's ready to move on, she lets him know with a small noise, so he can climb on. If he gets left behind, she'll come back for him; when he gets too big to ride on her, but not big enough to make every tree crossing safely, she'll even stretch herself between two branches to make a monkey bridge for him. The small infant is nursed, of course; but when he's old enough to eat solid food, his mother will only rarely (and perhaps even then only accidentally) pull a branch or leaf down to let him feed.

Mothers also protect their infants from the attentions of other females, who engage in what has informally been called "nursemaid" or "auntie" behavior. The newborn howler is of great interest to the group's infant-less females. They may simply remain close to the mother for hours at a time, watching; they may nose or touch the infant; they may try to pick it up. Usually all this attention is quite unhelpful and even annoying to the mother, who never asked for a nursemaid in the first place. But once I did see an infantless female place her arm around and her body partly over a mother and infant as a summer rain grew harder.

Juvenile howlers occasionally play with each other, in a simple-minded way — chases, wrestling, tail-pulling. Adults are involved in play only when they're the butt of a juvenile joke. Most nonhuman primates, particularly those of the Old World, socialize extensively by grooming each other (picking bits of dirt, dead skin, and so on out of each other's fur with mouth and fingers). Howlers seldom groom; even mothers groom their infants very little. Since the grooming serves in other primates to remove parasites, its absence in howlers may explain why the howlers have such a hard time with botfly larvae infestations. Extensive social interaction may be unnecessary for howlers in most regards; but in this case, it appears they could use more than they have. (Melvin K. Neville [personal communication] observed an apparently higher incidence of grooming among red howlers in Venezuela, and also observed no botfly problem. There may, however, simply be fewer botflies in the Venezuelan habitat.)

AGGRESSIVE ACTS

Hostile (or, more technically, *agonistic*) behavior occurs within the clan even less often than positive behavior — sporadically at most. The low incidence of hostility may result partly from the way it's handled at first appearance, in juvenile play-fighting. Juveniles usually stop nipping and slapping when they begin to get hurt; but if their fighting becomes serious, an adult male will usually emit a sharp grunt, at which point the juveniles cease all action. It isn't clear whether their response to the male's grunt is entirely learned or has an innate basis; but frequent repetitions of the grunt-and-stop sequence among juveniles may be

18

sufficient to instill in howlers learned limits to adult aggression against their own clansmen.

Among the group's adults, the most frequent of infrequent hostile responses occurs when an animal accidentally leaps onto another's back, or onto an already occupied limb that can't support two. Howlers seem properly sensitive about their balance and stability of support, since the ground may be 100 or 150 feet down; an upset howler will often snap at the intruder. A mother may also snap at or cuff a too-attentive "auntie"; I've even seen an adult male do the cuffing. In contrast to this unusually "fatherly" behavior, I've also seen an adult male squeeze a young juvenile until it screamed, with no apparent provocation. Collias and Southwick (1952) once saw a male bite an infant's tail in half and hurl the baby to the ground.

These latter incidents *are* unusual behaviors. Some students of primate psychology object to the citation of unusual behavior, on the grounds that it misrepresents the usual behavior of the species. Homicide and suicide are comparative rarities in human society, too, but they're considered significant in framing personality theories, particularly as they bear on the question of innate aggressiveness in humans. Just so, examples of howler aggression within the group are mentioned to indicate that these animals aren't entirely peaceful, but have the potential for aggression under certain conditions.

The isolated males mentioned earlier may represent an even stronger case of within-group aggression. No one has ever observed a howler being driven from a group by his fellows, but there he is, out in the jungle, all by his lone. This occurrence of isolated males is doubly surprising, because howlers don't show the sharp competitiveness and rigid dominance structure displayed by certain other monkeys. No one has witnessed any fights to the death, or even any spats leading to serious injury among individual adults; no struggles for mates, no squabbling for food. Such behavior seldom occurs in primates having clear dominance hierarchies, either; but the howlers attain this relatively peaceful state without even an apparent rigidifying of social structure. Chivers (1969) suggests that howlers may be getting more combative toward their fellow clansmen as the island population increases; he reports a 15 per cent incidence of "scarred, or freshly torn, lips" among adult males as evidence. But he doesn't report having seen any battles in which these split lips presumably originated.

Altercations between howler clans, however, are not hard to find. Although a physical clash between two clans, with hand-to-hand combat, has never been reliably reported, howlers do react violently when another group approaches anywhere within several hundred feet. The reaction and counterreaction consist mainly of what howlers do best: they howl.

19

Robert Ardrey (1961) makes the encounter fit for a Disney film:

> When two groups sight each other, each on the fringe of its territory, all break into total rage. Males, females, juveniles and infants become ants on a hot plate, leaping through the branches, scudding through the tree-tops, screeching, barking, chattering in frenzy. The forest cathedral becomes a green asylum for its insane inhabitants, and the howls of apparent melancholia become the shrieks of the truly demented.

This is a pretty example of Ardrey's literary talent, but it doesn't describe usual howler reactions. When one group's nearby presence does become known to another (by smell, by incidental noises, or by the first group's howls at another provocation), the second group is likely to *stop* any activity, rather than leap about furiously. Then one or more adult males will begin the bark leading to the roar and howl of the full-throated vocalization, joined in by the other males. Adult females and occasionally older juveniles may add their barks and high-pitched chatter. The males of the second group will usually respond, and the cries of both groups may alternate or continue simultaneously from several minutes to an hour or more. During this time, monkeys in each group may move about cautiously, sometimes closer to and sometimes farther away from the other group; but their vocalization is likely to be their only clear sign of disturbance. If two clans accidentally find themselves unusually close together, some monkeys may shake branches or move about in apparent agitation; but they usually manage to stay so far apart that howling suffices to express their distress. Ultimately, both groups will subside into grumbling and feeding, or one group will turn in its path of progression and make a slow retreat. The remaining group may vocalize for several minutes more without reply from the retreating group; then it will either move into the trees just vacated, remain where it is, or itself retreat in the direction from which it came. In no case will one group pursue another.

These vocal exchanges between groups leave no casualties, but they do help to keep strange howlers out of the territory inhabited by each group. Much has been made of the territoriality concept recently, because it seems to offer a biological basis for certain cultural phenomena among humans; but considerable confusion exists about the howler's version of territoriality. Howlers don't act as though they've built a fence or drawn a border, and then go tearing around the perimeter looking for invaders. Rather, they're born into a group that is familiar with a certain part of the jungle; in following the group, they presumably learn the location of food trees, lodge trees, and arboreal pathways in that piece of jungle, and turn back from unfamiliar territory. These pieces of familiar territory overlap somewhat, so that two or more howler groups occasionally come into contact. When they do, their reactions give no observable sign of territorial possessiveness but rather a display of irritability like that shown by a human when someone invades his "personal space." As Carpenter (1965) has said of howlers, *they defend the place where they are* — an idea quite distinct from defending a big hunk of real estate.

Much has also been made of the observation that howlers "defend" their territory only against other howlers, and don't react to intrusions by other species, such as white-faced cebus or capuchin monkeys. This isn't quite true. Howlers do usually save their best howls for other howlers; but in several instances I've seen howlers move away from capuchins in the same tree, stop a group progression from one tree to another when capuchins came near, and sometimes even vocalize at capuchins. This isn't really surprising. Even if capuchins don't compete much with howlers for food, they are distinctly unpleasant animals in their natural habitat. They chatter altogether too noisily; they shake tree limbs, and sometimes break off and drop branches with an annoying crash; they do not respect howlers' branch-rights, and will sit down on the same limb even if it's in danger of snapping. If you lived in a tree, would you want a band of white-faces to move in next door?

Ivan Sanderson (1957) has suggested of the howler that "If the countries of South America ever decided to federate or wished to choose a common emblem, this might well be the best animal to select as typifying the continent, roaring his individualistic defiance at the world, emblazoned in red-gold on a green jungle treetop against an azure tropical sky." Sanderson is either unaware of, or too embarrassed to mention, the howlers' alternate means of defense, though it might make the animals even more appropriate for certain national emblems. Very simply, when a threatening figure such as a human being is on the ground, the howler will move directly over him and then release a load of urine and watery dung. The first time an observer is the object of this treatment, he feels insulted and betrayed — he feels the howlers' meanness has no limit. After a while he becomes accustomed enough to the practice to move out of the way, and begins to wonder how this easily avoidable maneuver can be of any value to the howler. He wonders until the day he discovers a howler's hidden presence overhead by the gentle rain of excrement all around him.

Several writers have argued that this foul behavior is not intentional, that the howlers let go only because they're nervous or excited. Anyone who believes this should be placed unprotected beneath a hostile howler group several times before he makes his final judgment. Both male and female adults have been observed repeatedly to move with care from distant to nearby limbs and discharge their loads of excrement in close proximity to the observer, before returning to their original positions. Carpenter once built a blind under a group's likely line of march, to observe them unseen. The howlers paused over the blind, each in turn, defecated, then continued on their way.

21

more monkeys, also apes:
primate diversity

*Early in 1933 a small band of monkeys was imported
from Singapore and liberated in this natural jungle more
or less as an experiment. Not only did this little band of
immigrants from far off Asia decide the jungle was satisfactory but they set up their own government, ruled by a
chief and took over the jungle so completely that it was
soon found necessary to construct a cage to protect visi-
tors from the jealous monkey inhabitants.*

— Leaflet from Monkey Jungle,
22 miles south of Miami, Florida

"Carpenter has a good thing going with his research on howlers," our
friendly neighborhood Congressman might tell the National Science
Foundation, "and the Canal Zone is American soil. But don't go handing
out grants to study foreign species, understand? When you've seen one
monkey, you've seen 'em all. If anybody feels like gallivanting around to
look at something different, let him go to the zoo."

Most behavioral scientists seemed to feel likewise for two decades after
Carpenter's pioneering work with howlers. (Their attitude was helped
along by the interference of a world war and the practical difficulty of
mounting field expeditions, as compared with doing laboratory research.)
No major effort was made to study other primate species in the wild,
with the exception of Carpenter's own observations of gibbons; and the
howler data, along with Sir Solly Zuckerman's baboon studies in the
London Zoo, strongly influenced numerous scientific and popular treatises
on What Primates Are Really Like. The territorial howler, the tyrant
baboon with his harem — why, we can see the same behavior in Florida's
Monkey Jungle! In human society! Primates all, and all brothers beneath
their multicolored skins!

The gibbons and Sir Solly's baboons will shortly be given their due.
First, let's tell our Congressman a little about zoo studies. The zoo primate is in a strange environment, tremendously simplified in comparison
with his own wild homeland, even when zookeepers do their best to
supply him with "natural" surroundings. His physical wants are met
easily; his area of travel is grossly limited; and he is likely to have been
raised not by his own parents but by the zookeeper's daughter. So he
will probably be crazy, to begin with; even if he isn't, his behavior will
be abnormally restricted to little more than playing, copulating, or fighting. A zoo may be quite instructive about the physical form of various
species. But if you're interested in primate *behavior*, a visit to the zoo is
rather like going to a lunatic asylum to laugh at the inmates.

Nor can the howler be accepted as representative of wild, "natural" primate behavior. Primates include about two hundred species, hardly brothers under the skin and mostly distant cousins at best. Not only the physical form but the behavior of each species is distinctive. This significant fact has been made clear by a major resurgence of primate field studies during the past few years. In reviewing the recent findings (made by psychologists, zoologists, anthropologists, and representatives of several other disciplines), we can use howler behavior as a benchmark, in order to note important similarities and differences; but the howler is no more an ideal model of a social monkey than any other species. So many different kinds of monkeys and apes have by now been studied in detail, or are being studied presently, that we'll look at only a suggestive range of primate behaviors.

GROUP COMPOSITION

Let's start again with social cohesiveness. Most primates do live in stable groups, and in many species the size of the group is not much different from what you'd typically find in howlers. But an Asian ape, the gibbon, and two New World monkeys, the callicebus and the night monkey, regularly live in nuclear family units only — mother, father, and one or two young. At the other end of the scale, the hamadryas baboons of Ethiopia may gather in sleeping troops of several hundred animals at night, though the troop breaks into smaller units during daylight hours.

The proportion of adults to juveniles and infants in a group varies in different species according to birth rates, maturational rates, and survival rates; but there is often a disproportionate ratio of adult females to males, perhaps 2 or 3 to 1. This recurrent oversupply of females in many primate groups has intrigued primatologists ever since Carpenter first gathered reliable data on it in howlers (he called it the "socionomic sex ratio"). K. R. L. Hall and Irven DeVore (1965) explain it rather simply. It's not the result of male duels to the death, as some writers have speculated; males don't duel to the death under natural conditions, among howlers or baboons or any other primates studied except man. Nor can it be accounted for as the result of young males being driven out of the group by the old tyrant, or of old males being driven out by the upstarts, though an occasional lone male is seen. Instead, the disproportion is mainly a matter of maturational rates. Females mature from half again to twice as quickly as males among most primates; and since primates have relatively short life spans, *adult* females may outnumber *adult* males considerably, even if the total number of males — adult, juvenile, and infant — in a group is about equal to the total number of females. Add to this that males seem more likely to become isolates, that males are more likely to be killed defending the group when predators abound, and that some younger mature males are misidentified as juveniles because their sexual maturity isn't as obvious as in a pregnant, estrous, or child-carrying female, and there you have the socionomic sex ratio. (Hans Kummer [1968a] reports only about 10 per cent more adult females than males among hamadryas baboons. But in that species, younger animals of both sexes take on a distinctive sex role rather early, so he counts every animal from three and one-half years on. Because he starts his count of sexually typed animals at the same age for both sexes, the numbers come out almost equal.)

Among many primate species, groups are virtually closed units, as with howlers. Additions are made mainly by births; strangers are not welcome; departures are likely to be permanent. Among gorillas and even more so among chimpanzees, groups are rather fluid. George Schaller (1963) observed several instances among gorillas in which adults of both sexes, as well as an occasional juvenile, switched groups with little or no trouble. Vernon and Frances Reynolds (1965) describe chimpanzee groups in the Budongo Forest of Uganda as "constantly changing membership, splitting apart, meeting others and joining them, congregating or dispersing." Some of these behaviors seem random; others involve group transfers as an animal's life condition changes. A female in heat becomes an attraction for wandering males, thus forming what Adriaan Kortlandt (1962) calls a "sexual group." When she gives birth and is no longer attractive, she associates with others in her condition; a "nursery group" results. When no estrous female is present, males find little in mothers or children to attract them, and so they may travel in all-male bands. Larger groups, containing males, females in heat, mothers and young, typically are attracted together by a particularly bounteous food tree. Jane Goodall (1965) reports that mother-and-young families are the only completely stable "groups" she has seen; any other relationship may break off without notice, and an animal in any other category may travel by himself if he has no strong reason to travel with other chimps.

SOCIAL STRUCTURE

Within primate groups, substantial differences in social structure can be observed. Few species seem to have a much looser structure than the rather free-form howler clan; but many primates show a tighter group organization, founded upon a dominance hierarchy. Dominance hierarchies have been observed in various birds and mammals, starting with barnyard chickens (from which came the alternate term of "pecking order"). The most dominant animal in a group may get first crack at food or sexual mates, or may determine group movements. He may also be able to display hostility toward other group members without being aggressed against in turn. The less dominant animals may make a show of subordinance, or redirect their annoyance toward group members still lower in the hierarchy. When Walt Whitman said he could turn and live

24

with the animals because "Not one kneels to another," he knew not whereof he spoke.

Dominance in primates was first studied extensively by Sir Solly Zuckerman (1932), under unfortunate circumstances. Sir Solly, a distinguished British zoologist, managed to observe baboons in the wild for a few days in the 1920's, but he did most of his research on a large hamadryas baboon colony in the London Zoo. To organize a zoo colony properly, he would have had to know much more about baboon social life in natural surroundings than he was able to learn in a few days. One bit of helpful knowledge would be the slightly greater number of adult females than adult males in the wild hamadryas troop. Another would be the fact that peaceful relationships in a hamadryas troop are structured on adult males' recognition of each other's exclusive rights to certain females, these rights being built up gradually from before the time a female is sexually mature. And another would be the baboon troop's insularity: baboons usually react negatively to strange baboons.

What Zuckerman began with at the London Zoo was about four times as many adult males as females; males captured from several different troops, and thus unfamiliar with each other; males thrown together with no time for the peaceful establishment of rights to particular females. What Zuckerman got were vicious fights between males, fights over females and even *against* females and young — baboons mutilating and killing each other until hardly any baboon colony remained. In the process, Zuckerman also saw males repeatedly presenting "sexually" to other males, and this looked to Zuckerman like sexual perversity, though it was most likely a stereotyped communication pattern referring to geographical movement rather than sex. In his famous book, *The Social Life of Monkeys and Apes,* Zuckerman presented a picture of the dominant male baboon as absolute tyrant, monopolizing all available sex partners, destroying opponents, always craving sex, sex both normal and perverted. Until recently, his work has been the definitive picture of baboon social life, and for many the definitive picture of natural primate social life, from which man escaped by supreme acts of will and morality.

Following Zuckerman's lead, baboons were long thought to be particularly stern practitioners of the rule of dominance. The top male had his harem, which he defended against all comers; subordinate males virtually starved, if they weren't killed or driven into the lonely wilds. But that myth has been at least partly shattered: neither hamadryas nor savanna baboons are anywhere near as hierarchy-oriented in their natural state as their zoo behavior had suggested. Indeed, even when a distinguishable dominance hierarchy has been found to exist, researchers have often had to use sophisticated statistical techniques to be sure which animals are dominant over whom, and under what circumstances (Bernstein, 1970).

The savanna baboons of South and East Africa display clearer domi-

25

nance patterns than most primates, but even their behavior is remote from the heights of despotism. Normally, competition for food is nonexistent; males' infrequent disputes for other reasons are brief and usually noninjurious. Hall and DeVore (1965) report that the most dominant males in a group do tend to monopolize sexually receptive females during the peak of each female's estrus period. But Thelma Rowell (personal communication) detected no such monopoly in the groups she observed; even in Hall and DeVore's groups, dominant males shared estrus females with subordinate adult males and older juveniles when the females were coming into and going out of heat.

Nor does dominance in the savanna baboon always follow the traditionally assumed single-line pattern, from the top male to the second and so on down, in such other prerogatives as grooming or aggressive displays. Rowell (1969) found adult males of forest-dwelling groups to move from one group to another so often that no stable hierarchies could be established. Among groups where hierarchies exist, the dominant position is often held jointly by two or three adult males, acting in concert, though singly each of these males may be subordinate to other animals in the group. Members of such an alliance come to each other's defense when attacked by another male; they don't compete even for scarce food tidbits provided by human observers. They obviously can't share the same female simultaneously, but their alliances appear to withstand occasional sexual competition. Such dominance alliances probably develop over extended time periods in most groups, but Hall and DeVore observed one situation in which a very subordinate male of one group moved to another group, quickly allied himself with one of the more dominant males there, and thus began a presumably happy life as joint top dogface.

If a savanna baboon does attain dominant status, he acquires certain responsibilities along with his ambiguous privileges. His principal obligation is to protect women and children. When the group is on the move, dominant males typically remain at the center, surrounded by mothers and infants, with subordinate males on the periphery. At a sign of danger, the dominant males move immediately to the front of the group to face the threat — not only with their bark, but with their daggerlike canine teeth. As with howler males, both dominant and subordinate savanna baboons also protect the group from internal aggression: if an older juvenile is roughing up a younger one, or if two females have become angry at each other, an adult male will usually break up the dispute before it escalates, either by growling or by chasing the offending party away (Hall and DeVore, 1965).

Group structure and dominance relationships are arranged rather differently among hamadryas baboons, the species involved in Zuckerman's zoo studies. In the wild, hamadryas groups exist on three levels (Kummer,

1968a). The *troop* contains as many as several hundred animals, who usually sleep in the same area and leave together in the morning. They then split into several *bands* of thirty to ninety animals, who remain loosely associated during daytime activities. Presumably both the troop and the band serve useful defensive purposes; the troop may also develop partly because a shortage of suitable sleeping space forces large numbers of animals to sleep in the same area (Kummer, 1968b). Each band is further organized into several *one-male units*, typically composed of one adult male and one to four females with young. The band's subadult and young males who have no females of their own may follow a one-male unit at a distance, or they may simply remain in the general area foraged by the entire band. Around 20 per cent of a band's adult males at any one time are mateless.

Zuckerman identified the one-male units as "harems," and the name still seems somewhat appropriate, though some harems contain only one female. The male leader keeps his eye on his entourage and permits little association, sexual or otherwise, with other males. A venturesome female is likely to be rewarded with a bite on the neck from her leader. But the harem is not built up through brutal combat, as Zuckerman thought; nor is it quite as closed as it appeared to him in the zoo. The one-male group is likely to begin with a young male's adoption of a one- or two-year-old female, still sexually immature and still several years from childbearing age. He mothers her, he keeps her close to him and brings her back if she tries to run away, until a firm social bond is established. Only later will sexual activity begin. The male may then acquire other mates in the same way, or take over a mature female who has been "let go" by an aging male. Hans Kummer saw little indication that harems are broken up through fighting, but the older males seem to tolerate their females' moving gradually farther from them, until the females may affiliate with younger males. The old males, as they give up certain sexual prerogatives, gradually take over direction of the entire troop's travel — expending their energies as executives rather than as breeders.

TERRITORIAL BEHAVIOR

Territoriality, in the sense of staying in a home range that overlaps little with other groups' home ranges, and of somehow defending one's immediate location from infringement by other groups, is not nearly as widespread among primates as Carpenter thought when he found it in the first two species he studied at length, the howler and — halfway round the world — the gibbon. Perhaps a more frequent pattern is the one observed by Phyllis Jay (1965) among langurs, the sacred Hanuman monkeys of India. In the population Jay studied, each group of langurs stayed in a home range that overlapped with the home ranges of other groups, and largely within a core area that didn't overlap with others.

Groups seldom met, partly because adult males produced a "deep, resonant 'whoop'" when ready to move to another area (somewhat as howlers roar before they move in the morning). But when groups did meet, conflict didn't occur; the smaller group gave way to the larger. (Under different environmental conditions, Suzanne Ripley [1967] observed troops of langurs apparently seeking each other out for battle, but territorial issues did not seem to be involved.)

In savanna baboons too, a group's home range overlaps considerably with areas sometimes traversed by other groups, while core areas are fairly exclusive. When two groups do meet, for instance at a water hole during the dry season, they may act nervous toward their newfound neighbors, but they usually don't roar, bare their teeth, or otherwise display hostile intent in the howler manner. One baboon group may gradually creep away, and some entire groups appear dominant over other entire groups in this way, at least partly on the basis of group size; but the whole interaction is polite, with no chasing allowed (Washburn and DeVore, 1961). Waterhole sharing under such circumstances may well be necessary for species survival. Howler hostility toward other groups is perhaps not a requirement of primate life but a luxury.

A weird modification of territoriality is practiced by the callicebus or titi, studied in Colombia by William Mason (1966, 1968). Callicebus monkeys live in small family groups; the parents display their mutual attraction by sitting together and entwining their long tails at eventide. Each family group usually stays in its home range, with several such families occupying delimited areas of a small woods surrounded by open savanna. Groups coming into contact vocalize strenuously, and may charge each other with a great display of hostility. So far, they appear howlerishly territorial; indeed, titis show even less overlap of group territories. But during a female's estrus, something extraordinary happens. When two groups meet for an aggressive interlude at the edges of their respective territories, this usually monogamous and homebody female may ignore her own mate's sexual advances and wait for the rival male to come satisfy her, or she may even move out toward him. Her own mate naturally displays signs of annoyance, and may attempt to interfere, but often she's able to enjoy a brief copulation with the other family's male, after which she returns to her husband with virtually no marital repercussions. Perhaps her mate is by this time already contriving his own liaison with another titi's woman. The promiscuous but group-centered howlers would surely deliver a moralistic roar at the very thought of such behavior, were they able to think upon morality.

Among apes, the gibbon seems unique in its strong territorial defense. Orangutans have been too little studied, and their societies perhaps too

28

disrupted by all the forces that have pushed them toward extinction, to say much about their apparent lack of territorial behavior. Gorilla concern about territory is rather casual (Schaller, 1963). The home ranges of adjacent gorilla groups usually overlap a great deal, sometimes completely; encounters between groups elicit only slight excitement and perhaps a staring contest between males, with a little chest-beating sometimes thrown in. Schaller has seen two groups bed down and sleep for a night side by side, then go their separate ways in the morning. Intergroup antagonism among chimpanzees, including territorial defense, simply has not been observed. Each loose "community" of frequently interacting chimps apparently remains mostly in one several-square-mile home range, but individual animals exhibit no proprietary feelings toward this familiar area. The Reynoldses several times watched groups, which spent nearly all their time in one area, spontaneously travel "fast and noisily" into the heart of another area usually occupied by a different set of chimps. No hostile reaction ever occurred on either side.

When large numbers of chimpanzees gather in a small area around a common food source, the animals appear extraordinarily excited at the sight of so many unfamiliar faces, and sometimes stage what have been called "carnivals." Many animals vocalize simultaneously, and males drum on tree trunks for hours at a time. The Reynoldses (1965) describe "chimpanzees coming and going in all directions, some to and some from the centers of hubbub. . . . Sometimes whole valleys along a stretch as much as a mile would resound and vibrate with the noise." The carnivals occasionally last into the night (as all good carnivals should), and sexual activity may reach unusual heights. It's indicative of chimpanzee distinctiveness that although howlers roar at unfamiliar howlers in attempted repulsion, chimps treat similar occasions with excitement, curiosity, and what really appears to be delight. Further, though chimps do call out briefly and drum on trees while traveling, this doesn't seem to space out or prevent group contact, as with other primates; instead it may attract them together.

PARENTAL ATTENTION

The howler gives about as little attention to its young as any true primate can get away with; in several other species the attention is substantially greater. In the langur, "auntie" behavior has been highly developed. Females of all ages are immediately attracted to a newborn, and begin to take it from its mother a few hours after birth — in Phyllis Jay's words (1965), "gently manipulating, nudging, and smelling the infant." When the infant indicates discomfort, another female (or perhaps the mother) will take it. Jay has seen as many as eight females handle the infant on its first day of life. Older females seem more competent

29

than younger at this baby-handling, but as Jay points out, "Because langur mothers allow other females to hold their infants, no langur female is completely without experience in infant care." Furthermore, "auntie" behavior often turns into "babysitter" behavior: one mother may deposit her infant with another mother, and at times a single mother may sit with several infants for a good part of the day.

Among a few primate species, paternal behavior is notable. The night monkey father, for instance, apparently spends most of his waking time carrying his infant. By the age of three weeks, the night monkey infant goes to his mother mostly to be suckled, and spends the rest of the night riding on his father's back. The callicebus father behaves rather similarly. Martin Moynihan (1964) suggests that this may be a useful division of labor for such monogamous family-grouping primates. But it would cause problems for species such as the howler, where no child knows its own father and where infants may outnumber adult males.

In at least some groups of Japanese macaques, adult males take care of the group's juveniles. They don't merely protect the juveniles from attack, as with savanna baboons; they don't adopt female young in mate relationships, as with hamadryas; and they don't carry young infants around, as with night monkeys. Instead, a male will take over a year-old juvenile of either sex when the mother has had or is about to have a new baby. According to Junichiro Itani (1959), the male hugs the yearling, "takes it on his loins, or walks with it; when sitting, he will groom it." This paternal care declines after the female delivery season has ended, but it may be repeated again the following year, particularly for juvenile females or those who are "especially undergrown and weak." Most juvenile males by this time have formed their own play groups.

"CULTURAL" VARIATION

The adult males' relationships with juveniles may deliver benefits in both directions. Associates of the Japan Monkey Center have encouraged groups of monkeys to come out of their usual mountainous forest habitat to more humanly accessible clearings by "provisioning": they supply the monkeys with sweet potatoes and other interesting foods. Even before provisioning began, considerable differences existed between food preferences of various groups. For instance, some groups dug for edible roots; others did not. Provisioning made possible experimentation with the development of such apparently "cultural" differences in behavior — patterns learned and handed on rather than inherited (Kawamura, 1959). Itani passed out candy to one group; the older animals refused to eat it, but the juveniles were more venturesome, and candy eating soon spread throughout the group's juvenile population. Mothers still in close contact with juveniles began eating candy too; so did the more paternal males. Infants then learned from their mothers. The less contact an animal had with the innovative juveniles, the slower he was to pick up the candy habit. At the end of a year and a half, 51 per cent of group members were confirmed candy eaters.

In another group (Kawamura, 1959), one juvenile female spontaneously started washing sweet potatoes before eating them. Again, other juveniles and then their mothers picked up the practice. But in this troop, adult males had no close "paternal" relationships with juveniles, so the males went on eating dirty sweet potatoes. In still another instance, M. Yamada began giving wheat to the group; this time an adult male was first to accept the new food. Shortly the group's dominant males picked up the habit, then the head female; and from there it spread downward to the whole clan. Some Japanese monkeys even invented a way to separate the wheat from the chaff, so to speak (Frisch, 1968). The wheat was usually poured out onto a sandy beach, and the monkeys had a hard time making a meal of wheat without getting a mouthful of sand too. So they began tossing the mixture into the sea. The sand sank, and they scooped the wheat off the water.

The founding of another cultural practice may have occurred in chimpanzees. Goodall (1965) observed chimps making and using tools, by trimming twigs that they then thrust into termite holes, so they could draw out and lick off the clinging termites. Only the chimpanzees in Tanzania's Gombe Stream Reserve have been seen to use this method of catching termites. Young chimps there appear to learn the practice from their elders, so it may well be that one lucky or brilliant chimp developed the practice, which then spread to other members of the chimpanzee community by imitation. In other areas, chimps have been reported to thrust sticks into beehives and then lick the honey off; whether the two practices are culturally related isn't known. The Reynoldses, in an area where both beehives and termite nests are present, never saw chimps bother either one.

Chimpanzees in particular show a variety of other social behaviors: complex greeting patterns, social facilitation (hyperactivity of various kinds in the presence of several other chimps), sexual and aggressive displays. Indeed, the chimpanzee may prove to be, despite its extremely loose social organization, the most "advanced" social animal besides man. The Reynoldses (1965) have suggested that the chimps' apparently loose social structure really reflects their relative advancement in social behavior: because they can communicate so efficiently from a distance, and can remember intermittently occurring social relationships (as indicated by variations in greetings to more and less familiar animals), they needn't maintain tightly organized groups with constant visual contact. Just so, a loving and confident husband might be observed to remain farther

31

from his wife at a party than an uncertain and jealous husband from his. But perhaps we need more research on both husbands and chimpanzees before we accept either hypothesis.

As with howlers, the social behaviors described in this section consume only a small portion of primates' time and energy — even among chimpanzees. Social animals they may be, but the nonhuman primates are still far less wrapped in a social world than humans are. However, the behaviors I've mentioned aren't just trivial curiosities, a sort of Believe-It-or-Not of the primate world. They are all functional aspects of living behavior patterns that have enabled many different primate species to maintain themselves for several hundred thousand years or more. Socialness is important for the primate, even though his small brain is not constantly concentrated upon it.

how the primate got his gregarity: origins of social motivation

The main factor that determines social grouping in subhuman primates is sexual attraction. Females attract males and males attract females.

— Sir Solly Zuckerman
The Social Life of Monkeys and Apes

My daughter Heather, long before she could talk, showed a fierce fascination with other children her size — shouting to them across rooms crowded with adults, grabbing at them as they passed in supermarket shopping carts. Her reaction was so enthusiastic, so free of attempt to win parental favor, that it appeared almost instinctive. Then again, it might have come from her equally vigorous appreciation of herself in a mirror, projected outward onto similar objects (but why did she like her reflection, other than because it seemed to her another child?); or from the pleasure she got out of child-sized toys; or even from her mother pointing out other infants with the cry, "Bay-bee! Bay-bee!" Who knows?

No one can really know, since human babies are complicated creatures reared in a complex world, and since child development researchers are ethically constrained from reducing either complication or complexity experimentally. So the nature-versus-nurture controversy, at least as applied to humans, is hardly a fit topic any more even for junior high school debating societies. Separating the factors in any meaningful way is simply impossible. But wait — who should be available but the relatively simple nonhuman primates, in their relatively simple environments, and with little protection of their rights against drastic experimentation? They may not be of much direct help in explaining my daughter, but perhaps field and laboratory studies of their behavior can help us deal with broader questions raised by her enthusiasm for other children: Why are so many primates attracted to each other? Why do they group together? What are the bases for primate sociability?

SEX AND SOCIETY

Zuckerman's early hypothesis (1932) is still influential among nonspecialists: society is founded upon sexual copulation and sexual competition. "Reproductive physiology is the fundamental mechanism of society," he declared — particularly of primate society, since he assumed that primates lack a breeding season and are thus continually interested in sex. Sir Solly devised this position not from reading Freud but from observing his zoo monkeys, who had nothing much besides sex to be social about.

Carpenter had made more reliable observations, from which he developed a more subtle explanation of sex's role in primate society (1942). His idea was not that sexual desire dominates primate life, but that the social bonds between males and females in a group are repeatedly reinforced through the year by the reward of frequent sexual activity. This would be particularly effective in holding groups together if they practiced the kinds of "rotating mateships" found in howler and rhesus monkeys, because in such situations a female rhesus, for instance, "may be possessed by all the *more dominant* males in her group during estrus, and with each one social affinitive relations may be strengthened by the coincident positive conditioning (or learning) occurring during copulations." In other words, all the adult females in the group keep all the adult males happy (or at least the more important males), and all the males keep all the females happy, so they all live together in one big happy family.

The view of sex as the center of primate society remained attractive enough for a distinguished anthropologist, Marshall Sahlins, to write in 1960:

> The powerful social magnet of sex was the major impetus to subhuman primate sociability. . . . Subhuman primates are prepared to mate at all seasons, and although females show heightened receptivity midway through the menstrual cycle, they are often capable of sexual activity at other times. Most significantly for the assessment of its historic role, year-round sex in higher primates is associated with year-round heterosexual social life.

Sahlins qualified his remarks with the acknowledgment that "certain Old World monkeys . . . do have seasonal declines in breeding without

33

cessation of horde life," but he insisted that in general, sexuality pervades nonhuman social life throughout the year.

Carpenter many years earlier had noted in howler females a distinct estrus period, not just a period of "heightened receptivity." He was therefore much more careful to qualify his hypothesis about sex and sociability (Carpenter, 1942):

> It must be concluded that strong attachments between individual monkeys or apes may be formed and persist without overt and primary sexual activity, unless we make identical the social and the sexual behavior. Through reciprocal play, through mutual grooming or through communal feeding, social relations and statuses are acquired and these learning processes are strongly motivated and reinforced by reciprocal interactions of drives and their incentives other than sexual.

As masses of data have recently become available showing either the distinct periodicity of a primate species' sexual behavior, or the year-round low level of sexual activity in many primate groups, the assumption of sex's primary role in sociability has largely been abandoned; and these other rewarding aspects of social life have been given more and more weight. It's clearly pleasant for the infant primate to have the attentions — the nutriment, warmth, protection — of his mother; pleasant for the young primate to play with his fellows; physically pleasant for most primates of any age to be groomed (as with human back-scratching). It may also be rewarding to see other members of the group defend oneself, perhaps oneself to join in defense, against intruders or predators. When sexual behavior occasionally happens, that should be rewarding as well; but it is not the ultimate and unique gratification of social life. As Carpenter says elsewhere (1940), "Almost every phase of behavior of which a primate is capable enters to some degree into the determination of its 'gregariousness' and the qualities of its complex social behavior."

FUNCTIONS OF SOCIAL LIVING

Whether social behaviors are pleasurable to the individual or not, they may promote survival of the species. Recent writers on primate sociability have chosen to emphasize this feature: the *functional* basis of group living. If a social behavior is more functional in preserving species existence than a nonsocial one, evolution is more likely to "select" the social; and there are good reasons to believe that social life is and has been highly functional for most primates. This doesn't necessarily mean that evolution has implanted a social instinct into every monkey and ape, though we'll explore that possibility later. It may only mean that the primate's physical structure predisposes him to social living, makes socialness either an easier or a happier way of life than isolation — for instance, because an animal has a back that feels good when it's scratched, or is so physically disorganized at birth that he must cling to his mother for months, being strongly rewarded by social contact all the while. Or it may mean developing the capacity to transmit traditional patterns of functional behavior: through social communication, through imitation, or through parental reward or punishment of certain acts.

The usefulness of primate social grouping is many-faceted. Childraising may be more effective, because the infant may not only get attention from several adult group members at various times, but also has the opportunity to learn coordination and sex-roles safely in play with other infants. Further, in case of the mother's death, adoption by another group female may be possible. Growing adolescents have the opportunity to observe various adult roles that may help them mature behaviorally with fewer mistakes. Adults have more opportunity to find sex partners when a partner is desired, and indeed more opportunity for any kind of social stimulation when and if they need it. The group may not only protect the individual from immediate danger, but may help him to cope with potential dangers by teaching him, at least through example, about his environment: what foods to eat, what organisms and natural phenomena (eagles, nettles, bogs) to avoid. Trial-and-error learning may be useful for the laboratory rat, but it could be deadly for the isolated primate.

Because different primate species live in different environments, the same forms of behavior are not universally functional. Development of varying functional responses to varied environments may account in large part for behavior differences between species, as well as for variations of group behaviors within species. The Reynoldses (1965) have suggested that chimpanzees' relatively large size and their dependence on fruit are at least partially responsible for their loose social organization. Bands of twenty to thirty chimps may form in areas where ripe fruit is heavily concentrated, but at other times and places such a large band could hardly avoid starvation. Mainly ground-dwelling monkeys show, on the whole, distinctive general behavior patterns not found in mainly tree-living monkeys — for instance, the clearer dominance hierarchies of the savanna baboon, which some writers have suggested would be the most useful social organization for defense against ground-dwelling predators. The same baboon species may encounter fewer predators in the forest, and so shows the much looser social structure observed by Rowell (1969). A related species, the hamadryas, may encounter such severe survival problems in the harsh Ethiopian environment that its social structure in some ways is even stricter than that of savanna-dwelling baboons, though more fragmented as well. (On the other hand, as Washburn and Hamburg [1965] note, different adaptations are possible even within similar environments. For instance, patas monkeys, "unlike baboons, have adapted to ground life by speed rather than by size and social organization.")

The origin of primates' ancestors in trees rather than on the ground was itself probably a significant factor in the development of strong social motivation, simply because the infant had to cling so closely to its mother for so long a time before it could safely venture out into the tricky arboreal environment. At the same time, Hall and DeVore (1965) have suggested, development of the abilities necessary to respond to a complex social life may in turn be the source of much primate adaptability to the physical environment: if a primate can change his behavior to suit his neighbors, he should be able to change even more easily to suit a new but relatively stable climate or geographic area.

SOCIAL BEHAVIOR IN THE LABORATORY

With all this talk of functionality and evolution, the word "instinct" may keep bobbing around in the back of your head. Has evolution been so impressed by the functionality of group living that it has implanted a seed of gregariousness in us all, monkeys, apes, and men? How do we answer that question? Well, we can't go depriving human children of social contacts, or stripping their environment to the bare essentials, to see if gregarity remains. But we can do — and have done — such things to monkey children.

Much laboratory work in this area was initiated by Harry Harlow and his colleagues and students at the University of Wisconsin. Harlow is well known for raising infant rhesuses on imitation mothers, shaped from heavy wire screen that sometimes remained bare and sometimes was upholstered with terry cloth. The infants (now we can say, "Of course!") vastly preferred the cloth-covered mother even if she was milkless while the bare-wire mother had a milk-dispensing "unibreast" in mid-thorax. Perhaps less well known is a later Harlow study in which the infants were given a choice of *two* cloth-covered mothers, one with unibreast and one without. Some infants had a brown nursing mother and some a green nursing mother; the non-nursing mother got whichever color was left. All good humanitarians and Martians should be glad to know that color of mother made no difference to the infants. More significantly for our purposes, preference for the nursing mother lasted less than four months. After that, though the young monkeys were still nursing, they spent roughly equal amounts of time with the nursing and non-nursing mothers. Harlow (1962) concludes, "Certainly nursing and activities associated with the breast are not variables underlying the persistent, relatively inextinguishable affectional bonds of the infant for the mother." All good behavioral psychologists, who've attributed human social attraction

36

mainly to maternal reduction of such "basic" drives as hunger and thirst, should be properly dismayed.

Harlow's research has settled no arguments about the existence of monkey social instincts. The clinging reflex that predisposes the infant rhesus to "love" the cloth mother is not complex or long-lasting enough to account for social behavior by itself. But Harlow has made clear that a social instinct, if it exists, is not enough for social life. His infant rhesuses, raised for six months or more with an artificial mother, developed serious disturbances, particularly in their social behaviors: they withdrew into themselves when faced with more sociable monkeys, or fiercely attacked other monkeys who had undergone even greater social deprivation. Sexual behavior, the most obviously biological and "natural" of social behaviors, was just as severely blocked as other social responses. Harlow delights in telling how carefully his socially deprived females had to be coaxed and coached by experienced males before they ever conceived. Once they became parents, these females were often miserable mothers with their firstborn, completely ignoring the infants or grinding their faces into the wire mesh of the cage. Infants raised without mothers but with other infants seemed to develop somewhat more normally; and the miserable mothers, having contradicted all assumptions about maternal instincts with their firstborn, generally became capable mothers with their second. In each case, social "instincts" had to be supplemented by social contact with a real live responding primate before something approaching normal social behavior could emerge. As Harlow says about the sexual development of his socially deprived males, both "yearning and learning" are essential — both social motivation and social experience.

William Mason, a former colleague of Harlow's, has approached the development of primate sociability from another direction. Mason (1965) hypothesizes the existence of an optimal stimulation level in any primate. When the degree of stimulation rises above the optimum, the primate will try to reduce it; when stimulation falls below the optimum, the primate will try to increase it. This basic idea, shared with several other psychologists, is distinctly different from the more popular drive-reduction theories, in which the organism is assumed to strive perpetually for a minimal level of stimulation.

Mason demonstrated how this hypothetical process of maintaining optimal stimulation operates, through a series of simple experiments. He dressed two experimenters in different costumes, each with a sort of abstract primate mask over his face. One costume was always associated with the experimenter's quiet holding of a baby chimpanzee to his chest; the other costume was always associated with the experimenter's playing with (tickling, bouncing, gently pushing) the baby chimp. Given a choice, the chimps generally preferred the play-person over the holding-person by a considerable margin. But in an unfamiliar room, which presumably raised the chimps' overall arousal level, they usually didn't want to be aroused further by play; they preferred the person in the holding-costume. (This preference decreased, however, as they became more familiar with the unfamiliar room.) The same was true in other disturbing situations, such as when a young chimp was removed abruptly from its cagemates.

Mason uses the data from such experiments to explain at least partly the primate's preference for social companionship. A world of inanimate objects could become very boring very quickly; other living organisms provide the most complex stimuli. Other organisms with which one is familiar — the members of one's own group — could provide the most pleasing alternative to too much stimulation or too little. This is particularly true of the young primate, who can turn to his familiar mother in time of excessive stimulation, and to his playmates when more stimulation is needed. Even if adult life in the group becomes rather tame, the primate has received so many rewards — so many hours of optimal-level existence — from the group as a child, that he is unlikely to leave it without hesitation as an adult. Besides, there's nowhere else to go. A solitary life would be even more boring, and an existence of flitting from one strange group to another too upsetting.

But what of primate species where adult group life is not so tame — where an aggressively dominant animal may at least occasionally threaten or chase or bite his subordinates? Wouldn't his offensive behavior severely strain the group's social ties? Michael Chance and Clifford Jolly (1970), using Mason's hypothesis, argue that the reverse may be true. Initially, a subordinate animal may scurry away from his attacking leader, who has raised his stimulation level too high. But as time passes and the attack is not pursued, the subordinate animal's stimulation level will drop to the preferred optimum, and he should therefore be attracted more strongly than before to the source of this recurrent pleasure, his exciting leader. In the words of many a harried spouse or parent, "Well, at least life is never dull with him [or her] around."

INNATE SOCIAL RESPONSIVENESS

Other research indicates that a primate needn't play with others, or be groomed by them, or have sex with them, to find them rewarding; all he may need is a vision of another primate like himself. Robert A. Butler (1965) has conducted numerous studies in which a monkey housed in an opaque box is taught to perform tasks for the reward of getting a quick look at laboratory goings-on, or at a picture, or perhaps at a cagemate in an adjacent pen. Although the monkeys will work for a sight of just about anything (perhaps to raise their stimulation level to optimum),

38

they appear to prefer looking at other monkeys, particularly at familiar monkeys, and more particularly at sexual mates — though males may prefer to look at a strange female rather than at their own mates, "especially if the stranger is in full sexual coloration"!

The reward value of social sneak-looks has been explained by some writers in terms of secondary reinforcement: the monkey has been satisfied in the past by sexual mates, or has been played with by his cagemates, so he gains an associated pleasure merely from seeing them. Butler rejects this idea, because monkeys will persist at tasks for long periods with no primary rewards to strengthen the "secondary" visual one, and because very young monkeys — one to two weeks old — seem to find such visions rewarding too. One of the most convincing demonstrations of Butler's point, and indeed one of the most convincing indicators of innate social responsiveness in primates, is a set of studies done by Gene Sackett.

Sackett (1966) raised infant rhesus monkeys from birth in individual opaque cages. Each monkey never saw another monkey and saw humans only during its first five to nine days of life, when it had to be hand-fed. One wall of each cage was a projection screen, and beginning at two weeks of age, the monkey was exposed to various projected color slides on this screen. Sometimes the experimenter himself turned the slides on and off; sometimes the monkey, after a brief initial exposure to the slide, could himself turn it on repeatedly for as many as five minutes, by touching a lever in the cage. The monkeys' preference for particular kinds of pictures could be gauged either by how often they pressed the lever when they were able to control the length of the slide's exposure, or by what behaviors they showed when the experimenter controlled the exposure of a particular slide. Month-old monkeys showed no differences in preference. But older infants showed a clear preference for pictures of other monkeys, particularly infant monkeys, rather than for control pictures such as sunsets, trees, or "a pretty adult female human." Between ages two and four months, negative responses ("fear, withdrawal, rocking, and huddling") were given especially often to pictures of a threatening monkey; but "this apparently innate fear response to threat stimuli" started declining midway during that period, presumably because the threats were never carried out. Pictures of monkey infants elicited more playing than any other stimuli, though the threat pictures were accompanied by almost as much play. The threat and infant pictures each generated more overall activity than any other types of monkey pictures (mother-infant, sex, play, etc.); these "other-monkey" pictures in turn generated more activity than the non-monkey control pictures.

Maybe seeing humans during the first week of life, or seeing the fur on its own body, could predispose the infant monkey to prefer other

39

anthropoid forms on the screen (though why not the pretty female human?). But such experience would not account for its preferring to see an infant monkey, since it had never seen its own face — a distinctive cue for identifying infancy, in the pictures — nor for its showing fear responses at pictures of threatening monkeys. Furthermore, when Sackett allowed other infant rhesus monkeys to look at one of several live adult monkeys of various species (in a more complicated apparatus known as the Sackett Self-Selection Circus), the infants generally preferred monkeys of their own species, and particularly females. Since the infants had been removed from their own mothers shortly after birth, had seen no other monkeys since, and did not resemble adults of their own species either in color or in facial appearance, their preferences are hard to explain as the result of learning (Sackett, 1970). Sackett seems to have found, as he suggests, clear evidence for certain rather general types of innate social response tendencies, both positive and negative, in at least one primate species. Whether similar innate tendencies are present in other primates will be answered by further research. Whether such innate response tendencies exist in humans may never be definitely known.

Is primate social behavior determined primarily by heredity or by environment? However dull or uncontroversial the answer sounds, it must be: by the interaction of both. As with various other organisms studied by ethologists, primate behaviors seem to have evolved in such a way as to interlock with the environment. Given certain environmental and social cues, certain heredity-based behaviors will emerge and will undergo subsequent modifications by the environment. Given a drastically different environment, such as a zoo or laboratory, these behaviors will emerge only in stunted, disorganized form, will emerge as perversions of "natural" behavior, or will be inhibited from development in any recognizable form. Primates differ from other organisms in that these emergent behavior patterns show more modifiability, more possibility of "cultural" variation as a function of variations in the social and nonsocial environment. This relatively greater modifiability itself suggests a major lesson about the basis of primate sociability: such sociability is not tied to one single factor or type of factor, but expresses a complex interaction of factors. Harlow's research has destroyed the idea that positive reinforcement from breast or bottle is the basis for human sociability; DeVore, Washburn, and other field researchers have finally overturned the idea that sex is the single key to primate sociability. These single-factor hypotheses may be good for generating aphorisms, or for starting a field of research on its way from infancy, or for giving the lazy writer convenient cubbyholes in which to fit his accumulation of disorganized facts. But we must now accept the necessity for far greater intricacy in our explanations of social life, among monkeys and apes as well as among ourselves.

40

the human primate:
generalizations to homo sapiens

How like to us is that filthy beast the ape.
— Cicero
De Natura Deorum

What does all this information about nonhuman primates add up to? Some scientists would argue that it's simply interesting in its own right, a description of yet another chunk of the universe; that science admits no scale of values which renders one topic more important than another; that we needn't worry about any further implications of our findings, as long as we understand monkeys or apes better than before; and that therefore you might as well study monkeys as, say, humans. I wouldn't dismiss such a position altogether, because I do find monkeys and apes interesting and entertaining in themselves — at least as interesting and entertaining as some people I've tried to study. But I'd still have to say that this is not enough: that at least as a social psychologist, and at most as a human being, I must search the nonhuman primate data for whatever information will help in understanding the world's most social primate.

I do not, however, fall into that small but intense crowd who feels that primateness is all — that mankind is ruled by his primitive primate passions, and that with knowledge of his evolutionary kinfolks' behavior we can plumb him to his depths. Nor am I, on the other hand, among those who, like the anthropologist Leslie White (1949), feel man to be so qualitatively superior to other primates that we can ignore them altogether. Though this may sound like mass-media mugwumpishness, I must conclude that neither extreme embodies the most tenable position, which of course I am now ready to offer, in four parts.

BIOLOGICAL SIMILARITIES BETWEEN
HUMAN AND NONHUMAN PRIMATES

Undoubtedly, the nonhuman primates resemble us more in physical form and physiological function than do any other organisms. So if we're to gain any useful knowledge about humans from animal studies, we might best turn to these primates. Experimental psychologists have long argued the validity of using rats as analogs for humans, because both organisms learn — both show persisting behavioral modifications as a result of experience. But beyond this similarity, without which any fairly complex organism in a very complex world couldn't exist, there's probably little important resemblance. Between the rat's slow modification of behavior after repeated trials and rewards, and a human's one-trial learning of a multitude of memories, there may be an unbridgeable gap. Köhler's

41

classic studies of "insightful" ape problem-solving (1927) suggest at least somewhat greater similarity in learning potential between us and other primates than between us and rodents. Greater similarities also seem to exist in such things as curiosity level (for most primate species) and amount of unstructured play — a worthwhile sort of behavior for incidental learning.

That we do need to turn to other species for certain information has already been emphasized. We don't permit ourselves to do certain things to humans, even in the interests of science, that we can do to captive monkeys. We can't find natural human social groups anywhere near so simple in structure as nonhuman primate social groups, and we can't create really primitive human groups artificially. But information about the effects of biological endowment on such simple social groups may be useful to us in tracing our own psychological history. Other primates have had to face some of the same problems as we, and have had some of the same opportunities, based on similar physical structure and developmental patterns. Both human and nonhuman primate infants, for instance, are born unable to care for themselves, and must have parental attention over a period of years to survive. This means there's a longer time in which learned behaviors can be passed from one generation to another, and in which opportunities for large amounts of social reinforcement abound. Also, the lack of efficient biological defense measures in both human and nonhuman primate adults means a greater necessity for mutual defense. Also — there are several dozen *also s*, based on such biological similarities as these. Some of the other primates' simple responses to such similar problems and opportunities may be the very ones with which we began our initially slow but gradually accelerating march to civilization.

ENVIRONMENTAL SIMILARITIES BETWEEN
HUMAN AND NONHUMAN PRIMATES

Certain nonhuman primates live in environments that appear similar to those in which man's immediate ancestors and early man lived, and in which man's basic social patterns may have developed. Man's direct ancestors may not have closely resembled today's primates, but some were arboreal, as most primate species are today. Early *Homo sapiens* very likely existed rather like present-day savanna baboons in many areas, traveling on the ground and hunting for food during the daytime, sleeping in trees at night. (Adolph Schultz [1961] has pointed out that many areas where early man lived had too few caves to maintain an adequate population of "cavemen.") Early man was not an individualist living in his own cozy hole or camping with his family under the stars. Most ground-dwelling primates live in groups; this is one of their major defenses against possible predators. If early man had a cave, he probably shared it; if he lived in the open, plenty of other men were around — at least if we can judge from what works for the baboon or rhesus. Man then gradually made various discoveries that enabled him to take advantage of other types of surroundings. But as with his biological structure, his early environment must have played a major role in forming the social patterns that gradually became elaborated into those we use now.

DIFFERENCES BETWEEN HUMAN AND NONHUMAN PRIMATES

Paradoxically, certain differences we observe between our social relationships and those of other primates may reveal more than the similarities about our own social psychology. Given somewhat similar biology and similar early surroundings, why are the nonhuman primates as different from us in behavior as they are? In trying to discover why these differences are so great, we may be able to develop questions about human social behavior that we'd never have imagined if we'd limited ourselves to studying only humans. Maybe later we can develop answers to these questions.

Perhaps the major questions, from which many answers may flow, are: Why can we talk when other primates can't? What is it about us in particular that has both allowed and compelled all human groups, even the most "primitive," to develop complex languages, while other primates have failed to go beyond a few dozen strongly stimulus-tied sounds and gestures? What differences did this crucial distinction make in the early as well as the later social life of man? The first of these questions has already received the beginnings of some convincing answers (Bastian, 1965; Lancaster, 1968). Other primates not only lack vocal apparatuses capable of complex speech, but also lack certain elaborations of brain structure characteristic of humans. Evolution apparently has not endowed them with such brains because in their environments and with their patterns of living, speech-enabling brains would be of little advantage. As with the howler, most primates can get enough to eat and drink, and a decent place to sleep, with hardly a "word" to or from their fellows. Even species that have the capacity to acquire a simple symbolic language, such as the chimpanzee (Gardner and Gardner, 1969; Premack, 1971), apparently have not utilized this capacity in the wild; and until they find such capabilities useful, evolutionary processes will not select animals whose linguistic capacity is unusually high. These answers still need a great amount of detailed research support; but already, by getting into the vital human topic of language, we can see how stimulating the differences between us and the other primates may be.

DIFFERENCES AMONG NONHUMAN PRIMATES

Perhaps even more paradoxically, the behavioral differences we find not between humans and other primates, but among the various species of nonhuman primates themselves, may help us understand our own be-

43

havior better by making us more reluctant to apply any findings about animal behavior directly to human behavior. I've already mentioned the frequent assumption that a human behaves like a slightly more complex rat. The assumption has also been made occasionally that any significant behavior found in wild primates will appear in some form in tame humans. These assumptions don't seem to include the recognition that because the many species of nonhuman primates show such wide ranges of behavior among themselves, no one behavior can be attributed to man until that behavior has itself been studied in man and established as part of his repertoire. Those who apply primate findings directly to man still fail to appreciate what primatologists have known for many years: that behaviors are species-specific, that species variability is not only physical but also behavioral and psychological. Some primates appear to defend a "territory"; some howl at others on sight; some don't care. Some monopolize mates, or monogamize them; others live in pleasant promiscuity. Some show distinct dominance structures; others display apparent democracy (though not necessarily with female suffrage). Some pass their babies around; others protect or overprotect. Out of all this, where is man? Who can say? Who dare try? Some do try — see the next section — but none should. Primate studies generate many questions about humans, and perform very usefully in that function. The answers should be obtained from humans themselves.

Even if the nonhuman primates were sufficiently cooperative to resemble each other more, we should not forget how much our generalizations from their behavior must be limited by their overwhelming differences from man. Not only their speech centers but their entire forebrains are vastly more limited than those of humans, not only in size (which may not be significant in itself) but in structure and function. The biological relationship is not as close as the fundamentalists fear; even the anthropoid apes cannot locate a common ancestor with us closer than one or two million years back. Nonhuman primate females do not naturally show continuous sexual receptivity; human females do, at least in a manner of speaking. Nonhuman primate babies never display that interesting evolutionary invention, the social smile, which certain stimuli will elicit automatically in human babies at ten to twelve weeks of age. When other primates do defend their "territory," they stop at its edge; they do not engage in crusades into enemy territory, defensively killing and raping the opposition. The search for novelty in other primates is not absent, but it is muted in comparison with man. Man's dissatisfaction apparently did not come from losing the easy availability of food and drink; that came *after* he was dissatisfied, and *because* he was dissatisfied, as the Good Book says.

We so often insist that every bit of knowledge discovered by science must mean something for humans, that it may be hard to accept the lack of such immediate meaning in research on primates or other animals. But again, the lack of direct applicability — the fact that I cannot list for you all the positive contributions that primate research makes to humanity — should not conceal its great heuristic value, its capacity for revealing to us important questions we must ask about the foundations of human social psychology. To know whether a particular motivation observed in gorillas also occurs in humans, how strong it is in humans, whether it may be strengthened or weakened or deflected and in what manner, we must turn to the empirical study of man himself, however much more complicated that may prove to be. But monkeys and apes, by their very unlikeness to us, will compel us to make this complicated effort.

instinct and logic: the ardrey approach

> *Prostitution (the offering of sexual favors in return for material benefits) exists in the animal world among the Primates. Since man is a Primate, we must therefore recognize that prostitution is a part of our over-all inheritance from our furry ancestors. As such, it can never be discarded as long as our species survives, no matter how much wishful thinking we indulge in. When a modern girl marries for wealth and/or status . . . she is simply obeying a powerful female instinct shared by our cousins the gibbons and monkeys and baboons for many millions of years. We can no more suppress prostitution than we can any of our other inherited instincts.*
>
> — Letter to *Playboy*, March 1967

Curiously, the increasing evidence for behavioral diversity among primates has been accompanied by increasing public acceptance of the idea that humans share certain basic instincts with nonhuman primates and other animals. In particular, Robert Ardrey's proclamation of man's "territorial imperative," described as "an inherent drive to gain and defend an exclusive property," has captured adherents all the way from the superpatriotic right to Eldridge Cleaver and the Berkeley radicals of People's Park.

Ardrey's professional background is in dramatic writing, but he has spent fifteen years studying the animal behavior research literature, and his knowledge of the field is impressive. However, this knowledge has not tempered his enthusiasm for styles of argumentation that his literary experience should have taught him to avoid, and for simplistic explanations of human behavior that would render any drama lifeless. Konrad

45

Lorenz (1966) and various other students of animal behavior have displayed similar shortcomings in discussing human social behavior; but the inadequacies of logic and evidence are particularly vivid in Ardrey's work. His favorite fallacies may serve as good examples of how not to approach human social psychology from the orientation of nonhuman behavioral observations.

NAMING AND EXPLANATION

Ardrey seems to assume, as did William McDougall (1908), that giving a name to a category of behaviors necessarily increases our understanding of those behaviors. Ardrey has so far argued that various organisms possess instincts for aggression (*African Genesis*, 1961), for territorial defense (*The Territorial Imperative*, 1966), and for dominance-submission relationships (*The Social Contract*, 1970). In each case, he applies these instincts to the discussion of human behavior mainly by repeated insistence that humans do have such instincts (e.g., "We act as we do for reasons of our evolutionary past, not our cultural present" [1966, p. 5]), and by citations of particular behaviors that he feels express these instincts ("If we defend the title to our land or the sovereignty of our country, we do it for reasons no different, no less innate, no less ineradicable, than do lower animals [1966, p. 5]). But what more do we know about the institution of private property, or the display of patriotic sentiments, after we are given Ardrey's new labels? We can surely do much to explain the existence of such behavior patterns by noting the daily usefulness of territorial possession to the individual owner, or the importance of nationalistic ideologies to the maintenance of the individual's acquired values. What more is added by such catchy words as "territoriality"?

Ardrey does suggest one line of evidence for human territoriality that might give the concept some explanatory usefulness. He cites animal data indicating that a territorial defender fights more vigorously the deeper it is into its own territory. He then argues that this "mysterious enhancement of powers which a territory invariably summons in its male proprietor" should give the owners of a family farm more energy to do their work than if they were merely paid workers on someone else's land (1966, p. 103). If such a "mysterious enhancement" of human energy could be demonstrated, Ardrey might indeed claim some advantage for his hypothetical instinct; he makes a valiant try, by comparing American family farm productivity with Soviet collective farm productivity. He fights a losing battle, however, with such complicating factors as the greater American use of modern farm machinery, the role of agricultural colleges and extension services in American farm development, and finally the increasing efficiency of America's large-scale, paid-worker agribusiness enterprises over the rapidly disappearing family farm. Sim-

46

ilar difficulties intrude when he claims that the arousal of ancient territorial instincts is reflected in the scientist's willingness to make "available to the art of murder the most intricate secrets of his trade" during wartime; in Ardrey's own personal distress over the bombing of Pearl Harbor; and in the valiant response of various peoples to the invasion of their homeland. In each case, too many complications of learning and material interest and personal values enter to make any predictive use of territoriality possible.

Ardrey also tries to use labeling as explanation in his postulation of three great needs that supposedly pervade all organic life: security, stimulation, and identity, in ascending importance. Territoriality, he says, satisfies the need for security, by supplying a place of retreat; the need for stimulation, since the animal can stroll up to its territorial borders any time and get into a lively fight with its neighbors; and, preeminently, the need for identity, by giving the animal his very own plot of earth to call home. Dominance hierarchies satisfy the three needs somewhat similarly, as does war; but love, Ardrey feels, is too boring to fulfill the need for stimulation, and it also exacerbates one's identity problems (1966, pp. 333–338).

What is the evidence for these three needs? Ardrey cites a scattering of ambiguous animal observations to support the first two. Had he but known, he could also have cited William Mason's experimental data (1965) on chimpanzees, as well as research on humans by such psychologists as David McClelland (McClelland et al., 1949) or Donald Fiske and Salvatore Maddi (1961), all of whom have hypothesized the organism's need to maintain an optimal level of stimulation, neither too much nor too little. The third need, identity, is proposed by Ardrey solely on the basis of his own inspiration, and I can think of no data from any source that would support its widespread existence among nonhuman organisms. Ardrey here relies upon rhetoric rather than data (1966, p. 171):

> The animal seeks to differentiate himself from all others of his kind . . .
> the social animal belongs to a group differentiated from all other groups;
> and within that group he requires a territory or a rank of status or a
> perching or resting place, acknowledged as his alone, which distinguishes
> him from all other members of the group. He has achieved identity.
> Through a fixed and unique relationship with something larger or more
> lasting than himself — the pebbles in a stream bed, the herd grazing on
> a slope — he has defeated the pressures of anonymity which myriad life
> continually brings to bear on the individual's psyche.

Or this (1970, p. 195):

> Why a Douglas fir will grow to its maximum height, why a chicken will
> struggle for her highest possible rank in the pecking order, why a man

47

will sacrifice fortune for fame . . . all are avenues to identity in one's own eyes and the eyes of others.

Ardrey might just as well have argued that all organisms, from the slime mold on up, have an immortal Christian soul. He would have explained about as much that way, and would have been able to call upon at least as much evidence. In the hands of such theorists as Erik Erikson (1968), identity has proven a useful concept in discussing human behavior; but extending the concept to plants and animals seems hardly more than a literary exercise.

IDENTITY BY ANALOGY

Ardrey does not usually take a human phenomenon such as identity and generalize it to animals; more often he works in the other direction. Either way, however, he is given to taking very different phenomena, applying the same term to all of them, and thereafter assuming — indeed, insisting in the most extreme terms possible — that they are identical. This amounts to making a crude analogy that by itself might be useful in helping the reader to understand a complex process, and then proclaiming that the analogy is in fact a simple description of truth.

One of the most misleading uses of this procedure is again in the realm of territoriality. The howler monkey and the gibbon display behavior more resembling territoriality than do most primates, and are used as two of Ardrey's main examples. But the gibbon's territoriality involves a single small family defending a space against other families; the howler's territoriality involves a group of as many as 40 or 45 individuals defending a space against other groups. With which kind of territoriality are humans supposed to be imbued? Ardrey vacillates between one and the other, without acknowledging his vacillation. At times he endorses private property and the family farm as embodiments of territoriality; at other times he speaks instead of a man's love for his country. If we are howlerlike in our territoriality, there is no reason to condemn (as Ardrey does) a completely communistic nation for its contradiction of human territorial needs. In fact, if this group form of territoriality requires only a defining of borders to determine how territoriality is expressed in the individual's thinking and behavior, we might define the entire world as our "territory" and all men as our territorial brothers, thus rendering the very concept of territoriality completely meaningless for humans. On the other hand, if our territoriality involves the gibbon's family attachment to a small piece of land, defended strenuously against close neighbors, there would be no basis for national feeling, for urbanization, for any sort of life other than that of the primitive homestead. Ardrey seems to side somewhat more with howler-type territoriality, judging from his rejection of the nuclear family as a basic primate pattern

48

and his discussion of the larger-than-one-family "biological nation" as the height of social development, analogous to the human nation-state. But his simultaneous defense of private property and the small farm indicates his continuing confusion. The confusion is only increased by his recent references (1970) to personal space (the distance that an individual prefers to maintain between himself and other individuals during social interaction) as "the portable territory," and by his assertion that maintaining symbolic or "psychological space" is sufficient to satisfy whatever needs the occupation of physical territory was originally supposed to satisfy.

An even more extreme confusion strips *aggressiveness*, a key word in Ardrey's books, of any significance. "What is aggressive is the disposition to dominate, to seek one's ends whether or not by forceful means," he says at one point (1970, p. 288). A page later, he throws caution to the winds:

> The force that presses on us is as large as all vital processes. . . . This is the aggressiveness that many would deny. It is the inborn force that stimulates the hickory tree, searching for the sun, to rise above its fellows. It is the inborn force that presses the rosebush to provide us with blossoms. It is the force, brooking no contradiction, directing the elephant calf to grow up, the baby starfish to grow out, the infant mamba to grow long. . . . The gasp for air, the grasp for the nipple, or if we are a newly dropped wildebeest calf, then the shaky following of our mother, represents for all of us the first commandment of independent life: that we come to terms with our environment. And so, as our bodies are born, our drive to dominate comes into overt being.

If indeed all vital processes from the grasp for the nipple to the bursting forth of the rose blossom can be called aggressiveness, who can deny Ardrey's thesis that man and beast and plant are all dominated by the drive to dominate? And, having agreed with Ardrey, who can then explain the exhibition of any one behavioral pattern rather than another by the concept of aggressive drive or power instinct? The word that means everything conveys no meaning at all.

RULES OF EVIDENCE

Ardrey often writes as if different rules of evidence apply to the study of human behavior than to animal behavior. He shows a weakness throughout his books for anecdotal reports or casual observations by amateur naturalists, rather than for the more careful and sophisticated studies of trained researchers. He has controlled this weakness more and more with regard to animal behavior, until in *The Social Contract* (1970) he depends largely upon data collected by eminently reliable observers who have used appropriate scientific procedures. (He still skimps over or ignores data he does not like, but he is perhaps only a little more guilty in this regard than many scientists.) Unfortunately he continues to rely, as far as human data are concerned, almost entirely on his own intuitions, personal emotional reactions, and admitted prejudices.

This is not entirely Ardrey's fault. Systematic observations of humans in their "natural" habitats are quite scarce, as the final section of this chapter indicates. Studies of human infants isolated from birth, which might provide evidence for the existence of unlearned territorial urges in the same way that Gene Sackett's studies of rhesus infants suggest innate social response patterns, are of course unavailable. Evidence for the selective advantage of territorial or dominance behavior during human evolution is also lacking, though Ardrey occasionally speculates about such possibilities. He is not responsible for the absence of such information on humans; but he is responsible for concluding, on the basis of extremely unreliable information, that human behavior is dictated by exactly the same processes as he sees in the animals for whom he has reliable data. He is also responsible for largely ignoring the anthropological, sociological, and psychological data, collected by other means than naturalistic observation, that often appear to contradict his central theses.

HUMAN AND ANIMAL MORALITY

Ardrey writes as if the same rules of morality apply to humans and to other animals. He frequently employs a pattern of argument in which he imputes human morality to lower animals, then insists that man is moral only when he behaves similarly to those animals whom Ardrey sees as moral. A notable example is his contrast between "the harshest of all primate authorities," the baboon oligarchy, center of "an authoritarian society of compulsion and compliance, threat and punishment," and on the other hand various truly territorial primate societies, which "tend toward the equalitarian, exhibit the lowest gradients of dominance, present the fewest examples of physical conflict or punishment, and while attaining a maximum of social solidarity and cooperation, sacrifice a minimum of what a human being would call personal freedom" (1966, pp. 221–223). In fact, this "voluntary association of partners" in the territorial society is said to possess "something resembling the personal dignity which man so prizes." A shining example of the territorial primate is, naturally, the noble and dignified howler, who "has achieved a most perfect inward amity," and within whose society "peace is unbroken," males refrain from attacking females, and "neither do females suffer from quarrels with each other." All this is in preparation for Ardrey's recommendation that humans recognize and live according to their own territorial instinct, on a nationalistic and capitalistic model.

A danger in imputing moral characteristics to nonhuman organisms is

50

that one's moral judgments may bias one's descriptions of animal behavior. As indicated previously, baboons do not live the life of harsh tyranny and frequent punishment that Ardrey (like Zuckerman before him) suggests. As for howlers, females *do* aggress against each other at times; so do males against females, males against males, adults against infants, juveniles against each other. Such aggressive behavior is infrequent and seldom becomes a serious matter, but occasional nipping and growling, slapping and biting do occur within the howler group. The statistical incidence of physical aggression among howlers may be significantly less than among savanna baboons; we do not yet have adequate statistical evidence that it is. Ardrey presents no such evidence, nor does he offer persuasive support for his general contention that nonterritorial monkeys are somehow meaner to each other than territorial ones.

Another difficulty with such discussions of animal morality is that one's definition of what is moral and what is not may change sharply with a simple shift in point of view. In *The Social Contract*, Ardrey has become much more admiring of primate tyranny. The territorial imperative now turns out to be only one aspect of the innate "drive to dominate." Another valuable aspect of this "will to power," according to Ardrey, is the establishment of social hierarchies, with the most distinguished primate practitioners being those previously nasty baboons. The "alpha males" or natural leaders of such social hierarchies possess an innate "magnetism" that holds the group together. Establishment of the dominance hierarchy supposedly reduces in-group fighting, and the alpha male provides the focus for the group's identity, thus satisfying the greatest need of all. Let us then go and live like the moral baboons.

The main problem with all this moral talk, of course, is that observations of what animals *do* hold no significance for what humans *should* do. Ardrey apparently feels that humans should own their own property; that they should avoid physical aggression toward those who respect their property rights, but should attack those who do not; that they should defer to individuals obviously more talented or "naturally dominant" than they. Because various animals behave as he thinks humans should behave, these animals are therefore moral, even if they have no choice in behaving as they do. And because moral animals are territorial, hierarchy-oriented, and aggressive only toward out-groups, humans should behave likewise. Such arguments culminate in Ardrey's discussion (1970, p. 404) of "the religion of animals, a set of assumptions accepted without question by an entire species." This is a topic about which you might wish sometime to consult your dog or cat.

EXCEPTIONS TO THE RULE

Finally, Ardrey appears to accept without question the old saw that the exception proves the rule. In science, no exception proves a rule; exceptions demand that the rule be modified or rejected. Ardrey often encounters clear exceptions to his sweeping hypotheses; but rather than changing hypotheses, he usually prefers to explain how a particular exception has no status anyway, or to ignore the exception altogether in his enthusiasm for more examples of the general rule.

In *African Genesis,* for example, Ardrey stated, "Every primate species so far studied — with the significant exception of the gorilla — maintains and defends territories." He explained the gorilla's annoying lack of territoriality by saying the animal was nearly extinct anyway, an evolutionary dead end — "a sorry paradox of architectural incongruities." By the time *The Territorial Imperative* appeared, many more primates had been studied which were not territorial, and this time Ardrey did modify his territorial rule to include dominance hierarchies: "An effective social organization in primate groups will be achieved through territory, or it will be achieved through tyranny. Contemporary research has revealed no third way." The amended rule was not, however, free of exceptions. As he admitted later in the same book, the chimpanzee displays neither territorial concern nor genuine tyranny. But the chimp, according to Ardrey, is "an evolutionary failure" just like the gorilla. The chimpanzee has, of course, survived until the present; and every wild mammal in the world besides and possibly including man may soon be extinct at the hands of man. Ardrey apparently has not seriously considered these points.

Exceptions to the territorial rule among humans are dismissed just as summarily. Ardrey suggests that the Jews have not displayed proper territorial responses, because so many went without protest to the gas chambers during World War II. They showed no aggressive reaction toward those who deprived them of life and liberty because, according to Ardrey, "what we have described as a Jew has been nothing other than a de-territorialized man." Once the nation of Israel was re-established, its Jewish inhabitants remained Jews no longer, but became truly territorial animals. The Italians were likewise poor at territorial defense during World War II, not because territorial defense is an acquired rather than an inborn response, but because Italy has never been a true nation. It is instead, Ardrey says, a society held together by the pleasures of intragroup hostility. France was apparently a true nation during World War I, so Frenchmen fought valiantly; but sometime before World War II, France too became a "society of inward antagonism," so the French lost their ability to repel territorial intrusion (1966, p. 238).

Ardrey's ingenious explanations for admitted exceptions to his hypotheses may divert our attention from many exceptions he fails to mention. On the animal level, evidence is increasing of substantial variation among nonhuman primates not only between but within species — evidence that the savanna baboon is not always compelled to develop strong dominance hierarchies, that the langurs who are nonterritorial and non-combative in one natural setting may aggressively invade neighboring home ranges in other settings, and so on. Among humans, the exceptions are surely endless. Ardrey attributes North Vietnam's ability to withstand the American onslaught to the extra strength given its inhabitants by an intrusion into their territorial space; but he is silent about the apparent lack of such extra strength among the South Vietnamese. Ardrey says that although the sense of territoriality is inborn in humans, the specific territory about which one feels territorial must be carefully taught. Why Ardrey now lives in Rome, rather than in the Chicago he presumably learned to love as a boy, remains a puzzling idiosyncrasy, unless his learning about art or income taxes has outweighed his learning about territory. The mobility of Americans in general is a mystery that he never discusses. He sometimes calls other primates "evolutionary failures" because they now occupy only a small area of the world. One could argue equally well that humans are successful in an evolutionary sense precisely because so many have been willing to give up their territory, to strike out into the unknown, to see what's beyond the next hill or the next ocean. Having a house, owning land, can serve useful functions; but humans seem in no sense bound to their property by any indissoluble link, and all the better for them.

Let me repeat: the behavior of our closest animal relatives varies so greatly, with regard to territoriality and social dominance as with everything else, that we cannot attribute any animal "instinct" to man on the basis of its being omnipresent in nature. In observing man himself, one is struck less by a uniform concern for some such aim as territory than by man's astonishing capacity for variation and innovation. Perhaps man does have a few vague inborn tendencies to develop some expression of certain general categories of behavior — territorial, social, aggressive, altruistic, who knows? But as Ruth Benedict (1934) wrote, such tendencies if they exist are mere "pin-point potentialities, and the elaboration that takes place around them is dictated by many alien considerations." Not only the diversity of human cultures, but the diversity of individual behavior patterns within each culture, should be sufficient evidence that any such potentiality can either flower in vast and motley profusion, or die unborn.

But hold on: maybe one overriding instinct *is* present in all the primates for Ardrey to write about, an instinct that all people should recognize as natural to the whole human race. Nearly every kind of primate I can recall (though I may have overlooked some, since right now I'm a little drowsy) works at getting food most of the morning, then knocks off for a rest and perhaps a quick nap sometime between 11 A.M. and 2 P.M. Therefore I propose that Robert Ardrey's next book be titled *The Siestal Mandate.*

53

the natural behavior of people: human field studies

Indeed, as most of us who work with human personality realize all too well, one has to forego experimental control long before one gets to the matters that are of real importance in psychology.

— Raymond B. Cattell, in J. M. Wepman
and R. W. Heine (eds.), *Concepts of Personality*

With few exceptions, the many years of laboratory experimentation on monkeys and apes have told us much less of consequence about primate behavior than the past decade of naturalistic studies. Roger Barker (1968) argues that careful studies of humans in their own usual surroundings, undisturbed by scientific manipulation or experimental interference, will also reward us handsomely. Barker sees the tons of studies of humans that involve some kind of control by psychologists as substantially misrepresenting human behavior. Laboratory control makes it appear that the human immediately emits a response to every stimulus, since the psychologist can demand or force the response; but Barker finds that humans usually respond overtly to only about half the social stimuli they encounter. In a classic experiment by Barker himself (Barker, Dembo, and Lewin, 1941), children who were experimentally frustrated often regressed to earlier behavior patterns. But many years later one of Barker's students, Clifford Fawl (1963), found that frustration actually occurs in the typical child's life infrequently, and when it does, it doesn't necessarily or consistently produce regression or any other predictable response. Barker (1965) suggests that studies of intelligence may also be giving us highly artificial data; despite the millions of intelligence tests taken, we have "almost no information about the intellectual demands the environments of life make upon people, and how people respond to the 'test items' with which they are confronted in the course of living."

MIDWEST, KANSAS

To remedy such serious shortcomings in our knowledge of humanity, Barker (along with Herbert Wright and several fellow researchers) set up a "field station" in a small Kansas town in 1947. It has been going ever since. "Field station" doesn't denote a special kind of architectural structure or equipment, but only the particular location where long-term scientific observations of behavior are conducted, somewhere out in the real world. Midwest, Kansas (a code name) was chosen as the location for the field station for several reasons. It was small enough to make observation of the town's entire life possible on a broad scale (pop. 750, including 119 children). It seemed representative of the "core American culture" (making an almost perfect score on a formal scale to measure that concept — and listen to a Rotary Club speech: "Midwest is but a step removed from the noise and discomforts and distractions and vices of the major centers. Midwest offers unexcelled opportunities for quietude of mind and growth of soul, for time to listen to the morning song of the brown thrush in the berry patch, the gay note of the meadowlark, and the whippoorwill's mournful note in the valley at eventide."). The town's citizens were favorable to the research, and the town was fairly close to the University of Kansas, where Barker teaches (Barker and Wright, 1955). Several of his coworkers actually took up residence in the town, as a vote of confidence and as a means of "leaving the natural habitat undisturbed" by hit-and-run studies from outsiders. The resident staff members participate in community life, not too much or too little — just enough "to achieve behavioral 'protective coloration.'"

A substantial amount of Barker's research time in Midwest has been devoted to answering such questions as just what constitutes a "behavior unit" or "behavior episode," the basic distinguishable element of observable behavior (he figures the 119 children of Midwest "engaged in about 100 thousand episodes of behavior each day, over 36 million in a year"), and listing the town's "behavior settings," discrete situations where particular patterns of behavior occur consistently. Midwest has 1,445 family behavior settings and 585 public behavior settings in all, the public ones centering on Clifford's Drug Store. A fascinating diagram and list of these public behavior settings is presented in Barker and Wright's *Midwest and Its Children* (1955), with hours of occupancy for each during a whole year: 18,525 hours for Clifford's Drug Store, 208 hours for Hopkins' Cream Station, 11,900 hours for the Saturday Night Dance. The occupancy patterns of private and public behavior settings seem almost a poetic description of the human condition: "The amount of time spent in community settings increased from infancy to adolescence, where it amounted to almost half the waking time of adolescents; it declined in adulthood and old age."

The really crucial parts of the Midwest research are extended minute-by-minute behavior records for specific individuals — all children so far, because adolescents and adults are more inclined to be skittish under observation. (The best seller of the century may be written when someone conscientiously applies Barker's observational techniques to adult sexual behavior, instead of depending on Kinsey's secondhand reports or Masters and Johnson's artificial laboratory studies.) Barker and his associates have done single full-day observations of twelve Midwest children who ranged from two to ten years old, plus various studies of shorter duration.

OBSERVATIONAL PROCEDURES

Barker's observational methods are in several ways strikingly similar to those used by observers of nonhuman primates. Rather than skulking behind the bushes, the observer stays unobtrusively near the subject, behaving in a friendly neutral fashion. The parents already know about the study, and the child himself is told what is going on; he may even have seen other children being studied. For thirty minutes at a time, the observer notes everything he sees the child do, where it happens, in what context it occurs, the child's apparent emotional reactions, and how he performs the action — resentfully, thoughtfully, enthusiastically. (In this last assessment Barker parts company with behaviorists and *nouvelle vague* novelists, because he feels that even a biased guess about internal reactions is better than no inference at all, and that the several biases of the several observers over a day may well cancel each other out anyway.) Then the first observer is relieved by a partner and goes off to dictate a more extended account of the thirty minutes of behavior he has seen, as well as being "debriefed" by another worker. After further additions to the record by each observer in turn (as many as eight or nine different observers in a day), the child's entire day-long record, fourteen or more hours of waking behavior, is assembled.

The amount of detail and the extensiveness of such a behavioral study are indicated by one published behavioral record, Barker and Wright's *One Boy's Day* (1951). Starting at 7 A.M. and ending at 8.33 P.M., 420 normal-sized book pages tell what Raymond Birch, seven years and four months old, did on April 26, 1949. As the book says, "It was a Tuesday. The temperature ranged from 61 degrees in the morning to 84 degrees in the afternoon. During most of the day the sky was partly overcast. Nothing out of the ordinary happened in Midwest during this day."

That beginning is auspicious — rather like a Truman Capote "fact novel," or an Andy Warhol movie. Unfortunately, a seven-year-old boy's day is, on the whole, of little interest to anyone besides himself:

> 7:03. He pulled on his right sock.
> He picked up his left tennis shoe and put it on. [Left sock had gone on at 7:01.]
> He laced his left shoe with slow deliberation, looking intently at the shoe as he worked steadily until he had it all laced.
> 7:04. He put on his right shoe.
> He laced up his right shoe. Again he worked intently, looking at the shoe as he laced it.
> His mother called, "Raymond, do you want an egg for breakfast?" in a pleasant, inquiring tone. Raymond responded very sleepily, "No." His voice showed no irritation or resentment; he just answered in a matter-of-fact, sleepy way, "No."

Things liven up a bit later in the day, such as at 10:27 when he knocks his pencil-box off the desk at school, or at 4:14 when a toy tire with which he's been playing almost rolls down the stairway leading to the ladies' restroom at the courthouse. But all in all, Raymond's day would win no prizes for excitement.

Nonetheless, Barker is quite right in claiming the importance of this kind of record — and claiming that it may be even more important in a hundred years than it is now. As he suggests, we'd probably be much better able to understand the influence of technological, political, and economic changes on human life if we'd had similar records of children's behavior at various points during the past several hundred years. We do not; but future psychologists and historians will, if the work of Barker and his colleagues continues.

CHILDREN AND PARENTS

Certain of Barker's findings, abstracted from the masses of data which the Midwest field station has collected, are of more immediate interest. Some of the results are not surprising: for example, children in Midwest interact much more with their mothers than with their fathers (Dyck, 1963). But others are unexpected: even when father is home from work, he has less contact with the child than does the mother and is relatively uninfluential in the child's behavior. He does play almost as much with his child as mother does, however, and "seeks to express himself" to the child more — seeks "to share his activities, his thoughts, and his feelings with the child." Perhaps Dad realizes the child doesn't know what he's doing most of the day, and wants to explain.

A child's life in Midwest seems rather more idyllic in quantitative terms than many psychologists would predict. Clifford Fawl, in his study of "incidents experienced as disturbing by children in their natural habitats" (1963), found that the study's twelve Midwest children averaged 5.4 disturbances per hour, most of them mild in intensity (only 3.2 per cent were rated as strong). Over 88 per cent of these disturbances lasted less than a minute. Barker and Wright's study of Midwest children (1955) also reflects a largely pleasant existence, with conflict involved in only about 5 per cent of social behaviors, and conjunction ("ordinary social intercourse without joint enterprise but with 'a meeting of minds'") accounting for 62 per cent. However, actual cooperation occurred only 3 per cent of the time. All these percentages, it might be noted, are similar to what one would likely find in howler monkey social life, though the howler has not received such close statistical treatment.

Barker and his associates have also opened a field station in Yorkshire, England, in a little town called Yoredale, similar in size and other characteristics to Midwest (Barker and Barker, 1963). This gives them a chance to make behavioral comparisons between American and British children, plus comparisons of child-adult relationships. They find, for instance, that British adults are four times as likely to deprecate, disapprove, or belittle children as Americans are; twelve times as likely to threaten punishment or scold children; twelve times as likely actually to punish; eleven times as likely to be "distant with children (unconcerned, indifferent, inattentive, unaware)." British children are more distant in turn, more polite, less affectionate to adults than are American children. However, on the whole, behaviors of British and American children, and their relationships with adults, show many fewer national differences than might be expected.

ENVIRONMENTAL PRESSURES

One particularly intriguing discovery, made both in the Midwest-Yoredale comparisons and in a comparison of a big and a small American high school, demonstrates the influence of the community environment upon the degree of community participation, among both children and adults (Barker, 1960, 1965, 1968). Yoredale has fewer behavior settings than Midwest, and almost twice as many people; so there are usually more people in any one Yoredale behavior setting. The big high school had more behavior settings than the small, but also many more students — so again, more people per behavior setting. Any behavior setting, according to Barker, exerts some pressure to behave; but the more people are there, the more can act only as onlookers, watching others do the behaving. That's just what happened in these two instances. Students in the small high school were more involved in group activities, filled important positions much more frequently, felt more challenged, generally felt they were accomplishing more of value to themselves, even though the big-school students had much more to do and many more facilities with which to do it. Midwest inhabitants — children as well as adults — also filled responsible positions more frequently than Yoredale inhabitants, were busier, undertook more difficult tasks. For example, "On the average, every Midwest adolescent acts in a play, works in a store, teaches a Sunday school class, plays in a basketball league game every three weeks; Yoredale adolescents occupy such positions every eleven weeks, on the average" (Barker, 1960).

According to Barker, these differences in activity occur not so much because the people in different settings have different internal motivations, as because any behavior setting holds "claims" on people that must be fulfilled; and the fewer the people to a setting, the more versatile and active they must be to meet these claims. The behavior setting is not a neutral arena where any behavior can take place; to some extent it limits and forces the kinds of behavior that can occur within it. People, Barker suggests, are the medium through which the behavior setting functions.

Barker speculates that the resourceful, independent American character has been shaped by the great number of "undermanned" behavior settings that have existed during the nation's development. "But now," he says, "things are changing. We are becoming a nation of overpopulated settings. It is likely that in the Midwests of the United States of America underpopulated settings are making their last stand" (Barker, 1960). And what happens when the population explosion really blows up, when all the behavior settings are packed? Will most of us sit around watching a few people behave on television, and will even those few on television spend most of *their* private time watching somebody else do something else on television? From the study of a couple of high schools, several Sunday schools and Rotary Clubs, and two little culturally related towns, I doubt that Barker has found all the answers to the question of why civilizations rise and fall. I doubt that overpopulation of behavior settings explains, for example, the fate of Rome. But he certainly has presented a provocative alternative to the speculations of Toynbee, Gibbon, and William F. Buckley, Jr.

OPPORTUNITIES AND CHALLENGES

Barker and his coworkers at the University of Kansas are not entirely alone in studying human behavior in naturalistic settings. Such researchers as Robert Sommer (1969) are busy observing people's use of space in libraries, classrooms, and other locales, partly in hopes of obtaining information that will promote better design of the human environment. Various researchers (see Craik, 1970) have been watching the travels of mental patients through the wards, in hopes that their "natural" behavior, uninfluenced by the psychotherapist's intervention, may reveal something useful about mental illness. William Soskin and Vera John (1963) have studied the spontaneous talk of adults over long periods, by attaching small radio transmitters to volunteers and setting them loose to interact in vacation resorts. (Unfortunately, the transmitting apparatus was not completely miniaturized, and an antenna sticking up from behind a person's shoulder itself causes a little spontaneous talk.)

These studies of natural human behavior — natural in the sense that it isn't dictated or directed by an experimenter, interviewer, or tester — do not at the moment represent the major wave in social psychology, or even the coming wave. They have so far delivered few major discoveries about human behavior. And they do have their own problems. For instance, the sheer volume of the data often leads Barker to resort to simplistic quantitative summaries, such as counting the hours spent on certain activities. Such quantification may misrepresent the intensity or the quality of concern. We may be fervently interested in something and give it rather little of our time, because of institutional pressures or culturally specified ritual duties — loving Bach, but spending more time driving to work. In such instances, greater use of subjective reports may be valuable, as well as more comparisons within categories instead of between: Bach versus Johnny Cash, rather than Bach versus bathing.

Barker does make certain quantitative distinctions regarding intensity of motives, but he needs to find better ways of representing and discussing the *qualitative* differences in behavior that, as he argues, the experimentalists have already too much ignored. (On the other hand, quantitative measures of Bach versus bathing, for instance, may give the lie to a person's conscious misrepresentation of his interests.)

So far, the contributions of such studies appear to have been mainly in methodology. They have prepared us for bigger studies to come, by developing ways of recording behavior units, isolating behavior settings, and discriminating among various behavior categories. Barker's initial inspiration seems to have come at least partly from ecologists and naturalists who study animal behavior; but his own methodologies have been developed to such an extent that the naturalists might now usefully turn to him. The study of nonhuman primates could benefit from his quantification methods, from his distinctions between self-initiated and other-initiated behaviors, from his techniques of comparing American and British children only in similar settings so that basic behavioral dispositions can be distinguished from environmentally initiated behavior differences (as different primate species have already been compared in a few studies), and in general from his attention to the interactions between physical environment and social behavior. Several of my earlier statements about primates were based on rough approximations of what Barker has closely approximated with humans — the amount of time spent in conjunctive social activity, the comparisons of aggressiveness between species — and such rough approximations for the other primates need to be honed down fine. It might also be worthwhile to compare the quantitative incidence and intensity of aggression in human groups versus other primate species, though here we get into another sort of problem with which Barker has not dealt successfully so far: the problem of indirect preparations for aggression, of great differences in level of overt aggression during official peacetime and official wartime — again, the general problem of human complexity. Perhaps now that he has developed so well the techniques for studying overt human behavior in natural contexts, he should start asking his volunteers afterward what they were thinking while he was studying them. You can't ask gorillas, but that's no reason to avoid asking humans.

Whatever their problems and however unproductive of dramatic discoveries they have been so far, Barker's studies are undeniably important. The experimentalists seem willing and eager to apply their laboratory findings to general human behavior, without knowing much of anything about nonlab behavior. People like Ardrey see patterns of territoriality and aggression in humans, without really looking at anyone but their friends and relatives, and even then only through a fog of preconception. Many important behavioral changes in our individual lives, which social psychologists might wish to study in connection with such broadscale phenomena as cycles of war and peace, birth rates or suicide rates, simply go unmeasured and unmarked by us all — changes in time spent with each other, in treatment of children, in preferred forms of affectionate display, and so on. Barker has gotten a really good start in dealing with such behaviors only in children, and the gaining of comparable information on adults will surely be a difficult process, particularly when it touches upon such potent subjects as sex, aggression, prejudice, and psychological defensiveness. But at least we have a start.

According to Barker (1968),

> psychologists know little more than laymen about the distribution and degree of occurrence of their basic phenomena: of punishment, of hostility, of friendliness, of social pressure, of reward, of fear, of frustration. Although we have daily records of the oxygen content of river water, of the ground temperature of cornfields, of the activity of volcanoes, of the behavior of nesting robins, of the rate of sodium iodide absorption by crabs, there have been few scientific records of how human mothers care for their young, how teachers behave in the classroom (and how the children respond), what families actually do and say during mealtime, or how children live their lives from the time they wake in the morning until they go to sleep at night.

Perhaps through the efforts of Barker and other researchers who share his concerns, we will not too long from now know as much about these human phenomena as about the incidence of grooming in baboons, of howling in the howler. We have no cause to alter the howler's cries or to increase the baboon's grooming. But the more we know of human life, the better we will be able to make it more than a tedious string of behavior units, largely determined by haphazard behavior settings.

3
everyday extremists

the right side of dallas:
a psychological inquiry

Folly is a more dangerous enemy to the good than malice. You can protest against malice, you can unmask it or prevent it by force. Malice always contains the seeds of its own destruction, for it always makes men uncomfortable, if nothing worse. There is no defense against folly.

—Dietrich Bonhoeffer
Letters and Papers from Prison

I once knew a Dallas woman in her late twenties — let's call her Mrs. Apperson — who dragged her husband and children to John Birch Society chapter meetings once a month. "I have had two honors in life," she told me gravely, "a proposal of marriage from a very fine man, and an invitation to join the John Birch Society, which accepts only people of intelligence, courage, and high moral character."

Mrs. Apperson's marriage was virtually without blemish. Not only did her husband join with her in Birch affairs; she assisted him enthusiastically in his duties as Republican precinct chairman. In an autobiographical sketch she wrote,

> The greatest shock and disappointment in my life was the realization that the communist plot the Birchers "rave" about, was not fantasy. We have tried to find error in the logic of Robert Welch; it is impossible — he is supported by history. . . . The majority of Americans, who regularly read *Life, Look, S. E. Post, The New Yorker,* and *Time,* know that I am "dangerous," "militant," "dogmatic," "unrealistic," "extremely queer," and "subversive" (for am I not a member of the John Birch Society?).

Unfortunately for my own preconceptions, Mrs. Apperson showed few signs of extreme queerness. She did enjoy telling people she belonged to the Birch Society, to see their reaction: "Their expression, it's very amusing, and they sort of do a double take, and sometimes it takes several months of thinking about it before they can venture to ask us why we joined." And she did talk about liking people "as specimens"; but so might any well-adjusted psychologist. She also kept a gun and a dog at home to protect herself, and "everytime I hear a sound, I go see what it is"; but so do many non-Birch Dallas housewives. Mrs. Apperson wasn't completely satisfied with life; someday when her children were older she wanted to resume her college education, which had been interrupted by marriage. But for the time being she found housewifery congenial, as long as it left her time to read everything published by the JBS. (For a while she had subscribed to *The Daily Worker* too, to learn President Johnson's plans in advance.)

With the modest exception of her political beliefs, Mrs. Apperson was a normal, pleasant, attractive woman. Even her politics were unexceptional until the year before I met her; previously, said Mrs. Apperson, "I didn't even know what conservative and liberal meant." She had realized only recently that her parents were Republicans, though "I suppose they brought me up to be conservative." They could hardly have anticipated the magnitude of their success.

Another Dallas acquaintance first came to my attention when he was reported to be recruiting members of his Sunday school choir for the Birch Society. This moral gentleman, whom we might call Mr. Baldwin, turned out to be a JBS chapter leader. He was also a Republican precinct chairman, having become aware of "the danger this country is in at the present time" only during the Goldwater presidential campaign. That election night "really was like a nightmare to me. . . . After that I couldn't sit still and not do anything about it any more." So he sent in a coupon he clipped from a JBS advertising supplement in *The Dallas Morning News*. Mr. Baldwin held a college degree, an advanced white-collar position in a national corporation, and a responsible lay position in his church. Yet, he said, "I am viewed today, by the opinion molders and attitude makers of society, such as newspapers, T.V. and radio commentators, important members of government, as an extremist, right wing fanatic, hate-monger, war-monger, etc., since I still believe firmly in God and our U.S. Constitution."

Mr. Baldwin's father was also well-educated, a professional man, "firmly Christian and pro-American," and had never objected to Mr. Baldwin's JBS activities: "I think he cares that much about me that he would tell me if there was something that's bad" about the organization. Mr. Baldwin's late mother had felt likewise, though she was "not as serious" about politics as his father; his own wife could be described similarly. Other than Birch activities, Mr. Baldwin's favorite spare-time pursuit was playing and reading with his children. He felt they respected and loved him, but he said they required firm discipline, "since both are very active and healthy."

Mr. Baldwin told me, "A democracy is the most vicious type of dictatorship there is." Asked for a definition, he said, "A democracy is where 51 per cent of the people can get together in a group over here and say okay, we're going to vote to strip the other 49 per cent of all of the rights and everything they have. That's where you have democracy. Which in this country we're degenerating very rapidly into now, by letting anybody vote who can't even write their name." He felt "this whole civil rights thing is a fraud," but said no, the Communists haven't infiltrated it: "They control it, they've created it."

Mr. Baldwin displayed no signs of psychological abnormality, except perhaps a little grandiosity of thinking. After describing the ideal government he said, "I would hold, *if necessary*, a high position in this government, but I would prefer not to" (his emphasis). He worried that he was too introverted, but he came across as a big-talking extroverted Texan. He thought perhaps he'd like to go into business for himself (he was in his early thirties), but found his present job generally satisfactory. If you made clear at the start that you had no plans to join his Birch chapter or his church, Mr. Baldwin would probably make a good neighbor.

VOLUNTEER RECRUITMENT

Neither Mrs. Apperson nor Mr. Baldwin were among my neighbors in Dallas. During the years that I taught at Southern Methodist University, most people in my social circle were at least willing to give democracy an even break, and several were solidly liberal. One neighbor did have a vast pile of low-grade rightist tracts stored in his apartment, and eagerly handed out free copies to me and the rest of the neighborhood; my favorite barbecue stand was run by one of the state's most radical rightists. But it generally doesn't pay to use one's neighbors or restaurateurs as research subjects, and I didn't.

In Dallas, however, the student of extremist politics can eliminate personal acquaintances and still have a vast research population. Dallas may not be the most rightist urban area in the United States; I'd give either Houston or California's Orange County the edge. But with H. L. Hunt, Major General Edwin A. Walker (U.S.A., Ret.), Dan Smoot, *The Dallas News*, and the Southwestern Regional Headquarters of the John Birch Society as leading attractions, it seemed to me a prime location to study the psychology of rightist extremism.

Nevertheless, you can't just walk up to a JBS chapter chairman and say, "Hi, I'm a psychologist, I'd like to study your members." Bircher legend has it that psychologists are out to send all true patriots to a mental institution in Alaska, or at least to hook American youth on a diet of pornography, pot, and permissivism. A few researchers have circumvented the Birchers' queasiness by infiltration, by sending their clean-shaven graduate students out to join the local chapter. But this procedure usually yields only information on what goes on at meetings (very little) and what Birchers say (the same old things), not what they think or feel or how they got that way. One group of social scientists attended a rightist convention and handed out questionnaires, but the returns were probably somewhat unrepresentative, and the questionnaires were limited in content. They'd have to be, or hardly anyone at a rightist convention would answer them.

Instead, I read the letters-to-the-editors columns of the Dallas newspapers for several months — a painful experience, after a while — and clipped any letter with a far-right tone and a local address. (*The Dallas News,* which fancies itself as a sort of Southern Baptist *New York Times,* also prints frequent rightist letters from such remote locations as Birmingham, Alabama, and Conway, Arkansas.) My criteria for far-rightedness were based on current social scientific definitions: belief in substantial infiltration or control of major American institutions by Communists; advocacy of extraconstitutional, extralegal means to achieve rightist political aims. I excluded letters that were solely segregationist; racists and rightists overlap, but not entirely. Letter-to-the-editor writers as a whole differ in certain ways from the ordinary population, according to several studies; but the differences did not seem crucial for my research. The Birch Society in particular may contain very few non-letter-writers, since all members are given monthly assignments to write to newspapers about specified topics.

Once I had a list of names, I started sending out letters myself. Again, I couldn't very well start off by saying, "Since you're an extreme rightist, would you please appear at my office tomorrow." So I capitalized on a concern I share with many rightists: the questionable validity of the short-answer opinion questionnaires so much used by professional pollsters. My letters began:

> You are probably familiar with recent criticisms of public opinion polls (the Gallup Poll, the [Texas] Belden Poll, etc.). These polls have been criticized for asking questions which could be easily misinterpreted, for not allowing a person to clarify his answers, and for other things. As a social psychologist interested in opinions, I personally feel that some of these criticisms of opinion polls are correct. But little scientific research has been done to find which criticisms are accurate, and whether the polls should be changed in some way or restricted to private use.

Then, after making clear that I'm the type of psychologist who studies *normal* people, the plea: "Volunteers are needed for this scientific research project. Because you are active in community life, or have recently expressed your opinions to a local newspaper, I am asking for your assistance." This assistance consisted of coming to my office for three two-hour sessions of questionnaire answering and interviews; a modest financial inducement was offered in return. No mention was made of my interest in extreme rightists, and in fact the letter was sent to a number of liberals as well, since I needed a comparison group to make sure whatever I found about Dallas rightists wasn't true of Dallasites in general. (I wanted a comparison group of extreme leftists, but if any such crittur existed in Dallas at that time, he didn't show himself to the local newspapers.)

This appeal seemed quite persuasive. Over half the right-wing men to whom the letter was sent agreed to participate, and over 60 per cent of liberals, men and women. Only about 18 per cent of the rightist women volunteered; whether they feared rape, brainwashing, or that Alaskan boobyhatch wasn't clear. At any rate, the overall response level was surprisingly high, considerably reducing the danger of selective bias. Perhaps the nonvolunteers of both sexes included a disproportionate number of *really* far-out rightists, afraid to talk with any representative of the normal world; but other nonvolunteers may have been among the less involved, belonging to rightist groups mainly for social reasons and not interested enough to discuss their opinions at any length. Most who actually came appeared suspicious at first, but warmed up when they found I wouldn't argue back and wasn't a government agent. (One young man spent about as much time questioning me as vice versa, because he was sure I belonged to some nefarious liberal cabal such as the Ford Foundation. He was never quite convinced otherwise, and remained in the study only after much coaxing; he said as little as possible. On the other hand, one liberal lady took a good look at the first questionnaire, decided too many "Birch-type" statements were included to be a coincidence, and walked out, despite my graduate assistant's protestations of our innocence.)

The first time each volunteer came in, my assistant gave him a series of questionnaires: typical public opinion poll items on various social and political issues, measures of "pre-Fascist" tendencies and racial prejudice, and a political knowledge quiz. A week later, I gave the volunteer a TAT (Thematic Apperception Test), which involves making up stories to fit a set of ambiguous pictures, designed to reveal basic motivations and concerns. (I also gave a few volunteers the Rorschach Inkblot Test, but it seldom revealed enough to be worth the time.) During the second and third sessions, I also questioned volunteers extensively about their political and related opinions, taking off from their earlier questionnaire responses; and asked for certain personal information, including a written autobiography. All this was designed to indicate how extreme these people were, on what issues and for what reasons (Elms, 1969).

RIGHTISTS OUTSIDE THE BIRCH SOCIETY

A majority of the extreme rightists whom I studied were not Birchers. One gentleman, whom I'll call Mr. Field, said the JBS couldn't "do anything but help bring greater awareness on the part of the American voter to the true consequences of the actions of many of the people now in high places of the government as well as the so-called Communist element," but added, "The trouble is that those kinds of organizations have a tendency to pull in the lunatic fringe." He felt he hadn't missed much by not belonging: "I've only seen two of their publications and they were borrowed. I didn't spend a particularly great amount of time on them. Most of the stuff I saw I already knew, put it that way. It was nothing new to me and therefore with a limited amount of time I more or less skipped through it."

Mr. Field argued, as Mr. Baldwin had, that the civil rights movement was run "to a great extent by racial agitators who laid down the plan thirty years ago, thirty-five years ago" as "part and parcel of the great so-called proletariat revolution." He believed a conspiracy of "people in New York" was responsible for "processing the mentality, the mental attitude of the American people" to accept Castro's takeover of Cuba, the Communist takeover of China, and the attempted Communist takeover of the Congo. Rather than being "processed" by the mass media, he read "weeklies and bi-monthlies which are privately circulated." He had stopped going to church "because unfortunately so much of what I heard being said made me a little upset, so I got mainly into abstaining from church going but still being religious so-to-speak." Instead he read *Plain Truth* magazine ("Gosh, it's so right, how could it be wrong?") and listened to radio sermons by Garner Ted Armstrong, who "has more to offer than most of the preachers in the pulpits who are discussing sociological phenomena and things so unrelated to religion, even going so far as to inject political matters into the pulpit." Mr. Field was retired from military service and was now working in an executive business position. He displayed no noticeable peculiarities, other than still being single at forty-two.

Another non-Bircher, a lady in her early thirties, I'll call Mrs. Stevens. Her favorite extrafamilial activity was the round of speeches she delivered to ladies' clubs and PTA's about the impending loss of our freedom via the graduated income tax and creeping socialism. With several other women she had handed out leaflets to shoppers, blaming "wasteful government spending" rather than greedy grocers for higher food prices; she had testified at state hearings that certain high school textbooks were

67

socialistic; and she was active in local Republican politics. Her spare time was filled with rightist books, Communist books (for kicks), and tapes of rightist speakers. Mrs. Stevens had a college degree, had built "a good life" with her husband, didn't like housework but said she was trying to give her children a good home. She felt her attitudes toward society had been particularly influenced by the last few verses of Matthew 25: "Inasmuch as ye did it not to one of the least of these, ye did it not to me."

An oil man, who'll be called Mr. Downey, said he had his first big strike when he was thirty and had since hit eighty-six dry holes straight. He said he knew JBS members — "architects, lawyers, engineers, all of 'em are well-educated people" — but was coy when I asked whether he belonged too. The point was academic. He included Lyndon Johnson in the "extreme left wing," thought "most professors and most preachers have embraced the rather radical left wing," and said, "Fulbright speaks of shades of gray. . . . I think that gray is dirty white." He felt somebody had "sabotaged" Goldwater's campaign, "somebody besides the Democrats." He believed the admission of Communist China to the United Nations was a "damn moot question. What the hell, the Communists have control of the United Nations anyway, so what difference does it make if another Communist nation's in there?" He complained that following the 1964 election, "we have what you can call a true democracy, that's true: there's 60 million people, 60 million voters that are ruling the other 27 million, whose ideas are given absolutely no consideration." (Twenty-seven million people voted for Goldwater.)

Mr. Downey seemed particularly sensitive to government regulation of business, specifically the oil business. He said he'd become a conservative when the Wagner Act was passed, establishing the National Labor Relations Board. But he also referred to his reaction when, as a GI in Germany during World War II, he saw the Russians

> beat old men and women and force them into trucks, there in Germany, take them back to Russia. Their people had been captured by the Germans, taken to Germany as slave laborers, lived there for a number of years. The Russians sent a detail over to round those people up and take them back to Russia. I saw those people screaming, crying, begging not to be put in those trucks. I saw the Russian soldiers beat them with the butts of guns and force them in, all back to Russia.

Mr. Downey had graduated from college before the war. He said his major was "playing poker, shooting dice, having fun. B.B.A., run and play with B.B.A. [Bachelor of Business Administration]. I didn't learn a cockeyed thing, I don't think." He had wanted to be an engineer, his father insisted on business, and now that his own sons and daughters were in college, Mr. Downey was letting them make their own career

68

decisions. He believed his children "think of me as affable, too easy going, and perhaps not too bright. Believe they are fond of me in spite of not having too much respect for me." He was indeed an affable, voluble man, with a rich sense of humor. He'd had a "very satisfactory married life and I wouldn't change partners if I had it to do over again." He had gone through several extreme ups and downs in the oil business, but showed little bitterness or frustration; he was still hard-working on the job, relaxed and generous off it. His occasional outbursts of hostility were directed only toward the remote federal government and toward people he didn't know, such as college professors and the Reds.

As with the Birch lady who began this chapter, so it was with the rest of these Dallasites: only their political stance struck me as strange. Otherwise, in the words of another rightist volunteer, "All the people that I know that belong to the Birch Society work for a living, and most of them go to church regularly and they have children and go out and water the lawn. You know they're not running around bombing houses and making midnight phone calls." Or as a matronly lady told me, "All the people I know that belong to that society are very nice people. I mean, really, they are. I can't see where they are really radicals or going around doing anything awful. All they're doing is trying to promote patriotism." Or as Barry Goldwater was fond of saying about the Birchers (quoted in Frommer, 1964), "They are the finest people in my community. . . . Birch members are generally impressive, intelligent people."

PSYCHOLOGICAL DIFFICULTIES
However, not all the rightists I interviewed would make as good an advertisement for Mental Health Week. Several had relatively mild or well-controlled psychological problems; two were in worse shape. Among the former was a gentleman whom I'll call Mr. Hansen. Mr. Hansen believed that Eleanor Roosevelt was a member of ninety-one Communist organizations; that she sent diplomatic notes to Canada to allow entry for couriers "carrying the money for the Communist Party in the United States," as much as $400,000 at a time in counterfeit bills printed in England; that she personally assisted Julius and Ethel Rosenberg in having an atomic bomb mechanism dismantled, "taken through North Dakota and over the North Pole" to Russia. Mr. Hansen did not make up this story from whole cloth; he said he'd heard it (with supporting evidence) from "the head of naval intelligence" at a closed-door briefing of defense plant personnel in 1945. Mr. Hansen had previously been a Democratic precinct worker for thirteen years, but he accepted the story immediately and "just flipped over" from Democrat to Republican.

> At the time, being an admirer of Roosevelt, you can imagine how you'd feel. I was in my thirties and idealistic, and to have this guy get up and

just make all these statements that Eleanor Roosevelt was the center of Communist activities in the United States, and she was independent of Franklin Delano Roosevelt, she was the stronger of the two, it was through her direct intervention that they had stolen the atomic bomb from us — Ye Gods! . . . It was something that I'll remember, I guess, as long as I live.

Mr. Hansen was usually quite a jovial character. At the time I talked to him, he held a responsible position in a religious and charitable organization: "Most of my work is dealing with people, and I believe that I enjoy this work more than any other I have ever done." He was happily married (after an earlier divorce) and was well pleased with his children. He was a member of the John Birch Society, but had refused to work either for the JBS or the Republican party during the Goldwater campaign because he felt Goldwater was not a "true conservative." Mr. Hansen's father had been dead for many years, but if he were still alive Mr. Hansen felt he would be considered an "ultraconservative." His mother, whose active life at eighty he took great delight in describing, was "ultraliberal"; that is, she thought "medicare and all those programs . . . are great things."

Mr. Hansen did have one psychological abnormality: periodic feelings of intense depression, which he felt might be hereditary because his father had had them and because "health or money can't be blamed." He had learned to live with these feelings; when he felt a spell coming on, he turned to methodical, nonsocial work, and waited out the two or three days the depression lasted. A curious affliction, but apparently not serious; and these episodes appeared to have had no influence on his political beliefs.

Mr. Maxwell had greater problems. He was desperately afraid the collectivists had already taken over the country; he spent virtually all his spare time reading extremist tracts, attending extremist lectures, and writing bombastic letters to the newspapers. All this began shortly after (he said) his mother wrecked his marriage, got him fired, and drove him to consider suicide. He had publicly threatened to kill himself, but when that didn't help, he began seeking "answers" in the public library, until he stumbled across a book of rightist essays. He had since become a devout believer and propagandist, but still felt he was "desperately in need of a psychotherapist" to help him "strengthen my pride, my self." Even in delivering his tirades against our collectivized society, against virtually everyone who didn't agree with him completely on the desperate shape of the nation, Mr. Maxwell was terribly fearful that he was creating a bad impression, that he wasn't convincing, that he was not communicating his ideas clearly. He was right.

Then there was a man I'll call Mr. Whiteside. He'd never felt any particular interest in politics until, in his early sixties, he broke his hip

70

and had to quit his job to convalesce. With time on his hands he dropped in on something called the National Indignation Convention, and thereafter

> began to get literature, I began to get what you can't get from the newspapers and the radio and television. If you get any information regarding anything that is pro-American in the way of fighting the world conspiracy, you've got to take it from the grapevine . . . patriotic organizations such as the Christian Crusade, the Christian Nationalists, the Christian Anti-Communist Crusade and of course, the National States Rights party.

He attended Birch Society meetings for a couple of years, but didn't join since he couldn't afford the dues. He had since come to believe the JBS to be a front for the International Zionist Conspiracy, directly financed by prominent Jewish bankers.

Mr. Whiteside got through half of *Mein Kampf* before it was due back at the library, was greatly impressed, and became a hanger-on and general handyman for the Dallas chapter of the American Nazi Party — distributing leaflets, picketing Jewish speakers, publicizing appearances of George Lincoln Rockwell. I haven't heard from him since Rockwell's assassination, but if the Dallas Nazis have broken up, I'm sure Mr. Whiteside has managed to find congenial activities. Even at the time of his greatest participation in Nazi affairs, his interests were diversified; he spent several hours a week actively fighting income taxes and fluoridation, both as Communist/Jewish plots.

Mr. Whiteside's background differed somewhat from that of the other rightists I've mentioned. He'd had a spotty education, had worked at low-level jobs all his life, and even owned a criminal record, having been given a long-term suspended sentence and a large fine some years back for hitting a neighbor over the head with a crowbar. Self defense, he said. His relationships with brothers and sisters had been extremely bitter and occasionally violent throughout his life; as for his own children, "they resent my participating in patriotic programs and activities. For all practical purposes, we are now under communism, but they are so brainwashed with the Jew controlled news media that they refuse to believe the ridiculously heinous things planned by the world wide Jewish conspiracy for our beloved Nation." My other rightists also resented people like Mr. Whiteside. His is the type, they said, that gives extremism a bad name.

Does Mr. Whiteside really have anything in common with, say, our good housewife Mrs. Apperson, other than their antipathy toward communism? We need to build up to that question slowly, so let's save it for later. A simpler question: do radical rightists have anything in common with the lower primates who dominated our previous chapter? You might spot a few apparent similarities: the chest-pounding of gorillas, the

71

howlers' roars at strange members of their own species, a certain rigidity of thinking in all three. But the real similarity lies in social psychologists' frequent attempts to achieve a little perspective by studying organisms different from the common ordinary run of mortals. When we look at human beings in their everyday average complexity, it's terribly hard to discern how our biological inheritance bears upon our current behavior, or how we developed such intricate structures as our present set of political attitudes. Find a monkey or a volunteer different enough, and the complexity may be sufficiently simplified, the basic influencing factors sufficiently delineated, to give us our first toehold on understanding.

Indeed, rightist extremism has appeared so simple to many writers that both the professional literature and popularized treatments abound with "explanations" of the phenomenon. But the explanations have been astonishingly short on facts; few psychologists have studied real extremists up close. The tendency has instead been to pontificate upon the public utterances of extremist leaders, which may not be at all indicative of what the bulk of their followers (or even they themselves) think. It's one thing to live out your extremism on stage, to get paid and wined and maybe womaned for it. It's quite another to go about your daily life thinking extreme thoughts and making extreme statements with nothing much coming to you in return, except perhaps an occasional punch in the mouth. The motives of such "everyday extremists," the bulk of the rightist movement, are both harder to understand and potentially more interesting than those of the Robert Welches and Billy James Hargises, who derive obvious benefits from their eminence. The everyday extremists may ultimately help us to understand, in spite of themselves, not only how their own radicalism was born and nurtured, but how our political processes as a whole can be shifted toward a new rationality.

the little old lady in tennis shoes and how she grew: theories of rightist extremism

No, his discomfort was not of a political nature and must have had deeper roots, down in one of those reasons which we call irrational because they are buried under layers of self-ignorance.

— Guiseppe di Lampedusa
The Leopard

The least sexy *Playboy* cartoon in recent memory had a bearded analyst showing a Rorschach inkblot to a middle-aged man, who pounds on the analyst's desk and shouts: "I see creeping socialism, chiselers on relief and the erosion of fiscal integrity in government!"

I didn't laugh; it sounded too familiar. Not long before the cartoon was published, I had interviewed Mr. Whiteside, my Dallas Nazi, beginning with the Rorschach test. To reveal a rather unrevealing clinical secret, most people see a large chunk of the test's first inkblot as a bat. Hermann Rorschach could hardly have done better if he'd dipped a real bat in ink and slapped it onto the card. But when I held it out to Mr. Whiteside, he immediately responded, "It looks like an eagle." Pause. Then: "It looks like the U.S. emblem." And when I gave him a sheet of tracing paper so he could trace what he saw, he sketched the Great Seal of the United States — eagle, shield, and all.

PROJECTION AND DISPLACEMENT

Mr. Whiteside and the *Playboy* cartoon both exhibit a process that is central to the most popular psychological theory of rightist extremism. If the inkblot doesn't really show creeping socialism or the Great Seal, then the person who sees it that way isn't describing it realistically — he's projecting his own concerns onto the blot. If a rightist sees Reds under his bed and Communist conspiracies in the White House, with no reliable information to support his views, chances are he's engaging in projection on a wider scale, projecting his own private problems onto the whole political scene.

Sigmund Freud (1896) first developed the concept of projection, describing it as a process of defending oneself against disturbing self-knowledge. He also discussed (1894) a related psychological defense, displacement, in which a person redirects an emotion from its appropriate object to an inappropriate one, again for self-protection. Projection and displacement are often used simultaneously: if your long-haired son is insufferably insubordinate, but you can't beat him up for fear of what your wife and friends would think, you may begin to view all hippies as violent anarchists and take fierce delight in excoriating them.

Freud did not apply these concepts directly to the individual's acquisition of a political ideology. That was left to Harold Lasswell, a political scientist trained in psychoanalysis. By locating former political figures in mental institutions and by applying psychoanalytic interview techniques to active politicians serving as anonymous volunteers, Lasswell was able to probe far more deeply into the private motivations of politically oriented persons than anyone had before. He came up with a neat formula: $p \} d \} r = P$, which means that private motives are displaced onto public objects and then rationalized in terms of the public interest, to produce the conscious behavior and attitudes of the Political Man. As Lasswell saw it in his first book, *Psychopathology and Politics* (1930), virtually any important political orientation could be traced to repressed infantile motives.

One of Lasswell's case histories, the case of F, is particularly instructive because it involves a man who would today be considered a radical

73

rightist. Lasswell called him a "soldier-patriot." After an early career in the Army and the Secret Service, F was given command of a group of secret military police during World War I. When fellow officers interfered with his policies, he began to complain that someone was putting ground glass in the camp bread, and that camp officers were in league with the Germans. He was referred to a psychiatrist, who apparently didn't help; soon after, F went on the lecture trail. "The enemies of his country were his enemies, and he denounced them up and down the land. . . . F was a moving spirit in the opposition to the covenant of the League of Nations because the name of God was not mentioned in it. His argument on the point is said to have impressed President Harding." Projection and displacement worked well here, according to Lasswell: F was able to dispense with his symptoms of personal persecution "by reinforcing his identification with the interests of the nation and God, and displacing his suspicions upon more generalized foes."

In F's case, Lasswell saw fairly immediate causes for the persecutory feelings that were redirected onto political objects. In other cases, involving various political beliefs and activities, he looked further back. Contemplating "the prominence of hate in politics," for instance, Lasswell suggested that "the most important private motive is a repressed and powerful hatred of authority, a hatred which has come to partial expression and repression in relation to the father." This pattern of the child turning repressed father hatred outward onto political authority figures may or may not be the most important basis for political behavior, but it has certainly become the most widely used formula for tracing the influence of displacement and projection in political extremism, both right and left.

In *Psychopathology and Politics* and later works, Harold Lasswell was very helpful in redirecting attention from the classic and simple-minded political science view of political man as essentially rational, toward a view of political behavior as shaped strongly by private and often irrational motives little related to the actual "issues" or even to the actual "personalities" of politics. Unfortunately, Lasswell's approach was itself too simplistic: he found it hard to credit political activity with any basis other than those primitive unconscious motives that were central to Freud's early theories. Freud had already introduced important revisions into psychoanalytic theory even before Lasswell's book was published (Freud, 1926), and the revisions tended to emphasize the conscious, reality-oriented elements of behavior that Lasswell so heavily discounted. But it was Lasswell's view of Freud, rather than Freud's own developing ideas, that largely infused psychological approaches to political behavior, particularly extremism, during the next two decades. Even a biography of Woodrow Wilson presumably coauthored by Freud in the 1930's, but apparently written almost entirely by William Bullitt (Freud and Bullitt,

1966), saw the overriding mark of childhood experience in every manifestation of what was said to be Wilson's extremely moralistic and egocentric approach to world politics. This pattern was used by many more writers than Bullitt: take a politician or a political movement, usually one you abhor, and search for the underlying motives not in any realistic current concerns, but in Oedipal hang-ups and unsatisfied dependency needs and anal fixations.

The main variations in political psychologizing up to 1950 were rather banal accounts of group suggestibility and political instincts dating back to McDougall's primitive social psychology, or occasional oddities such as Wilhelm Reich's revelation (1946) of the origins of fascism. Reich, an apostate psychoanalyst, saw personality as consisting of three layers: a superficial social layer, in which "the average individual is restrained, polite, compassionate and conscientious," and whose political expression is liberalism; a middle layer, presumably the Freudian unconscious, which consists of "cruel, sadistic, lascivious, predatory and envious impulses," and which is expressed in fascism; and the deepest layer, or "biological core," in which "man, under favorable social conditions, is an honest, industrious, cooperative animal capable of love and also of rational hatred," and which produces "all that is genuinely revolutionary, all genuine art and science." All this becomes entangled with Reich's worship of orgasm and his hostility toward the machine age, until we ultimately learn that "fascist mysticism is orgastic longing under the conditions of mystification and inhibition of natural sexuality." Reich's view was not persuasive to most psychologists, though it appears to have been partially resurrected in recent years by the further reaches of the New Left.

THE AUTHORITARIAN PERSONALITY

Psychoanalytically based explanations of rightist extremism, particularly in terms of Lasswell's emphasis on repressed hostility toward the father, reached their full flower in a 1,000-page book called *The Authoritarian Personality*, written jointly by sociologists, social psychologists, and psychoanalysts (Adorno et al., 1950). The book reported a large-scale postwar study of the kinds of persons who would be most susceptible to Fascist movements in the United States. The Fascists had been beaten abroad, but the authors feared the possibility of an internal takeover much as had happened in Germany, and wanted to know both whether potentially Fascist personalities were present in significant numbers in American society, and what produced such personalities. Little effort was made to suggest the social or political conditions that might lead to Fascist control of America; the assumption was that men on white horses were always available, and that the crucial variable was how many ordinary people would respond to their call. The researchers used an impressive

75

combination of techniques, emphasizing successively refined personality and opinion questionnaires, plus psychoanalytically oriented interviews of high and low questionnaire scorers. They studied college students, Rotarians, imprisoned felons, housewives, unionists; and they found the personality type they were looking for.

Plato had already partially identified the type: "Such a man would be brutal to slaves, instead of treating slaves with disdain, as a man properly educated would do; but he is gentle to the freeborn. He would be very obedient to rulers, with a passion for rule himself, and for honor. . ." (*Republic*, Book 8; Rouse translation, 1956). In addition to these key features of submissiveness to those higher in authority and cruelty to those lower, Adorno and his colleagues noted in their pre-Fascists a general ethnocentric or prejudiced outlook, expressed particularly in anti-Semitism; a rigidity of thinking; an intolerance for ambiguity; an unusual repressiveness toward direct expression of one's own impulses; and similar symptoms that all seemed to hang together in one authoritarian syndrome. The character of the authoritarians' thinking is indicated by the sorts of questionnaire items with which they agreed: "Obedience and respect for authority are the most important virtues children should learn." "Most of our social problems would be solved if we could somehow get rid of the immoral, crooked, and feebleminded people." "Most people don't realize how much our lives are controlled by plots hatched in secret places."

Adorno and his colleagues paid more attention than earlier students of extremism to social factors that influenced the expression of authoritarian trends in specific behaviors, but their idea of how these trends originated sounds familiar. The future authoritarian was raised in a home in which his expression of basic passions was rigidly limited and frustrated, particularly by his father. He responded both by identifying himself with the paternal authority figure (warding off parental hostility by becoming Daddy's little man), and by repressing his feelings of hostility toward his father, bottling them up to be expressed later toward minority groups and disliked authority figures.

During the rightist revival of the past decade, the conclusion often has been announced that Birchers and their ilk are nothing more nor less than authoritarian personalities with a slightly revamped vocabulary. Adorno and his colleagues did see substantial correspondence between authoritarianism and the political conservatism of the late 1940's, but the relationship was by no means perfect. The main questionnaire measure of authoritarianism, known as the California F Scale, correlated only moderately well with a questionnaire on political and economic conservatism — not nearly so highly as the F Scale's correlations with measures of anti-Semitism or ethnocentrism. Current rightist extremism may

76

very well be related to authoritarianism, but anyone who assumes an identity between the two had better have more support than the thousand pages of Adorno et al.

However, these variables may have been more closely related even in the Adorno research than the statistics indicate. The research has been sharply criticized, particularly on grounds of agreement response set — the possibility that many participants agreed with items on the F Scale not because of any truly Fascist personality trends, but because they tended generally to agree with somewhat ambiguous statements set down in cold print. The F Scale is full of these ambiguous statements ("If people would talk less and work more, everybody would be better off"), and all its items are scored positively: if you agree with any statement for any reason, you're one point higher on authoritarianism. The conservatism questionnaire also contained ambiguous items, but some were liberal and some were conservative in content, so that a general tendency to agree would get you only a middling score on conservatism. Therefore scores on the two scales, affected sometimes by real authoritarianism or real conservatism, and sometimes (but more often on the F Scale) by agreement response set, wouldn't necessarily show a close relationship even if all true authoritarians were also strong conservatives. Whether they were or not remains an unanswered question, as far as the subjects of *The Authoritarian Personality* were concerned.

SOCIOLOGICAL HYPOTHESES

Another question that fortunately remains open to debate is how authoritarians would actually respond to a strong Fascist movement in America. Some did get a trial run during the McCarthy era, which lent a fresh urgency to studies of rightist extremism. Support for Joe McCarthy seemed to be traceable to certain social, religious, and geographic categories, so theories of extremism began at this time to acquire a distinctly sociological tinge. It wasn't so much a defense against generalized anxiety or repressed childhood conflicts that produced the authoritarian/pre-Fascist/far-right/McCarthyite; it was his social group's status problems. (Plato was again first here, explaining the origin of the authoritarian type in terms of the child who "hears his mother grumbling that her husband is not one of the governing class and so the other women look down on her.")

This sociological view was given its most influential expression in a book edited by Daniel Bell, called *The New American Right* when it was mainly concerned with McCarthyites in 1955, and *The Radical Right* in its "expanded and updated" 1963 version, by which time the visage of the enemy was more sharply defined. By this time, too, the sociological view had become sufficiently assimilated into popular mythology for then-

California Attorney General Stanley Mosk to stereotype the Birchers and other rightists with one memorable phrase: little old ladies in tennis shoes.

The little old ladies in tennis shoes had presumably seen better days. Social security checks might crimp their style now, but once they had enjoyed champagne and golden slippers, or at least the respect of other people. How could they restore their hard-won, hard-lost status, with a minimum cash expenditure? Simple: attack those who now enjoyed high status; display a thoroughgoing patriotism impossible for the newly status-rich to achieve. At the same time those the sociologists call "up-mobile," who had moved suddenly from sneakers to imported leather, wanted to relieve their own long-felt status frustrations and, particularly if they were of third- or fourth-generation immigrant stock, felt impelled to establish themselves as the truest Americans. So both became over-patriotic, hostile toward the United Nations and the Eastern intellectuals and anyone else who could be made to sound un-American.

The main proponents of this view, Seymour Lipset (1963; Lipset and Raab, 1970) and Richard Hofstadter (1963, 1965), have used the term *status politics* to distinguish such movements from *class* or *interest politics*, which involves economic issues only. Interest politics may diminish in importance during affluent times, when most economic problems seem solved or solvable; but as Lipset (1963) says,

> in status conflict there are no clear-cut solutions. Where there are status anxieties, there is little or nothing which a government can do. It is not surprising, therefore, that the political movements which have success-fully appealed to status resentment have been irrational in character, and have sought scapegoats which conveniently serve to symbolize the status threat.

Here we have displacement again, but of recently aroused class hostilities rather than of family conflicts. The objects on the receiving end of the displacements have also changed since the days of *The Authoritarian Personality*'s Jews and zoot-suiters. Racial and religious minorities are no longer acceptable targets in much of the country, as mass media, churches, and educational institutions have stressed the unfairness of such prejudice. But Communists enjoy little such immunity, partly be-cause their foreign associates have been a real threat in the past and are potentially dangerous even now.

Psychologists often seem to see humanity as a classless society, and pay less attention to status concerns than they should; so we owe our gratitude to the sociologists for pointing out the contribution of such variables to extremism. But there's one major problem in explaining things in terms of sociological categories rather than of definite childhood (or even adult) experience. The *degree* of feelings of psychological dis-

78

possession, or of status anxiety, or of whatever is considered necessary to send someone off into extremism, is rarely specified — only the groups in which such feelings are presumably strongest. I'm not one for unnecessary quantification, but surely quantitative factors must be important here, or else practically everyone in our society, everyone who had suffered any social slight, would be a Bircher. In fact, just about everyone does seem to have made the radical rightist list at one time or another on a sociological basis. Nelson Polsby (1963) found, in the seven chapters of *The New American Right*, all the following groups named at least once as sources of the far right (the earlier ones are the more popular):

> New rich, Texans, Irish, Germans, middle class, Catholics, Midwesterners, lower middle class, up-mobile, less educated, "cankered intellectuals," old family Protestants, "shabby genteel," recent immigrants, downmobile, minority ethnics, Old Guard G.O.P., ex-Communists, Midwest isolationists, lower class, small town lawyers, auto dealers, oil wildcatters, real estate manipulators, small businessmen, manual workers, elderly and retired, rentier class, youth, Southern Californians, South Bostonians, fringe urbanites in middle-sized cities, transplants to city, Polish Catholics, hick Protestants, patriotic and historical group members (e.g., DAR), Scandinavians, Southern Protestant fundamentalists, soured patricians, small town residents, neo-Fascists.

And that's only in one book.

POLARITIES OF RIGHT AND LEFT
Recent psychological discussions of the right have added status anxieties to the list of neurotic problems that can be projected or displaced, but have otherwise shown little innovation. Attempts have been made to improve upon the standard hypotheses by including leftists and rightists on the same continuum (Eysenck, 1954; Rokeach, 1960), without much success. One recent approach, however, seems to fall largely outside the traditional patterns of causation.

Silvan S. Tomkins (1963) talks instead about "ideo-affective resonances," which are simpler than they sound, but more ambiguous. According to Tomkins, if our parents treat us in such a way that we feel it important to express our individuality and develop our human potential, we will acquire a humanistic orientation that makes us more sensitive to, more likely to resonate with, left-wing attitudes and beliefs. Left-wing positions, he says, stress man as an end in himself, man as of ultimate value simply through his fulfillment of the potentialities inherent within him. But if our parents insist on our conforming to norms, to absolute standards of behavior, and appear to value us only to the extent that we conform, we will develop a normative orientation that makes us resonate more toward right-wing positions. Tomkins feels rightist positions are based on the idea that man is himself neutral in value, and gains value only by conforming to a norm or achieving an objective value that is independent of him.

These developmental patterns sound rather similar to the origins of "democratic" and "authoritarian" personalities as described by Adorno, except that Tomkins doesn't hypothesize repression and later projection or displacement for the rightists. That could be a step forward, because the repression-projection sequence is hard to observe directly anyway; but unfortunately he doesn't give any better account of how parental treatment gets translated into ideo-affective resonances. The really provocative thing about Tomkins' ideas is that he sees right and left orientations as extending far beyond our political views. How does right-wing mathematics grab you? Do you resonate to left-wing athletics? Rightist sex? Leftist Rorschach interpretation?

Tomkins has studied rightist and leftist orientations in detail with reference to the choice of math as a career. He finds

> a polarization between right-wing mathematicians, who were attracted as children by its certainty and discipline, by the possibility of knowing what the right answer was and whether they had attained it; and left-wing mathematicians, who were attracted by its novelty and promise of excitement and its "wild, unaccountable spaces."

Rightist mathematicians feel that mathematical axioms, numbers, transformations, somehow have an existence independent of man's thinking, have always been there and were just waiting to be discovered. Left-wing mathematicians feel mathematics should be viewed as an end in itself, a highly intellectual form of play whose rules have been invented by man.

Right-wing mathematicians may, of course, be completely apolitical or even politically leftish, if their political education and circumstances dictate; but a thoroughgoing normativist would presumably be more comfortable on the right in both math and politics. Tomkins does allow for cases in which a child has, for example, a right-wing mother and a left-wing father: if the mother buys the family clothes and the father pontificates upon current literary fads at the breakfast table, the child may very well grow up with a conservative taste in clothes and a passion for innovative literature, as well as other peculiar mixtures of preferences and ideologies. Tomkins reports no data on whether left-wing men are more likely to marry right-wing women, or vice versa, or neither; or whether happier is the child who results from such miscegenation.

In fact, Tomkins has published few data so far on any of his hypotheses, though some results indicate, for instance, that Young Trotskyites are more likely to be left-wing on his measurement scale and Young Americans for Freedom more right-wing (William Domhoff, personal communication). Tomkins is quite persuasive in his logical analyses of

80

diverse fields of human endeavor into right-normative, left-humanistic approaches; I hope his empirical studies will be equally revelatory, because the displacement-projection view of rightist extremism seems to have considerable limitations. But Tomkins' neat classificatory scheme can also lead to dismaying trivia. In one study (Tomkins, McCarter, and Peebles, 1965), he adapted an item from his test of right and left polarities for administration to a group of Princeton undergraduates, five days after the assassination of John F. Kennedy: "If you had to describe the total experience [of the assassination] as one which smelled bad or as one which left a bad taste — which would it be?" The results: "Although the majority do not cry [at assassinations], there is a significant increase in not crying among 'smellers.' Of those few who say the assassination leaves a bad smell, 90% (10) do not cry and 10% (1) do, whereas of those who say the assassination leaves a bad taste 62% do not cry and 38% do." Quickly, now, your response to this study: bad taste or bad smell?

the functions of attitudes:
how extremism benefits extremists

You tell me whar a man gits his corn pone, and I'll tell you what his 'pinions is.
— Mark Twain, quoted in Justin Kaplan,
Mr. Clemens and Mark Twain

One hypothesis about the origins of right-wing extremism beloved by the rightists themselves is simply that they command the truth, that they possess a special knowledge or special moral sense that enables them to recognize the real threat to our nation. (Some rightists say other people also know the truth, and are just too lazy to act on it; but I don't think anyone who really believed the Birch version of current history would sit around waiting for the Reds to come slit his throat.) Given the difficulty of assessing Real Truth, this sort of explanation for ideological leanings is always a possibility, but it seems rather unlikely in the case of the rightists.

For one thing, most rightists severely limit their intake of information to sources whose preference for fantasy over fact is easily demonstrable. Their occasional forays into nonrightist sources often center upon the most biased publications of other extremes, such as *The Daily Worker* or the Black Muslim press. National news broadcasts and mass-circulation newspapers, which have their own biases but which might forestall wilder flights of fancy, are either avoided or approached with ideological filters so dense as to admit only gross distortions of the source's actual point of view.

Several nonright writers have suggested that, at least on strictly factual

81

questions, radical rightists are well informed. Maybe so, if you compare them with the general disinterested public. But when I matched my Dallas rightists against the comparison liberal group (whose interest in politics was perhaps not quite as intense) on a series of factual items — such as the United States population, the names of prominent government officials, the ratio of military to nonmilitary expenditures in the Federal budget, the capital of North Vietnam — the liberals came out slightly better, and neither group did particularly well. On questions of highly charged ideological significance, such as the distinction between a democracy and a republic, or the authors of the United Nations charter, the rightists were abominably misinformed, though some could cite specific page numbers of obscure congressional publications to support their contentions. The rightists' political extremity may have driven them to learn more than usual about a few peculiar aspects of politics, but their political knowledge seems to have played little role in pushing them toward political extremity.

SHORTCOMINGS OF PREVIOUS HYPOTHESES

Unfortunately, those leading psychological and sociological theories of extremism discussed in the previous section seem to work little better than the rightists' own hypothesis. If unconscious psychological conflicts or status anxieties need be present in only mild degree to precipitate extremism, then it's hard to see why most of the population remains unextreme. If extreme psychological problems, or extreme status concerns, are necessary (as most authors imply), then it's just not the case that all extreme rightists show such extremity of causal factors.

Take the sociological explanations first. Daniel Bell (1963) summarizes them in terms of dispossession: the extreme feel they have lost social status or have been prevented from gaining it; they feel alienated from society, powerless, frustrated; and they think they will get everything back by being tough on pinkoes. Several studies of rightists have lent support to this kind of reasoning, by showing greater occupational mobility among rightists than average, or more job dissatisfaction or more discrepancy between social class and income. But others have not. For instance, Raymond Wolfinger (Wolfinger et al., 1964) found participants in a Christian Anti-Communist Crusade Anti-Communist School to be at least as "status stable" as the national average. They didn't appear unusually alienated; they felt themselves more politically efficacious than the national average; and even within this group of anti-Communist crusaders, status-stable businessmen and professionals were distinctly farther to the right than the upwardly mobile. In my Dallas sample as well, extreme rightists hardly differed from liberals on occupational mobility or job satisfaction: practically everyone, right and left, was mildly dissatisfied.

82

Next, let's take the psychologists' hypothesis of inner hang-ups projected outward — paranoid tendencies, high hostility levels, and so on, that must be dealt with externally because they can't be tolerated as a part of one's own personality. Again, the formula fits certain specific cases neatly: several of Lasswell's, quite a few of Adorno's, even some of mine. But as a general hypothesis it doesn't work, simply because there are so many nice, next-door-neighborly, psychologically stable rightists around who seem to have no personality problems big enough to make them extreme, and never did. Wolfinger describes his Christian Anti-Communist Crusaders not as "social or psychological cripples," but largely as responsible businessmen and professionals, participants in many different community organizations: "The Crusaders' beliefs about the extent of internal subversion may be regarded as paranoid, but, despite the deviant quality of some of their political attitudes, they are functioning members of society." Mark Chesler and Richard Schmuck (1969), who interviewed over sixty Midwestern "superpatriots" and comparison groups of conservatives and moderates, report that the superpatriots "were not generally psychotic, irrational, or severely disturbed. Most of them seemed to be pleasant, considerate, and law-abiding. They were comfortable and happy with their familial relations . . . they were not suffering from excessive anomie and did not feel especially powerless."

I could say pretty much the same about the Dallas group. Two out of twenty-one far rightists, a proportion not much different from the national average, had what appeared to be severe psychological problems. Several others (but no more than among the nonextreme liberals) had minor problems or had experienced difficulties in the past, now apparently resolved either with or without the help of their political opinions. The majority seemed to be psychologically healthy and stable, and appeared never to have been otherwise, if I can believe extensive interview material, autobiographies, TAT's, and several Rorschachs. The projective hypothesis looks very useful for some cases; but it's not enough. Even in combination with the sociological hypotheses about status anxieties, it's not enough. Too many rightists are left with nothing to explain them.

FUNCTIONAL HYPOTHESES

Here a more general approach to the functions of attitudes is helpful. The extremists are distinguished mainly by their attitudes; their behavior is seldom more extreme than writing crank letters or voting for political crackpots, and even then attitudes underlie the behavior. The concept of attitude is central to social psychology; many writers call it the most important single concept in the field. As social psychologists most often define the term, an *attitude* is a learned predisposition to behave in a consistent way, usually favorably or unfavorably, toward a particular class of objects. (Opinions are often discussed as a somewhat more specific version of the same thing, or as verbalizations of attitude.) In Chapter Five we'll talk about how attitudes can be changed. Research on extremism is one of the important ways to study how attitudes are acquired and maintained.

Most hypotheses about the development of attitudes assume they are functional: an attitude must be useful to the individual in some way, or he wouldn't accept it or keep it. You could make a long list of how particular attitudes serve useful purposes — how developing the "proper attitudes" helps little Johnny to avoid getting spanked by his parents, how voicing a love of pro football helped cousin Junie get a husband, and so on. It seems more productive to group these specific instances of usefulness into several broad functions of attitudes, as various psychologists have done. The grouping proposed by Daniel Katz (1960) and the one developed jointly by M. Brewster Smith, Jerome Bruner, and Robert W. White (1956) are among the most convenient.

Smith, Bruner, and White worked out their categorization during a study of attitudes toward the Soviet Union, but it's easily generalizable. They talk about three major functions of attitudes. *Object appraisal* refers to the usefulness of attitudes in helping a person "size up" objects and events in the environment from the point of view of his major interests and material needs, as well as in helping him maintain a stable picture of the world and how he fits into it. Without attitudes, a person would have to decide anew, by trial-and-error, how to respond to every slightly different experience or stimulus he encountered. With attitudes, he can usually refer the new and different to an already established attitude category, and respond to it efficiently. The quotation from Mark Twain at the beginning of this section refers to the object appraisal function. Attitudes do help us get our corn pone, by helping us make the appropriate responses to our world more easily; and we're likely to maintain those attitudes that help us get our corn pone best.

Second, Smith, Bruner, and White suggest a *social adjustment* function of attitudes, in recognition that other humans behave differently toward us, and we toward them, than toward the rest of the objective world. Our attitudes help us get along with other people — help us to become accepted, liked, loved, or help us to discriminate ourselves from those we dislike. Opinions of the weather are used to assist social adjustment perhaps more frequently than any other expression of attitude; but political opinions, expressions of religious faith, and ethnocentric views obviously can serve the same function very well if they are used "properly," to ease our relationships with the good people of the world and to widen the gap between us and the bad guys.

The third function, *externalization*, is best exemplified by the projection and displacement processes discussed earlier. Our attitudes toward the outside world sometimes serve no more useful purpose than helping us deal with inner psychological problems. By feeling hostile toward hippies, we can keep a tighter lid on direct expression of our own forbidden sexual impulses; by denouncing dirty books, we can both keep the lid on direct expression and get our kicks indirectly, through our loving condemnation of filth.

Attitudes don't usually fall neatly into one or the other of these categories. But the categories can be helpful when we look at what a particular attitude is doing for a person — whether it mainly serves reality demands (object appraisal), social demands (social adjustment), or inner psychological demands (externalization), or two or three in combination.

Katz's categorization largely duplicates Smith, Bruner, and White's, but he does add one more category that is somewhat distinct and therefore useful: the *value-expressive function*. Not only do attitudes help a person defend against anxiety, help him cope with psychological weaknesses; they can help express his own sense of himself and what he most highly values. Much has been made recently of identity problems, à la Erik Erikson; and attitudes are an essential part of our identity. They establish to ourselves, as well as to others, what we are and wish to become. Smith, Bruner and White's discussion of "inner psychological demands" focuses almost entirely on neurotic if not psychotic demands, and the idea of an "externalization" function of attitudes, essentially a defensive maneuver, reflects this. Katz's extra category emphasizes the more positive psychological demands that attitudes can also serve. (Brewster Smith's recent [1968] broadening of the social adjustment function, to one of "mediation of self-other relations," does much the same thing.)

FUNCTIONS OF RIGHT-WING ATTITUDES

How do radical rightist attitudes serve all these functions? Object appraisal first: Mr. Downey, our oilman, could argue that his attitudes bear directly upon his material interests and that they sprang originally from his observations of the real world. Even when attitudes don't accurately reflect objective reality, they can and obviously do reduce the chaos for rightists. Particularly if one's tolerance for ambiguity is low (as was characteristic, for instance, of Adorno's authoritarians), it should be very helpful to have a Communist bag in which to shove one large chunk of the world's people and politicians, and an all-American bag in which to shove a smaller but higher-grade chunk, without worrying about inbetweeners. And according to a good part of what these rightists read and hear from their limited sources of information, this is the right, true, and ultimate way to subdivide the world.

Rightist attitudes serve the social adjustment function better or worse according to the kind of society in which you live. Our Mrs. Stevens, who preached to PTA's about creeping communism, apparently drew an enthusiastic response wherever she went in Dallas, and was regarded highly by all her friends for her noble defense of free enterprise. But I'd guess that if she tried the same speech before PTA's in the university town where I now live, she'd not only run into some pretty abrasive situations but would find her friendships limited mainly to lower-status social circles. (Her attitudes could then help remedy her plight, by making her feel decidedly superior to all those nincompoops who couldn't see a Commie if he was tweaking their noses.) Social adjustment is the function the sociologists are usually talking about.

For several years I mainly used rightist examples to illustrate the externalization function to my social psychology classes, until I found that a substantial number of rightists didn't exemplify it. But externalization is probably the most important function for the real rightist kooks, from Lasswell's soldier-patriot to my American Nazi, Mr. Whiteside. When rightist attitudes work to relieve neurotic conflict or to keep a psychotic break unbroken, they fulfill the externalization function.

None of these functions by itself provides a sufficient basis for the far-right attitudes of most of my Dallas volunteers. But any set of political attitudes will serve all three functions to varying extents — not only rightist attitudes, but leftist, moderate, apathetic, anything. The puzzle is not what the Dallas rightists' attitudes were doing for them: for most, the attitudes seemed to be serving the common ordinary functions of any common ordinary set of political attitudes. The puzzle is why the attitudes had to be so extreme.

In a place like Dallas, the answer may simply be, why not? Radical rightism is already solidly established in the Dallas social and political structure, for various historical reasons; it has a firm voice in the city's biggest newspaper; so for those just now discovering politics, it's probably as open an option as any other ideological position. The Birch Society and its literature are easily accessible (an American Opinion bookstore was located three blocks from the SMU campus when I was there); friends will accept your membership; nobody will fire you; even the local Republican party seems heavily infiltrated, if not run, by Birchers. So why not indeed? No neurosis needed, no abnormal status problems — just a reasonable concern about what's going on in the world, a desire to understand it better with the least expense of time and effort, perhaps an interest in doing something useful and stimulating with your leisure time. What'll it be — the Women's Christian Sewing Circle or the Christian Anti-Communist Crusade?

IDENTITY AND RIGHTIST EXTREMISM

But even in Dallas not everyone has taken the path into the Birch grove, so maybe a little more is involved. The data I have at hand don't suggest much else specifically, so let me just speculate for a few paragraphs, with the assistance of Daniel Katz's idea (1960) that attitudes may sometimes play a value-expressive function. Most of the Dallas rightists I interviewed had been raised to honor the conservative values — preservation of home, country, God. But they weren't content to do their honoring in peace and quiet. Even those with no loose screws or status hang-ups were disturbed by social pressures to conform, by the increasing homogenization of society (they too!), and by their own lack of significance. They had good jobs, substantial incomes, comfortable homes, most of them; but so did everyone else they knew. Each really wanted to make a name for himself, not to become famous but to be known as a distinct individual. This desire, as much as economic selfishness, seemed to be behind the frequent references to "individualism." Political moderation, even moderate conservatism, would hardly bring forth their faces from the crowd.

Their jobs or household roles had not given them the sense of distinct identity that they sought. They could have looked beyond work to the traditional hobbies: stamp or coin collecting, woodworking, amateur musicianship, sports. In this time of experts, many Americans stake a claim on self-esteem through their hobbies, through their development of something more than casual knowledge of at least a minor piece of the universe. But simultaneous trends in opposite directions seem to be rendering such hobbies unsatisfying for many. On the one hand, the problems of our civilization are now so grave as to make most hobbyist bywaters embarrassing in their triviality. Even though one man alone can do little about world famine and nuclear proliferation, shall he turn completely from such issues to Scott's Stamp Catalogs? On the other hand, more Americans than ever before are now largely free of major *personal* worries about financial and physical security, while at the same time they have more ready access than ever to televised amusements, pop music, and other cheap thrills. An escalation of expectations about entertainment has occurred in America during the past decade, not only among the young. Instant kicks have become an important criterion for the continued allotment of time to any nonwork pursuit. It it's not more fun than television, at least, why bother?

For those who have found few thrills in numismatics or home workshops, politics itself may become a new hobby. Genuine expertise in history or political theory, even at an acceptable amateur level, is gained only with painful and often boring effort. But the mass media, by publicizing and personalizing politics and by analyzing complex events in five-minute doses, make politics look like a satisfactory substitute both for more serious but boring hobbies and for more trivial but entertaining ones. The rightist organizations take things from there.

Radical rightism is a sort of quick-and-easy mail-order diploma way to gain political expertise, while its conspiracy theories supply the requisite titillations. The JBS and similar sources provide "factual information," "in depth," which for the uninformed reader can have all the excitement of a televised spy drama. Their publications often resemble a hyper-*Time* magazine, or worse, a political pornographic sex manual, entertaining and "educating" simultaneously at the shallowest level. But the reader is not just getting his personal kicks, with a little learning on the side as gravy; he's helping to save the Nation, and after that the world.

So why don't more people embrace radical rightism? Partly because its benefits are still outweighed by major social and personal disadvantages in many parts of the country. What good is an identity that others view with scorn? In such areas, probably the only persons who adopt the far-right role are those truly driven, by neurotic problems or otherwise. They may very well fit the extreme patterns that psychologists and sociologists for years have presented as the only patterns. But they are not the only, and perhaps not even the most representative, rightists in the country.

Talk about multiple causation is by now a cliché in psychology, but a cliché gets that way sometimes because it is the most apt expression of a pervasive truth. If you look at radical rightism as a national phenomenon, the data point to multiple causation. My Dallas Birchers cannot be explained as a group, and often not even individually, by reference to a single influence such as the externalization of neurotic conflicts, or the displacement of status anxieties. They must be looked at not only in the context of these relatively extreme problems, but with regard to the ordinary, everyday concerns and interests of surely a majority of the population: the need to be someone recognizable, to enjoy life, to get a firmer grasp of a complex world. They must also be considered with regard to the particular social environment they inhabit — in this case the Dallas environment, which is so accepting of rightist politics that Birchism can become a simple hobby designed to deal with these normal concerns and interests.

Most of these people show only one extreme characteristic besides their politics, namely, living in Dallas — and even that's not necessarily as crazy as it may seem to the non-Dallasite. Nor is Dallas unique. Dozens of other cities exist, large and small, where the politics of the local communications media are monolithically conservative, and where those same everyday concerns about identity and enjoyment and understanding become daily more and more pertinent to substantial segments of the populace. From such common breeding grounds, rather than from occasional extraordinary combinations of authoritarianism, anomie, and paranoia, are likely to come our future legions of political reaction.

the leftist as extremist:
communism and radical activism

*Once an angry man dragged his father along the ground
through his own orchard. "Stop!" cried the groaning old
man at last, "Stop! I did not drag my father beyond this
tree."*

— Gertrude Stein
The Making of Americans

Until recently, social psychologists have seldom studied radical leftists in their own right. Psychologists are themselves much more often political liberals than conservatives, so they may have perceived leftists as less peculiar or threatening than rightists, or they may simply have had a harder time finding leftists whom they considered genuinely extreme. Those who wrote about leftist radicals without studying them up close usually explained their existence via another of Plato's hypotheses (*Republic*, Book 8): the radical is merely the son rebelling against his father's values. This hypothesis has been nursed along for years by rightists and has been given new life recently by the sociologist Lewis Feuer (1969); but in America, at least, it has not proven very useful.

PSYCHOLOGY OF COMMUNISM

Among American Communists, a more typical pattern seems to be rebellion against maternal strictures. The late Robert Lindner (1955) described one Communist patient, "Mac," who had been raised by a puritanical step-grandmother and a fundamentalist grandfather. From his grandfather's stories of immigration's hardships, Mac acquired the social indignation that would later be strengthened by his own hard knocks; from the harsh treatment his step-grandmother dealt him, he built up a fund of repressed hatred toward all society. Smith, Bruner, and White (1956), in their study of attitude functions, used another Communist as their prime example of externalization. He'd had great difficulty with pathological anxiety, insecurity, and hostility dating from childhood, when his vicious mother had succeeded in "rubbing it in how poor they were and how the children were bringing disgrace on the family." His later Communist beliefs allowed him, like Mac, to satisfy his long-repressed aggressive urges in acceptable form: he could shock people, disturb their complacency, and enjoy thinking about the destruction of American society, all with the idea that such events must occur before a new and greater Communist society could rise from the ashes.

In Dallas I encountered another case of extreme leftism which may have begun as these did but then followed a different pattern of psychopathology. Mr. Hewitt's mother had always been very much the boss in the family, but he wouldn't say enough about her or his father to provide a basis for psychoanalytic speculation. By late adolescence he had developed what he described as a "very serious emotional disturbance," centered on the conscious level around intense feelings of rejection by a girl he hardly knew. He was hospitalized briefly, and went through three different psychotherapists in two years. After the third course of treatment "went bad," he developed an intense depression, which extended through early adulthood and involved a virtual withdrawal from social contacts. Toward the end of this period, Mr. Hewitt became interested in politics and joined several groups with a "strong leftist trend," including some later officially designated as Communist front groups by the United States Attorney General. (Mr. Hewitt was not living in Dallas at the time.) He also campaigned actively for Henry Wallace's presidential candidacy. He said his work in these groups helped him significantly in overcoming his depression and restoring his ability to interact with other people. After a time he began to feel too deeply involved in the front groups, and when an opportunity developed for a move to Dallas, he terminated his memberships and his leftist activities. He had apparently not fully recovered, and suffered a somewhat milder recurrence of depression in Dallas. But by the time I interviewed him, Mr. Hewitt had overcome his major psychological problems and had returned to political activity, on a much less intense level and only in liberal Democratic affairs.

Gabriel Almond (1954), in the one extensive psychological study of United States Communists, provides further evidence not only for psychopathological roots but for the key role of the mother. In an extensive questionnaire survey of ex-Communists (current members were unavailable, and in any case might include so many FBI agents as to invalidate the results), he found that nearly 60 per cent of the entire sample and 75 per cent of the middle-class respondents had joined the party substantially to satisfy "neurotic needs." In a number of case histories of Communists given to Almond by various psychoanalysts, the most common problems involved "chronic" rebellion and hostility on the one hand, and neurotic withdrawal from personal relationships on the other: "Among the American first-generation native-born of foreign parents a quite frequent constellation was one in which the father was weak and the mother dominant, and in which joining the party appeared to symbolize a revolt from the mother and a search for a strong father." However, in other cases the rebellion was against an authoritarian father, fitting the Platonic explanation. Some cases even centered upon "intense sibling rivalry." Almond concludes that no standard relationship exists between neuroticism and communism — that a combination of any of the usual neurotic patterns, plus exposure to Communist party activities, plus certain other interacting factors, can produce party membership.

90

Furthermore, as our discussion of rightist attitudinal functions would suggest, Communist activity need not involve neurotic trends at all. In the United States, where communism has long been considered the ultimate in political deviancy and is severely persecuted, neurosis seems almost a prerequisite for the middle-class rank and file. But in other western countries studied by Almond, particularly France and Italy, neurotic needs were distinctly less important in motivating party membership than other factors — the values of one's reference groups, the material benefits promised or delivered by Communist programs to one's social class, the personal benefits of being a paid Communist activist. The same was true of American high-echelon party members; and obviously it would be even more true in a Soviet-bloc nation, where Communist ideological acceptance could very handily serve all attitudinal functions, not just externalizing ones.

THE RADICAL STUDENT LEFT

During the past few years, psychologists have been studying student radical leftists much more enthusiastically than they ever studied Communists. Not only have the students stirred up enough trouble to make the country at large see them as a problem worth studying; not only have they been getting into the psychologist's own hair, by complaints about his personal teaching methods or about the "dehumanizing" effects of his research and assessment procedures; but perhaps most importantly, they're *there*, right in the psychologist's own backyard. For decades psychologists have relied on college sophomores as a major source of research subjects; now the sophomores are both convenient and important. Not all the psychologists' problems are solved by the easy availability of this interesting subject population, however. It turns out that the most convenient hypothesis available, that same old adolescent-rebellion-against-dad chestnut, works even less well with the New Left than it did with Communists.

In the early 1960's I wrote a slightly autobiographical novel that was, I like to think, ahead of its time. Its hero is a college humor magazine editor who fights a running verbal battle with the university administration over its denial of student rights. The climax comes when the hero's editorials inspire an ROTC rebellion and a joyous student riot, during which the administration building is set afire and the local business district is wrecked. An associate dean, trying to fix responsibility, tells my hero he has no just grievances against the university but is merely redirecting his antipaternal hostility onto the educational authorities. My hero rejoins with a description of the excellent relations he has always enjoyed with his own rather rebellious father and bohemian mother. But he's expelled anyway, for publishing a dirty joke in his humor magazine.

91

Publishers' readers found the novel hard to believe. Where in America, after all, were students demanding a role in university decision-making processes? Who really gave a damn one way or the other about ROTC? What student would ever dream of burning down a college building? Those questions distressed the readers so much that they hardly bothered with the novel's paradoxical protagonist, who went around making trouble for the campus establishment wherever possible but who claimed he was trying to redeem the university; who insisted he was not only not rebelling against his parents' values but was actually carrying their values into action; who was depicted as a bright, capable, resourceful young man rather than a bitter and frustrated screwball. Perhaps I was a better psychologist than novelist in this instance: the novel was never published, but studies of radical leftist students during the mid-1960's repeatedly showed them to share my hero's basic qualities.

Other factors besides psychological ones surely contributed to the spread of leftist student activism, as much as to the growth of the radical right. Leftist activism might have remained as rare through the rest of the decade as at the time of my novel, had it not been for such phenomena as the Vietnam War, the increasing affluence of the college population, and the expansion of the publish-or-perish ethic among university faculties and administrations (Lipset, 1968). But given these social and economic and historical changes, why did only a particular fraction of American college students become leftist activists? Psychological studies of student activism have attempted to answer that question.

An excellent example of such studies is Kenneth Keniston's investigation (1968) of a dozen participants in Vietnam Summer 1967, a project intended to arouse the public to rise up in protest against the Vietnam War. Keniston's study was loaded in favor of demonstrating competence among the participants, since they had been chosen to work in the project's national office. But they were not drawn by high salaries or personal publicity, as they received neither; and in many ways they resemble less highly selected young radicals in other studies. Further, Keniston was able to collect much more extensive psychological data from them than has usually been possible.

He found these left-wing activists — rather extremely left by most standards at that time — to be complex characters. They were quite open to psychological exploration of their own motives (in sharp contrast to many rightists); nonparanoid; not strongly devoted to an abstract ideology, but to "belief in a set of basic moral principles: justice, decency, equality, responsibility, nonviolence, and fairness." They were all going beyond anything their parents had ever done in political action (even in the case of the small number with "radical" families), but most felt a strong sense of continuity with their previous family history. When one was asked by his parents to come home and talk about what he was doing, he told Keniston, "I'm looking forward to really trying to explain to them the kinds of things I feel, that I am a very personal embodiment of what they are, what they created in a son and what they brought me up to be."

Rather than suffering from status anxiety, these young activists seemed to have "learned to enjoy the openness" of living with an uncertain future. Their previous family life had usually been comfortably warm, with mothers "achievement-demanding" but not threatening, fathers seen not as domineering but in an ambivalent light: "highly ethical, intellectually strong, principled, honest, politically involved, and idealistic," but also sometimes "unsuccessful, acquiescent, weak, or inadequate." If any of father's characteristics was rejected, it was not his principles but his failure to act upon them. Keniston's activists frequently reported an early sensitivity to "the issue of violence, struggle, and conflict" (both within themselves, for instance in feelings of sibling rivalry, and outside the family), and a consequent desire to control it; but such retrospective reports about a distant childhood can easily be distorted by present concerns. Their descriptions of recent adolescence are probably more reliable: unusual "turmoil"; feelings of outrage when parents tried to control their lives, after having raised them to be independent and free-thinking; few neurotic symptoms. Any such symptoms, any feelings of strong hostility towards parents, faded as the adolescents settled down to several years of academic and extracurricular success in high school and college. But during this period of relative political quiescence, of conformity to the expectations of parents and society, they found that such success failed to advance their own high principles. "This sense of having tested the psychological possibilities of one way of life and found them wanting," Keniston suggests, "was a prelude to their becoming radicals."

Radicalization itself was not a sharp break for any of them, but gradually followed direct confrontations with the inequities of American society (slums, war, prejudice, etc.), and personal acquaintance with an individual who could serve as an effective radical model. Although their own socioeconomic backgrounds were generally comfortable, Keniston's young radicals did not feel particularly guilty about their affluence; they were much more likely to feel "indignation, disillusion, and anger" at finding others deprived of what they themselves enjoyed. Having a sense of personal responsibility dating from childhood, encountering highly committed radicals who were already working to remove the inequities, they followed, and awoke to find themselves radicals too.

Keniston's approach to the psychology of these young leftists is more impressionistic than precise, and his conclusions are based on a small and in some ways clearly unrepresentative sample. But on broad points, on points easily checked by statistical information, other research on radicals of the same period has largely supported him. Much of the "harder"

93

data have come from Berkeley, not only because it was the first major center for young activists in America, but also because it is a center for survey-taking, attitude-measuring social scientists. In several instances, campus researchers have descended upon Berkeley protesters in the very midst of their protests. In other cases researchers have obtained arrest lists after mass sit-ins, and have subjected the participants to extensive follow-up questionnaires. Similar research tactics have been applied to activists at other schools and at noncampus demonstrations.

With an occasional exception, the results of these separate studies have proven to be quite similar (see Sampson, 1967; Keniston, 1969). Militant leftist students have usually been characterized by relatively high grades; independence in thought; greater devotion to intellectual pursuits than most undergraduates display; less likelihood of becoming dropouts; majors in the people-oriented social sciences and humanities, rather than the more money-oriented areas of engineering and business administration. Their parents typically have been more highly educated and more liberal than the parents of moderate or conservative students, though nowhere as near as radical in belief or action as the leftist students themselves. The young radicals have most often come across on motivational questionnaires and in interviews as being moved by high principles, by "optimistic idealism," not by self-interest. This is not just a question of the self-images they try to project to others, but of their usual approach to personal and social issues. One Berkeley study (Haan, Smith, and Block, 1968) presented activist and nonactivist students with a set of moral problems developed by Lawrence Kohlberg to indicate a person's general level of moral judgment. More than good intentions are necessary to exhibit a high moral level on Kohlberg's measure; a person must have a genuine command of subtle moral complexities. The Berkeley activists on the whole showed distinctly more advanced moral development than nonactivists did. The sort of activist studied in most of the research we've reviewed (identified by Jeanne Block [1968] as "continuity" activists for their feelings of continuity with broad parental values and with their own personal pasts) scored highest of all in terms of Kohlberg's developmental categories, making decisions on the basis not only of legalistic considerations but of abstract philosophical principles.

All this may sound like a picture of the student activist as perfect human being. Indeed, after reviewing much of the data noted here, political scientist Christian Bay (1967) has concluded that "every new human being is potentially a liberal animal and a rebel," that the more a child is raised so that he has a low anxiety level and the freedom "to develop according to his inner needs and potentialities, the more likely that a capacity for political rationality and independence will develop" — i.e., the more likely he will become a left-wing activist. Bay admits that leftist views can occasionally be neurotically motivated, but he argues that political activism and neuroticism (including such symptoms as "constant worry about popularity or career prospects") are *more* likely to be found together the *farther* a person is from the political left.

This kind of statement has been hard for other social scientists to take, arguing as it does that certain specific political values are more consonant with psychological health than others. We can say on the evidence that student activists are more likely than not to be psychologically healthy, but Bay's argument about leftist radicalism as a necessary outcome of ideal personality development is another matter. It may look that way now, but times change. As Bay notes, various studies during the 1920's and 1930's showed radicals to be more intelligent than conservatives; but instead of proving a close relationship between radicalism and intelligence, such studies may have indicated a tie between intelligence and accurate perception of the current sociopolitical environment. Just so now: our social problems may appear to demand, in many instances, radically progressive solutions, and the students who are brighter and psychologically freer to assess these problems objectively may be more likely to adopt a radical stance. But problems are solved or transformed as history advances, and the radical leftism that strikes these young people as so appropriate to the solution of current problems may be altogether invalid in other circumstances.

THE SUPEREGO TRIP

Furthermore, although accurate perception of problems may be *necessary* for their solution, it is not always a *sufficient* basis for problem-solving. Young leftist radicals may be more prone than others to base their assessment of our difficulties on object appraisal, but they may also pursue social solutions in order to further their own social adjustment (seeking the "right ons" of their fellow activists), to resolve identity problems, or even to attain something akin to externalization. Robert Jay Lifton (1968), in analyzing the Communist Chinese cultural revolution, identified a process that he called "psychism" — the effort to control external reality mainly through internal psychological maneuvers which are little related to that reality. Lifton stressed attempts to induce technological change through efforts of will, as when the Chinese people were led to believe that a combination of backyard pig-iron smelters and sheer enthusiasm could substitute for modern factories, or when Mao Tse-Tung declared that the quality of agricultural land is irrelevant to crop production: "there is only unproductive thought, there are no unproductive regions." More recently, Lifton (1970) has somewhat hesitantly suggested that a process similar to psychism may at times be found in the young radicals of other nations including our own, though our radicals are unconcerned with or even opposed to the technological advances that (in illusory form) are central to psychism.

I think perhaps a less formal and more general term would be appropriate for the domestic version of this phenomenon: the *superego trip*. A superego trip is behavior that makes you feel you've accomplished something morally good, something that indulges your superego, even though you've actually had little or no effect on the objectionable external conditions that provoked you to act initially. A person can take a superego trip while sitting in his chair, by thinking heavily about how he and all those other young (or young-thinking) people are on the side of right, which must therefore ultimately prevail. He can take a superego trip — and simultaneously launch dozens of other people on theirs — by writing or speaking of the impending death and revolutionary rebirth of the nation, without presenting any explicit programs for the transition. He can even take a superego trip by going out and really *doing* something — "trashing" the repressive college administration's windows, say, or tossing a few ineffectual firebombs at police stations and thereby turning most of the community against him, while he dreams about rolling the revolution on.

The superego trip is in some ways the opposite of projection. Projection involves trying to cope with internal problems by attributing one's own failings to external reality. When you take a superego trip, you're trying to cope with external problems by creating a sensation of internal triumph, a feeling that all's right with the world because for the moment all is right inside you. Projection and the superego trip are similar in that neither really solves the problems toward which it is directed; it merely conceals the problem's continued existence.

Since most radical activists are reported to be psychologically healthy, projection may play no major role in their personalities. But standard assessments of psychological health would probably miss even relatively heavy reliance on the superego trip as a means of dealing with social problems. Indeed, the practiced superego tripper would probably do well on paper-and-pencil tests of moral sensitivity that require him to recognize a moral issue and to suggest a solution, but that do not require him to execute his solution. I won't argue that radical activists are unusually prone to superego trips, though their high level of concern with moral issues may make them so. But even given equal amounts of such tripping-out among radicals and status-quo moderates, it is the radicals whose goals would suffer most. Lifton's analysis of the Red Guard movement in China indicates that psychism can quickly assume a major (and eventually disastrous) role in a radical movement; and I see sufficient evidence of superego-tripping among even the best of our own young radicals to make me worry about the effect of further psychological research reports that assure them without qualification of their moral purity. They may possess moral purity in unusual abundance; but when they concentrate on actions that do little more than assert its existence, they may well be foreclosing their role in building a more moral world.

OTHER PSYCHOLOGICAL PATTERNS

Not all young activists are sufficiently concerned about a moral world to share even the potential for a superego trip. Most available studies of student leftists have been of the early committed or the highly committed: the ones who were there at Berkeley when it all started, the ones who stuck to their Vietnam protests through public apathy and official harrassment. But with the easy availability of sex-and-politics underground newspapers, with the institutionalization of the rebel subculture on many campuses, I wouldn't be surprised to find a significant number of "fun activists," similar in some ways to the "fun Birchers" of Dallas: people looking for kicks, for something to do with their time, something more provocative than the deadly dull Young Democrats and Republicans but more consonant with their rather vague political orientations than the Young Americans for Freedom. Nor would I necessarily expect these people to be the bright, highly competent youths the "early modern" activists proved to be. Smith, Haan, and Block (1970; Block, 1968) seem recently to have found at least a few such people at Berkeley. As contrasted with the "continuity" activists who accept certain general parental values and view their own Spock-inspired upbringing relatively favorably, these "discontinuity" activists or "dissenters" flatly reject their parents' values and see their own muddled pasts, filled with a combination of parental indulgence and parental demands for public conformity and achievement, as something to escape. Furthermore, they score miserably on the Kohlberg moral development scale, operating mainly according to a "naively egoistic orientation" (Haan, Smith, and Block, 1968). These "dissenters" seem in part an updated hippie or yippie version of the "alienated," "uncommitted" young people Kenneth Keniston studied several years previously at Harvard; they are usually so politically uninvolved that I won't discuss them in detail until the next section. But in the superheated political atmosphere of a polarized college campus, they may find their own private goals best expressed in political controversy. In protests they are likely not to be striving for the realization of high political principles, but objecting to the frustration of their immediate desires by official regulations or by the demands of university scholarship. The continuity activists seem more likely to carry on their programs of protest after the spectacular local controversies have died down; but they may ultimately become the main object of official repression initiated by the dissenters' unprincipled confrontations with authority. (The dissenters may not be the only source of leftist violence, however; see Chapter Nine.)

97

Finally, one should not assume that all the highly principled, intelligent, psychologically stable youths in our country are left-wing activists. Given the Indochina War and other massive social wrongs in which the nation has recently and historically indulged, they may find it hard to resist being driven leftward into protest. But Block, Haan, and Smith (1968, 1969; Smith, Haan, and Block, 1970) found a number of "constructivists" in their Berkeley–San Francisco State sample, students active in "restitutive work aimed at relieving social ills" but "infrequently involved in organized protest," who appeared somewhat similar in personal and background factors to leftist activists. (Block et al. do note a suggestive difference between the parents of the two groups: the constructivists saw their parents as mainly prohibiting self-expression or self-assertion, while the activists felt their parents were most concerned with suppressing aggressive behaviors.) And Larry Kerpelman (1969, 1970) has recently found right-wing student activists on several northeastern campuses to be as intelligent and emotionally stable as left-wing activists. Sustained political activism of whatever kind may demand personal qualities that, at least in certain social environments, loom larger in the total personality pattern than the qualities determining specific ideological commitments.

the moderate as extremist: middle-of-the-road dogmatism

Fear and dull disposition, lukewarmness and sloth, are not seldom wont to cloak themselves under the affected name of Moderation.

> — John Milton
> *An Apology for Smectymnuus*

Professor Bay is not the first man to conclude that psychological health leads naturally to a particular political stance. The widespread criticism of left and right extremes itself reflects an unvoiced assumption that the perfectly normal individual is perfectly moderate in his politics, neither too liberal nor too conservative, seeing a little good perhaps in both sides but The Good in neither. Even scientists who view their research on extremism as value-free may carry this bias toward moderation, unbeknownst to themselves. Indeed, moderation is so little thought of as a bias — the mean in politics as elsewhere is so much seen as golden — that discussing moderation in terms of extremity may seem at first only a silly play on words.

98

Political moderation, in the sense of hewing close to the fuzzy dividing line between the two major political parties, certainly appears to be a reasonable ideological position for much of our population. It's likely to cause the least interpersonal friction in most social environments; and it's likely to strike many people as the only realistic response to the world that their daily newspapers and newscasts structure for them, to the world which their parents and schools have held up to them as the proper myth since their early years. Substantial research evidence indicates that most people develop their broad political orientation by the end of adolescence, much of it perhaps by early puberty, and thereafter tend to ignore or misinterpret contradictory information (Hyman, 1959; Campbell et al., 1964). In large areas of the United States, contradictory information has not been easy to come by anyway, unless you knew where to look, or looked for it particularly hard.

But the world's problems are becoming both increasingly difficult, and increasingly difficult to ignore. The threats are daily more threatening; the usual remedies daily prove less palliative. When the political extremist demands either destruction of the threats or a new society that will creatively cope with them, he's at least indicating his recognition that the threats are genuine and are too significant to be ignored. But as our troubles become more and more immoderate, some people seem to insist all the harder on business as usual, on restraint until the troubles go away, or on gradual escalation in the face of imminent disaster. Under those circumstances, might not the psychologist be entitled to wonder whether "moderation" can serve an externalization function in the individual personality at least as well as rightist or leftist extremism can? If in particular a person insists on his moderation with great passion, berating any who diverge from the middle of the road because he sees all positions to left and right as falling in the gutters, might not the psychologist appropriately respond by starting to investigate the possible existence of "extreme moderation"?

Psychologists have not so responded. Their studies of college students' ideological commitments, for instance, have been directed almost entirely toward left and right polarities. (Larry Kerpelman [1970] has studied both moderate and politically inactive students along with his rightist and leftist activists, but he hasn't examined the extremes within any of these.) The middle-range students are typically assumed to pursue strictly utilitarian goals, such as getting a job or a husband; and utilitarian goals, though distasteful to many academics, are thought easy to understand without resort to psychodynamic hypotheses. But might not some students become short-range utilitarians for reasons other than materialistic utility? In the face of the massive crises obviously bearing down upon the personal futures of us all, why should anyone make a

heavy commitment to money-making and to an evanescent personal
security?

ANXIETY AND "MODERATION"

One answer is evident in a recent paraphrase of John Milton: "The
middle of the road is where the yellow stripe is." People may fear not
only the problems of the world, the horrible future opened up to us by
war and pollution and overpopulation, but also the extreme responses to
these problems — the leftism or rightism that might be the answer, but
that might also get us into even more trouble. Rather than examining
specific proposals from "extreme" sources, such people may turn off all
thought of them, in order to avoid any divergence from the careful and
compulsive moderation that has left them alive and not too badly
wounded so far. Major innovations in welfare or education or judicial
procedures must be rejected firmly, not because they head in any particular direction but because they are too different from what we have.
The incumbent president must be supported, however distasteful and
wrongheaded his policies may seem. His replacement from either party
must be the least disturbing, most status-quo candidate.

One widespread symptom of neurosis doesn't possess the bravura
qualities of the syndromes that draw popular audiences to psychiatric
casebooks. It is known as flatness of affect. It may be observed, for instance, in responses to the Rorschach Test (Klopfer et al., 1954): rather
than seeing anything particularly happy or sad, interesting or disturbing
in the inkblots, the patient describes a picture of consummate dullness,
of colorlessness even when the inkblots are particularly colorful. He
often turns out to be afraid of his own impulses, so afraid of getting himself in trouble by being overly enthusiastic or sexy or aggressive that he
lives instead a life of steady monotony.

Monotonous people usually don't get studied, or if they do their case
histories don't get published. This seems particularly true of the compulsive political moderate. I think he's there, because I can see him supporting many of our more inept politicians; I can read his letters in many
to-the-editors columns outside Dallas; and I've interviewed a couple of
students (from a small sample of assorted moderates, liberals, and
radicals on the University of California's Davis campus) who share some
of his characteristics. But psychologists and other social scientists have
spent so much time on the psychological weaknesses and strengths of
right and left that nobody has the data to tell me how widespread this
breed of extreme moderates might be. Perhaps they are no greater in
percentage terms than the really driven rightists in my Dallas sample.
Perhaps they are at least a substantial minority of the silent majority.
At times I suspect they may be running the country.

100

There *is* considerable information on the political independent, who is not necessarily an extreme moderate but sometimes may be. At any rate he seldom turns out to be a rational actor in politics. According to the most comprehensive study of American voters available (Campbell et al., 1964), independents

> have somewhat poorer knowledge of the issues, their image of the candidates is fainter, their interest in the campaign is less, their concern over the outcome is relatively slight, and their choice between competing candidates, although it is indeed made later in the campaign, seems much less to spring from discoverable evaluations of the elements of national politics.

The kind of moderate I've been discussing may actually be *very* interested in the campaign and the candidates, but have as little real basis for his interest or his voting decisions as these "independents." Neither group is what it seems.

Herbert Hyman (1959) has suggested that "special dynamics might lead to extreme adherence to parental politics, despite other broadening tendencies." The data he discusses involve the strong adherence of certain Jewish college students to parents' ethnocentric views, but the psychodynamic pattern he proposes sounds as though it could apply in case of parental moderation as well. The Jewish students he cites appeared to "have a need to exhibit excessive devotion so as to repress hostility to parents," and couldn't "objectively criticize parents without suffering guilt." Apparently we've returned here to the traditional situation where the son becomes a political extremist because he hates his father; but the outcome is rather different. At an unconscious level, the son's pattern of thought might go this way: "Extreme left? Oh shame! Extreme right? Dad would kill me! But extreme moderation? I'm safe, and Daddy will love me always, and my politics will never threaten *him!*"

I doubt that all extreme moderates follow this particular pattern. Any difficulty with impulse control, leading to the necessity for confining behavior to a rigidly narrow range, would seem to be enough. In effect, the extreme moderate would be identical to the neurotic leftist or rightist in clinging tightly to a set of political externalizations that help him live with his inner nonpolitical problems; he has simply found the political center more useful for this purpose than either end of the spectrum.

POLITICAL ALIENATION

There is one other direction to move in the political arena if you want to control your emotions particularly strongly; that direction is *out.*

Plenty of research evidence is available here, so much so that this seems the main political route traveled by the neurotic. Perhaps it is merely easier to detect than the compulsive pursuit of centrist politics; but whatever its strength relative to extreme moderation, opting out is a very popular maneuver.

One simple index of that maneuver is consistent failure to vote. Political scientists have devoted much study to nonvoters, and have found numerous indications that their psychological health does not measure up to that of the voting populace (Kornhauser, 1959; Lane, 1959). Nonvoters are on the whole more socially isolated, more dissatisfied with their communities and their jobs, more apathetic generally. They exhibit higher levels of chronic hostility and anxiety than voters, but tend more often to cope with such feelings by an intense passivity. As Robert Lane notes, our society in the past has been rather more apolitical than most of Europe, and "One of the little-appreciated benefits of such a culture is the low premium on politics for the anxious and neurotic." The recent growth of certain elements within both far right and far left indicates that this situation may have now changed; but among large segments of the population, political involvement still seems to be avoided as anxiety-arousing rather than anxiety-reducing. (It also happens that those low in education and social class are more likely to be nonvoters. But they often face enough real obstacles to political participation, without our needing to hypothesize psychological problems as well.)

Nonvoters are apt to be pretty quiet. But Kenneth Keniston (1965) and others have studied small numbers of people, usually college students, who are vociferous about their nonparticipation in the American political process, and indeed in the American cultural process generally. Keniston has called them the alienated, the uncommitted; many show characteristics that would now identify them as "hippies." Keniston argues convincingly that their alienation does not merely express their own psychological difficulties, that plenty of things exist in America to turn them off. But a special personality constellation appears to make them more prone to alienation than to the response of doing something about the whole mess.

Keniston views the usual pattern of causation largely in psychoanalytic terms. The alienated youth has likely had a talented, domineering mother and a weak father; the son therefore is able to triumph in the Oedipal conflict, winning the mother's affections and intimacy. But it is a "disastrous victory," because he has relinquished maternal warmth in return for a "devouring" mother whose emotional demands he can never really satisfy, while at the same time he has lost all hope of a respect-worthy father with whose maleness he can identify. As a result, the child grows up rejecting the values of the father who failed him so terribly (in sharp

102

contrast to the value-accepting activist youths Keniston studied later); rejecting any kind of commitment as resembling his stultifying relationship with mother; rejecting any sort of competition, whether in personal relationships or as represented in "the competitive business ethos of American society," because it was his childhood competition with father that brought disaster upon him. Political ideology itself, whatever the brand, is rejected as involving both too much commitment and too much competition with alternate positions. Indeed, the alienated concur with many psychologists in seeing political ideologies as "rationalizations for more sinister personal or class interests, attempts to put a good front on selfish motives."

Jeanne Block and her associates (Block, 1968; Block, Haan, and Smith, 1969), in their study of Berkeley leftists, found somewhat similar personality patterns in their "discontinuity activists" or "dissenters," but didn't find it necessary to hypothesize a particular Oedipal relationship. The dissenters, as previously noted, are semi-hippie types who are at least temporarily active on the Berkeley political scene; but their political stance appears largely an application of the alienated viewpoint to personally involving issues (such as the military draft, or administrative regulations on student behavior.) Again, their mothers are likely to have been dominant in the family, more highly educated than the fathers; and it is the children, rather than the fathers, who seem to bear the responsibility for displaying family accomplishments, through their carefully managed public behavior. The male children may fail to identify strongly with their weak fathers, and then later reject both father's relatively conservative political values and the profit-oriented world in which he works. Indeed they tend to reject anything involving the public display of socially acceptable behaviors, whether political or otherwise, perhaps as too much resembling the stage-managed childhood behavior into which they themselves had been forced. Their own model for behavior appears to be not parental principle, but parental self-gratification: the parents used their children for their own ends, and though the dissenters try to avoid using other people in the same way, their goal is still self-gratification and not the good of mankind.

If Keniston's alienated youths and Block's "discontinuity activists" were simply seeking to avoid ideological commitment, and had no motivation to reject American marketplace values wholesale, they might well have taken a position of compulsive moderation. Moderation itself can involve a strong unwillingness to make a clear-cut choice; but it is not an explicit and public *rejection* of choice, as with these youths. Is moderation then any more valuable than hippiedom or political polarity, any more likely to save or renew our civilization? That is our next, and last, question about the hyperenthusiasms of left, right, and center.

103

the end of extremism:
"cures" and cautions

The world acquires value only through its extremes and endures only through moderation; extremists make the world great, the moderates give it stability.

— Paul Valéry
History and Politics

We are now faced with two extremes of opinion. One says that extremism of both left and right should be wiped from the face of the earth. The other says that one's own brand of extremism should be preserved and promoted, but that all other forms of extremism should be wiped from the face of the earth. Being a reasonable person, I'll take a more moderate view myself: while both opinions have some value, I hold certain reservations about each.

But should I even discuss this question? Or should social psychologists keep their mouths strictly shut about such issues, simply study extremism, provide others with the facts, and avoid questions of value, including the question of eliminating extremism? I could evade *that* set of questions by simply saying, "All right, I'll speak here as a private citizen." But I have already asserted certain values simply by choosing to study social psychology: values including open discussion and rational consideration of issues. Under certain circumstances, extremist politics can affect the preservation of these values; so I think that even as a social psychologist, I have a right and a duty to speak my mind here, as long as I can bring social psychological theory and data to bear on the question.

ORIGINS AND WORTH OF POLITICAL OPINIONS

First, however, I must make clear that in considering the elimination of certain extremisms, I am not concerned with the value of any particular political opinions, but with the ways in which the opinions are held. The beliefs of the Birchers about the U.N.'s inefficacy, or of the New Left about the insidiousness of the military-industrial complex, may appear exaggerated or faulty to some, but they must be challenged or supported through other means than psychological hypotheses. The fact that in some cases such beliefs are based on externalization of repressed conflicts does not by itself invalidate the beliefs. The same is true of views that may appear to us noble rather than reprehensible, but that also derive from neurotic trends. Albert Schweitzer's devotion to the welfare of poor Africans, for instance, may have been in part an expression of long-standing private conflicts; but even if that were the case, it does not negate his actions' worth (though basing one's good deeds on irrational motives may sometimes lead one to overlook more pressing needs among

104

one's beneficiaries). Furthermore, some attitudes that appear silly here and now could be of great worth within certain realities, and may already have been at other times and places. Witness, for instance, the "fanatical" anticommunism of many Hungarian and Cuban refugees.

The real problems, from a social-psychological view, involve the implications of the individual bases for holding these attitudes, opinions, or beliefs. If an attitude is held on the basis of what Smith, Bruner, and White (1956) call the object appraisal function — derived, that is, from the individual's perception of objective reality — you really can't condemn it very harshly, though you might try to change certain misleading aspects of the individual's "objective" reality, such as the newspapers he reads. Attitudes held for reasons of social adjustment may be unfortunate at times, but if no other motives entered in, such attitudes would likely be fairly reasonable (though perhaps a little shiftier than most.)

But attitudes held for intense personal reasons — projected or displaced onto the outer world from unresolved neurotic conflicts, or fastened upon to bolster a weak and threatened sense of identity — can cause real trouble. For one thing, their possessors are likely to be particularly intolerant of competing views. If you've committed your psychological stability to a particular ideology, you may not take kindly to the voicing of alternative ideologies. If your grasp on your stability, your identity, or your moral purity is tenuous, you may react with fear and hostility even to the modest compromises of which democracy is typically made. If owning and using guns is a central and crucial feature of your masculinity, you may see even minor gun-regulation laws as savage threats to your manhood. If the lid on your own dangerous sexuality is held down with the assistance of your daily denunciations of pornography, court decisions protecting literary works may seem pacts with the devil himself, to be resisted with all your Christian vigor.

Not only are externalization-based attitudes likely to be particularly rigid; they are likely to encourage the acceptance of political leaders entirely on the basis of gross appearances. If your attitudes are based on unconscious fear, you may welcome with open arms the demagogue who panders to that fear, without being able to make the finer discriminations about his other policies and virtues (or their absence) that you'd have considered in better days. Further, you may be so wrapped up in your own problems and in what your attitudes can do for them, that you are unable to see the problems of your neighbor, or of the slum dweller whom you never meet anyway, or of the starving and envious billions of other continents. As with neurotic resolutions of problems generally, your externalized opinions may benefit you in the short run, while building toward an explosion in the not distant future.

If opinions based on externalization and ego maintenance rather than rationality are very widespread, democracy itself is in serious jeopardy.

Governments "by the people" work on the assumption that individuals will seek their own long-term self-interest and will make judicious allowance for the interests of others. If too many are so absorbed in the immediacy of their own psyches that they cannot do so, the popular vote can destroy the democratic process that it once embodied. Aristocratic criticisms of "mob" motivations have long been available; but now we have empirical data indicating that substantial numbers do not vote logically or rationally, even in their own self-interest. Indeed, they often do not know the facts that would permit them to vote in their own most selfish economic interests; they vote instead on the basis of just such irrational motivations as we have discussed. The greater part of the vote may still be accounted for at least roughly by material self-interest; but that is no real consolation. Short-run material self-interest itself may involve a psychological retreat from other threatening realities, and it is unlikely to serve effectively the true long-range interests either of the individual or of society.

POLITICAL EXTREMISM AS FUN

Then there are the fun seekers. No one seems to have seen these as a serious threat, until occasional members of the New Left began manning barricades instead of negotiating with the Dean. But, if my Dallas data are representative of very many other American cities, fun seekers of the right as well as the left may indeed come to threaten the effective operation of our major institutions. The constructive side of political action is seldom fun. Few people are beguiled by the idea of working to relieve the poverty of others, or to pursue the slow road to disarmament. The politics of discord, of hawkishness, of conspiracy, on the other hand, fall neatly into the entertainment patterns of television and movie melodrama. If such selfishnesses were aimed instead at arts and crafts, at private fantasy, even at religion, they could be pursued without being terribly bothersome to others. Their indulgence through politics is likely to get people hurt.

There is also the problem of "entertainment escalation," perhaps particularly among the more alienated elements of the New Left. Just as the literary-artistic-cinematic avant garde has devoted much of the twentieth century to progressively more radical and more short-lived innovations; just as segments of the hippie culture have moved on to bigger doses or wider varieties of drugs to get a more perfect high; so the political forms already tried seem to give less and less satisfaction to some, and the only possible outcome is an unending string of innovation — whether sit-downs in the streets, or Molotov cocktails through the Dean's window, or nude-ins at the national political conventions, only time and impulse will tell.

Not that I am accusing young leftists in general of such a pattern. As I

106

indicated earlier, most studies of the New Left to date suggest that it includes substantial numbers of the nation's more rational, creative young people, people whose resourcefulness is likely to be directed at techniques for producing valid change, if they can control their own superego-tripping. But the New Left has also, at least until very recently, remained new enough and exciting enough to attract more than its fair portion of the McLuhan Generation, imbued since childhood with the importance of appearance over substance. These "dissenters" have now rejected the appearance their parents sought, but it is still the shallow appearance of newness and delight that they pursue; and these youths, once involved in politics, are likely to produce a deadly upward spiral of excitement. The rightists, perhaps because they are after all conservative, have so far not engaged in so fast an escalation of expectations; but when Ronald Reagan palls, can George Wallace be far behind? Once the Supreme Court is purified of its most extreme comsymps, why not hang the President from a sour apple tree?

CURES FOR EXTREMISM

Again I must stress that extremism is not necessarily bad in itself; one usually cannot judge, without careful study of the people involved, whether it is based on the externalizations and fun-seeking that disturb me, or on something more substantial. Those New Leftists who share high principles, healthy personalities, and grave disappointments in the uneven course of American democracy should not be condemned simply because their politics are farther left than Hubert Humphrey's; nor should the young black nonviolent activists who have pushed the civil rights movement farther in ten years than in the previous ninety. Staunch moderates who can be influenced by facts are surely necessary too, as a stabilizing counterbalance to the pendulum swings that even the psychologically sound activists may initiate.

But given that some extremism is subversive of democratic institutions, and is thus counterproductive in the long run even for its adherents, what can we do to eliminate it, to "cure" it? One common assumption, heavily favored by historians, is that we have had extremism before, it subsided then, and it will again. But that is a poor assumption to make unless we can demonstrate specific consonances between the causes of extremism then and now, as well as showing that the seeds of its earlier destruction are again waiting to sprout. In fact, the conditions necessary for extremism-as-fun, particularly the large amounts of leisure time and the easy mass-media access to political models and pseudo-expertise, were never present to more than a limited degree at any earlier time in our history. Further, the very presence of these extremism-for-fun fanatics in significant numbers makes the growth of extremism-as-neuroticism more likely than before, since the fun seekers not only sup-

107

port the extensive extremist apparatus that offers an easy path for externalization, but may become personal models for neurotics seeking a syndrome.

Politics itself, under the pressure of media needs, is yearly becoming a more prominent television spectator sport, nearly equal to pro football in offering outlets for repressed rage, and presenting many more outlets for public mischief. As politicians aim the conventions and the campaigns more and more toward sheer audience appeal, we're likely to get not only more entertainers as politicians, but a search for more and more entertaining politics. If these political shows become more and more extremist as a result, the psychologically aberrant will be close behind.

FACTUAL AND THERAPEUTIC APPROACHES

When public officials and secular sermonists do consider ways to eliminate extremism, a favorite method is to present the facts. Such fact-oriented campaigns — Negroes aren't *really* inferior; Earl Warren is *really* a good American — have usually been rather dull, and therefore are hardly likely to attract either the externalizers or the fun seekers whose conversion we might desire most earnestly. Harold Lasswell (1948) once suggested that we utilize film and television to help mold the "democratic character," by showing in concrete detail the lives of those unfamiliar people whom we have always distrusted for their strangeness, and by demonstrating in dramatic form the values we should all pursue in human relations: "We can turn the globe into a village and familiarize every villager with the facts of life." But even with ample technical and artistic expertise on call, I wouldn't count on these educational documentaries to replace such delights as Communist conspiracies in the fantasies of many; and they are likely to turn off the political neurotic entirely. In Marcel Proust's words (1932), "The facts of life do not penetrate to the sphere in which our beliefs are cherished . . . as it was not they that engendered those beliefs, so they are powerless to destroy them; they can aim at them continual blows of contradiction and disproof without weakening them." Experimental evidence (Sarnoff, Katz, and McClintock, 1954) suggests that factual efforts to change the ideological views of neurotics, for instance on racial prejudice, may actually generate a boomerang effect. The neurotic, alerted by the truth campaign that his protective shell is under attack, may develop even greater rigidities of defense.

It's possible, as Sarnoff and his colleagues suggest, to apply more careful therapeutic techniques in certain cases: to explore the neurotic bases of beliefs with the individual patient, attempting to deliver enough insight into his condition so that he himself will see the foolishness of his attitudes. But such an approach, if handled without particular sensitivity, and surely if attempted through a wide-scale broadcast media approach,

108

is again likely only to raise the extremists' defenses (as with the Birchers' hostile attitude toward mental health programs.) Further, therapy seldom changes the extremist's objective or social environments, either of which may be giving implicit support to his views or exacerbating his neurosis. Perhaps if it were continued long enough, a campaign to convince people that extremism is crazy would diminish the number of blatant political extremists by driving them into other areas of endeavor or other styles of politics, just as the popularization of Freudian concepts has led most neurotics to avoid conversion hysteria and to fasten upon complaints less easily dismissed as simple-minded neuroticism. But that kind of campaign would hardly dent the number of fun-and-games extremists (except perhaps for a few who would switch to the joys of amateur psychiatry instead), and it might make the rest merely more cynical about the "mainstream" politicians who would countenance such a campaign. Any effort to convince people that *moderation* may be neurotic would probably never get off the middle of the road.

CHANGES IN CHILDRAISING AND SOCIETY

There is also the long-range possibility that if we change our childrearing techniques, we will eliminate neurotics, or at least authoritarian ones. This seems to have been the hope communicated to many readers by *The Authoritarian Personality*. Doubt still exists, however, about just which childrearing practices produce authoritarianism and how much. (One set of studies [Mosher and Mosher, 1965] found that mothers' own attitudes, rather than the childraising techniques they used, were largely responsible for children's authoritarian or ethnocentric attitudes.) And of course quite a few parents *have* tried nonauthoritarian methods of childraising, à la Benjamin Spock, and what did they get — extremists! I won't complain too much about the Spockian "extremists," although some of them seem disturbingly attracted to the fun-and-games sort of political action that their alienated fellows enjoy. What I do want to emphasize is that when you manipulate childraising techniques, you never know what kind of adult politics you're producing until it's already too late for your generation to do anything about it. Who would object to producing masses of people with more "ego strength," less neuroticism, more seriousness of purpose, and yet at the same time a saving sense of humor; with a humility that yet permits creativity, and a gracious resistance to group pressures? I'm sure that if we were able to raise a whole generation of such youths, we'd be far down the road toward eliminating externalized extremism. But not even if we were all Benjamin Spocks could we guarantee such results.

As for those growing masses of fun-and-games extremists, you obviously can't cure them simply by increasing the number of sewing circles and photography clubs. Society itself must be redesigned for genuine satisfactions in work, in family life, in individual creativity, if it is not to be destroyed by its own leisure time. I will not propose a new social design; presidential commissions and philosopher-sociologists already own a near-monopoly on such enterprises. What the available psychological data indicate — what little data exist — is that just as with the massive problems of the Negro poor, fractional measures of relief are unlikely to achieve anything important. New ways of life and newly regenerated social environments are in order, to replace the cultural and human-relations slums in which too many people now live. If we can create the interest in life and the sense of personal value which seem to have been missing for so many of these people before they discovered extremism, we may find we have many fewer serious, incurable extremists than we thought — in much the same way that, according to Thomas Pettigrew (1961), Southern whites include many "latent liberals," apparently deeply prejudiced until the social support for prejudice is removed. But it probably will be much easier to provide the necessary social support for integration, over the years, than it will be to take our automated, overgrown, money-grubbing civilization and make it really *interesting* again — so interesting that whites and blacks have no difficulty discovering the fulfillments and fascinations that can justify their lives, on the job and off.

When I said social psychologists are working to help solve the problems of humanity, I didn't say they'd make the job easy.

4

acts of submission

milgram's myrmidons:
two experimental scenarios

Myr-mi-don. 1. Class. Myth. *one of the warlike people of*
ancient Thessaly who accompanied Achilles, their king,
to the Trojan War. 2. (l.c.) one who executes without
scruple his master's commands.
     — The Random House Dictionary of the English Language

Suppose your name is Arthur Krumholz and you live in New Haven and
you are sitting at home reading *The Register* as usual and you come upon
a two-column display ad (see page 112).

A little flashy for Yale, you think. But — well, hell, why not? So you
send in the coupon. A couple of weeks later, you get a phone call. This
young man says he's calling for the Memory and Learning Project at
Yale, and he wants to know whether you can come tomorrow evening
at eight. How about nine, you say, since you eat dinner at 7:30. He says
okay and gives you directions.

The next night, you drive through the fancy arch by the art gallery,
right into the heart of the Old Campus, and park your car outside one
of those old stone buildings, Linsley-Chittenden Hall. You stroll through
the first floor hallway until you see another guy, middle-aged uncle type,
bumbling around like he doesn't know where to go. "You looking for the
memory experiment?" you say, and when he says yes you point to what
you think is the right number: "This door here, looks like."

Just then the door opens, and a young, serious-looking guy in a
scientist-type lab coat pokes his head out. "I'm Mr. Williams, Dr. Milgram's associate — which of you is Mr. Krumholz?" You say, "That's me,

Public Announcement

WE WILL PAY YOU $4.00 FOR ONE HOUR OF YOUR TIME

Persons Needed for a Study of Memory

*We will pay five hundred New Haven men to help us complete a scientific study of memory and learning. The study is being done at Yale University.

*Each person who participates will be paid $4.00 (plus 50c carfare) for approximately 1 hour's time. We need you for only one hour: there are no further obligations. You may choose the time you would like to come (evenings, weekdays, or weekends).

*No special training, education, or experience is needed. We want:

Factory workers	Businessmen	Construction workers
City employees	Clerks	Salespeople
Laborers	Professional people	White-collar workers
Barbers	Telephone workers	Others

All persons must be between the ages of 20 and 50. High school and college students cannot be used.

*If you meet these qualifications, fill out the coupon below and mail it now to Professor Stanley Milgram, Department of Psychology, Yale University, New Haven. You will be notified later of the specific time and place of the study. We reserve the right to decline any application.

*You will be paid $4.00 (plus 50c carfare) as soon as you arrive at the laboratory.

112

sir." So he tells the other fellow, "Then you must be Mr. . . . ?" "Wallace," the other guy says, "is this the Memory — " "Would you please step this way," says Mr. Williams. You and Wallace follow him past a little anteroom into a very big, very impressive place with heavy curtains and wide mirrors on the walls, fancy microphones hanging on booms from the ceiling, chairs and tables grouped in several spots — like how you imagine a professional broadcasting studio must look, a radio studio since there are no TV cameras. A lot of money behind all this.

In fact, Mr. Williams now says, "Before we do anything else, let me pay you." As he writes out a check for you and one for Wallace, he continues: "Of course, as in all experiments, the money is yours simply for coming to the laboratory. From this point on, no matter what happens, the money is yours." You and Wallace nod and sign the receipts. Very official.

Then Mr. Williams points to a couple of books on the table, with something about learning on the covers. He starts talking about how there are lots of theories on memory and learning, and of course sometimes it helps to reward a person, and sometimes it helps to punish him. "But actually, we know very *little* about the effect of punishment on learning, because almost no truly scientific studies have been made of it in human beings. For instance, we don't know how much punishment is best for learning — and we don't know how much difference it makes as to who is giving the punishment, whether an adult learns best from a younger or an older person than himself — or many things of that sort." Williams goes on, sounding like he really knows his stuff, and says tonight he wants one of you to be the teacher and the other one to be the learner. "The way we usually decide is to let you draw from these two pieces of paper on which I've written the two positions. If this is agreeable with both of you. . . ."

Well, hell, you think, I don't want to get punished for learning — but me, a teacher? You sort of nod your head tentatively, and so does Wallace: sure, it's about as agreeable as anything. Each of you picks out a wad of paper. Mr. Williams says, "Would you open those and tell me which of you is which, please?" "Teacher," you say with a silly grin. Wallace looks at his and says, "Looks like I'm the learner." Poor guy — he doesn't look like he could learn his way out of a paper bag. Nice guy, but slow.

"All right," says Mr. Williams, "the next thing we'll have to do is set the learner up so that he can get some sort of punishment." He walks toward the anteroom, and uh-oh, you think as you notice the shock generator for the first time: a big black machine on the table by the wall, with lots of switches and dials and things. Williams says, "Would you step out here with me, please?"

So into the anteroom you all crowd. Mr. Williams sits Wallace down in a straightback metal chair with arms on it, and shows him a little switchbox on the counter in front of him, and explains that when he pushes one of the four switches, it'll light up a light in the other room to tell the teacher how he's answering the teacher's question. Sounds reasonable, you think, until Mr. Williams tells Wallace, "If you make an error, however, you'll be punished with an electric shock." Then he asks you to help him strap Wallace's arms down to the chair arms with leather straps, "to avoid any excessive movement." Wallace laughs sort of nervously and so do you. You strap Wallace's arms pretty loose; Mr. Williams tightens them up, both arms, like an electric chair. Next he puts a sort of metal bracelet on Wallace's bare arm, with wires attached to it, and says it's an electrode and the wires are attached to the shock generator in the next room. Then Mr. Williams takes a tube of white stuff and squeezes some under the electrode and says it's electrode paste, "to avoid blisters and burns." "Is there any danger?" says Wallace, and Mr. Williams says real cool, "Although the shocks can be extremely painful, they cause no permanent tissue damage." "Oh," says Wallace. "Oh-oh," says you.

Then back you go into the big room, leaving Wallace strapped into his chair, his hand resting on the switchbox, the electrode on his arm. The boss closes the door on Wallace and sits you down in front of the shock generator. Now it looks even bigger, a very fancy precision machine, with 30 lever-type switches in a row, a little red light above each one and a big purple light that goes on when the boss flips the power switch. And under the long row of switches, you notice the labels: 15 volts, 30 volts, 45 volts, all the way up to 450 volts, with words under the numbers: "Slight Shock," "Moderate Shock," "Strong Shock," "Very Strong Shock," "Intense Shock," "Extreme Intensity Shock," and in red, "Danger: Severe Shock," and then several red x's — these when it gets up over 400. God, you think, I hope Wallace is smarter than he looks.

Mr. Williams is telling you how you're supposed to read a list of word pairs over a microphone to the learner, RED BARN and FAST TRAIN and so on, and then you're supposed to start again with just the first word of the pair and give him four choices for the second word. If he picks the right one, if he lights up the right number in the little box on top of the shock machine, fine, and you go on to the next word till he gets them all right. If he misses a word, you give him a shock, you flip one of those switches. Mr. Williams picks up another electrode and puts it on your arm with a little electrode paste and asks if it's okay to give you just a sample while you close your eyes and guess how strong it is. He pushes down a switch, and damn, it hurts so much you open your eyes, as the little red 45-volt light goes on and a buzzer buzzes and a dial needle flips and Mr. Williams lets the switch up. You'll start at 15 volts, Mr. Williams says, and each time the learner misses, you move to the next switch up the line, and tell the learner before you press the switch what voltage you're going to give him. You look at the list and think, okay, it's short, ten pairs of words. Mr. Williams says he's going to be making notes on the learner's progress, and he sits down with his clipboard in front of more machines at a smaller table, and tells you to begin.

Well, it doesn't go too well, the first time through. That dumb Wallace gets the first word right, then he misses a couple, then another one right, then 3 or 4 more before he gets one right again, and before you know it you're at the end of the list and he's getting 105 volts. You try to make the shocks short, and you praise him when he's right and ask him to do better when he's wrong. He doesn't have any microphone so you can't hear him, but he keeps making the numbers light up in the little box, so you guess he's okay.

Then Mr. Williams comes over and says that's fine, and takes the list of words and gives you another list. *Thirty* pairs? Oh brother, oh God — and he says to start at 15 volts again, and give the next shock higher every time the learner misses, and when you get to the bottom of the word list start over again, until the learner learns all the pairs correctly. All of them? Maybe I could be a better learner than Wallace, you think, but boy am I glad I'm not in his shoes right now. Please begin, says Mr. Williams, and sits down at his little table.

This time Wallace is terrible. He gets maybe two or three out of the first ten, and you have hopes, and you're saying come on Wallace, that's it baby, till he misses a string of about five, and you're up to 105 volts again, did I hear something through the wall? You wait a moment, you listen: nothing. You read the next word, carefully, and he lights up the light and it's wrong, so you push the 120-volt switch, ZAP! and Wallace yells so loud you can hear him through the wall, "Hey, this really hurts!"

You turn and look at Mr. Williams, but he's just making notes and doesn't even look up. You think, what have I got myself into for four bucks? You wait a little more and Wallace is quiet. You think, well, let's try one more and see what happens. This time Wallace gets it right, that's a good boy, so you try another one and it's wrong. You look at the shock board. Strong Shock, it says, 135 volts. Well, let's try to do it fast, maybe it won't hurt so much, ZAP, and you can hear Wallace groan. So at least he didn't yell, he's going to take it like a man. Another wrong one, 150 volts, ZAP, and Wallace yells, "Experimenter, get me out of here! I won't be in the experiment any more! I refuse to go on!" Oh, God, well, it's over. You turn and look at Mr. Williams again, and he looks up and then goes back to his notes. You say, "He says he won't go on." "Please continue," says Mr. Williams, and keeps on writing, glancing at the small machine in front of him. "But he doesn't want to go on." "Whether the learner likes it or not, you must go on until he has learned all the pairs correctly. So please go on."

What to do? The next word is "white" and Wallace is supposed to

115

guess "horse" and that's pretty easy, so you try it, and damned if he doesn't get it right. Another word and he misses, and you look at the shock board. 165 volts! Well, maybe he's feeling better now. Maybe he's getting used to it. ZAP. "Get me out!" yells Wallace, "I'm through, I quit!" You look at Mr. Williams. He says nothing. "Just be calm," you tell the microphone. "Just concentrate." You read another word, and there's a slight pause and you think maybe Wallace isn't going to answer any more. But then his number lights up and it's wrong. Well, wrong is wrong. ZAP. "I can't stand the pain!" Wallace cries. Another word, wrong, ZAP, "Yaaaaah!" screams Wallace. The shock board now reads Very Strong Shock. 195 volts. Another word, wow, he gets it right, can he still think? Another word. Wrong. ZAP. Another. Wrong. ZAP. Another, wrong, ZAP, and Wallace is screaming louder now. Just do your job, you're thinking to yourself, do *your* job, and Mr. Williams is doing *his* job, and Wallace is doing *his*. If the stupid idiot wants out, why does he keep answering the questions? Another word wrong. Well, this is getting sort of ridiculous. The shock board says 255 volts, Intense Shock. Am I going to kill the guy? Who would they send to the chair, me or Mr. Williams? You sit looking at the shock board.

After a bit, Mr. Williams says, "Did the learner make an error?" "Yeah." "Please go on," says Mr. Williams. "Maybe we'd better take a look at him," you say. "The experiment requires that you continue," says Mr. Williams. "Okay," you say, ZAP and Wallace is screaming bloody murder. Another one wrong, ZAP, 270 volts; another word, right for a change, probably just lucky, another one right, hey, that's cookin', baby, maybe he's smartening up. Another word. Wrong. Well . . . ZAP. "I can't stand it, lemme out of here, I won't go on," screams Wallace for the dozenth time, really hysterical now. "You hear what the guy is saying?" you ask Mr. Williams. "The experiment requires that you continue." "Well, I dunno about that," you mutter, but you read the next word. Wrong. You look at the shock board. 300 volts and the next one is going to be over into Extreme Intensity Shock. This is really going too far, damn science anyway. ZAP. "Aaaieeee!" screams Wallace. "I absolutely refuse to answer any more. Get me out of here! You can't hold me here. Get me out! Get me out of here!"

"Well, you heard him," you say to Mr. Williams, "that's it." "The experiment requires. . . ." "Yeah, I know, I know, but the experiment's no good if he won't answer anymore." "It is absolutely essential that you continue," says Mr. Williams. "Essential for what? What's it going to get you when this man passes out?" "You have no other choice, you *must* go on," Mr. Williams says. "Well, friend," you say as you stand up, "you can just get yourself another man, because I've made my choice, I'm going right out that door."

Mr. Williams stands too, and says, "If you don't continue, we'll have to discontinue the experiment." "Damn right you will," you say, "and here's your check." "Keep the check," says Mr. Williams, "it's yours for coming. But I would like you to answer a few questions now," and his assistant Mr. Elms comes in from somewhere with several questionnaires while Mr. Williams goes off to take care of Wallace.

Elms asks you how you feel right now, what's your religion, political party, how much education have you had, stuff like that. Then there's a picture you're supposed to tell a story about, looks like an oldtime schoolmaster ordering his flunky to whip a student in front of the class; and a plexiglass clock dial thing you're supposed to set the hands on to show how much responsibility you had for what happened to the learner, and how much Wallace had, and how much Mr. Williams had. Well, hell, Wallace was just dumb, he couldn't help that, so you give him just a little responsibility, and you split the rest 50-50 with Mr. Williams.

Then Mr. Wallace comes out of the anteroom, rubbing his wrists, a little sweaty but still alive anyway, with a foolish grin on his face. "God bless you, boy," he shouts, "you had me shaking in there!" "Gee, I'm sorry," you start to say, but he interrupts: "No, forget it, if I'd been teacher I'd of done the same — just the luck of the draw — I just got excited when you started reading off all those high shock levels. No hard feelings — it really didn't hurt bad at all." And Mr. Williams says some people do get excited, he should have told both of you that the shock labels like Intense Shock and so on don't actually apply to humans, the machine was originally made to use on small laboratory animals like mice and it's perfectly safe. And he tells you how helpful you've been, and thanks both of you very much and says you'll get a complete report when the series of experiments are over, and Wallace shakes your hand, and everybody smiles, and you and Wallace walk out into the hall and Wallace laughs and jokes around a little and says very pleased to meet you, so long, and walks off in the other direction.

And that's your first psychology experiment.

Other scenarios are possible. For instance, suppose that after 300 volts, when the learner says he won't answer any more questions and Mr. Williams says to go on, you go on to 315 volts, 330 volts, ZAP! And the learner lets out a really bloodcurdling shriek, and screams out, "Let me out of here! Let me out of here! You can't hold me here! Letmeoutletmeoutletmeoutletmeout!" And he doesn't answer, doesn't light up any number on the little choice-board, and you say, "Now what?" Mr. Williams says, "If he doesn't answer within five or ten seconds, count it as a wrong answer." You giggle a little and the guy still doesn't answer, so ZAP! No noise from Wallace, no answer; you read the next word, no answer, ZAP, not a peep, 375 volts, *Danger: Severe Shock* in red letters, no answer, and this time you laugh out loud as you zap him, and then you sort of guiltily wipe the smile off your face and turn to Mr. Williams to see if he noticed, if he's grinning too. But he's not, he didn't see you, so you read another word, no answer, ZAP, and you let go with a real belly laugh while the buzzer goes ZAAAAAAP. This is crazy, why are you laughing, do you *like* this stuff? Next time you pause a little before you zap, and Mr. Williams says, "Please go on," so you do, choking your giggles, ZAP ZAP ZAP, and you can just imagine the learner going Scream Scream Scream, but there's not a sound coming through the wall. Before you know it you're up to 450 volts, no more switches to throw, no higher shocks, and you turn to Mr. Williams and say, "Is that all? Hey, maybe I'd better check; the guy could be dead, you know," and you chuckle at your own joke. "Just continue to use the final switch," says Mr. Williams. So you read another word, no answer, ZAP, 450 volts, another word, no answer, ZAP. Mr. Williams says he thinks that's enough. You sit there looking at the shock generator, trying to get a cigaret out of the pack in your pocket, while he goes and gets the learner who comes out rubbing his wrists and grinning a foolish grin.

But nobody would behave as we supposed you just did, would he? That's really a pretty far-fetched scenario, isn't it?

obedience as situational response: proximity and other variables

Thou hast seen a farmer's dog bark at a beggar,
And the creature run from the cur:
There, thou might'st behold the great image of authority;
A dog's obeyed in office.

> — William Shakespeare
> *King Lear*

The scene into which you have just supposed yourself, if you're an obedient reader, is a dramatic rendering of an experimental situation devised by Stanley Milgram (1963, 1965b). The thoughts attributed to you are hypothetical; but the sequence of events described was faced (with certain variations) by more than a thousand adult New Haven volunteers in the early 1960's. And what about the shocking behavior attributed to the man sitting at the shock box? Would anyone really complete the second scenario, obeying the cruel scientist absolutely and shocking that poor strapped-down victim into hysteria or coma? How many would even go so far as the first scenario, continuing to flip the shock switches all the way up to 300 volts and almost to Extreme Intensity Shock?

Milgram himself, and those who assisted him in the research, found the answers to these questions astonishing. Others who heard the results second-hand found them incredible. When Milgram made the first formal presentation of his findings to a group of Yale psychiatrists and other psychologically oriented professionals, he described the circumstances of the experiment (though not in as vivid detail as here) and handed out diagrams of the shock generator's control board, asking the audience to indicate the likely behavior of a typical set of volunteers. (Not only was Milgram getting expert opinion to corroborate or contradict his own earlier predictions; he was also collecting evidence to counter a familiar phenomenon in psychological research, the I-could-have-told-you-*that* ploy.) Forty psychiatrists responded. They predicted in general that most volunteers would quit at 150 volts, when the "learner" first demanded to be let loose; that fewer than 5 per cent would go as high as 300 volts; and that about one volunteer in a thousand would go all the way to the end of the board, 450 volts. These forty psychiatrists included several of the most prominent men in their profession; Milgram could hardly have assembled a more expert group to make such predictions. (A group who might consider themselves more expert, fourteen Yale senior psychology majors, had already predicted similar results.) But their estimates were wrong. They didn't even come close.

VARIATIONS IN PROXIMITY

Milgram actually created several different predicaments within his one basic experimental design, and the results depend somewhat on the situation, so I'd best describe these variations before revealing the sad truth about the behavior of his volunteers. Milgram called the situation described in the two scenarios the "Voice Feedback" experimental condition, the results of which he used as the baseline for later experiments. In another condition, "Remote Feedback," the situation was very similar except that the "learner's" screams could not be heard. At 300 volts, he pounded on the wall, and gave no further answers via the light-box; at 315 volts he pounded again, and was silent thereafter, whether he was shocked or not. In a third condition, "Proximity," the "learner" sat at his own table in the same room as the "teacher" volunteer, 1½ feet away and with his back turned. He could not only be heard but seen, twitching, jerking, and occasionally turning his head to scream at the teacher. In a fourth condition, "Touch-Proximity," the learner again sat close to the teacher, but no electrode was attached to his arm; the experimenter explained that to receive the shock the learner must rest his hand on a metal plate on the teacher's table adjacent to the shock generator. The learner again demanded to be set free at 150 volts, and refused to put his hand on the shock-plate thereafter. Thus began a wrestling match, with the teacher physically forcing the learner's hand onto the shock-plate for each shock. (The teacher was protected from shock himself by a plastic wrapping over the learner's hand and arm.)

For those wondering how Milgram escaped lawsuits from several

119

hundred damaged "learners," I should note that the learner never received a single shock. The only person to be shocked was the shocker, the "teacher," who got his sample 45 volts early in the experiment to show him the shock generator really meant business. In fact, a great deal of the experiment was not what it seemed. Milgram was never interested in studying memory and learning; he was concerned with the psychology of obedience to authority. The "learner," that other volunteer, bumbling Mr. Wallace, was neither a volunteer nor a bumbler, but a paid experimental confederate and quite a good amateur actor, in private life a working accountant. The Mr. Williams who apparently ran the show was not a psychologist, but a high school biology teacher who looked sterner than he really was. Even Mr. Elms, the assistant who helped with the interview at the end of the session, was often really Stanley Milgram. I called people on the phone to make appointments during the initial months of research, and I did start out as the assistant interviewer, so my name continued to be used for a while after I moved on to other things, in order not to confuse anybody. (I also played the experimenter during several trial runs before the experiments officially got going, and Milgram played the learner-victim. But I looked too young, and Milgram was temperamentally unsuited to being a victim, so he hired people who better fit their roles.)

Now the results. In the Remote Feedback conditions, with the learner audible only when he pounded on the wall, twenty-six out of forty volunteers obeyed the experimenter completely, even administering the 450-volt shock three times as ordered. *All forty* volunteers went at least to 300 volts, the point where the first wall-pounding was heard. Five volunteers stopped there, four more gave the 315-volt shock and stopped, and the other five who quit did so by 375 volts. In the Voice Feedback condition, when the victim could be heard grunting, groaning, and screaming as in our earlier scenarios, the number of obedient subjects hardly changed: twenty-five of forty went all the way through 450 volts. (A fresh set of forty volunteers was used in each experimental condition.) The psychiatrists, remember, said one person in a thousand would get this far. Those volunteers who refused to obey completely did, on the average, quit a little earlier in Voice Feedback than in Remote Feedback, but not by much — particularly when you consider the dramatic difference in the victim's show of suffering.

The learner-victim's presence in the same room did reduce obedience considerably, though it wasn't as great a deterrent as one might expect. In the Proximity condition, sixteen volunteers displayed complete obedience. Even in Touch-Proximity, the condition that required vigorous arm-wrestling to keep the victim's hand on the shockplate, twelve volunteers wrestled him all the way to the end, and several others held his hand on the plate through repeated increases in shock before they quit.

What are we to make of all this? Did the volunteers simply see the whole experience as unreal, and trip laughingly through the shock series to play the experimenter's little game? Laughter, yes: almost half the one hundred and sixty volunteers in those first four conditions laughed or smiled upon occasion while they were delivering shocks, and fifteen went into uncontrollable seizures of laughter. But nobody seemed to be joking. Their laughter appeared anxious, tense, perhaps an irrepressible discharge of tension from an unbearable conflict: obey the experimenter or listen to the victim? Tension was even more unambiguously expressed in groaning, hairpulling, sweating, lip-biting; hands trembling as they pushed the switch; stuttering as the "teacher" continued his lessons. Most volunteers later described themselves as having felt moderately to extremely tense and nervous during the experiment; some who described themselves as hardly nervous at all had shown obvious signs of tension during the shock series. The fully obedient volunteers reported themselves as reaching even higher levels of nervousness than those who refused at some point to go any further.

For virtually all volunteers, the experimental situation was very real and quite believable. They were making real decisions, with real consequences for real people — something seldom true of laboratory psychological experiments. Nearly all seemed to feel genuine conflict about which outer pressures and which inner motivations to obey. When I interviewed forty volunteers again several months later, one man who had obeyed completely said he'd begun to have doubts about the reality of the situation halfway through the experiment, and several others (obedient and defiant) said they had begun to wonder about it after the experiment was over — after they had seen the learner unharmed. But such recollection of doubt may well have served a defensive function, excusing them from having behaved so abominably during the experiment. Questions of credibility seemed hard to come by when volunteers were in the midst of a quite busy, quite anxiety-provoking round of "teaching" and "punishing." Milgram's results cannot be accounted for by the possibility that participants treated the whole thing frivolously.

So we have a set of authentic responses from a group of apparently ordinary Americans, many of them willing, even in the face of agonized cries for help from their victims, to go on zapping on command. True, the closer they were to the victim, and the more signs they had of his distress, the less willing they were to impose the highest available levels of pain. But a substantial number obeyed the experimenter even when he commanded them to engage in what amounted to close-quarter assault on a seemingly innocent bystander. Can we now generalize from this reality to the reality of the world beyond the laboratory, and argue as

Milgram (1965b) does that a great fund of obedience exists in "the kind of character produced in American democratic society," ready to engage in "brutality and inhumane treatment at the direction of malevolent authority"? Can we conclude that we share, though perhaps in smaller measure, the worst tendencies of Nazi German society, ready to come to the fore when a George Wallace or a Spiro Agnew accidentally or otherwise becomes President?

INSTITUTIONAL AUTHORITY

Not at all, some critics of the Milgram study have answered. Yale University is the most prestigious institution in New Haven; the Social Interaction Laboratory in which these studies were held itself appears awesomely professional to the layman; and within it a Yale psychologist was conducting a legitimate research study. Why shouldn't the volunteers obey him implicitly? He certainly wouldn't let the "learner" be seriously hurt, and if the man *were* hurt, it would obviously be Dr. Milgram's or Mr. Williams' responsibility and not the "teacher's." The teacher, after all, was only following orders.

Several volunteers offered just these reasons, in later interviews, for their behavior. So did Adolf Eichmann. The Third Reich was a rather more prestigious institution for most Germans than Yale University is for *any* New Havenite. It was engaged in an important endeavor, establishing German hegemony; and Adolf Hitler's authority and prestige were doubtless hundreds of times greater than then Assistant Professor Stanley Milgram's were at the start of his experiments. (Milgram has recently come up a bit.) Besides, hardly anybody saw the Jews after they got on those boxcars and rolled away; and anyway, Adolf made it clear that they deserved what they got. Mr. Williams *said* to shock the man, after all, and why should he say so if the man didn't need it? That guy Wallace did look pretty dumb, anyway, and he was lousing up the experiment with his poor performance; he got what was coming to him. ZAP.

Further, not everything in Milgram's original experimental situation was needed to gain the obedience of many volunteers. After Milgram had completed several experiments, the Yale Sociology Department, which had kindly loaned him its fancy and expensive Social Interaction Laboratory, decided the laboratory was needed for something else. Milgram had to move into the basement of the same building, where several large empty spaces were converted into a set of small experimental rooms. They were neat and clean but hardly matched the splendor of his earlier locale. To make sure that his later studies could be reasonably compared to his earlier ones, he did the entire Voice Feedback study over again with a new crop of volunteers. His results hardly differed from the original Voice Feedback condition.

Milgram also redid the Remote Feedback condition, in an even more disparate locale: a marginally respectable suite of offices in a run-down building adjacent to Austin's haberdashery in downtown Bridgeport, about 20 miles from New Haven. A cheap world map hung on the wall and checkered cotton curtains covered the windows. The same equipment and staff were used, and volunteers of similar ages and occupational backgrounds were procured in the same manner. No reference was made to Yale University. A fake name, "Bridgeport Research Associates," was used instead, and if volunteers asked, they were told it was a "private firm conducting research for industry." The number of fully obedient volunteers dropped from twenty-six at Yale to nineteen at Bridgeport (out of forty), but the difference is not statistically significant. Several participants indicated their own doubts about the auspices of the operation. One, for instance, later wrote Milgram an account of his thoughts during the experiment: ". . . Should I quit this damn test? Maybe he passed out? What dopes we were not to check up on this deal. How do we know that these guys are legit? No furniture, bare walls, no telephone. We could've called the police up or the Better Business Bureau. I learned a lesson tonight." The lesson for Milgram was that many people in his samples, and probably in the country as a whole, will display frightening levels of obedience upon minimal indications of institutional authority.

As yet we have no experimental data indicating that America is unusual in this. In any organized society, children must at times learn to obey the instructions of those who presumably know more about a situation than they do. How strongly different cultures instill such obedience in their members, and to what extent cultures teach their members to judge certain authoritative commands as illegitimate, have not been studied quantitatively. In the midst of the Milgram studies I applied for a grant to set up an obedience laboratory in Germany, so we could gather data that would allow us to compare German and American obedience levels (and to compare the behavior of contemporary German youth with that of their war-implicated elders). Whether because of my minimal command of German or because the implications of Milgram's research were not yet apparent to the granting agency, my application was rejected.

Since the My Lai massacre, people may be much more willing to believe that similarities between American and German obedience levels are worth studying. American soldiers at My Lai not only showed far higher levels of destructive obedience than participants in the Milgram studies; they may have demonstrated the importance of an additional factor that enabled Milgram to generate such a terrible willingness to obey in the laboratory. Seymour Hersh (1970) quotes one My Lai participant as saying afterwards:

> It was like going from one step to another, worse one. First, you'd stop the people, question them, and let them go. Second, you'd stop the peo-

ple, beat up an old man, and let them go. Third, you'd stop the people, beat up an old man, and then shoot him. Fourth, you go in and wipe out a village.

Milgram put the long row of switches on his shock machine mainly so he could measure obedience quantitatively, in terms of the highest shock switch a volunteer was willing to push. But this arrangement also happened to allow the volunteer to increase his level of destructive obedience gradually. If Milgram had built only a single 450-volt switch into the shock machine, demanded that each volunteer administer 450 volts to the victim the first time he made a mistake, and then had the victim yell his most blood-curdling shriek in response, he might have found very few people willing to administer even one shock and hardly anyone willing to give a second one.

Not only did the series of increasing shocks permit a degree of emotional acclimation or desensitization to the victim's cries; they also showed the volunteer that no punishment was forthcoming for increasingly vicious behaviors — indeed, that the authority in charge welcomed such behaviors. Baron and Kepner (1970) have noted several studies other than Milgram's in which the absence of punishment for normally prohibited behaviors has led to increasingly serious violations of such prohibitions. Increasing levels of unpunished aggression over a period of weeks (apparently mixed with increasing levels of frustration) ended in the appalling viciousness at My Lai; increasing levels of unpunished — indeed, officially sanctioned — aggression against Jews in Nazi Germany led easily into the Final Solution.

IMMEDIACY OF VICTIM

So far we've been concerned with the question of why Milgram got any obedience at all. Once he found he could get a great deal, he concentrated on factors that might either increase or decrease the degree of obedience elicited. We'll deal with one such factor, the volunteer's own personality, in the next section. Milgram's main concern, however, has been with the situational determinants of obedience: aspects of the environment that, regardless of variations in volunteers' personalities, influence overall levels of obedience. We've already discussed one situational factor, the general experimental setting — whether the research is conducted in a sumptuous scientific laboratory, a crowded set of basement rooms elsewhere in the same university, or a fly-by-night commercial office suite. Such variations can make a difference, but not necessarily a large one. The other obvious situational determinant in the studies we've reported so far is the proximity, physical and psychological, of victim to volunteer.

Milgram had observed in early pilot studies with Yale undergraduates

124

that volunteers often avoided looking at the shock victim, by averting their eyes or twisting their heads away, even though the victim at that time was always partially concealed by a silvered glass. In his later experiments, Milgram intentionally varied the visibility and audibility of the victim (what he calls in general the "immediacy" of the victim). As we've indicated, he got roughly the differences he expected: less obedience the more immediate the victim. The same effect has been noted anecdotally in observations of military actions: for instance, it seems psychologically much "easier" for combatants to drop bombs or napalm from a great height onto the suspected enemy than to thrust a bayonet into the vitals of an unarmed person, unless the My Lai sort of habituation has already occurred.

Milgram (1965b) has proposed several different factors that might account for the immediacy effect. One possibility is that "as the victim was brought closer, the subject became more aware of the intensity of his suffering and regulated his behavior accordingly." Milgram discounts this because volunteers in all conditions were similar in their later descriptions of how much pain the victim had suffered. Rejection of this factor may be premature, however, since a ceiling effect is involved: nearly all volunteers even in the Remote Feedback condition attributed the highest pain level possible on the scale Milgram used. Milgram instead suggests the importance of a related factor: the amount of "empathic cues" available in the different situations. The more clearly the volunteer can perceive the victim's state, the better he can imagine himself in the victim's place, and the more strongly motivated he may therefore be to do unto others as he would prefer to be done unto. The victim's immediacy also should make it harder to use the defense mechanism of denial. Particularly in the Remote Feedback condition, in which only some little lighted numbers and a couple of thumps signify the victim's existence, it may be easy, as one volunteer said, "to forget that there's a guy out there. . . . For a long time I just concentrated on pressing the switches and reading the words." When the victim is up close, you can hardly ignore him, and your switch-flipping is obviously hurting him; you can't be on the fence any longer. The ghettos can be ignored more easily than the next-door neighbor's sick dog.

Milgram also speculates that when the victim is actually in the same room, it's important not only that you can see him, but that he can see you — perhaps shaming you, making you more self-conscious or inhibited in your switch-flipping. Further, it's no longer necessarily you and the experimenter against the guy in the other room; it may be you and the man sitting beside you against the experimenter six feet away. You "have an ally who is close at hand and eager to collaborate in a revolt against the experimenter."

Finally, Milgram suggests that you're likely to have learned earlier in life not to hurt someone who is close enough to punch you in the nose, but that such caution doesn't extend to more distant figures. (Did you ever drop waterbombs from a hotel window?) I would add that with the victim sitting right next to you, the possibilities might look better for actual role reversal: the experimenter might get up and say, "All right, switch chairs please, and Mr. Wallace will now shock Mr. Krumholz for a while." Some volunteers indicated at the end of the experiment that they thought such a role reversal would or should take place. As far as I know, no one kept track of whether more people thought that way in the Proximity conditions than in the Remote and Voice Feedback conditions; but such differences in assumptions may very well have been present.

VARIATIONS IN VICTIM AND EXPERIMENTAL CHARACTERISTICS

The volunteer's feelings toward the victim may be manipulated more directly, and Milgram has done so in other experiments (Milgram, in press), for instance by having the victim shout at some point that he has heart trouble and is afraid of a heart attack. This reduces obedience somewhat, but doesn't eliminate it. Also, volunteers themselves may change their feelings toward the learner and the experimenter, to justify their obedience or defiance. I found in the later interviews that obedient volunteers described the learner's personality in distinctly more derogatory terms, and the experimenter's personality in much more positive terms, than did defiant volunteers. Maybe that's one reason they were more willing to obey in the first place. But it's at least as likely that under the pressure of the experimenter's commands, they sought to justify their obedience to themselves by seeing the learner as dumber and weaker, and the experimenter as smarter or more beneficial to mankind, than they had initially.

The experimenter himself is clearly as important a feature of the experiment as is the victim. In the studies already described, the experimenter was always a few feet away, watching to make sure obedience occurred, and prodding the volunteer at any hesitation. But what if, as is often true in real life, the authority figure is more remote or temporarily absent?

Milgram ran one study in which the experimenter, after giving the necessary instructions, said he had to get back to his office in another part of the building, but that he would occasionally telephone to see how things were going. In another study a sign instructed volunteers to switch on a tape recorded message when they entered the laboratory, and they were given all instructions without ever seeing the experimenter in person. Obedience dropped sharply in both cases. For instance in the experiment with the telephone connection, only nine volunteers out of forty were fully obedient, as contrasted to twenty-six in the comparable condition with the experimenter present. Further, several volunteers in the experimenter-absent condition gave the victim lower shocks than they were supposed to, sometimes the lowest shock possible, and then lied to the experimenter on the phone that they were going up the shock board as directed. (Similarly, several volunteers I interviewed later, when asked if they had ever shot at anyone in military combat, said they had fired guns, "but not at anyone." One said he had simply shot in the air.)

GROUP STUDIES

The situation may also be altered by having the volunteer work as part of a group rather than by himself. In one study, Milgram (1964a) ran a control group in which the volunteer, as usual, was the only "teacher," but this time was allowed to choose the shock level he was to administer for each error, rather than being directed to increase the shock level gradually. Most volunteers stayed in the lower ranges of the shock board, 15 to 90 volts; only two went beyond 150 volts, at which point (in this experiment) the victim shouted about his heart condition. Then Milgram ran an experimental group in which two extra hired confederates were added. They were presumably volunteers as well, and the situation was set up so that the real volunteer became one of the three "teachers." One "teacher" read the words to be learned, another checked to see whether the learner's answer was right or wrong and then gave him the right answer, while the third — the real volunteer — administered the shock for wrong answers. All three were allowed to recommend which level of shock to give, with the lowest level taking precedence; the two fake volunteers kept recommending higher and higher levels. Under such group pressure, only four volunteers stayed in the 15 to 90 volt range; another nine went to 150 volts; and the other twenty-seven went on beyond the heart-attack warning, including seven who caved in completely to the pressure of their "fellow teachers" and administered the full 450 volts.

In a further study, the two actors were again present as additional "teachers," but this time one actor pushed the shock switch, moving higher and higher in accordance with the experimenter's commands, while the real volunteer merely read off the words to be learned. It was made clear that the experiment could not continue without the real volunteer's participation, that he was an integral part of the experimental procedures; so he presumably shared a substantial amount of the responsibility for the victim's agonies. But in this condition Milgram got virtually unanimous obedience: thirty-seven out of forty cooperated all the way to the highest level of shock. And so do chemists and secretaries trudge daily to their tasks in the napalm factories.

Milgram has by now conducted many permutations of these situational variables. The really astonishing thing about all the research he's done, from a psychological viewpoint, is that he has produced such great variations in obedience not by choosing people with different personality patterns, but by putting similar samples of people in different situations. As Roger Barker's work in Chapter Two indicated, the environment itself places heavier demands on us than we usually realize. As Chapter Three suggested, the environment can legitimize and encourage behavior in "normal" individuals that we would otherwise expect only from clear "abnormals." Milgram's work has done more than any that I know of to dramatize these situational influences, and to explore their possible baleful effects upon behaviors that could ultimately be disastrous for us all.

obedience as personal response:
the role of individual differences

Obedience is a curse. That is what makes Germans.

— Gertrude Stein
Yes Is for a Very Young Man

The forty volunteers in each of Milgram's experimental conditions were quite similar to every other forty volunteers in age, sex, and general occupational category. This sameness of certain individual variables, and the randomness of others, made it possible for Milgram to draw his conclusions about situational variables. If he'd used forty Yale sophomores in the Touch-Proximity condition, and forty middle-aged Rotarians for the Remote Feedback condition, he could hardly have said anything about behavioral differences between groups — whether they were situationally determined, or determined by any or all of the ways in which Yale sophomores differ from Rotarians.

A large pool of potential volunteers was built up before Milgram started running his main experiments. Each experiment's set of forty volunteers could therefore be selected to include 20 per cent professional, 40 per cent white collar (sales and business), and 40 per cent skilled and unskilled workers; and within these occupational categories, 40 per cent in their forties, 40 per cent in their thirties, and 20 per cent in their twenties. Most volunteers were men, and only men were used, except in one later experiment that included only women. (Their level of obedience was about the same as for men.) An impressively varied assortment of people volunteered, ranging from grade-school dropouts to Ph.D.'s, from unemployed laborers through many types of skilled workers to the highest professional categories. Motives for volunteering obviously varied as well. Some mainly wanted the $4.50 for an hour's work; some were mainly curious; some wanted to help science; some seemed to enjoy the prestige of participating in a Yale University enterprise.

The method of recruiting made little difference: the several hundred who responded to Milgram's newspaper advertisement appeared similar in background to several hundred more who responded to a form letter giving the same information in similar language. The language in Milgram's form letter seemed to me so crassly commercial that I thought it might be scaring some people away, so I wrote a more high-toned letter that we sent out in a test mailing of two hundred. It said things like, "We hope you will seriously consider taking part in this project, since the result may be of considerable scientific importance," and it delivered twenty responses — roughly the same percentage as with Milgram's brassier letter, which we continued to use thereafter. Because only 10 or 11 per cent of the people who got the letters responded to them (and because only a small percentage of those who saw the newspaper ad sent in the coupon), the ones who came may well have differed in unknown ways from the population as a whole. However, because they were volunteering for an experiment on memory and learning rather than for an obedience study, and because those who did come displayed a wide range of motives, Milgram's findings probably aren't very unrepresentative of the population as a whole.

But personality differences, though perhaps not pronounced between experimental groups, were obviously a substantial factor within each experiment. When twenty-four men are willing to shock a helpless victim with high levels of electricity, while sixteen men flatly refuse under the same circumstances, chance alone is not likely to determine who is obedient and who is defiant. When the situation is made so stressful that all but a few men refuse to participate, what streak of subservience or sadism characterizes the few and not the many?

PERSONAL CHARACTERISTICS OF VOLUNTEERS

In the interviews held immediately after experimental participation, Milgram asked volunteers questions about their military experience, political affiliation, and the like. Republicans and Democrats were not significantly different in obedience levels; Catholics were more obedient than other religious groups; the better-educated were more defiant; those in the more "moral" professions such as law, medicine, and teaching showed greater defiance than those in the more technical professions such as engineering and the physical sciences. The longer one's military service, the more obedience — except that former officers were less obedient than those who had served only as enlisted men, regardless of length of service.

The picture of a schoolmaster commanding his assistant to whip a student, especially drawn for the study, yielded little useful information. It was included so that volunteers might project their unconscious or unstated feelings of guilt, remorse, sadism, and so on into the story they

129

made up about the picture (much as in the Thematic Apperception Test). But they generally gave pretty ordinary stories, and — strikingly — seldom commented on any resemblance between the picture and their own present situation.

To obtain more detailed information on personality differences, I invited a number of Milgram's volunteers to come back to Yale, several months after their original participation, for a two-hour interview (Elms and Milgram, 1966). Milgram's overall results suggested that a certain percentage of volunteers were on the fence, in terms of possible personality bases for obedience: if they happened to be in the situation where they merely heard the victim yelling, they shocked him; if they both saw and heard him, they didn't shock him. Others seemed to have a more personal commitment to defiance regardless of the specific situation; a few bangs on the wall from the victims were all they needed to quit. Still others had such strong predispositions toward obedience that they obeyed even if it meant slamming the victim's arm down onto the shockplate. To sort out the personality characteristics leading to obedience or defiance somewhat more clearly, I interviewed twenty people who had defied the experimenter even when the cues to do so were relatively mild (these people were mainly from the bump-on-the-wall Remote condition, with a few from the Voice Feedback condition), and twenty who had obeyed even when the victim was sitting next to them, or even when they had to press his arm to the shockplate.

I tried several ways of getting useful personality data from each of these people. For one thing, I gave them the MMPI (Minnesota Multiphasic Personality Inventory), a widely used list of several hundred statements with which a person's total number of agreements and disagreements supposedly shows whether he tends toward paranoia, schizophrenia, psychopathic deviancy, homosexuality, or several other unfortunate conditions. I suspected that an obedient volunteer, for instance, might show psychopathic tendencies, because the presence of a strong conscience (lacking in the psychopath) would probably interfere with shocking people. But I found that obedients and defiants don't differ significantly on the MMPI measure of psychopathy, and now that I think of it, it's also true that a psychopath might not put much stock in obeying orders, as the obedient volunteers do. Paranoids supposedly have a high level of repressed hostility, so maybe they'd be better shockers; but then they might distrust the experimenter and refuse to obey him — so again it's not really a surprise that defiants and obedients showed no significant difference on paranoia. You can find the same contradiction, as applied to behavior in the Milgram experiment, for just about every scale of the MMPI; and in fact I didn't get significant differences on any of the twelve standard scales. The only one that did differ noticeably was intended to measure "social responsibility" (Gough et al., 1952); defiant

130

volunteers were more responsible, as you might expect. Or might you? High scorers on this scale are supposed to be more willing to accept the consequences of their own behavior, to show "greater concern for social and moral issues," to feel a greater sense of obligation to their peer group, all of which might describe the ideal defiant volunteer. But high social-responsibility scorers are also supposed to be dependable, trustworthy, "more compliant and acquiescent," "less rebellious and recalcitrant." Now, is that or isn't that an obedient subject? Oh, well — the MMPI took only about half the interview session.

Then I asked each man to "tell me the most important things about yourself," and let him talk. Here the reader may exercise his psychological acumen: which of these answers are from defiant subjects and which from obedients?

> A: I'm a good worker; I provide for my family; I work hard; I work for my father, and there's no harder boss than your own dad. I don't go out and bum around like some of the guys do, I don't have time. The only bad things about me, I do get tied up in my work — I promise the kids to do something, take them somewhere, and then have to cancel because I get called out on a job.

> B: I enjoy my job. I have an enjoyable family, three children. If I had it to do all over again, I might choose another profession, for financial reasons. . . . I like hunting very much and fishing. I like to grow flowers around the yard — I like to raise a vegetable garden, primarily because I like fresh vegetables.

> C: I feel disappointed at the lack of opportunity provided by the social-intellectual climate of society for me to make contributions I feel capable of making. . . . I have turned for consolation to the comforts of family life and financial accomplishment. I still remain hopeful a position may present itself in which I can better take advantage of what I feel is my intellectual ability. I have not turned bitter. I have a generally low opinion of the intellectual level of humanity.

> D: I'm basically honest. I believe in the hereafter, God and everything — I'm a family man, a good provider. I'm 38, honest with myself, with my neighbors and so forth.

If somebody can see any noticeable pattern distinguishing them, or the other volunteers in my files, then somebody is a better analyzer of open-ended responses than I am. A and B were obedient, C and D were defiant. Most volunteers felt they weren't perfect, felt some disappointments in life, could see some cause for optimism, liked their wives and kids; several drank too much; and there appeared to be simply no consistent differences between obedients and defiants. Whenever there was a defiant volunteer who did charity work for slum children, there was an obedient subject who was active in a civil liberties organization. Whenever an obedient forgot to mention his family as being of any importance in his life, a defiant did likewise.

131

There was no good evidence among these people for the scapegoating or frustration-aggression theory of hostile behavior, either. The obedients seemed to lead neither more nor less frustrated lives than the defiants. Arnold Buss (1966), using a similar shock machine to study aggression rather than obedience, has purposely frustrated volunteers to different degrees, and finds no real differences in their willingness to administer strong shock. Russell Geen (1968) has found immediate frustration to provoke delivery of higher shock levels, but only if obvious cues for strong physical aggression (such as a film of a savage prize fight) are presented as part of the situation. Such cues were not present in the "scientific" surroundings of the Milgram situation. Scratch another good idea.

AUTHORITARIANISM AND OBEDIENCE

Following that open-ended question on the "most important things about yourself," I asked thirty more specific questions, and here we got several differences. Obedient volunteers reported being less close to their fathers during childhood than defiants did. Obedients described their fathers (but not their mothers) in distinctly more negative terms. As children, obedients usually had received either spankings or very little punishment, while defiants had often been punished either by severe beatings or by some kind of deprivation — of love or dinner. Slightly more obedients had served on active military duty (Milgram had found an even clearer difference here, in his short post-experiment interview); among these veterans, nearly every obedient said he had shot at men, and every defiant subject denied it. Obedients saw the "Memory and Learning" experimenter as clearly more admirable, and the learner as much less so, than did defiant volunteers.

Part of this may sound familiar, if you recall the discussion of *The Authoritarian Personality* in Chapter Three. Authoritarians were reportedly more distant from their stiff authoritarian fathers as children; they presumably would be more at ease in the military; they should see people occupying positions of authority in a more favorable light than those in inferior positions. Nor do we have to depend entirely on these indirect indications of authoritarianism, since I mixed the original Authoritarian F Scale into the MMPI. Here we get a big difference: obedients are significantly more authoritarian than defiants.

The problem does arise that less-educated people have been found to be consistently more authoritarian than the well-educated, and that Milgram had found less-educated people more obedient. So instead of authoritarian personalities producing obedience, lack of education could be producing both. But even after educational level was statistically controlled for, the more obedient subjects were still more authoritarian on the F Scale. Anyway, we should not lightly dismiss the fact that low education goes with obedience, whatever the relation of both to the F Scale.

Maybe a poorly educated person agrees with more F items because some of the items sound pretty dumb, as several writers have suggested; if so, the relationship between education and F scores would be a rather trivial finding. But the willingness of a poorly educated person to inflict grievous harm on an innocent bystander isn't trivial, whether it's because he's ignorant or what.

Obedience to authority does not appear to be absolutely synonymous with authoritarianism, at least as Adorno et al. saw it. The authoritarian is reported, for instance, to idealize his parents; but the obedients did the opposite, at least with regard to their fathers. Authoritarians typically report receiving strict discipline as children; obedients report rather spotty discipline. It's true that the obedients were asked about their fathers' characteristics here and now, and maybe most had come to see Dad in a more realistic light, as the authoritarian SOB he really was. But there's still room for doubt as to whether obedience and authoritarianism are entirely one.

Nonetheless, the relationship between obedience and some elements of authoritarianism seems fairly strong; and it should be remembered that the measure of obedience is a measure of actual submission to authority, not just what a person says he's likely to do. Too much research on authoritarianism, and too much criticism of it, has been at the level of paper-and-pencil responses, which don't necessarily get translated into behavior. In Milgram's experiments we have people either obeying or refusing the demands of authority, in a realistic and highly disturbing situation; we find that most of the few personality measures which discriminate obedients from defiants involve the sort of thing Adorno and his associates sifted from a large mass of very different kinds of measures and called authoritarianism. So it looks as if those researchers in the late 1940's really had something, something that can be translated from abstract tendencies into actual authoritarian behavior: submitting to the man in command, punishing the weaker subordinate.

Of course we knew it all along, didn't we? We knew it about Germans, anyway: how Germans had cherished authoritarian ideologies during a good part of the past hundred years; how German childraising, German character development, led to ugly behaviors in adulthood. But those were Germans, a peculiar breed of humanity. These are Americans, and their ancestors include English and Irish and Italians; their religions run the gamut and so do their occupations and their socioeconomic statuses. Look around you: whose basic character is obedient and whose defiant? How about yours?

HYPOTHETICAL SITUATIONS AND REAL BEHAVIOR

One small indication of how hard it is to tell, without going through a Milgram experiment — how hard it is to predict a man's behavior from what he says he'd do — is the sad story of a questionnaire I devised, the last thing I gave my interview volunteers. It consisted of ten situations in which a person was faced with a choice between obedient and defiant behavior, altruistic or self-serving responses, punishment or mercy toward others. One situation that seemed fairly easy for most volunteers to decide negatively was this:

> An eccentric millionaire, whom you have read about in the newspapers, calls you and invites you to his home. There he tells you he wants to take revenge on a beautiful woman who has refused to marry him. He offers you five hundred thousand dollars, all taxes paid, if you will throw enough acid in this woman's face to scar her permanently. He will arrange all the details so there will be no clues to trace you; the reason he is asking you to do it is because he wants someone who has absolutely no connection either with him or with the woman. Would you do what the millionaire asks in return for the five hundred thousand dollars?

Other situations seemed to present more problems: one that asked whether the volunteer would share his family's bomb shelter and short rations with neighbors during atomic attack; one that presented a dilemma involving a good student caught cheating on an exam; and one that went:

> Assume you are a soldier in the American Army in World War II, and your troop unit marches in to take over a German village. Although the people are poor, there is a fine schoolhouse in the village. Your commanding officer orders you to burn the schoolhouse down, in order to show the Germans that the American troops mean business. The villagers beg you not to burn it down, since the village children would have no place to attend school. Will you burn the schoolhouse down or not?

The answers were mostly unimaginative, but some were at least entertaining, and a few fulfilled my expectations for obedients and defiants. For instance, on the last question above, one obedient volunteer replied, "If an officer says you burn it, you burn it. You may not like to, but you burn it." Another: "Burn it down — I'm a soldier." "We will burn the schoolhouse down — I answer from experience." One obedient volunteer even quoted from "The Charge of the Light Brigade" in justification. But, sad to say, defiant subjects agreed to burn the schoolhouse just about as often; and a few obedients suggested other outcomes — for instance, that a fatal "accident" might happen to the commanding officer when he had his back turned. The fallout shelter question generated even more division of opinion; but the division again was not along the obedient-defiant dimension. Some defiants would sternly keep people out; some obedients seemed surprisingly soft-hearted. One obedient chuckled his way through an answer: "I don't know what you would do — feed them to the dogs — lock the door. I'm only joking — but realizing we can't live through this like that, I'd keep them out." (Would you use force to keep them out?) "Yes. I would shoot 'em! Just joking. . . ." And finally he said, "Actually I would let them in anyway. When the situation came, we don't know how we'd react to it."

That seems a pretty fair statement, because in these imaginary situations, obedients and defiants together ran the gamut from kindness to cruelty, obedience to defiance, selfishness to selflessness. Of course we know that in the crucial circumstances of Milgram's laboratory, the obedients zapped their way to the end of the shock board, while the defiants stopped the show. But we'd never know it from the questionnaire. One man who had been completely obedient in the Touch-Proximity condition described himself, in response to a hypothetical situation, as "the kind of guy who tries to dodge a squirrel with a car, and looks back to see that the next guy doesn't hit him." Another Touch-Proximity obedient, who said he put himself through college by working summers in a slaughterhouse, "standing knee-deep in blood," answered nearly every hypothetical question in the kindliest fashion, disobeying authorities and ignoring his own self-interest repeatedly (in imagination) to come to the aid of others. Perhaps he and several fellow obedients were trying to restore their own good self-image, or their image in the interviewer's eyes, by answering the questionnaire so altruistically after having behaved so despicably in the experiment; but there was little indication that this was the main concern of most respondents.

Lawrence Kohlberg (1969) has presented another group of Milgram's volunteers with a set of imaginary moral dilemmas, emphasizing not so much *how* they say they'd behave as *why*. He finds that of the few who base their decisions on general moral principles, most were defiant in the Milgram study, while most of those at a more restricted level of moral development obeyed the experimenter completely. But even Kohlberg's procedures, as far as I can tell, wouldn't produce very accurate predictions of behavior over the entire range of proximity conditions. My own questionnaire was considerably worse in its predictive power; and most short-answer psychological tests of "behavior" and personality resemble my questionnaire more than Kohlberg's, both in their emphasis on what a person says he'll do instead of why, and in their inability to predict actual behavior. The moral seems clear: the further you get from overt behavior in a genuinely involving situation, and the closer you get to armchair speculation (even if it's a person's speculation about his own probable future behavior, or the speculations of forty expert psychiatrists), the higher the likelihood of ending up with the wrong answers. Milgram had constructed a reality that divided men on an important behavior; I had constructed a questionnaire that looked as though it should yield similar divisions. But however I analyzed the answers to this questionnaire, forward, backward, upside down and sideways, the obedients

135

and the defiants just weren't much different. That wouldn't have bothered me much, except that I knew they really *were* different, dammit!

the sin of conformity:
laboratory studies of group influence

The land of the free! This the land of the free! . . . Why,
I have never been in any country where the individual
has such an abject fear of his fellow countrymen.

— D. H. Lawrence
Studies in Classic American Literature

Milgram's obedience studies were not the product of an isolated genius creating a radically different body of research. They came out of a heavily worked vineyard within social psychology, the field of experimental conformity research. Milgram's virtue is that he has drawn new wine from old vines. But conformity research itself has not been unproductive; it has even had its vintage years.

A few years ago, the word "conformity" was bandied about so often and in so many contexts that it was left with hardly any meaning beyond a vague connotation of opprobrium. Even current dictionary definitions are looser than they might be: "being in harmony or agreement" (*Webster's New World Dictionary*, 1962), "compliance or acquiescence" (*Random House Dictionary of the English Language*, 1967), "action or behavior in correspondence with current customs, rules, or styles" (*American Heritage Dictionary*, 1969). Your agreement with me that $2 + 2 = 4$ wouldn't be evidence of conformity, the way psychologists see it; the bohemian's rejection of common "customs, rules, or styles" wouldn't necessarily be evidence against his conformity; and acquiescence as a result of physical force had better be called compliance rather than conformity. Agreement with another person as the result of logical arguments or elaborate emotional appeals has also seemed to psychologists to fall into a somewhat different psychological category. Psychologists usually define conformity as the act of behaving similarly to a group's majority, as a result of simple expressions of opinion by group members. It's not that the group is doing something you'd do anyway, even if there were no group; it's not that they're berating you or threatening you or delivering oratorical declamations at you; they're just stating a judgment and you're going along with it because that's what the group says.

THE AUTOKINETIC EFFECT

Several early studies of group influence didn't really make such a clear distinction between conformity and persuasion, freely mixing simple judgmental statements with more complicated attempts at influence. The first important research on what we now would call conformity behavior, though it was then referred to as "formation of social norms," was done by Muzafer Sherif (1936). He seated volunteers, singly or in small groups, at one end of a darkened room, with a stationary point of light at the other end. Under such circumstances the light will soon appear to start moving; this is known as the "autokinetic effect" ("self-moving"), since the light really remains stationary and appears to move only because of the volunteer's own perceptual processes. Left to himself (and not told the light isn't moving), a person will establish his own norm of apparent movement: he'll see the light moving only within a rather narrow range of distances and directions. Sherif found that when several people are placed together and are asked to announce aloud how much the light is moving, most will come to agree on the amount of movement over time. Establishing such a group norm is actually a case of "mutual conformity": group members start off with no standards or with individual standards of movement, and are influenced by each other's statements until they agree closely on the light's movement.

Sherif's technique of reducing the group's operations to a bare minimum, and of using a task for which no norms exist outside the experimental laboratory, was much more susceptible to experimental manipulation than previous methods of studying group influence. But his results were not really surprising, either to the participants or to other psychologists. The autokinetic situation offers no real basis for judging what scale to measure the perceived movement against anyway, and other people are as likely to be "good" estimators of movement as oneself. So because their judgment is the only external reference point in the situation, why not use it to decide on your own scale? Conformity it may be, but of a relatively innocuous kind. Further, the sort of conformity involved – a mutual influence that ultimately establishes a group norm where none had previously existed – is rather different from most of our daily experiences with group influences, where long traditions are often involved and where even the new groups we form are likely to be so similar to previous groups that we can carry over old norms bodily.

THE ASCH STUDIES

Fifteen years later, Solomon Asch (1951, 1956) began to publish the results of research on another conformity situation, results that were not only surprising but that to a greater extent duplicated our experience with the groups we join – perhaps our experiences with society itself. Again, a situation ingenious in its simplicity: the volunteer finds himself sitting with seven or eight fellow students, all ready to participate in a visual discrimination study. The experimenter holds up two cards, one card with one vertical line on it and one card with three, and asks the students to say which of the three lines on the one card is the same length as the one line on the other card. Each student announces his choice in turn, our volunteer being next to last; because the differences in the lengths of the three lines are quite noticeable, everybody agrees on the answer. The experimenter holds up successive pairs of cards, with still other lengths of lines, but the pattern is always the same: everybody chooses the one line out of three which is the same length as the line on the other card.

Soon, however, the first student to respond makes a mistake, picks what is obviously the wrong line. The other members of the group, for some strange reason, make the same mistake. What is our hero, alas, to do — tell it as he sees it or go along with the group, dissent or conform? Whichever he does, the experimenter moves along without pause to other cards, other lines; and occasionally the group members agree with our hero on the right line. But most of the time, over and over again, they choose a line that is definitely wrong, sometimes the wrongest line possible. They aren't demonstrative about it, they aren't disturbed at dissent; they just continue to answer dispassionately, whatever the volunteer does. And each time, the volunteer faces the choice: are his eyes right, or are the seven or eight pairs of eyes that belong to his fellow volunteers?

Knowing already about the occasional deviousness of social psychologists, you may immediately suspect (quite rightly) that those seven or eight other volunteers are paid shills of the experimenter, and that they've agreed in advance to agree on the wrong answers, to see whether the one real volunteer will go along or not. Most real volunteers didn't suspect; they believed the situation was as it appeared to be, and they became obviously upset at the conflict between what their own vision told them and what other group members reported. (If this conformity research, in particular, resembles Milgram's obedience studies, it should; Milgram worked as Asch's assistant for a year at Princeton's Institute for Advanced Studies.)

Asch's findings were as startling upon first publication as Milgram's obedience results were later. Three-fourths of the volunteers apparently ignored their own eyes and went along with the group at least part of the time; 27 per cent agreed with the group most of the time (on eight or more out of the twelve wrong group judgments). Only 24 per cent stuck with their own perceptions. In a control study, less than 5 per cent of volunteers tested alone chose anything other than the right line, and then only once or twice at most.

"Horrors!" a good many of Asch's readers seemed to think, "here we have a breed so conformist it will look at black and see white, if only the group says so! Conformity at its worst — blind, slavish conformity! Thank God, at least, for that virtuous 24 per cent who retained their own independence!"

138

But as it turned out, the nonconformists were not completely without guilt, and the conformists still saw black when they looked at black. They just *said* it was white. The contradiction between group judgment and personal judgment seemed highly stressful for practically everyone who participated, whether they remained confident that their own judgment was correct, or gave in to the group every time. Very few really came to think they were seeing things the way the majority was seeing things. A few did get so confused that they pretty much ignored the visual cues of the lines themselves, and simply took the majority version as accurate. Still others continued to see the lines as they really were, but went along verbally with the majority, for various reasons. Some independents never had major doubts about their own judgments, though they found their announced disagreements distressing; they speculated that the group might be subject to an optical illusion that didn't affect them, or that the rest of the group had misunderstood instructions. Other independents thought perhaps they themselves had misunderstood the instructions — that maybe, for instance, they were supposed to be judging which lines were similar in width, not length (though all lines were of the same width). But they weren't sure enough to change, and blundered ahead giving the right answers. Still others were pretty sure the group knew what it was doing, but just couldn't see any reason to change their reports of what they themselves saw, because they'd never had cause to distrust their vision before. As one volunteer told the group, "You're *probably* right, but you *may* be wrong!"

The behavior of the nonconformists in this situation is readily understandable: the experimenter had asked them to pick the right answers, and to help science, show their own intelligence, defer to the presumably powerful experimenter, or fulfill a commitment that they had voluntarily undertaken, they picked the right answers. The behavior of the conformists seems less immediately explainable. Asch lists several reasons given later by the conformists themselves: belief in the legitimacy of majority rule in a democracy, for instance, or a kind of "logical" calculation (if they're right and I disagree, I'm wrong; if they're wrong and I agree, everybody's wrong, so what?). One might even speculate that some volunteers were responding less to the current situation and the apparent demands of the current group than to much earlier conflicts, "transferred" to the present situation à la Freud — though Asch's post-experiment interviews were not designed to probe so deeply.

But what appear to be the main reasons for conformity, not necessarily identified as such by the conformists, work down to a small group of motives. Different psychologists have called the motives by different names, but they fall essentially into two categories. In one, the motives for giving answers acceptable to the experimenter are similar to those of the non-conformists; but rather than depending solely on their own senses to determine the correct answers, the conformists defer in part or whole to the group's judgment as well. We're very much accustomed to using the judgments of others to augment our own, when we don't have first-hand information or when a stimulus is ambiguous. In the Asch situation, the habit seems to carry over for a portion of the volunteers, even though the stimuli are unambiguous. Two reliable sources of information are, after all, in direct conflict, so why reject one source — the social one — entirely?

So some defer to group judgments to help them judge objective stimuli. For others, the group may be an even more important source of information in judging themselves. Both our self-esteem and our self-identity come in large part from the voiced or unspoken reactions of others. Social relationships play a major role in human life for many reasons, and the only reliable way to judge your own efficacy in such relationships is to see how others respond to you. In the Asch situation, volunteers were often fearful of seeming strange or silly to the rest of the group; some even reasoned that if they behaved so stupidly in this temporary group, they would behave similarly and suffer similar consequences outside the group. "I hope you didn't think I was different," volunteers said after the experiment; "I like to be one of the boys, so to speak"; "For a while it [disagreeing with the group] made me feel funny; it seemed as though I was a fool"; "They probably think I'm crazy or something." These statements came despite the fact that the group never indicated any thought that the real volunteer was strange or lunatic; in this respect the group was quite artificial. The response such nonconforming behavior would likely get in a "real" group is illustrated by another Asch experiment, in which sixteen genuine volunteers and one paid stooge participated together. The real volunteers, when asked to judge the length of the lines, of course agreed consistently on the right answers; the lines were, after all, pretty easy to match. But at a certain point the stooge began giving wrong answers, minority-of-one answers, just as in the other experiments. The real group just laughed at him, laughed repeatedly and with great glee. Those minority-of-one volunteers in the usual Asch groups not only accurately perceived the lines on the cards; they appear also to have accurately perceived the likely group response to any dissenting judgments.

SITUATIONAL AND GROUP DETERMINANTS

As with obedience, the particular situation at hand can make a big difference in how many people conform and how much. For one thing, the issue on which one is being pushed to conform can be crucial. The judgments demanded in conformity studies have ranged from which two pictures have the same number of paratroopers dotting the sky, to which of several arrangements of thumbtacks look more "friendly," to whether volunteers believe they could be happy without any friends at all. (Richard Crutchfield [1955] and others have built machines which can present many different kinds of visual stimuli or opinion items in rapid sequence, so that a battery of conformity situations may be used in one session.) In each case, the volunteer has no information from the group except its majority vote; he decides to dissent or conform on that basis. The general finding about such variations is that the more ambiguous the stimulus, the more conformity occurs and the easier the conformity is on the volunteers (the less conflict or anxiety) — the Sherif autokinetic situation being about as ambiguous as possible and the Asch line-judging situation being about as unambiguous. A related factor is how far out the group's judgment is. If the stimulus is rather unambiguous and if the group's judgment is way off, volunteers will likely show less conformity than to a more reasonable but still wrong judgment. But through most of the range of possible judgments, at least some volunteers seem willing to tag along. In a study by Read Tuddenham (1958), for instance, volunteers working by themselves never estimated that people over 65 constituted 60 per cent or more of the United States population; but over half the volunteers in a group situation agreed with the group that this was the correct percentage. In the same study, only 2 per cent of the non-group volunteers agreed with the statement, "I could be perfectly happy without a single friend," but 40 per cent of a volunteer sample in a group-influence setting agreed with the statement after the rest of the group did.

Characteristics of the group make a difference, too. A group whose members are seen as more attractive, more competent with regard to the issue at hand, or higher in status generally, is more likely to induce conformity. The group's size is important only up to a point. Asch eventually found that he didn't need to pay eight or nine assistants every time he tested one real volunteer; three assistants could elicit just as much conformity. (Two assistants got noticeably less and one assistant even less than that.) Perhaps this leveling off of conformity, once you go beyond three group members influencing one, happens partly because the unanimous agreement of larger numbers begins to look a little suspicious; perhaps partly because (as some volunteers have indicated) the response pattern of a larger group looks too much like one instigator leading his flock of sheep into error, thus reminding the real volunteer of his own sheepish tendencies.

All these conclusions are predicated on a unanimous group influencing the lone volunteer. Give him a single ally, in a large group or small, and his likelihood of conformity drops drastically. Give him an ally who abandons him midway, and his likelihood of conforming jumps back toward normal. But if the ally can give a convincingly urgent excuse for leaving the scene, other than growing dislike for the volunteer or withdrawal from group pressure, the volunteer is likely to retain a good bit of the backbone with which his now departed buddy invested him.

INDIVIDUAL DIFFERENCES IN CONFORMITY

Certain personality and demographic factors also influence conformity, but just how is not always clear. In various studies using a single type of conformity measure, a considerable assortment of personality variables have been found associated with conformity. But such associations have then usually turned out to be absent or contradicted in other studies, although since different experimenters have seldom used the same personality measures, it's a bit hard to tell whether even the contradictions are contradicting whatever was originally studied (see Mann, 1959). Among the individual-difference factors most often found in these one-conformity-measure studies are that women are more conforming than men; that older people are more set in their ways and less conforming to the temporary group than the young; that the stupid are more conforming than the smart; and that authoritarians are more conforming than nonauthoritarians. But each of these differences has been found not to apply in at least some conformity situations.

An Australian researcher, Graham Vaughan (1964), tried several rather different ways of eliciting conformity in the same set of volunteers. He found that about 80 per cent conformed in some situations but not others, so that they couldn't be described as having any general conformity trait that could then be correlated with other traits. Vaughan feels, probably rightly, that most conformity-and-personality studies have exaggerated the relationships involved by locating personality characteristics that are important in determining one particular kind of conformity behavior, and then generalizing to conformity in all situations. Vaughan found only about 10 per cent of his volunteers conforming in all four of the conformity situations he used, and about 10 per cent consistently remaining independent of conformity pressures. Several factors differentiated these two groups: the independents were higher in intelligence and in assertiveness (on measures separate from the conformity situation); conformists were higher on measures of authoritarianism and dogmatism. However, even Vaughan's results are not without their problems. For instance, one of his conformity measures was the student volunteer's response to a request to turn in an extra class assignment by a deadline — behavior that would appear to partake more of obedience to authority than of social conformity, and that might be contaminated by other little-related factors such as procrastinatory tendencies. So Vaughan could be underestimating both the amount of general conformity and the number of personality factors related to conformity.

142

Attempts have also been made to relate conformity to certain national or cultural differences. Herbert Barry (Barry et al., 1959) has speculated that in hunting and fishing subsistence-level cultures, individualism and assertiveness would be most likely to promote survival, while in pastoral or agricultural subsistence-level cultures, compliance and conservatism would best guarantee survival. To test this hypothesis, J. W. Berry (1967) administered a simple modification of the Asch line-judging technique to adults of the Temne culture of Sierra Leone, whose food supply is mainly dependent on a yearly rice crop, and to adult Eskimos of Baffin Island, who are hunters and fishers entirely. A sample of Scotsmen was used as a sort of Western-culture control group. As expected, the Temne sample was highly conforming, the Eskimo almost completely nonconforming. The Scots were rather closer to the Eskimos than to the Temnes, as any Englishman might have predicted.

Stanley Milgram (1961), prior to his obedience research, did a cross-cultural study of conformity in Norway and France. He carefully selected volunteers in both countries so that such background factors as age, educational level, and social class were fairly equal. The volunteers were asked to participate in another modification of the Asch situation, in which they judged the relative length of musical tones heard on earphones. The instructions were delivered in the appropriate language by a native speaker; five other volunteers were presumably judging the same tones over a microphone system. Actually these other judges' responses were taped and only the one volunteer and the experimenter were present in the laboratory. Quite consistently, the Norwegians conformed more to the "group" judgments than the French — 62 per cent of the time versus 50 per cent in the basic experiment. When subjects in a separate experiment were told the tone-judging results would be used in designing accurate safety signals, conformity was slightly lower but the Norwegians were still ahead, 56 per cent to 48 per cent. When the situation was changed so that the real volunteer didn't have to announce his judgment aloud, French conformity dropped sharply to 34 per cent; Norwegian conformity less so, to 50 per cent. Milgram was able to increase conformity, on the other hand, by tape-recording snickers and belittling comments ("Are you trying to show off?"), supposedly originating from the group, which were played from a second tape recorder whenever the volunteer made an independent judgment. Norwegian conformity jumped to 75 per cent, French to 59 per cent. The Norwegians just took the criticism, but in France, over half the volunteers talked back when criticized, and two "became so enraged they directed a stream of abusive language at their taunters." Overall, 12 per cent of Norwegian volunteers conformed completely to the group, but only 1 per cent of French volunteers; 25 per cent of the Norwegians showed "strong independence," compared with 41 per cent of the French. Milgram suggests a relationship between these results and the "highly cohesive" Norwegian society, oriented toward social responsibility and group identification, versus the politically unstable, low-consensus French society, with a "tradition of dissent and critical argument."

COUNTERFORMITY

Hollander and Willis (1967) have suggested that Milgram's results need not indicate any virtuous independence from group pressure on the part of the French, but that a good many Frenchmen might instead be what social psychologists call "anticonformists" or "counterformists." Whereas nonconformity or independence, in or out of the conformity laboratory, refers to doing your own thing regardless of group pressure, counterformity refers to doing the opposite of whatever the group is doing, just because the group is doing it. For the true independent, social pressure is either irrelevant or (more often) is not the critical factor in his behavior. But the counterformist is as dependent on the decisions of the group as the conformist is. He has to know what the group feels, so he can do something different — and he will do it even if the group is right.

Many people suspect their children, or youth in general, of being counterformists (so a song in The Fantasticks warns you not to caution your children against putting beans in their ears). There are good theoretical reasons for postulating the existence of counterformists in conformity situations, but experimenters have seldom run across consistently anticonforming individuals. Robert Frager (1970) has observed occasional anticonformity behavior in an Asch-type situation among Japanese college students, and finds it correlated with feelings of social alienation; but no one to my knowledge has found enough American counterformists to see what their problems might be. It probably wouldn't be hard to set up a laboratory situation that would temporarily generate a lot of counterformists: make the volunteer fighting mad at the group just before the line-judging starts, or present the group as Birchers and use only Maoists as real volunteers, or vice versa. But I don't see what that would prove, other than that social psychologists can waste a lot of time being inventive.

The search for counterformists has come, I suspect, from more than abstract theoretical considerations alone. Psychologists seem to grow uncomfortable if they go on condemning one category of person too long; and a good bit of the conformity research has implied, if not stated, condemnation of conformists. On the other hand, we all like to think of ourselves as rather independent-minded. (Even the conformists themselves, in the studies that took the time to ask them, seldom praised their

144

own conformity, and conveniently forgot or overlooked most of it.) So who else can we condemn to make up for our rough treatment of the conformists? Well, those hypothetical counterformists are definitely baddies — nonthinking troublemakers who don't even have the graciousness to go along with the group, which after all is right *part* of the time.

THE USES OF CONFORMITY

Conformity has been a popular research topic among social psychologists for several of the same reasons as rightist extremism — e.g., they don't like it and would like to undercut its rational bases or find ways to discourage it. But the psychologists have usually been careful (perhaps as a result of Asch's own thoughtful analyses) to grant the validity of conformity in certain situations. Obviously someone who allows all his behaviors to be determined by the group is a spineless ninny. But partial conformity to the group's standards can save us a lot of trouble, and permits enough efficiency in unimportant things to leave us time to make our own important decisions. A little less time spent on developing one's own unique artistic style, I daresay, would give us a rather larger quantity of substantial art; and if you don't worry too much about whether your clothes are sufficiently avant-garde, you might be able to put a little more time into serious reflection on your own place in the universe, or whatever else you care to reflect seriously about. It is the content rather than the form of art or thought or life that can be seriously damaged by conformity.

Social conformity can on certain occasions even lead to a positive good. Such occasions have not often been studied; but Stanley Milgram (1965a) modified his obedience situation to provide us with one example. In his Voice Feedback condition, remember, twenty-six out of forty volunteers were completely obedient to the experimenter's commands to shock the protesting learner. Milgram ran another forty volunteers through this same basic condition, but added two more "volunteers," really paid confederates, who divided up the job of "teaching" with the real volunteer. When the "learner" yelled at 150 volts that he wanted out, one fake teacher refused to go any further, and walked away from the shock board. At 210 volts, the other fake teacher did the same, saying, "I'm willing to answer any of your questions, but I'm not willing to shock that man against his will; I'll have no part of it." So the real volunteer was left at the shock board to complete the experiment, and the experimenter told him it was essential that he do so.

Here, experimenter pressure for obedience conflicts with group pressure for disobedience. The volunteer could be a nonconformist, and shock the victim for the sake of science; a few people did. (One obedient volunteer sounded like the more self-righteous independents of the Asch studies: "Momentarily I was ready to go along with them. Then sud-

145

denly I felt that they were just being ridiculous. What was I doing following the crowd? . . . They certainly had a right to stop, but I felt they lost all control of themselves.") But thirty-six out of the forty volunteers in this experiment conformed to the behavior of their peers, and defied the demands of the experimenter to continue — about as high a level of defiance as Milgram ever got. Other factors obviously intrude: for instance, the volunteer sees the fake teachers quitting and getting away with it. But the important feature here is that an effective situation for *positive* social conformity was created, one which, in Milgram's term, "liberated" the volunteer's more humanitarian impulses. With a little more of that kind of social pressure and that kind of conformity in the world, it might be harder to fight a war than to stop one.

experimental ethics: issues raised by obedience research

Science leads to powers whose exercise spells disaster and nuclear weapons are not the deepest of these. In the great strides in the biological sciences, and far more still in the early beginnings of an understanding of man's psyche, of his beliefs, his learning, his memory and his probable action, one can see the origin of still graver problems of good and evil.

— J. Robert Oppenheimer, quoted in
The New York Times, May 23, 1956

Psychology thrusts no new moral dilemmas upon us. At most, by increasing possibilities of prediction and control, it demands that we attend more seriously to the solution of old moral and philosophical dilemmas.

— Raymond B. Cattell
The Scientific Analysis of Personality

In most of Milgram's research, complaint volunteers engaged not in constructive but in destructive obedience, and seemed willing to abdicate their moral responsibility as they did so. But of course they were not freed from moral responsibility just because the experimenter demanded that they obey; neither the moral codes of most modern religions nor the deliberations of such bodies as the Nuremburg tribunal would grant them that freedom. Milgram, in exploring the external conditions that produce such destructive obedience, the psychological processes that lead to such attempted abdications of responsibility, and the means by which defiance of illegitimate authority can be promoted, seems to me to have done some of the most morally significant research in modern psychology. A number of ministers who have based sermons on this research, and the Germans and Israelis who were the first to publish translations of Milgram's papers, apparently agree.

But by an odd twist of moral sensibilities, the Milgram studies have themselves been more extensively attacked on ethical grounds than any other recent psychological research. Part of the criticism has come simply from coffee-break moralizers, who feel their own vague personal codes of ethics to have been somehow bruised. But the studies have also been used as stepping-off points for serious discussions of the psychologist's ethical responsibilities, both to his research participants and to society at large.

Psychologists had not ignored the moral and ethical issues involved in experimentation prior to Milgram's research. The American Psychological Association's *Ethical Standards of Psychologists* has gone through several editions, with another major revision in progress (Ad Hoc Committee on Ethical Standards, 1971). Several APA divisions have additional codes of ethics, or committees to investigate ethical violations; and a good many college psychology departments have their own machinery for policing the ethical practices of faculty and student researchers. An APA committee investigated Milgram's obedience research not long after its first appearance in print (holding up his APA membership application for a year in the meantime), and judged it ethically acceptable. But the criticisms have continued, partly because the APA code is foggy enough to allow for wide differences of opinion, partly perhaps because really clear cases of violation seldom come along and some psychologists were looking for a convenient battleground. One's moral purity is hard to establish nowadays without a good fight.

The first and most widely published criticism of the Milgram studies, by Diana Baumrind (1964), raised several key issues. Milgram (1964b) has published a careful rebuttal of her specific points, but the general issues hold implications for other psychological research as well, and are worth considering at length.

THE ISSUE OF "ENTRAPMENT"

Is the psychologist ever justified in leading a volunteer into a situation the volunteer has not anticipated and to which he has not given his prior consent? It's tempting here simply to generalize from good medical research practice and argue (as Baumrind does) that the volunteer should always give his "informed consent" in advance, that he should be told what's going to happen and what the dangers are so he can decide whether he really wants to participate or not. This may be feasible when you want to inject a bacillus into people, because telling them about it won't do much to the bacillus one way or the other. But if you want to study the conditions under which a volunteer will obey an authority's

147

orders, you'd better not tell him, "I want to see when you'll obey me and when you'll disobey me," or you might as well go play a quick game of ping-pong instead. The same is true for social conformity experiments, and in fact for a large proportion of the questions studied by social and personality psychologists.

This doesn't mean that deception in psychological experiments is a trivial problem, or above reproach. Misrepresentation or lying, in the service of science as well as anywhere else, is both unfair and possibly damaging to the recipient of the lie, and may ultimately harm the deceiver's interests as well. As more and more deception is used and becomes known in psychology, potential groups of volunteers are likely to build up layers of distrust toward any kind of unusual or particularly demanding situation, for fear of suddenly being told something like "Smile, you're on Candid Camera!" Not only will this inhibit spontaneous behavior; not only does it cause serious public relations problems for psychologists (particularly with their students); it also renders the results of many psychological experiments even outside the laboratory thoroughly suspect. I would distrust the results of any new social-psychological experiment using student volunteers from Harvard, Yale, Michigan, or several other over-researched universities, unless I knew much more than most experimenters learn about how the volunteers actually saw the experimental situation. Many researchers now make an attempt to question volunteers after an experiment about their perception of deception; but the attempt is often directed more toward reassuring the experimenter about the efficacy of his cover story than toward obtaining useful information about the incidence of doubt.

What can be done, then, to protect both volunteers and psychologists? An easy suggestion is to reduce deception to a minimum. Some psychologists have gone the other way: I know of a study where the volunteer was led to believe he was helping the psychologist dupe another volunteer who presumably thought he was helping dupe a third volunteer (and maybe there was a fourth one in there somewhere), when of course only volunteer number one was really being fooled and the others were experimental confederates. It may have been vital to go to such lengths in that particular case; but I think it's safe to say there's much more deception going on than need be. Part of it is simple one-upmanship; the psychologist feels good knowing a few things the volunteer doesn't know. I've done research myself in which I laid on perhaps twice as much deception as was necessary, to make the experiment more stimulating to my potential readers. I can say now that I wasn't mature enough then to know better, and that I won't do it again, and that I hope others won't either. But is that enough?

Herbert Kelman (1967) and others have suggested that we might instead resort to roleplaying: tell our volunteers what we're trying to study, and then have them go through the experimental situation while pretending they don't know what it's all about. This approach assumes that sophomores and other volunteers already know all there is to know about their own probable responses in real life, *or* that they will do the same things in a simulated situation as in a realistic one, both of which are patently wrong. I've already mentioned two occasions within the Milgram series alone that indicate the likely invalidity of such role-playing studies: the fact that nonparticipants, even highly trained psychiatrists, are miserable predictors of real participants' responses, and the discovery that Milgram participants, asked to describe what they would do in other situations of destructive obedience, often gave answers totally discrepant with their behavior in the obedience situation. Maybe they would do all those things; but I prefer to believe their real behavior, even in a laboratory experiment, over their roleplayed behavior. Milgram also asked volunteers in another study (1965a) what they'd be likely to do in the basic obedience situation, without actually putting them through it; nobody said he'd go higher than 300 volts, though of course many real participants went to 450 volts. Roleplaying looks like one of the worst of many possible resolutions to the deception problem (see also Freedman, 1969).

So we have a set of studies such as Milgram's, which must involve some deception if they are to be done at all. Once we've limited that deception to the necessary minimum, is that all we can do? Just say, "Oh well, deception is necessary," and drop it?

No, we can still do a couple of things. One is to make it clear to the volunteer that any time the experiment becomes distasteful to him, calls upon him to do things he would not willingly do, he can get out of it. In a medical study this might not be very useful, if the patient is already under anesthesia or has his belly open or a needle in his spine. But for consenting adults in a psychology experiment, it can be made a live option throughout, and a number of college psychology departments make it an alternative to "informed consent." In the Milgram study, all volunteers were explicitly told at the beginning that they were being paid simply for coming, not for completing the experimental procedure, and they were paid in advance to free them from financial pressure to continue. In other types of experiments where willingness to obey is not an issue, volunteers can also be told repeatedly that they are free to stop at any time during the experiment.

We can also tell the volunteer, as soon as possible, what has been going on: undeceive him, so he won't go around still believing the misrepresentations. This can often be done most feasibly immediately after the experiment, particularly with college students who are likely soon to scatter to the four winds. Such a practice may still create difficulties where an experiment is spread over an appreciable time: participants are likely to talk to other people about their experience, if it is of any interest at all. Careful studies have shown that even when students sign agreements that they won't tell, volunteer performance may change significantly from those who participate early in an experiment to those who participate late. What Milgram initially did was a reasonable compromise: he told volunteers as soon as their participation was over that the victim hadn't gotten nearly as much shock as they'd thought. Then Milgram waited for several months, until the bulk of the studies were completed, to notify participants fully of the experiment's purpose, the extent of the deceptions, and the early results, as well as emphasizing the value of their participation. Volunteers who participated after the experimental series was further along were told immediately afterward exactly what was going on.

It's sometimes tempting not to "dehoax" volunteers at all. That way, presumably, word doesn't get out about the study before it's finished, the volunteer isn't made to feel like a fool for having been duped, and psychology isn't given a bad name by publicizing all those deceptions. According to this reasoning, maybe I shouldn't write anything about deception here. But word *will* get out sooner or later anyway, if the psychologist makes any effort to circulate information on his research, as he properly should, or if he trains his students at all in the techniques that research involves, as he also properly should. Better the word get out intentionally and in context, than be publicized as an exposé several years later. If social psychology gets a bad name simply from the dispassionate or even sympathetic description of its research techniques, it will surely have earned that bad name. I don't think it has earned such a name; as I've said, experimental deception is sometimes a legitimate means to legitimate ends, and it can be presented to volunteers in that light. Deception will remain a technique to use in minimal fashion, only when nothing else will get the requisite information. Most psychologists have enough ethical distaste for deception as such to avoid it when possible, and maybe greater publicity about it will force the rest to devise alternate means of study. But deception need not be thought of as a mortal sin in and of itself.

THE ISSUE OF PSYCHOLOGICAL INJURY

The question of whether it's all right to make the volunteer feel like a fool by telling him you've tricked him brings me to another of Baumrind's points: Milgram's assailing of volunteers' "sensibilities." He upset them emotionally, pushed them into a situation where they could only obey and then hate themselves for it afterward, and all this was "potentially harmful because it could easily effect an alteration in the subject's self-image or ability to trust adult authorities in the future."

The phrase "adult authorities" suggests how Baumrind really sees

Milgram volunteers: she is a child psychologist and the volunteers are all children at heart, unable to resist the experimenter's wiles and therefore needing protection by someone who knows better, namely Dr. Baumrind. But of course the volunteers are actually grown men, in full legal possession of their senses and their wills, undrugged and faced with no physical force. If they could do nothing but obey, Milgram would have no experiment. But they *can* do something else (as the victim, by his protests, seeks to remind them), and a goodly number of them do; it's their choice, not Milgram's. The experimenter does demand that they obey, true; but if he is an "adult authority," they are adult moral agents in their own right. As Milgram (1964b) says, "I started with the belief that every person who came to the laboratory was free to accept or to reject the dictates of authority. This view sustains a conception of human dignity insofar as it sees in each man a capacity for *choosing* his own behavior. And as it turned out, many subjects did, indeed, choose to reject the experimenter's commands, providing a powerful affirmation of human ideals."

Several psychological studies have been conducted where the volunteer undergoes certain morally questionable manipulations with no choice on his part. He is falsely told that he has homosexual tendencies or that he is stupid or is repugnant to some group of respected people. Baumrind herself (1967) has placed small children in situations where they are sure to fail a task, in order to observe their responses to failure. One might be able to justify even these kinds of manipulations, if they are absolutely necessary to an important scientific enterprise and if great care is taken to alleviate afterward any misimpressions that the psychologist may have created in his volunteers. But I would still have doubts about such techniques, simply because the element of choice has been removed. The element of choice remains continually present in the Milgram situation; and choice, after all, is what makes morality.

Baumrind is distressed not only because Milgram puts his volunteers in a situation where (she says) they can do nothing but obey, but also because he gets them extremely excited and anxious and upset, because the whole situation is so "traumatic." Their disturbance, of course, is another sign that they recognize a moral dilemma; I for one am glad that few if any delivered shocks to the victim with cold impassiveness. But did Milgram have any right to upset them at all?

An unfortunate tradition within certain regions of social psychology dictates that social interactions under study should be stripped of any real-world referents. The dynamics of a small group discussion, for instance, may be studied by isolating volunteers in separate cubicles and having them pass notes to each other through little slots, in this way conducting a slow-motion argument about an issue of absolute triviality. Such studies have their partisans, but I am not one and I have avoided

151

discussing them at any length in this book, since their social relevance seems minimal. It's possible to conduct research without raising a participant's blood pressure or arousing his slightest concern; but since the important aspects of human life often involve concern and heightened blood pressure, I don't feel researchers should avoid them.

Volunteers may not always want their concerns aroused, and we must keep the rights of the volunteer constantly in mind. But such considerations are not completely impervious to other demands. Just as the conformity experiment participant faces a conflict between objective and social information, the psychologist who wishes to study humans faces a conflict between the general value of his research, not only to "science" but to humanity at large, and the possible harm that participation may cause to his volunteers. He has a strong obligation to reduce negative effects to the minimum. But must he, as Baumrind demands, cancel his experiment if he cannot eliminate every possibility of "permanent harm, however slight"?

Most serious students of ethics at some point reach the conclusion that there is more than one source of ethical obligation, whether they approach ethics from a religious viewpoint or a philosophical or even a scientific one. You cannot use absolute words in talking about moral obligations toward the individual or toward society; you cannot insist on either the "greater good" or "the individual good" with any degree of certitude. When the bulk of psychologists come to that realization, and begin transferring their psychological investments from their own personal moral codes to a hard critical consideration of professional ethical complexities, perhaps we'll attain a more honest confidence about the resolution of our perplexing ethical decisions than we hold now. But absolute certitude, I doubt. The medical profession, with a much longer history of trying to deal with such issues, hasn't got there yet, and doesn't seem about to.

Milgram, as Baumrind herself indicates, was concerned with a very important social problem, one which has been directly implicated not only in the physical destruction of millions of people during the twentieth century alone, but with the moral abdication of millions more. The ethical case *for* his upsetting several hundred people in the laboratory in order to study this problem seriously is surely much better than the case against, though neither can at this point be established absolutely. He does have an obligation to minimize any long-term negative effects of such upsets as thoroughly as possible. Has he done so?

Baumrind, reading Milgram's two-sentence description of his procedure for alleviating volunteers' emotional tensions in his first report, didn't think so: "In view of the effects on subjects, traumatic to a degree which Milgram himself considers nearly unprecedented in sociopsychological experiments, his casual assurance that these tensions were dissipated before the subject left the laboratory is unconvincing." But the tension-dissipation procedures were in fact anything but casual; they were, as far as I know, nearly unprecedented in sociopsychological experiments. The standard procedure in other sorts of experiments involving deception has been a straightforward explanation of what the study was all about, with the assumption that this would relieve any disturbances; in most cases it probably has. A few experiments, such as Asch's, have also involved discussions with the experimenter and sometimes with his confederates afterward, to clear up any misunderstandings and to further alleviate any obvious distress. Milgram went well beyond that. As I've indicated previously, the volunteer was told post-experimentally that the machine could not administer shocks harmful to humans; the victim came out in a very friendly mood, explaining he had been overly excited but not hurt; he stressed he had "no hard feelings," shook the volunteer's hand at least a couple of times, and often said he would have done the same in the volunteer's shoes; and the experimenter explained that the volunteer's behavior was by no means unique and indeed was what was expected in a memory-and-learning experiment. Between experimenter and "victim," a very effective job was done of relieving whatever tensions the volunteer had accumulated during the experiment. Baumrind actually complains that the experimenter was too nice: "the subject finds it difficult to express his anger outwardly after the experimenter in a self-acceptant but friendly manner reveals the hoax." But the volunteers seldom indicated any thought of anger at this point, and whatever anger existed was soon dissipated by their relief at not having hurt the "learner," or by the volunteer-accepting (not self-accepting) manner of both experimenter and victim. All this was reinforced later when volunteers received the written description of the experiment's true purpose. As Milgram says of this report, "Again their own part in the experiments was treated in a dignified way and their behavior in the experiment respected."

But Milgram didn't stop there; he had an extensive program of evaluating the effectiveness of these tension-relief procedures, in addition to the on-the-spot evaluations at the end of each volunteer's participation. For one thing, a short questionnaire was mailed to each volunteer along with the written report of the research results. Most returned the questionnaire and most indicated a continued positive response to their participation; only 1.3 per cent indicated any negative feelings about it. In my separate interviews with forty volunteers, conducted before the report was sent out, I questioned them about whether they had subsequently "felt bothered in any way about having shocked the learner," and probed gently about such things as guilt feelings or bad dreams. Only two people indicated even mild concern. Indeed most obedient volunteers were willing to participate again, as either teacher *or* learner.

A majority of the defiant subjects interviewed were also willing to return to act as teacher again, though they had refused to do so at some point in the original experiment.

I didn't question these volunteers extensively about their feelings toward the obedience research, but a psychiatrist not otherwise connected with the studies did interview another forty in depth a year after their participation, purposely choosing those who seemed most likely to have suffered psychological harm from their participation. His conclusion (as quoted in Milgram, 1964b): "None was found by this interviewer to show signs of having been harmed by his experience. . . . Each subject seemed to handle his task (in the experiment) in a manner consistent with well-established patterns of behavior. No evidence was found of any traumatic reactions." A recent obedience study by Ring, Wallston, and Corey (1970) found a similar absence of lingering disturbance following experimental participation, as long as volunteers were told — as in the Milgram studies — that the victim was not actually harmed and that their own experimental behavior was appropriate.

In view of all these precautions and all the evidence that they were effective, I'd say that the Milgram research, far from being attacked for ethical shoddiness, might well be held up as a model of how one should proceed in conducting a serious experiment on serious human problems, with full consideration of the ethical issues involved in experimentation. If there's anything I'd complain about, it's that Milgram made it too easy for the obedient volunteers to ignore the ethical implications of what they'd done, by assuring them that other people did the same kinds of things and by implying that this was acceptable behavior. Maybe he should have left them a little more shook up than they were.

This raises the issue of what people consider to be psychological harm. Baumrind's position, again, is, "I do regard the emotional disturbance described by Milgram as potentially harmful because it could easily effect an alteration in the subject's self-image or ability to trust adult authorities in the future." Along somewhat the same lines, Herbert Kelman (1967) has argued, "In general, the principle that a subject ought not to leave the laboratory with greater anxiety or lower self-esteem than he came with is a good one to follow." Milgram rightly responds to the latter part of Baumrind's statement by noting that people should *not* indiscriminately trust authorities who order harsh and inhumane treatment. But what about this matter of self-esteem? Maybe the volunteers didn't have bad dreams later, or develop any neurotic symptoms as a result of shocking the learner; but surely some recognized the weakness of their own ethical systems, realized they'd proven themselves poorer human beings than they had previously thought? And aren't you unjustly harming a person when you lower his own evaluation of himself in this way?

154

Stanley Coopersmith (1967) and other psychologists have observed in some individuals a "discrepant" or "defensive" self-esteem, which is not based on accurate assessment of the individual's own behavior and indeed may be concealing truths about the person that he'd be better off knowing. I see no obligation for the psychologist to strengthen or maintain such defensive self-esteem, though if his actions are likely to weaken it he should be prepared to help the individual find more realistic bases for rebuilding a positive self-image. Self-esteem is another of those things that looks like an absolute good at first, to the ethics-oriented thinker looking for absolute goods, but that may prove at least partly illusory.

THE ISSUE OF INFLUENCE

Some would continue to reject such a view, arguing not only that psychological researchers should "do no harm," but that they should avoid intervening in an individual's behavior uninvited even if the behavior's continuation is likely to damage the individual's own interests or the interests of others. Kelman (1965) puts this in rather strong terms: ". . . for those of us who hold the enhancement of man's freedom of choice as a fundamental value, any manipulation of the behavior of others constitutes a violation of their essential humanity." He grants that manipulation is sometimes necessary to achieve good ends, but insists that "even under the most favorable conditions manipulation of the behavior of others is an ethically ambiguous act." Certain critics of psychology extend this argument not just to manipulating others' behavior, but to collecting information on others' behavior. One writer has gone so far as to suggest that a psychologist may be acting unethically simply by using his psychological skills to draw inferences about another person in casual interaction — much as it is a serious crime for a prize-fighter to hit a private individual with his fists.

Such critics are, however, demanding that psychologists observe a moral absolutism that is found in no other field of human endeavor. Sound moral judgments cannot be made in the abstract, and when we try to make them in reality, there are nearly always conflicting claims on conscience, as Kelman (1967) recognizes. Psychologists in some cases (for instance in testing employees of certain governmental agencies and private corporations) may indeed have gone too far in invading personal privacy; but even privacy has no absolute moral guarantees. As Ross Stagner (1967) argued in testifying before a congressional committee on the creation of a National Social Science Foundation:

> . . . great social dangers cry for investigations which may be blocked by excessive emphasis on the right of privacy. Consider the case of the rapist, the violent criminal. As a youth he may certainly object to "prying questions" which might reveal his explosive, destructive, antisocial tendencies. Yet society is clearly entitled to look for measures to protect

155

women from his hostile sexuality. A loaded way to phrase this question is to ask how we balance the right of the young man to privacy against the right of the woman to walk safely in the streets. A more defensible question is: how can social scientists gather the data which we so desperately need, the basic information for the prevention and correction of violent behavior, with proper consideration for the right to privacy?

That should be language Congress can understand. If you think rapists and crime in the streets have been too much abused, look at it as a question of whether we should guarantee absolutely the right of the potentially destructive authoritarian against a confrontation with his own personality, or whether we should give some weight to developing means to prevent the manning of more gas chambers and concentration camps. Or would the moral absolutists still bar the psychologist from research on such problems, and trust their own moral indignation to keep the next six million away from the cyanide showers?

I am not here advancing the you-can't-make-an-omelette-without-breaking-eggs line. Omelettes aren't necessary foodstuff and human personalities are not eggs for the breaking. But psychologists do have important work to do; human behavior must be understood, if man himself is to survive in any dignity; and I do not see that anyone has any clear right to noninterference with his private person as long as the psychologist takes full care to do the minimum of probing and influencing necessary for his investigations, and to maintain the psychological health of his research participants.

Not only can one justify imposing certain unpleasant experiences on psychological research participants; one might even argue that the experience these people undergo can sometimes be a moral good in itself. As I've noted, Milgram did not falsely attribute any despicable qualities to his volunteers, as has occurred in a few studies; it happens to be quite true that the obedient volunteers were willing to shock innocent human beings upon command, and each volunteer proved this to himself. Should we instead leave people to their moral inertia, or their grave moral laxity, so as not to disturb their privacy? Who is willing to justify privacy on this basis? Who would have done so, with foreknowledge of the results, in pre-Nazi Germany? Do we not try to wake our friends, our students, our followers or leaders from moral sloth when it becomes apparent, and are we bound to use our weakest appeals when we do so? Who now condemns the Old Testament prophets for having tried to arouse people to the evil within themselves? Milgram doesn't claim prophetic stature, but his experiments may similarly awaken some of the people involved. It's true that these people didn't *ask* to be shown their sinful tendencies; but people rarely do. That's why ministers lure people with church social functions, why writers clothe their hard moral lessons

156

in pretty words and stories, why concerned artists blend morality and estheticism: because people prefer not to face the truth about themselves if they can avoid it. I have heard the other side of this argument, come to think of it: the argument that a certain group of people doesn't want to be educated, that maybe they'd prefer to remain in happy ignorance, and therefore should be left to their familiar pattern of life. Yassuh, massa.

The thrust of such arguments in Milgram's case is that he was simply too effective in bringing volunteers into dramatic confrontation with their own conflicting moral trends and their own weaknesses. We don't hear the same complaints about other psychological studies, or about most public speakers or writers or teachers or preachers, because they seldom move their audiences enough to make complaints worthwhile. Plenty of ministers, 1 am sure, would be ecstatic over the possibility of giving their congregations such a harrowing contact with their own immoral inclinations as Milgram has done, and would feel the process producing this experience to be truly heaven-sent. (In fact, one doctor of divinity who was a research volunteer asked Milgram afterwards whether he would put some of the good reverend's divinity students through the procedure, and let the good reverend in on the results. Milgram, feeling a bit of doubt as to the ethics of such a procedure, said no.)

The Beatles once sang, "I'd love to turn you on." Thousands of moral advocates would love to turn their own audiences really on, at least for a few moments. Milgram has done just that, though most of his volunteers seem to have possessed sufficiently firm psychological defenses to backslide into their old ways again soon after. I wouldn't contend that the obedience studies are *justified* by such self-revelations as I've been describing. I *am* arguing that the studies' justification in terms of adding to our knowledge of authoritarian behavior and destructive obedience is not invalidated by any taint of questionable ethics through the induction of such self-revelations.

Further, it's impossible to avoid upsetting someone, lowering someone's self-esteem, sooner or later, if you do any significant research and publicize it. I didn't tell my rightist volunteers in Dallas what I thought of the bases for their political activity; but when they read this book, as I hope some will, they may feel a bit less self-esteem at finding they're either projecting inner conflicts or easing their social relationships or just getting their kicks out of rightist activity, instead of doing it because it's the most rational position around. Diana Baumrind is going to lower at least a few parent volunteers' self-esteem, when her conclusions that their childraising techniques produce personal characteristics not valued by our culture eventually filter out into the popular press. Some psychologists seem to hope their research can continue in a vacuum, can be

157

bound up forever in the small-print journals and thus never help or hurt anyone, so that they needn't consider whether it's moral to do such research or not. They need to examine the ethical implications not only of their research, but of their wish to keep it as private knowledge.

Any research influences its participants, and some would not choose that influence. I've done research in which I tried to persuade people to stop smoking, and I've never heard any criticism of it on ethical grounds, but obviously it could so be criticized; it involves tampering with people's opinions when they don't necessarily want to be tampered with. I do generally try not to change anyone's behavior except through rational appeals, through overcoming psychological defenses which themselves are ultimately harmful; and the same could be said for Milgram's studies. But we might still get arguments on the morality of it all, from the tobacco companies if nowhere else. Any worthwhile research *must* influence its audiences, both the primary audience of participants and the secondary audiences that get the information through mass media, teachers, and community leaders — though again, even among the secondary audiences, some would just as soon not be influenced. Influence itself is neither moral nor immoral; it is a vehicle for ideas and feelings, and the content rather than the vehicle is what should be judged. In the case of Milgram's studies, I cannot see that the content of the influence, insofar as it got across, was anything but supremely moral.

THE ISSUE OF ULTIMATE VALUE

Baumrind finally comes down to arguing that although certain ethically ambiguous actions may sometimes be justified (as in medical research "at points of breakthrough," where harm to volunteers could be outweighed by benefits to humanity), *no* psychological experiments are of sufficient worth to warrant the slightest ethical risk. Although she agrees that Milgram's research deals with an important topic, she sees his methods as trivializing it: the psychological laboratory and Yale University's prestige together induce such high levels and unique patterns of obedience that the results are in no sense generalizable. We've dealt with this sort of argument before, pointing out that other volunteers were almost equally obedient in a non-university setting with a minimum of prestige, and that anyway many other institutions in our society have the potential for inducing at least as much obedience as Yale and its psychologists can. Further, our future obedience in contravention of ethical standards may be more and more commanded by appeals based on respect not for the traditional authorities, but for the authority of science and technology: obey, so that society can cope with the population explosion, the expansion of the cities, the shortcomings of the gene pool. Studies of obedience to scientific authority may be even more useful in the long run than studies of obedience to governmental authority.

158

So maybe a good word can be said for the value of Milgram's research. But what of the broader position advanced by Baumrind (who is mainly a clinician rather than an experimentalist) — the idea that psychological experimentation as a whole is so worthless that its value can be counted zero in any moral equation?

Psychologists are often inclined to exaggerate the immediate importance of their work, particularly when applying for research grants. But this entire book is an argument for the *ultimate* significance of experimental social psychology and related empirical work. Only if we confine ourselves to piddling trivialities that affront no one's moral sensibilities in the slightest, are we likely to fail to influence the development of human civilization in radical ways. Obedience to authority, for instance, is only one aspect of social psychological efforts to understand the conditions of human freedom and control. The whole area of experimental persuasion is crucial here too, and discoveries in this area could be potentially as dangerous, or more so, than the ultimate nuclear weapon. People can't be held down by fear of destruction forever; but a really smoothly persuaded person *likes* having been persuaded, so why should he ever rebel?

Such possibilities raise all the problems the physicists have faced: "value-free science," cooperation with governments, individual freedom to pursue or not to pursue a potentially destructive/beneficial line of research. Social psychologists have not yet actually devised the principles or methods that would allow them to wreak vast changes upon society; they haven't yet gotten their fingers burned seriously, as the nuclear scientists did in the blasts of Hiroshima and Nagasaki. So most psychologists have hardly begun to work through the moral implications of their research. Even the most serious and responsible among them, such as Herbert Kelman, have so far come up mostly with very limited and tentative formulations. Of those who do announce their concern, too many seem to play around with problems of good and evil mainly to raise their own self-esteem. We must all look at the moral implications of our field for weightier reasons than that; and once we are looking, we must pay much more attention to the problems of moral ambiguity, and to our individual *and* collective responsibilities as psychologists, than anyone in the field has paid so far. We have our experts on response set and cognitive inconsistency and small-group dynamics; it is time we began producing our ethical experts as well. We don't rely merely on intuition to decide whether our experimental results are statistically significant; no more should we rely entirely on our moral intuition. We may occasionally seek expert mathematical advice on our statistical problems; and perhaps we should likewise look outside our field for moral inspiration. But the religionists and the philosophers have their own ethical hang-ups, so I'm afraid they'll be of no more than peripheral use as

159

expert consultants. The severe criticisms of Milgram's morally important research for its presumed immorality indicate that *somebody* needs to straighten out our moral sense, or at least make it a good bit less curvilinear than it is presently. And this somebody had better start working on the problem now, before we really do have the ability to get ourselves and mankind either out of the frying pan or into the fire.

5

how to convince friends
and influence people

which softsoap gives the whiter brainwash?
introduction to attitude change

> *The woman said, "The serpent beguiled me, and I ate."*
> — Genesis 3:13

In my moonlighting career as a frustrated novelist, I once began a manuscript which starred a social psychologist. The usual scientific combination of careful research and sheer luck enabled him to develop a set of nonsense syllables whose repetition rendered any listener absolutely open to persuasion. He could now change anyone's attitudes, toward anything, at any time. Naturally, my hero was a responsible man, seeking only the greatest good for all humanity. So of course I planned in the rest of the book to depict his gradual corruption and ultimate downfall, as he made puppets of his friends, seduced truckloads of beautiful women, and became dictator of the world.

Actually I stopped writing before the novel got that far. Science fiction has often seemed to me a good way to say certain things that need saying; but fantasy, never. And a social psychologist who can change any attitude at will is sheer fantasy.

Such fantasies are not, however, original with me. The myth of the all-powerful persuader is ancient and widespread. The myth's prime embodiment has been Satan in all his guises. But others have substituted for him on occasion: the medieval sorcerer with his potions and spells; the irresistible hypnotist (Svengali or Mandrake); and now the psychologist, whose scientific skills have surely given him the secret of complete

161

control. The myth seems as alluring as that other dream, the ability to influence the physical world mentally, whether through prayer, three wishes, or psychokinesis. Of the two concepts, most people probably find it easier to believe in absolute powers of persuasion, since they see human wills as far more insubstantial than wood and steel. Even in circles where the latest demonstration of "mind over matter" is taken as a joke, vast claims of mind over mind often induce both acceptance and anxiety.

I am not thinking only of the popular press. Many otherwise intelligent and rational men have displayed astonishing credulity concerning methods for inducing credulousness in the masses. For instance, when Aldous Huxley (1958) "revisited" *Brave New World* to see how far we have moved toward his classic dystopia, he expressed particular horror at the new persuasive techniques, which he saw as fully justifying his own most dire predictions. And who should turn up to fulfill Huxley's predictions but that ole debbil social psychologist?

> . . . unfortunately propaganda in the Western democracies, above all in America, has two faces and a divided personality. In charge of the editorial department there is often a democratic Dr. Jekyll — a propagandist who would be very happy to prove that John Dewey had been right about the ability of human nature to respond to truth and reason. But this worthy man controls only a part of the machinery of mass communication. In charge of advertising we find an anti-democratic, because anti-rational, Mr. Hyde — or rather a Dr. Hyde, for Hyde is now a Ph.D. in psychology and has a master's degree as well in the social sciences.

Huxley was here concerned with the "motivational analyst," who might soon discover the unconscious symbols that would sell any product, and whose techniques applied to politics might guarantee the electorate against ever hearing the truth about anything. At other points, Huxley expressed equal anxiety about Pavlovian techniques applied to brainwashing; "subliminal projection," which he wanted to outlaw before it could hit its full stride; and various other mechanical and chemical changers of attitudes, such as sleep-teaching and LSD. All these techniques and others being developed, he felt in 1958, could soon make absolute dictatorial domination of public attitudes "completely realizable."

The writer who predicts doom can thereafter find satisfaction either in doom's fulfillment or in its avoidance through his help. Huxley's 1939 *Brave New World* had not noticeably changed the drift of modern civilization in the decades since; so Huxley, with only a few years left to him, chose to believe instead that his direst predictions had been confirmed. But writer's pride did not motivate those who made the claims Huxley accepted. The powers of motivational research and subliminal perception were proclaimed mainly by those with financial interests at stake. The great brainwashing scare, on the other hand, seems largely to have been propagated for ideological reasons.

MOTIVATIONAL RESEARCH

Motivational research (MR) is a term loosely applied by public relations men, advertising agencies, and a scattering of psychologists to their attempted use of psychoanalytic concepts in advertising campaigns. Depth interviews, individual and group free-association sessions, projective tests, and related procedures have been employed to discover the unconscious or preconscious motivations associated with consumer behavior, in hopes that advertisers can manipulate these motivations to promote sales. The attitude-changing efficacy of MR-inspired ads has been trumpeted not only by the motivational researchers themselves but by their best-selling critics, notably Vance Packard. His book *The Hidden Persuaders* (1957), now approaching its fortieth paperback reprinting, was an excited survey of "the use of mass psychoanalysis to guide campaigns of persuasion." Packard occasionally laughed at the motivational researchers' claims, but more often he viewed their powers with great alarm. Perhaps the discovery that "baking a cake traditionally is acting out the birth of a child," and that therefore the cakemix manufacturer should let the housewife add her own eggs and milk, represents little threat to our free will; but what of those motivational researchers who market political candidates, religions, entire ways of life? Most ad men are nice guys, according to Packard — "But when you are manipulating, where do you stop?"

Packard didn't realize that the motivational researchers had hardly been able to get started. MR data were generally kept secret, so as not to give business competitors any advantages; but the research that was described sufficiently for independent evaluation seldom deserved to be called research. Concepts of research design and efforts at quantification were nil; consumer interviews were often conducted by unqualified personnel, in such brevity that even a professional psychologist would have been able to deduce little from them. The sweeping claims about consumer motivation often made by MR specialists seemed in most cases to derive as much from their own personal fantasies as from anything their research told them.

Further, the basic assumptions of motivational research were highly questionable. Our daily decisions, including consumer decisions, may indeed rest partly on unconscious motives. But these motives and their relationships to the outside world are likely to be very individualized, hard to discover, unreliable, and difficult to manipulate. The consumer may not be entirely rational in all his purchases, but that doesn't mean his irrationality can be conveniently channeled through a mass advertising campaign. Nor does any good evidence show that motivational researchers have been able to do so. Instances can be cited in which an

163

ad man followed a motivational researcher's advice and apparently increased his company's sales by several million dollars as a result. But several million dollars may mean changes in the behavior of only a small fraction of an advertising campaign's audience. Such changes may derive instead from the layout director's artistic inspiration, or from competitors' stupidities (perhaps induced by their own MR men), or from sheer good luck. Neither advertisers nor motivational researchers like to waste their time with carefully controlled experiments, and they do not publicize their failures.

The Hidden Persuaders goes on selling, but hardly anyone in the advertising world mentions motivational research today. Even without careful assessment of the results, ad men seem to have concluded that MR failed to deliver on its promises. Or maybe they've just moved on to new fads. Individual consumer interviews are still used in combination with quantitative surveys to assess product "images" or to obtain advance reactions to proposed advertising campaigns; advertisers and their hired social scientists still pay obeisance to psychological theories, Freudian and otherwise. But Oedipal conflicts and oral-dependency needs now remain largely in the ad man's own private therapy sessions, rather than being offered as the key to unlock the minds and pocketbooks of the nation's consumers.

SUBLIMINAL STIMULI

Subliminal perception is another technique that has provoked in Huxley, Packard, and innumerable journalists delicious fears of wholesale persuasion. Our senses register more than we consciously perceive, the argument goes, so maybe whatever doesn't get through on the conscious level hits hard at the unconscious level. Perhaps by flashing words on a movie or television screen in tiny fractions of a second, imperceptibly or "subliminally," the advertisers could catch us with our guard down. Or so they hoped.

Psychoanalytic theory does refer to certain processes that screen out disturbing events from conscious perception before a person realizes they are there, and other processes that make the person more sensitive to objects and situations touching directly or symbolically upon his unconscious concerns. Because these hypotheses allow more explicit predictions than many others in psychoanalysis, researchers have worked hard at trying to support or contradict them experimentally for thirty years. Thirty years have made the researchers much more sophisticated methodologically, but have provided no conclusive answers to the question of whether subliminal perception actually occurs. The researchers who prove it does happen have kept a mere step ahead of those who prove it doesn't, and I wouldn't bet on their keeping even that little lead for long.

Various technical and conceptual problems confound the assessment of subliminal effects. A "subliminal" stimulus is one which an observer reports perceiving less than half the time it appears. So what is technically subliminal part of the time may not be so all the time, or to all observers (since individuals differ in perceptual thresholds), or under all circumstances. Further, an observer may be able to perceive something without being able to verbalize it, particularly if it is vague or on the threshold of perception. He may not even be sure, after the experience, that it ever occurred. But this doesn't mean his later behavior will be unaffected by such light touches of stimulation, particularly if they're at least a bit pleasant or a bit unpleasant and are repeated often. Finally, observers may be reluctant to report what they really did see, if, as in the experiments on conformity, they feel it might mark them as odd or might differ from what others see. This was a serious problem in several early studies whose "subliminal" stimuli were sexy words or drawings.

So we remain uncertain as to whether subliminal perception occurs at all. We should hold ourselves even more uncertain as to whether subliminal perception sells goods or candidates any better than supraliminal perception, because as usual the advertising men have not backed up their claims with adequate data. We have no good reason to assume that fleeting, vaguely apprehended messages should be more persuasive than carefully presented, clearly perceived ones — except for the idea of sneaking things past our guard. Advertisers who suspect their products are useless may be right to peddle their wares through the least rational means possible. What puzzles me is why, if they've heard of unconscious perception, they haven't heard of unconscious defenses too. If an advertisement is stupid and annoying, the unconscious is not likely to show any more tolerance toward it than the conscious. Perhaps some MR–based sex symbol ads would come across better if the audience couldn't see them; I'd certainly feel better about plenty of products if their commercials were invisible. But it seems quite doubtful that unconscious perception is superior to, or even anywhere close to par with, conscious persuasion processes. (Unless maybe somebody is right now protecting his techniques from further scientific investigation by flashing split-second messages at me, saying "SUBLIMINAL PERCEPTION IS TRASH.")

BRAINWASHING

The irresistible persuader doesn't always rely on subtlety or secrecy. The most frightening modern version of the myth is one of frontal attack, of brute physical and psychological force: brainwashing. Wholesale confessions of anti-Party sins during the Soviet show trials of the 1930's, the conversion of thousands of American POW's and anti-Communist intellectuals into Red Chinese lackeys — what combination of savagery and sorcery can twist so many good men into evil?

The twists involved have more often been of printed truth than of human wills. Curious, isn't it, that hardly anyone besides the Communists is ever accused of brainwashing? The world is simpler if only the enemy makes such drastic efforts to convert his prisoners; and, in a strange way, the world seems simpler too if the enemy can convert only through magical powers — perhaps helped along by mysterious drugs or hypnosis, but magic nonetheless. Reports by people who'd rather understand the Communists' behavior than make up tall tales about their deviltry, however, generally agree on two deflating but useful conclusions.

First: brainwashing is far less effective than it has usually been painted. Few American prisoners during the Korean War showed substantial attitude change in the directions demanded by their captors (Biderman, 1962; Schein et al., 1961). The much more extensive "thought reform" programs directed toward Chinese intellectuals during and following the consolidation of Communist rule seem to have been only partially effective, mainly influencing those under thirty, and even then were not necessarily enduring (Biderman, 1962; Lifton, 1961). Among the Russians too, confessions appear seldom to have been based on genuine changes of heart; "permanent" change probably occurred chiefly in those executed shortly after the trials. The surprise is not that brainwashing has sometimes been successful, but that the maximal efforts put into it have produced such minimal results.

Second: the essential element in the occasional success of brainwashing, particularly as practiced by the Chinese, is plain old hard work. Neither Oriental tortures, nor sophisticated psychological techniques such as hypnosis, nor mystery drugs, nor Pavlovian conditioning were the crucial factors. What made any change possible was that the brainwashers slaved to make themselves the sole source of every satisfaction for the psychological functions served by their victims' attitudes.

One group of researchers calls the basic elements in brainwashing "debility, dependency, and dread" (Farber et al., 1956). The victim is usually subjected to semistarvation, to physical abuse, to experiences that create intense fatigue and that lower his resistance to disease. He is cut off from friends and family; the letters he receives are carefully censored so that only statements promoting dissolution of normal social contacts remain. He is also explicitly threatened — with death, with injury, with damage to his loved ones; with permanent incarceration; with undescribed and unknown dangers. In his tightly controlled environment, only his captors can give relief. In effect, they return the prisoner to an early state in which he had needs but no attitudes to help satisfy them. If he adopts his captors' attitudes now, they can relieve his debility by giving him good food, comfortable quarters, medical treatment; they can satisfy his desire for social relationships by becoming more friendly and perhaps by returning him to the West; they can alleviate his dread by eliminating the threats and the tortures, mental and physical. Having

166

disrupted his sense of a continuous identity through their intense and deliberately confusing interrogation procedures, their insistence upon public self-criticism, and their destruction of his old social reference points, they may now be able to provide him with a new or substantially modified identity, based upon the Communistic attitudes and values that they hold before him daily.

The brainwashing victim's attitudes were formed originally to serve the broad range of psychological functions discussed in Chapter Three. Those attitudes can be eroded and perhaps eventually obliterated if they repeatedly and drastically fail to be functional; other attitudes, suggested by the captors, may then be internalized because they are immediately, strongly functional. Such a process of destruction and replacement through manipulations of functionality may never be completely effective, since attitudes seem often to possess a powerful inertia which may carry them through any attack on their present functionality, and since (as was particularly obvious in Chinese attempts to convert American POW's during the Korean War) an outside manipulator may be unable to discover all the internal functions served by a particular attitude. But with time, effort, resources, and power, significant change can surely be induced. Complete change may not be necessary anyway — just a shift in perspective, a new willingness to cooperate overtly with a political structure whose own dogmatic rigidity may make it relatively insensitive to attitudinal subtleties and internal reservations.

But where is the magic, the ultimate attitude change agent, in all this? At tremendous expense, complete environmental control of a few people can induce them to undergo varying degrees of attitude change. So what? Clearly, entire populations cannot be similarly converted to an enemy ideology. Nor can the environments of whole nations — even China itself — be controlled sufficiently to maintain extensive permanent attitude change, even in the small number of people a government could afford to send through its thought control centers. There are many in any nation, of course, who do not care what ideological faction is in power, as long as their own comfort remains or increases; and in twenty-five years, a whole new generation whose brains were "clean" from birth can be educated to revere a government from whom many genuine blessings flow. Neither of these circumstances, however, is evidence that the Chinese government has succeeded in brainwashing several hundred million people, as is often claimed. George Orwell and others have suggested fanciful methods of controlling the attitudinal environment through mass media techniques; but I suspect they vastly underrate the power of human ingenuity to find ways to disregard communications of any kind, mass or individual. Our parental population is now discovering that even the environmental control they thought they had over their own children was far from complete enough to induce the attitudes the parents desired, or to maintain such attitudes beyond childhood.

167

Attitude change is not a matter of grand techniques that render any audience helpless to resist, immediately and reliably. Attitude change occurs through various processes, generally in small doses and in patterns that are hard to predict. Most psychologists who study attitude change have stopped searching for the philosopher's stone, the one big answer. They seek instead, as in other areas of social psychology, for the many limited answers that one day will provide the basis for a general synthesis – a synthesis that itself will surely give no one the single key to change, but will inspire greater appreciation for the sheer complexity of human psychology.

Even the possibility of a general synthesis may strike fear into those accustomed to thinking in terms of *The Manchurian Candidate* and *1984*. But although attitude change may sometimes involve brainwashing and doublethink, it is also the stuff of human progress, the medium of mankind's psychological growth. The great and small movers and shakers of our race have necessarily bent themselves toward changing the attitudes of their own and succeeding generations. Some have done so more effectively and some less, but in few cases could they rely solely upon the simple logical appeal of their arguments; they had to be persuasive as well as right. Still less now, when the marketplace of ideas is so glutted, can we simply develop our own good idea and wait for people to come to it. We must seek the best means of driving that idea home, despite heavy competition. This doesn't mean that knowing the right techniques will enable bad ideas to drive out good; psychologists have found the appearance of truth to have its own persuasive value. It does mean we should know more about how to appear truthful when we are so, to present the truth so that it looks true, and to appeal to those qualities in our audiences which will enable them to accept the truth for what it is.

We therefore turn from the fantastic to the pragmatic, from the extraordinary to the eclectic, in order to locate the most useful knowledge about attitude change. When I speak of attitude change research as helping to advance truth in the world, I don't mean to suggest that every psychologist who studies attitude change tries to convince his audiences of the great truths as he sees them. To get any research done at all, psychologists tend to work on rather trivial attitudes, which can be changed measurably in an hour's time. When they do try to change "major" attitudes, these tend to be the kind in which most people have a rather shallow investment – as in the old joke where the lady says, "My husband makes the major decisions in the family and I make the minor ones; he decides whether Red China should be admitted to the UN, while I decide how to raise our children." But although the limitations of such studies are obvious and require certain correctives, you should not be deceived by their smallness. They are often aimed squarely toward the elucidation of the basic processes underlying the effectiveness not only of advertising but of teaching, preaching, political campaigning, child-raising, courtship, legal advocacy, serious writing, friendly and unfriendly argument. Name an area of social life, and research on attitude change should eventually help you to deal with it better.

HOVLAND'S RESEARCH

A few scattered experimental studies of attitude change were conducted in the 1920's and 1930's. But the field was quietly revolutionized by Carl Hovland, beginning during World War II and continuing through his postwar work at Yale University. I met Hovland only once, at a get-acquainted party for psychology faculty and graduate students during my first semester at Yale. I felt flattered when he insisted on questioning me and other new students about our budding research activities; looking back, I think he may have been trying to judge the prospects for attitude change research in the years following his impending death from cancer. He must surely have known that his own influence on those years would be great. Hovland was only forty-eight when he died, but during his fifteen years in attitude change work, he organized the field, did much of its basic research himself, and set many other researchers out in the directions they and the field are still largely following.

Hovland's special talent lay in identifying the essential elements involved in attitude change, and in devising simple experimental procedures for studying these elements independently and in combination. He began not with any strong guiding principles, but with a quite pragmatic orientation. He was in the Army; the Army during World War II had a lot of draftees on its hands who weren't sure what they were fighting for. The Army wanted to indoctrinate them as rapidly as possible, since they should be better fighting men for believing in the American cause. The problem was not to change ideologies, as with "brainwashing," but to mobilize available values in support of a particular war. So the Army's Information and Education Division devised several indoctrination films and other materials, presenting the American and Allied case against Hitler; the Research Branch of the Information and Education Division was told to evaluate the effectiveness of these films; and the Experimental Section of the Research Branch of the Information and Education Division was told to develop experimental techniques for making such evaluations. Hovland was in charge of the Experimental Section's research programs.

Hovland and his colleagues in the Experimental Section (Hovland et al., 1949) mainly made straightforward comparisons of specific indoctrination materials. Show one group of draftees a movie on the Battle of Britain; show another group nothing; measure both groups' attitudes toward the British allies, to see whether the movie was better than nothing. Or show the Battle of Britain movie versus a Battle of Britain filmstrip, and see which changes attitudes more. This sort of study still accounts for most applied attitude change research, and it was quite useful in measuring the worth of the Army indoctrination programs. But a good advertising agency could do as much; and regardless of who conducts such studies, they rarely improve our general understanding of attitude change. Too much happens in a Battle of Britain movie, too many differences can be found between a particular movie and a particular filmstrip, to know what's responsible when attitude change does occur.

CONTROLLED VARIATION

The Hovland group really began to understand general attitude processes through their work with controlled variation: starting out with the same stimulus materials and systematically varying a single element to determine its effect. One such study, which deals with the effects of time lapse on a persuasive message, exemplifies Hovland's usual experimental design. He first gave a questionnaire to ten Infantry Replacement Training Companies, asking both factual and opinion questions about the conduct of the war — size of the German Air Force, whether the men felt the British were doing their fair share of fighting, and so on. Then half the companies were shown the Battle of Britain indoctrination film, designed in part to make attitudes toward the British forces more favorable. A week later, several companies that had seen the film and several that hadn't were given a second questionnaire to determine the film's short-term effects. After eight weeks more, the remaining companies were given the same second questionnaire to check for long-term effects. Changes from before the film to after, on both factual and opinion items, were then compared for everyone: those who had seen the film and those who hadn't, those measured after a week and those measured after two months.

Here, time was the key variable. But it's possible, using this basic design, to study the effect of many other variables on attitude change. For example, you could give a pre-exposure questionnaire, show your film, then show a rebuttal film to some people and not to others before you give the post-exposure questionnaire. Or you could tell some soldiers the film is an independently made Hollywood production and others that it's an official U.S. Army film, to study the effect of sponsorship. Hovland used the same procedure in various studies during and after the war: a pre-measure of attitudes, then a persuasive communication incorporating a specific experimental variation, then a post-measure.

In the study of time effects, Hovland found that the Battle of Britain film was more effective over the short term than the long term, as long as only accuracy of factual responses was considered — a result in concordance with other research on recall of factual information over time. But in terms of opinion change, the film was more effective over the long

170

term. Thus, the soldiers who saw the film became rather more favorable toward the British role in the war than the soldiers who didn't; but they were even more favorable nine weeks after the film than one week after, whereas the attitudes of soldiers who hadn't seen the film remained fairly constant as time passed.

Such a finding raises more questions than it immediately answers. What was there specifically about the time lapse that increased the film's effectiveness? Did the forgetting of factual information have anything to do with the changes in opinion, or did seeing the film make people more sensitive to other positive material about Britain that they encountered later, or what? Hovland's intuitive answers to such questions were often brilliant, but his final reply was always: let's take our guesses and build them into experiments.

Over several years Hovland gathered enough interesting questions and enough tentative answers to develop a systematic program of postwar research. He identified four categories of variables that are crucial in any attitude change situation (Hovland et al., 1953): the communicator, the communication, the audience, and the audience's response. Hovland said less formally that he was concerned with *who* says *what* to *whom* with *what effect*. During the rest of his life, he proceeded to explore experimentally several of the more important variables in each of these categories; many other psychologists have since added their efforts to what he began. The following sections will explore representative studies of *who, what*, and *to whom*, as well as one aspect of *what effect* that may be directly related to the delayed effectiveness of the Battle of Britain film: attitudinal inoculation. Research on another aspect of audience response — role playing — has become so inextricably involved in the evaluation of general attitude change theories that it will be saved for Chapter Six.

jefferson versus lenin:
communicator credibility

We believe good men more fully and more readily than others: this is true generally whatever the question is, and absolutely true where exact certainty is impossible and opinions are divided.

— Aristotle
Rhetoric

No matter what you want to persuade people is true, you're better off having a good man deliver your message. That's a useless truism for most of us, since John Aldens are seldom available. We must speak our own piece and hope the word gets across, regardless of how the audience sees our personal qualities. But advertisers have the money to hire Aldens of any size, shape, and color; and because they so often have little to say and less reason for their audience to believe it, they've tried hard to learn which kinds of speakers are effective regardless of the message. Psychologists too can use a variety of mouthpieces to deliver an experimental communication, or they can vary a speaker's obvious attributes almost at will. With this freedom, they can study the role of the communicator in persuasion, as well as what he says and how he says it.

Certain communicator characteristics emphasized by advertisers have impressed psychologists rather little, perhaps because of their obviousness. The communicator's ability to arouse audience interest is one such advertiser-stressed quality. Statuesque beauty queens, Rock-Hudsonesque announcers — the audience must pay attention before the message can get across. I survived three semesters of graduate-school statistics not because appeals to cherish the Smolgorov-Kirlov test of randomness are inherently persuasive, but because Professor Robert Abelson is a brilliant and outrageous punster. We had to be alert to catch the puns as they came, and during our alertness he taught us statistics. Indeed, he may sometimes have demonstrated unawares another maxim well known to advertisers: communicators should be interesting but not too interesting. Unlimited cleavage sells sex, not cars. Comic genius may create hysteria rather than profits.

Social psychologists have generally assumed that the communicator must arouse audience interest, without testing that assumption empirically. Indeed, they have often seen speaker-induced differences in audience attention as an annoyance rather than as an effect worth studying, and have tried to equalize such differences between experimental conditions. Psychologists usually have the audience's attention anyway: it's typically a volunteer audience, self-selected to expose itself to whatever the experimenter throws at it; and it's likely to be on tenterhooks, wondering what will happen next in this mysterious psychological investigation. No wonder, then, that interest levels are fairly equal in the various conditions of the typical experiment, or that it's usually easy to equalize the degree of interest when necessary. But though this assured audience attention often helps the laboratory psychologist, it may also frustrate attempts to use his results in the attention-hungry world of practical persuasion outside the lab.

PRESTIGE AND CREDIBILITY

Let us assume that the advertiser or Administration Spokesman can, with considerably more effort, attain the same attention levels as the psychologist. Are all communicators now on an equal footing? Aristotle said no: the good man, the prestigeful speaker, the credible communicator obviously has the edge. Aristotle did little more than state this as fact, and give the quality a name ("ethos") that professors of rhetoric, if not psychologists, still employ. A host of rhetoricians over twenty-odd centuries, and of psychologists over twenty-odd years, have filled in the details.

Hovland crystallized the issue for psychologists. Several dozen experimenters before him had studied "prestige suggestion" by attributing an opinion to a prestigious figure and measuring the effects on an audience, as compared to the effects of the opinion with no such attribution. Of course, prestige suggestion was more effective, since the audience was given no other information for or against the opinion. If one commercial says "Smoke Camels" and another says, "Joe Namath says 'Smoke Camels,'" the second commercial should sell more cigarets than the first. But what, Hovland wondered, about the more normal situation, when the advocate of a position actually presents arguments in favor of it? Will his personal characteristics influence the acceptance of his arguments, i.e., affect his general credibility? (*Credibility* as Hovland used the term includes not just prestige, but whatever influences a person's believability in persuasive situations. Lyndon Johnson may have had high prestige as president, but he suffered from a credibility gap nonetheless.)

Hovland and Weiss (1951) studied this question by measuring attitudes pre- and post-experimentally on such topics as the feasibility of atomic submarines, and by having volunteers read arguments either for or against the topic between measures. The arguments sometimes appeared to come from a highly credible source such as J. Robert Oppenheimer, sometimes from a low-credibility source such as *Pravda;* they were written so that they could have come from either source. The volunteers not only believed the arguments came from where the experimenter said they came from, but obediently accepted the arguments much more when they were attributed to the highly credible source than to the low.

Or rather, the volunteers responded that way right after reading the arguments. In this and other experiments, the immediate effects of credibility differences wore off in a few weeks, to such an extent that attitudes ended up at the same level regardless of the original source's credibility. Hovland suggested that after several weeks, the audience no longer spontaneously recalled where they had heard the arguments for or against a position, and therefore showed only the lingering effects of the arguments themselves. A good logical argument for banning nonprescription antihistamines is still a good logical argument, whether you saw it in an excerpt from *Look* or from *The New England Journal of Biology and Medicine* — as long as you don't remember it came from *Look* or *NEJBM*.

In another study, Kelman and Hovland (1953) gave volunteers a strong reminder of the source of the arguments, shortly before remeasuring their attitudes. This time the superiority of the highly credible source continued even after several weeks. Perhaps, Hovland (Hovland et al., 1953) speculated, if a communicator were tied so closely to his message that he'd be spontaneously recalled whenever the topic came up, this "sleeper effect" of gradual decay in credibility-induced differences wouldn't happen: Barbra Streisand arguing against nose jobs, say, or Hubert Humphrey urging parents to give their children unusual middle names, or the "head of naval intelligence" (p. 69) revealing his secret data on Eleanor Roosevelt's supposedly scarlet past. But nobody I know of has experimented with such an effect.

Those early credibility studies by Hovland and his associates looked so nice: not only were the good rewarded by being more persuasive and the bad punished by their ineffectiveness, but as a little extra fillip to delight sophisticated psychologists, the silly audience forgot where they'd heard all that stuff after a while and showed no further effect of credibility.

Then the complications set in.

EXPERTNESS AND TRUSTWORTHINESS

Hovland, as conscientious as Freud in exploring the full import of his basic concepts, identified the first complications, though he didn't fully test them. Credibility, Hovland said, is not one indivisible quality. A communicator may be credible because he is expert, or because he is trustworthy, or possibly both at the same time, or maybe even because of a few other factors as well. Expertness, of course, involves how much he knows about what he's talking about. But there are at least a few sneaky rascals in the world who know a lot and still tell you only what they want you to believe. So you must also take account of the communicator's willingness to be honest with you, to tell it like he really thinks it is. That's trustworthiness.

The early experiments on credibility didn't distinguish between these two factors experimentally. Robert Oppenheimer would probably have known more *and* been more honest than *Pravda* about nuclear submarine development. Expertness is easier than trustworthiness to vary independently, and researchers have often varied it — either by describing the communicator's credentials as great or minimal, or by actually demonstrating his expertness somehow just prior to his persuasive speech.

But how do you study trustworthiness independently of expertness? You could try quoting from someone like Benjamin Spock on issues outside his area of competence; but his trustworthiness might still be hard to separate from other factors. Dr. Spock is such an expert on children that some people might see him as an expert on life itself, and thus expert on the facts of atomic testing, on the Vietnamese War, on anything affecting human lives. Such ambiguity is likely to be present any time you refer to well-known trustworthy people in your experiments. If trust-

174

worthiness is to be examined in its own right, it must be varied in other ways.

Advertisers have had their own problems with trustworthiness, and their temporary solution has also been useful to psychologists. The advertisers found that their audiences had lost their innocence; even the most apparently trustworthy figure is now seen as unreliable if he's willing to appear in a commercial. He must be cashing in somewhere, and if he is, he's not necessarily telling us what he truly believes. It took the advertisers years to realize that John Wayne was chipping away at his own trustworthiness every time he endorsed a product. Once they did, their initial response was to use ordinary housewife and home-from-the-office types in dramatized endorsements. If Natalie Wood says she washes her delicate undies in New Blue Cheer, she's obviously lying for pay; if Mrs. Myrtle Gorfunkle, a weather-beaten frump from Great Falls, Montana, says the same, well, maybe it's true. Of course Mrs. Gorfunkle might need the cash even worse than a movie star, so the advertisers turned to the candid camera shot. Mr. Orval Hotchkiss drives up to a Shell station and demands Super Shell with Platformate, insisting to a doubting station attendant that he'd never buy any other kind of gasoline. Whereupon the attendant says, "Mr. Hotchkiss, would you believe you're on camera right now?" "Oh, pshaw," says Mr. Hotchkiss, with just the right degree of surprise.

Since Mr. Hotchkiss is not saying all those things to make money, or to influence the television audience intentionally, the audience should assume he truly loves the product he endorses; he's highly trustworthy. No expert, maybe — he even claims he doesn't know what Platformate is, except by golly it works — but you can really *believe* a man like that. Or so the advertisers hope.

EXPERIMENTS ON TRUSTWORTHINESS

Increasing trustworthiness by means of "candid" or overheard conversations is so simple-minded a procedure that it's not surprising psychologists overlooked it nearly as long as the advertisers did. Elaine Walster and Leon Festinger (1962) experimented with it first. They invited Stanford coeds and student wives to participate in a "nationwide study of the therapy process," which involved listening to and evaluating a "psychotherapy session." Half the participants were told in advance that the two therapists being evaluated knew a live microphone was carrying their words to an audience — the "aware" condition; the rest were told the therapists didn't know — the "candid" condition. While the therapists waited for their patient to arrive, they conversed casually about several topics, and each managed to incorporate a six-minute persuasive speech into his remarks, since they were not therapists at all and their "live" therapy session was a taped experimental stimulus. The therapists then engaged in a desultory exchange with the "patient," after which research participants were asked to rate the therapists and to give their opinions on several local issues, including the topics upon which the therapists had expounded. For topics with which participants felt little involvement (e.g., "Husbands should spend more time at home," directed to single coeds), the "candid" condition showed no superiority over the "aware" condition. But with topics likely to elicit strong personal involvement (e.g., "Husbands should spend more time at home," directed to wives of students), the candid condition produced significantly more attitude change.

Why? When a speaker talks about something that doesn't really interest the audience, he's not likely to be trying hard to influence them, even if he knows they're out there. But if what he's saying is personally relevant to the audience, then he just may be trying to manipulate them for a reason of his own — unless he doesn't know anyone is listening. It's as if the volunteer wives listening in the aware condition thought to themselves, "I'd like to believe what this therapist is saying, because he's endorsing something that sounds good to me — the idea that husbands should stay home more, for the psychological health of the family. But he knows I'm here. Does he really believe his own arguments, or is he trying to con me? He knows I'm going to rate his therapeutic performance; is he trying to get in good with me by saying things that sound nice?" Whereas the wives in the candid condition might think, "I'd like to believe what the therapist says, and because he doesn't know I'm here he's got no reason to be fooling me; so I'll accept it as honest opinion." Instant communicator credibility.

These thoughts from the audience are only guesswork; Walster and Festinger didn't question people afterward about their reactions to the therapists' conversation. But other studies suggest the same process: people reject a tempting argument when they're afraid of being conned. For instance, in an experiment not involving overheard statements, Judson Mills and J. M. Jellison (1967) showed volunteers a speech supposedly given by a politician running for office. The politician's main line was that a bill should be passed to triple the license fees of tractor-trailer trucks. One volunteer group was told that the politician gave this speech to a railway union local; another group was told he gave it to a long-haul truckdrivers' union local. The first group accepted the politician's arguments much less readily than the second group. Like most of us, they had apparently learned not to trust a politician when he tells an audience what they want to hear.

Now, suppose you've got a message you want an audience to accept, one that you assume they'll want to accept, but you can't easily set up a "candid" or overheard-message situation. How else can you convince them you're not conning them? The experimental data suggest at least two procedures that might increase your trustworthiness.

First, try being honest about your persuasive intentions. In one study (Mills, 1966), the experimenter started off telling volunteers something they probably wanted to hear — that he really liked them. If he then tried to act as if he weren't interested in persuading them, while he went ahead with a persuasive message, he got little attitude change; the audience probably smelled a con job. But if he told them bluntly that he *wanted* to persuade them of his position, he got substantially more change; he was obviously being honest, even though his intention was to persuade. On the other hand, if he started off saying he disliked the volunteers, he was more effective if he then said he didn't care whether he persuaded them than if he said he wanted to. Again, obvious honesty won out over evil intentions.

Second, try using a communicator who has no selfish reason to advocate your position — indeed, who may be harmed by it. Koeske and Crano (1968) fabricated statements from General Westmoreland saying either that American bombing of North Vietnam had "reduced the influx of men and military supplies to the South" or that the number of United States casualties in the war had "far exceeded that reported in the U.S. press"; and statements from Stokely Carmichael saying either that a lot of police brutality goes on in Negro neighborhoods or that "often Negroes have not taken the initiative required to benefit from civil rights legislation." In each case, the second statement, an incongruous and non-self-serving one, induced much more opinion change than the first. For the same reasons, I think, former Marine Commandant General Shoup has often been quoted by Vietnam war critics; and the Birchers like to quote Communist sources about how nefarious the Communists really are. The effect may rest partly on the presumed expertness of the speakers about their topic; but much of it seems to come, as Koeske and Crano suggest, from the audience's feeling that "If *he* says *that*, it's probably true" — that a speaker would say something which flies in the face of his own interests only if it were really, without a doubt, absolutely the gospel unadulterated.

PERSONAL ATTRACTIVENESS

Expertness, trustworthiness: enough credibility? You can make yourself or your spokesman an acceptable speaker in several other ways; one factor-analytic study (Schweitzer and Ginsburg, 1966) statistically analyzed credibility into over a dozen different communicator characteristics. But the only other factor that has received more than minimal research attention is *personal attractiveness*. As a credibility component, personal attractiveness refers not to pretty girls attracting more attention, but to your adopting somebody's opinion because you like him and want to be like him, or want to keep on his good side. This is, for instance, one of the presumed bases of the child's identification with his parents in psychoanalytic and other theories. If personal attractiveness increases opinion acceptance, then greater attractiveness should produce more attitude change; and there are many ways to increase attractiveness.

Propaganda analysts have called one technique "flogging a dead horse." The speaker shows he shares his audience's virtues by denouncing some sin they all love to denounce, before he drives his real persuasive message home. Walter Weiss (1957), for instance, worked with a group of volunteers who very much favored academic freedom but were fairly neutral about fluoridation. He gave them two news articles, apparently from the same newspaper; one endorsed academic freedom and the other denounced fluoridation. Then he measured their opinions. The anti-fluoridation article was more effective when the pro-academic freedom article came first than when the articles were reversed. Apparently the audience decided the newspaper was more worth believing on one issue if it had already taken their side on another.

Timothy Brock (1965) used a similar technique in a real setting, a paint store in Pittsburgh. Brock's assistants were part-time salesmen, trained to give a standard spiel to any customer shopping for certain kinds of paint. Depending on the experimental condition to which each customer was unknowingly assigned, he was encouraged to buy either a higher-priced or a lower-priced paint. The clerk said either that he had himself recently used with great success a quantity of the recommended paint equal to the amount the customer wanted, or that he had recently used twenty times as much of the recommended paint, also with great success. The measure in this experiment was not a checkmark on an attitude questionnaire, but whether the customer bought the recommended paint. Customers were of course much more easily persuaded to buy the cheaper paint. But regardless of price, the clerk was more successful if he said he'd used a similar amount of paint than if he said he'd used much more than the customer wanted. In this case, the clerk's similarity to the customer was competing directly with a dissimilarity that might indicate greater expertness (using more paint), and similarity won hands down. On other issues and in other situations, maybe, expertness could be the key to persuasion; but who wants a smart-aleck paint salesman?

Some people may; the expert salesman did sell paint, though not as much. Experimenters occasionally ignore the fact that communicator credibility exists only in the eye of the beholder. It is not assigned by the experimenter, nor do particular people possess the same level of credi-

178

bility for all audiences. Certain characteristics may *generally* be associated with increased credibility in a particular culture: in ours, maleness, higher social class, middle age, among other things. But even these general characteristics are by no means foolproof, and you can now find plenty of peole who will reverse them. Don't trust anyone over thirty; venerate the flower child over the hardnosed expert; view drugs as the source of wisdom; accept the poor black as the only honest man. Various audiences may have been misled or betrayed in different ways; they may have learned to recognize different cues indicating the kinds of expertness that are really helpful and the kinds that are just a pretentious display of erudition. Whatever their experience, it won't be the same for everyone, and credibility will be no less varied.

INTERACTIONS BETWEEN
COMMUNICATOR AND CONTENT

Communicator credibility is further complicated in that it is frequently *interactive* rather than *additive*. You can't measure how credible a speaker is to a given audience, and how acceptable a message would be without the speaker, and then combine your two measures to find how much attitude change will occur when that speaker delivers that message to that audience. Communicators don't just attach their value to any communication arithmetically; they're likely to change the meaning of the message simply because *they* said it. Solomon Asch (1952), for example, attributed the statement, "I hold it that a little rebellion, now and then, is a good thing, and as necessary in the political world as storms are in the physical," either to a high-credibility source, Thomas Jefferson, or to a low-credibility source, Nikolai Lenin. (They were high and low, anyway, to most of his American volunteers.) Then, rather than merely measuring quantitatively how much the statement was accepted depending on its presumed source, as earlier researchers had done, Asch asked his volunteers to write their interpretations of the statement. The differences in interpretation were substantial. Volunteers who thought Jefferson made the statement wrote about "new ideas in government and politics"; "discontent and dissatisfaction as indicative of a healthy awareness of what is going on"; the founding of third parties; "an upheaval in personal political opinions within a party." Those who thought the source was Lenin said that he was justifying the Russian revolution, that he "based his statement on the Marxian dynamic concept of society," that he "meant rebellion in the sense of outright revolution within a country," that he was endorsing "frightening" actions and purges of the old order. Opinions toward the "Jefferson" statement were clearly much more favorable than toward the "Lenin" statement; but they did not represent increased favor or disfavor toward revolution per se. A different pitcher created a whole new ball game. Such an effect is not necessarily permanent; under other auspices at a later date, the same people might reinterpret the same statement quite differently, and indeed Asch reports such instances. Nor is the effect absolute: whether Jefferson or Lenin says 2 + 2 = 4, most people will see the statement similarly. But because many opinion statements are ambiguous, and because the audience uses whatever information they can to interpret such statements, the reputation of the speaker will mean more than just a certain additional degree of acceptance or rejection.

In fact, it may be that only in a setting such as the typical advertisement does communicator credibility work as straightforwardly as psychologists originally conceptualized it. When John Wayne says, "I favor absolute adherence to the U.S. Constitution," and a black Harlem housewife says, "I favor absolute adherence to the U.S. Constitution," the listener may hear two quite different statements. But when Wayne says, "Buy this soap," and the black housewife says, "Buy this soap," we can look to the effect of their relative credibility on message acceptance without worrying much about who means what. Soap is soap.

BOOMERANG EFFECTS

And what if Nikolai Lenin says, "Buy this soap"? Does that mean only that fewer people buy the soap, or that some in the audience give up soap altogether, or that somebody tosses a Molotov cocktail into the nearest soap vat? In the precise technical terminology of psychological research, mightn't we get a "boomerang effect" instead of positive opinion change?

In none of the research mentioned so far did boomerang effects occur, at least for any experimental group as a whole. Even communicators whose credibility should seem really low to many volunteers — Lenin, *Pravda, The New York Daily News* — have usually produced either zero attitude change or even a little positive change, not a shift *away* from the position advocated. Because common-sense everyday observations, as well as political lore about "the kiss of death," seem to suggest otherwise, psychologists have several times purposely set out to induce a boomerang effect; and more often than not they have failed. The boomerang is not as straightforward an instrument as it may appear.

One particularly ingenious study of boomerang effects did succeed in part, and it also had the advantage of being a field experiment. Robert Abelson and James Miller (1967) staged the experiment in Greenwich Village's Washington Square Park during several pleasant weekend summer afternoons in 1963. Martin Luther King's March on Washington was coming soon; several sit-ins against discrimination in the building trades had recently occurred in New York. Into this setting came one researcher, known to insiders as the Stooge, who sat down beside the first lone bench-sitter he saw. Soon a second researcher, the Experimenter, strolled up to the chosen bench-sitter, whom we shall call the Mark. The Experimenter announced that he was from Survey Research Associates (he had a clipboard, a microphone, and a tape recorder to prove it), and that he wanted to interview the Mark about discrimination against Negroes in employment. He asked the Mark first whether he favored "the recent demonstrations by Negroes against job discrimination." If the Mark said yes, as most did, the Experimenter asked him to fill out a scale showing how strongly he favored the demonstrations. The Stooge, sitting on the same bench, was asked to do likewise.

The Experimenter then started to interview both Mark and Stooge about their feelings on job discrimination, fair employment laws, and related issues, alternately questioning either the Mark or the Stooge first. The Stooge replied with a series of standardized responses, all anti-Negro but varying somewhat in tone. For example: "Forced integration in employment will undoubtedly lead to friction on the job, which makes it economically unsound." In addition, the Stooge preceded his own answers by commenting on the Mark's answers. In the "Neutral Remarks" condition, his comments were innocuous: "I listened carefully to this man's remarks." In the "Insulting Remarks" condition, designed to provoke a boomerang effect, the Stooge said such things as "That's ridiculous," "No one really believes that," "That's just the sort of thing you'd expect to hear in this park."

Sometimes a crowd would gather during these proceedings, but not by accident: they were three to five additional confederates of the experimenter, depending on how many could get to Washington Square that day. Their job was to be attentive when the Mark spoke, and to insult the Stooge mildly when he spoke: "Oh, no!" "That's absurd!" "I disagree!" "Tut-tut-tut!" The crowd was included to underline for the Mark just how obnoxious the Stooge's views were, according to community standards — hopefully to exacerbate the boomerang effect. Occasionally a real person, which is to say a nonconfederate, would join the crowd; but such people usually added nothing to the situation, except for one apparently psychotic woman who grabbed the Experimenter's microphone and started "broadcasting" her own schizophrenic views of the world situation.

The experiment's results: a boomerang effect. Whether a crowd was present or not, Marks insulted by the Stooge were significantly more favorable to the civil rights demonstrations after the interview than before, moving *away* from the Stooge's position. Uninsulted Marks also showed favorable change, but mainly in the crowd situation. The latter sort of change can't really be called a boomerang effect, because it wasn't a response to an odious communicator. Instead the crowd appeared, by its opposition to the Stooge, to have pushed the Mark in the direction of the group's standards — moving him positively toward their views, not negatively away from the Stooge.

The boomerang effect among insulted Marks seems to satisfy our expectations of what should happen in such a situation, but working out a good theoretical explanation for it is another matter. Abelson and Miller speculate that Marks might have been trying to retaliate against the Stooge for his nastiness, by showing him how much they really disagreed with him on the final questionnaire. That might well account for boomerang effects in politics, where voters can indeed get back at the fat cats or the Commies by defeating the candidates they endorse. But such an explanation doesn't work in the present experiment. Abelson and Miller included another experimental variation, in which the Stooge either stayed while he and the Mark each filled out the final attitude scale, or else gave a plausible excuse and rushed off into the anonymity of New York City before the Mark was given the final scale. If it were a case of Marks avenging the Stooge's insults by showing him he had unleashed a backlash, then Marks should show more boomeranging attitude change when the Stooge stayed than when he left. But they didn't.

Perhaps instead expressions of opinion were being used in this study to assert the Mark's identity. He certainly didn't want to be confused with that sneering bigot; so on the scale which the Experimenter, and possibly the crowd, would be seeing shortly, he placed himself as far away from the Stooge as he could reasonably get. Communicators can help serve the object appraisal function of attitudes, by being expert; and the social adjustment function, by being trustworthy; why not the value-expressive function too, by giving the audience somebody good to identify with or somebody bad to identify away from? Several of my Bircher acquaintances seemed to use communicators in just this manner. The politicians and writers they favored often had shown themselves to be untrustworthy and inexpert in various ways, but nevertheless voiced the values the Birchers themselves felt it proper for public figures to advocate.

One other possible basis for credibility comes to mind here, although it has nothing to do with boomerang effects and although I know of no direct evidence for it. Certain communicators may be credible to certain people because they serve an externalization function so neatly. They may possess no factual reliability, may have betrayed their followers or allies repeatedly, and may generally display a character so foul that even a real neurotic would have a hard time identifying closely with them; but oh, what they say makes him feel *so* good! Mr. Whiteside, my Dallas Nazi, was disturbed enough about the German Nazis' final solution to deny that it had ever happened. But he seemed to love reading about it, loved the words of those who promised to destroy the Reds and the Feds and the Niggers and the Jews. Credibility works its small wonders in many ways.

182

media and messages:
persuasive content

Some praise at morning what they blame at night,
But always think the last opinion right.

— Alexander Pope
An Essay on Criticism

Whenever a reporter is assigned to cover a Methodist
conference he comes home an atheist.

— Journalists' proverb, quoted in H. L. Mencken
A New Dictionary of Quotations

When I was an undergraduate, The Pennsylvania State University had 3.3 male students for every female. Telephoning a girl for a date, therefore, required considerable advance planning. First, when should I call her? Not too long before the event, or she might be reluctant to commit herself; not too short a time before, or she would surely have a date already — or be embarrassed to admit that she didn't. Should I call her in the daytime, when she probably wouldn't be in anyway and I'd have to give her roommate my name, thus frustrating my plans to call the next several girls on my list; or in the late evening, when she'd already have been called half a dozen times; or in mid-evening, when the dormitory phone lines would inevitably be tied up by ten thousand boys calling three thousand girls? And if I did get through, what should I say? Build up the coming attraction, or play it down in favor of her company; ask first, bing, right off the bat, with all small talk later, or try a long build-up, maybe so long she'd get bored; attempt to be brilliant, funny, sophisticated, affectionate, cool, or my own ineffable self; try to be spontaneous, or prepare a script in advance (my high school romances having been largely literary); take no for an answer and hope for better luck next week, or insist on this week; give the impression there are other girls who'll do as well, or tell her that for me she's the only woman alive?

And all that was only for a date.

Had I but known, I could have rationalized at least part of my wasted effort by pretending to be conducting research on that aspect of persuasion usually described as "content." You might think psychologists wouldn't be interested in such trivial content as a college date; but when they investigate persuasive content, they're usually not so much concerned with what the communicator is saying as with how he says it. The question is not whether a date with him really would be a desirable thing, but whether he says this explicitly or implicitly, when in his speech he says it, whether he asks for the date first and then provides

183

supporting reasons or vice versa – all the variables I unknowingly worried about in that dormitory phone booth, when I thought I was concerned only with the company of Katie or Ellie or Marcia or Alice.

MESSAGE CONTENT AND FORMAT

In some ways this concern is similar to Marshall McLuhan's (1964) emphasis on medium rather than message, but the differences are more important. The medium itself may indeed be the principal message in certain artistic productions or entertainments; it is seldom so in communications designed (with any sort of competence) to be persuasive. Further, any one communication medium can be used in many ways, and various different media can be used in essentially the same ways, to convey a specific persuasive message. Psychologists have been much more interested in the effects of varying patterns of presentation than in the technological developments that allow these patterns to travel more quickly or to greater distances.

There are those who discount the influence of communication format almost entirely. "More powerful than armies is an idea whose time has come," according to Victor Hugo and others; "The tide of history is with us," according to the Soviets and others; "Damn debates about tactics; we have the truth and we will triumph regardless," according to various leftists, rightists, and others. Peculiar, then, that armies still exist, that so many apparently good ideas have been lost amid the erratic tides, that so many people at any one time believe in unmitigated falsity. Certainly some ideas have a greater immediate appeal than others; but without benefit of superior rhetorical skills, they may quickly fade into obscurity. The number of "great" scientists and philosophers who have also been outstanding literary stylists is hard to explain by chance alone. Perhaps their linguistic ability enables them to examine and evaluate subtle ideas more easily, so that they waste less time on the poorer ones; but perhaps too, similar concepts in less skilled hands do not convert enough of us deeply enough to attain the status of "greatness," or the influence they might deserve.

A few psychologists have compared the relative persuasiveness of different concepts or recommendations, in such terms as "strength." More attention should be devoted to this prime ingredient in message content, because without it there would be nothing to communicate and because the wrongheadedness, stupidity, or cleverness of what a man has to say clearly does influence his message's persuasive effectiveness. But once you go beyond format to comparisons of specific messages, you begin mixing the study of psychological processes with philosophy or literary criticism or some such thing; and most social psychologists, as disrespectful of disciplinary boundaries as they are, seem to feel they have enough to do in studying message format. They don't argue that the meaning of

184

the message is unimportant, as McLuhan often seems to; they do feel their time and their skills are better devoted to the *way* the meaning is communicated, and to what this means for its acceptance or rejection.

When I was still taking psychology courses rather than teaching them, the chapters and lectures on attitude change were filled with specific recommendations about the format of the persuasive speech, deriving largely from the early research of Hovland and his colleagues (Hovland, Janis, and Kelley, 1953). You should state your conclusions explicitly if your audience is low in education, implicitly if it's well-educated; you should present only your side of the issue if the audience already tends to agree with you and isn't likely to run into counterpropaganda later, but you should acknowledge the other side of the issue too if the audience starts off disagreeing or will likely hear contradictory arguments later; and so on. In their recognition that communication format interacts with such variables as audience characteristics, such recommendations were a considerable advance over previous simpleminded prescriptions for persuasion, hardly changed from Aristotle; but inevitably, they in turn have proven too simple to be useful. It's hard these days to know what to tell a student who, let's say, wants to write a series of really persuasive articles endorsing population control for the college newspaper. Psychologists have found so many complicating factors in persuasive format that I have to recommend reliance mainly on journalistic art.

PRIMACY AND RECENCY

Consider, for example, a central issue in the study of communication content: primacy versus recency. Psychologists have most often studied attitude change by presenting one set of volunteers with one communication, another set with a somewhat altered communication, and measuring the differential effect. But suppose any *one* volunteer hears from *two* opposed speakers, or even more? In a jury trial or a televised debate between Presidential candidates, for instance, does it make any difference which speaker gets his licks in first?

Frederick Hansen Lund convinced himself so well that it did make a difference, that in 1925 he proposed a Law of Primacy in Persuasion. Not many social psychologists today go around proposing Laws, particularly on the basis of only one experiment; I'm not sure whether Lund was naive or just pugnacious. In his experiment, he gave several different groups a mimeographed set of arguments on one side of an issue — defending monogamy, or attacking protective tariffs, or even attacking monogamy — then measured their attitudes. He then gave them a set of mimeographed arguments on the other side, and another attitude measure. People didn't change their opinions of monogamy much one way or the other, but on the remaining topics, a distinct primacy effect occurred: the first set of arguments presented, on whichever side of the

185

topic, was much more influential than the second. Thus originated the Law of Primacy in Persuasion.

At this point I wish to propose a Law of Nonreplication in Attitude Research: any time anyone finds a clear, unambiguous result, chances are somebody else who does a similar study will get the opposite result, or no result, or at least something different from the original. This law usually works not through random variation in attitude change data, though it sometimes looks that way, but rather through the first researcher's failure to appreciate the role of important variables, which the second researcher either controls for or stumbles across during his own research. Whether Lund was naive or pugnacious makes no difference here; in either instance, he wasn't watching everything that was going on, and his experiment, rather than supporting a general law, turned out to be only a special case. His law stood for twenty-five years because almost no one bothered to do research on the primacy-recency question; then it dribbled away as other data began to come in, showing all sorts of other special cases where recency was stronger than primacy, or primacy worked only part of the time, or neither one worked with any consistency at all. As a notable example, Hovland and Mandell (1957) used Lund's own sets of arguments, but found a primacy effect in only one of three groups tested. Using more current issues with several other groups, they found considerably stronger *recency* effects than primacy effects.

What had Lund overlooked? Out of several available possibilities, the one first proposed by Hovland and Mandell may still be the most likely. Lund was a college professor, delivering information to students; he presumably had some prestige via his professional role, and the students were predisposed to absorb what he had to say. So when he passed out the first set of arguments, the audience took it without a grain of salt, not realizing that anything more was coming. When the opposing set of arguments came, they awoke to the realization that Lund was acting outside his normal professional role, that he was engaging in some kind of unexplained hanky-panky. So they either paid much less attention to the second set, knowing it wasn't a lesson to be learned, or else they accepted it much less than the first, knowing Lund wasn't placing his authority behind it. Loss of credibility, at least in attitude experiments, is not completely retroactive; so the material presented before disillusionment set in retained its advantage.

Has Lund's Law of Primacy been succeeded by another Law — perhaps a Hovland's Law of Recency? No, but Hovland (1957) did come up with the soundest and most cautious proposition I've seen in the primacy-recency controversy: "When two sides of an issue are presented successively by different communicators, the side presented first does not necessarily have the advantage." Sometimes it will and sometimes it won't. Since Hovland, numerous researchers have tried to develop support for some kind of primacy-recency principle that's a little firmer; and perhaps in light of their several dozen additional experiments, a revision of Hovland's Proposition is appropriate: "When two sides of an issue are presented successively by different communicators, the side presented *second* does not necessarily have the advantage."

DISCREPANCY EFFECTS

Another problem in persuasive content has generated nearly as great a battle as primacy-recency, but appears to have attained greater uniformity of results, if not greater theoretical clarity, over the years. Suppose I'm a Penn State sophomore and I've finally gotten a date with a genuine girl and I feel the need for a little more physical contact than a handshake. Or, more seriously, suppose I am a black militant and I've finally gotten the ear of the national news media and I want to add some genuine food to the diets of the nation's black children. Do I make a sweet little request for just a bit more than I had before, or do I go for broke? Attitude researchers deal with such questions in research on attitudinal *discrepancy* — the size of the difference between what a persuasive speaker advocates and what his audience already accepts. The question of discrepancy effects is neither artificial nor narrow in application, as the primacy-recency issue turned out to be; it should concern nearly everyone who ever needs to persuade someone else.

The first important studies of discrepancy reached conclusions that various militants seem to have learned well, but that I never dared test as a Penn State sophomore: the more you ask for, the more you get. Maybe you don't get as high a percentage of what you've asked for if you ask for a lot; but if you ask for everything and get half, isn't that better than asking for half and getting three-eighths? Hovland and Pritzker (1957) gave volunteers a persuasive message — on the time needed to discover a cure for the common cold, for instance — that argued for only a slight change from the volunteers' previous position. Other volunteers got a similar message which argued for a moderate degree of change; still others, for a sizeable amount of change. Quite consistently the amount of change went up as the amount asked for went up. Other researchers have gotten similar results with a considerable assortment of volunteers and topics.

But before you draw up your own list of nonnegotiable demands, before you do a Portnoy and ask the next good-looking girl you meet the most outrageously lewd request you can dream up, be warned that later research has added several qualifications. First — this applies to the early studies too — attitude researchers who've tested discrepancy effects have on the whole tried to sound reasonable and logical; they have not purposely advocated the absurd. Even when they're argued that the

187

most healthy amount of sleep is none at all, they've tried to put a good face on it. Second, when Hovland and others found attitude change consistently increasing as the amount of change demanded went up, they were usually using highly credible communicators — people a volunteer would find much easier to believe than to ridicule, no matter how far out their messages got. With low-credibility communicators, the most effective message usually argues for a position moderately distant from the audience's real one, not far out. When Stephen Bochner and Chester Insko (1966) tried to persuade people about the ideal number of hours of sleep, they found that a "Nobel prize-winning physiologist" got volunteers to change most when he advocated one hour of sleep a night; the "director of the Fort Worth YMCA" was most effective at three hours. When Aronson, Turner, and Carlsmith (1963) tried to change college students' rankings of nine snippets of modern verse, they found that an essay attributed to T. S. Eliot was most effective when it argued for the greatest change. The same essay, credited to Miss Agnes Stearns, an education student at Mississippi State Teachers' College and cousin of the experimenter, was less effective overall than in its Eliot guise; and it was even less effective in its extreme form than when it argued only for middling change.

Third, the discrepancy effect Hovland got with relatively non-ego-involving topics doesn't work very well with high-involvement topics — as he predicted. When people are faced with an argument downrating their own personality characteristics, for instance, they're willing to go only a moderate distance in agreeing; when they listen to arguments downrating an unfamiliar person, on the other hand, they're influenced most by relatively extreme statements (Eagly, 1967). Fourth, there's that term *relatively extreme:* most studies of message discrepancy have involved only a few levels of discrepancy, none of them definitely far out. It's easy to achieve real extremity on some topics: in arguing for less sleep, you can't go lower than zero. (Even the influence of the Nobel physiologist dropped off somewhat when he argued for no sleep at all, although he still had enough influence at that point to lower volunteers' opinions significantly below their previous seven to eight hours.) On other topics, it may be hard to guess in advance what a volunteer will really see as extreme; so the studies that have reported the most change with the most extreme arguments may just never have gotten very far away from moderation.

DISCREPANCY AND BACKLASH

The really discerning Penn State sophomore might read all these qualifications, and still ask, "So what — what have I got to lose?" No matter how far out the arguments, or how ego-involving the topics, no researcher yet has obtained a significant *negative* change by advocating a highly

188

discrepant position. The amount of positive change may drop below what it would be with a moderate position; it may even drop to zero; but it doesn't boomerang — it doesn't get worse than it was to begin with.

This is the only point in these discrepancy studies at which the laboratory results seem to me to part company with reality. There really are girls who will not just not go along with an indecent suggestion, but who will slap you in the face and never speak to you again — definitely a worse situation than you started out with. Some newspapermen, I'm sure, do get converted to atheism at Methodist or Baptist or Church of Christ conventions. There really are white Americans, apparently in plentiful supply, who not only refuse to consider black militant demands, but who grow more negative to any black requests as a result; and both black and white Americans who respond to young activists of either race likewise. The differences between the laboratory situations that don't produce boomerangs and backlashes, and the real-life situations that do, may partly involve the reasonableness of the arguments (insults are usually carefully avoided in the lab), partly the degree of ego-involvement possible, partly the brevity of laboratory presentations versus the long-term repetition — and sometimes escalation — of demands outside the lab. Differences clearly exist, though they're not necessarily unresolvable.

However, I don't want to imply that backlash is the only result of "extreme" demands in the real world. It may be that most racial backlashers are already prejudiced anyway, and just show their bias more clearly in response to a discrepant speaker. The people who complain most about modern youth may have had a good bit of authoritarian hostility dammed up inside and are just letting it out onto the first good target. Among whites in general, even in the South, at least a little evidence (Pettigrew, 1969) shows greater positive change toward Negroes during and after periods of racial controversy than during "quiet" periods, despite the statements of some whites that such controversies "hurt the Negro cause." I'm reminded of a Feiffer cartoon (1962) that shows two Negroes arguing in a restaurant within hearing distance of two whites: "Don't give me that handkerchief-head pacifism! It's time for the Afro-American to meet violence with violence!" "Nonsense! Non-violent resistance is the most effective weapon the Negro *has*. Why surrender it?" After several minutes of this, the whites tell each other, "We'd better integrate immediately!" "God, yes! Before those *extremists* take over!" Whereupon the two blacks privately congratulate themselves on another job well done.

The pattern suggested by Feiffer differs from that of any discrepancy experiment I know, but it's worth trying. What does happen if, instead of having one communicator deliver an extreme speech and then measuring his influence on an audience, you have two speakers on the same side — an extreme one and one who's only moderately different from the audience? Does the extreme one soften up the audience for the moderate one? Does he, in Sherif's term (Sherif and Sherif, 1967), shift listeners' "latitudes of acceptance" to such a degree that they'll accept the moderate speaker's message, though they wouldn't have accepted it if the moderate speaker had been alone? Under what circumstances, if any, does the extreme speaker poison the atmosphere so much — expand listeners' latitudes of rejection to such a degree — that they reject even a moderate position they would have accepted before? I'm not at all sure that the more extreme persuasive speakers of our time would accept scientific answers to such questions. But the questions are important; they are relevant to the proper conduct of our public life; and I see no reason why they cannot be answered scientifically.

the persuasible person: individual differences in attitude change

You can even fool some of the people all the time.
— Abraham Lincoln, quoted in A. K. McClure,
Lincoln's Yarns and Stories

There's a sucker born every minute.
— attributed to P. T. Barnum

I'm just a girl who can't say no.
— Oscar Hammerstein II
Oklahoma

The mythical perfect persuader is usually an object of fear. The companion myth, the completely persuasible person, has traditionally been the butt of malicious fun, although pathos or even tragedy often waits in the wings. The simpleton who'll believe anything at the drop of a hat, the dumb blonde who succumbs to anyone at the drop of her skirt, seem hugely satisfying to the common man, who often has good reason to doubt his own powers of resistance. A variant on the legend has the fool, who after all resembles the common man more than anyone else, believing whatever he's told but ultimately profiting from it: Jack and the Beanstalk, the Beverly Hillbillies, the Good Soldier Schweik. Psychologists have also recognized the sucker's existence, but not seeing themselves as common men, they have felt little reason to view him sympathetically.

In real life, absolute pushovers are nearly as scarce as perfect spellbinders. But even casual observation will show you that some people respond more quickly to persuasive appeals than others, and succumb more often. What is it in these people, rather than in the communicator or his communication, that makes them bite even when their immediate associates refuse the bait? Psychologists try to answer that question when they study both *general persuasibility,* a broad individual predisposition to accept any sort of persuasive communication, and *specific personality differences,* which may predispose a person to accept particular kinds of arguments in certain situations.

GENERAL PERSUASIBILITY

General persuasibility is itself a relative concept, not an absolute one. Obviously you can't tell whether a person is generally persuasible merely by telling him he should drink Geritol and waiting to see if he responds. Whether he says yes or no, you'll learn only how he responds to a particular attitude-changing situation. On the other hand, you can't measure his response to every variety of persuasive appeal and every opinion topic possible, or you'd be testing him forever. The people who study general persuasibility have tried instead to include a relatively wide variety of persuasive appeals and topics in any one study, selected to represent a substantial percentage of the persuasive encounters that do take place in the real world.

The basic study of general persuasibility was conducted by Irving Janis and Peter Field (1959a). They measured volunteers' opinions on five different topics, then presented the volunteers with a set of persuasive statements on those topics, followed by another attitude measure similar to the first. A week later the same volunteers were given another set of persuasive statements opposing the first set on every topic, and finally a third attitude measure like the first two. The persuasive statements varied not only in content — ranging from General Von Hindenburg's status as a German democratic leader to the career prospects of Jack O'Keefe, an imaginary television comedian — but also in attributed source (newspaper columnists, medical researchers, etc.) and in type of principal appeal, with various statements stressing logical, emotional, social, or other considerations involved in accepting the statement's content.

If a trait of general persuasibility were nonexistent, attitude changes back and forth among the positions advocated by these messages should be largely unrelated. If general persuasibility *did* exist, predisposing people to change their attitudes no matter what, the amounts of attitude change induced by different appeals should be positively related to each other. And indeed, thirty-nine of forty-five possible correlations were positive: general persuasibility at work.

Or probably at work, anyway. Janis and Field, despite their wide variety of topics and appeals and sources, used only brief printed communications; they avoided the truly wild appeal; they used only

191

topics that college students would find of little immediate personal relevance. No one has gone farther than they in varying attitude-change formats; but somebody should, to find out just how general Janis and Field's general persuasibility is.

The concept has been checked in other ways, for instance by using no real persuasive appeals at all, merely a series of checkmarks indicating how certain other people feel about a long string of attitude positions (King, 1959), or by using brief tape-recorded messages from several people endorsing a particular position on each of several topics (Abelson and Lesser, 1959). Both these methods got results similar to Janis and Field's: a general persuasibility factor influenced at least a portion of volunteers to show at least a little attitude change no matter what the communication. But the factor was usually weak, and its effects could probably be washed out by all sorts of other circumstances.

SPECIFIC PERSONALITY DIFFERENCES

One such circumstance is the existence of personality traits that not only influence a person's general persuasibility but also make him more or less responsive to particular types of persuasive messages. Research on the contribution of personality traits to attitude change is plentiful; it has, however, shown more promise than useful results. Perhaps this is because it seems so easy to do. Run a simple opinion change study; toss your volunteers whatever personality tests you have at hand; calculate a fast correlation — and presto! Hypomanic people are more persuasible than hypermanics. Or less. Or nonsignificantly different until you omit a few volunteers for very good reasons and run the correlation again by a different formula.

Not all the research is done that way. In a few cases, somebody has expended enough time and effort and experimental imagination to tease out the tricky relationships that really exist between important personality factors and important categories of attitude change; and other people have come along with enough additional research support to guarantee that the initial discovery wasn't altogether unique. Further, empirical expertise in the area is increasing fast, particularly as guided by the systematizing hand of William McGuire (1968, 1969a). But you still have to be pretty careful what research you buy and what you turn down, because the number of lemons and bad apples peddled here is considerably higher than the general public — or the scientific public, for that matter — has a right to expect.

What personality characteristics can you rely on to influence attitude change, and in what ways? First, a clarification: to attitude researchers, "personality" includes not only such usual considerations as temperament and neurotic traits, but also such ability factors as intelligence. We'll consider the ability factors first, for good reason. Psychologists have identified at least two steps in attitude change: comprehension and yielding. If you want to change someone's opinion, you must make him understand your position before you can have any success in getting him to accept it. And the two don't necessarily go together. One of the most sweetly inane pop songs of the late 'fifties argued, "To know know know him is to love love love him," and maybe in his case it was so; but it doesn't necessarily follow. A greater truth is found in the popular expression: "I know it but I don't believe it." Comprehension without acceptance is worthless; acceptance without comprehension will likely produce only attitudinal garbage, as witness the curious versions of religious doctrine that many of the faithful create for their own personal use. Tertullian's dictum, *"Credo quia absurdum"* ("I believe because it is absurd"), enjoys little popularity among attitude change researchers.

ABILITY FACTORS

How then does intelligence influence attitude change? Curiously, the most frequent finding has been a zero relationship between the two: apparently, persuasibility is not affected by intelligence (Hovland and Janis, 1959). But only apparently. Intelligence can work two ways: it can enable your audience to comprehend your message, and that's good; or it can enable your audience to knock holes in your arguments, and that's bad. If you've got a fairly normal population and a fairly normal message, the effects of intelligence may very well cancel each other out. If you've got a difficult but solidly constructed message, higher intelligence should lead to greater attitude change; but psychologists don't usually use such messages. If you present a simple message with little support, then the lower a person's intelligence, the more likely he should be to bite; he can understand it without being very bright, and the less bright he is, the less critical he'll be. Psychologists do use such simple and unsupported messages frequently, not in persuasion studies but in conformity experiments, where only a brief statement about the opinions of a group's majority is given. In those experiments, acceptance of the majority opinion has consistently been found to increase as intelligence decreases.

Other possibilities exist at the extremes. The complete idiot wouldn't be able to understand enough of any message, no matter how simple, to accept it. At the other end of the scale, William McGuire (1968) has suggested that the completely omniscient individual, God Almighty, would long ago have evaluated every possible argument for anything and would have already accepted or rejected it on its merits, so you can't change Him now, however powerful your logic. If you feel like praying, don't waste your time on rhetorical niceties; just pray.

At least one other factor seems to be involved in the comprehension of persuasive messages: fantasy ability. Janis and Field (1959b) first measured fantasy ability in relation to attitude change, using such questions as: "When you imagine things that might happen to you in the future, do you picture them in your mind almost as if they are real?" They found that the better a person says he is at fantasizing vividly, the higher his general persuasibility is likely to be. They suggest that the talented fantasist should be better able to imagine all the good things that will happen to him if he changes his attitudes in the direction the communicator advocates. His greater ability to fantasize thus leads to greater motivation for change.

I've obtained evidence for a somewhat different process (Elms, 1966). I found again that more attitude change occurred in people with more fantasy ability; but what seemed important was *empathic* fantasy ability, the ability to imagine yourself in someone else's place, holding someone else's attitudes, rather than the ability to imagine all the goodies you'll get for changing. A person can understand a position intellectually without really caring to relate it to his current attitudes, maybe even without being able to relate it. But if he is able to try it on for size, to picture vividly how it fits in with the rest of his attitudes, or with his entire self-picture, he may be much more likely to accept it. It may bring rewards, and he may recognize that; but change is more likely to come from his ability to see himself clearly as holding the attitude, than from his ability to imagine particular rewards. If the new attitude fits, that is. If it contradicts his self-image, if it's out of place in relation to his other attitudes or is unlikely to serve any useful function in his personality structure, his fantasy ability should lead him to reject the message all the more promptly.

Other kinds of fantasy ability may be more important than empathic fantasy ability in certain attitude change situations. In my research, the main attitude change procedure was roleplaying — acting out the part of a person with a different set of attitudes — and that might well have exaggerated the importance of empathic abilities. Fantasy ability effects might also be confused at times with those of intelligence; but no significant relationship between these two ability factors appeared among my volunteers. Perhaps as definitions of intelligence are expanded by the work of such people as J. P. Guilford (1967), fantasy ability will be included as a component of intelligence. Right now, all we can say is that fantasy ability and verbally measured intelligence may both influence the comprehension phase of attitude-change efforts, but not necessarily in the same ways.

SELF-ESTEEM AND PERSUASIBILITY

What factors influence the acceptance or yielding phase? The one for which we have the most evidence is *self-esteem*. Self-esteem is defined and tested variously, but it involves mainly one's assessment of oneself

194

and one's personal characteristics, positively or negatively. The early findings, principally by Janis and Field (1959b), indicated a negative relationship: the lower your self-esteem, the higher your general persuasibility. This relationship, supported by a number of later studies, could originate in one of several ways. A person may think so little of himself and his opinions that he's eager to accept anybody else's. Or he may want to raise his self-esteem, thinks he can do so by garnering the praise and friendship of others, and tries to get them on his side by accepting their opinions. Or he may feel he's been kicked around so much already, and wants to avoid being kicked around any more, that he defends himself by identifying with possible kickers, thus blending in with the social environment. At the other end of the scale, the high-esteem person may think so well of his own opinions that he doesn't want anyone else's; or (as Arthur Cohen [1959] suggested) he may be able to sustain his high self-esteem only by defensively denying the truth of anything contradicting his self-picture, including contradictory opinions.

These suppositions are all based on the assumption that a particular self-esteem level developed first, and susceptibility to persuasion came later. Other assumptions can be made: for instance, that a person started off being highly persuasible, perhaps as a result of early parental demands, and then later, upon the realization that he was terribly gullible, suffered a sharp drop in self-esteem. Or a third factor could be influencing both self-esteem and persuasibility. Suppose somebody develops a heavy burden of guilt, arising from real or imagined transgressions. He may then simultaneously suffer a loss of self-esteem, as a result of recognizing how "bad" a person he is, and try to make things up to everyone he has sinned against by accepting everything they say.

Such ambiguities often arise from research that statistically correlates attitude change measures with personality measures: even in the unlikely event that you find a positive relationship, how do you know which causes the other, or whether they're both caused by something else? Some research has been directed toward clarifying the direction of causation, by experimentally creating a temporary drop in self-esteem in the laboratory, and then observing its effects on attitude change; in such situations, lowered self-esteem does sometimes lead to greater persuasibility. But the relationship between this "acute" loss of self-esteem and the "chronic" low self-esteem measured in other studies is unclear. All we know for sure is that as self-esteem goes down, persuasibility goes up.

Or do we? McGuire (1968) suggests that outside the laboratory the low self-esteem person is likely to be socially withdrawn, so that his chances of receiving, let alone comprehending, persuasive messages would be less than for the high self-esteem person. The relationship might therefore be at least somewhat curvilinear: little attitude change with high esteem, because of unwillingness to accept recommendations from others; moderate change at moderate levels of esteem; high change at low levels; little change again at very low levels of esteem, because of failure to get the message.

McGuire's hypothesis has not been tested; but Donald F. Cox and Raymond Bauer (1964) have found a curvilinear relationship between attitude change and self-esteem in a laboratory study, apparently for other reasons. They managed to get almost three hundred middle-aged women from several Boston-area Ladies' Sodalities to volunteer for a research project. Each lady was asked to rate the quality of two "brands" of nylon stockings (actually identical) on several dimensions. Then she heard a tape-recorded "salesgirl" give a brief speech on why Brand R was better than Brand N; then she was asked to re-evaluate the nylons. Everyone also filled out a measure of self-esteem. The ladies with moderate self-esteem changed most in response to the speech; those with high self-esteem changed considerably less. Those with low self-esteem changed least of all — in fact, almost as many changed in a negative direction, rating the salesgirl's recommended Brand R *worse* than before, as changed positively. It may be that the low-esteem ladies in this study were substantially lower in self-esteem than in most previous research, which involved such generally high-esteem groups as Yale under-graduates. If that was the case, Cox and Bauer's explanation of their unusual result sounds reasonable: people with very low self-esteem have psychological defenses "so brittle that they cannot stand the strain of contradictions or even implied criticism by another person." So instead of succumbing to pressure and thus upsetting the delicate balance that enables them to live with their low self-esteem, they refuse to change, or they may even boomerang. They may be pretty low, but they've still got a little pride.

In addition, certain special types of persuasive messages may be particularly appealing or tolerable to high-esteem people but not to low-esteemers, reversing the usual relationship. To test this possibility, Harry Gollob and James Dittes (1965) first gave a "Space Relations Test" to 165 Yale freshmen, assuring them it measured "skills of abstraction . . . highly related to personal effectiveness and professional success." The experimenters then led half the freshmen to believe they had performed miserably on the test, and the other half to believe they had performed magnificently. With their self-esteem thus temporarily smashed or ele-vated, everybody was given an opinion questionnaire, followed by an article on cancer research. Part of the article argued that we should spend money on "a widespread, diffuse program of many people working . . . in many different ways" to find a cancer cure, rather than on a massive crash program. Gollob and Dittes expected that this argument, a not very personally involving one, would elicit the usual relationship between self-esteem and persuasibility: the *more* esteem, the *less* change. It did.

196

The second part of the article argued that "At present the whole cancer problem seems almost hopeless," that one person out of four gets cancer, that it's getting worse every year, that it could happen to you, and that there's no really effective cure. Gollob and Dittes assumed the high self-esteem people would be strong enough to take this kind of argument without flinching, and might even accept it in part; but that the low-esteem people would reject the argument, because accepting it would mean further lowering their already depressed self-picture. "Not only am I a poor lousy slob in all those other ways," the low self-esteemer might think, "but now I'll probably get cancer, too." As expected, the usual relationship was reversed on the attitude items dealing with this part of the article: the *lower* their self-esteem, the *less* volunteers changed their attitudes about cancer's hopelessness.

AGGRESSIVENESS AND ATTITUDE CHANGE

Similar reversals on specific messages have been found with another personality variable that affects acceptance: general aggressiveness. Janis and Rife (1959), among others, report evidence of a negative relationship between aggressiveness and attitude change. A man with a high level of hostility is as likely to reject another person's opinions as to reject everything else about him. But Walter Weiss and Bernard Fine (1955, 1956) discovered that if they used particularly aggressive or punitive messages, such as arguments favoring harsh punishment for juvenile delinquents, hostile volunteers were much more likely to accept the message than relatively nonhostile volunteers. This was true whether the hostile tendencies were a longstanding aspect of the volunteer's personality, or a temporary reaction brought on by insults from the experimenter.

Most of the research I've mentioned so far in this section has been done on males. Research on women has generally revealed two things: they are more persuasible than men, and their persuasibility seems much less related to particular personality characteristics. Hovland and Janis (1959) suggest that both findings may derive from a cultural emphasis on female yieldingness, so strong that it washes out any effects of individual differences among women. But additional possibilities have been noted by McGuire (1968) and others. Women volunteers tend to choose personality questionnaire answers more on the basis of the answers' social desirability than men do, so the questionnaire results may not accurately reflect those characteristics of women which do underlie their persuasibility. Males usually create both the personality tests and the persuasive communications used in all this research; so maybe the personality scales aren't as sensitive to real differences in women as in men regardless of social desirability differences, and maybe the women are not as ego-involved in most of the persuasive topics — atomic submarines, medical research, General Von Hindenburg. Cox and Bauer's research, which did

197

show a firm relationship between self-esteem and attitude change in female volunteers, was an exception in using nylons as a topic. McGuire even suggests that women may be "(a) genetically more susceptible to social influence and (b) genetically less variable among themselves in this regard than are men" — an idea certain not to amuse either the DAR or Women's Lib. But then, McGuire is only a man.

PERSONALITY, PERSUASIBILITY, AND COMPLEXITY

Support for other relationships between personality and persuasibility has been rather more fragmentary than those I've already discussed. Authoritarian individuals may be more susceptible to authoritarian communications, as you might expect (Wright and Harvey, 1965). People who tend to differentiate sharply their perceptions, memories, and other cognitions may show more change upon reading a disorganized communication than people who tend to assimilate their cognitions into one big muddle (Baron, 1965). Et cetera, et cetera.

The personality-persuasibility field is another one that seemed so clear at first — attitude change goes down as self-esteem goes up — but then suddenly got messy when the researchers really began to work things over. Under such circumstances, as McGuire (1968) observes:

> The unsophisticated student is inclined to say . . . "Some people find a positive relationship between X and Y; others a negative relationship. The whole field is utterly confused. Is this supposed to be an objective science? No one agrees with anyone else. There are all sorts of contradictions."

But as sophisticated students have by now realized, there's no reason to believe personality factors *should* consistently show some kind of neatly predictable straight-line effect on attitude change. The fact that our needs or our neuroses predispose us to accept certain kinds of statements does not mean they will move us to accept any statement whatsoever. The fact that a personality trait has one effect on comprehending a persuasive statement doesn't necessarily imply that it will work the same way to promote yielding to the statement; McGuire argues rather persuasively that it will more often show opposite effects at those two stages. The observation that a personality trait works one way on attitudes in one person should not lead us to conclude that it will work likewise in another; the second person will probably differ from the first in many other personality characteristics, any of which may interact unpredictably with the trait we mainly want to study. Indeed, various aspects of the communicator, the communication, the person's own traits, and the entire experimental or real-life situation can all interact, cancel each other out, add to each other's effects, and/or lead to apparent and real reversals of effect, to produce an astonishing multiplicity of attitude change results.

198

At this point not only unsophisticated students but also ʋ. will may rightly throw up their hands in disgust. However, peʋ. still doing research on personality and persuasibility, as well as on ʋ. aspects of attitude change. They now recognize the existence of thoʋ. tricky interactions and confoundings and situational weightings and so on, but the field seems all the more challenging for this recognition of difficulty. They know it's a hard row to hoe; but that's never been a good reason to stop hoeing.

how to become crank-proof: resistance to persuasion

"But what I want you to be, Trot," resumed my aunt, " — I don't mean physically, but morally; you are very well physically — is, a firm fellow. A fine firm fellow, with a will of your own. With resolution," said my aunt, shaking her cap at me, and clenching her hand. "With determination. With character, Trot. With strength of character that is not to be influenced, except on good reason, by anybody, or by anything."

— Charles Dickens
David Copperfield

Despite all the research on attitude change, and all the techniques experimenters have devised to induce change, and all the data showing they *can* induce change, large-scale studies of attitude change among the general public have shown with discouraging frequency that people hardly ever change their attitudes. Whether the persuasive efforts have originated with political candidates, or with advertising agencies, or with presumably altruistic public health organizations, change has rarely been induced in more than a small percentage of any potential mass audience.

Several good reasons for this poor showing come to mind (see also Hovland, 1959). Large-scale attitude change campaigns are often directed at highly ego-involving attitudes, which are the hardest to change anyway. They cannot be forced on the audience, and so most people ignore them. They usually can't take account of personality differences that may affect acceptance. Even when they do reach an audience with the "right" appeals, the audience may be in very much the wrong mood for attitude change: worrying about bills, taking care of kids, listening to somebody else make fun of the communication. And chances are another attitude change campaign is waiting just around the corner, designed to move the audience in the opposite direction.

199

No wonder, then, that even the best work of attitude change researchers hasn't yet been translated into effective persuasion on a large scale. No wonder, too, that until recently little scientific attention has been paid to the development of *resistance* to attitude change. Nobody worked on fallout shelters when the major radiation threat was from watch dials.

ROSS AND RESISTANCE

Unscientific interest in resistance to unscientific persuasion dates much further back. For instance, in E. A. Ross's *Social Psychology* (1908), Chapter Five is titled, "Prophylactics Against Mob Mind." Ross wanted to protect his readers from the influence of sudden waves of popular opinion — in particular, from such things as "'holy rolling,' vegetarianism, wonderworking shrines, divine healers, table-tipping seances, frenzied religious revivals, land booms, speculations and panics, the Belgian hare mania, and the walking craze." He thought their political beliefs needed protection from "a costly wavering in dealing with money or tariff," "a fickle sentimental foreign policy," and "war fevers tending, perhaps, to national humiliation and loss of prestige." Resistance to these follies came, according to Ross, from such sources as the study of literary classics, participation in sports, and the "avoidance of yellow religion." Along with sections on such topics as "How to become crank proof," he provided a string of stirring little marginal comments, of which my favorite sounds like a modern-day Agnewism: "Shun the dithyrambic press."

Ross started off with the assumption that his readers already believed as he did. So when he proposed to protect them *from* such momentary aberrations of opinion as that "a cure for consumption is ready to be given to humanity, the flying machine is soon to displace the bicycle, or the manufacture of weather is about to begin," he was also proposing to protect them *for* belief in the worth of private property, small businesses, the Anglo-Saxon family structure, and "the great Protestant denominations." That's often the pattern followed by people who want to insulate others from attitude change. When I was sixteen, a kindly neighborhood lady who tried to encourage my intellectual development was much distressed that I should want to read Marx's *Capital*, because she felt I wasn't mature enough to resist ideological propaganda. She suggested I spend my time with the Bible instead. Other kindly ladies are still trying to get the California State Legislature to ban all grade-school textbooks that mention evolution — not because they feel school children are too young to think upon the origins of man, but because the evolutionary account might weaken the students' belief in the King James version. Some people may dream of the perfect attitude change technique, and some may look for the perfect patsy, but nobody wants a way to induce absolute resistance to all attitude change. They just want to prevent

200

others from accepting the persuasive messages to which they themselves object.

MODERN RESISTANCE RESEARCH

Psychologists as people must often feel similarly; but psychologists as psychologists have recognized a somewhat different kind of responsibility. They've done a lot of attitude change research during the past twenty-five years. The research may not have produced very effective change techniques so far, but it will eventually; and when it does, these techniques can be used by anyone who has a message to peddle. Psychologists could stop working on such research because somebody might misuse it. But attitude change is an important aspect of human social psychology, and it won't go away even if scientists ignore it. They could stress rational attitude change in their research, and many have. But just as with research on the "peaceful" uses of nuclear energy, research. on "rational" attitude change can be employed for less than rational purposes. So how else can they respond to their ethical dilemma? They can do research on techniques of *resistance* to persuasion. They can devise means not only to increase resistance to what psychologists don't like, but resistance to any form of persuasion an individual may wish to reject — just as their research on persuasive techniques may be used to advance any position an individual wishes to support.

Some have argued that any research on attitude change also gives us useful information about resistance to change; but things don't necessarily work out that way. Knowing that a speech with explicit conclusions is more persuasive to a poorly educated audience might lead you, if you don't really want to convince a poorly educated audience, to omit your conclusions; but that doesn't prevent somebody else from propagandizing the same audience and making his conclusions very explicit. And if we depend only on attitude change research for our knowledge of attitude resistance, resistance will always be at least one jump behind change.

Certain attitude change findings do help us recommend resistance strategies. If a speaker is relying on communicator credibility to get his point across, we might best counter him by attacking his credibility. If we're disturbed that cigaret ads appeal to the teenager by promising to increase his self-esteem, we might try associating cigarets with characteristics (stupidity, susceptibility to disease) that would lower his self-esteem, or we might try to build his self-esteem in other ways so he wouldn't have to rely on cigarets. If we see an extreme message tugging an individual along on what for him seems to be a low-involvement topic (he's sort of for population control, but he doesn't really care, and anyway some people say it's only an antiminority ploy), we might try to make the topic more highly involving. But these strategies for resistance are mostly rather hit-or-miss, after-the-fact maneuvers. Psychologists owe it to the world to provide something better.

An experiment conducted a few years after World War II pointed the way to something at least a little better. Arthur Lumsdaine and Irving Janis (1953) presented one group of volunteers with a one-sided set of arguments, contending that the Russians couldn't mass-produce atomic bombs for at least five years. Other volunteers were told the same, but they were also told the Russians did have certain nuclear capabilities, an acknowledgment that the issue had at least two sides. The two-sided speech elicited roughly the same degree of immediate opinion change as the one-sided speech. A week later, volunteers from both groups heard another speech by a different speaker, arguing that the Russians would be producing large quantities of A-bombs within two years. When opinions were measured following this speech, the volunteers who had heard the earlier one-sided speech were found to have retained almost no effect of either speech; the two had cancelled each other out. But the second speech had no cancelling effect on the volunteers who had earlier heard the two-sided speech; they retained almost as much opinion change from the first speech as a control group who never heard the second speech at all. Why? According to Hovland, Janis, and Kelley (1953), a volunteer who has heard the two-sided speech

> is already familiar with the opposing point of view and has been led to the positive conclusion in a context where the negative arguments were in evidence. In effect, he has thus been given an advance basis for ignoring or discounting the negative arguments, and thus "inoculated" will tend to retain the positive conclusion.

Inoculated? But some of the later arguments about Russia's great nuclear capability were barely mentioned in that first two-sided speech; some weren't mentioned at all; only a few were briefly refuted. Why should the two-sided speech induce more resistance to the second speaker, other than by making the first speaker seem more fair-minded? What was the audience being "inoculated" with?

With *weakened counter-arguments*, William McGuire suggested several years later (McGuire and Papageorgis, 1961) — just as people are inoculated with weakened germs to protect them from disease. You don't inoculate them with full-strength germs, which would give them the disease you want to prevent; and you don't give them the full-strength arguments against your views, for fear they'll be convinced by the other side right away. On the other hand, you don't keep people away from measles or smallpox germs altogether in hopes that they'll never get sick, since chances are they'll run into an infection accidentally

202

and have no defenses against it. Instead you use those weak germs, or even dead ones, to provoke the body to build up its own defenses in advance. Something similar may happen with attitudes. Those volunteers who weren't told anything good about Russia's nuclear potential proved to be pushovers the first time they heard otherwise. But inject them with a few weak arguments suggesting at least a modest Russian nuclear capability; sit back and let Nature's own psychological protective devices go to work — and all of a sudden you've got resistance to persuasion.

So began McGuire's inoculation theory of resistance. The medical analogy is not perfect — analogies never are, or we'd call them something else. But it has been amazingly productive of hypotheses and experiments. The Lumsdaine-Janis study only suggested the analogy; McGuire has carried it considerably further. Suppose, he suggests, the situation is not a contaminated one as in Lumsdaine and Janis' study, where the volunteers had probably already had at least a little contact with arguments on both sides of the question; suppose instead you have a germ-free environment. The body has never encountered disease; the psyche has never met contradiction of its basic beliefs. In this situation, body and beliefs will both look strong. Maybe they'll look even stronger if you provide supportive therapy — an apple a day for the body, a good word about Mom's apple pie now and then for the patriotic psyche. But let in a flood of germs or a nasty speech about how Mom's apple pie hardly rates in the bottom fifth percentile of all apple pies ever made, and blooie! The body falls. The patriotic beliefs are overcome. You needed prior inoculation here a lot worse than in the Lumsdaine-Janis study.

MC GUIRE'S RESEARCH PROCEDURE

But what attitudinal environment is truly germ-free? Has Mom's apple pie always been above criticism? Dad himself probably had a few unkind words to say about it now and then, not to mention your first-hand comparisons with Aunt Sue's pies and the local bakery product. How about religious beliefs? Maybe once upon a time they dwelt in an antiseptic paradise, but no more. McGuire had to test quite a few possibilities before he found an attitude category that had almost never been exposed to attack, even among college students: common health truisms. "Everyone should brush his teeth after every meal if at all possible." "Most forms of mental illness are not contagious." "The effects of penicillin have been, almost without exception, of great benefit to mankind." "Everyone should get a chest X-ray each year in order to detect any possible tuberculosis symptoms at an early stage." Given a scale ranging from "definitely false" to "definitely true," college students consistently rated such statements as "definitely true," and seemed hardly to consider that anyone would ever argue otherwise.

203

Then up stepped the Devil's Advocate, William J. McGuire. He told volunteers that they were participating in a study of "the relation between reading and writing skills," or of "analytic ability." Then he gave each volunteer several sheets of paper, with a health truism at the top of each sheet. The volunteer read the truism, then was presented with a defense of it. At times, the defense was "supportive," a statement endorsing the truism and telling why it's good — thus building up the truism even further, like building up the body with an apple a day. At other times, the defense was "refutational": several arguments *against* the truism were mentioned, followed by a refutation of each. A refutational defense is analogous to the weakened germs of inoculation: not strong enough to overwhelm, but strong enough to set the organism's own antibody-producing mechanisms into motion. Sometimes this refutational defense was "passive," sometimes "active." In the passive condition, the volunteer was given a set of refutations already written out, just as people are sometimes injected with antibodies produced by other people or by animals. In the active condition, the volunteer was told only of possible ways in which his beliefs might be attacked, and then was asked to write out his own refutations.

Then came the *real* attack — not just a few piddly sentences criticizing the truism, not a little dose of half-dead germs carefully cushioned by antibodies, but a thousand-word essay really lambasting X-rays or toothbrushing or penicillin or maybe even some belief that hadn't been mentioned yet. At times this attack came right after the defenses were introduced, at other times a few days later, to help answer the question: how long does it take to build up attitudinal antibodies?

REFUTATION-INDUCED RESISTANCE

First questions first: Are any attitudinal antibodies built up at all? Well, *something* happens. McGuire and Papageorgis (1961; Papageorgis and McGuire, 1961) found that a strictly supportive defense (saying only good things about the truism) initially added to the strength of the attitude, only to collapse under attack. McGuire departs from his medical analogy temporarily to call this the "paper-tiger" effect. But refutational defenses (mentioning possible lines of attack against the truism, then negating such attacks in advance) gave substantial protection against the later full-scale attack — much more protection than either the supportive defense or no defense at all. Passive refutational defense, in which the volunteer was given specific answers to specific attacks, were the best single way to induce resistance to stronger versions of those same attacks coming soon after the defense. But when the major attack was delayed by several days, the active refutational defense, which required the volunteer to think up his own answers, tended to provide relatively greater resistance (McGuire, 1964).

204

Why do the refutational defenses increase resistance? For passive refutation of arguments that reappear in the full-scale attack, the answer seems obvious: the volunteer is given convenient answers in advance to what he must deal with later. Passive refutation directed toward arguments that don't reappear later, and active refutation in general, work somewhat differently. Here's where inoculation theory comes into its full glory. Alerted that attacks are possible (and, in the active-refutation condition particularly, shown by his immediate unaided efforts at refutation that he hardly knows how to respond), the volunteer presumably begins to generate his own defenses — not just to the possible lines of attack mentioned by the experimenter, but to any kind of attack. If he has a while to think about the topic, and knows anything at all about the truism beyond the fact that he believes it, he should be at least partly prepared for whatever comes his way during the real attack. The active-refutation volunteer may not be quite as able to respond to the specific lines of attack mentioned previously as is the passive-refutation volunteer, who after all has been given a carefully worded rebuttal prepared by experts, but he'll have something ready. The passive-refutation volunteer, on the other hand, may not be quite as inspired to think up arguments against new lines of attack, because the lines of attack already mentioned to him in the refutational defense were so neatly handled by the experimenter. Furthermore, he's forgetting a little more of those experimenter-authored refutations every minute. The active-refutation volunteer meanwhile is just beginning to create his own refutations, even for the lines of attack the experimenter has mentioned, and he should be able to remember them that much longer.

Each protective device McGuire has developed possesses certain advantages and disadvantages. The supportive defense builds up the strength of the original attitude, but stimulates no thoughts of refutation against later attack. In the passive-defense condition, the volunteer is provided with several good models for refutation, but may be only moderately stimulated to create other refutations. In the active-defense condition, the volunteer should be very much stimulated to think up his own refutations to all sorts of later attacks; but he has no good models of what a refutation should be, and therefore must take quite a while to work out anything halfway useful.

The best way to induce resistance to persuasion might involve a *combination* of defense strategies. McGuire (1961) has tried that too. A combination of active and passive refutational defenses seems to work best when the later attack involves only arguments already considered for refutation; the volunteer has both read some good arguments against those lines of attack, and has had to think of some others by himself. But the combination doesn't work as well as the active refutational defense alone, when the later line of attack is an unfamiliar one. Apparently the combination is so reassuring that the volunteer just doesn't bother thinking up many defenses against novel arguments on his own.

So here's the picture so far: if you want your favorite Marine recruit to keep thinking America is the gosh-darndest nation in the world, or your closest long-haired friend to go on believing in the merits of the counterculture, and you know nobody will ever tell either of them differently, you'd better not tell them differently either. Just talk more about the Good that resides in the Good Old U.S.A. or in Consciousness III. If you think somebody may try to tell them different, but you're pretty sure you know what the arguments will be on the other side, you'd best spend your time both specifically refuting those arguments you know are coming, and at the same time provoking some refutational work in your audience. Try to do so often enough for the refutations to be fresh in the mind of green Marine or Con-III convert when the Devil appears. But let's say your hip friend has taken a 9-to-5 job, where he'll hear who knows what strange arguments in favor of squaredom; or suppose the Marine is headed for the mysterious Orient and a possible hitch in a Commie POW camp. Do you do the Polonius bit, the Lord Chesterfield letter? Heaven forbid — they'll forget nearly everything you tell them within forty-eight hours. Instead, you simply say, "Ole buddy, you know that the new consciousness is under constant establishment attack; you'd better start thinking about how you'll defend yours." Or, "My son the Marine, this is what the Reds may say about America; what say you?" Then you sit back and let them leave, and if they know anything about square thinking or America, they should be able to handle themselves better than you could guide them. You may need to jiggle their antibody producers with a postcard every now and then — about once a week, if McGuire's laboratory research can be generalized. But that's better than having to stage a daily confrontation.

ATTITUDINAL ANTIBODIES

All this, of course, depends on McGuire's inoculation theory being valid. Perhaps the inoculation analogy is false at bottom. Maybe more important psychological processes are at work that McGuire has overlooked. Two questions are relevant here: where are the antibodies, and what happens when we move from a germfree environment into a normal one?

McGuire's theory presupposes that certain conditions will stimulate the individual's own defensive processes, while other conditions will leave him completely open to attack. But what does a person have after a session of active refutation, let's say, that he doesn't have after a session of supportive defenses? What he should have, if the antibody analogy is correct, is a store of ready responses to most possible attacks on his opinion. These ready responses are presumably produced, over a period of hours or days, as a result of the individual thinking to himself, "Gee, I'm wide open to attack on this point — what *would* I say if somebody said this, or that, or therefore?" A Ph.D. candidate preparing to defend his dissertation in oral examination should be able to list for you quite a string of such responses, both specific and general; and if he wants to pass he'd better have worked through them thoroughly himself, rather than depending on his dissertation committee chairman to feed him the right questions and answers in advance. But when McGuire and others have tried to get just such a list of ready defensive replies from experimental volunteers, they've been surprisingly unsuccessful. Volunteers in the refutational-defense conditions are usually able to list slightly more arguments than supportive-defense volunteers, but not enough to be statistically significant and certainly not enough to account for the big differences in resistance to change.

Why, then, do the refutational defenses work so well? One possibility is that nobody has developed a good measure of attitudinal "antibodies." A volunteer may find it hard to list in the abstract a number of arguments defending his beliefs against unnamed attacks, and yet find such defenses sufficiently close to verbalization to be readily useful when he is attacked. Or he may harbor enough reservations, hesitations, and equivocations to block his acceptance of the opposing position, but still be unable to verbalize them explicitly.

Another possibility is that the refutations do something besides producing antibodies — something besides provoking the volunteer to produce his own supportive or refutational arguments. In his early research, McGuire suggested that refutations also weaken the effect of the opposing arguments, first by explicitly showing some to be fallacious and second by showing generally that arguments from the attack side are not all-powerful, that anybody's armor has chinks if you but seek them. McGuire hasn't explored this possibility in his more recent publications, perhaps simply because it has nothing to do with his inoculation analogy. But Ronald W. Rogers and Donald Thistlethwaite (1969) raised the possibility anew after failing to find evidence for the antibody hypothesis. They also suggested ways in which this alternate hypothesis could account for such effects as the inferiority of active to passive refutation when followed immediately by an attack, and active refutation's superiority if the attack is delayed a couple of days. The active refutation volunteer, who has to make up his own defensive responses, may well see them as inferior in immediate comparison with a carefully written and printed-out attack. But if the attack comes days later, all he may be able to remember is that he was able to think up *some* refutations to possible lines of attack, and thus the present attack may not look that overpowering. The passive-refutation volunteer is in a somewhat different position. If he's attacked right away, he has just read a set of refutations as carefully written and printed as the attack. But if the attack is held back for a while, he may be able to recall only that some experimenter could think up refutations several days ago, while here he is all by his lonesome, with the expert attack staring him in the face.

So passive refutation should provide superior resistance in the short run, active refutation in the long run; and that's what Rogers and Thistlethwaite found, just as McGuire had before them. But the volunteers who should have seen the strength or quality of the major attack as less impressive, according to Rogers and Thistlethwaite's formulation, did not, at least not enough to account for the resistance they showed — just as the people who should have produced more defensive arguments, in McGuire's formulation, didn't either. Percy Tannenbaum (1967), working within a different theoretical framework and using different measures of attack quality, *has* found evidence that refutational defenses weaken the perceived force of a later attack. But he doesn't find this process sufficient to account for the total resistance generated by refutational defenses, and suggests that McGuire may be right in also emphasizing the generation of defensive counterarguments. If attitude change hardly ever depends on a single psychological process, why should attitude resistance?

SEPTIC ATTITUDINAL ENVIRONMENTS

Then there was our other question: Do things work the same way in our usual germy attitude environment as in the germfree one of health truisms? Will refutational defenses help protect us more from change than supportive defenses, for instance with political attitudes where we run into half a dozen refutations every time we open a newspaper? In the early days of his resistance research, McGuire seemed to think so, because the data then suggested that people tend to avoid contradictory information whenever they can. It's a lot easier to spot a William Buckley column and not read it, than it is to detect a gang of germs and run away from them. So maybe most people wouldn't pay much attention to attacks on their favorite opinions, even if the attacks were freely available; and maybe the best way to induce resistance to a really strong face-to-face attack on those opinions would be to make people listen to a few weakened refutations, in the laboratory if nowhere else, so they'd start thinking seriously about how to answer the ultimate confrontation.

But more recent research (reviewed by McGuire, 1969a) strongly indicates that people *don't* consistently avoid information contradicting their own opinions, *can't* avoid much of it even if they try, and often even *seek out* contradictions — perhaps to maintain an optimal level of stimulation, if for no other reason. I know liberals who read William Buckley, Jr., just to get their adrenalin pumping in the morning. So chances are that for many important opinions, most people have run into more refutations already than the experimenter can write down; and if they still

208

need to develop defenses against change, the best defense may be a supportive defense. Fill them with facts, with authoritative support, with anything to make their opinions stronger and more sturdily based. If they've built up a strong set of opinions despite all those germs floating around, they need not fear sudden infection.

Cheryl Brown (1971) has in fact found that a supportive defense produced more resistance than a refutational one with regard to the controversial issue of population control. In her study, however, refutational defenses failed to produce any resistance for one of McGuire's health truisms as well as for the controversial issue; so perhaps other complications were present besides the controversy-truism contrast. Certain kinds of active refutational defense sessions may yet prove useful in inducing resistance on debatable topics as well as on platitudes. People may start overestimating the strength of their own defenses and the weakness of their opponents', after a few weeks of peace and quiet. They may also, when they go looking for criticisms of their own positions, seek out the most ludicrous, outrageous, and muddle-headed sources they can find. That could be one reason why William Buckley is more popular among liberals than Russell Kirk. So even opinions that apparently meet frequent challenge may be much flabbier than one might suspect; and if it's important that they withstand an accidental direct blow or a concerted surprise attack, a good refutational work-out in the resistance lab now and then wouldn't hurt. Or perhaps an exercise manual would do as well: *How to Add Weight and Muscle to Your Opinions in Ten Short Days Through a Balanced Informational Diet Plus Dynamic Tension.* Just sign on the dotted line; no salesman dare call.

6
the hobgoblin
of little minds

alice in dissonanceland: or,
attitude change through the looking glass

"I should see the garden far better," said Alice to herself,
"if I could get to the top of that hill: and here's a path
that leads straight to it — at least, no, it doesn't do
that — " (after going a few yards along the path, and
turning several sharp corners), "but I suppose it will at
last. But how curiously it twists! It's more like a cork-
screw than a path!"

— Lewis Carroll
Through the Looking Glass

The week had been a curious one for Alice. On Monday she'd attended the first meeting of a campus sex discussion group, where she was asked to demonstrate her embarrassment tolerance level by reading aloud a list of decidedly spicy words. That was easy enough; but the group itself totally lacked spice, so she did not return.

On Tuesday in Home Ec 33, sweet Mrs. Trimmins had tried to coax Alice into eating a fried grasshopper. Alice had finally nibbled a bit off one drumstick, which she promptly threw up. No more grasshoppers, thank you.

The next day in psychology class, Alice had volunteered for an experiment that turned out to be three times as boring as the sex discussion group: an entire hour of twiddling little wooden knobs. As if this weren't enough, the experimenter had then given her twenty dollars to spend

210

two minutes convincing the next volunteer that knob-twiddling was really a glorious experience. Alice took the money guiltily and exited fast, before the experimenter could begin twiddling anything besides his dinky wooden knobs. But he did ask her for a Friday date, and against her better judgment she had accepted.

Anyway, the world was supposed to end at 2 o'clock Thursday morning, according to Alice's roommate, so why worry? But of course it hadn't ended, though Roomie had prophesied its doom incessantly for weeks and had urged Alice several times a day to repent and join the Gospel Ship Heavenly Church, which would save all true believers from destruction. When Roomie had returned Thursday afternoon from her unfulfilled vigil at the church, she'd slumped into bed without a word to Alice, pulled the covers over her head, and hadn't so much as poked her nose out since.

Now Friday evening had come, and Alice sat dreamily before her mirror, practicing a misty look in her eyes and dreading the insufferably insipid date which would begin in 45 minutes — chess in the Student Union game room, of all things! Might that psychology experimenter secretly be continuing his research on boredom? How much money would he offer her this time, and for what? The possibilities so intrigued her that she hardly noticed the mirror itself growing misty. Alice started to wipe it clear, and suddenly found her arm elbow-deep in the mirror. She raised her eyebrows, whispered "Extraordinary!" then stepped carefully up onto the vanity and through the looking glass.

THE NAKED CAUCUS-RACE

Alice expected singing flowers and gloved rabbits, but instead she found herself standing at a side door of the university gymnasium. A sign over the door stated: ".EREH URHT SECAR-SUCUAC"

Through the door Alice went, bump! into a mutton-chopped old man. He emitted a soft "baah" upon impact, then regained his balance and announced, "Qualification trials this way, please!"

"But aren't I already qualified for a caucus-race?" Alice asked. "I mean, what sort of qualifications should one have?"

"Harrumph!" said Muttonchops. "As caucus-races may be distressing to the uninitiated, the International Accumulation of Caucus-Race Adjudicators has prepared a series of standardized stimuli for the pre-race assessment of each contestant's psyche. Please place these electrodes on your wrists, madam — face the projection screen — first stimulus!"

Alice turned toward the screen just as the first picture appeared: an elaborately detailed line drawing of a naked man, exhibiting his muttonchops full-face. The drawing was unlabeled except for a small "JT" in one corner, but the likeness was unmistakable. Without looking away, she said, "What a dirty old man you are!"

211

"Pay attention — second stimulus!" Alice blushed slightly in spite of herself as the next drawing flashed on: it was Alice, quite bare except for an awkward arrangement of her waist-length hair. She had no time to ask her inquisitor what looking-glass he had peered through to make that sketch, before a third drawing appeared of Muttonchops, Alice, and an array of similarly unattired adolescent girls, gamboling through an intricately landscaped garden. As the rest of the stimulus series followed in quick succession, the sketched Alice and her companions clustered around Muttonchops beneath a massive rose tree, submerged him beneath their flesh, then paired or tripled or quadrupled off with the man or each other to engage in an assortment of behaviors Alice had never dreamed possible. She watched in amazed fascination until a bell rang and Muttonchops said, "Qualification trials completed; you may join the caucus-race. Through that door!"

"But I really don't understand, sir — what *is* a caucus-race? Is it run naked? Do people really run, or do they — " She pointed to the blank screen. "Must *I* undress?"

"What a crude young lady you are," said Muttonchops. "Qualification trials do not a caucus-race make. Mind — no stopping until the race is won!"

Alice was now strolling through a tunnel lined with crates of marmalade. Well, it should be interesting, she thought; she had never been to an orgy before, and supposed it was something every young woman should try at least once. She was debating whether to remove a token stocking to show she was in the mood of things, when she emerged into a large hall, in whose center was a very dry swimming pool. Around and around the floor of the pool the caucus-race ran, and the participants were obviously nude to a man — or to an animal, since there was not a human among them. She noticed a small bear with a honeypot, and a pig carrying a lute, and a snub-nosed possum, and several other odds and ends of animality. Or bestiality: is that the game? she thought. Not altogether the kind of orgy I expected, but a girl must keep an open mind these days.

As she climbed down to the floor of the pool to join the race, however, she noticed that the honeypot bear had stitches running up and down his arms and legs. The dodo was covered not with feathers but with green terry-cloth, and all the other animals were also both stuffed and sexless. She smoothed up the blue stocking she had begun to remove, and nearly said aloud, "How disappointing!" But what came out was, "How delightful!" How delightful to join the toy animals in this merry though pointless race; how lovely to skip along without a care in the world; how curious, of course, that she had had to go through that nasty qualification trial for such an unexciting event, but now that she was here, tra-la, tra-la, what a beautiful caucus-race it was!

212

Suddenly a stern voice cried out, "Stop! Stop this caucus-race at once!" The Red Queen marched out onto the race course.

"But why?" said Alice. "We were having such fun, and the Dodo told us there'd be prizes for everyone afterward, and — "

"Silence, child — it's well past time for tea! Sit here, elbows at your sides, pinky out, and pour! Pour, and take a caterpillar before you pass the tray!"

The Red Queen had such an icy voice that Alice could hardly bear to listen; but the word "caterpillar" caught her ear. She looked down at the table before which they were now seated, and there beside the teapot was a serving-dish piled high with fat writhing caterpillars. "Oh, but surely," said Alice, "you don't expect me to eat a caterpillar! A fried grasshopper or a bread-and-butterfly, perhaps, but — "

"No frying, no butter! Chin up, chest out, toes straight, and eat!"

Alice ate, first one caterpillar, then another. Then she tried a third with ginger marmalade and a fourth with bitter orange. She was suddenly filled with a wild passion for caterpillars; only the Red Queen's stern gaze prevented her from absolutely stuffing herself. "Curiouser and curiouser," she thought: "Mrs. Trimmins could hardly get me to sample a single grasshopper drumstick, even seasoned with the sweetest words imaginable. The Red Queen, on the other hand, is treating me much too sternly to say the least; but I love every mouthful of her greasy green caterpillars! Will Looking-Glass-Land wonders never cease?"

"No mumbling at table, child — pay attention!" The Red Queen tapped at a huge pendant watch beneath whose crystal a rabbit's face and hands were visible. "You're late for your appointment with the White Queen — off with you!"

THE DORMOUSE'S EXERCISE WHEEL

"But I haven't finished the caterpillars," Alice began to say, when she found herself trotting along beside the White Queen inside a gigantic exercise wheel. It rather resembled those used by pet rats and guinea pigs, except for its size. The White Queen's features were somewhat softer than the Red's, and she spoke with embarrassed hesitation. "Finished what, child? Are you hungry?"

"Oh — not really," said Alice, continuing to trot as the exercise-wheel turned beneath them. "What does this wheel do? And doesn't it get terribly boring?"

"Naturally it does nothing, my dear. If we wished it to do something, we'd electrify it. Perhaps it does bore a little girl like you; but don't ever say that to the dormouse! You see, this is his very own exercise wheel, and I fear for his self-esteem if you should abuse it."

"Well, perhaps I shall," said Alice, "since my feet are getting tired and it *is* terribly dull *and* useless. I can't honestly think of anything *more* dull, except possibly that peg-twiddling psychology experiment I once did!"

"Hush, hush, it's the dormouse! If you speak nicely to him about the wheel, I'll give you half a groat!"

"Hm — well," Alice said, pausing because she didn't know what half a groat was worth. Rather little, she suspected, but still: "I'll take it. Oh, Mr. Dormouse, over this way, please — your exercise wheel is so divine, I simply love walking on it, the exercise is marvelous for my figure, the company is adorable, the view — "

No sooner had those insincere words left her mouth than she believed them heart and soul — and sole too, if she might be permitted a lame little pun, as her feet had suddenly stopped hurting. Exercise wheels, rat races — what a glorious way to spend the rest of one's life!

HUMPTY DUMPTY'S PREDICTION

The dormouse apparently had not heard her, for as he weaved his way nearer, his eyes three-quarters closed in sleep, he began to shout: "The sky is falling! The sky is falling! At precisely 6:32 P.M. this very November eleventh evening, today exactly, the sky will let go kerplop and we shall all be covered in clouds to a depth of 78.46 feet!"

"Oh, honestly, how do *you* know?" said Alice, miffed at his failure to acknowledge her praise. "And anyway, why are you shouting at me? What can I do about it?"

"I know," said the dormouse, "because Humpty Dumpty told me, naturally! But enough: top secret, restricted access, highly confidential, destroy after reading. Six-thirty-two tonight!"

"Such poor timing," Alice said, "it'll barely miss being on Walter Cronkite. But where can I find Humpty Dumpty?"

"The wall," said the dormouse drowsily. "To the wall!"

Alice had long felt sympathetic toward Humpty, who in the nursery rhyme suffered a cruel fate for no good reason. Here in Looking-Glass-Land he appeared whole; but perhaps the knowledge of his impending doom had driven him into this paranoid delusion about falling skies. As she approached him she asked as gently as possible, "Please, Mr. Dumpty, is what the dormouse said really true?"

"Six-thirty-two post meridian, Greenwich Observatory Time, no further comment," said Humpty curtly. A small group of hangers-on at the foot of the wall, including not only Tweedledum and -dee but several apparently AWOL members of the King's Horses and Men, echoed, "The sky will fall at 6:32; no further comment right now for you."

At that moment the Red Queen re-appeared. "Observe the time, child;

it's 6:31, and you'll be late for your chess date. Chin up, chest out, march!"

"Oh, all right," said Alice, trotting off in the direction of her looking-glass, "but I did so want to see the sky fall!" Even as she spoke, she heard a thunderous crash behind her. She looked back to see a horribly fractured Humpty Dumpty pick himself up from the ground — he was hardboiled, fortunately — and begin a Stentorian speech to the country-side. "My friends, the Nation has been saved this once, owing to the incredibly self-abnegating dedication of myself and my multitudinous disciples. But it shall not escape a second time, no, never! At 7:57 P.M., Friday next — "

Meanwhile the King's Men, white and red knights, dodoes and dormice were spreading through the landscape, shouting, "The sky *will* fall! The sky *will* fall! At 7:57 P.M., Friday next, the sky *will* fall!" Before she could reenter her looking glass, Alice found herself surrounded by as-sorted Dumptian disciples in full cry.

"Why are you all shouting so?" Alice demanded. "Didn't you see that it was Humpty Dumpty who fell, not the sky? How can you be such blockheads?"

At this remark they all leapt at her, and she stumbled backwards through the looking glass. Abruptly she was standing in the middle of the Student Union game room, where her date was waiting with a chess-board and a leer.

DISSONANCE THEORY BASICS

Pity poor Alice — for in this excursion through the looking glass she and her curious acquaintances were playing not chess, as Lewis Carroll origi-nally had it, but the game of dissonance reduction. The rules, initially devised by Leon Festinger (1959), at first appear as simple as the straight-est of paths. According to Festinger, people generally try to keep their knowledge of themselves and the world consistent. If two bits of knowl-edge (or what people treat as knowledge, including beliefs and opinions) happen to be inconsistent, the person holding them feels uncomfortable. He is therefore motivated to eliminate the inconsistency — or, in Fest-inger's terminology, to reduce the dissonance. The larger the number of dissonant relationships in a situation and the greater their importance to the person, in proportion to the number of consonant or consistent relationships, the greater his discomfort. The more dissonance he en-counters, the more motivated he is to get rid of it. He can get rid of it by lessening the importance he attributes to the dissonant cognitions, or by somehow adding more consonant cognitions to the situation, or by changing the cognitions themselves. Because some of the cognitions he changes may be attitudes, the study of cognitive dissonance quickly en-ters the area of attitude change. Nobody has ever argued that cognitive

215

dissonance reduction is the basis of all attitude change, but some psychologists think it accounts for a very hefty portion. So Festinger's theory of cognitive dissonance has often been employed as a general theory of attitude change.

Indeed, dissonance theory has for the past decade been the single most influential theory of attitude change in social psychology — not because of the subtlety or sophistication of the rules summarized above, but because the imaginative application of these rules has produced many intriguing and persuasive experiments, often with results which seem quite the reverse of what common sense or traditional psychological theories might suggest. For some psychologists, tired of the old saw, "Why bother doing that research, since the results are so obvious?" the very nonobviousness of dissonance theory predictions has been the theory's most appealing feature. And it is their nonobviousness too, their curious inversion of common experience, that qualifies dissonance phenomena for Looking-Glass-Land. Each of Alice's preceding encounters was based upon a distinguished dissonance-reduction experiment; and each experiment has been cited many times to show that certain not-so-uncommon experiences in our own lives may demand a distinctly uncommon theoretical explanation. The results of such experiments are themselves so dissonant with our conceptions of normal behavior that they have produced attitude change in a large number of psychologists — attitude change toward acceptance of dissonance theory.

SEVERITY OF INITIATIONS

Alice's caucus-race experience, for instance, is based on a study by Elliot Aronson and Judson Mills (1959). Why is it, Aronson and Mills asked, that unpleasant experiences such as fraternity hazings often leave their victims even more firmly committed to the perpetrators than before? Common sense provides no good answers; indeed, it may wrongly suggest that a painful initiation will always turn the initiate away from the organization responsible. But dissonance theory has an answer. When the initiate undergoes a painful experience to get into a group, his perception of this painful experience is dissonant with any indications that the group isn't worth such trouble. He therefore reduces the dissonance by magnifying the group's spendors and ignoring its defects. Result: a loyal brother for life.

Aronson and Mills tested this hypothesis not by founding their own pair of fraternities, one with a tough and one with an easy initiation, but by inviting over ninety Stanford coeds to a sex discussion group. As each girl arrived, a male experimenter explained that she was about to join an ongoing group, but that to make sure she could "discuss sex freely," she must take an embarrassment test. For some girls (in the experiment's "mild initiation" condition), the test consisted of reading aloud five mildly sexy words, such as "virgin," "petting," "prostitute."

216

Other girls (in the "severe initiation" condition) had to read aloud twelve words, starting with "screw" and moving quickly to a string of four-letter obscenities, plus "two vivid descriptions of sexual activity from contemporary novels." Regardless of which initiation a girl underwent, she was then told she had passed the test and could join the group.

The group was not exactly a group, as it turned out: members supposedly "met" separately in several rooms, so nobody would be upset by face-to-face discussion. (The other members were really tape-recorded voices.) The girl was given her own room and her own earphones and was asked simply to listen to the other members for a while, because she hadn't read the assigned reading for the day. The taped discussion was far more boring than a caucus-race: members talked only about secondary sexual behavior in lower animals, said very little about that, and showed themselves to be appallingly inept discussants. At the end of the "meeting," the real girl was asked to rate both the group and its discussion on such criteria as interestingness and intelligence, after which the experimenter explained his true intentions.

How would the "mild initiation" girls experience this situation? They had said a few unexciting words, and then found the experience for which this qualified them to be hardly worth getting excited about. They should have felt little or no dissonance between their perceptions of the initiation and of the discussion; they should make little or no effort to alter their initial reactions toward the group. In fact, their reactions differed hardly at all from ratings made by control volunteers who went through no initiation of any kind: both rated the group and its discussion as rather dull and uninteresting.

But the other girls had gone through what the experimenters assumed to be a really stressful "initiation," which the girls then discovered to have qualified them for a really blah discussion group. The result should be much dissonance — dissonance that can't be reduced very well by denying the nasty initiation's painfulness, but that *can* be reduced by deciding this is a great group after all and its discussions are fascinating. In actuality, the severe-initiation volunteers didn't go quite that far, but they did rate the group and the discussion as rather neutral — not very exciting, but not as dull as the controls and the mild-initiation girls had said. Dissonance had apparently led them at least part-way through the psychological looking glass.

PERSUASIVENESS OF NEGATIVE COMMUNICATORS

Then there was Alice and the grasshoppers and the caterpillars. Remember that communicators with positive qualities tend to be more effective attitude changers than communicators with negative qualities, at least in the short run. Now, if you wanted to get Alice or somebody else to eat insects, wouldn't you try to be as nice about it as possible? Not so, say the dissonance theorists: as long as you can be obnoxious and still

217

get a person to consume at least one grasshopper, he should come to like grasshoppers more than if you act agreeable. Doing something unpleasant for an obnoxious communicator should be more dissonant than doing if for a charming communicator; and the dissonance can then be reduced by deciding that the experience wasn't so unpleasant after all. Honey may draw flies, but vinegar gets the grasshoppers.

First to test this hypothesis was Ewart E. Smith (1961), a researcher for the Army Quartermaster Corps, which had good reason to encourage people to like grasshoppers — not as a substitute for creamed beef on toast, but as an emergency food during war or disaster. An Army officer presented a tray of grasshoppers to various groups of Army reservists, acting "friendly, warm, and permissive" to some, "formal, cool, and official" to others. The formal manner produced more enthusiasm about grasshoppers, as dissonance theory predicted. But couldn't such results come from differences in communicator credibility, rather than from differences in dissonance arousal? A "friendly, warm, and permissive" Army officer might seem pretty freaky to those reservists; real Army officers are supposed to be "formal, cool, and official."

Nonetheless, the Quartermaster Corps and Philip Zimbardo liked the idea behind Smith's experiment; so Zimbardo tried it again, in a new improved version (Zimbardo et al., 1965). For one thing, much greater care was taken to assure that the communicator (an ROTC Brigade Commander this time) stayed within his military role when speaking to reservists, even though he displayed positive personality characteristics to some volunteers and negative ones to others. For another thing, college students in a nonmilitary setting, as well as reservists in a military setting, were studied. The results again supported dissonance theory: people who ate grasshoppers at the urging of the negative communicator began to like the idea of eating grasshoppers significantly more than those who ate at the urging of the nice communicator. This effect was more noticeable with the Army reservists than the college students, again indicating that Army reservists don't expect either officers or ROTC Brigade Commanders to be nice guys; but the college students were also influenced in the right direction.

Such experiences as Alice getting a half-groat for praising the dormouse's exercise wheel will be saved for a later section, when they can be given loving care. Needless to say, dissonance theory predicts the unexpected: the more money somebody gets for lying, the less he'll believe himself. Several oil-loving Congressmen apparently haven't gotten the word.

DISCONFIRMATION OF PROPHECY

Finally there was the case of Roomie retreating to her bed when the world didn't end as expected, versus Humpty Dumpty rushing to proclaim his beliefs to the world after being likewise discredited. Leon Festinger recognized that the prophet proven wrong may reach the heights of dissonance; and he also realized that many prophets in history have not succumbed to mere facts. In the intriguing book *When Prophecy Fails*, Festinger, Henry Riecken, and Stanley Schachter (1956) reported their infiltration of a Midwestern doomsday cult whose prophetess had predicted that on a December 21 some years ago, great floods and earthquakes would destroy civilization. Death or serious injury would come to all but the cult's faithful, who would be rescued by flying saucers from another solar system. Prior to the big day, the cult made little effort to recruit followers; indeed, its members maintained considerable secrecy. According to Festinger, cult members had no reason at that time to feel dissonance between their beliefs and reality, and therefore no reason to try reducing dissonance by adding new consonant elements, i.e., adding other believers, to the picture. But on December 21, reality abruptly changed: it refused to permit the predicted world destruction. The group quickly reversed its secrecy policy, began calling newspapers and wire services to proclaim its beliefs, and entered a phase of active proselytization, welcoming potential cultists with eager arms. Such behavior is quite puzzling, Festinger argues, without dissonance theory to explain it. Prediction and reality were grossly dissonant, and nobody in the group was sufficiently psychotic to deny either that they had predicted a specific date for the world's end or that the world continued to exist. So they began as speedily as possible to reduce their massive dissonance, by seeking broad social support – support which would agree with them that they were really right all along, and indeed had saved the world from destruction through their faith and purity. After all, hadn't they ripped all the zippers and snaps and brassiere-hooks off their clothes in preparation for boarding the anti-metal flying saucers? Didn't that display unsullied devotion to Truth?

So there we have dissonance theory: a path that leads straight to the Hill of Understanding, overlooking the beautifully variegated Garden of Attitude Change. But look! – what are those corkscrew bends ahead?

theories of consonance: consistency and attitude change

Contradiction, an absurd remark, the sight of a dissenter,– anything, sets me a sneezing and if I begin sneezing at 12, I don't leave off till two o'clock – and am heard distinctly in Taunton when the wind sets that way at a distance of 6 miles.

— Rev. Sydney Smith
Letters

Beneath the dull exterior of every attitude change researcher beats the heart of a psychological Einstein — or at least of someone who dreams Einsteinian dreams. He may have done perfectly adequate small-scale experiments on specific variables for years; but the day will dawn when all those data look so scattered, so strung-out and individually trivial that he just has to unite everything into one great sweeping theory of attitude change. Kinnicutt's Doctrine of Attitudinal Confluence! Falkenberg's Plasmatic Principle of Opinion-Belief Ontogeny! The entire field's problems are solved, and his name is made forever.

I haven't quite reached the grand-theory point in my career, so I can still afford to be flippant about it. But many people have arrived there already, and more are showing up every day. You might expect that anyone trying to promulgate a serviceable attitude change theory would attempt to be at least as inclusive as those who've proposed theories of attitude development. The functional theories of Daniel Katz (1960) or of Smith, Bruner, and White (1956), for instance, propose that we develop and hold attitudes because they are useful to us in meeting the demands of objective reality, of social relationships, and of our own inner psychological economy. Now, if we *develop* our attitudes to serve these various functions, it would seem reasonable to assume that we *change* our attitudes to serve these functions better.

Oddly enough, the most popular attitude change theories during the past decade have ignored most attitudinal functions. They have concentrated instead upon one particular kind of inner psychological demand: the need for consistency. Festinger's theory of cognitive dissonance (1957) is the prime example of such consistency theories, but it was by no means the first or last. Before we look more closely at dissonance, several other consistency theories warrant at least brief treatment.

All these theories share the assumption that human beings attempt to maintain some sort of psychological consistency. This is hardly a new idea. I haven't run across specific mention of it in Plato or Aristotle, but amateur and professional cogitators have dabbled with the concept for centuries. Even in the young field of social psychology, it dates back at least to 1925, when Frederick H. Lund wrote of "the *ideal of consistency.* . . . We feel called upon to be consistent in the same way as we feel called upon to be rational. Once we have committed ourselves we frequently dare not change our positions lest we should be challenged with our former statements."

HEIDER'S BALANCE THEORY

Fritz Heider had apparently begun to think of consistency as an ordering principle in human behavior at about the same time, but he made no formal statement of his concepts until the 1940's (Heider, 1944, 1946). Heider places his balance theory within the framework of the seventeenth-century philosopher Spinoza's *Ethics*, though if you weren't looking hard for a similarity between the two you'd probably never find it. Spinoza proposed that a person will love whatever aids him in his quest for perfection, and hate whatever interferes. Heider proposes that a person will develop a "liking relationship" toward anything that enjoys a "unit relationship" with whatever the person values — unit relationships including such things as physical or psychological proximity, belonging, or causality. Heider sees this sort of situation — the person holding positive feelings toward anything positively related to something else about which he holds positive feelings — as psychologically balanced. If a wrong sign exists somewhere in that triangle of relationships, a negative instead of a positive, Heider sees the situation as unbalanced; and "If no balanced state exists, then forces toward this state will arise." The person will start changing his feelings, or his perceptions of relationships, to balance the situation, at least as it exists in his own thought processes. For instance, if a man likes a girl whose boot heels rip the carpet in his magnificent new Porsche, he might balance this unfortunate situation by coming to dislike the girl, or by coming to dislike the Porsche, or by deciding the damage wasn't really her fault anyway — the fault lay instead with the fashion designers who forced her to wear those boots, or the cheap European labor who made those shoddy carpets, or the smog that weakened the carpet fibers. The possibilities for restoration of balance are limited only by the perceiver's imagination, though presumably some paths to balance are easier to see and therefore more heavily used than others. At any rate, psychological forces to restore balance will persist until imbalance no longer exists.

Heider speaks of his general system, including his balance theory, as a "common sense" psychology (1958); and he appeals mainly to common sense for support of his hypotheses. A few research studies have also lent direct support. For instance, when people are asked how they feel about hypothetical "balanced" and "unbalanced" situations, they generally prefer the balanced (Harari, 1967). But not always. Common sense systematized is not necessarily either common sense or useful psychological theory.

A major problem with Heider's balance theory is the lack of specified limits on the possibilities for restoring balance in an unbalanced situation. Maybe some situations really have no such limits, but that doesn't improve the theory's predictive usefulness. Further, Heider's deliberate ambiguity in defining the "liking" relationships and the "unit" relationships that form the basis for balance has left the theory open to easy confusions. Leon Festinger has pinpointed one such confusion with a simple example: If I like chicken and chickens like chickenfeed, must I also like chickenfeed or else feel imbalance? Well, you might respond, Festinger's liking of chicken is a different kind of thing than the chicken's liking of chickenfeed. (It isn't, at least in broad terms, since both like some kind of food.) Or maybe Heider was just talking about human-type affection, not chicken-type affection. Or maybe Festinger really does like chickenfeed indirectly, because it fattens the chickens he likes to eat; he just prefers to wait until it's converted into white meat. Any or all of these possibilities could be true, but Heider hasn't given any hint of how to incorporate them in his theoretical model. Liking is liking, and there's no way to discriminate one unit relationship from another when the time comes to decide what's balanced and what isn't.

Even when Dorwin Cartwright and Frank Harary (1956) represented the Heiderian system graphically, and applied the mathematical theory of linear graphs to it, they were unable to depict such subtleties as different kinds of liking. Indeed, they made even clearer the unsubtlety of the whole system by representing all positive relationships, whether liking or unit, by solid lines between two points, and all negative relationships by broken lines (Fig. 6.1).

Figure 6.1

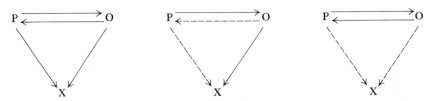

The left hand graph tells us that person P likes other person O, O likes P, P likes object X, and O likes object X (or maybe P or O owns object X, a unit relationship). In these circumstances everybody's happy and the situation is balanced, unless perhaps object X is the Hope Diamond, owned by O but passionately desired by P. The middle graph says P likes O, O dislikes P, P doesn't like X but O does. This situation is unbalanced, mainly by P liking O; so maybe we can predict he'll start disliking O and thus produce balance, because any other change would require still another change before balance is reached. But Heider doesn't say that's a good reason for predicting a particular change. The right hand graph shows P and O in mutual admiration, while mutually hating something else. Such mutual hatred of a third party is often the basis for mutual admiration, and the situation is balanced. Theoretically, anyway: if I dislike tall grass in the back yard only mildly and my wife hates it with a passion, the potential for trouble remains.

CONGRUITY THEORY

Charles Osgood and Percy Tannenbaum (1955) have attempted to deal with such differences in intensity, in the version of consistency theory

222

they call congruity theory. They allow a person not simply plus or minus attitudes about various people and objects, but a range of attitude intensities from +3 to −3, with zero in the middle. The person feels no pressure to maintain congruity between any two objects holding plus or minus values, unless he learns of a relationship between them. If he does notice the relationship — if, for instance, he discovers for the first time that Paul McCartney has thought seriously about walruses and in fact praises them highly — then he'll feel some pressure to move his attitudes concerning McCartney and walruses toward equilibrium, congruity, or in Heider's term, balance. He not only will want to feel the same general way about the two related objects, either positive or negative, but will want to feel *quantitatively* the same way. If he'd rated both McCartney and walruses −1 on his attitude scale all along, no problem. But if he'd previously rated McCartney +3 and walruses −2, he'll now start moving them along his attitude scale until their rating is identical. He might suddenly decide walruses are fabulous and rate them +3 just like McCartney; or he could henceforth rate McCartney as objectionable (at −2) as the walruses have always been. But Osgood and Tannenbaum argue that attitudes don't work quite that way; instead, the original attitudes toward both McCartney and the walruses should change. They feel the more extremely rated object will show less change in its rating, but it will move along with the less extreme one. McCartney won't be completely downgraded for liking those smelly beasts, but he'll drop somewhat, while the walruses will show a proportionately greater change in the positive direction. I will not give the formulas for calculating such changes: suffice to say that eventually Paul and the walruses should both come out at +1, at which point they may all legitimately stand up and sing "I Am the Walrus," because they have become attitudinally equivalent.

In testing this more precise version of consistency theory, Osgood and Tannenbaum found that a few corrections were necessary. One whose necessity is particularly obvious is the correction for incredulity. Clearly, if Paul McCartney (+3) were to say, "Lawrence Welk [−3] really turns me on," anyone who had rated them that way would say, "Come on, now, you're putting *me* on," and would show rather less attitude change toward both than would normally be predicted — at this extreme, no attitude change at all. Welk would need a few pleasant words from less positively polarized objects, say Glen Campbell or Arthur Fiedler, before Paul's pleasantries could do him any good.

Another correction Osgood and Tannenbaum introduced is the assertion constant. If McCartney says something nice about walruses, or if the Pope puts in a good word for Joe Bananas, it seems reasonable that the speaker would change less in the audience's estimation than whoever is spoken about. Osgood and Tannenbaum, after collecting actual data on the way volunteers changed their ratings in such situations, calculated that the speaker should change .17 less than the spoken-of (in addition to the change otherwise predicted), on a seven-point scale. That's real precision.

Precision is precisely what gets congruity theory into trouble. When you lay your statistical neck on the line to the second decimal, at the present state of research in social psychology, you can be sure it will be chopped off. In their initial studies, where they could tinker with assertion constants and such to achieve a good fit between hypotheses and data, Osgood and Tannenbaum were able to obtain high correlations between the way things should happen and the way they did. But nobody else has been able to come up with anything near the predicted results since. More often than not, the results have tended toward the general direction predicted by congruity theory, but certainly not the specific quantities predicted. We're almost back with Heider's bare pluses and minuses.

Well, not quite. The qualifications Osgood and Tannenbaum introduced may turn out to be of general value even if their quantifications don't. What a speaker says may very well change the audience's estimation of him as well as their estimation of the object he says it about, though their view of the speaker doesn't usually change to the same degree as that of the object. People may simply not believe an egregious inconsistency, rather than trying to convert it to consistency. And there surely are some quantitative differences in the intensity of attitudes that should make a quantitative difference in consistency resolution. Osgood and Tannenbaum just haven't quite found the quantities yet, or all the other variables that might alter the quantities in any specific situation.

ABELSON AND ROSENBERG'S BALANCE THEORY

Further advances in qualification, if not quantification, have been made by Robert Abelson and Milton Rosenberg (1958), in their theory of balance or "psycho-logic." They suggest first that when a situation appears to the observer as imbalanced, he will try to restore balance in the least effortful way, psychologically speaking; and second, that he can restore balance not only by changing particular attitudes or perceptions, but also by such devices as "differentiation" and "transcendence." Differentiation is splitting one object in an inconsistent relationship into more than one perceptual element, and then seeing the relationship with one of these elements as balanced. Paul McCartney may groove to the sexy mating calls of the bull walrus, but neither he nor I like walruses in general. Transcendence moves the other way. McCartney likes those filthy walruses? Well, as the song says, I am you as you are me as we are they and all are one together, if you want to take a broad view of things.

224

Finally, Abelson and Rosenberg find they can't make good predictions about attitude change based on consistency alone, but have to allow also for a *hedonic force,* an impulse toward the psychological maximization of gains and minimization of losses. The relationship of this "new" force to consistency maintenance first became apparent in Rosenberg and Abelson's (1960) classic situation comedy, "Fenwick and the Art Display."

Fenwick was the imaginary rug department manager in a Midwestern department store. Each volunteer in Rosenberg and Abelson's experiment was asked to imagine himself as the department store's owner, who strongly valued high sales volume in every department of the store. All volunteers were also told to imagine that "Displays of modern art in department stores *reduce* sales volume; Fenwick *plans to mount* such a display in the rug department; Fenwick in his tenure as rug department manager has *increased* the volume of sales." As if this weren't enough to induce acute psychological imbalance in any Midwestern department store owner, some volunteers were asked further to imagine that they personally liked both modern art and Fenwick; others, that they liked Fenwick but not modern art; still others, that they liked neither Fenwick nor modern art. Everyone was then presented with a set of three messages from various "store officials," each arguing that the situation was not quite as it seemed. One official said he had good data showing that "modern art displays actually *increase* sales volume." The second said he'd heard reliably that Fenwick wasn't really going to mount a modern art display. The third said his information showed that "Fenwick really has *failed* to maintain sales volume in the rug department." Volunteers were then asked how much they saw each of these last three messages as pleasing, persuasive, and accurate.

In some instances these messages, if accepted, would have increased the imbalance in the whole situation, therefore making it more difficult for the volunteer to reduce the imbalance by his own efforts. In other cases, endorsing a single message would eliminate imbalance. The main prediction was that volunteers would be much more likely to accept the message that restored balance with the least effort on their part. That's what happened, almost. The "almost" is where the hedonic force comes in: the straight consistency prediction didn't work very well when accepting the easiest route to consistency would lead to less sales. For instance, if volunteers were supposed to believe that the disliked super-salesman Fenwick was going to mount an obnoxious art display that would hurt sales, and then were told Fenwick had really been a lousy salesman all along, they were reluctant to accept such a message. They preferred instead to believe that Fenwick would somehow decide against the art display in the end. The latter choice left them with the imbalance of disliked Fenwick being a super-salesman; but if he's still moving those rugs, what's a little personality clash among profit-sharers? So Rosenberg and Abelson arrived at the conclusion that *both* motivation toward cognitive balance *and* the striving to maximize gains and minimize losses must be taken into account in such situations. The two forces can at times work in the same direction, and produce perfect balance. But sometimes they will work at cross-purposes, and balance will be partly sacrificed to achieve greater gains and fewer losses according to criteria other than consistency.

AFFECTIVE-COGNITIVE CONSISTENCY

Milton Rosenberg (1968) has moved ahead on his own to develop hypotheses about a somewhat different kind (or, he feels, a different level) of consistency: affective-cognitive consistency. Most consistency theories stress harmony between various cognitions: *beliefs* about two or more objects or situations; *perceptions* of relationships; *knowledge* of events that do or don't seem to follow from each other. Even if emotional reactions such as liking are included, they are given no special treatment. Rosenberg is particularly concerned with the occurrence of consistencies between beliefs about an object and feelings about the object. If the object is seen as helping to attain desired goals, then feelings or affect toward the object should be positive. If it's seen as blocking desired goals, the associated feelings should be negative. That's the way things usually happen, in fact, and such a relationship need not necessarily involve consistency motives. Many learning theorists, who stress the effects of reinforcement or reward rather than consistency, assume that a person will feel good about something that has brought him satisfaction in the past because the pleasurable feelings of satisfaction will generalize from the original occasion to later similar situations. But Rosenberg hypothesizes that the reverse sequence can happen too, in a sequence unknown to reinforcement theories: if a person feels good about something to begin with, he should also come to believe that this something will help him attain valued goals. Let's say George Wallace's fairy godmother appears before him and tells him that forever after, he's going to be just crazy about Negroes. Rosenberg would predict that before long, George will not only love Negroes but will also perceive them as being instrumental in helping him win high political office, helping him get along better with his family, helping with whatever else George has in mind.

Fairy godmothers are few and far between, and feelings don't usually change in advance of beliefs. But Rosenberg (1960) played the role of fairy godmother in an experiment with hypnosis. He measured volunteers' beliefs and feelings toward various issues, and found substantial affective-cognitive consistency. Several days later, he hypnotized each volunteer individually and told him he would henceforth feel quite differently toward one issue, for instance:

When you awake you will be very much in favor of Negroes moving into white neighborhoods. The mere idea of Negroes moving into white neighborhoods will give you a happy, exhilarated feeling. Although you will not remember this suggestion having been made, it will strongly influence your feelings after you have awakened. Only when the signal to remember is given will you remember . . . and only then will your feelings revert to normal.

The volunteers were then awakened and taken to a second experimenter. He was presumably running a separate study, but he in fact remeasured their beliefs about how the crucial issue could help or hinder their attainment of important goals. Nothing had been said about any of their beliefs during hypnosis; only their feelings had been mentioned. But posthypnotically, the beliefs followed obediently along, changing generally in ways that would restore consistency with the newly-reversed feelings. When the change of feeling was maintained posthypnotically for a week, some volunteers apparently reorganized their beliefs to match their feelings so thoroughly that they didn't quite return to their old beliefs, even after they were told how they had been manipulated. Rosenberg suggests that in the meantime they may have found some really good reasons for feeling as the hypnotist had suggested, or that perhaps in some cases volunteers felt that changing back to their old attitudes in response to the dehoaxing would be inconsistent with their pictures of themselves as stable types who always changed their attitudes for good reasons. In any case, the ties between feeling and belief seem to be close no matter which changes first.

Rosenberg (1968) has added several interesting specifics to his hypothesis of affective-cognitive consistency. But in general terms, his thinking is not so different from Spinoza's, in suggesting that men come to love that which helps them to attain perfection; or from Heider's, in extending Spinoza's philosophy to all liking and unit relationships. Nor is Rosenberg, it seems to me, really so different from the functionalists, who suggest that we hold attitudes because they help us cope with the internal and external world. Positive attitudes toward those things that promote our conscious goals should certainly be helpful in coping — so much so that both Katz and the Smith group list such attitudes first in their respective functional categorizations. The functionalists are not very specific about how the link is formed between an attitude and the objects with which it deals; maybe Rosenberg can help there. But the functionalists do have a lot to say about how attitudes are useful in other ways than maintaining consistency; maybe there they can help the consistency theorists to arrive at a more generally useful account of attitude change. Dissonance theory, to which we now return, may need such help most of all.

dissonance is a four-letter word: alternatives to consistency

Nothing that is not a real crime makes a man appear so contemptible and little in the eyes of the world as inconsistency.

> — Joseph Addison
> *The Spectator*

With consistency a great soul has simply nothing to do.
> — Ralph Waldo Emerson
> "Self-Reliance"

Your hypnotist has just told you that when you awake you will remember nothing about cognitive dissonance or consistency theories, until he says the magic words: "Alternative hypothesis." Awake.

I'm sure you don't recall my mentioning anything about an experiment where one bunch of college girls (the severe-initiation volunteers) had to read aloud a set of dirty words before they were admitted to a sex discussion group, while another bunch (the mild-initiation volunteers) qualified for the group merely by reading aloud several mild sex-related words. The group discussion itself was designed to be insufferably dull, but the dirty-word girls rated it rather more favorably afterward than the clean-word girls. How would you explain such a curious outcome?

Well, you say, maybe the girls who read the dirty words aloud didn't know what some words meant, so they said nice things about the discussion group to ensure their remaining in it long enough to find out. After all, the girls might think, if the experimenter is so careful that he gives them a screening test beforehand, he might kick them out if they act either dumb or bored.

Or maybe the girls saw the dirty-word "embarrassment test" as just that, a test, and were happy they'd passed — so happy they rated the group discussion more favorably than it deserved. The girls who read the clean words hadn't really accomplished much, so why would they feel happy?

Or maybe those sexy words got the severe-initiation girls all hot and bothered, and after that *anything* about sex sounded good to them. If thumbing through Webster's Unabridged can titillate a horny adolescent, there's no telling what a sex discussion group might do, however boring the sexually unaroused experimenters intended it to be.

Or maybe the girls really *were* embarrassed at having to read those nasty words to a male experimenter, wanted to show him how clean-minded and academic their interest in sex truly was, and found a dull, academic discussion of sex precisely suited to their purposes. "I may pronounce dirty words at your request, sir, but what I really love is the

abstract scientific consideration of sexuality, as represented in this discussion I'm rating so positively. So if you think I'm an easy lay because I
can read 'screw' without blushing, think again!"

Or, possibly, the girls who had to read the dirty words got really
anxious about the entire procedure, and were so tremendously relieved
at the absence of obscenities in the discussion itself that they gave it a
good rating in sheer gratitude. Likewise, the degree of pleasure you feel
when you stop banging your head against the wall depends on how hard
you were banging in the first place.

Or, just maybe, when the severe-initiation girls heard the boring discussion they reasoned so: "Oh, wow, what a Mickey-Mouse discussion
this is! But I had to say all those dirty words to get into it — that must
mean it's really going to liven up as everybody gets to know each other
better. Also, the others may be holding back because I'm a new girl —
but since that initiation showed me it's not going to be a Mickey-Mouse
group forever, I'd better say nice things about it to make sure I'm kept
in." Whereas the mild-initiation girls might think, "Gee, this is a Mickey-
Mouse discussion, isn't it? But that was a Mickey-Mouse initiation, too,
so what could I expect?"

The magic words are: "Alternative hypothesis."

Oh, yes, you remember now — everything can be explained by cognitive dissonance theory! The severe-initiation girls feel dissonance between the fact that they had to say dirty words and the fact that the
discussion they thus qualified themselves for is boring. They reduce the
dissonance by deciding the discussion is really interesting. The mild-
initiation girls feel no dissonance between saying a list of inoffensive
words and hearing a drearily inoffensive discussion; no dissonance, no
attitude change. You do remember now — dissonance theory can explain
it all!

DISSONANCE THEORY AND ALTERNATIVE HYPOTHESES

Alternative hypotheses are the necessary bugaboos of social psychological
research. Every good psychology major learns early in the game that he
gets points for spotting how an apparently decent experiment may have
delivered its results in very different ways than the experimenter thought.
In social psychology particularly, the behavior studied is often so complex that the various possibilities for explaining one result are myriad.
So the fact that Aronson and Mills' data on severe and mild initiations
(1959) may be accounted for by at least a half dozen other post hoc
hypotheses besides their own dissonance one is not unusual. (Nor, incidentally, are these other hypotheses the worse for being post hoc. The
fact that somebody thought of them after the experiment rather than
before doesn't affect the likelihood of their being true.)

But if you looked at a variety of the more prominent experimental

229

studies advanced to support dissonance theory, you might conclude, along with a number of people outside the dissonance camp, that dissonance experiments are particularly prone to alternate hypotheses. Two reasons for this proneness come to mind. First, dissonance experiments are often quite ingenious, designed to demonstrate the "nonobvious" or to produce conclusions different from what any other theory would predict. It's certainly praiseworthy to try to show how your theory differs from others, and a little ingenuity is always helpful in livening up undergraduate social psychology courses. But the trickier an experiment gets, the more likely it is to involve additional variables that enable another theorist to jump in and say, "Aha! Through the operation of this particular subsidiary variable, I can explain your results with my theory at least as well — maybe better — than you can with yours!"

Second, dissonance theorists often seem to concentrate on their hypotheses about dissonance so hard that they fail to give sufficient consideration to other factors that may be involved in personality and social relationships. They know dissonance doesn't account for everything, but they're so concerned to demonstrate that it accounts for *something* that they tend to overlook even obvious alternative hypotheses while designing experiments that will fulfill dissonance theory predictions. It's the experimenter's duty to eliminate as many alternative hypotheses as he can in advance, by careful experimental design; but dissonance experiments seem often to be so narrowly conceived with dissonance in mind that post hoc alternative hypotheses are needlessly encouraged. Take the Aronson and Mills study. I happen to know from other contexts (e.g., Aronson and Carlsmith, 1968) that Elliot Aronson is a keen thinker and an expert in experimental design, as well as perhaps the most persuasive proponent of dissonance theory still in the business. (Leon Festinger has moved on to other fields of study.) That being the case, why did Aronson and Mills choose dirty words and sex discussion groups for their study of mild and severe initiations? Wasn't it obvious that reciting four-letter word lists can have a variety of effects on adolescent girls, and that some of these effects could produce the same apparent end result as dissonance arousal and reduction? I can only surmise that the dissonance hypothesis seemed so impressive to the experimenters at the time that it temporarily blocked out other notable alternatives.

THE SEVERE INITIATION HYPOTHESIS REEXAMINED

When that happens, it's often necessary to do further experiments, to try to eliminate or verify some of those other alternatives. Harold Gerard and Grover Mathewson (1966) set up just such an experiment, designed to eliminate at one blow several alternatives to Aronson and Mills' conclusions and thus to leave dissonance reduction as the most likely explanation for the positive effects of severe initiations. Gerard and Mathewson first removed the previous study's sexual overtones, upon which the majority of alternatives (see Brown, 1965) depended. They did this by putting girls through an "initiation" that consisted not of repeating dirty words but of experiencing a sequence of varied stimuli — a spray of perfume from an atomizer in the experimental booth's ceiling, a sequence of slides of great art, a recorded excerpt from Copland's "Billy the Kid," and finally a series of three electric shocks, ranging from ticklish ("mild") to strong enough to hurt ("severe"). Aronson and Mills had assumed their dirty words would shock the volunteers; Gerard and Mathewson made sure the shocks were genuine. All girls then heard a recorded excerpt from a boring discussion.

In addition, the experimenters attempted to eliminate the "relief" hypothesis (Brown, 1965), the "harder you butt your head against the wall the better it feels to stop" idea, by telling only half the girls that the procedure was a kind of initiation into the club that had presumably recorded the discussion, a club dealing with "the problem of morals on university campuses." The initiation procedure was said to be necessary to eliminate "those girls who would let their emotions run away with them during a discussion." All other volunteers were told simply that the whole procedure, including the recorded discussion excerpt, was a "psychological experiment which involves your being exposed to a variety of different kinds of stimuli." Presumably if Aronson and Mills' results had depended on reactions of relief at hearing a boring discussion after a series of disturbing stimuli, even girls who had no thought of initiation procedures would rate the discussion more positively after painful shocks than after mild shocks. If the crucial process was instead one of reducing dissonance between a painful initiation and a disappointing preview of the club's activities, then girls who knew nothing about the club shouldn't duplicate the earlier results, because they shouldn't be trying to reduce such dissonance.

Finally, Gerard and Mathewson wanted to eliminate from further consideration the so-called "afterglow" hypothesis (Chapanis and Chapanis, 1964), the idea that the girls who "passed" the severe initiation felt pleased at their success and generalized their pleasure to ratings of the group. Gerard and Mathewson revised the original procedure here by telling some girls they had successfully qualified for the discussion group, and by telling other girls nothing.

That final manipulation didn't work quite as expected. Regardless of whether they got a mild or a severe shock, the girls who weren't told whether they had passed the initiation rated the group and the discussion more favorably than the girls who were told they had succeeded. This finding supports neither the "afterglow" hypothesis nor the dissonance hypothesis. It does suggest to me that the not-told girls in particular may have thought they'd better rate the group favorably or they wouldn't be let in.

The other manipulations worked rather smoothly. Ratings of the group and its discussions were higher after severe electric shock than after mild, following the same pattern as in the Aronson and Mills study — as long as the girls thought they were being assessed for discussion group membership. This result eliminates all alternative explanations in terms of erotic arousal, embarrassment, and other things sexual (unless the electric shocks happened to set some well-placed nerves tingling). On the other hand, when the shocks were delivered explicitly as part of a psychological experiment rather than as an initiation procedure, severe shocks did not induce higher ratings of the discussion group — in fact, the severe shocks were followed by *lower* ratings than the mild shocks. Gerard and Mathewson suggest that, because the uninitiated volunteers had no dissonance to reduce, the unpleasantness of the shocks merely generalized to the ratings that followed immediately; whereas when dissonance did exist between painful initiation and pallid discussion, the effort to reduce dissonance substantially outweighed this generalization effect and produced higher ratings, just as Aronson and Mills had originally argued.

Gerard and Mathewson's study is an impressive example of clearing away inappropriate alternatives. I hope similar care in design will be built into further research on the complexities of dissonance reduction, and for that matter into research on other postulated attitude change processes. But I'm still bothered by one possibility that Gerard and Mathewson themselves hint at without meeting head-on: the possibility that dirty words in the Aronson and Mills study, as well as severe electric shocks in the Gerard and Mathewson study, functioned importantly as cues that whatever the discussion group was doing now, some really hot stuff was ahead. Why have a girl say such dirty words, or sit through such jolts of electricity, merely to qualify for a namby-pamby discussion group? There *must* be more to the group than meets the ear!

This is the "Mickey-Mouse" alternative I mentioned earlier. Mild initiation plus Mickey-Mouse discussion equals mild ratings; severe initiation plus Mickey-Mouse discussion equals fascination, wonder, and good ratings pending further development. The girls who were told nothing about the club had no idea that further discussions were planned; so they rated today's discussion relatively low, whether they'd gotten shocked hard or not. But the girls who thought the experimental procedure was a screening device may have used their ratings for other purposes than to render accurate judgments or to reduce dissonance. They may have said pleasant things about the group and its discussion to insure that they weren't kicked out. And who should want more to stay in the club — girls who felt all they needed to qualify was the ability to tolerate a little buzz of electricity, or girls who had been told indirectly that these discussions of campus morals sometimes got so hot and heavy that they were comparable in effect to a triple zap of high voltage? I leave the question to your lubricious imagination.

At this point I should be ready to bring forth my own experiment, supporting or negating the final unscathed alternative. I've thought about it, but I haven't done it yet. There are so many experiments to be done, so many alternatives to be bolstered or undermined, that everyone I know has a much bigger store of free ideas than of statistically defensible results. But give me a little time: if nobody else has really wrestled with the Mickey-Mouse alternative to cognitive dissonance by the time this book is out, I may toss my lab coat into the ring.

PROPHECY DISCONFIRMATION
AND DATA CONTAMINATION

Laboratory experiments are not the only support dissonance theorists have claimed. They also see dissonance reduction as a guiding force in many of the everyday affairs of mortal man, even in his visions of immortality. But here too dissonance theory seems at times to have acted simultaneously as an inspiration and as a set of theoretical blinders, so that the dissonance explanations of available data are both novel and suspect. The most prominent example is a spectacular one: the study titled *When Prophecy Fails*, by Festinger, Riecken, and Schachter (1956). The basic situation was described earlier: a Mrs. Keech predicts mass disaster on a specific date, when flying saucers will rescue the faithful; disaster falls short of its promise; Mrs. Keech and her disciples, their faith shaken but still strong, rally forth to recruit new members to reduce their own dissonance.

Festinger and his fellow researchers didn't start or stop with the Keech cult in analyzing dissonance reduction and proselytization. They suggest, while admitting the lack of good evidence, that a number of great and small religious and cultist movements throughout history have shown similar patterns: explicit prophecy, heavily committed followers, explicit disconfirmation of the prophecy, and (if enough faithful are sufficiently close to give immediate mutual social support) redoubled efforts to recruit new faithful, so as to reduce dissonance through increased social confirmation of their beliefs. One of our foremost proselytizing religions, Christianity, might seem a good candidate for such an analysis. Several people (for instance, Joel Carmichael in *The Death of Jesus*, 1962) have argued more or less persuasively that Jesus predicted the immediate coming of a material kingdom of heaven on earth, within the lifetime of his close followers. That sounds like a sufficiently specific prediction, sufficiently contradicted by later events, to invite the hypothesis that

Christian evangelism in its early postcrucifixion days was mainly an attempt to reduce dissonance, on the same order as Mrs. Keech's post-disconfirmation attempts to win the ear of the broadcasting networks and wire services.

But as Festinger says, we just don't have precise enough information on earlier historical movements, including Christianity, to be sure what happened. If we are to believe that dissonance reduction is responsible for any proselytization, we have to believe it of the Keech movement first, because Festinger and his associates were there to collect the information they felt was needed to confirm the dissonance hypothesis. The necessary conditions for dissonance arousal, as Festinger defines them, were all present. The crucial question becomes whether proselytization follows a pattern predictable only by dissonance theory, or whether — again — the data fit alternate hypotheses as well or better. Festinger says proselytization did occur in a sequence that would be puzzling if judged by other theories or by common sense: relatively low-level recruitment before the big event, then a dramatic increase in proselytization immediately after complete disconfirmation of Mrs. Keech's main prophecy. If that really was the pattern, I think it would be hard indeed to explain by anything besides dissonance theory. But we have considerable evidence — apparently neglected by Festinger in the heat of his attempts to establish the value of dissonance theory — that the sequence of events was otherwise.

Mrs. Keech, according to When Prophecy Fails, began "receiving" messages from outer space several months before she acquired her first follower. As of early June of the year in question, she had one adherent; several more joined the fold later in June. As of August she had eleven semidisciples, but after her first predictions of a saucer landing proved erroneous, nine dropped away (two of whom later rejoined the movement). Then came her predictions about the imminent destruction of most of the inhabited world. There followed several overt attempts to recruit adherents in late August and early September, but Mrs. Keech still had "only a few followers" as of the end of October. At about this time a group of fifteen or so students were recruited en masse into the movement; at least two more enthusiastic nonstudents also joined in late October. A couple of others joined in November.

Meanwhile, two authors of When Prophecy Fails joined the group in October, the third apparently in early November, and four of their trained assistants joined the group over a ten-day period in the latter part of November. None of these new "members" were viewed by the group as casual acquisitions. Coming unannounced and having had no previous contact with any group members, they seemed confirmation that Mrs. Keech's message was getting through to the world without direct

234

proselytizing. Several researchers got into the group only through fabricated stories which suggested to Mrs. Keech that they had been getting confirmatory messages from space. One last trained observer joined the group on Christmas Day, four days after the major disconfirmation of Mrs. Keech's prophecies. He was seized upon eagerly as a genuine spaceman and was pumped for several days to see whether he bore any explanatory revelations.

So this was the situation: The group went through a relatively slow initial build-up, then a rapid increase of strength in late October and November, including seven social scientists disguised as members; then apparently no new members at all in December, until the single "spaceman" walked in several days after the disconfirmation. Efforts at proselytization *had* been made between the time of Mrs. Keech's prediction and the time members really began flowing in. Then for several weeks the group, its membership artificially swelled by undercover researchers (who ultimately constituted almost one-fourth of the group's "hard-core" membership), didn't need to make recruitment efforts. The December drought that followed may have gone unremarked as the group made intensive preparations to be saved by the saucer-men. Then the preparations were completed, the day came, and nothing happened. Do we need dissonance theory to explain the fact that several members, suddenly realizing that no new recruits had arrived recently (not even any researchers), began again to proselytize?

Festinger acknowledges that infiltrating eight researchers into a group with only twenty-six other members creates problems. But he staunchly maintains that he and his fellow researchers "at no time . . . exercise[d] any influence whatsoever on proselytizing activity. We were meticulously concerned with this point and we were completely successful in avoiding any impact on our major dependent variable," i.e., on proselytizing. They may indeed have refrained from proselytizing themselves; but their very presence should have served to dampen proselytizing efforts by others, and to accentuate the contrast when, with the advent of December, both true and false converts stopped coming. Festinger does argue convincingly that much of the information collected by his researchers could not have been gained without all those infiltrators, and the data they collected (including the group's reactions to the infiltrators) are truly fascinating. But we may pardonably wish for a test of his hypothesis that is less contaminated by the method of data collection.

PROPHECY FAILS AGAIN

Our wish may have been granted in a study titled "Prophecy Fails Again," by Jane Allyn Hardyck and Marcia Braden (1962). They investigated a group identified as the Church of the True Word: one

235

hundred and thirty-five men, women, and children who secretly built fallout shelters beneath a small southwestern town, and who retired to the shelters when their leader prophesied that a nuclear world war was imminent. Most stayed in the shelters for forty-two days, despite poor ventilation and worse plumbing; and when they emerged the war had not taken place. The group meets all the criteria set forth by Festinger in *When Prophecy Fails* for generating great dissonance and for its reduction through proselytization; but members of this particular group did virtually no proselytizing after disconfirmation of their prophecies. Indeed, they expressed indifference to Civil Defense officials' attempts to give them an award, and "turned away curious tourists who asked to see their shelters."

So the dissonance theory prediction in this case was apparently disconfirmed. How do Hardyck and Braden, dissonance theory believers both, reduce their dissonance at this disconfirmation? Naturally, they proselytize — by publishing an article arguing that dissonance theory is really right after all, but that the Church of the True Word differed in certain important respects from the "Lake City" group which Festinger studied. For one thing, the Church of the True Word had over three times as many members. Hardyck and Braden speculate that maybe under those circumstances it would be easier to get social support for disconfirmed views by staying within one's own social circle than by proselytizing:

> . . . interacting with others who had survived the same disconfirmation and who had emerged with their beliefs unshaken would be the best sort of support an individual could have. On the other hand, talking to the skeptical would be very likely to introduce new dissonance, since the person approached would probably reject one's attempts at influence and counter with arguments of his own.

This idea isn't included in the original dissonance formulation, but of course theories are made to be modified. More important, it seems to limit the amount of proselytizing that will follow disconfirmation of prophecies: members will presumably try to recruit others only until they have a total large enough to make them more comfortable within the group than out. At what point between thirty-four and one hundred and thirty-five this optimal group size may be, Hardyck and Braden do not guess. But the optimal size sounds too small to have accounted for the early expansion of Christianity, or of most other "doomsday" groups Festinger cites as possible beneficiaries of dissonance reduction.

Another difference Hardyck and Braden note is that the Church of the True Word suffered much less ridicule from the press and public after disconfirmation than Festinger's group. Waiting for flying saucers to deliver you from evil is silly; fearing nuclear war and building fallout shelters is rather more acceptable, as Civil Defense officials recognized when they bestowed their public service medal on Church of the True Word members. If you aren't ridiculed, you should feel no need to convert; if you *are* ridiculed, you should want to go out and convert your criticizers, to get them off your back. However, I don't think Hardyck and Braden can have their cake and eat it. If talking to the skeptical is "very likely to introduce new dissonance," as they put it in their first argument, then the group more criticized by outsiders should withdraw further into itself and *not* go around proselytizing, as the Lake City group did.

The other obvious difference between the Lake City group and the Church of the True Word, though Hardyck and Braden don't stress it, is the nature of each group's formation. The Church of the True Word was built up gradually over several years, and seems to have attained some stability of membership before the disconfirmation of its prophecies. Further, the group's size was not artificially inflated by infiltrating researchers; Hardyck and Braden collected their data by interviewing townspeople and occasional defectors while the group was underground, then by talking to group members after the disconfirmation and the exodus from the shelters. Mrs. Keech's Lake City group, on the other hand, was formed within about five months and most members were acquired within little over a month, including seven or eight obviously intelligent, well-educated, and keenly interested "adherents" who joined at very convenient moments. That must have been a heady experience for Mrs. Keech and her compatriots, one which they apparently tried to duplicate after the big letdown. But it was an experience quite dissimilar to that of the Church of the True Word, and so was the subsequent reaction. In neither instance was dissonance necessarily the key factor; other factors unfortunately overlooked because of the concentration on dissonance reduction might well have been firmly in control.

COMMITMENT TO INCONSISTENT BEHAVIORS

One line of research does exist in which dissonance or inconsistency may be the most important influence on behavior and attitude change. This line was represented earlier by the grasshopper-eating experiment. An authority figure demands that you eat a grasshopper, but provides little reason to do so. The authority figure is an unpleasant person and your eating the insect at this SOB's behest is obviously a crazy thing to do, unless — hmm — well, maybe it's a pretty tasty insect after all! Various other experiments have established a similar pattern involving some simple behavior whose performance is inconsistent with another element in the situation. A child is induced to eat spinach, even though he has already announced that he strongly dislikes it (Brehm, 1959); a teenage girl is asked to rate two pop records, is given the one she likes less, and is asked to rate them again (Jecker, 1964); a child is shown a group of toys, is warned mildly or emphatically not to play with the one he likes best, and then after he has been left with the toys for a while is asked again which one he prefers (Aronson and Carlsmith, 1963). In all these cases, researchers have found attempts at inconsistency reduction to be a crucial variable, and I have little reason to doubt them. Such studies seldom show the complexity of the Aronson and Mills dirty-word experiment, or involve the tricky human relationships of doomsday cults. They usually are so narrowly circumscribed that the volunteer would find it hard to come up with an interpretation of the situation much different from what the experimenter had in mind when he set things up: namely, inconsistency so obvious that the volunteer feels it should somehow be straightened out. Why avoid playing with a toy you were only mildly warned against, unless you don't really like it that much? Why eat spinach without being forced to do so, unless it really is good for you? (Elliot Aronson [1966] once published a *New York Times Magazine* article advising parents of resistant offspring to "Try a Little Dissonance.")

What I'm suggesting (along with such people as Milton Rosenberg, 1966) is that although dissonance theory does not nearly begin to account for the broad and complex situations of attitude change to which Festinger and others have often applied it, it may be useful when the situation is so carefully delimited that inconsistency is an obvious and comparatively important factor in the eyes of the person involved. I'm sure the dissonance theorists themselves won't be too happy with this attempt to narrow their domain; and anyway it cannot be done by fiat, either on their side or mine. Instead, we need more experiments that contrast hypotheses drawn from dissonance theory and from other sources, applied to both simple and complex versions of controlled events or situations.

That may sound like a rather vague suggestion, which will allow me not to draw any conclusions for several years. But a sinuous string of such experiments has already been conducted to determine how roleplaying induces attitude change. As you may have been able to tell from my frequent suggestions to imagine yourself as this or that — to picture yourself as a research volunteer in one case, as a howler monkey in another — roleplaying intrigues me, regardless of the role it may play in tests of dissonance theory. So in the next section I shall digress for a time on the general topic of roleplay effects. But the digression leads ultimately to a major battle between supporters of dissonance theory and competing approaches, so it may not only indulge and entertain me, but provide a basis for converting the battle's heat into light.

238

the power of pretense:
self-persuasion through roleplaying

*We are what we pretend to be, so we must be careful
what we pretend to be.*

— Kurt Vonnegut
Mother Night

Richard Nixon's first real success in life came as an interscholastic debater, and he has never really lost the competitive debater's style. According to one unsympathetic biographer (Costello, 1960), Nixon's high
school debate coach felt "disturbed" at his skill: " 'He had this ability,'
she said, 'to kind of slide round an argument instead of meeting it head
on, and he could take any side of a debate.' "

During my own career in college debate, my usual partner was cast
very much in the Nixon mold. He too was best at evasive tactics rather
than frankness, and he easily defended whatever position the debate
coach assigned him, not only with facility but with pleasure in his skill
at being all things to all audiences. He might have done well in politics,
but he went into advertising instead. I think I've seen him once since
graduation, not in an advertising office but starring in a televised cigaret
commercial — his smile, his tan, his expertly modulated voice, all pushing
the product with absolute urbanity.

I doubt that my former colleague really cared for the particular
cigaret he was peddling; during our debating days he never found it
necessary to believe what he said. Nixon, too, seems adept at saying
what he thinks a particular audience wants him to say; and although not
everyone finds his performances convincing, he has been good enough
at them to gain the presidency. The ability to say things sincerely at any
given moment, without feeling any strong need to believe them now or
ever, must be of great value to a politician. Look what happened to Barry
Goldwater, who apparently felt he had to say what he believed and vice
versa.

Goldwater is by no means alone in lacking the ability to ignore the
commitments inherent in one's own words. I've watched many college
debaters, assigned by the coach to defend an unpopular position, become
more and more favorable to that position as they've argued it throughout
a school year. Actors who play a single role for a long period, particularly
those who try to lead the character's life onstage both externally and internally (as with the Stanislavski Method), sometimes report persisting
changes in their own personalities after the stage role has ended. Pascal
refers to a similar process more than once: for instance, "If one acts
long enough as if one believes, the grace of faith will eventually be
given." Romantic novelists have made a mainstay of the cruel deceiver

239

who ends up loving the intended victim of his or her hypocrisy. The city slicker who gets hoodwinked into buying his own scheme has enjoyed similar popularity in movies and TV situation comedies. In each of these cases, the person for a time plays a role, some aspects of which are contradictory to his own beliefs; and this roleplaying leads ultimately to at least partial internalization of the assumed role, to a degree of real belief in what was only pretense before.

THE INFLUENCE OF ROLEPLAYING

Roleplaying has been intentionally manipulated to induce attitude or personality change since the 1930's, when a brilliant eccentric named J. L. Moreno (1946) developed the therapeutic technique of psychodrama. In psychodrama, a patient may play the role of himself before an audience of other patients and therapists, with a supporting cast drawn from the audience; or he may engage in role reversal, for instance playing his wife while his wife or another person plays him. Such play-acting, according to Moreno, often induces insight into one's own problems and beneficial changes in personality and behavior.

Other therapists now use roleplaying without the theoretical and procedural trappings of psychodrama, not only to induce change in the patient but to enable him to practice the changes before using them in real life. In addition, roleplaying has spread to various nontherapeutic settings. Arbitrators have attempted to induce greater understanding between management and labor during contract negotiations by having company executives and union leaders reverse roles for a time. Student nurses or student teachers may be asked to act out professional roles under the guidance of their instructors, to inculcate properly "professional" attitudes before they are set loose on real patients or students.

Why does roleplaying change attitudes? The practical users of roleplaying, particularly the psychodramatists, have often spoken of it as an almost mystical process, with few suggestions as to specifics. Others have tried to present it in a strictly rational light: "When a labor leader sits in management's chair, he sees the problems management must face, so he becomes more reasonable in his demands." But of course most ordinary persuasive messages can present such information too. Why should roleplaying in particular deliver this information so effectively — if it really is effective?

In college debate, I thought the controlling factor was exposure mainly to a single side of one issue for a long period. The debater was occasionally exposed to the other side for a half hour, when he had to sit through his opponents' speeches in an actual debate; but he spent much more time by himself or with his partner, seeking out new arguments and authoritative quotations to buttress his own case. Reading through newspapers and magazines, he quickly dismissed articles supporting the opposing side; or if he didn't feel like sorting through the material himself, he could buy manuals full of quotations neatly segregated on each side of the topic. In addition to all this one-sided exposure, winning a series of debates in defense of a particular side could make a debater more enthusiastic about the merits of that side. Festinger and associates might predict that losing would produce stronger endorsement of the defended position than would winning, because a change of attitudes could ease the dissonance resulting from a loss. But I didn't know enough about dissonance theory at the time I was debating to think of such a peculiar possibility.

The question of how roleplaying works is not an idle one. Nor does it deal merely with theoretical abstractions, of interest only to debaters and psychodramatists. We all roleplay a great deal during our lives, and are changed at times by the roleplaying. The child at first may pretend to accept Mommy's and Daddy's preachments to placate them, but he often comes to believe the preachments himself so firmly that his adolescence becomes a battleground between adult needs and childish superego. The recruit may go in hating the Marines, and come out proudly singing "The Halls of Montezuma" — not necessarily as the result of a severe initiation, but because his constant forced repetition of the standard leatherneck line has left its imprint on his own opinions. The young business executive may mouth the slogans of his superiors while secretly sneering at their innate fuddy-duddiness, only to find himself a fuddy-duddy in short order.

PERSUASION BY EXPERIENCE

You might assume, from the sheer volume of research on direct persuasive attempts, that in the typical attitude change situation a communicator delivers a speech and an audience responds with change. But when I've asked college students to describe recent major and minor instances in which they've undergone attitude change outside the laboratory, I've gotten few reports saying, "I heard a speech by so-and-so that changed my whole outlook on that topic." What I got most often was, "I felt that way about the Vietnam War and then my best friend got shot so now I feel this way," or "I thought girls were kind and gentle until this one bitch really dumped on me, so now I don't think so any more." These college students may have been influenced by the current rage for experience, the veneration of feeling over thinking. But my guess is that most people undergo substantial attitude change in the same way: through getting hit over the head by life, through having their faces ground into the facts of existence. Although such direct experience can sometimes be a poor basis for changing an important attitude, its power to induce a sense of inner conviction is undeniable.

Roleplaying is a controlled, artificial, diluted form of experience, but

241

it can be much more of an experience than listening to a speech. Role-playing may be a rather slight experience, such as endorsing a new product in twenty-five words or less (or even simply printing the product's name on a sweepstakes coupon, as in recent advertising practice); or it may be the experience of living a role all of one's waking days for years. But it is not passivity, which seems in most situations to be the enemy of real attitude change.

Getting one's face ground into the facts of existence may sound like a good reason to change attitudes; but we need a better understanding than that of why roleplaying — and by inference, real experience — is so persuasive. Few attempts have been made to study the influence on attitudes of actual roles in a natural setting. The best of these is a study by Seymour Lieberman (1956), who surveyed a large number of factory workers concerning their attitudes toward management and unions. A year later, after several workers had been promoted to foremen and others elected as shop stewards, he surveyed those particular individuals again, as well as control groups of workers who resembled them on various factors but who had remained ordinary workers. The control groups had retained ordinary worker attitudes, but the union stewards had become more pro-union, the foremen more anti-union and pro-management. Unfortunately Lieberman's research cannot tell us why the workers' changes in role led to such attitude changes; too many variables in this natural situation had to go unmeasured and uncontrolled. Such difficulties are particularly apparent in a second phase of Lieberman's study, in which he returned once more after a year and a half to find that over a third of the foremen he had previously questioned had been demoted to ordinary worker status again, as the result of a national economic recession. Whereas the foremen who were still foremen had become even more pro-management, the ex-foremen had generally returned to their pre-foreman attitudes. Did such changes in attitudes result from changes in role, or simply from gratitude on the part of the foremen who were kept on, and anger on the part of those demoted? We know too little about the situation to draw a conclusion.

EXPERIMENTS IN ROLEPLAYING

The ability to draw conclusions can often be improved through a set of carefully controlled experiments. Irving Janis and Bert King began the roleplaying set with two studies, ostensibly of "oral speaking ability" (Janis and King, 1954; King and Janis, 1956). Each volunteer either listened to another volunteer present a persuasive speech, or gave a speech himself, endorsing an opinion distinctly different from his own. Sometimes the speech giver was handed a detailed speech prepared by the experimenter, and simply delivered it verbatim. Sometimes he was allowed to look over this prepared speech to get an idea of what to say,

242

but then was required to improvise his own speech. The people who listened showed relatively little attitude change afterward; so did the people who delivered the prepared speech. But those who improvised their own speeches, who really roleplayed creatively, showed substantial changes in their own attitudes, in the direction of what they had been saying.

Why? Janis and King thought the improvisers might be paying more attention to their own words. But a group of listeners required to make careful notes on the speech showed no more attitude change than those who just listened; so differences in attention seem an unlikely explanation for the differences in effect of these particular speeches. Perhaps the improvisers were happier with the job they had done, and so were inspired to accept the words that had made them happy. But when King and Janis measured speechmakers' satisfaction with their own performance, those who read verbatim were happier than the improvisers. So feelings of success fail to explain the results here any better than in the severity-of-initiation studies.

Then what's so effective about improvisation? Perhaps people can understand persuasive messages easier if they have a chance to translate the messages into their own words? Sometimes, perhaps, but in Janis and King's research, the messages were so easy to understand and the volunteers were so well educated that such translation shouldn't help that much. Janis and King suggested two other reasons for a person's increased receptivity to improvised arguments and illustrations of his own: he may see himself as a more trustworthy, less manipulative communicator than other people, and he knows better the kinds of arguments that would really convince him. "In effect, the customer is not simply asked to examine the ready-made material in the original communication but is given scissors, needle, and thread to hand-tailor the material to suit himself."

Janis has developed the idea of hand-tailoring further in later research, as we shall see. The idea of the roleplayer as his own most trustworthy communicator hasn't really been given the attention it deserves. The idea I had as a debater, that roleplayers change mainly because they're self-exposed to much more material on one side, was not explored by Janis and King; they explicitly equalized the amount of information shown to all volunteers during the roleplaying period, to eliminate one complicating factor from what could easily have become as uninterpretable a study as Lieberman's. But this idea of self-exposure to only one side of an issue will arise again, in slightly different form, as our discussion of roleplaying expands.

What sorts of material might the improvisational roleplayer hand-tailor to convince himself? For one thing, said King and Janis, he might be more likely than a nonroleplayer to have "vivid anticipations" of the positive consequences arising from adoption of the new attitude. Perhaps he dreams of the social approval he will gain; perhaps he thinks merely of the financial aspects of coming to sound more like the boss. Janis and King had no way to be sure their volunteers were anticipating any such incentives; but a few years later, William Scott (1959) did an experiment — under the guise of a debate tournament, coincidentally — that encouraged some roleplayers to anticipate good things and discouraged others.

Several classes of students were invited to participate in Scott's debate tournament, with losers eliminated after each round and with the winners of three consecutive rounds to get twenty dollars apiece. Entrants were assigned to argue for or against one of three topics (for instance, the continuation of the fraternity-sorority system), regardless of whether they agreed or disagreed with the assigned position. Each first-round winner was to continue on to a second round and, if he won that, to a third; no prize money was awarded until after the third. The whole affair really *was* a debate contest, except that round one was fixed: winners were decided not by skill but by random choice, unbeknownst to the debaters. This random assignment of winners was necessary because those who genuinely performed better might be more set in their attitudes, or more intelligent, or more of something else that would have confused the results. Scott was not interested in personality differences between good and bad debaters, but in the effects of rewarding (or increasing the anticipation of reward for) a public expression of attitudes.

Scott found that the randomly assigned winners changed their attitudes positively toward their assigned side more than did either the losers or a control group that didn't debate. This was true whether the debater's own original position had been on the same side as his assignment, on the opposite side, or neutral. Those who debated on the opposite side had the most room to change as a result of their debating/roleplaying, and they changed the most. The changes in attitude did *not* occur as a result of the judges' endorsement of particular arguments or positions; in rendering their decisions, the judges referred only to the debaters' speaking abilities, not to what they said. Instead the determining factor appears to have been sheer cash.

ROLEPLAYING AS A SOURCE OF DISSONANCE

At about the time Scott was studying debates, Leon Festinger was thinking seriously about roleplaying and reward. Suppose hand-tailoring and vivid anticipations of incentives aren't involved at all, Festinger suggested (1957); suppose what roleplaying really does is to create dissonance. The roleplayer says one thing, but believes another: dissonance! How does he reduce this dissonance? Well, if he says his thing in public, or into a tape recorder, he can't very well take it back; that would involve losing face, or breaking time-honored commitments, or some such abomination. So instead he changes his attitudes to coincide with his public statements, and poof! — no more dissonance. Why did I say that? Because I believe it, of course. Why do I believe it? Because I said it.

A neat alternative hypothesis, that. With no other data available, it could explain Janis and King's roleplaying results as well as Janis and King's own speculations did. Scott's results were not yet available, or Festinger might have hesitated at the next step: he began to speculate about how rewards for roleplaying could affect attitude change. If Janis was right, Festinger reasoned, offering a big reward for roleplaying should produce bigger attitude change than a small reward; anticipation of incentives should be all the more vivid. But what if somebody starts feeling big dissonance between what he believes and what he says during roleplaying, and all of a sudden you wave a twenty-dollar bill under his nose? Instead of telling himself, "Why did I say that? Because I believe it," the roleplayer's line might quickly change to, "Why did I say that? Because I'm a poor starving student who needs a twenty-dollar bill, that's why!" If he can justify himself through cash, he doesn't need to justify himself through actual opinion change. If he can't tell himself he's saying it only for the money — if he gets no money, or just a little — then he should still have to reduce dissonance, by accepting the position he's roleplayed.

So the issue between Festinger's dissonance theory and Janis' incentive theory was joined. As Festinger saw the Janis position, more money for roleplaying should produce more attitude change; whereas according to Festinger, more money should produce less change. All he needed was an experiment to test the alternative hypotheses. With typical ingenuity, Festinger and a Stanford undergraduate, J. Merrill Carlsmith, promptly supplied the experiment.

This is the most famous dissonance experiment of all. Reprinted multitudinously, summarized in dozens of texts, filmed and broadcast over National Educational Television, it has stimulated at least thirty later studies. The vocabulary changes once more, so that Festinger and Carlsmith (1959) speak of "forced compliance"; but it's still a form of roleplaying. A male undergraduate volunteers for a study on "Measures of Performance." When he gets to the laboratory, he finds himself required to put twelve spools onto a tray, take them off, put them back on, off, on, for half an hour. Then for another half hour he turns forty-eight square pegs on a pegboard, each one a quarter-turn at a time, with one hand only, while the experimenter makes notes. That's the experiment.

Or so the volunteer thinks. When it's over, the experimenter explains that it's really a study of anticipatory set: some volunteers are told nothing beforehand, while others are told by an experimental accomplice disguised as a volunteer that it's really an intriguing, enjoyable, exciting experiment. Then the performance of the two groups will be compared. The experimenter adds, "Now, I also have a sort of strange thing to ask you." He pauses a bit, then goes on with "confusion," "uncertainty," and "a degree of embarrassment," according to Festinger and Carlsmith: "The fellow who normally does this for us couldn't do it today — he just phoned in, and something or other came up for him." So they're looking for somebody who can tell the next volunteer what fun the experiment is; would the student who has just gone through the whole excruciatingly boring thing oblige?

He'll be paid for his work, of course. It'll only take a few minutes but they'd like him to "be on call in the future, if something like this should ever happen again." So they'll pay him a whole dollar — or, believe it or not, a whole twenty dollars, depending on whether he's in the low-money or high-money condition. (Volunteers were actually given the money at this point so they would believe it, but the experimenters took the cash back when the experiment was truly at an end.) The real volunteer, who now thinks he's a fake volunteer, is then led into an adjacent room, where a girl is waiting whom he thinks is a real volunteer but who is really a fake volunteer. The experimenter walks off and the real volunteer starts recounting to the fake volunteer the delights of the experiment upon which she will soon embark. His remarks are secretly taped by a hidden recorder. The experimenter comes in again and leads the girl to the peg-board, while the real volunteer is directed to another office to participate in a previously announced survey of all psychology department research volunteers. Here he is quizzed about his feelings toward the pegboard "experiment" (this is the measure of attitude change in the study), is dehoaxed, and is gently relieved of his money.

Festinger's idea, again, was that volunteers would feel dissonance between their own perception of the pseudoexperiment's boringness and their statements to the girl pseudovolunteer about the pseudoexperiment's interestingness. If they got twenty dollars for such statements, the twenty dollars would count as a big consonant element in the situation, and should outweigh the dissonance sufficiently to eliminate any need for attitude change. But a mere dollar wouldn't provide much consonance. They'd tell themselves, "Why did I say that experiment was so much fun? Gee, I guess it really was sort of okay after all."

Some volunteers didn't take quite this road to dissonance reduction. They simply told the girl they'd been hired to convince her that the boring experiment was fun, or got her phone number so they could explain everything later. But most performed as expected: the twenty-dollar volunteers showed no greater love for peg-twisting than did a non-roleplaying control group, while the one-dollar volunteers, although they didn't really become ecstatic about the experience, gave it significantly higher ratings than either the twenty-dollar people or the control group.

So the alternative hypothesis was supported, and Festinger's dissonance theory reigned supreme, and perhaps we should simply let it reign. But might we once again be overlooking additional variables, which are more crucial to Festinger and Carlsmith's experimental situation than dissonance is? Say the magic words: "Alternative hypothesis."

the twenty dollar misunderstanding: roleplaying and reward

I can' help wonnerin, maybe I done somethin wrong. Maybe I coulda fix it up so's we unnerstan each others better an don' git all hung up on that mothahhumpin hunner.

— Robert Gover
One Hundred Dollar Misunderstanding

Twenty dollars for two minutes? Wages haven't been so good since the days of Mamie Stover. The experimenter did mention something about being on call; but he hemmed and hawed so much, saying things like, "If you couldn't make it, of course, we wouldn't expect you to come," that there's no telling what he had in mind. Maybe more twenties for more two-minute sessions — who knows?

Mamie Stover is not fiction's only financially resourceful prostitute. In Robert Gover's little novel, *One Hundred Dollar Misunderstanding* (1960), the protagonists are an upper-middle-class white college boy and a strictly bottom-class but quality black call girl named Kitten who's looking for an "invessment" — a wealthy steady who'll keep her supplied with money in exchange for good treatment. White boy and black girl expand a one-shot deal into a busy weekend, but he and she have very different ideas about whether the arrangement is for love or for a hundred dollars cash — and very different ideas on many other things as well. I've heard black activists complain that Gover himself doesn't understand Kitten any better than his hero does; but I still see the book as an excellent illustration of the easy confusions that can arise between the givers and receivers of money and services. That may be why William McGuire (1966) christened the controversy over Festinger and Carlsmith's roleplay experiment "The Twenty Dollar Misunderstanding."

Critics of the dissonance approach to roleplaying have cited at least three ways in which Festinger and Carlsmith may have misunderstood volunteers' reactions to large and small rewards. Researchers sympathetic

247

to the dissonance approach have cited at least three ways in which the critics may have misunderstood the operation of dissonance in Festinger and Carlsmith's study. To minimize our own misunderstanding, we'll consider these several possible confusions in a fairly orderly way, hitting the high points and leaving the side issues to several exhaustive (and exhausting) surveys in the professional literature. Misunderstood volunteer reactions will be examined first.

SIMPLE INCREDULITY

Early critics (e.g., Chapanis and Chapanis, 1964) argued that the twenty-dollar volunteers understood Festinger and Carlsmith only too well: they refused to believe they'd get twenty dollars for a two-minute persuasive speech. They were quite right, of course, because the experimenters never had any intention of letting them keep the money. And if the volunteers didn't believe they could keep the cash, any dissonance interpretation based on the assumption that they did believe must fall.

This simple incredulity argument was relatively easy to counter. Arthur Cohen (Brehm and Cohen, 1962) simply did another roleplay experiment in which he paid Yale students as little as fifty cents or a dollar to write a pro–campus-police essay, at a time when Yale police were in great disrepute among students. Cohen found that the fifty-cent volunteers became significantly more favorable to the police than the one-dollar volunteers. Surely, he argued, no Yale student would view a dollar as an incredibly large reward for such a task. Yet the results were the same as in Festinger and Carlsmith's study: the less money, the more attitude change. Criticism dismissed.

EVALUATION APPREHENSION

College students are capable of a greater range of reactions to psychological manipulations than merely simple incredulity. Students know from personal experience and campus rumor that psychologists are tricky bastards who are always diagnosing people, or trying to get people to reveal their true nature, or doing experiments that measure something — anything — besides what they say. Even when a student wouldn't ordinarily be much more concerned about getting a dollar to do a task than getting fifty cents, he may start feeling concerned when the greenback comes from a psychologist.

Milton Rosenberg (1965) has christened such concern about the psychologist's intentions "evaluation apprehension," and has suggested that it could easily account for the negative effect of increasing rewards in roleplay studies. If a volunteer is worried about what a psychologist thinks of him, he's likely to get more and more worried, the more money the psychologist offers him to say something he doesn't believe. And the more worried he is, the more he may try to present himself in the best

248

possible light, for instance by refusing to show any attitude change that might indicate gullibility or naiveté or lack of will.

Rosenberg sought to combat evaluation apprehension's effects on attitude change by sharply separating the experimental roleplay situation from the attitude-measuring situation. The volunteer might not want to show the prying psychologist that his attitudes had been changed through roleplaying, but he might be quite willing to reveal his·new attitudes later to someone else who wouldn't know he'd ever felt differently. Festinger and Carlsmith had partially separated roleplaying from measures of change, but in such a way that volunteers might still feel the experimenter would soon discover their change. Cohen had made no separation at all. Rosenberg carefully set up his experiment so that volunteers would think their roleplaying was performed for a nonpsychologist, in a different location, for altogether different purposes than those of the psychologist who finally measured their attitudes. Under these circumstances, relatively purified of evaluation apprehension, Rosenberg found that a five-dollar reward for roleplaying brought *more* attitude change than a fifty-cent reward, not the lesser change predicted by dissonance theory. Rosenberg titled his research paper, "When Dissonance Fails."

People may also feel apprehensive about being evaluated by nonpsychologists. James Tedeschi (Tedeschi, Schlenker, and Bonoma, 1971) has proposed that most apparent dissonance effects can be explained as the individual's attempts to maintain credibility in the eyes of his public audience. If others stop believing him as a result of his apparent inconsistencies, he will lose whatever influence he might otherwise have over them; so he may attempt to stage-manage their impressions of just how consistent he really is. This "impression management" hypothesis may indeed account for the outcomes of various dissonance experiments; but it does not explain the results of Rosenberg's or other studies where disguised assessment techniques detected genuine rather than fake attitude change.

SUSPICION, GUILT, HOSTILITY

Milton Rosenberg emphasized the volunteer's conscious resistance toward displaying attitude change to the experimenter. Irving Janis proposed that larger money rewards might generate various negative emotions which would block attitude change, even if the roleplayer wasn't trying to resist. By 1960, Janis had tightened up the rather casual early references he and Bert King had made to the way the roleplayer "hand-tailors" his arguments to convince himself. Janis now proposed that everybody, in making decisions, spends at least a little time mentally reviewing or "scanning" the various positive and negative incentives associated with each specific choice available. The roleplay volunteer is asked in effect to engage in "biased scanning" — to look at the positive incentives and only the positive incentives on only one side of the issue. We do our own biased scanning every day, in order to defend our current opinions against bothersome change. The roleplay situation differs in that we're asked for a time to bias our attention toward support for the side opposed to ours. Janis assumed further that greater rewards for roleplaying should motivate the roleplayer to do his biased scanning more intently — unless the money aroused guilt, suspicion, or other emotional responses which can interfere with biased scanning's effectiveness.

Would larger rewards always create such interference? Maybe, if they were really preposterous; otherwise, it would be up to the experimenter to create his own problems. If he acted embarrassed and asked the volunteer to lie for him, ten or twenty dollars might be pretty disturbing. If he seemed to be working for a good cause and had a plausible reason for his largesse, big money should instead generate good roleplaying and more attitude change. Festinger and Carlsmith might have created a test of money's negative effects on biased scanning; what Janis now needed was a test of its positive effects as well.

Enter Alan Elms, a first-semester graduate student looking for a good research topic. I had studied Janis and King's now classic roleplay research, as well as monkeys and apes, in C. R. Carpenter's undergraduate social psychology course; and I had been heavily engaged in my own biased scanning over the previous seven years, every time I prepared a debate case. When Professor Janis mentioned his preliminary work on roleplaying and reward, I knew I'd found my research topic. He felt his initial procedures needed some revision, and he also was interested in conducting not one but two experiments at different locations, with certain variations in procedure and communication content. He didn't want to come up with results that depended heavily on the peculiarities of Yale attitudes toward psychologists, or on the unconscious biases of an overenthusiastic experimenter — overenthusiastic on either side of the experimental controversy. So I signed on to set up an experiment at a non-Yale location; J. Barnard Gilmore, another graduate student who was rather more sympathetic to dissonance theory, was hired to carry out an experiment at Yale. Leon Festinger happened to be in town one day, and kindly took time to discuss the general design we were working on; he made several suggestions and agreed that what we had so far should be properly dissonance-arousing. While Janis and Gilmore refined the Yale procedures, I made several anxious trips by city bus out to a suburban community college named Quinnipiac, to obtain the cooperation of its only psychologist in recruiting volunteers. I also tried to make out with the psychologist's student secretary; fortunately the experiment was more successful.

The two experiments (Janis and Gilmore, 1965; Elms and Janis, 1965) shared several elements of design. Volunteers were asked to write an essay favoring a position most would normally reject. Some volunteers were paid a substantial sum, others only a little, for their roleplaying efforts. Half were told the sponsoring agency was a highly respectable group; the other half were told the sponsor was a group whose motives might be questionable. Again, Janis's idea was that with a trustworthy sponsor, more money should lead to more effective "biased scanning" during the roleplaying and therefore to greater attitude change. But with a sponsor of doubtful trustworthiness, more money could make the volunteer feel more guilty over his written support of an unacceptable position, more suspicious of the sponsor's real intent, more hostile about being manipulated — and therefore less likely to pay close attention to the position he was roleplaying.

Barney Gilmore told his Yale volunteers he was helping to conduct a survey either for a consortium of leading universities concerned with higher-educational problems, or for a new publishing company trying to build up its textbook market. As part of the survey, each volunteer was paid one dollar or twenty dollars to write an essay favoring additional math and science requirements at Yale. Hindsight suggests that this procedure was at best an ambiguous test of Janis' hypothesis. Undergraduate Yalies have traditionally been among the most business-oriented Ivy League students. They might view the universities more favorably than the publisher, but they wouldn't necessarily feel more guilt or suspicion at taking twenty dollars from a business representative than from an educational institution. The results suggest just such a reaction pattern: the university sponsor elicited more attitude change than the business sponsor (a result opposite dissonance theory predictions), but the twenty-dollar reward didn't produce either more or less attitude change than one dollar, whatever the sponsor. That doesn't mean an absence of negative reactions to the twenty dollars; it means those reactions weren't very strong and were distributed roughly equally between sponsors. Nearly all twenty-dollar volunteers did express some surprise or shock afterward at the size of their reward. Several also mentioned the twenty dollars as a source of "vague suspicions, guilt, or conflict," though such feelings were sufficiently overcome to play the role. As one volunteer said, "I feel like a bastard for going against my cause; but for twenty dollars, what the hell."

The research I carried out involved a somewhat sharper distinction between sponsors. I always represented myself as working for an opinion survey firm, but sometimes I told my student audience that my firm was working for the U.S. State Department, sometimes for the Soviet Embassy. In both cases, the object of concern was a proposal the United States and Russia were said to be considering, to send a number of American students to college in Russia to study "the Soviet system of government and the history of Communism" for four years. "Our Government," I said, "is somewhat skeptical about the value of this training and will not agree to the program unless it can be shown that a significant number of eligible U.S. students favor the plan. The Soviet Government wishes to go ahead with the plan for obvious reasons. Although our State Department believes the program might have some serious disadvantages, in addition to any advantages, it is withholding final judgment until an accurate evaluation of student sentiment can be made."

This was where my survey firm came in. We'd collect arguments that might appeal to college students, print the good ones in a pamphlet to be distributed nationwide, then take a poll — somewhat like a bond election where advocates of each side provide several arguments to be published along with the ballots. In this case, however, the Soviet Embassy was going to publish only the pro side; our State Department was naturally going to be fair about it, but had already gotten enough negative arguments and was now looking only for positive ones. Therefore, whether he was doing it for the USA or the USSR, each volunteer was asked to write only arguments in favor of shipping many American college students to Russia to be educated. His pay for roleplaying ranged from fifty cents to ten dollars. Festinger and Carlsmith may have had no trouble getting their twenty-dollar bills back, but in at least two cases I managed to retrieve my tens only by threatening to bring in the dean. The dean was also the one-man psychology faculty, my contact at the college.

The people who tried to keep their tens were all in the negative sponsorship condition. Many volunteers in this condition also appeared reluctant to write essays for the Soviet Embassy, though they had been assured that their anonymity would be protected; but only one refused completely. Some others took the money, wrote the essay, and then on an open-ended questionnaire afterwards accused me of trying to recruit members for the Communist Party or of trying to propagandize American youth. Most expressed great relief when I told them I wasn't really working for the Soviets. In the positive sponsorship condition, on the other hand, nobody tried to keep the money; several even tried to give it back before I asked for it, saying they were happy to write the essay without pay. These volunteers frequently reacted to the dehoaxing by saying they wished the State Department *was* planning a program to enroll American students in Russian universities.

The results were gratifying. When the Soviet Embassy was behind the roleplaying, people showed less attitude change for ten dollars than for fifty cents — rather as in the Festinger and Carlsmith study, though our story about Commie sponsorship was apparently so much more upsetting than theirs about sneaky psychologists that we didn't get much attitude change in the low-money condition either. But when the State Department "sponsored" the roleplaying, we got a little attitude change for fifty cents, and a substantial amount more for ten dollars — quite a significant amount more. More money produces more attitude change: a result dead opposite from dissonance theory predictions. Irving Janis's hypotheses about roleplaying as a matter of biased scanning seemed upheld and there was just no way the dissonance theorists could account for these results. Or for Janis and Gilmore's results, or Rosenberg's. No way. None.

Unless maybe Rosenberg and Janis and Gilmore and I had misunderstood the nature of dissonance all along, or at least had misunderstood the conditions that will produce dissonance and those that won't. If dissonance wasn't involved in our experiments, how could we expect dissonance theory to account for the results? No matter that Festinger and several other dissonance theorists had accepted our experimental situations as dissonance-arousing; many other dissonance researchers were ready to point out the nature of our misunderstanding. Again, I'll survey the three most prominent suggestions.

NO DISSONANCE FROM ANONYMOUS ESSAYS

Merrill Carlsmith, no longer an undergraduate assistant to Festinger but now a Ph.D. dissonance expert in his own right, proposed that the only really dissonance-arousing roleplaying is face-to-face speechmaking, as originally studied by Festinger and Carlsmith. A person must feel committed to the position he roleplays before he'll feel any dissonance between it and his private position; nobody feels committed to anything by writing an unsigned essay.

Such a position wanders away from Festinger's original definitions of dissonance, which said nothing about commitment; but again, any theoretical position requires occasional revision. It also ignores several previous studies (such as the pro-police essay experiment by Cohen) that employed essay-writing as the roleplay procedure and that supposedly delivered dissonance-supporting results. And it omits the reactions of such research volunteers as those in the Soviet sponsorship conditions at Quinnipiac College, who felt committed enough about writing an anonymous essay to be quite upset over their cooperation with the enemy. But Carlsmith, along with Barry Collins and Robert Helmreich (1966), felt the proposition was worth an experimental test.

They began with the standard Festinger and Carlsmith procedure: the volunteer is bored into stupefaction by a preliminary "experiment," then is told the research is really concerned with the effects of psychological set on performance. The new twist follows. Some volunteers are asked to tell the next "volunteer" what fun the experiment really is, and are given fifty cents or five dollars to do so. Others are told the experimenter needs ideas for an essay that he will write to convince future volunteers that the experiment is great fun, and he'll pay fifty cents or five dollars for such ideas. A face-to-face lie delivered to the next volunteer should produce much dissonance, which would be reduced by attitude change in the small-reward condition, or by money in the large-reward condition. An essay written only to give the experimenter ideas for his own essay should produce few feelings of commitment or dissonance, so that anything could happen — even more attitude change with more money.

That's what happened: results suggesting an incentive effect of greater reward in the essay roleplay condition, results suggesting a dissonance effect in the face-to-face roleplay condition. (Carlsmith, Collins, and Helmreich had carefully separated the roleplaying from the assessment of attitudes, so that Rosenberg's evaluation apprehension hypothesis couldn't be applied to the results.) Maybe we should leave the experiment there, with dissonance theory accounting for the effects of one kind of roleplaying, and Janis' incentive theory accounting for another — a neat slicing of the pie. But I'd rather not leave it there, because it seems clear to me that something else was going on. What else? Simply that Carlsmith et al., without resorting to "favorable" and "unfavorable" sponsors, had created conditions where volunteers would likely experience either considerable upset or relative calm as they performed their roleplaying, the upsets increasing with offers of greater money — and by "upset" I don't mean dissonance.

Consider the scene in the face-to-face roleplay situation. The experimenter says he needs a substitute assistant right away. He hurriedly rehearses with the male volunteer the lies to be told the next "volunteer," who turns out to be a girl. While the volunteer is lying to this girl, she quotes a friend as having told her the exact opposite. After a mere two minutes, the experimenter returns and cuts the volunteer's roleplaying short. Mightn't the volunteer feel a little more guilty about his lying, or a little more suspicious about the experimenter's real game, or a little more angry about the experimenter's interference with his performance, if he's paid five dollars instead of fifty cents?

Consider, on the other hand, the essay roleplay situation. No vital rush-rush job is involved; the experimenter just says he's been thinking of revising the essay he shows to experimental subjects, and needs new ideas for it. Some other volunteers are going to be asked to write their ideas down too, so it's not as if he's grabbing hold of our volunteer in absolute desperation. He tells the volunteer he can take five or ten minutes to do the writing, and actually lets him take up to seventeen minutes. No innocent young girl is sitting there ready to be deluded or to offer embarrassing contradictions; instead the volunteer has a peaceful quarter hour in which to write out a few arguments to help the experimenter in a

254

worthy scientific enterprise. Wouldn't five dollars be rather more motivating than fifty cents under such circumstances?

Milton Rosenberg (1966) has suggested that the time element is the most important factor here — that the face-to-face situation gives almost no opportunity for real roleplaying, for the actual contemplation of the new role. It may be more akin to the grasshopper experiment, where a quick action confronts a man with a contradiction between his public behavior and his private feelings, and nothing else has time to be important. The essay condition, on the other hand, is more along the lines of what most people see as roleplaying, more like the way we play roles in real life, with time to think about what we're getting into, time to consider the values we might promote by accepting a new attitudinal position. Although considerations of inconsistency between new opinions and old may play a part here, it's not the sort of inconsistency that a five-dollar bill would reduce.

NO DISSONANCE FROM HARMLESS INCONSISTENCY

I first met Barry Collins on the other side of a podium at an intercollegiate debate tournament, when he was still defending the honor of Northwestern University and I of Penn State. I beat him, too, though he went on to win the tournament — which is the way things go sometimes, in debating and in science. Collins has conducted or supervised well over a dozen roleplay and reward experiments by now, and has come up with such a mixture of results that nobody, including me, should be willing any longer to attribute roleplay-induced attitude change to any one phenomenon. Collins has been asking, "Well, what *is* dissonant about saying one thing and thinking the opposite?" and has tried to explore the most obvious possibilities (Collins, 1969). Maybe it's a matter of the human organism being constructed (through natural selection?) so that it functions smoothly only when it's saying and thinking the same things, as Festinger seems to feel; or of children being rewarded in our society for consistency; or of belief misrepresentation being viewed as sinful according to the Judeo-Christian ethic. But as Collins points out, lying is lying whether it's done face-to-face or in writing; people say one thing and believe another in Rosenberg's or Elms and Janis's experiment just as much as in Festinger and Carlsmith's. Maybe, Collins suggests, the abstract wrongfulness of inconsistency motivates no dissonance reduction; maybe the crucial factor is whether inconsistency will generate harmful consequences. For instance, will people criticize the roleplayer or make fun of him outside the laboratory for what he said inside, if he doesn't stick to his new position? If he thinks they will, perhaps he'll stay with it, unless he gets a lot of money to assuage the social hurt.

Collins and associates tested this possibility by making sure people outside the lab would know what the volunteer had said inside — for instance, by posting volunteers' signed essays on bulletin boards. But he got a clear dissonance effect in only one of several different experiments. More money led to higher attitude change in some cases, to no attitude change in others, but not generally to less change. The one instance of less change with more money occurred when Helmreich and Collins (1968) videotaped volunteers' roleplay speeches and told them the videotapes would be shown to a large class of fellow students. But here, contrary to expectations, the same "dissonance" effect occurred whether the volunteer was told he'd publicly have to stand by the videotaped position for three months, or was allowed to tape a second speech for the class in which he took back what he'd said in the first speech and explained the reasons for it.

So the possibility of being called names doesn't seem to hurt enough to produce reliable dissonance effects. But sticks and stones, and direct blows to the ego, may be more potent than mere words, so Collins ends up suggesting that dissonance reduction will produce attitude change in roleplayers only when the roleplaying may result in objective harm to the roleplayer and his fellows, or when it may damage his self-esteem. Many potentially dissonance-arousing situations have by this time gone down the drain; and Collins gives no guarantees that these two alternatives won't be sucked down with the rest. The first alternative seems to me inadequate to deal with the nondissonance outcome of such studies as Janis and Gilmore's, where adopting the roleplayed recommendations could have caused plenty of objective harm to the roleplayer and his friends by making it harder for them to graduate from Yale. The second alternative has been pursued in its own right by Elliot Aronson.

DISSONANCE BETWEEN SELF-CONCEPT AND BEHAVIOR

Leon Festinger identified the dissonance in his and Carlsmith's experiment as arising from the contradictory cognitions, "I believe the task is dull" and "I said the task is interesting." Elliot Aronson (in Nel, Helmreich, and Aronson, 1969) redefines the situation: "What was dissonant for most people (i.e., those with a high self-concept) is the cognition (a) 'I am a good and decent human being' and (b) 'I have committed an indecent act; I have misled another person.'" Aronson and associates argue that dissonance mainly comes from such inconsistencies between self-concept and behavior. In support of this position they quote with apparent approval another dissonance theorist, Dana Bramel: "Dissonance is a feeling of personal unworthiness (a type of anxiety) traceable to rejection of oneself by other people either in the present or in the past."

Festinger himself may well feel a heavy load of dissonance when he reads such lines. Where are his careful definitions of dissonant cognitions as any two cognitions considered in isolation, one of which follows from

256

the reverse of the other? Where are his examples of dissonance — getting drier and drier while standing in the rain, or smoking while believing that cigarets cause lung cancer? Such examples (and many others appearing in the experimental dissonance literature prior to Aronson's recent articles) do not involve self-concepts directly, and need not do so even indirectly unless you make sundry extra assumptions about how self-concepts are constructed and how information on one's behavior is interpreted.

Nel, Helmreich, and Aronson do seem to leave a little room for other sorts of dissonance, when they limit themselves to saying that "in the clearest experiments performed to test dissonance theory, dissonance . . . arose between a cognition about the self and a cognition about a behavior which violated this self-concept." Maybe in certain fuzzier experiments, Festinger's own basic concepts of what is dissonant and what isn't are still applicable. But by and large, Aronson appears to have stripped dissonance down until all that's left is what more old-fashioned psychologists have always called guilt. Aronson doesn't call it that, but the terms he uses to describe or define it share many of the characteristics of guilt, perhaps mixed with a bit of shame. Compare the earlier quotations with the way a prominent psychological dictionary (English and English, 1958) defines guilt: "realization that one has violated ethical or moral or religious principles, together with a regretful feeling of lessened personal worth on that account."

Certain qualifications introduced recently by other dissonance theorists, limiting the situations where dissonance will most likely occur, also sound like discussions of guilt — for instance, the qualification that a person must have felt free to decide whether to participate in an act before he will feel dissonance (Linder, Cooper, and Jones, 1967). As Nel, Helmreich, and Aronson say, "It is easy to see how the self is not really involved unless the subject himself has chosen to participate." As Adolf Eichmann said upon numerous occasions, "I am not guilty; I was only following orders." As permissive therapists may say in the future, "It's not guilt you feel at all, my friend, it's only dissonance, which may be eliminated in three ways: changing a cognitive element, changing . . ."

Nel, Helmreich, and Aronson established an experimental situation that did give volunteers free choice of whether to participate, but that varied the amount of dissonance — or guilt — in another way. The volunteers were University of Texas coeds who were strongly opposed to marijuana legalization. Each girl had initially volunteered for another kind of research, but was told on a pretext that her help was needed in preparing a videotape for use in a study of attitudes. She was asked to videotape a speech strongly endorsing marijuana legalization, and was paid fifty cents or five dollars to do so. In addition, each girl was told the videotape would be shown to a large group of students already in favor of legaliza-

tion; or that it would be shown to students already opposed to legalization; or that it would be shown to students who "really don't have any
opinion" about marijuana legalization and "don't even know very much
about it." The idea was that a person shouldn't feel very much discrepancy between his self-concept and trying to convince other people
about something they've already made up their minds about anyway; but
he should feel a lot of discrepancy — i.e., dissonance, i.e., guilt — at trying
to convince a naive audience to believe in something he privately abhors.
So, feeling this dissonance, he should change his own attitudes to reduce
the dissonance — or you could say he'll try to expiate the guilt by ra-
tionalizing that it's all for the audience's own good. If he gets five dollars
for roleplaying, he shouldn't need to change his attitudes much afterwards because the five dollars will have already reduced his dissonance
sufficiently. But a fifty-cent payment should make considerable attitude
change necessary.

Results: as predicted. The largest amount of attitude change by far occurred when the volunteer was supposedly speaking to a neutral audience
for a fifty-cent reward. None of the other conditions differed significantly
from each other; since there was no control group, it's unclear whether
the remaining volunteers changed at all. But Nel, Helmreich, and Aronson got the principal effect they were looking for.

One question occurs to me, though. When a person does something as
contrary to his self-picture as this pro-marijuana speech presumably was,
why does a five-dollar reward preserve his self-concept so neatly that he
hardly has to show any attitude change? Have we here a valuable new
technique for shoring up self-esteem — every time a ghetto resident
thinks something bad about himself, slip him a sawbuck — or do we have
instead an unfortunate mixture of new-style dissonance definitions and
old-style dissonance reducers?

I really doubt that a five-dollar reward was so consonant with each
Texas coed's self-picture that it relieved entirely the disturbance she
supposedly felt over hoodwinking a lot of innocent students into becoming pro-pot. But if we use the old word "guilt" instead of the newly
revised word "dissonance," and if we think back to what Irving Janis had
to say about the effects of guilt on roleplaying, a more plausible explanation of the results is at hand. The kind of audience you're speaking to
often does make a difference in your performance, as college debaters
soon learn: if you're convinced an audience is already firmly for you or
against you, you're not as likely to work hard at your speech as if your
audience is still open to influence. The girls speaking to the "naive"
audience were told the audience could be swayed by their speech; they
were also told the audience would be let in on the "true purpose of the
experiment" after a measure of their attitude change. So the girls in the
fifty-cent condition could roleplay enthusiastically for the sake of the

258

experiment, trying to sway a swayable audience without feeling much guilt about it; and the roleplayers' close attention to favorable arguments during the roleplaying might well sway their own attitudes too. But any guilt that was present should only be exacerbated, not reduced, by a five-dollar payment for ten or fifteen minutes' work; and such guilt should seriously interfere with the biased scanning that would otherwise lead to attitude change. The experiment wasn't planned with this interpretation in mind, but the results fit.

It should be obvious how I view the outcome of the Twenty Dollar Misunderstanding so far. I welcome the progressive narrowing of dissonance as defined by the dissonance theorists, though I hope it doesn't end up entirely as a polite euphemism for guilt. (Kelman and Baron [1968a] increase the euphemism's precision by calling it "moral dissonance," but they also allow for other forms of dissonance and other responses to inconsistency besides dissonance reduction.) I still see Janis's emphasis on the motivating effects of incentives, and on the interfering effects of negative emotional responses, as the best overall approach to the question of why roleplaying changes attitudes. Certain problems do remain, however. For instance, it has been difficult so far to find any consistent pattern in the number and quality of arguments produced by roleplayers in high- and low-money, high- and low-guilt or -dissonance conditions, though such patterns might be expected to occur if various incentives and emotional states do indeed facilitate or interfere with role-play performance (see Elms, 1967; Collins, 1970). On the other hand, recent research by Anthony Greenwald (1969, 1970) suggests that overt roleplay performance — essay-writing, speechmaking, or whatever — is less important to the final attitude change outcome than is the role-player's silent willingness to consider a new or usually ignored position. Greenwald prefers to call this the roleplayer's "open-mindedness"; but it could as reasonably be viewed as a shift in direction of the roleplayer's biased scanning, away from his usual biases and toward the assigned position. So we're back to the Janis hypothesis.

Perhaps our own scanning has become a little myopic during the past few pages of experimental confusion. Let us now back off and take one last view — an open-minded one, naturally — of attitude change theories as I think they should be viewed.

the final balance sheet:
dissonance and conflict

I never saw an instance of one of two disputants convincing the other by argument. I have seen many, on their getting warm, becoming rude, and shooting one an-

other. Conviction is the effect of our own dispassionate reasoning, either in solitude, or weighing within ourselves, dispassionately, what we hear from others, standing uncommitted in argument ourselves.

— Thomas Jefferson
Letters

True dissonance has been the Holy Grail of modern social psychology. It has never been definitely located but it has led to all sorts of interesting and useful discoveries on the side. Leon Festinger initially identified dissonance as a key determinant of human behavior more by logical analysis than by assembling a variety of laboratory and real-life behaviors that could not otherwise be explained. He argued that dissonance was tension-producing and bothersome, without asking anyone whether he felt bothered or tense in circumstances that were supposed to produce dissonance. Festinger insisted that dissonance-induced tension must lead to dissonance reduction, not because this was visibly the case in every situation where he could detect dissonance, but because he assumed dissonance arousal to possess the properties of a physiological drive such as hunger, which usually produces efforts aimed toward drive reduction.

Even hunger, the physiological drive upon which more motivational analogies have been hung than any other, is not a simple phenomenon, as such researchers as Neal Miller (1957) and Stanley Schachter (1968) have noted. Hunger does not necessarily come from an emptiness in the gut, nor is it necessarily satisfied straightforwardly by filling the gut. But food deprivation does produce certain internal sensations that most people identify as hunger, and a fairly limited range of behaviors usually result from hunger. So psychologists have been able to use food deprivation or subjective reports of hunger with reasonable reliability, when they want to study the motivating effects of what in scientific shorthand they call the "hunger drive."

Not so with dissonance. The necessary antecedent conditions for generating what Festinger assumes to be psychological dissonance are not at all as clear as his precise definitions would indicate. What usually happens is that an experimenter places people in a situation where he *thinks* they will feel dissonance, or where he thinks *he* would feel dissonance; he predicts what will occur if any attempts are made to reduce dissonance; and if what he predicted does happen in a fair number of cases, he assumes that dissonance has been aroused and then reduced. If what he predicted doesn't happen, he usually assumes either that dissonance wasn't aroused after all because of unanticipated peculiarities in this particular situation, or that it was aroused but that the participants in his study found some other way to reduce dissonance. He does not assume that dissonance as defined by Festinger never arises in any situation, or that dissonance was aroused but has no drive-reducing properties. Nor does he usually ask his research participants whether they actually felt any dissonance and then felt it reduced. Since participants in experiments involving other "drives" are often asked to report on their internal states, this reticence on the part of dissonance theorists seems somewhat odd. It may have arisen in part because Festinger's original formulation did not specify that a person had to be aware of inconsistencies between his cognitions in order for dissonance to start working. Perhaps it also comes partly from an unstated assumption that because even memories of dissonance might be tension-producing, complete dissonance reduction must leave no trace in the participant's thinking that there was ever anything to feel dissonant about.

I once asked several volunteers to report immediately after a hypothetically dissonance-arousing experience about how they felt during it. The situation, a roleplay experiment, contained enough explicit contradictions of participants' personal beliefs to present all sorts of opportunities for conscious dissonance; and their descriptions of their feelings were made so soon after the experience, with enough reminders of what they had just gone through, that repression would be unlikely to have wiped out all trace of unpleasant inconsistency feelings. Yet little mention was made of anything resembling Festinger's formal definitions of dissonance, such as believing one thing and saying another. Volunteers did express concern about the effects of the roleplaying on those who might hear it; puzzlement about the experimenter's intentions; pleasure or displeasure at their own acting ability — such a variety of responses, indeed, that the assumption of only one overriding response pattern would have been of little help in understanding the effects of their roleplaying.

INCONSISTENCY AS INFORMATION

Dissonance has by now undergone a number of redefinitions and qualifications, usually progressively narrower in scope. But as currently defined, it gives even less evidence than Festinger's original concept of working like the hunger drive to which Festinger compared it. No good evidence exists of physiological deficits associated with dissonance. So much evidence exists of cultural variation not only in what will eliminate dissonance, but in what will arouse feelings of inconsistency or dissonance, that any assumption of an inborn psychological tendency toward feeling dissonance as unpleasant and thus motivating is untenable. Such difficulties have prompted some psychologists (e.g., Kelman and Baron, 1968a, 1968b) to argue for a recasting of dissonance theory and related consistency theories in terms of information theory. The existence of inconsistency is no longer seen as having unique motivating properties of its own; it is instead a signal to the individual that his behavior may be working at cross-purposes with his beliefs or desires, or perhaps that he is heading for social trouble in a culture that insists upon consistency as an efficient means of promoting its own survival.

People surely do use inconsistency signals in just this way. In trial-and-error learning, the "errors" usually involve inconsistencies between expectation and outcome, and the learner revises his behavior accordingly the next time around. In logical calculation, inconsistency again means that something is wrong and must be straightened out. But situations also exist where inconsistency is defined as appropriate and where it is therefore not a signal for behavioral change. Roleplaying would often be such a situation. The roleplayer knows he has been specifically assigned to play a part, and mere inconsistency between his attitudes and his deeds in such a case should not be a major force for attitude change. Likewise in shaggy dog stories and in certain kinds of higher "art," we are freed from the necessity of regarding inconsistency as a warning sign.

Even in situations where inconsistency might have informational value, many other kinds of information can also prove useful in guiding social behavior and attitude change. Inconsistency may once in a while be the most useful type of information in a situation; much more often it may be subordinate to other categories, or even so trivial in context that it is overlooked. Judging from experimental data as well as from naturalistic observation, this seems particularly likely to occur when a choice exists between avoiding an inconsistency and gaining a major personal good — say, a choice between acting the introvert as usual and responding to the subtle advances of the most desirable girl at a party, or between maintaining consistency with your previous statement that the mayoralty of New York is the nation's most important job, and taking advantage of a really good chance that you'll be nominated for the presidency if you throw your hat in the ring now.

So if people are going to try to save the concept of dissonance by converting it from motivation to information, it seems to me they might just as well change to a more broadly framed model of all the kinds of information-processing that are vital to attitude change. If nothing of the sort were available, I might at this point suggest going back to Smith, Bruner, and White's (or Katz's) scheme of attitude functions, rephrased to predict that a person will change his attitudes when he gets information that one of his old attitudes is not properly satisfying the object-appraisal, social-adjustment, externalization, or value-expression function it's supposed to satisfy. But I don't need to suggest that, since Irving Janis has developed a theory of attitude change which includes all these considerations, plus some other useful information as well.

DECISIONAL CONFLICT THEORY

From his first idea of the roleplayer hand-tailoring his arguments to suit himself, and then his concept (shared with Hovland and, in one way or another, with many others) of attitude change as motivated by positive incentives, Janis (1959, 1968; Janis and Mann, 1968) has moved on to what he calls a "conflict theory of decision-making." The incentives associated with one attitude or action may conflict with the incentives associated with another; the adoption of a single attitude may entail conflicts between the positive and negative incentives which that attitude delivers; short-run incentives may conflict with long-run incentives. Janis sees the individual as totting up the large and small positive and negative incentives associated with each significant choice in any situation – systematically or haphazardly, as may befit his particular personality – and then taking the choice that delivers the optimal balance of positives over negatives. If an individual has already done this calculating, on however informal and unverbalized a basis, and has acquired an attitude thereby, he's likely to keep that attitude. The only way to change it is to introduce a competing attitude position, which is sufficiently attractive in comparison to arouse feelings of genuine conflict in the individual over which attitude to retain. So far, what I've described is not much different from Janis's earlier version of incentive theory. His conflict theory (developed in collaboration with Leon Mann) becomes more complex, and probably more useful, when he starts specifying the kinds of incentives a person is likely to consider and the times at which their consideration will be most crucial.

Janis identifies four major categories of anticipations that the individual will likely consider in making his choice between the old attitude and the new: utilitarian gains or losses for self, utilitarian gains or losses for significant others, social approval or disapproval, self-approval or disapproval. The first two include roughly the things Smith, Bruner, and White include in their "object appraisal" category of attitude functions: material rewards for you and yours. "Social approval or disapproval" and their "social adjustment" function appear to overlap completely. "Self-approval or disapproval" includes elements of their externalization function, and probably some features of Katz's "value-expressive" function as well.

If you asked a person contemplating an attitude change what he was taking into consideration in making his decision, he would likely mention factors that could fit into most if not all these categories. He would be very unlikely to arrange them in a neat balance sheet, with large and small pluses for the major and minor positive incentives, and large and small minuses for the negative ones. But you could certainly do so for him, as Janis has suggested, and such a balance sheet might very well indicate the likelihood of his choosing one attitude position over another. Let's say our person's name is Jack Jackson and he's recently married; a psychologist has just presented him with a taperecorded speech urging limitations on family size. Jack has always planned to have six kids, but he knows there are arguments for fewer, and he's willing to consider the possibilities — particularly since the psychologist is offering him a cash incentive to consider them. What might the small-family side of Jack's ledger look like?

Utilitarian gains or losses for self. If Jack stopped at two children, he might tell himself, he'd probably save $30,000 or $40,000 during the next twenty years, which he could spend instead on hi-fi equipment, cars, yachts, and other comforts for his middle age: a big plus. On the other hand, a mere two children couldn't provide him with many comforts for his old age: at least a small minus. But considering the way kids are nowadays, the fewer you've got the calmer your old age will probably be: big plus. And if everybody stops at two kids along with Jack, he might even have some decent air left to breathe in his old age: big, big plus.

Utilitarian gains or losses for significant others. Having only two kids would certainly make things easier for Jack's wife: another plus. But it might frustrate her maternal instincts, if modern women still allow themselves to have maternal instincts. Might help her keep her figure, though — Jack wouldn't mind if she got a bit fat and saggy, of course, but he knows *she'd* mind. And then the kids themselves would get more out of life in a small family; he's sure they'd enjoy a yacht. Furthermore, not only Jack but *everybody* would have air to breathe, and water to drink, and oceans to sail their yachts in.

Social approval or disapproval. Zero Population Growth would certainly appreciate Jack's help, and so would Paul Ehrlich. The parish priest might take a dim view of it, though, not to mention the Pope. And hadn't his mother always said she wanted a hundred grandchildren? They don't make maternal instincts like they used to. But his wife would probably approve, and so would his neighbors with the exotic rosebushes, and this psychologist who's sitting in front of him with a tape recorder.

Self-approval or disapproval. Well, he'd be taking a socially conscious action for almost the first time in his life. But it would transgress his own moral code, as received from the church: what was that about populating the earth? But still, he'd be contributing to the Greater Good — wow, me, Jack Jackson, contributing to the Greater Good!

ADDITIONAL SOURCES OF DECISIONAL CONFLICT

All these considerations could enter into Jack's decision on whether to change his favorable attitude toward large families. Irving Janis assumes a substantial amount of rationality on the part of human beings, so their decisions and their attitude changes will occur largely on the basis of such conscious anticipations of positive and negative incentives. But Janis allows for other possibilities. For instance, there are what he calls "pre-conscious affective charges" — emotional impulses of which a person is not presently aware, but which may influence his decisions and which he can recognize as his own if his attention is drawn to them. These include chronic emotional biases and momentary shifts of feeling, both based upon "emotional conditioning . . . and direct experiences of frustration and gratification . . . not wholly mediated by verbal thought sequences" (Janis, 1959). In considering a two-child family, such pre-conscious considerations might include a vague sense of oneself as pleasantly fitting the ideal all-American television-style pattern of Daddy, Mommy, Sis, and Bud; or on the other hand, an equally vague, unverbalized and unfocused feeling of unmanliness whenever one contemplates the use of prophylactics. Such feelings may be fleeting, or they may recur every time a particular issue is encountered. Janis's favorite example of a *momentary* emotional reaction that preconsciously influenced an important decision is found in Harry Truman's memoirs. Janis notes that the memoirs contain

> definite indications that following the news of the successful explosion of the A-bomb at Hiroshima, Truman's reaction was marked elation combined with enthusiastic optimism about the war being over soon, an emotional state that seems to have contributed to his decision to issue an order to General Spaatz "to continue operations as planned" for a second demonstration of the destructiveness of the A-bomb on hundreds of thousands of people in another Japanese city.

In other words, Nagasaki may have been bombed as the result of a transient euphoria whose influence Truman didn't realize, rather than after a careful evaluation of all the likely positive and negative consequences.

Also of possible significance are "unconscious affective charges," which Janis now sees as being a major consideration only in exceptional cases. Here he categorizes influences concealed from conscious awareness through repression or other defense mechanisms. Our potential father might, unknown to himself, see large families as fertile ground for various tempting patterns of psychological or physical incest. Or perhaps the small family would be a way of expressing long-hidden hostilities toward his prolific parents, whose lack of control over procreation denied him the childhood attentions to which he felt he was entitled. Janis thinks it unlikely that the attitude researcher will have to probe so deeply in most cases; but an attitudinal incentive buried that deeply will be particularly difficult for the attitude changer to manipulate.

Obviously with all these possibilities, it's no simple matter to add up all the pluses and minuses according to their relative size and get a final equation endorsing or rejecting a new attitude. There are further complications, too — for instance, the effects of short-term versus long-term rewards and punishments. The closer in time a reward is to a behavior, the more strongly it will reinforce that behavior, according to studies on rats and pigeons. But humans often learn painfully that succumbing to an immediate lure may get them into trouble later. That kind of learning is one reason why we have no more illegitimate pregnancies and impregnated brides than we do. So a particular attitude might come out very well on the balance sheet, and still not be accepted immediately by the individual, because he knows from bitter experience that he'd better think for a while about the remotest consequences he can imagine developing from this first step. He may even choose a course that results in more short-term pain or inconsistency, but that pays off better in the long run.

Again, the individual does not normally draw up balance sheets with all these considerations written out. But in assessing the relevant incentives, he does learn to do a substantial amount of what Janis terms "scanning" of his own memories and perceptions, and to seek out additional information that will help him to make the optimal choice. Ideally he uses unbiased scanning, assessments uninfluenced by irrelevant emotional tendencies or irrational impulses; but often his scanning is biased in one way or another. We've already discussed how an attitude changer may induce such biased scanning for his own purposes, particularly through roleplaying.

Roleplaying, in this scheme, will lead to attitude change only if the incentives it induces the person to scan are more positive on balance than the incentives associated with his previous attitudes. But the roleplaying may itself create a new incentive, if it involves any kind of implied or direct public commitment to the new position. Once attitudes are expressed vocally or in other behavior, people may expect us to honor our attitudinal commitments, and will often complain or call us bad names like "two-faced double-dealing hypocrite" if we don't. The possibility that this will happen can become a *negative* incentive associated with one's reversion to previously held attitudes. A related negative incentive can be created if the person actually does decide to accept the new attitude temporarily. Then, even if he doesn't express it publicly, he may find it a little hard to switch back to the old attitude, because if he did he'd have to admit that he had made a mistake or was wishy-washy — an admission that could do unpleasant things to his self-concept.

This is how Janis works certain "dissonance" phenomena into his theoretical structure: it may be that in some situations, where the incentives for adopting one side of an issue or the other are either very close to being equal or else are quite minimal all around, such a new negative incentive associated with inconsistency will be enough to tip the balance in favor of adopting the roleplayed attitude. But in most cases it will be only one negative incentive among many positive and negative ones. For some people it may not even be a big minus on the balance sheet, but

266

only a small one — or maybe even none at all, as witness Walt Whitman: "Do I contradict myself? Very well then, I contradict myself. I am large, I contain multitudes."

BALANCE-SHEET PLUSES AND MINUSES

The question arises: shall you adopt a favorable attitude toward Janis' balance sheet model or not? The positive incentives for adoption are several. First, it introduces no new hypothetical inborn drives for whose existence the proofs are mainly inferential and rather shaky. That people in general prefer to work toward pleasurable states and to avoid unpleasurable ones seems to me a very defensible assumption, with plenty of good experimental evidence as well as the abstract reasoning of many philosophers to back it up. When you add considerations about working for the good of loved ones, and for social approval, and for self-approval, you've pretty much covered the field of possible goals, even in such peculiar cases as the individual who prefers to maintain a negative view of himself and therefore approves only when he is being a brute. Janis so far has not worked out his own account of how such things as social approval and self-approval become goals, referring instead to the work of other theorists on these matters. But if he or someone else finds it necessary to modify the title of one of these categories because social approval, for instance, may become a negative value in certain courses of individual development, that shouldn't be difficult.

Second, the balance sheet is useful in determining the full range of incentives that might be significant for an individual in considering any potential attitude change. Asked why he has changed an attitude, he might well give you only a rather brief response identifying one or two incentives in a single category. But he can be asked about the importance of other possible incentives in other categories — and in at least some stages of research on the balance sheet he *should* be asked in considerable detail about all these categories, so we can learn what kinds of incentives are likely to be most important for a particular kind of decision-making or attitude change. (Janis and associates have already done this with regard to such topics as attitudes toward major surgery, cigaret smoking, and weight-reducing programs, using techniques of questioning ranging from relatively brief surveys to long-term psychoanalytic probing.)

Third, the inclusion of differential effects from short-term and long-term incentives enables us to predict, somewhat tentatively at present but perhaps with more certainty in the future, which points on the balance sheet may become real trouble spots following a definite decision, as a small minus associated with a new attitude grows into a big minus, or as a category of incentives overlooked altogether suddenly becomes very salient. Dissonance theorists themselves usually overlook such possibilities: once a person has made his decision between one behavior and another, or has publicly committed himself to one opinion or another, he is assumed to be unlikely to reconsider the decision, devoting his energies instead to finding ways to reduce any dissonances his new position may produce. Let's say, however, that a white Joe College has been away from home most of the time for four years and has either forgotten or at that distance has been able to repress recollections of the attitudes of his hometown family and friends. Now he has made a big decision about his future, and comes home to join the family business and to show off his beautiful black fiancée. Is he simply going to go around energetically reducing dissonance as everybody in town reacts negatively to the decision to which he has already firmly committed himself, or is he going to start reevaluating his decision, with that category of "social approval or disapproval" at the forefront of his thinking this time? The incentive balance sheet is not static; and although dissonance reduction may at times work to preserve decisions once they are made, few of our decisions are ever completely irreversible.

Several negative incentives intrude here. One is the difficulty of using the balance sheet in any precise quantitative way to predict what attitude changes will occur when. Even when only conscious incentives are taken into account, the balance sheet is likely to contain a multitude of pluses and minuses, not only of various sizes but varying in size from moment to moment, perhaps even changing in importance because an interviewer is sitting there insisting that they be made explicit. In some cases the pluses will so clearly outweigh the minuses for a particular choice that the immediate outcome will be clear. In many others, pluses and minuses will be close enough to equal, or the proportions of pluses and minuses will be similar enough with regard to several different choices, to make prediction well-nigh impossible.

Even if the balance sheet's pluses and minuses could be made more precise, several additional sources of complexity would still make pre- diction difficult: the possibility of preconscious and unconscious incen- tives; the differential effects of short- and long-term incentives; the possibility that certain kinds of incentives (particularly negative anxiety- producing ones, which we shall consider in Chapter Eight) will not show straight-line effects, increasing in motivational strength as they increase in size, but may even reverse their effectiveness as certain levels are reached. With all these intricacies, it looks to be a long time before the balance-sheet model is useful as anything more than an abstract repre- sentation of the psychological elements in an attitude-change situation.

But these negative aspects of the balance-sheet model suggest one last big plus in its favor. As I have indicated throughout this chapter and the previous one, the human attitude system is not a simple one, and attitude change cannot be induced or understood simply. Simplicity is a tempting thing to seek; the history of psychology is littered with the corpses of theories that proposed a single overriding motive force in human behavior. Simplicity of theoretical formulation makes it relatively easy to draw firm conclusions, to make explicit predictions, to promulgate the theory itself. But of course none of this is any guarantee of accuracy. Janis's balance-sheet model is a complex one; but so far, its complexities reflect the complexity of its subject, and are tied firmly to the complexities of the available data on attitude change. Most dissonance theorists would agree that attitude change is at least as tricky an affair as anything else in human psychology, and that other factors besides dissonance must always enter in. But most of their theorizing and research have gone into creating a picture of attitude change as single-minded as the motivational researchers' emphasis on the persuasive powers of sex.

SOCIAL CONSEQUENCES OF ATTITUDE CHANGE MODELS

What do all these arguments about attitude theories have to do with our society at large? I hope part of the answer is obvious by now: attitude change is a vital part of social change, and the more accurate our knowledge of it is, the better will we be able to ensure the social changes we must undergo to survive as a society and perhaps as a species. Controlling population growth, restoring a decent physical environment, limiting the role of force in human affairs cannot be brought about *by* force alone. The attitudes of millions must be changed, and effective change requires well-grounded, valid theory. Kurt Lewin's dictum is as applicable in the field of attitude change research as elsewhere in social psychology: "There is nothing so practical as a good theory."

Another part of the answer may be less obvious, but it is no less important for the *kinds* of social change our attitude change efforts may promote. A continued emphasis on dissonance or inconsistency as the basis for change will, it seems to me, make more likely the large-scale use of scientific techniques to induce irrational attitude change. The hallmark of dissonance research in particular has been change that is against the audience's best interests: change associated with less financial reward or less justification of other kinds, change that comes from greater suffering, change viewed by participants as immoral and reprehensible until they are first brought to induce similar changes in other people. I don't remember ever seeing a dissonance study in which the intent has been to develop ways of saving a person from his own foolishness. Instead, the tone is often one of observing with academic irony the absurd behaviors of which ordinary mortals are capable.

Janis's balance sheet model, while acknowledging this talent for absurdity, emphasizes the major role that rational processes *can* play in attitude change, and supports the use of change techniques that may produce a wide range of need satisfactions for the person being persuaded.

269

The balance sheet itself can be used in individual cases to overcome tendencies toward attitudinal narrow-mindedness and short-sightedness. Even biased scanning is usually employed experimentally to show a person aspects of an attitudinal position previously concealed by his own biases, not in order to trick him but to help him evaluate more accurately the different positions available to him.

Surely the maintenance of consistency can and at times does play a guiding role in the affairs of humanity; it is one of the most frequently cited bases for public policy. But though its role should be understood, consistency maintenance need not be encouraged by well-meaning psychologists whose development of manipulative techniques may ultimately serve purposes less benign than their own. Fortunately other bases for attitude change exist, and they deserve much more extensive exploration than they have so far undergone. We may yet attain a world where consistency is the least item of all on the typical balance sheet.

7
motivating people
and peoples

mc clelland's achievement:
a need for excellence

Obviously, if these older [Asian] societies are to escape
from poverty and misery, they must adapt their own atti-
tudes so as to include elements of the Western scientific
and technical outlook. They should also not exclude from
their thinking the optimistic view that animated the Eu-
ropean renaissance and the Western expansion of the
18th and 19th centuries. The basic idea that human
beings and human society are capable of improvement
through their own effort is essential to the success of any
program of development, an area in which the United
Nations has done much important pioneering work.
— U Thant, quoted in
The New York Times, May 21, 1967

Timothy Leary sits on one side of a long table, assembling small rocket
planes from Tinkertoy parts. The man next to him is manufacturing the
rocket planes at a slightly faster pace, so Leary glances occasionally at
his friend's handiwork to be sure of the next step. Both men are clean-
cut, dressed in business suits and conservative ties. Across the table,
a third man has taken off his jacket and is standing, so he can put
his rocket planes together more quickly. A fourth man stands at the end
of the table with a stop watch in his hand.

At the end of five minutes, the timekeeper announces that time is
up and assesses the competitors' output. The shirt-sleeved man has
clearly won. The timekeeper says, "This time, we'll be producing nuclear

tractors. I will give fifty dollars to whoever makes the most units within the next five-minute period."

"Fifty dollars?" says Leary's friend with obvious interest. No prizes had been given for rocket-plane production.

"Fifty dollars," the man says.

Leary's friend stands, strips off his coat, and announces plans to increase his output by 80 per cent. The man across the table, who hadn't quite reached his self-chosen rocket-plane quota, decides on a slightly less ambitious goal for nuclear tractor production. Leary appears as unaffected by the offer of money as he was by whatever motivated the third man originally.

What *is* motivating the third man? What moves Leary to assemble a few rocket planes and nuclear tractors, but no more? Why does a cash reward make such a difference to Leary's friend but to nobody else?

The scene comes from a film made by National Educational Television and the American Psychological Association several years ago (NET/ APA, 1963), well before Timothy Leary's face became familiar to the masses. The movie itself was a carefully staged demonstration of the workings of certain social motivations, and perhaps Leary's depiction of a man chiefly motivated by affiliation needs was accidental. But I suspect that David McClelland, who supervised and narrated the movie, tried to do at least a bit of typecasting when he chose the actors.

The film's primary concern is not the need for friendship. Its title is *The Need to Achieve,* and the third man is the exemplar of this need. He is hardly concerned with money as such, does not seek competition for competition's sake, and shows little dependence upon friendship while he works. He's mainly concerned with the high standard of excellence he has set for himself and his efforts to attain it. His plans for producing rocket planes are on the whole realistic, but influenced by optimism. He revises his estimate of nuclear tractor production according to feedback about his own recent performance. But always his thoughts are primarily about the attainment of that standard of excellence.

SOCIAL MOTIVES

We've dealt frequently with human motivation in this book. All psychology stands on the assumption that there are reasons for human behavior; and often those reasons are sought within the individual behaving organism rather than in the environment outside him. Assumptions about social motivation are usually no less crude than those dealing with gut-level motives, if they differ at all. According to various psychologists, people are moved mainly by a desire to reduce hunger, thirst, sexual swelling; or they seek to satisfy three or four basic kinds of needs, e.g., material, social, psychological; or they seek mainly to reduce dissonance, inconsistency, incongruity. The latter sort of assumption has gradually

272

acquired some of the complex dimensions that we might expect of an exclusively human, socially implicated motive. But along with most other motivational hypotheses, it is more often than not phrased mainly in avoidance terms — one seeks to lessen inconsistency, rather than actively to promote consistency. Furthermore, though the long-term focus on consistency motivation has revealed some of its complexity, this increase in theoretical sophistication may have been at the expense of other important social motives, which (with one or two exceptions) remain ill-understood.

Psychologists have made lists of needs or motives at least since the time of William McDougall. By far the most influential list in recent times has been that of Henry Murray (1938). From voluminous case histories collected at the Harvard Psychological Clinic and from masses of literature about human behavior, Murray extracted twenty manifest needs, seven additional possible manifest needs, eight latent needs, and various related psychological states. Several among these sound quite straightforward, such as *n* Sex ("*n*" denotes "need"). Others are more exotic in title if not in meaning: *n* Succorance, *n* Blamavoidance, *n* Sentience. Three major psychological tests (the Thematic Apperception Test, Edwards Personal Preference Schedule, and Adjective Check List) have been developed to assess the needs listed by Murray; many research programs have sought to study one or more of those needs. Disagreements have arisen and continue to arise as to how such needs or motives work — whether they continue to be dependent ultimately upon the "basic," "biological" needs, whether they really exert a driving force from within the person or are better conceptualized as ways of processing information from without. It does appear that individuals differ not only in their specific interests, not only in their somewhat broader attitudes, but also with regard to general orientations, which may be thought of as motives, as directions in which they are most easily moved, if not as genuine deficit needs. A person may, for instance, hold positive attitudes toward Democratic party policies, and may have a great interest in Rooseveltiana or Kennedyana that reflects these attitudes; but both interests and attitudes may be only partial reflections of his generally strong nurturant (nourishing, supportive, consolatory) motive. Nurturance has been little studied in any formal way; we'll discuss instead those social motives that have been investigated in some detail. We'll start with the most researched of all, *n* Achievement.

THE NEED TO ACHIEVE

The existence of a particular kind of motivation, distinct from all others and itself not an amalgam of several others, is difficult to discern with the naked eye, even with the psychologist's somewhat better trained and therefore even nakeder eye. McClelland narrowed Murray's original definition of *n* Achievement ("the desire or tendency to do things as rapidly and/or as well as possible") to include only the "desire to do a good job of work," to attain a standard of excellence (McClelland et al., 1953; McClelland, 1961a, 1961b). Then he set up a series of empirical tests not only to make sure this sort of motivation does indeed exist, but also to determine what its consequences are for those who hold it and for society in general.

The existence of achievement motivation was originally demonstrated through the Thematic Apperception Test. When known sources of motivation, such as hunger, are aroused, the stories told in response to TAT cards often reflect the storyteller's state of motivation — for example, he may more often mention being deprived of food, the hungrier he is. Likewise, McClelland tried to arouse volunteers' concern about meeting a standard of excellence, for instance by telling them the TAT could reveal "an individual's capacity to organize material, his ability to evaluate crucial situations quickly and accurately" (McClelland, 1961a). Under these circumstances, the volunteers told stories whose characters themselves were much more concerned with achievement than if the TAT were given under relatively neutral or relaxed conditions. Furthermore, some people seemed perpetually to display more achievement motivation than others, even when no one was talking about standards of excellence. Indeed, whole nations seemed to differ in the proportion of achievement themes found to be running through their myths, their children's readers, their poetry, and their pottery designs.

Lest this sound like an argument for the idea of "naturally lazy" Irishmen versus "naturally energetic" Scots, I must point out that McClelland assumed no inborn component of *n* Achievement. Differences in achievement motivation are presumably acquired through learning, largely during childhood. A psychologist with the non-nurturant name of Marian Winterbottom (1958) tested a number of eight- to ten-year-old boys for achievement motivation levels and then interviewed their mothers. She found that several anticipated differences between the upbringing of boys high and low in *n* Ach, such as amount and degree of punishment, were not confirmed. But the differences that did occur seemed rationally tied to the basic concept of achievement motivation. Mothers of boys low in *n* Ach often made the boys' decisions for them, and restricted their behavior in various ways. Mothers of high *n* Ach boys expected them to make their own friends, to do things for themselves, generally to become more independent and self-reliant at an early age (but at an age at which they were in fact capable of performing the expected acts). These mothers also rewarded their sons for such achievements with physical displays of affection more often than the mothers of low *n* Ach boys did. Other researchers (see Birney, 1968) have studied fathers as well, finding high *n* Ach boys' fathers to be emotionally warmer toward their offspring, more demanding of high achievement but less directive of how such achievement is to be accomplished, than low *n* Ach boys' fathers. Similar patterns have been observed in comparing children from different ethnic groups that stress early or late independence training.

FEAR OF FAILURE

Need for achievement is not all that may be instilled by parents interested in independent performance, however. Children who are punished or rejected for failure, rather than rewarded for their accomplishments, are likely to show both poor development of *n* Ach and a strongly developed *fear of failure* (FF). John Atkinson (1964) has explored the interactions of *n* Ach and FF, and finds it useful to view behavior in any situation that involves the possibility of accomplishment as a resultant of three factors: the person's degree of achievement motivation, his fear of failure, and the incentive value of success at that particular task. Atkinson and his coworkers (Atkinson and Feather, 1966) have developed and tested several relatively precise mathematical formulae involving different values of *n* Ach, FF, and the situation's incentive value; and several of their conclusions are intriguing. For instance, let's say you've finally become convinced that you must participate in political action at some level, but since you're not sure which level you should start at, an experienced activist has given you a list of possible political actions clearly labeled "EASY" to "HARD." The list begins with convincing your neighbors to vote for a local bond issue, and ends with completely revolutionizing the basic governmental structure of the United States. Just to get your feet wet, you try the local bond issue first, and you fail to change a single neighbor's vote. The question now is, if you stay in politics after that experience, will you try another easy action, or will you turn to a hard one?

Atkinson's calculations indicate that if you have high need for achievement and low fear of failure, you'll try another action labeled "EASY." If you have low need for achievement and high fear of failure, you're most likely to try something hard next. Why? Because a high FF person won't really care whether he succeeds at anything, just as long as he doesn't fail again; and if he's working toward something that's very hard to accomplish, he can feel it isn't really his fault that he's not getting anywhere. *He's* not failing; the problem is simply that it's damned hard to change the entire U.S. government. The low FF–high *n* Ach person, on the other hand, isn't afraid of failing at an easy action again, and the fact that he didn't turn in a decent level of performance the first time should motivate him to show he really *can* do well on the next easy action on the list. If he'd tried something difficult first and failed, however, he might well turn to a more obviously attainable goal, because occasional indication of success is important to him and he may suspect he can't succeed at the higher levels of difficulty.

All this assumes that the person will continue to engage in political

275

actions. If the high FF person can't find a task level at which he has little likelihood of failing, he's likely to drop out of the political scene altogether, because he's not much concerned to show accomplishment anyway. But the high n Ach person does enjoy achieving, as long as he has a reasonable chance to do so. At the same time, he doesn't see success at a task as genuine achievement unless there's a reasonable likelihood he could have failed. Given his choice, he should gravitate toward political goals that he has about a 50 per cent chance of attaining — say, the election of more competent congressmen. The odds are not so high against him that he'll rarely be rewarded with achievements; nor are they so low that he won't feel a sense of accomplishment when he does succeed. Nobody has studied the goal choices of political activists in terms of their achievement motivation (though Winter and Wiecking [1971] did find one group of radicals holding "responsible decision-making positions" to be relatively high in achievement need). The preference among high n Ach volunteers for a middling probability of success or failure has been verified by McClelland (1958) in observing the distances at which children prefer to stand from the target in a ring-toss game; by Bernard Weiner (1970) in giving college students a choice of geometrical puzzles with different levels of difficulty; and by Atkinson in several other contexts.

One context studied by Atkinson (1964) suggests immediate practical implications of such preferences. He found that sixth-grade students in a Midwestern city school system varied in their interest in and success at schoolwork, depending on a combination of their n Ach–FF levels and the sort of class they were in. Students high in achievement motivation and low in fear of failure felt greater interest in school, and actually performed at a "substantially higher level," when they were in classes where all the other students had similar abilities than when the classes contained a more typically wide range of ability. Presumably in the homogeneous class they saw their likelihood of success as closer to 50–50, and therefore were more highly motivated to succeed. In a heterogeneous class, they would see success over the weaker students as relatively easy, and their achievement motivation would be aroused correspondingly less. Students high in FF and low in n Ach were less satisfied with classes where other students were similar to themselves in ability, and performed less well than the high n Ach students in those homogeneous classes. They presumably saw their possibilities of failure as higher in competition with others like themselves, and indeed found this confirmed when their anxieties interfered with their schoolwork. Atkinson argues convincingly that fear of failure does not generally motivate one to do better; it inhibits.

Fear of failure has most often been measured by paper-and-pencil questionnaires (typically Mandler and Sarason's Test Anxiety Questionnaire [1952]). At least partly for that reason, FF has not figured importantly in the really dramatic studies of achievement motivation. The scoring techniques used to assess achievement motivation in imaginative responses to TAT cards can also be applied to other imaginative productions — not only children's readers and myths, but also motion pictures, novels, maybe even dirty jokes. This makes it possible for McClelland and his associates to measure, at least loosely, achievement motivation levels in other cultures and other eras than our own, even if no one has been there with a stack of TAT cards or a paper-and-pencil questionnaire. McClelland (1961a) has therefore been able to develop and test hypotheses about the workings of achievement motivation not only worldwide, but back at least as far as ancient Greece. (Some of these studies also utilize a graphic measure of n Ach, developed by Elliot Aronson [1958], which involves the degree of curviness, repetition, and other features in anything from doodles to abstract art. With this measure one can analyze the achievement motivation of present-day preliterate tribes or of prehistoric man. McClelland sees the graphic measure as even better than his verbal scoring techniques when nonwestern cultures are studied; but not all researchers agree upon its validity.)

ENTREPRENEURIAL ACHIEVEMENT

Once McClelland moves from the problems of measuring n Ach and discerning its childhood origins, his research focuses almost entirely on what might be more properly labeled n E Ach — need for economic achievement or entrepreneurial achievement, for initiating or improving business productivity. His measures of achievement motivation are particularly good at predicting success in the business world; for unclear reasons they don't predict success in scientific or artistic endeavors. One reason could be that many people high in achievement motivation don't enter science or the arts; such professions involve too much of a gamble for them, too little chance of high achievement. Business, according to McClelland, may represent the optimum compromise between risk and incentive for most young men — particularly those in the lower middle class, where n Ach is generally strongest in the United States.

McClelland also thinks the difference may lie partly in the relatively prompt feedback on success that occurs in the business world (through evaluation of weekly or quarterly or monthly profits), versus the much-delayed public or professional feedback characteristic of science and art. But scientists and artists have their own ways of judging their attainment of excellence during the ongoing creative process, which may sustain them even if the final product is not completed for years and even if the public critical response to that final product is rather mixed. I suspect that part of the problem instead is the difficulty of representing scientific and artistic achievement pictorially in such a way that people are likely

277

to tell imaginative stories about it in response to TAT cards – combined with the research psychologist's difficulty in deciding objectively what scientific or artistic achievement among other people really is, in all except the most outstanding instances. The failure to develop better ways to study the operation of achievement motivation in scientists and artists seems to me a major weakness in this area of research. Maybe that's only because I've always felt much more motivated to attain excellence in science and art than in business. But as our society grows in affluence, as monetary rewards become less and less differentiating and as overproduction becomes more and more a blight on our countryside, attention toward ways of increasing other sorts of achievement motivation will become essential.

The research on entrepreneurial achievement itself represents a high level of scientific achievement, and perhaps of artistic achievement too. McClelland (1965) has demonstrated that college students scoring high in n Ach are far more likely than low n Ach students to make their livings in entrepreneurial occupations over at least the next fourteen years of their lives. He has shown (1961a) that primitive tribes whose folktales are higher in n Ach are more likely to contain full-time entrepreneurs (traders, independent artisans, herdsmen who sell their animals) than low n Ach tribes. He has shown that increases in achievement themes in children's readers are likely to precede increases in a nation's economic productivity, and decreases in achievement themes to precede economic decline – usually by about enough years for the children thoroughly imbued with the readers' messages to grow to working manhood. He and his students (1961a) have even shown, by tabulating achievement themes in the works of such writers as Homer and Hesiod and by determining the geographic spread of Grecian urns at various periods, that the rise and decline of ancient Greek civilization were preceded by the same ups and downs in achievement imagery as he has observed among modern nations. Furthermore, McClelland makes a good guess as to why Greek achievement motivation, and thus the civilization itself, fell. It all started, he suggests, when middle-class Greek entrepreneurs became wealthy enough to turn their children over to slaves for their care and education. The slaves pampered the children, and performed the acts that the children might otherwise have been expected to do for themselves; and so self-reliance, n Ach, and Athens itself gradually declined.

CHANGING ACHIEVEMENT MOTIVATION

If childraising patterns are the crucial factor in the development of n Ach, might not a family or a nation profit by consciously raising its children with achievement in mind? Perhaps. But childraising is a pretty slow business, with reliable feedback far in the future; and no achievement researcher has publicly announced any successes, or even attempts,

278

along such lines. McClelland (McClelland and Winter, 1969) has instead tried to increase *n* Ach in adults.

How would you go about changing motivation in adults? Some people have tried to remedy the reading difficulties of teen-agers by forcing them to crawl like infants, on the theory that they messed up their brains early in life by crawling the wrong way. Would putting adults through a series of ring-toss games and friendship-choosing situations, and rewarding them with hugs and parental approval for making their own independent decisions, improve their *n* Ach? No more, I'd guess, than crawling really helps slow readers. Whatever the hypothetical similarities to the original infantile learning situation, teen-agers and adults are likely to react negatively to experiences that make them feel ludicrous.

But McClelland, though he thinks motives are generally acquired in childhood, does not ascribe to motives the depth or immutability they enjoy in, for instance, Freudian theory. Motives, McClelland says, are "*affectively toned associative networks* arranged in a hierarchy of strength or importance in a given individual." This means that when a person learns to react to certain stimuli with a particular pattern of emotionally loaded responses, he has acquired a motive; and the sort of pattern occurring most frequently in response to the various stimuli he encounters can be said to rank highest in his motive hierarchy. Some people respond frequently to their environment by thinking positively of how to attain a goal, how to meet a standard of excellence; they possess high achievement motivation, and they show it by talking spontaneously about achievement even when they're shown TAT cards. People typically learn such a pattern of thinking as children. But if they haven't, why not teach them to think that way as adults, especially when they encounter any sort of business-related stimuli?

High government and foundation officials must generally feel that motives are more complicated or mysterious than this, or that motivational changes are irrelevant to economic productivity. If they really accepted McClelland's conceptualization of motives, he wouldn't have had nearly as hard a time getting financial support for a fair test of his hypotheses as he did. Here he was, offering to train men in several underdeveloped countries to think achievement, and thereby to begin moving their nations' economies forward; and he was asking, comparatively speaking, for a mere pittance — a fraction of the cost of one malfunctioning F-111 fighter plane. But the Agency for International Development, our nation's official foreign aid agency, toyed with the idea for about a year and then turned him down. The Ford Foundation did likewise. Ultimately the work was supported at a rather low level by the Small Industries Extension Training Institute, an agency of the Government of India; even a good bit of that support was canceled in the midst of McClelland's efforts. What had originally been planned as a

279

massive test of achievement training among management workers in several Indian industries, three Indian towns, one or two regions of Southern Italy, and the entire nation of Tunisia, eventually turned into a comparison of the effects of a ten-day training course on fifty-one people in Kakinada and twenty-six people in Vellore, two small cities in Southern India, with bits and pieces of information from smaller efforts elsewhere. Those who wish to leap immediately from the laboratory to the halls of power will find the account of McClelland's own journey instructive if not inspiring.

Well, maybe they'll find it a little inspiring. McClelland and his Indian and American coworkers did get a training program going at the SIET Institute in Hyderabad; they did manage to train several dozen Indian entrepreneurs in the intricacies of n Ach; and they were even able to collect follow-up data in Kakinada, Vellore, and the "control" city of Rajahmundry over a two-year period. (The Carnegie Foundation came through with a modest grant for the latter, making up for a bit of what the Ford Foundation had withheld. Blessed be the entrepreneurs, for they would sometimes rather give money away than pay it in taxes.)

What were the Indian entrepreneurs taught, and what did they do with it, and what does it all prove about achievement motivation? First, they were taught how to get high n Ach scores on the TAT. That sounds reasonable, doesn't it? If you have high achievement motivation, you will make high n Ach scores on the TAT; so if you learn to make high n Ach scores on the TAT, you must have high achievement motivation.

That isn't quite as inanely circular as it sounds. People don't necessarily score high in n Ach if the psychologist says, "Tell me a story that involves a lot of achievement motivation." They have to realize that achievement motivation involves trying to attain a standard of excellence rather than just amassing a lot of money; that it involves taking realistic steps to attain goals, rather than just wishful daydreaming; that it involves such things as "taking personal responsibility for varied instrumental acts," rather than just waiting for the gods to do with you as they will. If a man learns well the elements a TAT story must include to rate high on n Ach, he's at least a little more likely to think about such things when he contemplates his own problems and opportunities.

McClelland took no chances on this latter possibility. A major part of the training course involved getting the volunteers to begin thinking about *themselves* in achievement terms. They were asked explicitly "to set realistic challenging goals for themselves." They took part in small group discussions of each volunteer's motivations, business opportunities, and future lines of action. They were asked to report regularly to Institute personnel about their progress after they had finished the course. In both Kakinada and Vellore, the volunteers on their own initiative set up "alumni" organizations, which involved frequent meetings of course graduates to discuss their progress with each other.

The results? The Kakinada trainees showed a significant increase in overall entrepreneurial activity in the two years following the course, the Vellore trainees a somewhat smaller increase, the untrained control subjects none at all. Trainees invested more money, hired more workers, and increased their gross income substantially more than the controls. McClelland figures that in two years, the forty-seven trainees for whom he has adequate data were responsible for creating 135 new jobs and for raising 376,000 rupees of new capital investments — these in two towns of a little over 100,000 inhabitants each. In terms of training costs for the entrepreneurs, he calculates that those additional jobs cost about twenty-five dollars apiece, and that the trainees' new investments cost roughly five to seven per cent to obtain — much less than typical government efforts using more traditional economic and technological approaches. McClelland admits that the city of Kakinada has not been appreciably changed by his relatively small-scale intervention in its economic life; but he is justifiably proud of the changes he has wrought in the lives of more than forty Indian citizens, mainly in the direction of making them self-reliant, industrious, productive citizens. Similar success stories have since been reported with n Ach training programs among Boston ghetto Negroes, middle-class blacks in Washington, D.C., and white businessmen in the economically depressed city of McAlester, Oklahoma. A small number of failures have also been reported, but the training programs in those instances were usually rather skimpy compared to the successful programs.

QUESTIONS ABOUT MOTIVATIONAL CHANGE

Now, how much is training in achievement motivation *as such* responsible for the success stories? Or as I put it before, what does all of this prove about achievement motivation? Several processes were at work in the Indian cities besides teaching the volunteers what n Ach means. The men were given a lot of special attention by outstanding American and Indian social scientists. They were taught how to investigate ways to begin new businesses, through government assistance and otherwise. They made new acquaintances among other volunteers, which enabled them to engage in joint enterprises and frequently to obtain financial backing about which they would otherwise never have learned. In a few instances at other locations, an attempt has been made to set up control groups who get similar attention without n Ach training; but the probable differences in enthusiasm between an n Ach trainer and a control-group trainer are difficult to eliminate, and the results of these comparisons are inconclusive. McClelland takes the position that the increase in entrepreneurial activity among trainees is the most important outcome, and in some regards that's true. But it's not true in terms of learning more about how n Ach works, or even in terms of the practical problem of how to design better entrepreneurial training courses. One curious finding in

281

the Indian studies is that trainees' n Ach scores declined by about 40 per cent over the two or three years between the training course and the final evaluation, and that trainees who became entrepreneurial successes declined in n Ach scores about as much as trainees whose entrepreneurial activities didn't change significantly. It looks as though increased thinking about achievement may not be as important as other factors, unmeasured by the TAT.

Furthermore, discrepancies in certain other motivational measures have suggested to McClelland himself that he never really changed the basic achievement motivation of his Indian trainees very much anyway. Those who were most successful entrepreneurially after the training were characterized by "an initial interest in being self-reliant and autonomous that was somewhat atypical for their society." In other words, they were already unusually high in certain crucial aspects of achievement motivation. McClelland feels the training served mainly to show these people how to direct their motivation most effectively, how to acquire the means to attain achievement goals. For those blocked by reality, frustrated by lack of access to the money or facilities or organizational power necessary to succeed entrepreneurially, it made little difference whether training in n Ach directed their attention to the means or not. They never attained their goal.

Recently I met a psychologist who had been doing research on achievement motivation for several years, and who had been drinking steadily for several hours. He announced that he had developed a much better questionnaire for measuring n Ach than the TAT or anything else heretofore. As he got drunker and drunker, he also insisted more and more vehemently that he was going to go home and burn all his research, since it was a danger to humanity. As soon as the military-industrial complex got hold of a really good measure of n Ach, he thought, they'd use it to develop training methods that would convert everyone into high achievers. All that is gentle and uncapitalistic and noncompetitive in our society would disappear.

I doubt very much that this gentleman's research is any more menacing than the available data on, say, attitude change or extremism. Judging from McClelland's work, nobody will be able to increase n Ach within broad sectors of the populace for a long time to come, whether the change efforts are directed at willing adults, unwilling adults, or unpredictable children. And even if our ability to develop n Ach does increase, as I assume it eventually will, I see little of the danger in it that my intoxicated acquaintance imagined. The world would be a sad place indeed if everyone shared a high level of entrepreneurial achievement motivation; but it would also be a pretty miserable place if no one did. The "underdeveloped" nations appear to be mightily in need of a good supply of industrious men interested in a standard of excellence. Within our own nation we now seem, willy-nilly, to have established childraising procedures or adolescent social pressures that militate against both entrepreneurship and standards of excellence among many of our most capable youths. A nation of ineptly operated hippie communes is no more my idea of the ideal than is a nation of GM's and IBM's. How we should decide who gets the n Ach treatment and who gets something else is, I admit, a genuinely puzzling question. But even more puzzling is the question of how humanity can survive if the spark of n Ach is permanently extinguished.

people who need people: motives toward affiliation

The ruling passion in man is not as Viennese as is claimed. It is rather a gregarious instinct to keep together by minding each other's business. Grex rather than sex.
— Robert Frost
"The Constant Symbol"

Hippies occasionally like to think of themselves as mutants. When they compare their own loving sensuality to the cold rigidities of their parents, they find it hard to believe the same gene pool is involved. They don't bother trying to square this dream of several million simultaneous love-oriented mutations with post-Mendelian genetics; they seem to feel, as did Carl Jung, that modern genetic theory is irrelevant to the dark processes of the unconscious. There they're wrong when they needn't be; they could talk about the possibility of broad motivational changes over a large part of a whole generation, and remain on firm theoretical ground. McClelland has in mind just such motivational changes, though with regard to n Ach rather than n Love, when he relates thematic shifts in children's readers to resultant changes in economic activity.

The hippies would not, however, find much actual data in the psychological literature concerning how to make people more loving, or even whether love is particularly important as a social motive. Henry Murray's list of twenty distinct manifest needs, seven possible manifest needs, and eight latent needs (1938) doesn't include a need to love or a need for love. Nor does love appear among his four "miscellaneous internal factors" or twelve "general traits or attributes." In describing the feelings associated with n Sex, Murray does list love — after "erotic excitement" and "lust"; his description of n Succorance includes such items as, "To be nursed, supported, sustained, surrounded, protected, loved, advised, guided, indulged, forgiven, consoled." But love is by no means the primary feature of either motive.

283

Murray obviously does not feel that love is all you need. The closest he gets to acknowledging it as *anything* you need is in the concept of *n* Affiliation, which he sees as a "positive tropism for people." The need for affiliation leads a person "to draw near and enjoyably cooperate" with others, "to please and win affection" of a valued person, "to adhere and remain loyal to a friend."

N Affiliation may seem to hippies and potheads and rock singers a rather inadequate representation of love. Timothy Leary was cast as the high-*n*-Affiliation man in McClelland's achievement motivation film, but what Leary preached during most of his public career was love. Perhaps Henry Murray, so careful in sorting out the necessities of human psychological life, misjudged the intensity or the quality of this one need in particular, and perhaps it's time for a rechristening.

Perhaps, on the other hand, what Leary and his sympathetic legions have called love is really closer to what Murray had in mind in discussing affiliation. The love the hippies speak of often appears so diffuse, so mellow, so tenuously connected to specific partners, that it may not deserve the same word used to describe the passions of Tristan and Isolde, of Arthur and Guinevere and Launcelot, or of the common millions who have tried to emulate them. Nor does it seem to match very closely that intense brotherly love which Christians have alternately called *agape*. When by love you mean the force behind the smiles that are traded within a temporary accumulation of warm bodies, *n* Affiliation may indeed be a better term.

Research on affiliation has fared a little better than that on love, but it's still sketchy. I'm not talking now of research on the question of whether man is innately gregarious; as I noted in Chapter Two, research on that issue is ethically and perhaps even realistically impossible. Nor am I referring to the question of a particular person's choice of people with whom to affiliate. That issue has received extensive empirical attention, under the title of "interpersonal attraction" or "mate selection"; but sociograms and fake computer-dating corporations have never really turned me on. Instead, I'm talking about the general level of *n* Affiliation within each individual: whether some people more than others are particularly attracted to people as people, and whether this attraction varies over time and circumstances, and what circumstances and times are involved, and what the results are of greater and lesser attraction. McClelland takes as given that some people are achievement-oriented; he wants to know when, and how much, and how come, and what happens next. Several of McClelland's associates and students have tried to answer the same questions about affiliation. But perhaps because people who burn to achieve something important in psychology are not likely to be very interested personally in affiliation, or perhaps because people high in n Affiliation are likely to be out affiliating instead of working in the psychological laboratory, the affiliation data have not accumulated nearly as fast.

AFFILIATION AND ANXIETY

Most empirical research on n Affiliation has, rather oddly, been directed toward affiliation produced by negative circumstances, instead of toward any evidence of bubbling warmth or general *Gemütlichkeit*. The first attempt to measure n Affiliation via TAT stories (Shipley and Veroff, 1952) focused on descriptions of loneliness, loss of friends or lovers, and other such interferences with affiliation. The first major affiliation experiments induced affiliation by scaring the volunteers; and this procedure of upsetting people to make sure they feel affiliative has remained more popular than any other. It's as if a group of researchers had decided to study the religious impulse almost solely by interviewing combat soldiers in foxholes. The results might be interesting, but they'd leave something to be desired.

This particular line of affiliation research was initiated by Stanley Schachter (1959). He worked mainly with college coeds, who were invited to come to his laboratory for an unspecified research project. When they arrived, each small group of girls found "a gentleman of serious mien, horn-rimmed glasses, dressed in a white laboratory coat, stethoscope dribbling out of his pocket, behind him an array of formidable electrical junk." He introduced himself as "Dr. Gregor Zilstein of the Medical School's Department of Neurology and Psychiatry. I have asked you all to come today in order to serve as subjects in an experiment concerned with the effects of electrical shock." Dr. Zilstein talked for a while about such matters as accidental electrocutions and electroshock therapy, then told the volunteers that as part of the experiment each of them must be given a series of electrical shocks.

Here the experimental conditions diverged. Girls in the low-anxiety condition were told the shocks might tickle or tingle but wouldn't hurt: "We will put an electrode on your hand, give you a series of very mild shocks and measure such things as your pulse rate and blood pressure, measures with which I'm sure you are all familiar from visits to your family doctor." Girls in the high-anxiety condition were told the shocks would hurt very much: "As you can guess, if . . . we're to learn anything at all that will really help humanity, it is necessary that our shocks be intense. Again, I do want to be honest with you and tell you that these shocks will be quite painful, but, of course, they will do no permanent damage."

In both conditions, Dr. Zilstein told the girls he'd need ten minutes to set up the equipment, and that meanwhile each girl could either wait

285

by herself in a room supplied with magazines, or could wait along with several other volunteers in an empty classroom. Because there might not be enough space to accommodate everyone in her first choice, each girl was asked to indicate on a questionnaire form how strongly she preferred to wait by herself or with others. Dr. Zilstein then removed his white coat, told the girls the experiment was over, and assured them they would receive no electrical shocks at all. The questionnaire asking whether they wished to wait alone or with others was, of course, the crucial measure, since Schachter was interested not in the effects of shock but in the conditions under which the need for affiliation would be most aroused.

After several such studies, Schachter concluded that the higher a person's anxiety, the more likely he is to seek out the company of others — as long as they are likewise anxious. Why? Not because anxiety reminds us how much we miss people, or how soon we are to depart this people-populated planet; but because being with people serves two key psychological functions. First is the direct reduction of anxiety. We are likely to learn that other people can often help us deal with fear-arousing situations; once we have learned this, their very presence may become fear-reducing. At least, we're likely to learn this if we're first-born children. Schachter discovered serendipitously that birth order interacts with anxiety: in his high-fear situation, the first-borns were much more likely than the later-borns to choose the company of other people while waiting for Dr. Zilstein to set up his shock apparatus. Other researchers have found similar contrasts between first-borns and later-borns. Schachter cites evidence, for instance, showing that first-borns are more likely to deal with chronic anxiety through such social means as psychotherapy, whereas later-borns are more likely to dissolve their anxieties in the nonsocial solution of chronic alcoholism. Schachter suggests that these differences develop because first-borns are more likely to have been overprotected by parents as children, and are therefore more likely to be fearful in later threatening situations; because first-borns are more likely to get positive attention from mothers, and therefore more likely to become dependent on people for approval and support; because later-borns are more likely to get kicked around by their first-born siblings, and therefore more likely to see the presence of other people as a mixed blessing at best. Such relationships are not one hundred per cent consistent; I'm a first-born and I'd guess I'm less affiliative than most of my younger siblings, in anxious times or otherwise. But maybe I was punched around a lot by older cousins. *Other things being equal,* as psychologists always say under their breaths, the presence of people with concerns similar to one's own is fear-reducing, especially to first-borns.

Why the qualification, "with concerns similar to one's own"? Partly because other people *are* occasionally interested in knocking you around, on the battlefield or in the business world, and their presence may produce anxiety rather than allay it. (Probably few girls in the high-anxiety condition were eager to affiliate with Dr. Zilstein.) But the qualification comes mainly from the other function of people that Schachter cites: they help you decide whether you're really feeling anxious, or whether you're just embarrassed or dumbfounded or what. Schachter (1964) has established convincingly in later experiments that humans don't identify their own emotions from internal sensations alone; they need information from outside as well, before they can definitely label their feelings. The situation in which they find themselves often helps them to find the right label; but if the situation is ambiguous or if it leaves open the possibility of several different emotional responses, another source of information is seeing how other people react to the same situation. As Dr. Zilstein continues to talk calmly about intense electrical shocks and helping science and curing psychotic depressions, you start feeling something, but what is it? If you're given a chance to wait with other people who aren't involved in the Zilstein study at all, they won't be able to help you answer that question. But other Zilstein guinea pigs will. They'll help most if you can talk to them about the experience; but even if you can't, maybe you can read the fear or anger or suspicion in their eyes.

These two functions of affiliative behavior — anxiety reduction and labeling of ambiguous emotional responses — have been identified as important in several other studies besides Schachter's. But the general scientific agreement on these points doesn't eliminate every difficulty associated with the research. For one thing, a person may not wish to confirm the nature of some emotional reactions by observing the reactions of other people with similar experience. Irving Sarnoff and Philip Zimbardo (1961) created what they called a "high-anxiety" condition by telling male college student volunteers they must suck on various objects while having their physiological responses measured. The objects included baby bottles, breast shields, big rubber nipples, pacifiers, and their own thumbs. When given a chance to wait alone or with other volunteers like themselves while the experimenter set up the measuring apparatus, these high-anxiety (or perhaps we should say high-shame) volunteers significantly more often chose to wait *alone* than did volunteers who were told they'd have to put several low-shame objects in their mouths — kazoos, balloons, whistles, pipes. Schachter says, "Misery doesn't love just any kind of company, it loves only miserable company"; and maybe that's true if misery wants company at all. Some kinds of misery would rather just go crawl into a dark hole.

POSITIVE AFFILIATIVE MOTIVES

Now we know a little about affiliative behavior in the service of anxiety reduction and emotional comparison. But what of affiliation for the sake of affiliation? Neither Schachter nor anyone else has made substantial experimental contributions to this question, so we're left mainly with correlations between TAT stories and other sorts of behavior. Following

287

that first TAT study of affiliation that emphasized loss and loneliness, most such research has emphasized story content dealing with friendliness, liking, "positive affective relationships" (e.g., Atkinson, Heyns, and Veroff, 1954). In one experiment (Atkinson and Walker, 1956) using a positive TAT measure of n Affiliation, high scorers were found to be significantly more sensitive to pictures of human faces than were low scorers, when the faces and various nonsocial objects were flashed on a screen so quickly that only a blur was visible. In another study (Lansing and Heyns, 1959), high-affiliation residents of an area in Michigan were found to make significantly more local telephone calls, to visit distant relatives somewhat more, and to write more letters than low-affiliation residents. (The researchers did not count letters mailed by research participants, or monitor their calls and out-of-town trips; they simply asked participants to report these behaviors. The researchers were able to obtain a record of participants' long-distance calls from the Michigan Bell Telephone Company, but found no relationship between that behavior index and affiliation. This raises a question as to the validity of the self-report descriptions of local telephoning and other behavior. On the other hand, as the researchers suggest, people who do a lot of visiting and letter-writing may not need to make as many long-distance calls to satisfy their desire for affiliation.)

Because no system has been devised to score doodles and pottery decorations for affiliation motivation, we have little indication of n Affiliation levels in preliterate or prehistoric men, except that we wouldn't be here if prehistoric man had felt no affiliative desires at all. But it is possible to score such verbal productions as children's readers for n Aff, just as for n Ach; so the scorers have once again gone rather far afield in their search for related variables. One such search began in the laboratory, where Elizabeth French (1956) demonstrated experimentally that when high-affiliation people are asked whether they'd prefer to work on a task with a competent stranger or with an incompetent friend, they nearly always choose the friend. High-achievement people do the opposite. She has also found, in terms of actual problem-solving efficiency, that high-affiliation volunteers do better when they see the situation as a group effort and are praised in terms of the group's smooth interpersonal relationships. High-achievement volunteers work better when the task is presented as mainly an individual effort, and when the group is praised for efficiency.

French's observations have been applied to Mexican businessmen by David McClelland (1961a), utilizing data collected by Fayerweather (1959). The Mexican businessmen Fayerweather studied were generally much more concerned than American businessmen with maintaining personal alliances, even if such alliances conflicted with business goals. The Mexicans also appeared to have relatively greater difficulty utilizing the criterion of efficiency when they judged business behavior. And fi-

288

nally, though they may perhaps have enjoyed their friends more, they also made a lot less money than the Americans. McClelland recognizes that pleasure can come from the satisfaction of other motives than achievement, and he isn't necessarily knocking Mexican businessmen by describing their friendly inefficiency. But he does warn his achievement school trainees that they can't have both achievement and affiliation to any great extent, and shouldn't continue if they prefer the company of family and friends over the triumphs of entrepreneurial success. Most hippies seem to have learned that lesson well. (Incidentally, John D. W. Andrews [1967] has located some Mexican business firms in which the key executives are high in n Ach; such firms grow much more rapidly than the more traditionally staffed ones. But more about that when we discuss n Power.)

McClelland has also found that high n Affiliation produces something besides friendly but inefficient Mexican businessmen: it produces children. In various nations, comparisons of recent birth rates with affiliation imagery in children's readers yield substantial positive correlations. McClelland thinks this relationship occurs mainly because high-affiliation people want more little people around the house; but I'd guess that feelings of affiliation between man and woman have something to do with it too, despite the pill and other modern methods of accident prevention. If the Great East Coast Blackout of 1967 could significantly increase the birthrate in one night, what might a year-by-year one per cent increase in n Affiliation achieve?

I've already noted the value of developing ways to measure and produce nonentrepreneurial types of achievement motivation, for those future years when our over-affluent society still needs quality and creativity but doesn't need massive increases in cash or consumer goods. Likewise we may benefit in the long run from research on finer differentiations of n Affiliation, and on means for encouraging certain aspects of affiliative motivation while discouraging others. What our overpopulated world needs now may not be more love but better methods to ensure that most people, particularly those fertile males and females who haven't developed a mutual plan for avoiding offspring, become nothing more than Just Good Friends.

people who help people:
tendencies toward altruism

If we resort to an indirect test, and ask Nature: "Who are the fittest: those who are continually at war with each other, or those who support one another?" we at once see that those animals which acquire habits of mutual aid are undoubtedly the fittest. They have more

*chances to survive, and they attain, in their respective
classes, the highest development of intelligence and
bodily organization.*

— Prince Kropotkin
Mutual Aid

Play another role. You are subject to grand mal epileptic seizures, and you fear the day when you have one at the wrong time and the wrong place, with no one to save you from disaster. But whenever you are "saved," you become embarrassed and even a little resentful; so you usually avoid appearing in public without close friends. Today no friends were available, but you've come to the university's psychology laboratory anyway, to participate in an experiment as part of a course requirement. You're glad each participant has been isolated in his own cubicle, since that lessens the possibility of embarrassment. On the other hand you feel a bit anxious, because no one is nearby to help in case help is needed. Only one other participant is here today. You've asked the experimenter whether others will come; he says that although they occasionally do, he thinks just the two of you will participate this time.

Now you're listening over the cubicle's intercom as the experimenter explains the procedure. He says he wants to learn about "the kinds of personal problems faced by normal college students in a high pressure, urban environment." He wants you and the other volunteer to discuss your personal problems freely; to increase your freedom of expression, he has set up this intercom arrangement and he's going to leave for a while. When he comes back, he'll give you a questionnaire about some of the things you've discussed. He says the microphones will work in only one cubicle at a time, with a mechanical relay activating each volunteer's mike alternately every two minutes. As the experimenter leaves, you start to mention to him your concern about possible seizures; but then you hesitate and he goes. Suddenly the "on" light for your microphone lights up, and the experiment has begun.

You start out hesitantly, mentioning a few minor problems in getting adjusted to the big city and to your courses. Particularly, you say, particularly you have this one problem whenever you're studying hard, taking exams, under pressure. Sometimes you have these seizures, you say softly, and they aren't pleasant. You sit for a moment, wondering how much you should say about them; then fortunately your microphone light goes off and the other participant starts talking.

He sympathizes with you, says something about how his aunt used to get fits. Then he begins a long story about how he finds it hard to meet new girls. The microphone relay cuts him off in mid-sentence. You start talking again, quietly at first, about girls and fraternities and things; and then you feel it coming on, and you find it hard to talk, hard to find your voice. "I-er-um-I think I-I need-er-if-if could-er-er-somebody er-er-er-er-er-er-er give me a little-er-give me a little help here because-er-I-er-I'm-er-er-h-h-having a-a-a real problem-er-right now and I-er-if somebody could help me out it would-it would-er-er s-s-sure be-sure be good," and your voice is getting louder and you are beginning to clutch at your throat, "because-er-there-er-er-a cause I-er-I-uh-I've got a-a one of the-er-sei — er-er-things coming on and-and-and I could really-er-use some help so if somebody would-er-give me a little h-help-uh-er-er-er-er-er c-could-somebody er-er-help-er-uh-uh-uh," and now you are choking and silently cursing the experimenter for leaving you alone like this, and you're screaming now, "I'm gonna die — er-er-I'm," and you're thinking, goddamn that guy in the other cubicle, why doesn't he come, why couldn't there be half a dozen guys here instead of one, and you shriek, "Gonna die — er-help-er-er-seizure-er — " and you choke again and that's all.

The empirical question at hand is: would you have been more likely to be saved if the other cubicles had been filled with half a dozen guys, or are you theoretically better off with only one possible rescuer?

John Darley and Bibb Latané (1968) say you are better off with only one. In a specific situation, it might be just your luck that that one is a baby-stomping Hell's Angel; but even there, you'd probably be better off with one Hell's Angel than you would with six. Darley and Latané have not used Hell's Angels as volunteers; neither have they used genuine epileptics. But they have found that on the average, when an ordinary college student finds himself participating in the situation above, and hears on the intercom what appears to be a terrified epileptic entering a seizure, the ordinary college student is much more likely to go to the epileptic's rescue if the college student is alone than if he is supposedly surrounded by several other participants in their respective cubicles.

DIFFUSION OF RESPONSIBILITY

Why should Darley and Latané play such a nasty trick on ordinary college students? Because they wanted to understand a very nasty phenomenon: the unwillingness of many people to assist their direly threatened fellow beings. The case of Kitty Genovese inspired them; a tawdrier inspiration would be hard to come by. Kitty Genovese did what any girl would do who was being repeatedly raped and stabbed in a public place; she screamed. And screamed, and screamed. *New York Times* reporter A. M. Rosenthal (1964) later found that at least thirty-eight people heard Kitty Genovese's screams and watched the attack from their apartment windows; but nobody went to her aid. Nobody even called the police until she was half an hour dead.

The Kitty Genovese case was the kind of public nightmare come true that makes newspaper reporters start calling psychologists. Some psychol-

291

ogists no doubt offered their usual quick answers — "apathy," "anomie," and so on — but Latané and Darley (1970a) instead began experimenting. They didn't try to reproduce the Genovese situation in its full horror; that had already happened, and *The New York Times* had already told us what the thirty-eight spectators had to say about it. Now somebody needed to sort out the crucial variables from the irrelevant ones. That's why people do experiments.

The first experiment was the one you've just roleplayed. The participant saw it from the other end: he was confronted with somebody choking to death during an epileptic seizure. The participant could sit and wait for another person to act, or he could try to help the victim himself. The crucial variable was whether the participant was led to believe he was the only person who could hear the victim's cries, or whether other participants were also apparently present. Sometimes there seemed to be four other people besides the real participant and the "epileptic"; sometimes one other; sometimes none. Everybody was actually on tape except the real participant. Every real participant who thought he alone could help the victim did go to help — 100 per cent perfect performance. When one other person was presumably available, a little over 80 per cent of real participants tried to help. When four others were supposed to be present, about 60 per cent of the real ones tried to help. Darley and Latané stopped there, but if the curve of probable assistance in relation to the number of bystanders kept going down at the same rate, you'd be close to a zero probability of help by the time you were in the vicinity of thirty-eight bystanders.

Newspapers in other parts of the country have often attributed the behavior of Kitty Genovese's silent spectators to the impersonality of life in New York City. I'm not a great fan of New York myself, and I think maybe the ordinary run of people in Kevil, Kentucky, or Dallas, Texas, or Davis, California, might have behaved a little differently under similar circumstances. But the participants in Darley and Latané's epileptic-seizure experiment all lived in New York City. Instead of asking why people didn't help, let's ask it the other way: why should between 60 and 100 per cent of these New Yorkers rush to help a person in trouble, even granting that the percentage went down the more people there seemed to be in the group? If New York City makes everyone cold and impersonal, that impersonality should linger even when the number of people in one place is reduced.

Darley and Latané did find that out of sixteen personality and background measures they obtained from participants, the only one significantly related to the speed of helping was the size of the community in which the participant grew up. The bigger his home town, the slower he was likely to be in rendering assistance. But this relationship didn't hold strongly enough among all the participants to account for the experiment's results; and it was not replicated in a later similar study (Schwartz and Clausen, 1970). Instead, Darley and Latané point to what they call "diffusion of responsibility and blame." If a person is alone when he's confronted with another's plea for help, he can't very well say, either to himself or to the victim, "Ask the other guy." He has to help if anyone is going to help; if he fails to help, all the blame falls on him. But if other people *are* present, he can see them as just as responsible for rendering assistance as he is; and if everybody fails to make the first move, so what? That other guy over there didn't do any more than I did!

Darley and Latané made it particularly easy for people to remain passive through such divvying up of responsibility and blame, because the experimental situation prevented the real participant from finding out what others were doing during the crisis. Only the epileptic's microphone was open; all the other cubicles were silent. In much the same way, all of Kitty Genovese's witnesses were peering out of apartment house windows, often darkened windows; none were in telephone communication with each other, or even knew each other's phone numbers. Should I help? Well, maybe I should — but *surely* one of those other guys has already done something by now. So why should I get involved?

OTHER PEOPLE AS EMOTIONAL CUES

Not all crisis situations carry this built-in impersonality, however. Sometimes you're face to face with other possible Good Samaritans, and you can see whether your victim is being aided or not. Diffusion of responsibility shouldn't lead to less total aid in such cases. People will help the victim as much as they can, and the more people are available, the more there are to help, right?

Wrong, for two reasons. First, there may be a maximum number of people who can help in such a situation, and once they are helping, all the others who are too slow or too doubtful of their own competency can stand back and watch the show. As in Roger Barker's studies (1960) of overpopulated behavior settings, the crisis that has more people than it needs generates a lot of spectators. If that were the only effect of increasing numbers in a public situation, the victim would still get all the help he needs; but Latané and Darley (1968) have suggested a second process that may again reduce the chances for help as the number of potential helpers grows. It's similar to the process Stanley Schachter saw as crucial in the arousal of affiliative motivation under stressful conditions: using other people's reactions to see whether you should be properly alarmed.

To study this process, Latané and Judith Rodin (1969) set up a situation described to volunteers as a market research study. Some people were tested alone; most were paired either with a friend who had also

293

volunteered, a stranger who had volunteered, or a confederate of the experimenter who did his best to look like a volunteer. A young woman calling herself a market research representative gave each volunteer a questionnaire to complete and then walked into an adjacent room, pulling a curtain shut behind her. After a few minutes of paper-shuffling, she was heard to climb on a chair, apparently to get at a high shelf in a bookcase that had been visible earlier. A loud crash followed, a scream, a thump as the lady landed on the floor, and then her moans: "Oh, my God, my foot . . . I . . . I . . . can't move it. Oh . . . my ankle. I . . . can't get this . . . thing . . . off me." More cries and moans, all in stereophonic sound from a tape recorder so that every volunteer would hear exactly the same thing. If the volunteer gave no help in two minutes, the lady recovered somewhat and audibly limped out another door, perhaps to find a more chivalrous gentleman who would assuage her wounds.

How many times did she need to go look for somebody else? A minority of times, if the volunteer was filling out the market research questionnaire by himself: 70 per cent of the unpaired volunteers went to the lady's aid. But when the experimental confederate was present, the proportion of helpers among real volunteers plummeted to 7 per cent. The confederate himself, of course, never offered to help; he just went on working. If "diffusion of responsibility" were the sole reason for the less-help-from-more-people effect, the confederate's indifference shouldn't be very inhibiting; the real volunteer should soon realize that now the buck has been passed back to him, and he should intervene. But most volunteers in this condition, though not entirely satisfied that the circumstances were normal, seemed to take the confederate's business-as-usual behavior as sufficient indication that they too were free from responsibility.

The confederate was paid to be impassive. When two real volunteer strangers were tested together, their mutual impassivity was not as great. But still only a minority helped the lady — 40 per cent of the pairs, if you generously include pairs where only one person helped. Pairs of friends did considerably better: in 70 per cent of the pairs, one or both intervened. It might therefore appear that two friends are at least as helpful as one person alone. But bear in mind that if help comes 70 per cent of the time when the potential helper is alone, then by strictly mathematical calculations help should come even more often when two people are available to assist — 91 per cent of the time, to be exact. So even the 70 per cent helping behavior of the two-friend pairs is worse than the single-person performance.

The differences between single volunteers and friends, friends and strangers, and strangers and confederates cannot be explained by assumptions about diffusion of blame and responsibility. But Latané and Darley's idea about the cue value of other people's reactions does seem to work fairly well. Is the lady's condition serious? If you're alone, the only way you can really tell is to go take a look. If somebody else is with you, you can look at him, to see how upset he is. The industrious stooge, betraying no reaction to the lady's alarm, shows you the situation isn't really as serious as you thought. The volunteer stranger may suggest cause for a little alarm, insofar as he's now looking at you to see how *he* should react; but because you don't want to appear excitable or uncool, you're likely to keep as straight a face as possible while you're looking at him, and he's likely to maintain his straight face as he looks at you, so neither of you sees much overt concern in the other's face. Friends may be more likely to display their feelings openly to each other, but they're still going to depend on each other in part for a definition of the situation. If they hold off responding until they supply a clear definition to each other, they may find that the lady in distress has already disappeared.

ADDITIONAL CUES FOR HELPING BEHAVIOR

This inhibitory effect of using other people as emotional definition-makers may not occur, though, if stronger cues are present. Irving Piliavin (Piliavin, Rodin, and Piliavin, 1969) staged a series of crises on the 8th Avenue IND subway in New York City, in which a man suddenly collapsed to the subway car floor in full view of his fellow passengers. The man remained flat on his back, motionless, gazing at the ceiling, either until somebody helped him up or until the subway pulled to a stop five minutes later. Sometimes he "smelled of liquor and carried a liquor bottle wrapped tightly in a brown bag"; sometimes he "appeared sober and carried a black cane." Piliavin estimates that about 4,450 people were involuntary subjects for the study, which involved 103 separate trials over a two-month period. Though several variables were studied, such as race of victim and of rescuer, the crucial one with regard to the earlier Latané-Darley research was the number of people in the victim's immediate vicinity when he collapsed.

The drunk introduced factors that may unnecessarily complicate our main concern with helping behavior. People could have been afraid he'd become brutal or obnoxious if he were assisted, and anyway a standard remedy for his condition is "sleeping it off." Even so, the drunk was aided in half the trials. The man with the cane seems more nearly equivalent to Darley and Latané's "victims" — and he got helped so often, sixty-two out of sixty-five times, that we have to turn to speed of assistance rather than to number of helpers before we can find measurable differences between experimental conditions.

If anyone is likely to maintain a poker face while somebody else drops dead, it's the typical New York subway rider. So the subway should be an ideal place to observe the phenomenon identified by Darley and

Latané as responsible for lack of helping behavior in face-to-face groups: using others' impassiveness to reassure oneself that a crisis is not serious after all. But in the Piliavin study, many subway riders did render assistance; furthermore, they were likely to render assistance faster, the *larger* the group of people in the victim's immediate vicinity.

Why were Piliavin's results the reverse of Latané and Darley's? Perhaps a crucial factor is that the latter never staged an experiment in which the subjects and the victim were in the same room together. On the subway, people couldn't assume the victim had already been taken care of by others; he was still lying there on his back, and the only rescue possible was from people within the subway car. People could look at each other to see whether the matter was critical; but even if other people were impassive, here was this poor guy still lying there, maybe dying, and the sight of him didn't get any fainter with the passage of time, as the distress cues did in Latané and Rodin's "Lady in Distress" study. The visible cues from the victim himself were in this case much less ambiguous than the facial expressions of onlookers.

PSYCHOLOGICAL BASES FOR ALTRUISM

All these studies have focused on determinants of aid to other people. This emphasis on benefiting others rather than oneself is what seems to most psychologists crucial in defining altruism. Altruistic behavior does not spring fully made from nowhere, absolutely uninfluenced by social pressures or thoughts of one's own benefit; if you want to define altruism that way, you've begun by defining it out of existence. But the primary intended gain should be for other people. If the doer does get anything out of it, that should be secondary, and perhaps even nonexistent or negative in his eyes at the time he aids another.

Altruistic behaviors have undergone a long series of status changes within psychology and related fields. At times altruism has been cited as an inherited characteristic of humanity, indeed as the basic evolutionary difference between man and other animals; but that now seems as hard or harder to prove than all the other assumptions about inherent human nature. The two major psychological frameworks of the last several decades, psychoanalytic theory and reinforcement learning theory, had no place for true altruism; because man works only to reduce his own drive arousal, he cannot by definition do anything mainly to benefit someone else. Even Henry Murray's need list (1938), which includes a variety of nonphysiological needs, doesn't quite manage to accommodate altruism. An approximate equivalence is found in n Nurturance, whose "desires and effects" are identified as: "To give sympathy and gratify the needs of a helpless O[ther]: an infant or any O[ther] that is weak, disabled, tired, inexperienced, infirm, defeated, humiliated, lonely, dejected, sick, mentally confused. To assist an O[ther] in danger." But all this serves mainly to satisfy one's own need to nurture, as strongly indicated by the emphasis on the inferiority of those to be helped. Nurturance is the white man's burden or the parent's obligation, rather than selflessly doing what needs to be done to help others, regardless of how it makes oneself feel. The physical relationship Murray sees as prototypical is: "To give the breast to an infant."

Altruistic behavior seems particularly resistant to being fitted into any general need schema. If you feel internally pushed to be altruistic all the time, as a person high in n Ach is pushed to achieve, you're unlikely to be much concerned with the true needs of your recipient; you may try to help old ladies across the street whether they want to cross or not. But this is not to deny the existence of altruistic behavior. It does suggest that genuine altruistic behavior is likely to occur only when an opportunity presents itself, rather than occurring because the highly altruistic person goes around making opportunities for himself to be helpful. On the other hand, it doesn't eliminate the possibility of individual variations in the level of altruistic responses. Some people avoid engaging in altruistic behavior even when the opportunity drags them by their feet. Others need only a gentle push.

Piliavin assumes that the apparently "altruistic" behaviors in his study were really mainly self-benefiting; he thinks the sight of someone in serious need of help created "an unpleasant emotional state" in his participants, which was then relieved by helping behavior. Piliavin didn't interview the participants, so he has no direct evidence that this is the case. Certainly one can deal with unpleasant emotional states in other ways besides helping. You can walk out (as some of Piliavin's participants did); you can ignore or deny the situation (as some may have); but you don't have to help (as quite a few also did). Some psychologists have postulated instead that genuine altruistic behavior is the accepted social norm when help is needed, and that help is therefore likely to be given unless other factors inhibit it, such as fear of being thought overly emotional. Darley and Latané (1970b) argue against this assumption, noting that our society actually has many diverse norms, some of which might promote altruistic behavior and some not ("Don't stick your nose in other people's business"). But it still could be that the norms supporting altruism strongly outweigh the others, at least under neutral circumstances.

Efforts have been made to elucidate these norms, partly by speculation, partly by paper and pencil tests, occasionally by experiment. Leonard Berkowitz (Berkowitz and Daniels, 1964) refers to a "norm of social responsibility," which tells us we have a social obligation to help those who need help. Ruth Leeds (1963) hypothesizes a "norm of giving," which stresses our obligation to help those who are so needy (because of age, infirmity, etc.) that they have no way of repaying us — indeed, they need help all the more because they *cannot* repay us. Both these norms, or generally accepted prescriptions for social behavior, will lead whoever internalizes them to perform helping behaviors that are unlikely to reap a reward appropriate to the amount of effort expended. Two other phenomena don't necessarily involve short-term rewards either, but do imply long-term benefit and therefore are not truly altruistic: Alvin Gouldner's "norm of reciprocity" (1960) and Melvin Lerner's "belief in a just world" (1966). The reciprocity norm tells us we should expect from others equal repayment for whatever benefits we provide them, and should feel obligated to repay them for whatever they give us. The belief in a just world is a generalization of such reasoning to the entire world or perhaps to the universe: everybody ultimately gets what he deserves in life, and whenever possible we should help the universe to ensure that people get what they deserve. If they're getting too high on the hog, we need to bring them down a peg; if they're getting short shrift, we need to give them a helping hand. There may be no possible way for us to benefit directly from our attempts to restore justice in this way, and so our behavior may look altruistic. But how are we to get our own just deserts if the universe fails to provide them for other people?

Little effort has been made to determine how extensively these various norms and beliefs are distributed through the population, in what intensities, and in what relation to actual behavior. The statement that a social norm exists is meaningless unless you know something about how it functions in the psychological processes of particular human beings. Berkowitz and Daniels (1963, 1964) have provided experimental evidence that something like the norm of social responsibility influences behavior in some instances; others have done the same for the other norms cited. But the relationships are at this point highly inferential, and as far as I know no one has attempted to order them — to show which norm is most frequently influential in behavior, which one next, and so forth.

Evidence does suggest that although certain norms may not be spontaneously engaged by occasions demanding altruistic behavior, they may become aroused if other people model the same behavior. Modeling behavior has been explored extensively in children, and occasionally in adults. James H. Bryan and Mary Ann Test (1967) found, for instance, that donations to Salvation Army kettles were increased substantially if a shill came along and tossed a nickel in the pot once a minute. Bryan and Test feel that "the bell-ringing Salvation Army worker, with kettle and self placed squarely in the pathway of the oncoming pedestrian, would seem to be reminder enough of one's obligation toward charity," and that the shill's effect is therefore more probably attributable to the arousal of shame than to the engagement of the social responsibility norm. But we may encounter so many reminders of social responsibility in a day that we screen many out in sheer self-defense; and it may really

298

take not only the kettle and the bell and the ascetic girl and the Christmas season to remind us of our duties, but also another living and breathing human being who really gives. (Jacqueline Macaulay [1970] found that donations to a bell-ringing Santa Claus were increased not only by a money-giving shill, but by a shill who blatantly refused to give money. Scrooge has long served to remind us of what Christmas behavior *shouldn't* be like.)

ALTRUISM AND EMPATHY

Living and breathing human beings may in some situations be all that's necessary to generate profound acts of altruism, with very little contribution from abstract social norms. Stanley Coopersmith (1970) has interviewed several individuals who risked their lives to save others from prison or death during the Nazi occupation of Europe, and he finds at least in their conscious thinking a definite bias against acting on the basis of general altruistic principles. They responded to immediate threats to the existence of a person well known to them; they felt that if they did not respond, a life would be lost. At the time Coopersmith interviewed them, these practical altruists expressed great enjoyment in being alive, in experiencing the pleasures of the flesh; in contrast, they had usually experienced hardship and adversity early in life. Perry London (1970), who studied another sample of rescuers, found them to share a love of adventure and some degree of "social marginality" — characteristics apparently similar to those identified by Coopersmith. Whatever the labels, this combination of alertness to life's possibilities and personal knowledge of its darker side may have contributed strongly to the empathy the rescuers felt with those they aided: they themselves could so easily have been facing the extinction of all earthly joys at the hands of the firing squad or the concentration camp commandant.

With empathy so strong, you may not need to be thinking about your social obligations or the general justice or injustice of the universe in order to feel impelled to commit an altruistic act. An imaginative intimation of the noose around your neck may be sufficient motivation to free the next person's neck. Indeed, Justin Aronfreed (1968) sees empathic responses as basic to all true instances of altruistic behavior; only then can the altruistic person be said to act mainly for the benefit of another, rather than in response to potential rewards or perceived social pressures directed toward himself. And under what circumstances does empathy develop and flourish? That could be the subject of another book. It *has* been the subject of other books, and deserves to be the subject of more, because empathy may turn out to be central not only to altruism but also to the prevention of destructive obedience, the promotion of attitude change through roleplaying, and a good deal else that's signifi-

299

cant in social psychology. Ultimately, perhaps, empathy rather than altruism may prove to be the essential characteristic that differentiates the social behavior of man from that of other animals. But that doesn't mean all humans are capable of strong empathy, or will never behave in anti-empathic ways. Proceed to the next section.

machiavelli's grandchildren: power and manipulativeness

Power certainly corrupts, but that statement is humanly incomplete. Isn't it too abstract? What should certainly be added is the specific truth that having power destroys the sanity of the powerful. It allows their irrationalities to leave the sphere of dreams and come into the real world.

— Saul Bellow
Mr. Sammler's Planet

Upon being sentenced to prison for possession of marijuana, Timothy Leary was asked by a *Rolling Stone* reporter whether he had changed his mind about hallucinogenic drugs. "Well," Leary replied, "they are sacraments given to us by God. I've always said they should not be used by everyone, maybe one person in a hundred. After all, it's a God Trip."

That Leary should cast himself as God is not surprising, since God is Love and love is affiliation and Leary is reportedly very affiliative. But perhaps the God Trip involves something more than affiliation. God is also God the Creator, and is pleased when his creations turn out well; so maybe Leary is really high on *n* Achievement after all. God also gave his only begotten son, etc.; so maybe the God Trip is essentially altruistic. Leary was certainly never reluctant to cheer up youthful lives through the blessings of psychedelia, even when he faced ten or twenty years in prison for his beneficence. Last, but hardly least, God is an omnipotent God, God the all-powerful. The First Commandment is an assertion of power, "You shall have no other god to set against me"; the next three are reminders of that power. The Christian description of heaven often includes a vision of eternal prostration before God's power, and Satan was cast down to hell because he dared compete for power. Could it be that Timothy Leary's ultimate quest is not for love but for power?

THE NEED FOR POWER

I have not given Timothy Leary a TAT and no one has content-analyzed his writings, so I won't answer that question even though his recent endorsements of political revolution make it reasonable. Power motivation is rather poorly understood anyway; in terms of empirical research, it

300

has come in a poor third to achievement and affiliation. (Certain related phenomena, such as power relationships in small groups and feelings of personal autonomy, have received considerable attention; see Minton, 1967.) One might expect more empirical research on the matter, since such diverse psychological theorists as Friedrich Nietzsche and Alfred Adler have assigned power-seeking a central role in human life. But it isn't considered polite in America to announce a concern with power, though you can freely acknowledge your affiliative and achievement orientations and can expect praise for most altruistic behavior. Power motivation is usually concealed as much as possible, and even psychologists admit its presence in their personalities as reluctantly as they might once have admitted an interest in sex.

Power-seeking has not been completely ignored by psychological researchers, however. Henry Murray employed the more polite term "n Dominance"; but under that name, power was the first need Murray discussed in detail. As n Power, it was one of the first motives studied along the lines of the McClelland model, after n Ach itself. Joseph Veroff (1957) administered the TAT cards to a group of student political candidates while they were waiting for the official vote count, and noted several ways in which their imaginative stories differed from those of other students whose power motives, if any, were presumably not so aroused. (Veroff defined power motivation as concern with "the control of the means of influencing another person.") But the possibility that student politicians may differ from their fellows on other criteria than n Power introduced a near-fatal ambiguity into Veroff's results. His scoring method for n Power was neither as often nor as productively used during the next decade as those for n Ach and n Aff.

A few interesting discoveries were made with the Veroff scoring method, however. According to McClelland's analysis of children's readers (1961a), "a combination of low n Affiliation and high n Power is very closely associated with the tendency of a nation to resort to totalitarian methods in governing its people." McClelland runs down the list of nations whose children's readers, below the international mean on n Affiliation and above the mean on n Power, anticipated dictatorships: Germany, Spain, Russia, Japan, Iraq, Pakistan, the Union of South Africa. He finds occasional exceptions, most of them reasonably explainable, one or two not (New Zealand?), and notes a somewhat different pattern in the United States: simultaneously high levels of n Power and n Affiliation. McClelland suggests that this combination doesn't lead to totalitarianism because our high n Affiliation "limits the extent to which people are willing to override the interests of particular others." But if the particular others are so black or yellow or long-haired that most people feel no desire to affiliate with them — what then, O nation of high n Power?

McClelland has also studied power motivation levels in private and

301

public executives from several countries. He finds no consistent differences in n Achievement between governmental managers and private-enterprise managers; but he does find the private ones generally much higher than the public ones in power motivation. The reasons for this are unclear. McClelland speculates that people high in n Power may find "obedience to arbitrary dictates from above (often for task-unrelated or political reasons)" personally objectionable, and thus may gravitate to private business where such arbitrary dictates are less frequent. But if most people in private business are high in n Power, such arbitrariness might well be *more* frequent. Andrews (1967), in his study of two Mexican firms whose executives differed sharply in power and achievement motivation, found the power-oriented firm to be "headed by a man who is generally very unpredictable. He runs his economic empire, playing the grand patron, rather like a feudalistic hacienda." This pattern, according to Andrews, "produces insecurity and anxiety, an atmosphere in which an executive can never be sure of what the results of his decisions or attempts at creative ventures are going to be." It is also associated with lower profits and much less business expansion than is the achievement-oriented pattern of operation in the other firm.

American businesses are not usually so clearly differentiated in need-orientation as these two Mexican firms; and since American executives tend to be high in both n Achievement and n Power, the most powerful executives' arbitrariness may often be dampened by their realistic assessments of probable success deriving from various policy decisions. But stronger power orientation is still likely to mean more abuse of power; so avoiding its abuse is unlikely to be the main reason why high n Power people go into business and lower n Power people into government bureaucracies. Maybe if we had more information about other motives, we'd find that the crucial difference lies not only in the private businessman's love of power, but in the public bureaucrat's greater orientation toward altruistic behaviors or nurturance — simply put, toward helping people rather than controlling them. Surely the motives of neither private nor public managers are pure (we have good evidence on the former from various Rockefellers, on the latter from Alexander Portnoy); but you don't need purity to get statistically significant differences.

RECENT STUDIES OF POWER NEEDS

Joseph Veroff's original study of n Power was a University of Michigan doctoral dissertation. But David McClelland's Harvard is no less concerned with power than with achievement, and so the major attempts to revise Veroff's n Power measures have been Harvard doctoral dissertations. One, by James Uleman (1966), centered on the motivations involved in winning games of chance, and in making other players lose; the findings may not be easily generalizable to broader categories of power.

The other was made by David Winter (1968), who aroused Harvard volunteers' interest in power by showing them a film of John Kennedy's presidential inauguration. Winter developed a TAT scoring method that discriminated between those so aroused and those not, and then validated the measure by comparing consistently high and low n-Power students on an almost uniquely Harvardian behavioral index: whether as freshmen having equal amounts of money, they did or did not "own or have access to such prestige possessions as the following: A television set; a refrigerator; a fully equipped bar; a car, motorcycle, or motorscooter; and wine glasses." Winter found that students high in n Power were indeed more likely to have possessed these things as freshmen. They were also more likely to have "participated in a college riot" — whether over general concerns about governmental power or over rules against having fully-equipped bars in dormitories, Winter does not say.

If we had no more information than this, Winter's scoring method for n Power could also be dismissed as too narrowly applicable. It might not even work at Yale. But Winter went ahead and administered the same measure to a group of adult, non-Harvard males. For middle-class males, somewhat similar correlations obtained: high n-Power men drank more, drove faster, read *Playboy* and similar magazines more often, and watched such vicarious displays of power motivation as *Mission Impossible* more frequently than low n Power men. They also held office in clubs more often, perhaps a direct indication of power-seeking. The Harvard high n-Power students showed a milder tendency to hold offices in student organizations; Winter suggests that on the Harvard campus, bars and cars deliver prestige more effectively. He also speculates that *either* "organized social power" *or* "vicarious expressive power through drinking and sex" may be the outcome of high power motivation; if one path is blocked, the second is taken.

Neither pattern held, however, for Winter's "working-class adults." Their n Power scores were on the average as high as those of Harvard students or middle-class males. But fewer held offices in clubs or even belonged to clubs, and their fast driving or reading sexy magazines didn't seem related to their n Power scores. Winter speculated that working class power motives might be expressed mainly through "participation in physical fights, or being a gang leader at the top of a dominance hierarchy." Perhaps he should look instead at the working-class male's behavior toward his wife and children, or at the politicians with whom he identifies, or at his treatment of individual minority group members — all the means by which authoritarians express their special concerns with power. Winter found no relationship between n Power and scores on the Authoritarian F Scale among Harvard students; but their scores on the F Scale are likely to be limited in range anyway, and probably less related to the intended content of the scale than the scores of a less sophisticated sample. Winter doesn't report giving the F Scale to his non-student volunteers, but it is known that overt authoritarianism tends to go up as socioeconomic class goes down; and maybe if you can easily exert your power over wife or kids or niggers or kikes you don't need to find another outlet.

Where does n Power come from? Winter has a few mildly suggestive data. High n-Power Harvard students reported greater admiration for father than for mother and more frequent siding with father in arguments; low-power students reported the reverse. High-power students had fewer brothers than low-power students, giving them, Winter suggests, "more exclusive possession of the young male role." But Veroff (1957) earlier had found no significant differences in total number of siblings, or in birth order, of high- and low-power subjects. Perhaps what really helps is having several sisters to boss around, thus accentuating the prerogatives of that male role. And the origins of n Power in women? The development of the women's liberation movement suggests the increasing relevance of such information; but so far as I know, no one has had the courage to collect it.

MACHIAVELLIANISM AND ATTRACTIVENESS

Of course picket lines and karate are not the only ways for women to exercise power. The phrase "womanly wiles" became a cliché for other reasons than mere alliterativeness. Nor is male power always expressed only through the channels of direct political control, vicarious identification with direct action, and petty authoritarianism. Richard Christie (Christie and Geis, 1968; Christie, 1970a) has identified a pattern of manipulative behavior that he calls "Machiavellianism," because many of the best items on the questionnaire he developed to assess predispositions toward this pattern come directly from *The Prince* or *The Discourses*. The Mach Scale includes such items as "It is wise to flatter important people" and "Never tell anyone the real reason you did something unless it is useful to do so." Machiavellianism has been found *not* to correlate with Authoritarian F Scale scores, in several different samples. Christie sees authoritarians as evaluating others in moralistic terms, on the order of, "Most people are no damn good *but they should be*" (as well as, I might add, "And I will make them good or kick them out of the human race"). Machiavellians, he says, evaluate others in opportunistic terms, e.g., "People are no damn good, why not take advantage of them?" People who score high on the Mach Scale do seem often to behave in just this way — as long as the high-scoring people are males. Females don't usually score as high as males, and their scores show little consistent relationship with manipulative behavior. A study by Jerome Singer (1964) suggests that this sex difference develops at least partly because women are able to manipulate without even trying to be Machiavellian.

304

Singer conducted his research at Penn State, my undergraduate alma mater, and I can testify personally to the truth of his main findings. Holding academic ability scores constant, Singer found that male students who scored higher in Machiavellianism were also likely to make better grades. In other words, given two male students with equal basic scholastic ability (as measured on verbal and quantitative college-entrance achievement tests), the student who took a more manipulative approach toward people was likely to do better in class. This is not to say that grades were based *only* on Machiavellianism; ability certainly contributes to college success. But Machiavellian tendencies also help, other things being equal — particularly for later-born males. Singer argues that first-born males, though they may want to be just as Machiavellian and therefore may score as high on the Mach Scale, are not as able to *act* Machiavellian, because of their now notorious tendency to be affiliative. If you depend heavily on others for approval, anxiety reduction, and so forth, you'll probably mess up many of your attempts to manipulate people; you will just not be sufficiently cutthroat. Speaking as a first-born, I'd add that first-borns may not need to be as manipulative within the family; they are older and bigger and can bull their way to their goals. Later-borns have to be devious if they're going to get anywhere. Why then should first-borns rank as high on the Mach Scale? Maybe because they learn to admire the deviousness of their younger siblings, even though they never get as much practice in deviousness themselves.

All this is characteristic of male students. Female students in Singer's sample scored as high as males on the Mach Scale, an unusual finding in itself. (Penn State, incidentally, has traditionally had a strong sorority system.) But once again the girls' Mach scores failed to correlate significantly with indices of manipulative behavior, such as getting better grades with equal abilities. Singer did find, however, that girls' grades didn't rest on their abilities alone; for first-borns, grades were positively correlated with physical attractiveness.

How did the girls use their endowments, and why only first-borns? As Singer points out, classes at Penn State often contain several hundred students, so a professor may know few if any students by name. If he picks any out on the seating chart, they'll likely be the pretty girls. He may also come to know by name a few students in the front rows, and a few who come up after class. If students have borderline grades at semester's end, the professor may be more likely to give the benefit of the doubt to anyone he remembers favorably. Singer found that the first-born girls sat in front significantly more often than later-borns and significantly more often came up after class. Furthermore, first-born girls appeared to be more aware of their own figures, insofar as they estimated their bust, waist, and hip sizes more accurately than later-borns, when warned in advance they could actually be measured after making their estimates. The first-borns also seemed more concerned about having the right kind

305

of body, in the sense that when they didn't know their estimates would be checked later, they consistently estimated their own body dimensions as closer to what they considered the ideal than did later-born girls. And the first-borns' estimates of the ideal measurements were closer to the norm for the entire group than were the later-borns' estimates, suggesting that first-borns were more sensitive to social standards concerning body size. Singer concludes that the correlation between grades and attractiveness in first-born girls doesn't happen accidentally; instead "it reflects, in part, a manipulative strategy using physique rather than Machiavellian procedures as the main tactic."

A strategy in part, yes. Any college professor sees his share of girls using physical attraction strategically, sometimes in as unsubtly Machiavellian a fashion as possible. But I suspect that part of the effect is still unintentional. First-born girls should tend to sit closer to the instructor and to try talking with him individually more often, not because they're being manipulative but because they're generally more affiliative and are in an anxiety-arousing situation, the classroom. They should also try to be physically attractive because in our culture that's one major way in which girls are supposed to promote affiliation. If they're close and attractive, and the professor gives them a better grade as a result, should they protest their unfair treatment?

MACHIAVELLIAN CHARACTERISTICS

The manipulative strategies used by male Machiavellians (and some females) seem to be as various as those suggested by Machiavelli himself — maybe even more so, because people have had plenty of time to develop new con games during the past four hundred and fifty years. The strategies are by no means unique to Machiavellians; other people lie and cheat and bluff and try to distract their opponents too. But Machiavellians usually do such things more effectively. They can't bluff or distract inanimate nature, so their talents don't work on anything but people; and they can't do much when rules and regulations are as rigid as inanimate nature (Geis and Christie, 1970). But give them a face-to-face situation where they have room to improvise appropriate manipulative strategies, and they're likely to take as much advantage of it as possible. The main characteristic that allows them to do so, according to Christie and Geis (1970), is their ability to avoid emotional involvements that distract them from the goal at hand. People low in Machiavellianism tend to get hung up on the ideological overtones or moral issues involved, or on the personalities of their opponents. The Machiavellians meanwhile are responding to those elements of the situation that will produce the result they desire, regardless of ethical or sentimental considerations; and so, at least in the short run, they get what they want.

What sorts of people are likely to be more Machiavellian? I've already mentioned that men typically score higher on the Mach Scale than women; this may come partly from our culture's emphasis on greater emotionality in women. Younger adults tend to be more Machiavellian than older ones, people involved in professional and service roles more so than those in business or assembly-line jobs, psychiatrists more than surgeons. Christie and Geis (1968) argue that such varying results as these may all come from the same source: jobs that involve handling people rather than things are likely to place a premium on the ability to manipulate people, whether that ability be present initially or developed on the job; and many more people maturing in postwar America have entered or have been trained for service occupations, which involve handling people. Increasing urbanism or cosmopolitanism also seems to have something to do with the greater Machiavellianism of the young (Christie, 1970b), but the reasons for this relationship aren't entirely clear. Singer (1964) found a sample of college professors at Penn State to be even more Machiavellian than their students. This could indicate that the students haven't yet completely learned the lessons necessary for survival in a service-oriented society, or it may only mean that college professors have to be pretty devious in order ever to get students to learn anything. Christie and Geis (1968) report that graduate social psychology students are more Machiavellian than any other segment of the population ever tested. As a social psychologist specializing in attitude-change research, I can confidently say that social psychologists score high on the Mach Scale only because their great knowledge of human behavior leads them to agree with Machiavelli's realistic evaluations, *not* because social psychologists want to manipulate anyone themselves. Perish the thought.

The term "Machiavellianism" probably has negative overtones for most people. But according to Geis and Christie (1970), "In no instance that we can recall have high Machs appeared behaviorally hostile, vicious, or punitive toward others." Furthermore, Christie and Geis (1970) suggest that high Machs could be of great value to others in certain situations — for instance, when an organization needs someone to bargain aggressively with outside agencies for its welfare or even its survival. Indeed, Machiavelli himself appears to have fulfilled just such a role in the Florentine Republic.

THE TROUBLE WITH n POWER

Whether the Machiavellianism of organizational representatives bodes well for the larger society, or whether a society's Machiavellian ambassadors are likely to serve the cause of international amity, is a different matter. Christie and Geis note that when the highly Machiavellian administrator tries to manipulate his subordinates, he may create "disaffection and problems of morale which can cripple the organization"; and I think such an analysis could be extended to other situations. The Machiavellian may often be working for worthy goals; but when his own unemotionality leads him to misjudge the emotional reactions of others, or when he begins to take more delight in his manipulations than in his goals, the outcome is likely to be trouble. This is likely to be still more true for the person high in n Power, a quality that may be related to Machiavellianism in some ways but that doesn't necessarily involve any talent for attaining interpersonal goals. The very definition of n Power (e.g., by Veroff, 1957) focuses on satisfactions derived from exercising power, not from what power accomplishes.

Attempts to satisfy n Achievement can generate valuable benefits for society as well as for the individual, as long as financial gain is not the sole measure of goal attainment. We can use well-built buildings, well-run transportation systems, carefully constructed printing presses. Society often benefits along with the individual in attempts to satisfy n Affiliation: love and friendship and good-neighborliness make the world a happier place and a less brutal one. Altruistic acts benefit society even more than they benefit the individual who commits them, by their very nature. But I cannot see what society has to gain from the getting or exercising of power for its own sake. Influencing others in the service of n Ach, even if it is done in Machiavellian fashion, may lead to useful outcomes; influencing others mainly in the service of n Power will, as with Christie's Machiavellian administrators or as in the autocratic Mexican firm, very likely lead to disharmony and inefficiency. Businessmen and government officials and university professors do need to exercise power at times, but if they begin to enjoy the exercise for itself, they begin to fail at their proper jobs.

David McClelland (1961a) has raised the question of whether a certain amount of n Power might be a prerequisite for successful entrepreneurship; he feels the evidence is inconclusive. But interestingly enough, Robert Townsend (1970), an extremely successful businessman, insists that to be successful, businessmen must ruthlessly cut out power-for-power's-sake practices and instead emphasize rewards for achievement. Without mentioning David McClelland, Townsend warns:

> Since the leader must lead the battle against institutionalization, it's to the leader that you should look for early signs of losing the war. Is he getting confused about who's God? Polishing up the image instead of greasing the wheels? Short-tempered before honest criticism? Are people hesitating before they tell him?

Townsend suggests firing or retiring any executive who shows these symptoms of the power bug. He's talking about private business, but government could surely benefit likewise.

I think my drunken acquaintance had the wrong enemy in mind when

308

he threatened to destroy his *n* Achievement research. The disaffected young have the wrong enemies in mind when they urge rejection or destruction of our achievement-oriented society, including the achievement-oriented university. Motivations toward achievement and toward power do often seem intermingled in our society; our public and private executives, from presidents on down, often seek public acceptance by presenting their power plays as noble achievements. But the two motives are distinguishable, and they produce different effects. Achievement motivation's effects are potentially constructive, but power motivation tends strongly, as Lord Acton recognized, toward corruption and worse. If *n* Achievement researchers have erred in their approach, it is less in studying achievement than in failing to spend more time studying *n* Power. Achievement motivation needs a little extra guidance; power motivation needs to be erased from the human psyche. In a world of power politics, power-seeking may sometimes serve achievement goals (as Donley and Winter's study of American Presidents [1970] indicates); but it remains an insidious diversion from the work at hand. The power need does not build; it dominates. Its epitome is not the private business but the thermonuclear bomb. If we fail to eliminate it — whether through those always attractive, always uncertain childraising changes of which psychologists often speak, or through the no less difficult alteration of adult motivational patterns — *n* Power may finally eliminate itself, by eliminating the species in whom it dwells. Because we are mortal, the God Trip is not for us.

8

the uses of adversity

experiments in anxiety: behavior under stress

I like a look of Agony,
Because I know it's true —
Men do not sham Convulsion,
Nor simulate a Throe.
— Emily Dickinson
The Complete Poems of
Emily Dickinson

Fear has lately come into considerable disrepute. Our schools and colleges must eliminate not only grades but all appraisals of performance, we are told, because comprehension and apprehension are mutually exclusive. Professional patients by the thousands welcome the Esalen Institute and its imitators, because their previous psychotherapists insisted on raking over unpleasant memories instead of celebrating the joy of life. Young revolutionaries threaten violent confrontations unless anxieties of every sort are immediately expunged from human society. Fear, they argue, is only a contaminant of human behavior, invalidating any social institution or system that makes use of it.

Neurotic anxiety, fear without an immediate objective source, must seem particularly useless and reprehensible from this viewpoint; and so Sigmund Freud (1895; English translation, 1962c) originally considered it. He saw neurotic anxiety as merely a converted form of sexual libido that has too long been blocked from expression, much as overaged wine turns to vinegar. If the libido were to be given its freedom, then, neurotic anxiety would disappear. But as Freud continued his research he found increasing evidence against this hypothesis. In 1926 (English translation,

310

1959), he concluded that neurotic anxiety is not soured libido at all, but serves essentially the same purpose as objective anxiety (the fear of real external threats). Anxiety, Freud now felt, is a signal from the individual's ego to his own psyche — a signal that an external danger is near, or that the id is insisting on demands which will get the entire personality in serious trouble, or that the person is about to do something which will outrage his superego. Objective anxiety, neurotic anxiety, moral anxiety: all serve as advance warnings of trouble, sufficiently bothersome in themselves to force the personality to head off the trouble before it arrives. If anxiety never occurred, life might feel more pleasant for a time; but in short order the individual would find himself in the middle of objective and psychological disasters so vast that his previous anxieties would seem a blessing by contrast.

So Freud concluded that anxiety is useful. That shouldn't be surprising, when you consider anxiety's prominent role in the development of the human race. Only within our lifetimes has mankind been affluent enough in substantial areas of the world even to think seriously of abandoning negative (mainly fear-arousing) incentives, and of relying only on positive motives to get the necessary work of the race performed. Nor has affluence changed the picture that much. Men still find short-range benefits, including the fleeting luxury of sheer laziness, to be powerful incentives for doing nothing. If fear were not there to get them moving, to energize and guide their unpleasant choices and painful efforts to save themselves, soon no one would be left to insist that love and kindness are always more effective. Even social psychologists would find it hard to stick to their jobs very long for the shake of sheer intellectual delight; they too need the motivations of economic worry, of nagging concern about the fate of a psychologically naive, but technologically sophisticated human race. As long as man lives in a real, unperfected world with other real, unperfected human beings, fear will play a valuable role.

Nevertheless, fear is not useful in all degrees or in all situations. At the highest levels, it can be physically incapacitating, disruptive of rational planning and behavior, destructive of social relationships. As a vital component of human life, fear has often commanded the attention of social psychologists, but they have wisely withheld either blanket endorsement or blanket condemnation of its role. Instead, they have attempted to determine its specific effects at varying levels and in various circumstances. When does fear generate appropriate thought and action, and when is fear itself something to fear?

Fear is fairly easy to produce in the laboratory — much easier to produce than joy, for instance. That may in itself indicate the relative importance of fear in human life and the need to study it. But fear's ease of production hardly solves all the problems of the research psychologist. Neal Miller (1959), for instance, has noted the difficulty of "devising situations that would really frighten eager young aviation cadets without terrifying generals and congressmen." Even if you can sufficiently calm the generals and congressmen to elicit their financial support, you may find an insurmountable barrier in your own conscience. The issues resemble those in Stanley Milgram's obedience research: you can't ethically study fear reactions by exposing participants to real danger; if you simulate a dangerous situation, you can't tell the participant it's only simulated, or he won't give you real fear responses in return; but how far are you justified as a research psychologist in subjecting people to distressing experiences without their fully informed consent?

Such a question must again be answered, I think, not in terms of absolutes but in terms of how distressing the experience is in relation to how generally beneficial the research is likely to be. When you are trying intentionally to generate high levels of fear, however, you may not be able to judge the full extent of distress until it is too late; and the benefits of your research may be ignored if too many fears are aroused beyond the circle of your participants. Both the possibilities and the problems inherent in systematic research on fear are illustrated in two studies that reached the limits of artificially induced anxiety.

SIMULATIONS OF DANGER

The first study was conducted by a research group from George Washington University. The group, usually called HumRRO (short for Human Resources Research Office), was established by contract with the U.S. Army, mainly for purposes of Army research. A HumRRO project headed by Mitchell M. Berkun (Berkun et al., 1962) was designed to study the injurious effects of psychological stress during battle, and to recommend to the Army ways of reducing such effects in its fighting men. The HumRRO psychologists perhaps could have marched into battle themselves with a well-chosen array of psychological tests; but such a procedure would have been beyond the call of duty for civilian researchers, and anyway it might have been difficult for the researchers to carry out their assessment techniques while they were under the stress of battle. As should be clear by now, psychologists are not immune to the phenomena they wish to study, any more than physicians are protected from disease. So the HumRRO team decided instead to set up several highly realistic simulations that would subject research participants to great stress without doing likewise to the psychologists.

The involuntary subjects were new Army recruits who had not yet started basic training. They were distributed singly to isolated outposts in a "large, desolate mountain area, undeveloped, dry, and rugged," designated as a military reservation. The recruits were told they were partic-

312

ipating in a test of "new concepts of atomic-age warfare" through "extremely wide dispersal" of untrained troops in a battle area. The experimenters mentioned that other units were testing live radioactive weapons and conventional artillery on the same reservation, and that a forest fire danger existed as well. These warnings set the recruits up to perceive the subsequent simulation as real.

Each man was left alone at his outpost, with supplies and a two-way "radio" that was secretly wired to the experimenters' command post. Occasional innocuous messages came in over the radio headset for about half an hour. Then the messages changed to warnings of danger. In one experimental condition, the reported danger was a forest fire in the recruit's immediate vicinity; to support this message, a smoke machine three hundred yards away started blowing smoke toward him. In a second condition, "an accident with radioactive material" was reported to have created dangerous fallout over the recruit's outpost area, and the needle on his radiation dosimeter began to swing as the report came in. In a third condition, the radio announced that live artillery shells were falling outside the official target area; a series of explosions, coming closer and closer to the recruit, showed him the unofficial target they were likely to hit soon. In each condition, the recruit was told over his headset that he would be rescued immediately by helicopter if he would transmit his location. But when he tried to do so, he discovered that the transmitter part of his radio had failed. After he had endured the emergency situation for twenty minutes without being able to send out a message, Command Post urged him to repair his radio immediately, and began giving him repair instructions. But he found that no matter what he did to the radio, it still wouldn't work. After another twenty-five minutes, an experimenter arrived and shoved a psychological mood questionnaire into his hands.

A series of control subjects were run in the same general area, but the only "emergency" they encountered was that their transmitter stopped working and they were told that no more food and water could be delivered to them until it was fixed. Because they had eaten and drunk their fill before the exercise began, they were not faced with any immediate crises, but did have some motivation to fix the radio, so their behavior could be compared with that of the soldiers motivated by fear of injury or death.

The radio repair job involved a series of distinct tasks: a wiring procedure that incorporated a standard mechanical ability test; an "exciter rejection" button that the soldier was told to push every time an "exciter indicator" light came on, thus giving the experimenters several measures of reaction time; and so on. Speed of correct performance of each task was recorded, unknown to the soldier; all his comments were also recorded, and his general behavior patterns were observed inter-

313

mittently from a circling helicopter, presumably searching for him in order to "rescue" him. Urine and blood samples were collected from each recruit immediately after the experimenter drove him back to the command post. Thus participants in each condition could be compared on several different measures of performance, physiological reactions to stress, and psychological indicators.

On physiological and psychological measures, participants in all three experimental conditions showed greater evidence of stress or anxiety than the control subjects; the threatening situations were experienced as genuine. Performance measures were another matter — not only performance in repairing the radio, but overall. Only the soldiers who thought they were being bombarded with artillery shells performed significantly worse on radio repair than the controls, mainly because a third of them ran away from their outposts instead of fiddling with the radio. Less than a sixth of the forest-fire subjects and less than an eighth of the radiation-accident subjects ran away. It's difficult to tell whether these differences came from greater fear in the artillery situation; the authors point out that running away was a more obvious means of escape in that situation than the others, because the shells were clearly coming from only one direction, whereas the radiation had presumably covered a general area and the location of the forest fire was somewhat ambiguous. Most forest fire subjects spent part of their time trying to locate the flames visually, and felt no need to run until the fire itself was close enough to be seen. Most radiation-accident subjects apparently assumed they'd already been exposed to the radiation and therefore might just as well sit where they were until they could be carried out for treatment. They showed little realization that longer exposure to radiation would have more serious effects; they just wanted to be damned sure the helicopter could find them so they could get to the hospital.

This set of simulations produced various interesting physiological data but not much useful behavioral data, with one minor and perhaps one major exception. The minor one was just mentioned: the evidence for passive responses to radiation hazards. This evidence suggests that civil defense education might stress appropriate responses to radiation exposure considerably more than it has. These soldiers hadn't undergone any Army training on radiation hazards, but they presumably had been exposed to the ordinary dosage of civil defense information encountered by the general populace; and this produced highly inappropriate responses. The possibly major behavioral observation involves indications that the radio repair task was frequently worked into a pattern of psychological defenses against anxiety, particularly in the artillery condition. This phenomenon was even more clearly observed in a final experiment, which simulated circumstances where the participant was not

314

threatened with physical damage himself but where he appeared to be responsible for serious injury to another person.

GUILT BY SIMULATION

The location was the same as in the previous experiments. Each recruit was left in an isolated bunker, where he was told he would assist in "a tactical training problem" by setting up a remote-control circuit for a demolitions training course in the canyon below. He had an intercom "squawkbox," but no other means of communicating either with the men setting up explosives in the canyon or with headquarters. When he finished wiring the remote control circuit as instructed, he was to throw a switch that would open the circuit for use. When he threw the switch, a large explosion resounded in the canyon, followed by a voice on the intercom: "Upstairs, can you hear me? Listen, if you can hear me, wait right there and don't touch anything. Listen, are you sure you did that wiring right?" This was followed by instructions to contact headquarters to get help for the injured man, who was said to be "hurt bad." At this point the soldier found that his transmitter was dead.

The intercom was still receiving, however. After five minutes, the intercom voice told him his messages weren't getting through and that he should try to repair the transmitter, since the survivors were having a hard time keeping the injured man alive. While the soldier was working away, occasional messages came in: more statements of urgency; mention that the Military Police would want to question him; finally, a statement that someone was coming to his bunker to do the questioning. Shortly, the experimenter arrived with a mood questionnaire, a Digit Backward Memory Span test, and the news that the whole situation was part of an experiment.

Control subjects were run without a simulated explosion but with instructions to repair the inoperative transmitter for innocuous purposes. The experimental subjects were this time significantly different from the controls on just about every physiological, psychological, and performance measure used. In fact, they reported significantly more anxiety on the mood questionnaire and were significantly worse on the performance measures than in any other condition in the entire series of studies. This doesn't necessarily mean that people feel more concern over injury to others than injury to themselves. In the other conditions, the possibility that the soldier could escape or be rescued without a scratch always existed, whereas in the final "demolition" condition the harm was already done — the soldier had hurt someone else seriously and he could expect to be punished for it as soon as a court martial could be arranged. So he quite properly felt more scared.

With little possibility of realistic escape in this situation, participants

315

resorted to an impressive array of psychological defenses. Maneuvers designed to deny responsibility, to allay personal feelings of guilt over misdeeds, are surely among the most common defenses (or "dissonance" reducers), beginning almost at the time a child learns to say no. The thoughts reported afterward by the "guilty" soldiers compose a familiar litany: "I did just as he told me"; "It wasn't *my* explosion"; "I thought it was just another of the explosions I'd been hearing"; "It's all a joke," "a dream." It was the victim's fault for messing with that TNT; it was all a coincidence; they must be talking to somebody else on the intercom, not me, not me. "They couldn't hold me responsible when I knew nothing about it" — nothing about electrical wiring, about explosives, about the Army, about anything.

DEFENSIVE TASK ORIENTATION

The trouble with all these rationalizations and denials and projections was that they didn't work. The voice on the intercom kept describing the seriousness of the injury, kept speaking right at the soldier in the bunker, kept telling him about those MP's who wanted to talk to him, kept demanding that he fix his transmitter so he could get through to a hospital. The participants' anxiety apparently continued to mount; and at this point many of them did what the artillery subjects in the previous experiment frequently did, and what some of Stanley Milgram's obedience subjects did. They began using their assigned task (which might normally be a rational response to a developing problem) as a defensive maneuver, to supplement and strengthen their other, solely internal defenses.

At times the soldier's concentration on the radio repair job helped his defenses by blocking out all other thoughts, particularly troublesome ones: "After a while, I almost forgot about it [the explosion and the injured man], I was so busy with the phone." (Recall the participant in Milgram's experiment who said it was easy "to forget that there's a guy out there [getting shocked]. For a long time I just concentrated on pressing switches and reading the words.") At other times, soldiers reported feeling that effective performance on the repair job would expiate their guilt: "It all bothered me less as time went on because I was trying as hard as I could." Or in other words, if I'm a good boy now, that shows I didn't really mean to do something bad before and maybe they'll go easy on me later.

Not every soldier reacted to the task in this way. Some found their anxiety increasing further as the repair job went on, partly because they found they couldn't do it and perhaps partly because the seriousness of their situation was still sinking in. But the opportunity to do something, anything, in an anxiety-arousing situation seems to have anxiety-reducing properties of its own, either because it interferes with other internal processes that maintain anxiety, or because we have learned in earlier situations that doing something — fight or flight or whatever — is more likely to save us from danger than doing nothing. Freud himself hypothesized that following the occurrence of anxiety as a signal of danger, the natural response is an effort to fend off the danger it signals, either realistically or through psychological defenses. Once you're doing something, you don't need the signal any more — unless whatever you're doing turns out to be worthless. For some kinds of danger, you may not discover that your actions are worthless for quite a while.

With their observations of work as a psychological defense, Berkun and his HumRRO associates were getting into reaction patterns that may have important social implications. Submerging oneself completely in busywork (or even in the demands of a creative job) is a frequent response to world tensions, to national political problems, to such menaces as environmental pollution and overpopulation. At times the work may make useful contributions to personal survival and, in a limited way, to the betterment of the human condition; it may be motivated in part by other factors too, such as abstract intellectual curiosity. But it's easy to use cultivation of your own garden as an excuse to avoid coping with the greater anxieties of the world situation. It may be even easier for some people to avoid such anxiety by working in a carefully altruistic but ineffectual way: "Look, World, I'm doing all I can — I'm giving my life so that others may know just a little more about the scent glands of the blue-eyed dragonfly. You wouldn't hit a guy who's already given up everything for humanity, would you?"

Learning how to overcome such responses would be more than make-work, much more than a defensive use of task orientations. We can't afford the waste of human effort that defensive task orientation involves, even if the man behaving this way can point to occasional accomplishments derived from his defensive activities. But when the first reports of the HumRRO research began to circulate, the criticisms started: no informed consent, too much stress, no real benefit to mankind, and so on. The American Psychological Association's Ethics Committee investigated and exonerated the researchers, partly because the recruits' superior officers had been fully informed of the experimental procedures and had judged the risks as acceptable, and partly because the researchers conducted post-experimental debriefing and clinical support sessions which apparently were effective in eliminating any lingering anxiety or guilt feelings in the soldiers. But by the time the investigation was concluded, the researchers' own morale had sunk very low and additional funds were hard to come by; so the research ended. It really does seem hard to scare "eager young aviation cadets" or Army recruits without also (rightly or wrongly) "terrifying generals and congressmen," or other psychologists, or newspaper readers.

Research on battle stress was not altogether ended with the closing of the HumRRO project, however. Generals and congressmen seldom object to the terrors of real war; and Vietnam has supplied a number of research opportunities. In one set of studies, Peter G. Bourne (1970) assessed anxiety levels in helicopter ambulance crews and Green Beret teams through both physiological and psychological techniques. These men kept anxiety at relatively low levels under combat conditions, using an assortment of psychological defenses that again prominently included task concentration. For example one crewman, "while flying out to a battle area to pick up casualties . . . would mentally review in minute detail every single action he would perform from the moment the helicopter touched the ground. In some ways it was as though he had taken the old Army adage that if you do your job right you will stay out of trouble, and extended it to cover even the intransigence of combat." Bourne adds no novel insights to the genesis or functions of this type of defense; but with the easy availability of foreign wars and the prospects of social strife at home, we may not need to simulate battle conditions in order to give it ample additional study.

TRAUMATIC CONDITIONING OF HUMANS

An experiment that allowed its subjects no opportunity to combat fear by task performance was conducted by Dugal Campbell, R. E. Sanderson, and S. G. Laverty (1964). They began their research by reviewing various experiments in which animals have been exposed simultaneously to a powerful electric shock and to a neutral stimulus such as a bell tone. Following these traumatic versions of Pavlovian conditioning, the animals usually show strong fear reactions whenever the bell tone recurs. The fear reactions are extremely long-lasting, even though the electric shock may never be paired with the bell tone again. Such data on animals have been used by analogy to explain the origins of human neurotic anxieties, but as Campbell notes, the analogy is not very precise. For one thing, the traumatized animals' anxiety reactions are usually elicited by a much more limited range of stimuli than are those of most neurotic humans. More significantly, the persistence of the animals' anxiety reactions depends upon being able to avoid the conditioned stimulus altogether or to escape from situations in which the stimulus occurs, whereas the anxiety reactions of neurotic humans continue to occur over time even though the stimuli that provoke them, particularly internal stimuli such as memories, may be inescapable. Finally, the experiences used to generate traumatically conditioned anxiety in animals usually involve great physical pain, whereas in humans physical pain appears to be present in only a small percentage of the traumatic experiences that underlie neurotic anxiety. Because the animal data had such drawbacks, Campbell and his colleagues felt that a better understanding of neurotic processes might

318

come from collecting controlled data on the development and resolution of traumatically conditioned anxiety in humans.

To obtain such data, they injected a drug known as Scoline into adult males undergoing hospital treatment for prolonged alcoholism. The alcoholics volunteered for the experiment with the understanding that it might lead to "a possible therapy for alcoholism." Scoline induces total paralysis of the skeletal musculature, including the muscles used for breathing; it is used in electroshock therapy to prevent convulsions and in abdominal operations to block interfering muscular reactions. In both these instances it is used along with a general anesthetic because it has no anesthetic properties itself; so the patient is usually out cold when Scoline takes effect. In the Campbell study, Scoline was administered while the volunteer was fully awake, lying on a hospital stretcher and listening to occasional beeps on a set of headphones. The volunteer was told in advance what the effects of Scoline might be, but he was not told exactly when it would be administered, and because it was given as part of a continuous series of intravenous injections he did not know when it actually came. His breathing abruptly stopped; he started to struggle, and found that he was totally paralyzed; the paralysis continued for about two minutes, as the earphones beeped away. (Several control subjects were given Scoline but no beeps.) Following recovery, each volunteer was interviewed on his reactions; virtually every participant said he had thought he was dying. In the words of the researchers, "the suspension of breathing was an experience that was horrific to a degree."

Before, during, and after the experience, measures were taken of such anxiety indicators as heart rate and galvanic skin response, each of which showed sharp changes. Similar measures were used as indicators of the conditioned anxiety response in later anxiety extinction trials, repetitions of the general situation in which the beep was played without administration of Scoline. Virtually every time there was a beep in these later trials, anxiety indicators would jump sharply. The conditioned anxiety response did not lessen during thirty extinction trials one day after the traumatic experience; it did not lessen during thirty more extinction trials a week later, or during forty more three weeks later. In fact, on several measures anxiety increased in intensity over time. The researchers were able to achieve temporary suppressions of the conditioned response by such procedures as playing the beep twenty times in quick succession. But after a one-minute pause the anxiety response returned at full strength. Nor was it elicited only by the beep. One subject, for instance, reported that "Whenever he entered the part of the building where he had been conditioned he took several deep breaths to reassure himself."

The experimenters in this case appear to have succeeded too well in inducing traumatic anxiety. Once they had conditioned anxiety to the beep, they couldn't make it go away. Perhaps if the subjects avoided beeps and the experimental building forever after, they might show no ill effects of their experience. On the other hand, they had undergone an experience that they saw at the time as bringing them close unto death, and this might have had effects of its own, independent of beeps. Maybe in some cases it gave them a deeper appreciation of life, as I've heard reported by some students who've experienced a bad acid trip. Maybe in other cases it added to their psychological burdens and drove them further into drink, as with other acid-tripping students whose bad trips drive them deeper into drugs. In a subsequent study (Madill et al., 1966) where the conditioned stimulus was a glass of beer or whiskey instead of a beep, a group of alcoholics did on the average reduce their total alcohol intake after the Scoline experience. But some were so scared by it that they took to drinking even more — in several cases turning to vodka because it didn't smell or taste like the beer to which their anxiety reactions had been conditioned.

The Scoline experiments did not involve social behavior directly, but the persistence of the conditioned anxiety responses they induced do appear to have analogs in social situations. Psychoanalysts have long assumed that childhood traumas can induce anxieties which persist into adulthood and which force the adult to seek surcease, if not in drink, then in religious or political outlets. The Scoline experience was similar, for instance, to the perception that psychoanalysts attribute to the child threatened explicitly or implicitly by his parents: grave danger to one's existence occurring when one is totally unable to take any protective measures. The child's pattern of psychological reactions to the danger may then recur every time he feels even mildly threatened by authority: extreme anxiety, followed by anger at his threateners, followed by repression both of his anxiety and of the anger that might elicit even greater threats, followed by identification with the source of danger and displacement of the hostility elsewhere. The Scoline experience was brief and not repeated, and once the volunteer recovered he found that the experimenters quite clearly were not interested in destroying him; so extensive defensive maneuvers of the kind that may seriously affect social behavior were unnecessary. But several volunteers did get so mad over the experience that they tried to frustrate their tormenters by increasing their alcoholic intake. Anxiety can be useful, but at its highest levels it may be hard to channel in the right direction.

What channels does fear follow in more social situations than a lonely army outpost or the depths of apneic paralysis? Does it help or hinder the social influence process, the relationship between doctor and patient, the binding together of a community's wounds after mass disaster? Do circumstances exist outside the laboratory in which anxiety is so traumatic that it ruins the individual's social life forever? Careful and complete answers to such questions have so far been blocked by the moral and procedural difficulties of research on human stress reactions. But a few social scientists have attempted to cope with the difficulties, rather than withdrawing into the scientific defensiveness of denying that the questions are important.

dental denial: fear and attitude change

An atmosphere of terror hardly encourages reflection.
— Albert Camus
"Neither Victims nor Executioners"

Words can create their own terror. Ministers of the gospel have long been expert at verbal terrorism: we are all despicable sinners, all condemned to the everlasting fires of hell, and likely to be struck down by God's wrath at any moment. One of childhood's tenderest prayers contains the astonishing line, "And if I die before I wake" — surely composed by some fiend who wished to invest not only the days but the nights of innocent children with panic. At times the Christian God may be a God of Love, but a majority of Sundays between my sixth and sixteenth birthdays were garnished with threats of eternal torture.

Priests and preachers and Sunday school teachers do not usually arouse such terrors out of pure sadism, of course. They are doing it for the good of people's souls. The good is expected to come partly from fear's purgative qualities, partly from its educational efficacy, but mainly from the likelihood of conversion. A sinner sufficiently frightened is a sinner won to faith in God. If heaven's golden streets fail to lure him, maybe the temperature of hell will scare him there. And lest he forget, the message must be repeated frequently: Mend your ways, amend your dangerous thoughts, or you will be cast into the pit like a dog.

Here we are back, for the moment, to the problem of attitude change — in this case attitudes changed not to attain consistency or positive incentives, but to avoid disaster. Preachers have not been alone in using fear to induce conversion; it would be hard to find any sort of professional or amateur attitude changer whose resources do not include fear. Some may be more inclined than others to use positive appeals — consumer-product advertisers, for example. But even they use fear so frequently that attempts to frighten the nation for the sake of a small increase in mouthwash sales seem an unexceptionable part of commerce.

Several political and racial groups have argued recently that because the nation has not responded to other kinds of attitude change appeals, they must turn to a campaign of fear. But they may have been deceived by the presumed success of mouthwash commercials. I suggested in Chapter Five that extreme demands may soften up an audience for more

321

moderate demands. Extreme fears may instead freeze the audience's attitudes solid. Our intellectual assessment of the distance of other political positions from our own may be quite a different thing than our response to sudden threats against our own being. Whites may be more willing to recognize Negroes as equals in certain regards following riots and massive demonstrations in other cities, but that doesn't necessarily mean the best way to get equal rights in a particular city is to threaten immediate destruction of the city's houses and businesses. Maybe that *is* the best way, speaking pragmatically rather than ethically; but even the pure pragmatist might do well to consider certain research data before he acts.

No social psychologist, as far as I know, has tried experimentally to influence public opinion on civil rights issues by using fear. Any temptation to do so would probably be quelled by the psychologist's own fear of public outcries or research grant cancellations. But the use of fear to induce attitude change *has* tempted public health experts, who are similarly faced with the public's impassivity toward conditions potentially damaging to many citizens. Will more people be impelled to stop smoking by a hard-sell description of tobacco's disastrous effects on the lungs, or by a soft-sell cartoon commercial? Will more people get a yearly checkup if they are threatened with sudden death, or if they are told only that good health comes easiest through preventive medicine? Research on changing public health attitudes is obviously praiseworthy, deserving of research grants and kind words from university trustees. So the psychologists who have done research on fear-induced attitude change have almost unanimously focused on health topics.

TOOTHBRUSHING AND FEAR AROUSAL

The seminal experiment dealt not with such dramatic issues as cancer prevention or heart disease, but with plain old ordinary toothbrushing. Irving Janis and Seymour Feshbach (1953) delivered three versions of an illustrated lecture on dental hygiene to three groups of freshmen at a Connecticut high school, and measured their attitudes before and after. Each lecture presented essentially the same factual information about how tooth decay develops and what should be done about it; but there were differences. The "low-fear" speech didn't say much about why tooth decay is a bad thing, and the slides accompanying it were innocuous: photographs of healthy teeth, X-rays and diagrams of cavities. The "moderate-fear" speech mentioned some dangers of decay, but in an impersonal and objective tone; the slides were photographs of modest oral problems. The "high-fear" speech was a dental nightmare: spectacular slides of tooth decay and mouth infections; frequent references to tooth-pulling, drilling out cavities, toothache pain; and such discomfiting statements as, "If you ever develop an infection of this kind from improper care of your teeth, it will be an extremely serious matter be-

322

cause these infections are really dangerous. They can spread to your eyes, or your heart, or your joints, and cause secondary infections which may lead to diseases such as arthritic paralysis, kidney damage, or total blindness."

Guess which group felt most worried about their teeth immediately after the speech? The high-fear group, naturally. And who reported the greatest acceptance of the experimenters' recommendations a week later? Not the high-fear group, but the low-fear group. Everybody, whether high, medium, or low, seemed to learn pretty much the same things from the speeches about the causes of cavities, the best type of toothbrush to use and how to use it. But at week's end, the high-fear students showed virtually no change in their tooth care habits. The low-fear students had changed significantly in the directions advocated; the moderate-fear students were somewhere in between.

Why did increasing the fear level reduce attitude and behavior change? You might think fear arousal would heighten motives to accept anything that promises to lessen the fear. You might think more fear arousal would raise the motivation higher, and that subsequent attitude change would increase likewise. But we've run into cases before where manipulations aimed at increasing motivational levels actually cut the amount of attitude change, by increasing various kinds of interference at the same time — the Twenty Dollar Misunderstanding being our major case. In Jani; and Feshbach's study, a little fear did seem to be a useful motivation. But a lot of fear may have gotten the students so upset that they just wanted to stop thinking about the whole thing — speech, slides, recommendations, and all. They might find it hard to ignore the speech while they were still in the experimental room, so they were able to answer questions about the speech correctly. But once outside, they could resort to the whole armamentarium of psychological defenses to reduce their truly painful anxiety: denial that such disasters could ever happen to them; rejection of the experimenters as lacking in expertise; misinterpretation of their own dental practices as being sufficient to forestall any danger; rapid forgetting of the recommendations; and so on. Janis and Feshbach suggest that such defensiveness might have been particularly likely in their study, because their recommendations on dental hygiene could easily seem inadequate to deal with the suggested dangers. Honestly, now, will using three rows of bristles instead of two really ward off blindness and arthritic paralysis?

FEAR APPEALS AND DEFENSIVE AVOIDANCE

Whereas low fear might promote attitude change, then, high fear might induce only a defensive avoidance of the whole tooth-care question. A reasonable explanation for Janis and Feshbach's results, perhaps; but they had little direct evidence that defensiveness was involved. The high-fear students did complain a lot more about the unpleasantness of the speech; but then, they had a lot more to complain about. Now, how can defensive avoidance be more directly measured — if it's really there? Several years later, Janis and Robert Terwilliger (1962) developed such a measure. This time they tried to convince adult volunteers of the dangers of smoking, by giving them a high-fear or a low-fear pamphlet to read. The low-fear pamphlet contained fifteen paragraphs gently noting that cigaret smoking may cause lung cancer, "a highly malignant disease which is extremely difficult to diagnose before it is too late for effective treatment." The high-fear pamphlet contained those fifteen paragraphs and seven more, on the order of: "Lung cancer necessitates drastic surgery. In only one out of three victims brought to the hospital will the cancer be localized sufficiently so that the cancerous lung can be removed. Of these, 85% will be dead within 5 years, most of them within 2."

The high-fear message was again less effective than the low-fear in changing attitudes, though the difference wasn't as large in this study. But the important thing here was the measure of defensiveness. While each volunteer was reading his pamphlet, he was hooked up to an "auditory feedback suppressor" — a pair of earphones plugged into a white-noise generator, which delivered a constant static loud enough to prevent the volunteer from hearing the sound of his own voice. As the volunteer read each paragraph aloud, he was asked to report what he was thinking; the auditory feedback suppressor had been found previously to reduce volunteers' censoring of their own self-reports. The volunteers' comments were taperecorded and later categorized by raters who didn't know which were from the high-fear condition and which from the low. The findings: high-fear volunteers as compared to low-fear explicitly rejected pamphlet statements significantly more often (for instance, "I don't believe that"), commented favorably on the pamphlet's style and objectivity noticeably less often (e.g., "That's an impressive way to put it"), and paraphrased statements about the dangers of smoking significantly less often ("So the idea in this statement is that the more a person smokes the bigger the risk he takes"). In several different ways, then, the high-fear volunteers really did appear to be defending against the anxiety-arousing communication; and so they failed to accept its recommendations to stop smoking. Janis and Feshbach's hypothesis appeared confirmed, and the status of their study as a psychological classic was preserved.

SHORT- AND LONG-TERM EFFECTS OF FEAR

An unfortunate effect of classic status is that people may begin to assign more weight to the "classic" than it was ever intended to bear. Janis and Feshbach had stated clearly that in different situations than the one they used, high-fear communications might be more effective than low-fear: for instance, where the main object of a speech is to get a quick audience response such as tossing donations into a passed hat, before defensiveness can become firmly established. But the novel idea of high fear inducing less attitude change found its way, almost unqualified, into multitudes of textbooks whose authors were hungry for psychological findings that challenged common sense. Not until several other studies offered support for common sense did Janis and Feshbach's qualifications of their findings begin to be taken seriously; and by that time most people had forgotten they'd made any qualifications at all.

One of the first studies to report something besides the high-fear–low-change pattern seemed to exemplify with unusual neatness Janis and Feshbach's idea about the differential effects of fear on short-term and long-term change. Howard Leventhal and Patricia Niles (1964) set up a booth at a summer Health Exposition in the New York Coliseum, attended by large numbers of people interested in health, cheap entertainment, and free air conditioning. Among a variety of exhibits and films on such topics as space medicine, diabetes, and glaucoma, the Leventhal booth offered a chance to participate in a "Health Education Program, Lung Cancer, Yale University." Those who wandered in were told they'd be exposed to one of three health programs, assigned randomly, for research purposes. Volunteers in the low-fear condition were given a pamphlet summarizing evidence on the dangers of smoking. In the moderate-fear condition they were given the pamphlet and were also shown a film dramatizing the case of a man who found he had lung cancer, who was told by a prestigious cancer specialist that smoking caused it, and who then prepared to undergo major surgery. In the high-fear condition the movie didn't end there; it went on into the operating room, where it showed the man's blackened lung being removed in bloody color. Most high-fear volunteers, according to the experimenters, "appeared deeply shaken" at this scene.

In all conditions, the experimenters recommended that every smoker who hadn't had a chest X-ray in the past six months should get one promptly, and pointed down the corridor to where a portable X-ray unit just happened to be parked. The pamphlet given to all volunteers also made the point repeatedly that people who quit smoking were much more likely to avoid lung cancer and live a long life. Promptly after exposure to the film and pamphlet, the experimenters questioned volunteers about how much of a relationship they felt there was between smoking and lung cancer, about whether they planned to cut down their own smoking, and about whether they planned to get an X-ray soon. In this study a measure of actual behavior (not available in either of Janis's studies) was also possible: the experimenters simply checked the records of the nearby X-ray booth when the Health Exposition was over, to see how many of their volunteers had really gone to get a chest X-ray afterward.

On one measure the results agreed with those of Janis: the low-fear people indicated significantly greater willingness to cut down their own smoking than the moderate- and high-fear people. But other measures followed the opposite pattern: moderate and high-fear volunteers were more likely than low-fear volunteers to agree that cigaret smoking causes lung cancer, and somewhat more likely actually to get a chest X-ray at the exposition. This isn't just another case of verbalizations being different from behavior: volunteers who said they planned to get an X-ray usually did, and those who said they had no such plans usually got no X-ray.

The difference between groups with regard to actually getting X-rays is statistically small, but in conjunction with the difference in announced smoking intentions, it does follow the direction Janis and Feshbach had originally suggested: quick and easy actions might best be motivated by high-fear messages, whereas behavioral changes over the long haul might be more likely after a less fear-arousing, less defense-activating communication. It would be nice if we could leave things right there, and recommend to all worthy fear-arousers that they should save their heavy guns only for hit-and-run campaigns, using softer words to induce lasting change. But one of the most irritating and valuable characteristics of serious scientists is that they're never quite content to leave things right there.

COMPLICATIONS IN FEAR AROUSAL

Howard Leventhal, for one, moved on from his first set of fear-arousal data to a series of other studies, so intriguing and yet so hard to account for in any simple fashion that William McGuire (1969a) suggested the need for "pretzel-shaped hypotheses" to describe "a pretzel-shaped reality." An early twist of the pretzel came at another New York exposition, this one held in Syracuse. (Leventhal's several years of duty in the U.S. Public Health Service are reflected in his predilection for field studies over laboratory work: if you aim to influence the general public, it may help to meet them on their own ground.) He and Jean C. Watts (1966) set up moderate- and high-fear conditions by using the same film on lung cancer as in the previous study. But they omitted the pamphlet, and in the low-fear condition they used another movie instead, this one simply presenting charts and diagrams on the dangers of cigaret smoking. In all conditions, the film included recommendations to give up smoking; and after the film, the experimenters also recommended that smokers get a chest X-ray every six months. An X-ray unit was again nearby, and the experimenters pointed it out.

When volunteers were questioned immediately after the film in this study, the three fear-arousal conditions yielded no significant differences in attitudes about smoking as a cause of lung cancer, or in announced intention to smoke less — although the previous study had found sig-

326

nificant differences on both measures, in opposite directions. Further-more, the *low-* and moderate-fear conditions in the present study moved a significantly larger percentage of volunteers to take chest X-rays than the high-fear condition did, though previously the *high-* and moderate-fear conditions had worked better than the low. Finally, in a survey of those participants in the current study who could be reached five months later, the *high*-fear volunteers significantly more often said they were smoking less since their research participation, contrary to the results on intent to quit smoking in the earlier study.

Where does that leave us? On such shaky ground that we'd better keep moving. In this study, low and moderate fear seem to have worked most effectively to promote a short-term behavior, X-ray taking, while high fear apparently produced greater changes in long-term behavior — the reverse not only of Leventhal's previous data but of Irving Janis' initial supposition. It may be that Leventhal and Watts' later survey results weren't that accurate: only a third of the original participants were reached, and those who were may have distorted their answers to a greater or lesser degree depending on their experimental treatment. Maybe the most vivid movie of all, the high-fear one, made it easier for those volunteers to remember Leventhal and Watts' strong concern with cigaret smoking when the researchers came around with their survey later, and therefore led the high-fear people more often to report having reduced their smoking whether they had or not, just to please the ex-perimenters. But whatever the post hoc possibilities, it looks at though the first easy answers to the fear arousal question were, to say the least, incomplete.

Leventhal and his associates have worked on several other possibilities that he hoped might make sense of the fear-arousal data. One possi-bility was that certain personality differences might either heighten or dampen the effects of the experimental fear manipulations, and that the distribution of these personality differences in different experimental settings might be sufficiently various to account for at least part of the contradictory results. Janis and Feshbach (1954) had found that volun-teers with relatively low chronic anxiety levels showed roughly the same attitude change whether they had heard a high-fear or low-fear speech; it was the volunteers relatively high in chronic anxiety who were moved more by the low-fear than the high-fear appeal. Presumably only those volunteers already somewhat anxious would have their anxiety raised enough by the high-fear speech to become really defensive.

Patricia Niles (1964) pursued this possibility in a study supervised by Leventhal, using the same combination of antismoking pamphlets and films as in the Leventhal and Niles study. Her main addition was a measure of each volunteer's general anxiety level and feelings of sus-ceptibility to disease. With this measure she categorized volunteers as either high or low in "vulnerability," and compared their responses to various experimental levels of fear arousal. Among low-vulnerability volunteers, the high-fear condition led larger numbers of volunteers to proclaim their intent both to stop smoking and to get a chest X-ray. (Unfortunately she made no follow-up measures, and no X-ray unit was nearby.) Among high-vulnerability volunteers, the medium-fear condition yielded more statements of intent to take both actions; high- *and* low-fear conditions were significantly less effective. These results are fairly consistent with Janis and Feshbach's, in suggesting that a combination of personal predispositions and immediate circumstances, rather than the circumstances alone, determines the effects of fear on attitude change. But for various other studies yielding inconsistent change results, we don't have the personality data that might enable us to reinterpret them successfully; and when the personality data are available, as in the Leventhal and Watts study, the effects of the personality variables are themselves inconsistent. They do appear worth taking into account, but still other variables are obviously at work.

One is the *specificity* of the communicator's recommendations. In a study of messages about tetanus, Leventhal, Singer, and Jones (1965) varied not only the fear-inducing content of the communication, but the amount of detail they used in describing how to get the needed inoculations. In this case, the high-fear condition produced greater verbal change concerning tetanus shots' importance and announced intent to get the shots than did the low-fear condition; but the numbers of high-fear and low-fear volunteers who actually got the inoculations soon after were not significantly different. The specificity of the recommendations did make a difference, however. When the experimenters left it pretty much up to the volunteers to plan how to get the shots, almost nobody got them, though the student volunteers presumably knew the location of the student health center where shots were given. When the experimenters carefully described the time and place where the inoculations could be obtained, and asked volunteers to figure out right then how to fit one of the available times into their own schedules, a significant percentage did go to get the shots. (At least some fear was necessary to energize them, though; other volunteers who were given the same specific recommendations but weren't given a fear-arousing message got no shots at all.)

A similar effect has been found in a study of changes in cigaret smoking conducted by Leventhal, Watts, and Pagano (1967). In that study, the effects of specific recommendations on how to go about giving up smoking were more obvious after several months than immediately following the experiment. People with the best of intentions, inspired by a high-fear message, started off strong in their efforts to quit smoking, but steadily backslid until they were up to their old habits again. Other people with the same intentions but with specific instructions from the experimenters on how to stay off tobacco dropped to a low level of smoking initially and remained there.

PRETZELS AND CURVES

Now you have some of the pretzel-shaped facts: high fear levels produce greater changes in attitudes and behavior sometimes; moderate or low fear levels produce the most change at other times. And where are the pretzel-shaped hypotheses? We're in luck, for both William McGuire (1969), who first suggested the pretzel analogy, and Irving Janis (1967) who first studied fear arousal, have come up with pretzelly explanations of all the data at hand, and maybe of all the data to come. The two hypotheses are as like as two pretzels, with only a few differences in the batter, so I'll describe them as one.

Consider a simple pretzel, lightly salted and a bit flat on the bottom. Let us take the height of any point on the pretzel's curves, measuring upward from the baseline of the flattened bottom, as the amount of attitude or behavior change produced by a particular communication. Let us also say that the point on the baseline from which we measure upward represents the degree of fear arousal built into the communication, with the level of threat increasing as we move along the pretzel from left to right. Curve ABC on our pretzel, then, would represent a situation where zero fear at point A also induces zero attitude change; mild to moderate fear arousal increases attitude change, up to the optimal point B; and higher levels of fear arousal again reduce change, all the way down to zero at point C — and perhaps even to less than zero as the audience withdraws from the whole topic or becomes hostile to the fear-arouser. Janis and Feshbach originally had this curvilinear relationship between fear arousal and attitude change in mind,

Figure 8.1

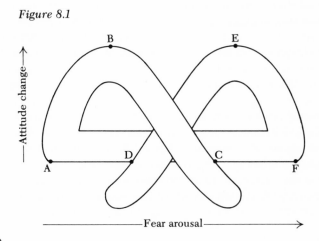

329

rather than a straight-line relationship where the lowest fear levels always produced the greatest attitude change. Both Janis and McGuire have advanced the same curvilinear relationship recently in more sophisticated form to account for the disparate results of the fear arousal studies. The "low" fear-arousal condition in Janis and Feshbach's study may have corresponded to point B, and the "high" fear-arousal condition to point C; whereas in at least some other studies where high fear induced greater attitude change than low, the "high" fear condition may have fallen at point B, and the "low" at point A. Unfortunately, the measures of fear arousal in different studies have been so various that it isn't really possible to be sure whether what was called "high fear" in one experiment may have really been "low fear" in another; but circumstantial evidence does suggest this in some cases.

If that were all there was to the Janis/McGuire or McGuire/Janis hypothesis, we'd merely need to develop a standardized scale of fear arousal and use it in every experimental and practical application of fear arousal henceforth. But there's another half of the pretzel there, to suggest that additional variables may interact with fear to change the shape and location of the curvilinear relationship between fear and attitude change. Let's say curve ABC represents a situation where the audience has previously heard little about the topic of the communication, such as tetanus. Curve DEF then might represent a topic with which the audience is all too boringly familiar, such as — at least today — the dangers of cigaret smoking. The usual warnings about lung cancer, even though they're relatively strong (point D), would be unlikely to move a confirmed smoker toward positive attitude change; they might even irritate him sufficiently to initiate greater smoking, in a perverse comeuppance to all puritans. But as the threat level in the communication reaches new heights, and particularly as novel arguments are introduced to reach those heights — for example, evidence of chromosomal danger from tobacco tars — he might perk up and begin to change his attitudes, more so as the evidence becomes more frightening, all the way up to point E. After that point, even the novelty of the message is no match for his fright, and he institutes new defenses that drop his attitude change back down to zero at point F.

Actually, William McGuire didn't have such a literal application in mind when he suggested the need for pretzel-shaped hypotheses. Both he and Irving Janis have been working with families of separate curves, rather than the double curve of the pretzel — with arrays of partial pretzels, if you want to push the analogy. Janis (1967) has arranged these families of curves in three dimensions (Figure 8.2).

However the curves are arranged, the essential idea is that no one line, straight or curved, can represent all the relationships possible between

Figure 8.2

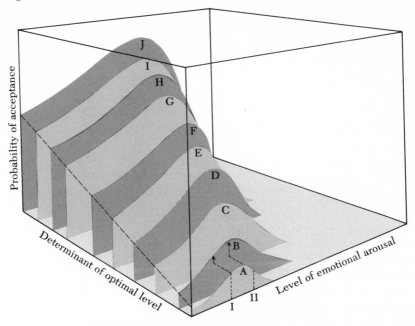

fear and attitude change; too many other factors can complicate the recipe. One such factor might be previous familiarity with the issue, as I've suggested. Different familiarity levels would then be entered along the "determinant of optimal level" side of the box, and the consequent relationships between familiarity, fear, and attitude change could be plotted as curves in the box — not necessarily the same set of curves as Janis uses in the illustration, but nonetheless a variety of curves rather than a repeated set of identical curves. Or you could enter communicator credibility as the "determinant of optimal level," or a particular person-ality factor, or any of a number of other things. For each, any substantial change in the contributing factor would be likely to alter the curve that shows how attitude change increases and decreases as the level of fear arousal varies.

Nobody has yet taken the time to study experimentally the family of curves that might be generated when several levels of a variable such as credibility are allowed to interact with several levels of fear arousal to produce attitude change. Perhaps the universe will turn out not to be shaped like a pretzel or half-pretzel after all. (Howard Leventhal [1970] argues instead for an information-processing model in which the indi-vidual responds to fear cues and to danger cues separately.) But the curvilinear hypothesis sounds plausible; and if it's right it could account for a lot of presently confusing data, as well as pointing the way for the practical use of high fear levels to induce attitude change without defensiveness. Watch for the needed experiments to appear soon. Too many people have put too many of their best years into fear-arousal research to let such a crisp, crunchy hypothesis go stale in the box.

the work of worrying: preparations for stress

He had now to penetrate regions that were not anesthetized and this he told her frankly, but he said that there was no danger at all. He apologized for the slip of the tongue he had made: in point of fact, he had not been near her brain, it was only a figure of speech. He began. The knives ground and carved and curried and scoured the wounds they made: the scissors clipped hard gristle and the scalpels chipped off bone. It was as if a tangle of tiny nerves were being cut dexterously, one by one; the pain writhed spirally and came to her who was a pink bird and sat on the top of a cone. . . . The surgeon, squeezing her arm with avuncular pride, said, "Good girl," as if she were a bright dog that had retrieved a bone. Her silent mind abused him: "You are a thief," it said, "You are a heartless vagabond and you should be put to death."

— Jean Stafford
"The Interior Castle"

Not long after the birth of our second daughter, my wife Roslyn was talking to a neighbor who was well into her first pregnancy. Roz asked, almost rhetorically, "Are you going to start prenatal classes soon?"

"Oh, no," said the neighbor, "I'm a big baby, and the less I know the better!"

Too many American women still feel that way. And too many doctors still feel likewise about their women patients. Maternity wards might seem good places to study the psychology of joy; but the ones I've seen were so full of drugged and dopey women fresh from delivery that they resembled opium dens instead. These women maintained almost total ignorance about their "interesting condition" until it was over; but ignorance in such cases is unlikely to deliver bliss. In addition to the physiological side effects of anesthesia on mother and more seriously on child, the procedure may generate adverse psychological side effects. In our time of liberated femininity, the woman is temporarily allowing herself to become an object again, rather than an active participant in the birth process. Her reliance on anesthesia allows her to enter labor without resolving ambivalent attitudes toward childbearing, which may hamper her postpartum recovery and her care of the new child. Finally, the awkwardness of anesthetic procedures usually prevents not only the husband's participation in but even his presence at the birth of his child. He often responds by anesthetizing himself with liquor and tobacco.

Roz is a psychiatric nurse, so she knew enough about the physical and psychological factors involved in childbearing to want to investigate natural childbirth procedures before the birth of our first child. The training program she found required joint participation of husband and wife, so I got educated too. I didn't have the proper equipment for part of the program — a series of physical exercises designed to increase control of the principal muscles involved in childbirth. But everyone shared in the circulation of information about the specific events to be expected prior to, during, and immediately after childbirth. For those who needed them, plenty of this-little-egg-gets-fertilized books and movies were available; but the most educational aspect of the program was the frequent discussion of all sorts of silly and serious questions, with unembarrassed answers coming not only from the two obstetrical nurses who coordinated the program but also from other prospective parents who were further into their nine months. Several women actually gave birth before the series of meetings ended, thus establishing that a baby really did come out eventually, and that everybody concerned could remain intensely conscious during the entire procedure.

A controlled study of natural childbirth training and its effects would require random assignment of participants to training and nontraining conditions, and the operation of at least one training condition with physical exercises but no information program, others with an information program but no exercises, still others with various combinations of both. Nobody has done that (though Darell Schregardus [Schregardus, Eichhorn, and Eichhorn, 1970–71] has made a beginning), so my assumptions about what worked and why it worked are guesses. The physical exercises did appear to help my wife, if ease of delivery is any indication; but they didn't help me. The information program helped everyone — particularly because of its specificity. As with experimental recommendations in several of the fear arousal studies, we were instructed in detail on the likely sequence of events and on what we should be doing during each stage to ensure successful birth. Our anxieties about pregnancy and childbirth, about whether we could get to the hospital on time and so on, were effectively harnessed to motivate our sticking to the information-and-exercise program, rather than just causing us to worry for nine months and then ask for an anesthetic. As we encountered each stage and found the recommendations useful, our anxieties never mounted to a disruptive level.

Research on the efficacy of such advance information *has* been conducted on one situation that typically involves even higher fear levels than pregnancy: major surgery. Irving Janis (1958) was again the first person to realize the possibilities of this research area: intense fear levels lasting over several days, sometimes weeks or months; sufficient numbers of potential volunteers with comparable physical afflictions; an environment under much tighter control than such other high-fear settings as large-scale disaster or military combat; the researcher's ability to blend into the surroundings, as just another professional asking questions to be used in the patient's treatment; the availability of useful independent data, including physiological measures and nurses' reports on patient behavior. Janis took direct advantage of all these possibilities in an intensive study of the preoperative and postoperative emotional state of twenty-two surgical patients in a large community hospital. He also utilized some of the possibilities more indirectly in a survey of one hundred and fifty college students who had undergone recent surgery, as well as in an extended study of one woman under psychoanalytic treatment, who entered surgery while the treatment was in progress.

The woman's case presented an unusual opportunity to explore reactions to surgery that were at least partially determined by unconscious processes. Janis notes a number of transference reactions (the woman acting as if the surgeon were an omnipotent father, or as if the nurse were a mother who punishes or indulges her child-patient), defensive maneuvers, and other neurotic patterns of thought and behavior focusing on the surgery — no surprise, surely, since several crucial aspects of Freud's theories about childhood sexuality involve loss of body parts. But a woman who comes in for psychotherapeutic treatment of severe neurotic difficulties cannot be used as a model of general reactions to surgery. At most, her case may be helpful in generating hypotheses to be tested by other means. Janis developed plenty of hypotheses, but he tested only two major ones in his other studies. Both involve the amount of preparatory information given to the patient before his operation; both hypotheses were rather well supported.

The first hypothesis says, "Persons who display an extremely high level of anticipatory fear or anxiety during the 'threat' period will be more likely than others to display intense fear of body damage during the subsequent crisis period, when exposed to actual threat stimuli." More simply, if you're very scared before the operation, you're apt to be very scared during the operation itself, although it turns out there's a little more to the proposition than that. The second hypothesis says, "Persons who display an extremely low degree of anticipatory fear or anxiety during the 'threat' period will be more likely than others to display

334

actions of anger and resentment toward danger-control authorities during the subsequent crisis period, when exposed to actual stress stimuli." You might think people who are very calm before an operation will be very calm during and after too; but Janis says they're more likely than other patients to get really mad at doctors and nurses when they find that the operation hurts.

Janis found both hypotheses supported by his data both from the college student survey and from the intensive study of surgical patients, though he found it necessary to qualify the second one by saying that low-fear people are likely to react angrily "only if they are exposed to relatively *severe* stress stimuli" during or following the operation. One apparent failure to confirm the second hypothesis (Johnson, Dabbs, and Leventhal, 1970) may have come partly from using patients whose operations entailed less stress, on the whole, than those in Janis's severe-stress category. Janis also found in general that people who showed "an extremely high level of anticipatory fear or anxiety during the 'threat' period" suffered from repressed neurotic conflicts not easily influenced by preparatory information from the hospital staff. That is, the really scared ones were anxious for other reasons than the operation alone, so talking about the operation with them in advance didn't help much. Those with an extremely low preoperative fear level, on the other hand, seemed seldom to be that way as a result of a specific personality pattern. Several low-fear patients had apparently displayed moderate or even high fear arousal upon previous occasions; so the present low fear level presumably came mainly from features of the immediate situation, particularly the patient's preoperative informational diet. But a diet that leaves the patient angry afterward can't be as good as his low fear suggests: either he's not getting enough of something or else it doesn't sit well on his stomach.

Implicit in all this is another Janis hypothesis, supported mainly by confirmation of the other two hypotheses: those whose preoperative fear level is moderate, rather than high or low, are less likely postoperatively to be *either* highly fearful *or* hostile, or upset in any other way. And how does a patient reach that moderate fear level in the first place? Through actively working over relevant information about his impending surgery.

HOW WORRY HELPS

Here Janis introduces the concept of "the work of worrying." Worry about an impending stressful event can help the individual to deal better with it when it comes, by forcing him to review the information he already has about the event, by motivating him to get more, and by leading him to develop contingency plans for coping with the expected stresses. Such mental activity is not particularly pleasant, and most people won't do it unless they really feel threatened. But if they don't do it, they

335

are left either to deny the threat as it looms ever more likely, or to elaborate their fantasy fears in ways that disrupt normal behavior much more than the time and effort it would take them to do the work of worrying honestly.

Preparatory communications about surgical operations both alert the patient to the unpleasant experiences he's likely to encounter, and give him some indication that either he or one of the professionals present can cope with whatever problems may arise. Normally, he responds with moderate concern about the unpleasant possibilities, and incorporates the coping information into his own set of realistic protective devices. If he already has a problem with neurotic anxiety, however, the preoperative communication's warnings are likely to exacerbate it, and the reassurances are not likely to alleviate his fears, fed as they are by a deep stream of neurotic concerns. So when he finds himself physically cut up and suffering from the rigors of recuperation, he'll probably display a continuation or heightening of his previous anxiety level.

But let's suppose he's not neurotic, and either is told very little of what to expect or is given a snow job about the operation: it'll be nothing at all, millions go through it every year, hardly a pinprick. Do you wonder that when the operation proves to be painful and his recovery slow and difficult, he becomes resentful and hostile toward the doctor, the nurse, and anybody else who helped spring this elaborate torture system on him unawares?

Janis's advice to medical personnel, then, is to give the patient pre-operatively "a *concrete, personalized picture of the outstanding danger events as the person will actually perceive them*" — to let him know what's likely to happen in the normal course of things, so he won't think he's dying every time he feels a twinge of pain, and won't suspect that every twinge of pain is the result of a planned program of sadism by the medical staff. Once the patient has this information, and a good indication of the help he can get if something out of the ordinary does happen, he can go to work to incorporate this material into his own thinking about his operation, and won't be taken by surprise when the necessary unpleasantnesses do occur. Here Janis's ideas about the work of worrying resemble McGuire's ideas about the development of resistance to attitude change. In both, the object is to prepare the individual so that his psychological stability doesn't fall apart at the first assault — by the surgeon's knife on the one hand, by a set of critical arguments on the other. In both, psychological stability is best preserved not by urging reliance on the word of some authority figure that "everything will be all right," but by giving the individual a sound basis for building his own realistic defenses against physical or psychological attack. Indeed, Janis and McGuire both use the term "psychological inoculation" to describe the effects of preparatory communications — effects that depend on the individual's own ability to develop protections against overwhelming stress, if he is given sufficient warning and sufficient knowledge to do so.

Janis's hypotheses may prove to be of considerable value to medical practitioners who wish to promote the total well-being of their patients. One group of practitioners (Egbert et al., 1964) has already tried his recommendations on a number of surgical patients in a controlled experiment at Massachusetts General Hospital, with impressive results. Not only were the psychologically prepared patients less troubled by negative emotional reactions after their operation than were nonprepared control patients; they also needed significantly fewer pain medications than the controls, and were released from the hospital an average of almost three days sooner than the controls (by doctors who were unaware the patients were in a psychological experiment). As in the childbirth training program, psychological preparation wasn't all that was involved; the experimental patients were also given instructions on how to avoid postoperative muscular spasms through relaxation, and how best to turn their bodies in bed to avoid further pain. Janis recommends such advice to give the patient a sense of active control over his recovery, but the fact that in this case such advice could by itself produce direct pain reduction renders the psychological effects of the preparatory communications unclear. No such confounding was involved in a study by Patricia Moran (1963), however. She found that describing to parents in advance what they could expect to happen during their child's tonsillectomy produced considerably greater parental satisfaction with the overall hospital experience, as well as less disturbance over hospitalization and surgery on the part of the children. Just as psychological preparation for childbirth can help fathers who undergo no physical exercise, so psychological preparation for a child's operation can aid parents who have no physical pains of their own to relieve.

WORRYING ABOUT SOCIAL ISSUES

Janis cautions about extending his findings from the hospital setting to other situations before they are carefully investigated. But he suggests that his conclusions about psychological inoculation may well be applicable to such circumstances as retirement, a spouse's terminal illness, or embarking upon a difficult and frustrating job such as Peace Corps service (Janis et al., 1969). Even broader applications are well worth consideration. Would public reactions to major social change be less negative if greater efforts were made to publicize well in advance the likelihood of such change, and the ways in which its undesirable effects on the individual can be softened? Are some conservatives right in arguing that destructive ghetto riots could have been avoided if government officials hadn't presented such glowing pictures of quick change via job training programs, Operation Headstart, and so on? Of course hospital patients do fairly often get genuinely poor treatment, and should complain about it if they want the hospitals to change; the same can be said for ghetto dwellers. But there are differences between complaints based on needless suffering, and complaints based on being grossly misled by authority figures about the probable outcome of their planned operations.

Perhaps, at the least, public officials and scientists and such should learn to be a little less rosy about their predictions. They should have already learned, since they've had plenty of object lessons by now. Negative public reaction to the Vietnam war, for example, appears to have been as much a response to too many disconfirmed "light at the end of the tunnel" speeches as to the war's actual conduct. John F. Kennedy's "Ask not what your country can do for you" speech might be viewed as a forerunner of the sort of communication Janis's research suggests: warning the populace of the dangers they face, not so they'll be frightened into voting for him but so they'll begin thinking about the hard decisions the entire nation must soon make, and begin devising realistic solutions for the nation's problems. Perhaps such speeches don't fit the mood of the country right now, and perhaps most contemporary political leaders would find it hard to make them. But as our difficulties burgeon and as every rosy speech becomes that much more likely to be disconfirmed, the price to be paid for today's rosy speech in the coin of tomorrow's uncontrollable anxieties and resentful anger may mount with unanticipated rapidity.

One obvious problem with trying to initiate the "work of worrying" about social problems is that the threat is not usually immediate. By the time it becomes immediate enough to motivate such mental labor as the work of worrying involves, the time may be too late for any actions to be useful. In the case of surgical stress, the problem is usually much more easily understood, and a specific date is set for the cutting to be done. So the patient has strong reasons both to worry and to direct his worry in a useful direction.

We can try to provide such reasons for worry to the general population, through frequent vivid depictions of the disasters that will befall humanity if prompt remedial action isn't taken. But here we return to the still unresolved question of fear-arousing communications and their optimal intensity. Perhaps certain of the steps that Janis recommends to cope with strong fears about surgery – particularly those involving specific recommendations for dealing with each stress as it arises – would help to keep public fears at a moderately strong but reality-oriented level, as they appear to have done in Leventhal, Singer, and Jones' experiment on motivating people to get tetanus shots. Janis has explored another possible way of attaining the same goal, though he has again used health issues rather than social ones: the technique of emotional roleplaying.

EMOTIONAL ROLEPLAYING

Emotional roleplaying differs from the roleplaying we considered earlier mainly in being designed to elicit an unusually high level of emotional arousal — in most cases, high fear arousal. By creating intense personal involvement with the fear-arousing message through roleplaying, Janis hoped to avoid the defensiveness that he had found previously in non-roleplay fear arousal studies. By harnessing the powerful motivating force of anxiety, he hoped to elicit even more attitude change through roleplaying than had been achieved in the past with financial or social approval motives. In establishing the conditions necessary to do this, he was also able to initiate for many volunteers the work of worry to a degree they would probably never otherwise have attained, unless they were actually facing a surgical operation. He did so by having the volunteer act out realistically an imaginary preoperative scene.

Leon Mann, who collaborated with Janis on this series of studies (Janis and Mann, 1965; Mann, 1967; Mann and Janis, 1968), usually played the doctor. Volunteers were college coeds who smoked at least fifteen cigarets a day. They were told the study was an effort to understand the emotional reactions of patients in a doctor's office without actually disrupting the work of a real doctor. At this point each volunteer in the roleplay condition was asked to imagine she had "a bad cough that was not getting any better," had been examined and X-rayed by the doctor previously, and was in the doctor's office today to hear the results of the X-rays. While Mann donned a white coat and a physician's mien, the volunteer was supposed to act like a patient. She was first to worry aloud to herself in the waiting room about the doctor's probable diagnosis, then to go in and talk with the doctor about "her" X-rays. The "doctor" showed her a set of lung X-rays, and told her she had a malignancy in the right lung, which must be operated on immediately, with only a "moderate chance for a successful outcome." The doctor phoned for a hospital bed, then gave the "patient" detailed information about reporting to the hospital the next morning and about the lengthy hospitalization she should expect. Finally, the doctor discussed with his patient her smoking habits and their probable connection with her lung cancer. He urged her to stop smoking immediately, and encouraged her "to speak freely about the difficulties she expects to encounter in trying to give up the habit at this time, now that she knows it is essential."

These roleplaying volunteers were compared with a control group who did no roleplaying themselves, but who heard a tape recording of one particularly dramatic experimental roleplaying session. The roleplayers' level of fear arousal was significantly greater (Janis and Mann described

339

their "tremors, trembling and flushing" while roleplaying as "far beyond the call of duty, even for whole-hearted adherents of the Stanislavsky method of acting"); they became much stronger believers in the relationship between cigaret smoking and lung cancer; and they were much likelier to announce their intent to stop smoking. Questioned a week after the experiment, the roleplayers reported an average decrease of more than ten cigarets per day, compared with the controls' decrease of five a day. At this time the roleplayers also made more spontaneous comments indicating that the work of worrying had been initiated in earnest: "If I'd kept smoking, I'm sure something would have happened to me, with my luck." "I've really thought about it — especially because Grandmother had cancer — there is a weak spot in the family."

Mann telephoned research participants again eight months later. The roleplayers were still smoking significantly less than the controls, and substantially less than before their experimental participation. When a female assistant, apparently not connected with the research, called again eighteen months after the experiment to do an "opinion survey," the roleplayers once more reported a significantly greater reduction than the controls — by now an average reduction of more than thirteen cigarets a day, compared with the controls' five. In few experimental studies has so brief an exposure to a persuasive experience induced such lasting change.

The usefulness of emotional roleplaying to induce action rather than apathy or defensiveness is suggested by another aspect of this research. It happened that just before Mann made the eight-months-after phone calls, the U.S. Surgeon General's *Report on Smoking and Health* (1964) was published. This report was generally followed by reductions in the current smoking levels of both roleplay and control volunteers, as well as reductions in smoking among the American populace at large. To learn what effect the Surgeon General's Report by itself would have on people comparable to the experimental and control volunteers, Mann called a number of other coeds from the same college, who were quite similar to the original sample in smoking habits and general background. These new volunteers reported a decrease in their smoking following the Surgeon General's Report; but after another ten months, they had backslid so much that they were smoking no fewer cigarets than before the Report's publication. The roleplayers, on the other hand, were smoking even less at the time of this final measure, eighteen months after their single hour of experimental participation, than they had smoked only two weeks after the experiment. Several roleplayers specifically said the experiment rather than the Surgeon General's Report was responsible for their decrease in smoking. One girl told the opinion surveyor: "The report did not have much effect on me. But I was in this other study. A professor was doing this psychological thing and I was one of the volunteers. And that was what really affected me. . . . He was the one that scared me, not the report."

Why was emotional roleplaying so effective here? We are daily bombarded with hundreds of direct persuasive appeals and demands for action — from politicians and advertisers, from ministers and friends, from wives and husbands and children, from salesmen and charity workers. We learn to shunt most of these aside, to protect ourselves from significant attitude change or active involvement in all but a tiny fraction of appeals. In most such instances, we are not defending ourselves from anxiety so much as from all the internal turmoil and all the external complications and all the just plain hard work we'd get ourselves into if we did respond to every demand. The work of worry takes time and energy just as any other kind of work does, and we must desensitize ourselves to most threats to keep ourselves from being worked to death, if not scared to death.

Anything that elicits major changes in behavior or attitudes, then, must stand out sharply from this background of daily persuasive noise. Intense personal experience appears most likely to stand out — the large experiences, or perhaps the small recurrent experiences, of our lives that vividly demonstrate the error or the rightness of our ways and direct us onward on the most reliable path. An impersonal authority's statement that smoking causes lung cancer is not that much different from myriad other impersonal statements we've heard and ignored. But to hear that *we* have lung cancer, even if the setting in which we hear it is imaginary, brings us into such direct confrontation with the possibility of our own extinction that we must try to cope with it. The fact that it's imaginary right now is all the better for us, since we still have time to prevent it. Some patients in Janis's hospital study were already too far gone for the work of worry to do them much good.

How can we bring enough people into the psychology laboratory to get their worrying mechanisms moving to deal with the threats of population, pollution, prejudice? We can't — so psychologists should start working right away outside the laboratory on better ways of promoting the widespread personal involvement, the feelings of a close brush with doom, that we need to generate in millions before the close brush becomes a head-on collision. The work of worry, properly directed, may help to cope with these threats realistically, once the threats are personally acknowledged; but too many people are still trying too hard not to feel threatened. They tell us that the X-rays are still too fuzzy and the doctor's white coat is only a costume from a television commercial. In the end they may require real bodies from real mass disasters after all. In the end.

341

behavior in extremis:
disaster psychology

*Here we may observe, and I hope it will not be amiss to
take notice of it, that a near view of death would soon
reconcile men of good principle one to another, and that
it is chiefly owing to our easy situation in life and our
putting all these things far from us that our breaches are
fomented, ill blood continued, prejudices, breach of charity and of Christian union, so much kept and so far
carried on among us as it is. Another plague year would
reconcile all these differences; a close conversing with
death, or with diseases that threaten death, would scum
off the gall from our tempers, remove the animosities
among us, and bring us to see with differing eyes than
those which we looked on things with before.*

— Daniel Defoe
A Journal of the Plague Year

A tornado hit Judsonia, Arkansas, in March 1952. Judsonia is near my
hometown of Batesville, but we were out of the state at the time, and
when we went to look over the area upon our return three months later,
a good bit of the obvious damage had been cleaned up or covered up.
But something terrible had obviously happened; it would take a long time
to clean everything up. In Judsonia itself, thirty-five people were killed
and nearly 400 injured, out of 1,100 residents; over 75 per cent of the
houses were destroyed or made unlivable. The entire county, never a
rich one, had suffered $3.5 million in damages. Several other tornadoes in
Arkansas the same day caused an equal amount of damage and killed
85 more people.

Worse tornadoes have happened. They have hit bigger and wealthier
communities than Judsonia. Judsonia's is a classic because three days
after it hit, a team of social scientists from the National Opinion Research
Center arrived on the scene and started a series of carefully planned interviews. They talked to officials in the area who had to deal with the
disaster and its aftermath, to local organization members who had to
make immediate response to it, and to many local residents selected by
systematic sampling techniques. The interviews and other data on the
Judsonia disaster, though never published in detail, have been crucial in
the development of hypotheses about disaster phenomena by C. E. Fritz
and E. S. Marks (1954), Allen Barton (1969), and others. According to
Barton, the Judsonia interviews "provide the most detailed and valid
description available to this day on a community disaster."

The research in Judsonia provided not only good data but a good example of the way modern disaster research is conducted. Prepared social scientists seldom happen to be at the scene of a disaster when it happens. William James found himself in Palo Alto during the great San Francisco earthquake and fire of 1906, and thereupon conducted what may have been the first disaster study by a social scientist (James, 1911); but his observations were at best rather casual. Better research has been done by people who have come into the disaster area from outside, anywhere from several days to several months later. Experimentation with disasters is ethically if not technically impossible; therefore, lacking direct observations of behavior in natural disasters, social scientists have had to rely almost entirely on interviews with survivors. Any single interview is not necessarily reliable on specific points, or even in general. But enough interviews selected without bias and carefully conducted, asking the respondent not only about his own behavior but about the behavior of those he observed directly during the disaster, can be highly informative.

Well over twenty thousand such interviews have been conducted by now — starting with the U.S. Strategic Bombing Survey of German and Japanese survivors in World War II and continuing through dozens of studies of tornadoes, earthquakes, floods, hurricanes, airplane crashes, community poisonings, typhoons, fires, explosions, blizzards, epidemics (Disaster Research Group, 1961). Much of this research has been sponsored directly or indirectly by the federal government, with the idea that a better understanding of reactions to comparatively limited disasters may lead to better preparation for civil defense against nuclear attack. But the data can be useful in other ways as well — for instance, in helping to prevent disastrous behavior during and after such unanticipated disasters as tornadoes, earthquakes, floods, hurricanes, etc., and more generally in understanding human behavior under conditions of strongly negative emotional arousal. A person facing surgery can give us information about responses to private disaster. A tornado or earthquake, as a public disaster, may expose distinctly different forms of behavior.

Occasional attempts have been essayed to make the disaster fit the theory: that is, to use disaster behavior in confirming what a theorist thinks he has already found elsewhere. For example, Leon Festinger (1957) applied cognitive dissonance theory to a comparison of the rumors that followed two major disasters in India. In the first instance, originally reported by Prasad (1935, 1950), rumors after an earthquake predicted still worse things to come — "fear-provoking" rumors, Festinger called them. In the second, reported by Sinha (1952), there was (according to Festinger) "a complete absence of rumors predicting further disasters or of any type of rumor that might be regarded as supplying cognition consonant with being afraid. Some of the rumors represented a slight exaggeration of the actual damage, while others were even of the hopeful variety." The crucial factor in the first instance, Festinger argued, was that Prasad collected the rumors outside the disaster area, "where a large number of people had the identical dissonance, namely, between cognition corresponding to the fear they felt and the knowledge of what they saw around them which added up to the cognition that there was nothing to be afraid of." These people therefore needed to reduce the dissonance by circulating "fear-justifying" rumors. Sinha, on the other hand, collected his rumors within the disaster area, where people experienced perfect consonance between their fear and the havoc around them; thus, no fear-justifying rumors were necessary. Festinger concluded that here again "dissonance reduction produced results somewhat contrary to what one would expect on the basis of the operation of other human motives."

Unfortunately, Festinger has given the data a consistency they did not exhibit in their original form. Prasad (1935, p. 11) noted extreme rumors *within* the disaster area as well as outside, some going so far as to predict the damaged city's complete destruction; these rumors gained substantial acceptance among inhabitants of the disaster area. (American researchers as well have often found the survivors of tornadoes, for instance, highly fearful that more destruction will soon follow.) Likewise, Sinha found various rumors of the "fear-justifying" variety among those whose fears were not at all dissonant with the destruction around them (e.g., "We have to suffer punishment for our sins. Worse days are ahead."). Prasad (1950) also noted some of the rumors prevalent in San Francisco immediately following the 1906 earthquake, including such non-dissonance-reducing "cognitions" as "A tidal wave had engulfed New York City at the same time as the San Francisco quake," and "The quake had set loose the animals in the zoo, and these were eating the refugees in Golden Gate Park." Dissonance theory seems less appropriate here than hypotheses dealing with such phenomena as latent sadistic impulses, or the need to lessen one's own sufferings by focusing momentarily upon the woes of others.

STAGES OF DISASTER BEHAVIOR

Disaster researchers generally have refrained, perhaps too well, from imposing ready-made theoretical structures on the data they encounter. Instead, the disaster literature is mostly descriptive, with occasional attempts to categorize observations and to develop hypotheses of limited scope to account for the behavior at hand. The most frequent categorizations of data have been in terms of time phases — ranging from the simplest three-phase sequence of Martha Wolfenstein (1957: threat, impact, aftermath) to the seven-phase listing of Powell and Rayner (1952), further developed by Dwight Chapman (1962: warning, threat, impact, inventory, rescue, remedy, recovery), with such in-between categorizations as Allen Barton's (1969: predisaster, warning, immediate unorganized response, organized social response, long-run post-disaster equilibrium). All such categorizations are somewhat arbitrary, but they can be convenient. I'll use the seven-phase sequence here to note recurring observations of disaster behavior, not because all seven phases are distinct and important in every disaster but because at least some behaviors in some disasters seem to fit best in one or the other of these stages.

Warning. In many disaster situations there are indications that a disaster is possible, considerably in advance of signs that it's really on the way. Agencies and officials responsible for disaster planning are often reluctant to emphasize such warnings of potential trouble, for fear of creating undue "panic" or public annoyance; without official underlining of the warnings, most people are inclined to dismiss them. Those who are not so inclined are likely to be neurotic, oversensitive to any possible danger; at best, their lives are going to be terribly inefficient because many more warnings occur than actual disasters. On the other hand, the tendency to ignore warnings, though it may be efficient and more often than not realistic, can have unfortunate consequences in "nonprecipitate" disasters (those which build up slowly), such as floods. People may become emotionally adapted to the presence of a warning at one level, then adapted to it again at a slightly higher level, then again — until the water is suddenly up above their heads. (Just so, the Birchers say, we have been swamped by the Communists — although the Birch simile is not usually floods but the lobster who fails to detect the slow increase in heat, until he's boiled red and dead.)

Threat. If the potential disaster continues to build, tentative indications of trouble turn into specific signs of its approach — either direct symptoms of the disaster itself, or communications of danger relayed by other people. Once the danger signs are unmistakable, most people will attempt appropriate steps to protect themselves and those for whom they feel responsible. But human powers of self-deception are at least as great in disaster situations as anywhere else, particularly if responding to the danger signals requires substantial trouble or expense. So there are often at least a few people who ignore the cues and determine to stick it out, gambling that neither hell nor high water will visit them today. Danger cues may also be assimilated to more ordinary happenings: the roar of the approaching tornado is just a freight train; the symptoms of mass carbon monoxide poisoning are only multiple hangovers; the floodwater seeping under the door is little Billy playing in the sink. People so unprepared, through their own denial or through their misreading of the

345

available information, may be the least able to cope with the disaster psychologically when it does arrive, just as in Janis's study of surgical patients (1958). Worry prepares and fortifies, even if it does not fully protect.

Impact. Among all their observations, disaster researchers appear to have been most impressed by something they failed to find: panic. Panic at the moment of impact, wildly irrational behavior without thought for others, almost never happens in natural disasters and is rare even in man-made ones. Mostly, behavior at impact continues to be reality-oriented, directed toward preserving one's own well-being and that of people nearby as best as possible. Depending upon the particular type of disaster, this may involve sitting tight or hiding somewhere or running away. The behavior may not be the best possible thing to do, but it is usually better than nothing and it is usually something that looks good at the time, rather than a result of uncontrolled impulse. One exception is where warning and threat are telescoped into a very brief time, perhaps only a few minutes. There, what looks like the best thing to do may be worse than nothing, because it brings people out into the direct path of disaster between safety zones, just as the disaster hits. In Judsonia, for example, the tornado injured proportionally more people who had about a minute's warning than those who had appreciably more or less (Fritz and Marks, 1954). But even the people with a minute's warning weren't panicking; they just happened to expose themselves to greater danger by starting protective measures without time to finish them.

Inventory. Barton's "immediate unorganized response" may be a better name for this phase, because people do other things immediately after a disaster's impact in addition to taking inventory. Their immediate inventory of the situation is usually wrong, anyway; they assume that only they themselves and their immediate environment have been hit. Thinking this, their first efforts are most often directed toward finding and rescuing other family members. This is the case even with many officials who have general community responsibilities in the disaster area, even firemen and policemen: the family comes first. Such behavior has been fertile ground for sociologists in particular, because it vividly illustrates the severe role conflicts inherent in our everyday lives, role conflicts whose potential consequences are usually avoided because not all our major social roles make pressing demands on us at the same time. In disasters, we may suddenly find ourselves bound to help wives, children, and the public simultaneously, urgently. Most disaster-stricken people, without malice aforethought, seem to take the position that "the public be damned" — at least until all family members are accounted for. Such searching about for family, without apparent plan, may be what gives less involved observers the impression of "panic."

346

Rescue. Sheer proximity may at times overcome the force of kinship ties in disasters, just as proximity can overcome the force of authority in obedience experiments. During the process of searching for family members, survivors may discover others who need help, and will often respond to their obvious needs. Once family members *are* located and taken care of, many survivors will turn promptly to assisting others, and by this time other people from untouched areas nearby may have arrived to lend a hand. A substantial number of rescue attempts usually occur during this continuation of the unorganized response period, when formal disaster-aid groups are still preparing to move. (Responding to the obvious needs of whoever is closest may sometimes hinder rather than help rescue efforts. A classic example [Wolfenstein, 1957] is the doctor in Worcester, Massachusetts, who rushed about after a tornado, trying to help now one, then another victim, so aware his help was needed that he never managed to finish helping anyone properly. He became so distracted at one point that he tied a tourniquet on a woman's arm with a cord that happened to have an electric iron solidly attached to the other end.)

During this and the next period some physically healthy survivors, most often those who have lost close friends or relatives or who have seen direct evidence of death and serious injury in other people, may display what is called the "disaster syndrome" (Wallace, 1956): apparent psychological withdrawal, physical passivity, the appearance of being stunned or dazed. In Dwight Chapman's words (1962), those exhibiting the disaster syndrome "are suggestible and passive, and medical workers observe in their docility a striking contrast to the more common querulousness of people who have suffered an ordinary street accident." Various writers have suggested that the syndrome represents a defensive withdrawal of attention from the surrounding physical and human destruction, so that the individual can come to terms with what he has experienced at a more manageable rate than full-blown reality would allow. Usually only a few hours seem to be needed for the person to begin catching up with the disaster; then the syndrome fades. Other evidence of persisting anxiety may be visible over several days, however: disturbances of sleep and appetite, nightmares, restlessness. At the same time, preexisting neurotic and even psychotic symptoms may at least temporarily disappear. The depressive may now feel appropriately punished for his sins, the man with repressed conflicts may find the social conditions that fed them now disrupted, and everybody may have to pour so much energy into survival and rebuilding that little is left to support former neurotic "habits."

Remedy. Within a few hours after most disasters in civilized countries, formal groups inside the disaster area are able to start imposing organization upon relief work. Outside groups, both private and govern-

347

mental, enter to begin dealing with less immediate and more long-range problems. General morale within the community is often remarkably high, as people find themselves working together on problems that for once appear to have simple and easily agreed upon solutions. With most people suffering from the same sources of deprivation, class and racial barriers tend to be lowered, and verily, in Defoe's words, disaster works to "scum off the gall from our tempers, remove the animosities among us," and "reconcile men of good principle one to another." Defoe was too much of a realist, though, to think it would last for long. "As the terror of the infection abated," he said of the plague, "these things all returned again to their less desirable channel, and to the course they were in before." Once the mud is cleaned up and the bodies laid to rest, enough people can find enough reason for their old differences to restore them once again; and what Wolfenstein (1957) has called "the post-disaster utopia" fades into memory.

Noble behaviors are often displayed during this time not only by disaster survivors, but by interested outsiders — at first from surrounding communities, then from other areas around the state, the nation, at times even the world. "Convergence behavior" is the general term here (Fritz and Mathewson, 1957); it includes the convergence on the disaster area of would-be rescuers, sightseers, and social scientists, as well as of solicited and unsolicited supplies. The sudden descent of thousands of people onto a little tornado-shredded town, however good their intentions, has its obvious dangers. They clog highways, get in the way of more competent assistance, disturb the survivors with their attentions. The convergence of supplies presents less obvious but no less real difficulties, as hundreds of volunteers must spend full time for several weeks sorting through rags and good clothes, warehousing old donated furniture, disposing of spoiled sandwiches. The problem is usually compounded by well-meaning but inept mass media, who broadcast the need for flashlights and baby cribs far and wide, with no way to stop the flood of flashlights and baby cribs after the first thousand or two. Perhaps appeals for supplies in all future disasters should be limited to one slogan: "Send money."

Recovery. The effects of a major disaster do not disappear once the rubble is picked up and the bodies are carried away and the survivors are fed and sheltered. The community may take many months, sometimes years, to reestablish some sort of "normal" living pattern. This pattern can never be identical to the previous one. Some residents may have died in the disaster, some buildings destroyed, some previously unsuspected behavioral tendencies — bravery, generosity, cowardice, officiousness — exposed for the first time and not easily forgotten again. But few if any people take the opportunity to build a completely new life. Most will

348

continue to live in the same area, will revert to the same personality patterns as before — including not only those related to racial and class differences, but all the little idiosyncrasies that have supported identity for a lifetime. Those few who do discover themselves during the disaster or who afterwards try to carry out disaster-induced compacts with God to be better people, ministers of the gospel, benefactors to the needy, seem so small in number or so quiet in their transformation that they seldom register on the social scientist's instruments.

Entire communities often show an unusual resurgence after disaster, a recovery so strong that the community is wealthier and more productive than it has ever been. Disaster researchers have invented a general term for this phenomenon, the "amplified rebound" (Fritz, 1961), and have been tempted by it to take Toynbee's "challenge and response" hypothesis of societal progress (1946) seriously. The postwar recovery of Germany and Japan from multiple man-made disasters is probably the most dramatic example of amplified rebound in history. But the fact that these nations received substantial outside help, and for many years redirected much effort and wealth away from the usual military channels, makes difficult an assessment of whether the amplified rebound depends upon distinctive psychological responses to disaster, or whether it would occur even without disaster wherever outside help and military budget-slashing occur. Most individual communities that have experienced dramatic recovery from disaster have also received unusual levels of outside assistance, particularly from the central government, so the issue remains unsettled.

If outside aid is indeed necessary, the amplified rebound may nicely illustrate an irony central to most disaster research. It is an irony that I have not seen noted in the disaster literature, though its separate elements are frequently remarked upon. Modern disaster research was initiated and funded mainly on the assumption that it would be useful in planning for civil defense and recovery in the event of nuclear war. It has indeed been extremely informative and often practically useful, both in revealing phenomena that occur with substantial frequency in disasters, and in negating longstanding but unfounded assumptions about disaster behavior. Yet many if not most of its major findings would be quite inapplicable to nuclear war, because of sharp differences between large-scale atomic bombardment and relatively limited natural or man-made disasters. The irony may turn out to be most telling with regard to the amplified rebound, inasmuch as massive outside aid to hydrogen-bombed communities after World War III seems a remote possibility. But the irony has other features, several of them potentially as gruesome for the survivors. Let us consider more closely our ultimate source of fear, our final disaster.

349

the psychological casualties of world war three: the ultimate disaster

"Do your studies demonstrate that American society can recover from a nuclear attack?"
"Yes! all except the people."

— Robert J. Lifton
Birds

In the year of the Judsonia tornado, a science fiction writer named Wilson Tucker published a short story, "To a Ripe Old Age" (1952a), and a novel, *The Long Loud Silence* (1952b). Both begin with the same anti-hero in the same circumstance: waking from a monumental binge in a fleabag hotel, he finds that a massive and mysterious disaster has hit the United States sometime during his several days and nights of drunken stupor. No one else in the hotel is still alive; no one is alive in the streets except a solitary dog. Then the short story and the novel abruptly head off in very different directions.

The short story's protagonist, George Young, is surprised to find that the dog talks perfect English, which it says George taught it through mental telepathy as he slept off his binge. George reacts with outrage to this story and drives the dog away. It is replaced by a flea-bitten but talking sparrow, and then finally by a magnificently bikinied woman. She is highly cooperative, but as they enter upon another extended binge, she has trouble maintaining her womanly form and gradually reveals that she is a scavenger from another planet, trailing after the Hunters who have by now eaten up everybody else on earth. They left George alone because he stank so badly from the whiskey in which he soaked himself at the height of his grand original binge. George is uncertain whether the scavenger "woman" will continue consuming whiskey instead of George, so he pumps her full of poison and locks her in a bank vault. But he has second thoughts. Fade to thirty years later: George is still drinking, still trying to hit upon the vault combination that will yield him the absolutely very last "woman" on earth.

In the novel he is named Corporal Russell Gary, and the dog does not talk. The girl Gary soon finds is an ordinary nineteen-year-old who enjoys the disaster because it has freed her to loot the city's jewelry stores of every diamond she can carry. Corporal Gary appreciates her willingness to prove in bed that she is older than she looks, but he views her jewelry collection with grim realism: diamonds are junk if they can't be traded for food or water or human services. He views everything else in the book with the same grim realism; while the short story was told with a half-deadpan, half-bawdy hilarity, the novel is a tough recital of life and death as they really are lived and died following a nuclear war.

350

Nuclear war, in this case, is mixed with botulism and pneumonic plague. The attack was weak enough to permit the nearly intact survival of American civilization west of the Mississippi; the western survivors now devote substantial energy to insuring that the plague-infested survivors east of the Mississippi never cross the river alive.

Corporal Gary has the right mixture of natural disease resistance, toughness, luck, amorality, and military skills to survive not only the collapse of society but the depredations of other survivors, who are interested less in rebuilding than in guaranteeing their own next meal. He loses the girl, but finally manages to cross the Mississippi west — only to discover he is still a plague carrier, the source of early death to everyone he meets and the object of a massive manhunt by the military police who control the remainder of the country. Gary recrosses the river east, and settles down bitterly to the task of keeping himself alive from day to day — by searching the ruins for canned goods, by sneaking through the countryside to avoid energy-consuming battles with other survivors, by killing anyone he does meet. Fade to many years later: Corporal Gary leaves his cave (houses are hard to conceal or defend) to grub for roots, field mice, anything edible; he runs into a trap self-baited by a naked woman; he manages to overpower her, and discovers that she's the girl he found and lost just after the initial disaster. At this point in the original manuscript, Tucker has told me, Corporal Gary dumped the woman into the pot of boiling water she'd prepared for him. Food is food, and hunters are hunters. But Tucker's editors objected to cannibalism among friends, so in the published novel Corporal Gary is left chewing on a convenient rabbit and planning to use the woman as bait to catch other survivors. Happy ending.

POSTNUCLEAR NORMALITY

Wilson Tucker's editors may simply have had weak stomachs. But even if they'd been tough enough to read closely the available scientific literature on disaster survivors, they could have argued against his original ending on the basis of empirical data. Survivors seldom attempt to harm other survivors, seldom even show such antiproperty behavior as looting. They help when they can; they rebuild as quickly as possible. Herman Kahn (1962a) has published a neat little table showing how long it would take American society to recuperate from a nuclear war, given a certain level of deaths — five years of recuperation after ten million deaths, for instance; fifty years after eighty million deaths. Even with extensive carbon-14 radioactivity remaining, which might make the environment "more hostile to human life for, say, 10,000 years," Kahn feels people could rebuild, could recover without superhuman effort, could once again lead "normal and happy lives." "The quality of life would not necessarily have been changed dramatically," he says at one point, and

351

adds at another: "While everybody's lives and thoughts will be affected by a war, the character structure of the survivors is unlikely to be changed in any startling fashion." Wilson Tucker's depiction of a survivor changing from a mild compassion and an interest in the restoration of American society, to a state of complete callousness and animal savagery, is obviously as much a fantasy as his story about the survivor who hears dogs talk and sees women transformed into alien scavengers.

It's an obvious fantasy, that is, if you limit your reading and thinking largely to "normal" disasters, or "traditional" military actions, or "short-term" psychological effects of nuclear war. When you let yourself think about other possibilities (as all good science fiction writers do); when you search the literature for unusual disasters, which may have something in common with massive nuclear attack; when you return to the survivors of Hiroshima and Nagasaki twenty years later — then you may begin paying more attention to the Wilson Tuckers and less to the Herman Kahns.

The postdisaster behaviors described by Tucker may not have appeared full-blown in any substantial group of modern survivors. But the seeds are there, waiting for fertile soil — the seeds both of Corporal Gary's savage egotism and of George Young's combination of fantasy, drink, and denial. If one conclusion can be extracted from all the research on fear-arousing situations, it is that human beings will generally try to cope realistically with danger if they can, and will institute psychological defenses against recognizing the danger if realistic action appears too difficult or too ineffective. Corporal Gary's reality-oriented behaviors were usually rather successful, although physical survival had its destructive effects on his psyche. George Young was in a worse situation; and whether we take his visions of conversational dogs and space-women as realities imposed on him by his author-creator or as fantasies of his own, his responses were about what might be expected of a man who awakes to find the rest of humanity gone. It's downright unrealistic to expect realism in such circumstances.

POSTWAR AND PREWAR DENIAL

Certain varieties of limited defensiveness are characteristic of survivors in less comprehensive disasters. The disaster syndrome itself, the temporary daze and apathy found in a minority of survivors, involves an elementary kind of defensiveness, a withdrawal of attention from what for the moment cannot be borne. The quick assumption of many survivors that they alone have been hit may also have its defensive functions: if only one house has been destroyed, plenty of help must be immediately forthcoming from everyone else.

The misreading or ignoring of danger cues before a disaster strikes is another sort of defensive maneuver, which protects oneself not only from

352

perhaps unnecessary fears, but from troublesome efforts to take realistic protective actions. Refusal to evacuate when threatened by a probable flood or hurricane is a common example. An even more common example may be found in the two hundred million people in this country who go ahead living their normal lives with only rare acknowledgment that a war could destroy everything they value. Herman Kahn (1962b) has himself urged the populace to "think about the unthinkable," rather than to go on ignoring all possibilities of nuclear war and its aftermath; and he has argued for such actions as constructing fallout shelters to reduce casualties in such a war. But he has also promoted a dangerous kind of predisaster defensiveness, it seems to me, by using his dryly optimistic calculations of postwar survival to argue against devoting more of our energies to the incomparably harder task of thinking about how to avoid war altogether. Kahn would certainly *prefer* peace, naturally; but since America could survive even a rather massive nuclear holocaust, we should continue to explore the usefulness of large and small atomic wars in achieving our aims. Maybe it would take a while to restore the buildings afterward; maybe American living standards would fall for a time to those of the 1930's; but normalcy will prevail.

The degree of predisaster denial present in Kahn's own thinking is difficult to assess. He does pay attention to criticisms of his position; he tries to use hard data whenever such data are available. But as Raymond Aron has noted in the introduction to one of Kahn's books (1962b), the ability to "neutralize" one's feelings about human suffering at least temporarily is vital to the nuclear war analyst's profession. The danger, of course, is that temporary neutralization of feelings may be so effective it interferes with adequate analysis of the problems at hand. What appears to me an extreme example of this process can be found in David Heer's *After Nuclear Attack: A Demographic Inquiry* (1965), prepared for the U.S. Office of Civil Defense.

Dr. Heer is clearly a responsible individual. He begins his discussion by noting that people sometimes defend against anxiety about nuclear war by not thinking realistically. Throughout the discussion he takes great care to note the different outcomes one might expect from nuclear attacks during daytime and nighttime hours, from attacks primarily on military targets (the "Spadefork attack," 18 per cent of the population killed) or on major industrial as well as military targets (the "Holifield attack," 30 per cent fatalities nationwide); he even admits that other official estimates run from over 50 to over 80 per cent fatalities. He cites possible sources of bias after each calculation he presents; he invites critical comments on his methodology. But it is not his methodology or his statistical biases or his careful tone that are the problem; it is his unvarying focus only on what his methods tell him. I generally feel that professional people should stick to their areas of expertise when they are trying to sound like professionals; but maybe one should renounce one's expertise altogether when one's professionalism leads to statements like these:

For the United States as a whole, the composition of the 1960 Presidential vote was 49.7 per cent Democratic and 50.3 per cent Republican and other. After the Holifield attack, the proportion Democratic would decline to 48.2 per cent and the proportion voting for the Republican and other parties would increase slightly to 51.8 per cent.

. . . after this [daytime Holifield] attack the proportion of the total population enrolled in school attending college would be reduced from 6.6 to 6.1 per cent.

. . . This figure of 7 per cent, derived from a formula which slightly overpredicts illegitimacy for the United States, probably represents an upper limit to the proportion of all births in the United States which would be illegitimate following a severe daytime attack. We conclude, therefore, that a very large increase in illegitimacy would probably not be a consequence of any foreseeable nuclear attack.

What Heer ignores, and what Kahn (1960, 1962b) and other optimistic nuclear war scholars (e.g., Nordlie, 1969) have treated spottily at best, is the nature of psychological reactions to such a war. They may be right in their calculations of population change and survival of resources. But if we're talking about a nuclear war of any real size, Heer's apparent assumption that normal behavior patterns will continue in the surviving portion of humans, and Kahn's airy assurances (1962b) that "most survivors would not go through as horrible a set of personal experiences as many Russians, Germans, Poles, Yugoslavs, Japanese, and others did in World War II," are almost surely wrong.

THE EGOCENTRIC SURVIVOR

Defensive denial or George Young–type fantasies will not be prominent survivor reactions for long after such a war. Limited psychological defenses may remain in effect until the terror of the moment and the subsequent grief can gradually be worked through; but if the survivors are to go on surviving, they must advance to meet the new world created by the disaster. Following massive destruction, those who respond most adequately to the objective reality around them will be most likely to survive; this was Corporal Gary's forte. Damn social proprieties; save whatever's yours and take what you can from others — this seems a much more likely response, and a much more useful one under the circumstances, than the act of sitting down and telling yourself, "I am a male thirty-two-year-old American citizen, college-educated, liberal on social welfare issues and moderately conservative on the preservation of Constitutional rights."

The self-protective pattern is apparent even in non–nuclear disasters,

354

as represented in the frequent postdisaster behavior of trying to rescue one's family first, and responding to the demands of other social roles only when the family is safe. Following a really massive nuclear and/or CBW war, few people are going to consider their families or themselves as genuinely safe for a long time; and during this time, they are unlikely to devote much of their attention to restoring civilization. If external conditions are as bad as in Tucker's book, cannibalism itself might not be as unlikely as his editors seem to have thought. Cannibalism appears to have been fairly extensive during the siege of Leningrad in World War II (Gouré, 1962), and has cropped up often enough in other cases of high deprivation to show that it's a very real possibility whenever war abruptly destroys food supplies over wide areas and leaves a mainly urban population to cope for themselves. Perhaps civil defense handbooks should include a few basic recipes for *Homo sapiens* stew, just in case.

The one point at which Wilson Tucker seems to me to have fared little better than Kahn or Heer is in his depiction of the survivors' psychological reactions to their own survival-oriented behavior. Corporal Gary, though psychologically sensitive in some ways, develops emotional calluses too fast and too deep to convince me — even if he is a combat veteran. People are willing to do many more things than they approve of doing; and what they disapprove in their own behavior may drive them, if not to dissonance, then to severe guilt, self-punitive thoughts, perhaps suicide. Even if a goodly portion of our material civilization survives the war, as Kahn thinks likely, few people may be willing to put up with it if they have to go through life with the load of guilt that they acquired at the outset by looking out only for themselves and their families.

SURVIVORS OF HIROSHIMA

Robert Jay Lifton (1967), who has made an extensive psychological study of A-bomb survivors, found this guilt — not only over what the individual didn't do for others, but guilt merely at surviving when so many died — to be a pervasive aspect of survivor psychology almost two decades after the Hiroshima and Nagasaki blasts. The survivors had responded to this guilt by closing off their emotions from others, by living a life of psychological suffering focused on death, by continually fearing their own deaths and seeing whatever pleasures they had managed to take from postdisaster life as counterfeit. Such reactions have occurred among the survivors of other disasters too — those who lived through the Nazi concentration camps, for instance. But the entanglement with death is particularly pervasive when nuclear weapons are involved, because radiation effects may not appear immediately — may indeed be expressed, as Kahn (1962a) says so casually, only in a somewhat earlier mean age of mortality than would otherwise occur. Kahn had not had the opportunity, when he wrote of nuclear war survivors leading "normal and happy lives," to read Lifton's description of the lives of Hiroshima survivors. Nearly twenty years had passed and they were not dead yet; but they anticipated death with every headache or bruise. In many cases they had married and borne children (perhaps had done so more often than the population at large, Lifton suggests, as a compensatory mechanism). But the happiness they might have enjoyed within the family was spoiled by the fear that their children had irreparable genetic damage, that they themselves might suddenly die of radiation disease and leave their children parentless. And always whatever joy might well up momentarily was poisoned by the guilt of survivorhood, summarized by Lifton in this terrible sequence of unvoiced thoughts and feelings:

> I almost died; I should have died; I did die, or at least I am not really alive; or if I am alive, it is impure of me to be so; anything I do which affirms life is also impure and an insult to the dead, who alone are pure; and by living as if dead, I take the place of the dead and give them life.

In some ways the survivors of Hiroshima and Nagasaki may have suffered more than the survivors of a general nuclear war. They soon found themselves surrounded by people who had not been exposed to the bomb, people who aggressively took over their businesses and their cities and who refused to let the survivors marry the outsiders' daughters. The survivors were tainted as others were not; they were often pointed out as peculiar specimens, were actively sought out by reporters and researchers, including Lifton himself. If everyone were exposed to nuclear war, no such discrimination would exist.

But in other ways the experiences of the Japanese survivors were deceptively mild. In the next war, it is unlikely that any major American or Russian or Chinese city will escape with nothing worse than a twenty-kiloton bomb explosion. More bombs and much bigger bombs mean far fewer people left to experience psychological problems; but their exposure to the sight of far more destruction, to tens of times as many mutilated bodies, means that the problems they do have will make Lifton's interviewees altogether obsolete in their puny concerns about death. The survivors of Hiroshima and Nagasaki often wandered out of the city into the countryside, finding undestroyed villages and whole people among whom to rest themselves; the survivors of a full-scale war will find the villages ravaged too, by wayward bombs or drifting fallout or chemical-biological warfare. The sight of corpses and of seriously wounded survivors is consistently reported (e.g., by Janis, 1951) as a major source of psychological disturbance in disasters; what if the corpses and near-corpses stretch to the ragged horizon and beyond? Hiroshima and Nagasaki are both fully rebuilt cities now, but little of the rebuilding was done by survivors of the atomic blasts, and many of the resources necessary for rebuilding came from outside. What if there is no outside, and no population of unaffected people eager to fill every occupational and residential gap a war makes? Lifton notes indications that many survivors had maintained themselves only at "a lower level of psychic and socioeconomic existence than one would have settled for had one not been exposed to the bomb," that some had apparently entered a "premature retirement." What if, rather than displaying Corporal Gary's aggressive bursts of survival-directed energy, the entire remaining population after World War III opts for a very premature retirement? Will even Herman Kahn feel like summoning them to their duties?

One of the most eloquent spokesmen for the view that nuclear war involves more than just greater destructiveness was Dr. Takashi Nagai, a radiologist who died of X-ray–induced leukemia six years after he survived the Nagasaki blast. Some people were already arguing then that a civilization could survive an extensive nuclear war with no great difficulty. Dr. Nagai (1951) asked, even before the full extent of the bomb's psychological damage was apparent:

Do they understand, have they investigated what it does to the heart and conscience and mind of those who survive? Do they have any knowledge of our society of spiritual bankrupts, now striving lamely to function as a community? . . . It is this spiritual wreckage, which the visitor to Nagasaki's wastes does not see, that is indeed beyond repair.

Let us be very optimistic: let us assume that millions of Americans would physically survive the final nuclear war. Who among them would survive psychologically, with wounds so minor that they could begin to rebuild and repopulate the earth? Perhaps some few would. But I fear that the qualities which enabled them to escape unscathed would be the very same ones which enabled the war to occur in the first place: namely, an incredible insensitivity and a first-rate ability to misuse their own human intelligence. Maybe in fifty years or so they could even get things back in good enough working order to stage World War IV.

9
toward peace

the initiation of hostilities:
human aggressiveness

But, just as there are animal bodies and human bodies,
that is to say, combinations of cells each of which, as
compared with a single cell, is as big as a mountain, in
the same way there are huge organized agglomerations
of individuals, which are called "nations"; their existence
simply repeats on an amplified scale the existence of the
component cells, and whoever is unable to comprehend
the mystery, the reactions and the laws of the latter, will
utter only empty words when he comes to speak of strug-
gles between nations.

— Marcel Proust
The Past Recaptured

War is man's most social activity. Given a fairly decent war, people will work together as they have never worked for a peaceful objective. World War II united more people for common aims than any other enterprise in history. Wars on this scale could not be fought or even dreamed of without the highest faculties man has developed: complex problem-solving abilities, technological inventiveness, the power of speech and all that speech implies. Altruistic acts are more rampant in war than at any other time. Men risk their lives to save battle companions and civilian non-combatants; they face death gladly for their country's greater good; mothers and fathers donate their sons to the cause, reluctantly perhaps but with pride. War shows man at his most human; no true parallel exists among the "lower" animals.

But is war necessary for the display of such humanity? Is war necessary

358

at all? William James argued (1911), before the outlines of the first great war became dimly visible, that it is not:

> The fatalistic view of the war function is to me nonsense, for I know that war-making is due to definite motives and subject to prudential checks and reasonable criticisms, just like any other form of enterprise. And when whole nations are the armies and the science of destruction vies in intellectual refinement with the sciences of production, I see that war becomes absurd and impossible from its own monstrosity. Extravagant ambitions will have to be replaced by reasonable claims, and nations must make common cause against them.

James granted that war generates pride and excitement, "strenuous honor and disinterestedness," and that it will not leave us until it is replaced with an alternative which engenders similar emotions. James himself proposed a sort of CCC or Peace Corps, "a conscription of the whole youthful population to form for a certain number of years a part of the army enlisted against nature." Although his proposal received wide circulation, it obviously did little to prevent the subsequent wars of the twentieth century. But James's vision, the idea of applying "prudential checks" to the "definite motives" producing wars, has enticed psychologists ever since.

The thesis looks simple: Because social psychological theory and research have been useful in understanding inter*personal* relationships, why not apply them also to inter*national* relationships? Nations are, after all, composed of people, and important decisions about international affairs are made by individuals or small groups of individuals. So why not jump from studying behaviors that affect two or three people at a time in the laboratory, to behaviors that affect two or three billion people at a time in the world at large? You will have attained the ultimate in relevance; if your work is any good, you may even help save humanity from Armageddon. No psychologist has ever won the Nobel Peace Prize, but it's there, waiting.

The reality is a good bit more complicated even than Marcel Proust's sentence structure. Specialists in history, political science, and international relations, who have won no peace prizes either, are quick to point out that nations are not merely agglomerations of individuals, and do not necessarily follow the laws of individual behavior, even if such laws exist. Structural regularities, geographical circumstances, legal and traditional relationships between national governments must all be taken into account. A nation is not the same as a person; it's — it's — well, it's a *nation*.

Social psychologists certainly should enter upon research into international relations with more than their usual humility. But it's hard to deny that people really are somehow involved in international affairs, and that they often behave as people rather than as abstract entities called nations. Some of the gravest problems in international affairs arise, indeed, when people come to think they are not people at all, but infallible embodiments of political abstractions. Psychologists shouldn't assume they know everything necessary to understand the workings of international affairs, or even that with their methods they can eventually discover all they need to know. Equally, however, they need not assume that they have nothing to contribute to the study of behaviors at the international level.

Why do people fight wars? Psychologists often turn first to the motive structure of the individual battler. Actually, war can at various times and circumstances satisfy most social needs: n Achievement, because in modern warfare a great deal of precise workmanship is required, from the assembly-line employee in a tank factory as well as from the nuclear physicist developing a better bomb; n Affiliation, because uniting to fight the common enemy may bring people closer together than they ever were in peacetime; and so on. But psychologists have been less interested in how a war already begun may satisfy multiple motives, than in what motives initiate war. The need for power is clearly implicated in the wars begun by ancient and modern dictators — as well as in those wars initiated or maintained by modern democratic leaders when no vital interest of the nation is at stake. Machiavellian tendencies may also contribute, to the extent that they can be successfully discriminated from power motives. Machiavelli himself recommended using war as a political device under certain circumstances, and surely war offers the greatest arena for exercising Machiavellian talents. But the need most often cited as a basis for war, and the one most argued about by combative social scientists, is one to which this book has previously directed little attention: n Aggression.

Because aggressive behaviors play such a large role in wars, it seems quite reasonable to assume that a need for aggression is expressed through war. Indeed, some readers may be surprised to encounter any doubt as to whether such a need is a necessary part of man's psychological equipment. Doubts do exist; and since assumptions about inherent and acquired aggressive needs may strongly influence any additional assumptions about human warmaking behaviors, I'd better air the main doubts right now. Scientific assumptions and data concerning human aggressiveness come in many subtle hues and outlines. Rather than exploring them all, I'll summarize them in terms of three commonly recognized types of hypotheses (cf. Daniels and Gilula, 1970): innate aggressiveness, aggression as a function of frustration, and aggressiveness acquired through social learning.

INNATE AGGRESSIVENESS

William McDougall (1908) argued that man has an inherited "instinct of pugnacity," which may be even "stronger in the European peoples than

360

it was in primitive man." One major argument for the existence of such an instinct, McDougall thought, was that tribal wars were still fought in such areas as Central Borneo for no other explainable reason: "If one asks of an intelligent chief why he keeps up this senseless practice of going on the warpath, the best reason he can give is that, unless he does so, his neighbors will not respect him and his people and will fall upon them and exterminate them." (Or as a certain commander in chief once put it, the United States must invade Cambodia or seem to the rest of the world a "pitiful helpless giant.") Following World War I, Sigmund Freud (1920; English translation, 1955) saw man instead as possessing an inherent drive for *self*-destruction. Freud developed this death-instinct hypothesis partly as a logical extension of his general drive-reduction model of personality, but also partly to explain much apparently irrational human violence that he felt was otherwise unexplainable. Aggression against others entered the Freudian picture in a roundabout way: the life instincts, keeping self-destruction at bay at least for a while, forced displacement of self-destructive impulses outward onto other people. These other people might well resent the idea that they were only the second choice on the destroyer's list; but the ultimate effect would likely be the same as with a pure instinct for pugnacity.

Konrad Lorenz (1966) and other ethologists have recently revived instinctual explanations of aggression with a greater degree of scientific sophistication; Robert Ardrey (1961) and other popularizers have once again reduced the sophistication to a McDougallian simplicity. In all these accounts, some sort of aggressive drive is assumed to be inborn, and drive level is usually assumed to build gradually until it must be discharged — against an "appropriate" target if possible, against a less appropriate one if necessary. The evolutionary advantage of such a drive is also insisted upon, though why it is advantageous for man to thirst after the blood of his fellow men rather than after food animals is not always spelled out. Ardrey depends largely on evidence that certain of our prehuman ancestors were hunters and/or killers of their own species; the Mark of Cain is then supposed to have been inherited by us, the warmongering descendants.

The presence of an inborn urge for aggression in humans is at least as difficult to establish as the existence of any other inborn human drive besides the overtly physiological ones. That our ancestors were capable of violence, or that the usually gentle chimpanzees today share a similar potential, shouldn't startle us; we are obviously capable of violence too. But *must* we periodically discharge some sort of stored-up aggressive energy? The evidence is moot. Violence can usually be shown to serve other functions than such energy discharge; and if it does serve other functions, an innate component need not be assumed. The innate tendency *may* be there, but it doesn't have to be, whatever the testimony of a prehistoric canine tooth or a stone axe embedded in a human skull.

uncertainty of generalizations from nonhuman species to humans already been treated at length; and even if generalization were pos-ს, such researchers as John Paul Scott (1958, 1967) argue as convincingly against innate aggressiveness in animals as other scientists have argued in favor. Finally, *even if it were all so* — even if we demonstrably did have an innate aggressive need, and even if this need were for some curious evolutionary reason primarily directed toward other humans — even then, wars need not happen, because the expression of such a drive could surely be controlled, diverted, shifted into new channels, much as man has done with sex. McDougall, Freud, Ardrey, and Lorenz all have admitted the possibility of such diversion, inasmuch as human beings are not always engaged in individual and collective strife. The unresolved question then becomes whether innate aggressiveness can be *entirely* expressed by other means than physical combat.

THE FRUSTRATION-AGGRESSION HYPOTHESIS

Upon the eve of World War II, John Dollard and several other Yale psychologists (Dollard et al., 1939) rejected Freud's apparently mystical death instinct, a child of World War I, and returned to Freud's prewar concepts about aggression. Frustration always leads to aggression, the Yale group announced; aggression is always preceded by frustration. Their hard evidence came largely from research on animals and small children, but their application was to lynchings and fascist dictatorships. When others noted exceptions to the frustration-aggression hypothesis in its absolute form, various group members (e.g., Miller, 1941) modified it to say something like, "Frustration *usually* leads to aggression; aggression is *usually* preceded by frustration." In that form, the hypothesis has generated much of the experimental work on aggression, in adult humans as well as children and animals, and it remains a strong contender in the aggression-theory battle under the current leadership of Leonard Berkowitz (1962, 1965). By now hundreds and perhaps thousands of college students and schoolchildren have been experimentally frustrated in any number of ways, from being interrupted while working arithmetic problems to having candy given to them and then taken back again. They have responded aggressively in any number of ways, from telling hostile stories on TAT cards to (rarely) punching the experimenter. Frustration has by no means always produced visible aggression in these experiments, but it seems to have done so considerably more often than not, particularly when the frustrator himself stays around to be aggressed against. When he isn't available, aggressive responses are sometimes directed toward other targets, as in classic Freudian displacement, but also sometimes not.

This occasional failure of frustration to generate aggression makes trouble for at least the original strong form of the frustration-aggression hypothesis; but it also raises intriguing possibilities regarding the permanent cessation of international hostilities. The Dollard group explicitly denied any assumptions as to whether the connection between frustration and aggression is inborn or learned. Certain consequences of its being learned are noted under the next subheading. Even if it were inborn the connection could presumably be modified, though the Dollard group argued that it could not simply be blocked through threats of punishment; the threats would themselves be perceived as frustrating the aggressive impulse, and would therefore further increase the level of aggressive motivation. For humans, a more effective way to interrupt the frustration-aggression sequence may be to redefine the situation originally seen as frustrating.

Shahbaz Khan Mallick and Boyd McCandless (1966) tried this with American third-graders. The children were asked individually to perform a series of easy block-building tasks, and were promised five cents per completed task. But another child, really an experimental confederate, kept getting in the way or "accidentally" knocking down the blocks. The interfering child then left, and the frustrated child either was given a chance to shoot a toy gun at a picture of a child resembling the frustrator, or was allowed to talk casually with the experimenter. During this conversation, the experimenter explained that the frustrater had been sleepy and upset and would probably have been more helpful if he'd been promised part of the subject's winnings. After the frustrated child engaged in symbolic aggression with the toy gun or heard the verbal interpretation of the frustrater's motives, he was permitted to take out his remaining aggressive feelings directly against the frustrater: he was shown a box with two buttons on it, and was told that he could help or frustrate the frustrater's own block-building efforts, which would soon begin in the next room, by pressing one button or the other.

The frustrater's initial interference with the volunteer's block-building did induce volunteers to behave significantly more aggressively with the button-box than control children who were never frustrated. The opportunity to shoot at a target resembling the frustrater did not reduce this aggressiveness significantly; but the experimenter's statements about the frustrater did. Volunteers who were given some good reasons for the frustrater's behavior reported liking him more afterward, and displayed significantly less aggression against him, than volunteers who got no such explanation.

Human beings respond automatically to few stimuli. Before frustration can lead to aggression, they must first see themselves as frustrated (blocked in some sort of goal attainment); second, they must see the frustration as intentional on the part of the frustrater (unintentional frustration has usually not produced aggression in the experiments where it has been studied); and third, they must define a particular behavior as an acceptable form of aggressive response. By changing their definition or perception of any element in this sequence, they may define frustration out of existence, render overt aggressive responses unacceptable to themselves, or at least greatly soften the degree of aggression they see as appropriate. On the other hand, a talented demagogue can reverse the process anywhere along the line: create frustrations where none really existed, blame an innocent bystander, or legitimize any form of destructiveness as a valid response to frustration. Words may never hurt you, but they have a lot to do with how many sticks and stones come your way.

AGGRESSION VIA SOCIAL LEARNING

Just as frustration may not always produce aggression, so may aggression come from sources other than frustration. Albert Bandura and Richard H. Walters (1963), in offering an extensive set of hypotheses about social learning, have proposed that a good deal of aggressive behavior comes from imitating social models. Little Eddie may kick the hound dog because it ate his fried chicken leg; baby Jack, freshly arrived upon the scene, may kick the hound too without knowing a chicken leg was ever involved. Why should baby Jack act at all aggressively against the hound dog, without any personal frustrations to impel him? Because he has learned in the past that imitating older brother Eddie often leads to good things; because Eddie laughed when he kicked the hound, so it looked like fun; because the hound dog yelped interestingly when it was kicked. Aggression can do plenty of other things besides relieving frustration, and the behavior of Eddie or other "models" will often reveal to the onlooker what else it might be able to do.

In the typical experiment on social learning and aggression, a child watches another person act aggressively, and furthermore watches him get a reward, a punishment, or nothing at all for his aggression. Then the child is given his own opportunity to aggress. If he has seen the model rewarded for aggression, chances are he will act aggressively too. If he has seen the model get punished, chances are he won't be as aggressive as the child who has seen aggression rewarded, or even the child who has seen nothing come from aggression. Bandura applies such findings to television dramas, where the child may see the villain get punished for his aggressions but is even more likely to see the hero rewarded for *his* aggressions — and who is the child more likely to imitate? (For the child old enough to discriminate fantasy from reality, however, violent television drama may serve other functions as well. Feshbach and Singer [1971] found that after viewing only such programs for six weeks, several groups of teen-age boys showed significantly less aggressive behavior than equivalent groups who had viewed mainly situation comedies and variety shows. Feshbach and Singer suggest that the violent programs may have helped these boys to control their aggressive impulses, permitting vicarious rather than direct expression of their pent-up hostili-

364

ties. But not all the groups studied showed these effects; and the general beneficence or harmfulness of televised aggression remains in doubt.)

Much wartime aggression is likely to be of the social learning variety. American combatants run into direct frustrations from the enemy much less frequently nowadays, particularly if the Americans are aggressing from the air. They may get occasional pep talks from their commanding officers, telling them that out there in the jungle are the gooks who've killed their buddies; the gooks are thus verbally identified as frustraters. But the soldiers probably don't need that, because most of their training tells them that if they follow orders appropriately, they'll be rewarded, and that if they don't, they'll be punished. They may perform the appropriate aggressive acts without feeling aggressive at all and without necessarily satisfying any aggressive motives. It's simply what you do to get ahead.

ALTERING AGGRESSIVENESS

This last form of aggression may sound particularly depressing; but it also leaves the most room for optimism about changing aggressive patterns. If aggressive motives are inherent, we can never expunge them entirely, even if we think we should; nor can we possibly eliminate all frustrations from the world. But we can, if we wish, do plenty to eliminate aggressive models and to change reward-punishment patterns for functional aggression. We may not do so; we may continue venerating violence in the mass media and on the battlefield, may continue rewarding the disguised violence of industrial pollution and environmental destruction. But we *could* do something to change all that, if we really wanted to.

The other hypotheses about aggression leave some room for optimism, too, although not as much. Frustrations can be dealt with by verbal redefinition or by actual removal of their sources. We may not be able to eliminate all of them, but we have the resources and the technology to eliminate those large enough to end in war. Even if aggression is bred into our bones, it may not have to be directed at human beings, or at animate objects of any kind. Inanimate objects may not always be appropriate vehicles for catharsis, however, as the experiment by Mallick and McCandless showed; and some objects may be better than others. So if we can't always eliminate aggressive feelings by redefining the situation, the frustrating event, or the frustrater's motives, we may need to put more effort into discovering what the nonhuman objects are upon which we can vent our hostilities most cathartically, without rewarding ourselves for being aggressive. I'll get back to such possibilities toward the end of the chapter. But even without novel ways of expressing aggression harmlessly, we may at least be able to remove international relations from the list of permissible aggressive outlets.

Some writers protest that we should leave humanity's aggressive impulses alone, because such urges account for most or perhaps all of human progress. If man never attacked problems or struggled against the environment, they say, we would be nowhere. These observations unfortunately confuse aggression with such distinct motives as n Achievement. But even if aggression is considered in its relatively pure form, I should say that I am not arguing for its complete obliteration. John Paul Scott (1967), among others, notes certain very useful functions played by mild aggressive behaviors. The yellow-bellied marmot, for instance, hibernates in the company of many fellow marmots without aggression; but once it emerges from its hole in warm weather, it becomes somewhat hostile toward its hole-mates. Such behavior leads the previously snuggled-together marmots to disperse over the area around their mutual hole, thus guaranteeing more effective feeding behavior. If humans felt no hostilities toward each other at all, if love were our only mutual emotion, we might spend most of our time clumped together in one big ball, like the hibernating marmots. That would be a rather impractical and unproductive way to live. But surely there is some reasonable middle ground between clumping together eternally and blasting each other into little pieces.

games nations play: simulations of peace

We have talked for decades with ever increasing light-mindedness about war and conquest, as if these were merely operations on a chessboard; how was this possible save as the result of a tone of mind which no longer pictured to itself the fate of individuals, but thought of them only as figures or objects belonging to the material world?

— Albert Schweitzer
Philosophy of Civilization

My colleague Robert Sommer one day became disturbed at the enthusiasm with which his young children were playing Monopoly. Opening night at the opera and hotels on Park Place seemed to him hardly representative of the realities that these children would soon face. So as a start at educating them in some other contemporary roles besides that of the Wall Street banker, Sommer suggested that one child act as a black player, with his own special rules. For instance, the "black" player got less money than whites when he passed Go, but when he went bankrupt the whites had to pay him welfare.

Sommer's children were soon arguing over who'd get to be the black player in each game — and also began showing increased appreciation of at least the simpler differences between real black and white social and economic opportunities. One thing led to another, until what was originally a slightly modified Monopoly game had become a very different "Blacks and Whites" game, with its own ghettoes and lily-white suburbs. After Sommer and Judy Tart (who collaborated on later stages of the game) sold it to *Psychology Today*, "Blacks and Whites" underwent still more changes, until it is now marketed not as a children's game at all but a means by which "each of us, rejoicing in his unique personhood, joins with other players in a community spoof on the artificialities of a racist tradition."

Games are commonly thought of as entertainment devices only; but as "Blacks and Whites" suggests, they can serve other useful purposes. Several business schools utilize business games to educate their students in the presumed realities of the commercial world; the military has long used war games of one sort or another for both training and strategy development. Military and civilian strategists together give strategic games heavy play in trying to determine how nuclear wars might be most effectively fought, without having to go through the necessity of fighting a nuclear war to find out. Finally, social psychologists and other social scientists sometimes use games as laboratory abstractions of social interchange, hoping to derive useful hypotheses about general social behaviors from the sorts of behaviors displayed within the game's narrow confines. They may even at times use games similar to those of the military strategists, although in such cases they are usually interested less in strategic outcomes than in the specific psychological processes that might produce such outcomes. A game used this way serves the same purpose as any set of experimental instructions designed to exclude the influence of certain variables and to control the influence of others.

ZERO-SUM AND NON-ZERO-SUM GAMES

The scientific study of game-playing behavior, both theoretical and actual, has attained heights of complexity that we need not attempt to scale here. One simple distinction can be usefully made before we go any further — between zero-sum games and non-zero-sum games. Poker and strip poker might be taken as prototypes of these two categories. Poker as most people play it is directed mainly toward winning money. What one player wins, others must lose, and at the end of the game the total wins and losses will add up to zero. Strip poker as most people play it is directed mainly toward sexual excitement (I would guess, without having made an empirical study of motivational arousal in strip poker). Though players "lose" socks and bras and so forth as the game progresses, other people don't win those items, and the principal outcome for a reasonably sophisticated set of players is not a set of pluses and minuses that equals zero but a set of pluses only, in terms of fun and good times and the simultaneous satisfaction of voyeuristic and exhibitionistic impulses. I can imagine strip poker games when instead the outcome would be an overall minus: where all the players come away terribly embarrassed and ashamed of their behavior, or are so hostile toward each other initially that they use their progressive exposure to make caustic comments about each other's bodies and motives. But whether it's a good strip poker game or a bad one, the outcome would rarely if ever equal zero.

Monopoly, in terms of the main criteria for winning and losing, is a zero-sum game. So are chess, checkers, and even games like basketball where the total points may be in the hundreds but where one team definitely wins ($+1$) and the other definitely loses (-1). Offhand I can't think of a commercially marketed non-zero-sum game, either for children or for adults.

International relations has often been viewed as a game. It has players, two or more in number. It has rules, not always observed but nonetheless understood by most players. It has moves, made by players individually or in concert. The moves deliver certain outcomes to the players: each nation sometimes wins and sometimes loses such things as natural resources, prestige, and lives. The game of international relations has no specific end point as most games do, or at least it hasn't come to one yet. But a specific end point is not one of the requirements of a game.

Simple-minded folk, including a substantial percentage of military strategists, often see international relations as a zero-sum game. Whenever the United States wins, Russia loses, and vice versa. But taking a broad view of possible consequences, the game of international relations is clearly a non-zero-sum game. If all nations lived in harmony and helped each other whenever they could, everybody would come out ahead. If one or more nations begins a nuclear war, we'll all end up with a minus score. So if you intend to try understanding international relations by using game-type simulations, you should at least begin with a non-zero-sum game.

By far the greatest number of attempts to simulate international behavior through games has been made, I would guess, by military agencies or under contract to military agencies. Not only because many have been zero-sum games but also because most have been concerned with how to fight wars, they will not be discussed in this peace-oriented chapter. But occasional game simulations have been aimed toward studying processes leading to peace; and they have typically been non-zero-sum games. You may find it easier to fight a war if you believe you can win; but you cannot produce peace if you think you alone will win.

A PACIFIST COMPUTER

One peace-oriented game study was sponsored by the Defense Department's Advanced Research Projects Agency. That may or may not explain why the peace strategy in this instance didn't work. The authors

(Shure, Meeker, and Hansford, 1965) didn't intentionally set out to prove that peace is impossible, but they did choose a rather extreme strategy for its attainment. Their entire operation was computerized, as experimental games frequently are. Computers aren't necessarily a part of such studies, but they can help keep track of fast game-playing, and in such cases as this one, they also make it possible to establish a programmed artificial player to compete against the real one. The real player in the Shure game didn't know he was playing against a computer; he thought his opponent was one of twenty-three other volunteers who came into the lab at the same time he did. The computer was actually playing twenty-four separate games simultaneously with these twenty-four players — another advantage of computers being their efficiency.

In each game, real player and computer were told that the object was for each of them to transmit as many single-word messages as he could through a common communications channel. The messages were provided by the experimenter; the channel could be used by only one player at a time. If both players tried to use the channel at the same time, an "overload" resulted, which meant that both players were charged "operating costs" until one or both withdrew his message. In each game, a total of three messages could be sent, if everything went smoothly; overloads cut down on the total number that could be processed. After several games were played, each real player (but not the computer) was paid a modest sum depending on how many messages he had sent.

In this situation, the obviously preferable game strategy for everyone would have been cooperation — taking turns within each game, alternating first turns from game to game — except for two further complications. First, each real player was led to believe he had two cohorts in other booths who were always urging him on to victory rather than to cooperation. (Actually, these urgings were also coming from the computer.) Second, all players were told that whoever played first in each game got to use the "jolt-back" action for the rest of the game. The jolt-back action was useful whenever the opponent was blocking the message channel by trying to send his own message: it both gave the opponent a painful electric jolt (supposedly; the opponent was of course the computer, who thrived on electric jolts), and also knocked the opponent's message out of the channel. The opponent could then jolt the first player back in revenge with another electric shock if he wished, but he couldn't knock the first player's message out.

How does this relate to peace and war? Mainly in that the computer who played all these games was a pacifist, firm but perpetually nonviolent. The computer always let the real player go first, so the real player always had command of the effectively violent jolt-back action; and the computer never used its own power to shock the real player. Instead, to force the real player to cooperate, the pacifist computer chose to lay its body down in the road, so to speak: it put its message in the channel as soon as the real player had sent his first message through, and refused to move out of the channel until the first player either agreed to let it have a full turn or else jolted it out of the channel with an electric shock. Meanwhile the real player's two simulated companions were urging him to make as much money for the three of them as he could, by refusing to give the opponent a fair turn.

Nonviolent resistance didn't come off at all well in this study. Out of 143 real players (all college students), 75 announced their intention to refuse their opponent his fair share from the outset; all but 4 of these stuck by their guns — or rather, their jolt-back buttons — through the first several games. Of the remaining 68, 54 succumbed to temptation or to the demands of their companions rather rapidly, and began jolting their opponent regularly in order to win the game. As the computer continued to resist nonviolently, somewhat less than a third of the participants came around to treating him fairly; two-thirds went on jolting to the end. Only 18 refused to shock him at all.

That old pacifist Friedrich Nietzsche once wrote (Kaufmann, 1968):

> And perhaps the great day will come when a people, distinguished by wars and victories and by the highest development of a military order of intelligence, and accustomed to make the heaviest sacrifices for these things, will exclaim of its own free will, "We break the sword," and will smash its entire military establishment down to its lowest foundations. *Rendering oneself unarmed when one has been the best-armed,* out of a height of feeling – that is the means to real peace, which must always rest on a peace of mind; whereas the so-called armed peace, as it now exists in all countries, is the absence of peace of mind.

A noble vision, but one that seems unlikely to be realized if Soviet or Chinese military leaders are anywhere near as heartless as Shure's American college sophomores. Neither Nietzsche's vision nor the total pacifism of Shure's computer, however, resembles the paths by which most psychologists would seek lasting peace.

SIMULATED GRIT

Charles Osgood, the social psychologist who developed congruity theory (Chapter Six), has for the past decade advocated what seems to many a sounder plan (Osgood, 1962, 1965). Osgood reasons that if the United States continues to seek nuclear superiority over the Soviet Union and vice versa, every increase in arms by one side will generate greater anxiety on the other side, resulting in a similar arms increase. But if the United States were to begin making a series of small conciliatory moves, each clearly announced in advance and each easily reversible if the Soviet Union did *not* respond, then the USSR might begin to reciprocate. If it did, the United States could make further moves, wait for the Soviets to respond further in turn, and in that way initiate a modest downward escalation of war preparations rather than an upward escalation. Once an atmosphere of mutual trust had developed with regard to this series of small conciliatory moves, then perhaps agreements on mutual inspection of weapons plants and weapons stockpiles could be reached, and major reductions of arms could be initiated with some confidence by both sides.

Osgood calls his plan "Graduated Reciprocation in Tension-reduction," or GRIT for short. Amatai Etzioni, who independently proposed a similar plan (Etzioni, 1962, 1967), has accumulated evidence suggesting that just such a procedure was followed by the Kennedy administration following the Cuban missile crisis, and that the Soviet Union responded appropriately. But Kennedy's death, the resulting change in administrations, and the heating up of the Vietnam War, among other things, interfered with the continuation of this "Kennedy experiment." It's also hard to judge whether the thaw in American–Russian relations following the Cuban missile crisis resulted from the GRIT–like moves, or whether entirely fortuitous circumstances (such as the distractions created by Mao and de Gaulle) were responsible. William Gamson and Andre Modigliani (1971), in a quantitative study of Soviet-American relationships between 1946 and 1963, found that whenever either side made a major accommodative move, the other side responded with a major conciliatory move, as predicted by the Osgood model rather than by more "hard-nosed" hypotheses. But again, these moves were not organized into an expanding conciliatory sequence; and the researchers' interpretation of specific moves as accommodative or conciliatory may be open to argument. Fortunately we have a more strictly controlled, though at the same time much more artificial, test of the Osgood GRIT plan, in a game study by Marc Pilisuk and Paul Skolnick (1968).

Pilisuk and Skolnick had two volunteers playing at a time. The volunteers were seated opposite each other at a table, with a partition between them so they couldn't directly see each other's moves. Each volunteer was given a board with five levers on it. Switch a lever to the left, and you reveal a picture of a missile; to the right, and you disclose a factory. Each game began with five missiles showing; during each of his five turns, a volunteer could "convert" one or two missiles to factories, reconvert factories to missiles, or leave the status quo undisturbed. At the end of the game, each player was told how many missiles and factories the other player had finally settled upon, via a light signal on his board. Then the next game began, toward a total of twenty-five games.

After the last game, each player was paid a penny a point for his total score, on this basis: following each individual game the player got one point for each factory on his board, plus two points for each missile he had in excess of the other player's missiles; he was docked two points for each missile he had fewer of than the other player. So the best outcome

371

possible for both players together would come from complete "disarmament" (five points apiece for five factories each), as might well be the case in the real world too. But if anybody had any missiles at the end of a game, a player would profit individually from missile superiority, and would lose points by being on the short end of a missile gap. In fact, if he ended with five missiles and his opponent with five factories, he'd do twice as well (+10) as in total disarmament and his opponent would come out in the hole (−5). Thus we have at least a rough approximation of the arms race's dangers and lures. Various other combinations of rewards and losses were possible with intermediate levels of disarmament on both sides; each player was given a list of the possible combinations and outcomes when the games began.

Several simplified arms-race strategies were tested. Some volunteers really did play against each other, and in these cases each player simply used whatever strategy he could devise. This condition ("natural pairs") might be compared to one of short-range expediency in the real world, with American and Soviet policy makers responding to changes in arms levels willy-nilly, depending on how they feel at the time. Other volunteers thought they were playing against each other, but were really playing against a simulated opponent. (Pilisuk and Skolnick don't say whether the simulated opponent was a computer; their experimental procedure was so simple that I suspect he was merely a graduate student.) Some players' simulated opponent played what was called a "matching" strategy, meaning that he ended every game with the same number of missiles and factories as the real player had maintained in the previous game. This strategy is somewhat akin to the pursuit of nuclear parity: whenever you add a line of atomic submarines, so does your enemy; whenever your enemy stops stockpiling cobalt bombs, so do you. Other people found themselves playing against a simulated opponent who used a "conciliation" strategy: he always ended a game with one less missile than the real opponent had retained in the previous game. This strategy is at least partially equivalent to the Osgood GRIT proposal: one side initiates small reductions in the arms race, and if the other side responds, the reductions can snowball into complete disarmament. If the other side doesn't respond, little is lost; if the other side continues to escalate, it's easy enough to get back on the nuclear bandwagon.

In addition to those three strategy conditions — natural pairs, matching, and conciliation — Pilisuk and Skolnick included in their design a sort of onsite nuclear inspection procedure. Half the real players in all conditions were told partway through each game how many missiles their opponent had already converted to factories. In this report, the simulated players were always completely honest: although two moves remained in the game, they kept until the end whatever number of missiles and factories they had revealed at "inspection time." Real players were not necessarily so straight: even if they had converted as many as four missiles to factories by inspection time, they could convert all those factories back to missiles by the end of the game, and thus perhaps gain nuclear superiority. Some did.

The other half of the players had no opportunity to deceive each other. They were given information about each other's moves only at the end of the game, when it was too late for either player to change anything. This is really a kind of inspection itself, since the end-of-game information about your opponent's behavior may help you judge what he's likely to do in the next game. In the real world, the big game is always in session and information about an opponent's previous moves are always of use. So the main difference between the "inspection" (information partway through game) condition and the "no inspection" (information at game's end) condition is that the former gave easy opportunities for deception and the latter did not.

Results: players in both the matching and the conciliatory conditions converted significantly more missiles to factories than did natural pairs players. Planned arms control triumphs over day-to-day brinkmanship. But the GRIT–type conciliatory condition induced no more disarming than the parity-type matching condition. "Inspection" during the game didn't increase disarmament in either the matching or conciliatory conditions; inspection produced significantly *less* disarmament than noninspection in the natural pairs condition, apparently because volunteers in this condition made deceiving each other a way of life. Pilisuk and Skolnick tabulated average numbers of missiles after each move for the various strategy conditions; the natural pairs average drops below three on the third move, then zooms back toward five by the fifth. Relatively little deception was found among real volunteers in the simulated-opponent conditions; the opponent's constant honesty apparently provided a worthy model for the real player's own behavior. The moral of this part of the study, I suppose, is that international inspection plans are worth less than nothing if they allow either your opponent *or* you to cheat. I can imagine the activity pattern in an H-bomb plant under a system of yearly inspection: every year, we spend the six months before inspection dismantling our bombs and facilities, and the six months afterward putting everything together again. Pilisuk and Skolnick didn't test a system of random spot-checks, but either that or direct constant monitoring, perhaps through remote sensing devices, might eliminate most of the Pilisuk-Skolnick inspection system's problems.

A striking discovery in several game studies (e.g., Pilisuk et al., 1965) is that natural pairs of players tend to "lock in" at either near-total cooperation or near-total competition over several game sessions — that is, they settle upon a consistently polarized pattern of behavior. In international affairs, the person locked into a hard-line approach is sometimes called a "hawk"; the one locked into a soft-line approach, a "dove." Pilisuk and Skolnick measured such tendencies by studying behavior in the last five of each player's twenty-five games. Anyone with at least twenty-two factories out of twenty-five at the end of these five games was labelled a dove; anyone with at least twenty-two missiles remaining, a hawk; anybody in between, a mugwump. The matching and conciliation conditions, whether with inspection or without, produced over 50 per cent doves and less than 15 per cent hawks. The natural pairs condition with no inspection and thus no deception produced low numbers both of hawks and of doves. The natural pairs inspection condition, where deception ran rife, produced *no* doves at all, and over 40 per cent hawks.

In this research, the experimental condition most resembling the GRIT proposal was clearly superior to the condition in which both sides were free to go on seeking nuclear superiority. But it was never significantly superior to a nuclear parity plan, which in reality seems not to have moved us very far toward disarmament even though the United States has occasionally endorsed it publicly. However, the GRIT proposal may yet turn out to be the best one after all; that it did not seem so in this game study could have been an artifact of the game's special rules. Recall that the simulated player in the conciliatory (GRIT) condition was programmed always to end a game with one less missile than the real opponent had held in the previous game. But the simulated player couldn't get any more conciliatory after reaching complete disarmament; he reached that state when the real player still retained 20 per cent of his original missile strength. The real player was likely never to attain complete disarmament himself, if he recognized or stumbled onto this situation; he got a higher score if he kept holding on to his one missile in every game. In reality, if the United States went down to zero missiles and the Soviet Union hung onto 20 per cent of its present stockpile, you can bet the Americans would bounce back up pretty fast, even if it were following the GRIT proposal to a T; so the most advantageous position for both players would be complete disarmament. Even when we reached that happy state, we wouldn't be limited to pushing the "zero armaments" button forever, as the simulated player was; the United States and the Soviet Union could surely think up many other conciliatory moves to keep each other happy.

THE UNREALITY OF GAMES

Of course this particular disparity between reality and the Pilisuk-Skolnick game is not the only one, nor perhaps even the most serious. All games, up to and including the most complex computer-calculated nuclear strategy simulations ever devised by the military-industrial complex, differ from the real world in many important ways. Most such games are two-person games, or at best two-sided, whereas in the real world a multitude of sides are competing, even including other nuclear powers. It is possible to devise and study games with several sides (see Rapoport, 1970), but very quickly the results of such N-person games become nearly impossible to decipher psychologically. Also, whereas one side of a game is usually represented by a single player or at most by a small group, most nations contain many differing factions, many contending internal pressures, many hawks and doves and mugwumps and various mixed breeds. Some gamesmen have tried to represent these contending pressures via computer simulations, but they have paid little attention to the interactions between intranation factions that may change the opinions and behavior of the contenders while the game is still in progress. Games usually do not generate extended high anxiety levels among the players, even when electric shock is involved; international relations may put the chief players under severe psychological strain for weeks or months at a time, occasionally with consequent neurotic or psychotic or just plain physical reactions that may result in disastrous leadership behavior. Furthermore, quite different psychological processes may be brought into play if you're sacrificing other people's bodies instead of your own cash. There may also be substantial national differences in game-playing and international-relations-playing with regard to such factors as risk-taking. If these are represented at all in laboratory games, they are likely to be represented quite crudely by asking one foreign student, say, to reflect the interests and reactions of all his countrymen as the game progresses.

All these qualifications, and many more that could be cited, should lead you to generalize from the gaming table to the conference table only with the greatest hesitation. But until the Osgood GRIT proposal is given a good extended trial between nations rather than between college sophomores, we seem to be left with that old choice: almost no systematic, unbiased knowledge at all about a vital aspect of our psychological and physical worlds, versus knowledge collected at several removes from reality. As long as you keep those removes in mind, I think you'll be better off with some knowledge than none.

the two-sided mirror: international misperceptions

My own belief is that Russian and Chinese behavior is as much influenced by suspicion of our intentions as ours is by suspicion of theirs. This would mean that we have great influence on their behavior — that, by treating them as hostile, we assure their hostility.

— Senator J. William Fulbright,
quoted by United Press International, April 5, 1971

375

When Americans speak to each other of Vietnam in years to come, they are unlikely to spend much time praising the bravery of our soldiers, or the might of our weapons, or even the cleverness of the politicians who finally extricated us from Southeast Asia. They are likely instead to ask each other: "How the hell did we ever get ourselves into that crazy mess in the first place?"

Hypotheses about innate aggressiveness won't help them much. Surely we don't need to go halfway around the world to express our pent-up hostilities; enough targets exist close at hand. Nor will research on games and simulations be of any great assistance. Game studies are usually structured on the assumption of a certain degree of rationality in the players; and any rational player would never have stuck with the Vietnam Game as long as we have. He probably wouldn't even have offered to play.

Nonpsychological explanations of our behavior are plentiful. They range from claims that the United States is fulfilling solemn treaty obligations or is defending an innocent nation against naked aggression, to claims that the United States is really motivated by overriding economic interests, is seeking to preserve markets for American industry as well as protecting vast supplies of rice and oil and even tobacco. These nonpsychological explanations largely appear to be also nonrational, and so require still more explanatory efforts by psychologists.

Discussions of war in terms of aggressive instincts focus upon the assumed rock-bottom foundations of human personality. Discussions in terms of game-playing focus largely upon the external structure of behavior, on what the observer sees the player do under various circumstances. But in between, other psychological processes may be going on, neither tapping instinctual human drives (if such there be) nor exhibiting themselves directly in overt behaviors. In analyzing war behavior, particularly the development of particular wars or particular antagonisms between nations, a number of psychologists have profitably remained at this intermediate level. Most have concluded that any recent international conflict, if its results were seen as clearly as game players can see their lists of rewards and losses for each possible move, would seem to the participants hardly worth playing. Since the participants usually go ahead and play anyway, these psychologists have concentrated on the misperceptions that might allow such peculiar behavior to continue.

MISPERCEPTIONS CATEGORIZED

Ralph K. White (1970) has found certain kinds of misperception occurring so regularly in international conflicts that he has gathered them into a neat list of six: the diabolical enemy image, the virile self-image, the moral self-image, selective inattention, absence of empathy, and military overconfidence. White has documented the occurrence of such misper-

376

ceptions in most detail with regard to the Vietnam War; and if future Americans really do want to find out how the hell we got into that crazy mess, they'll discover much useful data in his documentation. But Vietnam is by no means the only war in which Americans have misperceived reality; so in addition to certain of White's major Vietnam examples, we'll include a few additional observations in each category.

The diabolical enemy image. If your local television station still shows World War II–vintage animated cartoons on Uncle Bob's Kiddie Korral, take a look and you'll see an impressive collection of diabolical enemy images battling against Popeye and Daffy Duck. Ralph White grants that Hitler and occasional other figures may really have been diabolical, in certain figurative senses of the word; but not all our opponents can be as thoroughly evil as many of our citizens think they are. Following World War II, the Communists once again became the world repository of evil in the eyes of many Americans; and the only thing many of these same Americans know about the North Vietnamese and the Vietcong is that they are Communists. Vietcong atrocities have been seized upon eagerly by the Defense Department, perhaps manufactured at times if the reality was not sufficiently gory. Even when the atrocities have been real, as they often enough have been, our military command has imputed to their perpetrators the worst motives possible. White tabulated evaluative references to the Vietnamese enemy in two major public statements by President Lyndon Johnson and his Secretary of Defense Robert McNamara, made soon after large-scale American intervention began; 127 out of 130 references "were in terms of evil rather than good," and the remainder were ambiguous.

The virile self-image. This is the image of the hawk, of the hunter who promises to nail a coonskin to his wall, of the hard-hat construction worker who shouts homosexual epithets at peace demonstrators. White presents no content analysis of speeches by congressional defenders of the Vietnam War, but they have often contained appeals to manhood and accusations of cowardice as central elements in their demands for popular support of the war. Spiro Agnew seems to have had a virile self-image in mind when he referred to domestic opponents of the war as "effete snobs." Senator Richard Russell, late Chairman of the Senate Armed Services Committee, pushed the image of American virility to the ultimate when he said, "If World War III leaves only one couple alive on Earth, I want that couple to be American." Let's hope that the last man is not an effete snob, and that radiation fallout does not leave him virile in self-image only.

The moral self-image. We are not only strong, but good; God is on our side; we are defending freedom against oppression. Ralph White sometimes refers to the diabolical enemy image and the moral self-image combined as the "black-and-white picture." Most people would object to

377

being told they were thinking in black-and-white about anything; but for many Americans, shades of gray seem to end at the national border. Foreign policy is seldom defended on the basis of mere utility; we take actions abroad because they are morally just, and only secondarily because we stand to benefit from them. If our leaders wish, they can easily find the proper assortment of Carl McIntires and Cardinal McIntyres to bless their war policies.

Selective inattention. Even in a nation at war, with the news media under pressure to support official policies and perhaps hard put to collect independent information about war-related events, bits of data may pop up here and there that contradict the black-and-white picture or the virile self-image. Just as when in our personal lives new information contradicts our picture of ourselves and our world, we may find that the easiest response is to ignore the evidence, or to avoid listening to the people who are apt to tell us what we'd rather not know. Vietnam is a long way off, and the roots of the present war extend a long way back in time, so it's not hard to overlook a lot of information that might cast a very different light on the rightness of the war or on our likelihood of success. Life offers many options; why watch a bunch of goddam demonstrators on television when we can see a pro football game instead?

Absence of empathy. If selective inattention can work so well to remove us from the influence of naked fact, we shouldn't wonder about the human ability to ignore thoughts and feelings buried inside the enemy's head. Humans are capable of empathy, but they do have to work at it. In wartime, empathy is considered unmanly; it is likely to weaken the idea that we are pure and the enemy is evil; so why put any effort into it? Besides, those Vietcong are so far away and they talk different and they are a different color and eat strange things. In Vietnam we have enough trouble empathizing with our "friends," let alone our enemies. Considering that a few feet of distance and a thin wall can sharply reduce the number of empathic cues (as in Stanley Milgram's obedience studies), and considering that empathy often fails to produce altruistic behavior even when the victim is an innocent American student (as in the Latané and Darley studies), the really astonishing thing about American feelings toward Vietnam is that *any* American, for or against the war, feels *any* empathy toward the Vietnamese. Such remote empathy may be easily stilled; but that it exists at all may be grounds for mild hope.

Military overconfidence. The course of the Vietnam War has illustrated this variety of misperception more than any other. The light at the end of the tunnel has receded, always receded; the badly shattered Vietcong forces have always managed to regroup; devastating blows at North Vietnam and at the Cambodian and Laotian sanctuaries have somehow never been quite as devastating as planned. Not only public but private governmental estimates of American military effectiveness and enemy

378

weakness have often been filtered through rose-colored bombsights, as the Pentagon Papers attest (Sheehan et al., 1971).

THE BLACKTOP IMAGE

One element of military overconfidence has earned its own special term from White: the "blacktop image." This is the belief that the enemy really consists only of the opposing leaders; the "people" are presumably not hostile, but are being led astray or forced into war by the leaders. So the true Vietcong are assumed to be a tiny portion of the population, with no voluntary support from the peasantry; so the Russian people really aren't Communists or even Marxists at heart; so the Cubans will rise up in spontaneous rebellion against Castro if they are given a little encouragement. Odd, isn't it, how the Vietcong and the Russian leaders and Castro have survived in such hostile surroundings for so long?

The Vietcong and the Russian leaders and Castro are no strangers to the blacktop image either. The capitalistic bosses presumably dictate the behavior of the anticapitalistic American masses; the Vietcong flags of the far left are assumed to represent true mass sentiment in the United States. Indeed, a virtue of White's analysis of the Vietnam War is that he details misperceptions in all categories on all sides. The Vietcong surely underestimated, at the beginning of the American intervention, the military might that would be brought against them and the length of the American occupation. Their public statements appear greatly to overstate the degree of South Vietnamese peasant sympathy with their cause, as well as the degree of sympathy they have aroused in the United States and other nations. They deny clearly documented atrocities with as much innocence and outrage as the staunchest Bircher summons to deny the My Lai massacre. They too seem unable to appreciate the human feelings of their opponents — feelings that might, if recognized, help produce a stable negotiated settlement. The Vietcong's misperceptions may run less deep than the Pentagon's, but if so, it is not because of any special virtue on the Vietcong's part; it is at least partly because they are fighting on their own ground, among people very similar to themselves, in what has for twenty years been their own war and not someone else's.

INTERNATIONAL MIRROR IMAGES

The mutual misperceptions of international enemies often bear even more similarity than merely falling into the same general categories. They may be nearly identical, simply reversing the order of who is right and who wrong, who is good and who evil, who is manly and who cowardly. Both White (1961, 1965) and Urie Bronfenbrenner (1961), a Russian-born American psychologist, have called this reversal of international value judgments the "mirror image" phenomenon, and both have documented

379

it extensively. (Further documentation based on quantitative analysis of Cold War moves may be found in Gamson and Modigliani, 1971.)

Bronfenbrenner, who speaks Russian fluently and who "doesn't look American," first became aware of the mirror image in Russian and American mutual perceptions during a visit to the Soviet Union in 1960. At that time he spent several weeks making a special effort to talk with ordinary Russian citizens. The Soviet government would not permit systematic interviewing of its citizens by an American psychologist, so Bronfenbrenner didn't get a carefully distributed sample of respondents. But he did go out of his way to talk to people who didn't volunteer to talk to him — for instance, "I would enter a restaurant deciding in advance to sit at the third table on the left with whoever should turn out to be there." In these informal and quite unofficial conversations, Bronfenbrenner was startled to find that most Russians he encountered believed that "communism is the way of the future not only for themselves but for the rest of the world as well"; that "America is the warmonger bent on imposing its power on the rest of the world and on the Soviet Union itself"; that the American government cannot be trusted and that it exploits and deludes its own people, who are really not sympathetic to its regime; that American foreign policy is genuinely insane and might already have led to World War III, "were it not for Soviet prudence and restraint." Bronfenbrenner at first felt only that all this was a crazy way of looking at the world. Then he realized that most American citizens look at the world in just the same way, with only the names of the nations reversed. He then began to wonder about the craziness of *both* these world views.

MOTIVES FOR MISPERCEPTION

How does the warp develop in the mirror through which each side misperceives the other? Ralph K. White nominates as the main psychological processes those old standbys, projection and rationalization — old at least since the time Harold Lasswell first nominated them to explain the peculiarities of political behavior. White recognizes the contribution of intentional government propaganda, and Bronfenbrenner notes the self-censorship of foreign correspondents who want to keep selling their wares back home, as accounting for some of the common citizen's misperceptions. White also mentions the influence of roleplaying in making government officials gradually come to believe their own propaganda line. But not all the citizen's distortions come from the government or the media; some come from within himself. Not all the government leaders' and reporters' distortions are intentional manipulations of truth or products of roleplaying; many seem already to be believed by their promulgators when they are first voiced to the public. Such distortions are believed, according to White, because they are neat protections against conscious recognition of unacceptable impulses and self-knowledge. Projection enables us to impute everything bad in ourselves to the enemy; rationalization enables us to see as good those things we must recognize in ourselves. Other defenses such as denial and displacement may assist; anything will do, as long as it helps us continue to see ourselves as good and somebody else as bad.

But why should we need to use psychological defenses in the context of international relations? What sorts of self-knowledge do we need to conceal? At first thought, perhaps none; at second thought, the list may appear endless. Each of us has his own hang-ups; and just as some people cope with private hang-ups by externalizing them into the domestic political arena, others externalize them onto international politics. If you feel private doubts about your masculinity and have an army to command, it may be easier for you to prove your masculinity by plotting international military successes than by attempting success in your secretary's boudoir. If you have authority problems that you must displace away from the father who generated them, even Uncle Sam may be too similar to your father for comfort; but Uncle Ho or Comrade Leonid may unite just the right degree of authoritarianism and remoteness — and besides, few people in this country will complain about your professed hostility toward Comrade Leonid. It's always open season on foreign rulers outside the "allied" circle, for people who need to carry the hunt that far.

No good evidence exists, however, that most national leaders themselves maintain unusual levels of father-hatred. What then might they have in common that would make White's list of distortions not only likely but necessary? Power needs, for one thing. Given that overt displays of power motivation are considered improper in most cultures, and supposing that strong power needs are closely associated with political success in most modern nations (my guess), the outcome is likely to be a lot of government leaders searching eagerly for legitimate reasons to exercise power. What better reason than to protect the nation from that government leader over there who's exercising *his* power? And then what better reason for him to *really* exercise his power, than the fact that you're exercising *your* power? The mirror twists further.

The confusion between self-esteem and national accomplishment must also be important here. Each person's self-esteem rests upon several bases. One of these is typically his identification from earliest childhood with a particular geographical or political unit, or with several such units at different levels. He doesn't need any innate sense of territoriality to feel this; he is quite explicitly taught, in school and out, "You're a Walloonian, my son, and you should be proud of it!" Regardless of his own personal triumphs or failures, he can feel that on some higher plane he is sharing in the international success of his fatherland/motherland. As he protects his self-image by projection and rationalization and such, so must he protect the image of his nation, of which he is a part. He doesn't have

381

to change his behavior or his nation's, as long as he can believe the behavior is right. Particularly in the case of his nation, on whose overall behavior he probably has little influence, his ability to maintain an *inner* picture of goodness in contrast to another nation's evil is crucial.

Other motives for misperception could be cited: the need some people feel to maintain a simple picture of the world; motivations to behave like one's fellow citizens, although one's power needs or self-esteem problems may not be as intense as theirs; even the impulse to maintain consistency among one's cognitions. Once again the attitudes and beliefs people hold can be seen to serve a large variety of needs; once again they can all be seen as ultimately functional.

But once again you should realize that the functions served by any particular attitude need not be served by that attitude alone. It may be convenient for many people in this country to believe God is on our side and Satan on Russia's; but if that belief keeps getting us into trouble, it can be replaced by a more broadly functional and also more realistic belief. We have had occasional internationalists in this country ever since Tom Paine — people whose attitudinal functions were discharged quite nicely without adopting a black-and-white view of international relations. Various opinion polls, as well as frequent pronouncements by young people in particular, suggest that the number of internationalists is increasing. Certain personality types may still need to maintain international misperceptions more than other types; Pilisuk's game research (Pilisuk et al., 1965), for instance, suggests that "hawkish" players are likelier to rank high on the authoritarian characteristic of intolerance for ambiguity than "dovish" players. But even if we can find no prompt way to eliminate intolerance for ambiguity, we may still be able to guide the hawks into a fully functional hawkishness about literary criticism or scientific theory or bermuda grass rather than about international relations. Using domestic political action to satisfy motives irrelevant to politics is dangerous. Using international war preparations to satisfy motives irrelevant to international relations is suicidal. And suicide serves very few functions in the human personality.

giving peace a chance:
psychological anti-warfare

We can't have peace if we're only concerned with peace.
War is not an accident. It is the logical outcome of a cer-
tain way of life. If we want to attack war, we have to
attack that way of life.

> — A. J. Muste, quoted in Nat Hentoff,
> "Temptations of a Boston Atheist"

382

Every third week I take my two daughters to the preschool section of the Yolo County Public Library. There we jointly choose our next three weeks' assortment of picture books: Maurice Sendak and Dr. Seuss and Curious George if we can find them, otherwise a series of lucky and unlucky guesses about what might be tolerable to both generations through half a dozen readings.

Once we came home with a small book titled *The Minstrel and the Mountain: A Tale of Peace*, by Jane Yolen (1967). The book was set in large type, and it had a colored picture on every other page, thus qualifying it for the preschool section. But it distressed my daughters, because it depicted several battle scenes in which medieval soldiers hacked off other soldiers' heads and children battered each other with clubs. The illustrations were otherwise charming, and the book was well written, but I suspect it should have been labeled by the publishers, "For ages 35–45."

The plot concerned two kings who lived on opposite sides of a mountain. They set their armies to fighting because the king on the western side of the mountain envied the eastern king his sunrise, and the king on the eastern side envied the western king his sunset. An itinerant minstrel told each king separately that he had a plan whereby the other's kingdom could be taken. While the minstrel watched from the mountaintop, the eastern king and all his subjects crept around one side of the mountain, to find the western kingdom deserted; and of course the western king and all his subjects crept around the mountain's other side, to find the eastern kingdom equally deserted. Both kings thereupon realized their own foolishness and their essential similarities; and ever after, the two kingdoms exchanged locations yearly and got along beautifully together.

PACIFYING THE PRESIDENT

I responded to this moralistic little tale much more enthusiastically than my daughters did. After all, the minstrel had used as clever a bit of deceit as any social psychologist ever devised, in order to change the kings' attitudes toward war through a process very akin to roleplaying. Living for a time in each other's shoes, they saw each other's humanity and common problems in a new light, and thereupon commanded their subjects to lay down their swords. Having studied and used roleplaying as an attitude change agent for several years, I knew that the technique could indeed produce such mutual insights among competing members of management and labor, or among policemen and young people; and the possibility of employing it to reduce misperceptions among the world's contending rulers was intriguing. Give a social psychologist the slightest opportunity to imagine his pet phenomenon as the road to world peace, and his children will get no more child-sized fairy tales that evening.

But remind him of his own fairy tale the next morning, and he'll likely admit the crushing weight of reality. The world's leaders would be quite unlikely to sit down together and roleplay each other's problems, even if I asked them politely. Even if they did sit down and roleplay, the results would likely be close to zero: as I've already noted, certain sorts of politicians show considerable immunity to the usual effects of publicly advocating what one does not believe, and it would be just our luck to assemble such a set of politicians at our international get-together. And even if roleplaying did change our world leaders, did make them recognize their opponents as human beings with human problems, they'd soon be set straight again or else toppled from power by the congressmen, Joint Chiefs of Staff, Central Intelligence Agencies and such back home. If you're only dreaming, you might imagine the Joint Chiefs and the CIA also sitting down to roleplay with the Red Army Command and the NKVD. But the image of grown men running around Washington in Mao tunics and Muscovite black belts and Brooks Brothers homburgs is a little too much even for my trained imagination.

Many more psychologists than I have dreamed of promoting peace by altering the psychological processes of the world's leaders. But they nearly always come up against those same three problems: you can't reach the leaders in the first place; you can't influence them as effectively as you can ordinary citizens, even if you do reach them; and you can't change all the others who hold influence over them, even if you can change the leaders themselves. The proposal has several times been made, for instance, that all American Presidents be subjected to psychoanalysis or some other form of psychotherapeutic treatment. The proposal is usually based not on the assumption that all Presidents are crazy, but on the idea that a psychologically sound President would be less likely to break under the strain of office and more likely to assess the needs and fears of other nations accurately. The idea is a pleasant one, but I don't expect to see it put into practice during this century. Anyway, who would choose the psychotherapist – the President himself, or perhaps his cabinet? Can you imagine Billy Graham in a Viennese beard?

There are other variants on the same theme. Carl Rogers (1965) has hinted that a White House encounter group might help ease world tensions; William Schutz (1971) wants it to include Russian leaders too; Kenneth B. Clark has suggested in his presidential address to the American Psychological Association (1971) that world leaders should regularly be dosed with pacifying drugs. Such possibilities are intriguing to contemplate, but very unlikely to be realized. Even the most reasonable proposal for psychological treatment of national leaders is doomed to failure, not only because psychotherapy itself still has negative connotations for most people but also because national leaders unanimously

384

consider themselves so competent, stable, and wise that no psychological attention is needed.

For these reasons, the only psychologically oriented efforts at all likely to make our leaders less warlike will be those practiced far from the couch or the laboratory — for example, Charles Osgood's GRIT proposal. Once such a plan is accepted by a national leader and his associates, no psychologist need intervene to elicit the desired psychological effects, because the plan's reverse spiral of peace moves is explicitly designed to promote mutual trust in the leaders involved. Trust is a psychological characteristic, but if it can be established best through political moves rather than psychotherapeutic sessions, we'd better remove the psychologists from the scene and let the politicians get to work — at least until the time comes to hand out credit for success.

CHANGING THE SYSTEM

Psychologists and other social scientists have sometimes proposed not only a series of political moves, but changes in the entire international political system, in order to alter the psychological pressures facing potential combatants. It's easy to forget that one such change has been in effect since World War II: the United Nations. Despite its obvious political fragility, its founders hoped that the United Nations would provide a firm psychological foundation for worldwide cooperation and ultimate peace. Its fragility has lessened little if at all over the years; its psychological contributions have been small but genuine. National leaders must often have hesitated before pursuing solely their own nation's interest, lest they be condemned in the General Assembly. Models for international cooperation have been tested, sometimes discarded, sometimes revised and strengthened, within the organization's several agencies. And as various psychologists have noted, the very act of day-to-day association, joint labor, and off-the-record discussion among thousands of diplomats and their employees from over a hundred countries must surely lead to greater appreciation of each other's human rather than satanic qualities. Roleplaying is not the only behavior that promotes mutual understanding.

Nor is the development of the United Nations the only structural change in international relations that might improve the world psychological atmosphere. Amatai Etzioni (1969), for instance, has noted the value of buffer states or nonaligned nations in preserving the peace: when an array of such countries exists, leaders of superpowers can compete not in direct encounter but in trying to expand their influence among the uncommitted nations. "The floating vote is to be viewed as a reward that shifts to the favored side; the values according to which the floating vote shifts become the values the competing sides seek to promote, or at least seek to appear to be promoting"; and the value most advantageous to the nonaligned nations themselves is peaceful competition rather than international war. Social scientists cannot create non-aligned nations, but they certainly can point out to those who pursue peace the advantages nonalignment may have in mobilizing major international leaders' publicly pursued values in a peaceful rather than a combative direction.

Etzioni also endorses the value of regional international bodies, in establishing basic patterns for the imposition of international rules and for consensus formation. These may in turn lay the groundwork for "a process of upward transfer of power, rights, and loyalties to a central organ of the emerging world community." Some social scientists have urged going much further, much faster: establishing an international police force, they feel, would eliminate much of the anxiety that underlies the vicious circle of the arms race. If a leader or his followers are sure international transgressions will be punished by a higher body, they should feel less need to maintain their own protective arms, which are usually seen by other nations as sufficiently threatening to justify arms investments of their own. This is another tempting idea for the psychologist who wants to see his knowledge of anxiety reduction and reward put directly to work. But it seems to me that an international police force, under present circumstances, would mainly serve to generate even more anxiety, particularly among the leaders and citizens of the larger nations who now have little to fear from the disunited forces of the smaller nations. Before an effective international police force can be formed to reduce the anxieties and distrust that the world's people feel toward each other, some means must be found to reduce the anxieties and distrust that the world's people would feel toward any police force that might be used against their own nation. And the circle goes round and round.

PACIFYING THE PEOPLE

Clearly we cannot merely — merely! — change the world's leaders, or impose a new system upon their peoples from without; we must change the people themselves. Several times in this book I have mentioned what seem to me desirable psychological changes from the standpoint of individual relationships and intranational behavior — decreases in power motivation, for example, or increases in empathic responsiveness. These would surely serve us well on the international level too, if they could be implemented. Even though national populations hardly ever interact directly with each other, such shifts in sentiment and motives could do much either to force or to free national political elites to behave more sanely toward other nations. Probably it is at this level, in showing how to induce individual psychological change throughout an entire nation, that psychologists will make their greatest contributions to eventual world peace. That's only reasonable, since psychologists are most used to working at the individual or small-group level. In fact their would-be peacemaking proposals have been largely directed toward this aim of making the common citizen less warlike.

Perhaps a majority of these proposals have been designed to divert assumed hostile impulses from international targets. William James' "army enlisted against nature" (1911) was apparently so interpreted by much of his audience, though James himself assumed he was providing alternative occasions for pride and honorable behavior rather than for aggressiveness. Diverting aggressiveness has since his time provided the rationale for proposed international athletic competitions of various sorts (including a return to individual gladiators, representing each contending nation in an annual battle covered by worldwide television); for schemes involving joint exploration and exploitation of the ocean bottom, or alternately for visions of joint efforts to make the world's deserts bloom and burst into fields of wheat; and most recently, for dreams of the mutual or competitive exploration of space. I'm all for space exploration: a decent program would cost a good bit less than our current military budget, and with proper planning and publicity it could probably do a good deal more than it has to convey to the world's people both the merit and the unity of humankind. But I doubt very much that it can be defended as an effective displacement for the aggressive urges that cause wars — first because I'm still not convinced that man has any basic aggressive urges which must be displaced to avoid war, and second because man's thrust into impersonal space seems too remote from military actions to serve as a good symbolic displacement even if one were needed. The opponents of pornography might more reasonably argue that a good phallic space shot is needed once every week or two, to discharge the population's pent-up sex urges.

COMMON PREDICAMENTS

Earth Days and Whole Earth Weeks and such have recently drummed up support for a fight to preserve a decent worldwide environment, partly again with the idea of making that struggle an alternative to war. Perhaps some of this fight's proponents have the aggression-displacement hypothesis in mind, but it may be possible to justify such a battle in a better way than that. Specifically, the worldwide ecological crisis could be made to fit the pattern of the "common predicament," which social psychologist Muzafer Sherif (1966) has found effective in quelling antagonisms between groups and in promoting intergroup amity.

The temporary effects of common predicaments were observed by Daniel Defoe during the London plague, and were summarized in connection with various other disasters in Chapter Eight of this book. People

387

who had been mutually threatened by death or disaster were described as sharing a "postdisaster Utopia," in which old enmities were momentarily forgotten and social barriers of class and status had momentarily faded. But the postdisaster Utopia itself usually fades as immediate common problems are solved and as the mutual assistance practiced during the disaster is forgotten. Sherif attempted to determine exactly what elements of the common predicament contribute to favorable intergroup relations, and what devices might be used to extend those beneficial outcomes. Rather than studying disasters, whose effects cannot be controlled and whose victims may have established extremely complex relationships before the disaster, he developed a situation in which he could establish the social groups, stir antagonisms between them, create minor disasters, and watch the outcome closely. He founded a boys' summer camp.

More precisely, Sherif set up three summer camps, several years apart, to try out his evolving hypotheses about intergroup relations. The third and most extensively studied was at Robbers Cave, Oklahoma, so the research has come to be known as the Robbers Cave Experiment. Each time, the boys were eleven to twelve years old, selected by interview and observation for their psychological normality. They were white protestant middle-class healthy well-adjusted kids; Sherif wanted to avoid any overt excuses for antagonism. None of the boys were acquainted before they came to the camp. Once they arrived they were separated randomly into two groups, with no initial cause for ingroup loyalties or intergroup hostilities.

Loyalty and hostility were soon enough generated. "As though acceding to the boys' requests, the staff arranged a tournament of games: baseball, touch football, tug of war, a treasure hunt and so on, with prizes for the winning group." Competing against each other for prestige and treasure, the two groups quickly developed their own ethnocentrisms, their own flags and symbols, their own misperceptions of themselves and their opponents. Sherif found, for instance, that when he asked group members to estimate individual performance after each toss in a bean-toss game, the boys consistently overrated the performance of their compatriots and underestimated the performance of their opponents. Soon the camp staff couldn't control the hostilities: one group burned the other's flag, the other group seized the first group's flag in return, both groups began storing secret supplies of green apples, and despite Sunday morning sermons on brotherly love, the green apples were finally let fly in a surprise raid.

Having found that they could generate intergroup conflict rather easily, Sherif and the camp staff now stepped in with measures designed to promote peace. First they merely encouraged increased contact between the two groups — having them eat in the same dining hall, for instance. The meals rapidly disintegrated into what the boys called "garbage wars." Then Sherif reasoned: *If conflict develops from mutu-*

ally incompatible goals, common goals should promote cooperation." He therefore created several situations involving "superordinate goals," which could be attained only through the joint efforts of both groups. Some were relatively simple: a desired movie could be rented only through joint financial contributions. Others were more ingenious: the camp water supply mysteriously went dry, and all the boys had to join in finding the problem. The camp food truck failed to start when everyone was waiting for it to go get their picnic lunch, and both groups had to pull the truck with a rope to get it started.

Sherif found that a single effort to attain a joint goal had little effect in reducing group hostility. But repeated cooperative efforts over several days worked dramatically: friendships developed across group lines; joint enterprises were initiated by the boys even when cooperation wasn't necessary; unfavorable ratings of members in the opposing group dropped sharply. At vacation's end, the two groups chose to go home in the same bus rather than in separate buses, and the group that still had prize money remaining from the camp competitions spent it on malted milks all around. A happy ending for all — most of all for Muzafer Sherif. One wonders what the more avid watchdogs of psychological ethics would have had to say if his superordinate goals hadn't worked and all those kids had returned to the big city, ready for a *real* battle.

UNCOMMON PREDICAMENTS

Sherif's findings on the value of superordinate goals have been essentially duplicated in several other studies of small groups; and of course he would like to generalize his conclusions to large nations. Several difficulties arise, however. The main one is that the groups upon which the effects of superordinate goals have been demonstrated experimentally have usually existed for only a brief time — certainly not long enough to develop the history of chronic and acute hostilities enjoyed for many years by leading international combatants. The United States and Russia did work together on a superordinate goal during World War II, namely, defeating Germany; but the goodwill generated by that common enterprise was fleeting. The United States has also worked with some former enemies on a common goal after their defeat in war, namely, the strengthening of the "free world" to resist "Communist aggression"; we've had substantial joint success in reducing previous hostility between the Japanese and Germans on the one hand and Americans on the other. The fact that superordinate goals worked when pursued with our former enemies and failed with our former allies indicates that Sherif's conclusions can be applied to international affairs only with a good deal of qualification, and perhaps a hefty portion of historical luck.

Another difficulty is finding a common predicament sufficiently large and sufficiently general to unite the world. People often suggest that war itself is our greatest common enemy, and that by uniting to work against it we could simultaneously abolish war itself and build up mutual good-will. However, to say that the causes of war will be eliminated by joining together to eliminate war sounds sufficiently circular to me to suggest that it is an unlikely prospect. Others have suggested that what we really need is an enemy invader from outer space; *then* we would unite as one species to drive the invader away, and live in peace there-after. This solution appealed to me in my youth, but it strikes me now as less desirable. For one thing, I am no longer confident that we would win.

But there is still the war against environmental degradation, with which this discussion of common predicaments began. Surely, the argument goes, air pollution and DDT in the oceans and the disappearance of the world's forests threaten us all as menacingly as would an alien invader. If we would only unite in a worldwide program to keep the planet safe for humanity, peace and plenty would be ours evermore!

I endorse ecological sanity even more enthusiastically than I endorse the space race, for what that's worth to collectors of endorsements. But until the various federal, state, and local governments of the United States are much more firmly committed to environmental preservation, and until American private industry becomes much more severely re-stricted as to what it can do with and to our environment, and until a much larger portion of the American population is itself committed less to easy pleasures and more to conservation of irreplaceable natural and manmade resources than it has shown itself to be since the arrival of Europeans on this continent — until we have our own house in order, I doubt that we can use ecological enterprises as the superordinate striv-ings we need to foster world peace. The problem, as any rational Soviet citizen should be able to see, is mainly the United States. That's where most of the carbon monoxide and the DDT and all the other nasty side effects of unrestricted consumption originate. That's where most of the dwindling raw materials of many nations are being gobbled up to sup-port an ever-increasing population. The Soviet Union and other nations produce their own DDT and so forth, to be sure; their populations are increasing, and are asking for luxuries a little nearer the scale enjoyed by Americans; and anyway, regardless of who's *mainly* responsible, changes in the atmosphere or the oceans or the polar icecaps could genuinely threaten human life all over the earth within a generation. But common predicaments, I fear, must be rather more obviously common than the ecological one looks to be now, before they can be used to eliminate war.

PACIFYING EDUCATION

I have not discussed several more obvious ways of making national popu-lations more peaceful, particularly in terms of childraising and education. The same possibilities and problems intrude when we think of how to

390

raise children to be peaceful as when we consider raising them to be nonauthoritarian. We can eliminate toy guns and violence-inspiring television, and speak civilly to our children. But the precise combination of influence necessary to produce the child least likely to pursue international violence is still hard to predict, as our peaceloving Dr. Spock seems to have recognized in shifting his baby book gradually back to greater firmness. One recent comparison of national childraising patterns pointed out that Great Britain has participated in a good many more wars than Germany during the past century and a half, though the traditional childraising patterns in the former appear a good bit less authoritarian than in the latter.

A final suggestion may appear relatively trivial and lacking in psychological sophistication, but in view of Ralph K. White's emphasis on misperception as a basis for war, I think it may prove more important than it looks: our schools should greatly accelerate their moves away from distorted patriotism. Much of the basis for perceiving our own country as pure and enemy nations as evil is surely traceable to the black-and-white history and "civics" still taught regularly in most American elementary schools, in many of our secondary schools, even in a fair number of our colleges — and for that matter in schools the world over. Large numbers of our adult citizens remain so blinded by this early training (which is reinforced by innumerable newspaper editorials and political speeches) that they can conceive of no other treatment of history, and denounce any deviations from black-and-white as enemy-inspired. Many other adults assume that the young cannot appreciate subtlety anyway and would only become confused if exposed to it. Children do appear to grow in the ability to appreciate moral complexities as they advance in age and experience; but this is no reason to reinforce their early simplistic outlook with crude treatments of our national history. They can be taught to love our rocks and rills, to appreciate the value of free speech and the responsibilities that come with it, without hearing incessantly of our rightness and our victoriousness in every war, or of the wrongness and cowardliness of all our enemies. Patriotism need not be blind. If it remains so among the majority of our population, it will soon enough reduce to ruin the nation it seeks to praise.

Perhaps some readers will feel my plea is out of date, since many young people seem to be moving away from traditional patriotism by themselves, without having been educated to do so. The Vietnam War certainly has been very educational in showing our young that the nation can do wrong; but as an educational device, it has been slow to take effect and erratic in its application. Large numbers of our young seem to have learned little from it, continuing to accept the white-and-black picture of American involvement presented to them like a rehash of their grade-school history books by Presidents and congressmen. Others seem to have had the lesson applied much too harshly — reading in this war

the total evil of their own country and the unsullied virtue of their nation's enemies. War will not be ended by a simple reverse twist of the
two-sided mirror. The image remains two-dimensional and without human depth, whichever side we perceive.

revolutionary misperceptions:
sources of generational war

*With a world to be saved, or simply a life to be lived,
there is an overpowering urge to insulate yourself from
the nagging, nibbling doubts which seem to spoil every
confident hope and tarnish even the most ecstatic dream.
Dogmatic assertion is a great relief. To some, blind fanat-
icism is "beautiful."*

— Kingman Brewster, Jr.
"If Not Reason, What?"

I have come across a document which summons a new nation into existence and threatens that nation's enemies with war. The document is per-
meated with gross misperceptions, of exactly the kinds cited by Ralph
K. White in his Vietnam War analysis. Here are some representative
quotations and paraphrases from the document, appropriately grouped
in White's misperceptual categories.

1. *The diabolical enemy image.* According to the document's author,
whom we shall label *A* (for Author), the enemy nation runs by "Fascist
clock-time." Its government is senile; its businesses may be best described
as a Moloch with many teeth (flat "for grinding"); there is no real law
in the land; its major newspapers are worth using only as toilet paper;
the enemy has inflicted brain damage on many of *A*'s allies and has tried
to poison them with rotten food; government representatives once injected *A* himself with hepatitis. The enemy nation's chief law official is a
butcher; its chief executive is pictured as a *Tyrannosaurus rex* with a
fanged human face, pointed ears, and a snake's head at the end of his
tail.

2. *The virile self-image.* A writes passionately about his intentions to
build and defend the new nation, to liberate land in which his people
can do whatever they decide. In his nation, he declares, "there are no
writers — only poet-warriors." He exhibits his own fighting mettle by
reporting an incident in which he came close to blasting one of the
enemy with a shotgun; another incident in which "I felt that I was ready
to die over our right" to hold a piece of land; still another incident in
which his survey of the damage delivered upon his capital city by a fierce
storm led him to imagine himself as one of the enemy nation's great

generals, "inspecting the troops." *A* says his people will "build and defend the Nation by any means necessary." He prints diagrams of simple bombs and incendiary devices useful for sabotage, and demands that the enemy (as part of a peace settlement) "provide us with enough arms to successfully repel any and all invasions" by factions within the enemy nation "who fail to live by the treaty."

3. *The moral self-image.* *A* says he has no mixed feelings about the people of his nation; just as the enemy can do little but evil, he appears to feel they can do only what is right. True citizens of his nation, he feels, are so tolerant that they would not pass judgment on the folkways or morals of others (though he spends a good deal of his time passing quite negative judgments on the enemy). Those of his people who have been charged by the enemy with criminal acts are really only "prisoners of war" or "political prisoners"; they obviously are guilty of nothing except helping to found the new nation, and should be released forthwith. A citizen of the enemy nation accused of randomly bombing the enemy's buildings is seen as a worthy individual, someone with whom *A* can personally identify. A bystander killed by the enemy nation's forces in a border clash is venerated, though he apparently did nothing to help found the new nation; *A* says, "you ought to take your hat off when you hear his name." Even *A*'s attempt to blackmail potential allies into giving him a large amount of money to support his own political ambitions in the new nation is seen as perfectly acceptable; *A* clearly feels that anything he does, however criminal it might be considered in peacetime, is praiseworthy as long as he does it for his country.

4. *Selective inattention.* Much of *A*'s document could not have been written without selective inattention to the merits of his opponents and the transgressions of his own people. A few specific examples are particularly noteworthy. There is his demand that the enemy "Get off our Free Land," ignoring the fact that the land he then cites includes large parts of the enemy nation itself, inhabited for many years mainly by the enemy populace, and only recently invaded by a few of *A*'s compatriots. There is his description of one of his nation's holy places, which has been reported by other observers to be really quite shabby, as "the most beautiful place on earth." And there is also *A*'s argument that enemy entrepreneurs have "taken our culture out of the alleys and parks of our Nation and turned it into profits," even though his fellow artists voluntarily sold their products and even though most inhabitants of his nation have themselves happily encouraged the enemy entrepreneurs to package and disseminate these cultural products throughout both nations.

5. *Absence of empathy.* Though his nation and the enemy nation share many historic ties and, on the whole, a common cultural heritage, *A* refuses to acknowledge such commonalities. He urges children to kill parents who still feel allegiance to the enemy nation; he sees the military

forces of the enemy as merely paid to take orders, while of course all his own nation's forces are simply responding voluntarily. He now sees the enemy nation, despite its shared heritage, as an "alien country," and never credits even good intentions to its inhabitants. The enemy is never seen to share any motives, emotions, or aspirations which A himself experiences; the enemy is, after all, animal rather than human, and animals share no human emotions.

6. *Military overconfidence.* According to A, the enemy nation is dying, and he and his fellow citizens will joyously "dance on its grave." He imagines his compatriots as "thousands of soldiers resurrected from the Macedonian army hammering out their weapons," getting ready to crush the enemy "Dinosaur." Though his own people have relatively few material resources, he trusts that "the people will always be stronger than the [enemy's] technology." He feels his people can beat the enemy, if only they are urged to do so. He warns that if his peace terms are not accepted, the alternative will be the enemy's "total and complete death."

PIGS VERSUS PEOPLE

Sound like a familiar set of misperceptions? The enemy is called Pig Nation (another bit of diabolical enemy imagery); the abode of the good and strong is called Woodstock Nation; the author is Abbie Hoffman (1969), cofounder of the Yippies. Pig Nation of course is the United States of America (or Amerika, as Hoffman and other revolutionary leftists like to call it — more diabolism, Nazi variety, which removes a bit more empathy.) Or rather, it is the present United States minus what constitutes Woodstock Nation: most of the young people and various bits and pieces of geography, including "New Mexico, Arizona, Haight-Ashbury, the Lower East Side, Berkeley including the University of California, Ann Arbor, Michigan, the Boston Common, Rittenhouse Square in Philadelphia, Big Sur, Provincetown, Lincoln Park in Chicago," plus maybe the town of Woodstock, N.Y., and definitely the town of Bethel, N.Y., where the Woodstock Rock Festival actually happened and where "the Capital of our WOODSTOCK NATION" is therefore located. Presumably as other college campuses make the headlines, Hoffman will add their surrounding cities to the list.

Abbie Hoffman is by no means the first person to suggest the existence of a state of war between American youth and their elders, though he may have been the first to phrase it in terms of two distinct nations. The underground newspapers have been full of war talk for several years. *The Berkeley Tribe,* for instance, carried in one recent issue both a discussion of assaults on banks as "a sort of preliminary examination for the urban guerrilla in his apprenticeship for the techniques of revolutionary warfare," and a column on a man convicted of bombing several corporate buildings in New York City: "Call them the N.Y. Bombers.

Color them beautiful. Understand that they are a part of our history and a part of our future, a part of our lives. Live like them." Even Tom Hayden (1970), once a calm and clear-headed proponent of participatory democracy, now demands "self-determination for our internal colonies" and "Free Territories in the Mother Country." These territories would be used, according to Hayden, as "centers of constant confrontation, battlefronts inside the Mother Country"; and he adds, "All imperialist institutions (universities, draft boards, corporations) in or near the Territory would be under constant siege."

Both Hayden and Hoffman are intelligent men, and they frequently encounter real human beings in "Pig Nation," just as they sometimes encounter incompetents and self-servers in "Woodstock Nation." So they do occasionally voice doubts about their own purity as well as that of their followers. But the black-and-white picture Ralph White finds current among the citizens of other warring nations usually prevails in Hayden's and Hoffman's recent political writing. America is dying on its feet; it viciously attacks all those who would seek a new life; none of its institutions are worth saving; none of its leaders are worth following; its educational system teaches only lies; its mass media circulate only simpler lies. The nation's youth, on the other hand, want to hurt nobody, but are being forced into self-defense; their communal living will restore family life to sanity; their music is the only true art (as long as it's played for free); their sole motivation is love; none of their number is ever guilty of anything as long as Pig Nation is pressing the charges. Whether all the nation's youth are included in this benevolent vision is unclear. Hayden cautiously quotes a *Fortune* magazine poll that mentions three or four million students sympathizing to some degree with the New Left, then jumps to "our vast potential numbers"; Hoffman seems simply to include everyone who isn't a Pig, without ever being very precise about the defining characteristics of Pigs. The underground press relies heavily upon its version of the blacktop image: the People are with us, and only the capitalist fascist racist sexist pig leaders are against us; power to the People.

Large numbers of the nation's youth may in recent years have come to see themselves as belonging to a distinct subcategory of the general populace, but Woodstock Nation does not appear to have gained the allegiance of very many. Even among the college population, itself a clear minority of American youth, no more than a small minority currently share the bulk of Hoffman's warlike misperceptions. (This may be one reason for Hoffman's recently announced decision to cut his hair and seek power at the polling booths.) Many of the students with whom I have talked (informally or in a professional capacity) do enjoy rock music and have pleasant though fading memories of the *Woodstock* film; often they report having at one time or another demonstrated

395

against or even refused to serve in the Indochina War. But they can't see much reason to fight a war at home. Indeed, one of the most frequent questions I hear from students when I talk about the psychology of leftist student activism is "Why the violence?"

REASONS FOR VIOLENCE

For a while I found it hard to think of any helpful answers. It was easy enough at first just to say, "Well, there aren't that many violent leftists anyway," and go on to other things. But the incidence of violence has slowly mounted, and the verbal endorsement of violence among certain elements of the youth culture has escalated astonishingly. If we have nothing really resembling a state of rebellion or civil war right now, we may not always be so lucky. The processes leading to violent conflict within a nation clearly deserve as much attention from psychologists as the processes that promote war between nations.

Then it was easy for a while to say, "Well, the violent leftists are probably just the worst of the discontinuity activists." That's the term, remember, invented by Jeanne Block (1968) to describe alienated youths who flatly reject their parents' values and who use political activities to guarantee their sensual pleasures, rather than to promote the fulfillment of high principles. The strong element of hippie culture interwoven with the political tenets of the revolutionary left does indeed suggest the presence of the alienated in the ranks; and the burning of buildings can generate its own sensual delights. Robert Liebert, in a psychoanalytic study of Columbia University activists (1971), has suggested just this sort of differentiation between the motives of the "idealists," who "emphasize programs with 'realistic' and negotiable goals," and of the "nihilists," who "focus [their] planning on violence and disruption as ends in themselves, and as sources of pleasure if achieved." However, Liebert presents few specific data to support his inference that nihilistic activists are likely to have experienced erratic, discontinuity-producing family patterns early in life. Herbert Hendin, who also studied violent activists at Columbia from a psychoanalytic viewpoint (1971), did find among his sample an apparently high incidence of reported family relationships in which parents' surface warmth was combined with underlying emotional withdrawal.

But though such terms as "discontinuity activist" and "nihilist" may introduce useful conceptual refinements into the psychology of leftist activism, careless usage can also make them simply nasty names for anyone who doesn't act "responsibly." Judging from competent journalistic accounts of activists' personal backgrounds, such revolutionary leftists as Mark Rudd (Roberts, 1968), Jerry Rubin (Lukas, 1971), Bernardine Dohrn (Van Gelder, 1971), and Diana Oughton (Powers, 1971) do not fit the "discontinuity activist" or "nihilist" pattern of psychological de-

396

velopment at all well. I know less about Abbie Hoffman's early background; but his pre-Yippie work in mental hospitals, southern black schools, and fairly traditional political organizations does appear to contradict to a considerable degree the impression of discontinuity activism that one might get from his recent exhibitionism. So even if revolutionists do exist who began adult life deeply committed to social and political alienation, and hardly at all committed to any meaningful set of political principles, others apparently began as high-principled advocates of traditional values.

At times it was easiest of all to say, "Why not? Rubin and Hoffman and Dohrn and Rudd have at one time or another all been indicted on apparently exaggerated charges by the federal government; they have been subjected to incredible judicial treatment in Chicago and elsewhere; they have seen our leaders plunge us into the depths of what many view as an insane foreign war — why shouldn't they become so enraged that they threaten a few crazy actions of their own?" That sort of explanation may work pretty well up to a point. But rage is only a temporary form of insanity: nobody lives in a constant rage, and if he could, he'd be too ineffectual to cause much trouble. Even the "Days of Rage," in which a Weatherman faction went about smashing windows and cars and people after the Chicago Eight trial, were apparently planned rather coolly in advance. So sheer emotional discharge is not the explanation either. The question remains: Why has a small but influential segment of our well-educated and "decently" brought-up young people come to advocate violent revolution?

NORMAL MISPERCEPTIONS

One major lesson in Ralph White's analysis of wartime misperception is that men need not be evil or insane or momentarily blinded by passion in order to begin wars. Many otherwise normal human beings manage to convince themselves that it is fitting and proper to kill or maim fellow human beings for the sake of a political abstraction. They convince themselves by gradually developing a network of misperceptions that allows them to see themselves as wholly good and their opponents as wholly evil, their own cause as absolutely just and their opponents as so lacking in humanity that they can have no just goals. I suspect that the causative factors are similar, whether such misperceptions develop prior to international wars or prior to our would-be Second Civil War. Such factors include an upward spiral of claims and counterclaims, threats and counterthreats on both sides; some initially modest barriers to empathy (skin color and geographic separation internationally; age, changing culture, and different experiences with economic depression and affluence in the United States), which are soon heightened and strengthened by using the standard defenses of projection and rationalization and so on; problems with masculinity or identity or self-esteem that are more easily solved by group action than by individual effort. And in the same way that militarism becomes easier and easier to accept within a national population as the number of people grows who have already accepted it, so revolutionary leftism becomes progressively easier even for mildly radical youths to embrace, the more revolutionary leftists their campus or social circle contains. You don't have to be any crazier to become a gun-toting Brother waiting to start the revolution in Berkeley, than you do to become a gun-toting Bircher waiting to fight off the revolution in Dallas. Nor need you be any more accurate in your perceptions of the world around you and the people in it.

One notable misperception of the revolutionary left is that, although they themselves use the terminology of war and speak often of an ultimate shooting battle between themselves and the enemy, they fail to see that they are subject to the same psychological twists and turns as any other group intent on war. They recognize the presence of misperceptions on the other side, but fail to see the mirror image on their own side. Surely there *are* misperceptions on the other side, in profusion: dreams that only a few outside agitators are responsible for all student unrest (the blacktop image again); fears that youth has abandoned morality entirely; assumptions that a few well-placed National Guardsmen with firm trigger fingers will calm down everything in no time; and so on. Also, many actions on the other side to some degree justify youthful perceptions of the federal government as untrustworthy, of adults as resenting youthful freedom, of universities as continuing unreasonable regulations for sheer tradition's sake. The Johnson and Nixon administrations added two big loops to the upward spiral of hostilities by indicting first Dr. Spock, the Reverend Coffin et al., then Tom Hayden, Abbie Hoffman et al., largely for verbal opposition to Vietnam War policies. But revolutionary leftists have chosen to urge the spiral ever higher, instead of trying to clamp it down as they might if they were genuinely peace-loving. When they label all opposition as "pigs," regardless of the opposition's intent or level of argument; when they insist that there is no alternative to violence, although many alternatives remain in our political system; when they speculate upon the postwar utopia that will be founded upon the ruins of western civilization — then, I think, the revolutionists have gone far past the point of appropriate response to the shortcomings of our society. War fevers usually do pass beyond the bounds of rational discourse rather quickly.

REDUCING DOMESTIC MISPERCEPTIONS

Nor are those caught up in a war fever likely to respond rationally to discussions of their misperceptions. Many revolutionary leftists have been intent on spreading misperception as quickly and as widely as they can.

398

"Radicalization" is the game, and "radicalization" in the parlance of the revolutionary left most often appears to mean making other youths so angry at the authorities and so anxious about police retaliation that they too come to see all issues in black and white. This sort of misperception is the revolutionary left's stock in trade, since they would find few buyers for their visions of guns and glory without such perceptual distortion. Perceptual distortion may mean the death of the revolution in the end; but in the meantime, it can deliver many enthusiastic bodies to the cause. Power motives have rarely lacked importance in the leftist (or rightist) revolutions of other nations, as witness the almost inevitable clashes between the triumphant leaders; and we have little reason to doubt the presence of such motives in our contemporary combatants. Some, such as Tom Hayden, express occasional concern about their own enjoyment of power; but they drive on.

The revolutionary left is not alone in resisting efforts to cool the conflict. Conservative and opportunistic politicians continue to hope for benefits from a rightist backlash. A few moderate leftists seem to hope, like the pair of blacks in the Feiffer cartoon cited in Chapter Five, that demands more extremist than theirs will motivate the nation to accept their own nonviolent brand of social change. My suggestion then still seems reasonable to me: the Feiffer effect may work in some situations, but demands too extreme may so poison the atmosphere that all demands will be rejected — just as highly fear-arousing messages in the Janis pretzel model are likely to promote only defensiveness. Defensiveness, distortion, misperception — all work against any rational cause. For those who still seek to aid the nation and all its people, a worthier approach would be directing activist and antiactivist energies toward *accurate* perceptions of and *appropriate* responses to our massive unsolved social problems, while simultaneously damping down the passions that some hope will lead us to full-scale civil war.

Even if the most committed participants on both sides insist on holding to their misperceptions, many are left who are still far from armed conflict and who with encouragement could turn away from polarization entirely. Perhaps just as the causal processes involved in domestic and foreign misperceptions seem similar, some steps proposed to reduce international tensions may be effectively applied on the home front — perhaps even more effectively, because the antagonisms are so far generally weaker and the emotional ties are generally stronger between potential combatants. I suggest applying these steps only to reduce *mis*perceptions, not to subdue legitimate impatience with our national shortcomings. Once the distorted perceptions abate, our aroused young people will undoubtedly still find many objects in this nation for their protests, demands, and direct action. But they should then better be able to see what needs to be done and what can effectively be done, and to gain the necessary cooperation of those not so young or so impassioned. The reduction of misperceptions is not a means for the government or the various "establishments" to evade their responsibilities, but a way to increase the likelihood that they — and our other citizens, young and old — will live up to those responsibilities.

Because no foolproof procedure for ending wars has yet come from psychological research, it is unlikely that the following suggestions will prove to be sweepingly effective. But in each case they do rest at least loosely upon some of the psychological data and theory previously cited, and therefore might turn out to be more productive than policies directly opposed to such evidence. As in international relations, the major drawback to any plan of action will be getting the conflicting parties to recognize that aggressive behaviors are not as advantageous to either side as other alternatives. As in international relations again, the main persuasive force for adopting such proposals may be the less directly involved or more neutral parties, who are close enough to the conflict to see its dangers but far enough removed to see its stupidities. At the time of writing, many activists themselves seem to have retreated into apathetic neutrality, and under such circumstances the temptation may be strong to do nothing to eliminate the bases for generational misperception. But this may be precisely the situation we need to carry out policies that will head off future hostilities.

STEPS TOWARD PERCEPTUAL ACCURACY

First, individual efforts can be directed toward recognizing and advertising the misperceptions on both sides for what they are. Because misperceptions are necessary for the initiation and conduct of war, their repeated exposure should slow and ultimately help to end the hostilities. More hard information from social scientists on youthful activists (including revolutionaries) *and* on their opponents (including not only rightists, but moderates, conservatives, nonpolitical hardhats), particularly information that focuses upon their qualities as living, bleeding human beings, with similar fears and dreams, should help increase empathy and reduce images of evil. The commercial news media, without censoring themselves or being censored, could similarly help by increasing their explorations of the inner lives of people on both sides of the imagined generation gap — perhaps at the expense of generational "war stories," which must be misperceived by both sides to be perceived at all. Many underground papers may be beyond redemption by now, too much wrapped up in the war effort to quit purveying their *Pravda*- or *Daily News*-style distortions. But some might still respond to reader pressures that insist on fewer self-fulfilling prophecies about official repression, and more serious factual reporting from their staffs and correspondents. The nation needs alternative sources of news in addition to the large commercial newspapers; the underground papers gave promise of this at first and then failed miserably, as slanted "news" of the coming revolution seemed to excite their readers and increase circulation. Nonrevolutionary readers who fail to demand reasonable accuracy from the underground press are only indulging its worst characteristics. The same can be said of professors and politicians who fail to urge similar respect for intellectual honesty upon their respective constituencies.

Second, as the misperceptions decrease, a concomitant search should be conducted for an array of superordinate goals that can be pursued jointly by members of all generational groupings, regardless of their cultural differences. Preserving or restoring ecological balance has already come to the fore as one; with some deescalation of the rhetoric about race and gender, the promotion of equal treatment among all elements of the populace could be another. Even these opportunities for joint effort are often seen as battlegrounds, with misperceptions quickly developing on all sides. When your efforts are blocked, it seems easier to become angry than to keep on pushing with sweet reasonableness; the frustration-aggression hypothesis does after all possess some validity. But again, real success is unlikely to come from doing what is easiest, and if people are really more interested in keeping the world safe for humanity than in their own superego trips, they may be brought to oppose generational warfare and to stress the shared aspects of our major predicaments. Working jointly to save ourselves, we may find that Pig Nation and Woodstock Nation are one mixed good and bad but still worthwhile nation after all.

Third, perhaps before and perhaps after the two preceding moves have been initiated, the genuine combatants on one or both sides of the war might try initiating a kind of domestic GRIT plan. This may seem particularly inappropriate as applied to an attempted revolution or insurrection, because the opponents in such a case presumably are fighting over basic and unresolvable value differences. But Charles Osgood did not assume that opponents such as America and Russia had to share basic values before GRIT could work. GRIT is designed to build up mutual trust; once that is done, value differences can be explored and either resolved or let lie, as the opponents wish, without necessarily provoking further hostilities. The most committed revolutionaries are unlikely to promote any downward escalation of hostilities from their side except for tactical advantage; as Liebert (1971) suggests, once they are heavily into revolutionary activities they are likely to suffer enough hostile response from legal authorities to harden their initial misperceptions beyond correction. But the many youths who seem to have been only toying with revolution may be ready to move in other directions. It may take a change of administrations to obtain de-escalation on the government side; but any administration could make several relatively painless moves. (Some might render reelection a bit more difficult — but think of the eighteen-year-old vote!) One would be simply ending antiradical rhetoric, and perhaps even offering an occasional sincere good word for the virtues of student activism. Another, which has already begun in some states, would be banning deadly weapons among National Guardsmen and other police forces who deal with campus problems. (This policy can easily be reversed in local situations where revolutionaries actually engage in physical attack first; but such physical attacks might well be less likely under these circumstances.) An imaginative administration that really wants to forestall the spread of warlike perceptual patterns among our youth should be able to think of several dozen other GRITty moves.

Universities and colleges, which have heretofore changed their policies mainly in response to student pressures, could probably generate much goodwill among students, and perhaps save money besides, by periodically reexamining their general and specific policies with an eye toward eliminating the unnecessary and the uneducational. One useful phase of this reexamination, it seems to me, could be an annual or biennial quarter or semester in which students, faculty, and teachers jointly examine the purposes of higher education, and thereby — even if they emerge with different goals — at least come to recognize the honesty of each other's intentions. A smaller move (but one that might produce large rewards in insight, if my own benefit from lengthy interviews with students is any indication) would be establishing classes given by students to faculty and administrators in the subject students know best and cherish most: their own culture. Rock music, sexual ethics, political activism: many adults would benefit from just sitting at their desks listening, and asking occasional questions, while the students might gain educational insights of another kind by having to teach rather than learn for a change.

Parents might derive unexpected benefits from attending such classes, too, particularly if they are taught by other than their own offspring. Many seem to have acquired the idea that their children alone and without reason have invented a fantastic pattern of corrupt, immoral, and treasonous behavior. Perhaps a parental GRIT plan would be helped along also by establishing temporary amnesty periods at home: careful avoidance of condemnations or recriminations, and an emphasis on efforts to listen and try to find those points where assent is still possible. Between most parents and most children, agreement still *is* possible, in many areas of life and thought. The world has not changed as much in one generation as Margaret Mead, for instance, seems to believe. Young and old still share the same vocabulary, by and large; most parents and most children still seek a balance between security and change, between stimulation and quiescence; most parents and children continue to share the same essential values, though their mutual misperceptions may often conceal that fact.

Our nation remains troubled, fragmented, anxious about its own future, but the fragmentation can be overcome as misperceptions are straightened and as the real issues of our time gain our attention once again. I doubt that Woodstock Nation will ever truly see birth, because in the final analysis such a wrenching of our national structure is simply unnecessary for the attainment of the major goals of most citizens. America can still be spelled with a "c" instead of a "k," if its citizens give it — and peace — a chance.

10
the modest chapter

the eye in the microscope:
difficulties in studying people

*How do you picture science to yourself? "Oh, wonder-
working steed, build me a palace by morning," and by
morning there is a palace? And what if the problem has
been incorrectly stated in the first place? And what if
new phenomena turn up?*

— Aleksandr I. Solzhenitsyn
The First Circle

This is a short chapter. Maybe it's too short: social psychologists have a
lot to be modest about. But surely you've already learned a good deal
about our need for modesty during the previous several hundred pages,
so I won't review every painful detail.

The objectives of social psychology are far from modest: nothing less
than the complete understanding of man's psychological life among men,
and the ability to use that understanding to change man's social life,
presumably for the better. Our knowledge of and our ability to shape
individual social behavior are indeed increasing, just as our resources for
further increasing knowledge and ability — the professional journals, the
laboratories, and particularly the sheer number of research-oriented social
psychologists — grow yearly. Since World War II, we have learned more
about the areas encompassed by social psychology than man learned in
all his previous history. Both our aims and our interim accomplishments
support my first chapter's immodest claim for the field's social relevance.

Nonetheless, what we know now about the psychology of social man
is still too often tantalizingly incomplete or downright confusing. We

seldom have enough command of our competing theories to make them meet head-on in mutually exclusive predictions of research outcomes; and when we do, they usually bounce off each other harmlessly or strike only a glancing blow before they skid away into the bushes. Our once simple contradictions of common sense have become mazes of higher–order interaction effects. We seem to do much better at telling nonpsychologists where they're wrong than at showing them how to do things right. Knowing correctly that you don't know what to do is a much more relevant sort of knowledge than knowing incorrectly that you have the answers; but it is also a cause for considerable modesty.

In Chapter One I put our shortcomings mainly down to youth. The brevity of our field's existence is, I remain sure, a major reason for its lack of coordination and its frequent lapses from good sense. This reason is a very satisfying one for social psychologists to contemplate, because the remedy can be thought of merely as the passage of time. But we are hindered by other problems besides youth, and most of them require much more active efforts at solution. The central problem, which also happens to be our central advantage, is our object of study: people. Their sheer complexity, as I've noted upon several occasions, makes any discipline focusing upon human beings potentially far more difficult than any discipline dealing mainly with other phenomena. Add to the number of their brain cells and the diversity of their acquired behaviors the fact that people may behave in special ways because they are objects of scientific study, and you may begin to appreciate some of the pains the humanness of human beings can inflict upon social psychologists.

Making something the object of study typically changes its behavior. Perhaps the most well-known instance of this is also one of the most unlikely: Heisenberg's point that studying subatomic particles necessarily disrupts their actions to such a degree that precise observations can never be made. The subatomic particles don't care whether they're observed or not; it's just that the energy directed toward them during the act of observation interferes with what would otherwise be their "normal" behavior. Imagine, however, that you're inspecting the invisible universe with a scanning electron microscope and you suddenly come upon an intelligent eye looking straight back at you. The degree to which your observations may distort the behavior of whatever you're observing will have suddenly increased enormously.

That's what happens when you study humans instead of mesons. Not only do you disturb their behavior by pulling them out of their normal rounds and into the laboratory, or by injecting your own presence somehow into their normal world; in addition, they are likely to react quite specifically to their observations of being observed. Social psychologists have always realized this at some level, or else they wouldn't have gone

405

to such lengths to disguise the intent of their research from the participants. But only within the past few years have social psychologists really become aware that uncontrolled reactions of participants to being observed could interfere seriously with the main effects of experimental variables.

These main effects may suffer from other sorts of interference too, some of which have been subjected to intensive study. In discussing the Authoritarian F Scale in Chapter Three, I mentioned the problem of response set — the tendency to respond in consistent ways to psychological questionnaire items, regardless of actual agreement or disagreement with specific item content. For the psychologist who is attempting to measure authoritarianism or anxiety, the discovery that his questionnaire scores have been inflated by general agreement tendencies or by attempts to give only socially acceptable answers can be a serious setback. These response sets can be controlled, by such devices as using pairs of items matched for desirability, and asking the volunteer not whether he agrees with each item but which item of each pair he prefers most. However, until the psychologist realizes that a response set is influencing answers, his results may be seriously misleading.

Even more damaging, to the psychologist's ego as well as to his research, may be the discovery that he has been unintentionally biasing his own results, for instance by miscounting questionnaire responses so they come out slightly more favorable to his hypotheses. Observer bias is by no means unique to psychology; indeed, it was first detected in astronomical observations. But it may particularly distress the scientist who thought he knew enough about unconscious motivation to avoid its influence in his scientific work. And it doesn't stop with misreadings of the results, which can be corrected rather easily by using at least two independent data scorers or an automated data-recording device. Even the most scrupulous efforts to record data accurately can be wasted if the experimenter is unconsciously influencing the data before they are tabulated, by treating different volunteers in different ways according to his unrecognized biases.

Some of this differential treatment may occur equally across all experimental conditions, in which case it won't do much to misrepresent the phenomena the experimenter thinks he's studying. For instance, male experimenters have been observed to smile much more at female volunteers, and in general to treat female volunteers more "protectively" than male volunteers (Rosenthal, 1969). As long as male and female volunteers are distributed equally across experimental conditions, such experimenter bias shouldn't change the overall relationships of effects in the various conditions — though it may result in female data differing from male data across all conditions. But let's say the experimenter has predicted that a high-fear appeal will generate more attitude change than a low-fear appeal, and unconsciously acts a bit more pleasant toward volunteers in his high-fear conditions. He may indeed find his prediction verified, but not because of any differences between fear appeals; instead he is observing attitude change as a result of differences in communicator pleasantness.

Robert Rosenthal (1966, 1969) and others have demonstrated upon numerous occasions that experimenters can indeed influence their results unconsciously, though not all their examples are undisputed (see Barber and Silver, 1968). The means by which experimenters exert such influence are not altogether clear. Facial expression, body angle, word emphasis, and intonational patterns are only a few of the factors so far identified as transmitters of the experimenter's biases to his volunteers. Again, several fairly simple techniques have been developed to limit such biasing: for instance, the experimenter can tape-record all instructions, or he can distribute everything in printed form to the participants, or he can hire several subsidiary experimenters and have them give the instructions. But it may be hard to remove all biasing effects in these ways. The experimenter still must choose different words to record or to print as instructions in different conditions; and even his instructions to the subsidiary experimenters may indirectly influence the experimental participants, because what he tells his intermediaries may bias *them* to treat the volunteers in different ways (Rosenthal, 1969).

On top of all this, the fact that his research participants are people and not inert substances can multiply the experimenter's problems with his own biases. The volunteer doesn't just sit there being pushed around by the experimenter's smiles and frowns; at some level he's likely to be thinking, "What's he trying to tell me?" or "How am I supposed to respond to what's going on?" Milton Rosenberg (1965, 1969) has identified an important aspect of the volunteer's concerns in the experimental situation as *evaluation apprehension.* Martin Orne (1962, 1969) has spoken more generally of *demand characteristics,* or situational factors that guide the volunteer's responses in unplanned ways.

I've already discussed Rosenberg's idea of evaluation apprehension as offering an alternative explanation for part of the Twenty Dollar Misunderstanding results (Chapter Six). People who know anything about psychology are likely to worry that any psychologist they meet in a professional (or even perhaps nonprofessional) setting may be silently judging their sanity, their intelligence, or their psyche in general. Certain features of the setting, such as a substantial monetary payment for an unusual behavior, may be particularly likely to arouse this apprehension about being evaluated; and the more it's aroused, the harder a person may try to show the psychologist he's mentally healthy and strong — for

407

instance, by resisting the psychologist's persuasive attempts. Attitude change studies are by no means the only settings in which evaluation apprehension may complicate or distort empirical data; whenever situational cues suggest a heightened likelihood of evaluation, the volunteer's efforts to appear virtuous are likely to foul up the results.

The situational cues that arouse evaluation apprehension may be properly described as demand characteristics: they lead the volunteer to see the experimenter as wanting to get more out of him than the experimenter overtly asks for. Orne and others have discerned additional varieties of demand characteristics: cues leading the volunteer to assume that the experimenter wants him to behave in a particular way so as to verify the experimenter's predictions; cues indicating that the experiment is trivial and isn't worth putting any effort into; or even cues that the experimenter's aims contradict the volunteer's own values and should therefore be frustrated if possible.

Demand characteristics may not only confuse experimental results by operating differently in various experimental conditions, as Rosenberg suggests in the case of evaluation apprehension; they may also operate across all conditions, to misrepresent the applicability of experimental findings to the outside world. The experimenter may think he's doing an elegant and carefully controlled study of social perception, for example; but if the volunteer is paying more attention to various unintended cues about the experimenter's expectations than he is to the experimental stimuli, the results may be of very little help in understanding social perception in an experimenterless context.

The concept of demand characteristics lends itself easily to excess. Whenever someone gets results that contradict your assumptions, you can dismiss the contradiction simply by saying, "Obviously the demand characteristics of the situation were such that the volunteers responded to the experimenter's hypothesis rather than to reality." Furthermore, it's easy to forget that reality itself presents us with demand characteristics all the time: covert cues that other people want us to behave differently than they tell us to, or cues suggesting that a set of norms which might seem appropriate to a situation is really inapplicable and should be replaced by a different set. The presence of demand characteristics in an experiment need not invalidate it, unless the demands differ notably from what might be found in a similar situation outside the laboratory. (Orne and Holland [1968] seem to me to have overlooked such cautions in their enthusiastic application of demand-characteristic assumptions to the Milgram obedience research.)

How can psychologists cope with demand characteristics? They must first discover *what* demands are present in a particular situation; and the only way they can really do that is to ask the participants. Even if an

408

experimenter intentionally sets up a situation to include covert demand characteristics, participants may perceive things quite differently than he does; and it's their perceptions that create the demands upon them, not the experimenter's assumptions about their perceptions. So probably the best way to deal with demand characteristics is to interview participants carefully afterward about how they viewed the experiment (or, even better, to have somebody other than the experimenter interview them, since the postexperiment interview may be seen as making demands too), and then to set up the next experiment to eliminate or control as many implicit demands as possible. Other techniques for measuring the effects of demand characteristics have been suggested, such as the "nonexperiment" (Orne, 1969) — showing volunteers the experimental situation and then asking them how they'd probably respond to it, without subjecting them to the actual experimental treatment. But nothing except real experimental participation can fully reproduce the demand characteristics of that situation; so the people who worry about demand characteristics might better invest a large part of their coping time in improving postexperiment interviews than in developing fancier assessment methods.

"The people who worry about demand characteristics" now include, I'd guess, nearly every social psychologist in the country. Demand characteristics and other problems attributable to the humanity of researcher and researchee have provided a greater challenge to the steady progress of social psychology than perhaps any other factor since the field's founding. Such factors probably add enough static to experimental results to conceal many genuine effects; on the other hand, when they're working in the same direction as the researcher's assumptions, they may exaggerate real effects or even create apparent effects that aren't really there. My "law of nonreplication" — whenever one experimenter gets a clear result, the next experimenter is likely to get something quite different — rests not only on researchers' failure to recognize all the major variables influencing their research outcomes, but also on their failure to appreciate the influence of more subtle factors that act upon all participants in the research situation.

In spite of such confounding and confounded influences, however, there is reason for hope. A substantial number of social psychological research findings have been confirmed by additional studies in which demand characteristics and experimenter biases are likely to have differed considerably from the original ones. And as concern has risen about such matters, more and more researchers have begun to build into their research programs specific controls for these previously uncontrolled and undetected factors. Robert Rosenthal (Rosenthal and Jacobson, 1968; Rubovits and Maehr, 1971) has even managed to use something akin to experimenter bias creatively, apparently increasing children's intellectual abilities by telling teachers they can expect certain (really randomly selected) children to "bloom" academically in the near future. Although biasing phenomena in researchers and research participants may have seriously slowed the progress of social psychology in the past, the growing recognition of such phenomena should enable us to begin making advances substantial enough to support a genuinely realistic immodesty in the future.

cooperation and cooptation: making social psychology more useful

Malthus believed in artificially limiting population, but found that it could not be done by talking.

— Ambrose Bierce
The Devil's Dictionary

However great social psychology's social relevance may be, it will come to nothing if it is not put to use. Social psychologists have in the past left the job of finding applications for their knowledge mainly to other people; and other people have been notably slow either to realize the existence of that knowledge or to make good use of it. But during the last few years, largely in response to the demands of their students and other newly concerned elements of society, social psychologists have themselves begun seeking ways to ensure that their data and their theories will be properly applied.

Their attempts in certain cases may turn out to be counterproductive. Individual psychologists and professional groups have at times coupled demands for the application of social psychological knowledge with political demands little related to their professional expertise. Some have urged that the American Psychological Association itself become not only a professional and scientific organization but also a politically active one, much in the manner of the American Medical Association although on the other side of the political spectrum (see Sanford, 1970). Such pursuit of an overtly political role may well turn those whose policies are in most need of scientific correction strongly against any public role by social psychologists. But surely other means exist by which greater use of the field's existing knowledge, as well as increased development of those areas most likely to have a social payoff, can be encouraged.

I've already mentioned several problems that social psychologists face in getting their suggestions accepted by the people who could perhaps use them. There are, for instance, the difficulties involved in convincing government leaders that they personally are misperceiving American and foreign roles in cold and hot wars. There were McClelland's difficulties in raising funds for a program that would not merely distribute money to those who want it — the bureaucrat's simplest answer to all questions — but would change people's motivational patterns so they could help themselves (McClelland and Winter, 1969). Not only government leaders but anyone trying to cope with a problem on his own ground is likely to turn a cold eye toward the social psychologist who walks in with a new way of doing or looking at things.

How can we make ourselves more welcome? Perhaps a few more doses of modesty would help; but I'm afraid we've often been so modest in the past that no one noticed us. Perhaps we could use our own attitude-change techniques on those whom we wish to accept our recommendations; but effective attitude change usually requires, among other things, high credibility on the part of the communicator, and that's precisely what we're trying to convince people we have.

One recent report (Special Commission on the Social Sciences, 1969) suggests that part of the answer is educating people to the usefulness of the social sciences. Congressmen and Presidents may be hard to reach, once in office; but if grade-school and high-school children, college students, law students, adult-education students, and plain ordinary television watchers are taught more about what the social sciences have to offer, then when they encounter social problems — whether as ordinary citizens or as congressmen and Presidents — they may be more likely to think of social scientific findings as a possible part of the solution. Probably the best thing about such educational efforts would not be the communication of specific knowledge, which is likely to be superseded or considerably refined by the time the learner finds a use for it, but the communication of social scientific *ways of thinking* about social behavior, which may enable the learner more accurately to perceive which problems require social scientific knowledge, and what sorts of knowledge he needs.

Another proposal that might promote greater use of social scientific findings by people already in office, particularly in federal office, is the creation of a National Social Science Foundation (Harris, 1967; Mondale, 1967). The federal government already feeds considerable amounts of money to social psychology and the other social sciences through such agencies as the National Institute of Mental Health and the National Science Foundation; indeed, partly in response to the proposal for a National Social Science Foundation, Congress has recently obligated NSF officially to support research in the social sciences as well as in the physical and biological sciences. But a National Social Science Foundation would probably mean both a more equitable level of government support for the social sciences and greater visibility of social science

411

research in the eyes of the government's legislative, executive, and judicial branches.

The usefulness of social psychology will increase not only with better education of congressmen and other potential users about what it can do, but also with better education of social psychologists themselves. I'm probably fairly representative of social psychologists in seeking great precision of detail in my own research, but getting most of my information about research-relevant public issues from newspapers and other imprecise media. This means not only that social psychologists' attempts to apply their findings suffer from a lack of detail at the applied end, but also that they know relatively little about how to get their hopefully practical proposals implemented, whether at national or local levels. Several recent ideas could help with both these problems.

1. Nevitt Sanford and David Krech (1969; Sanford, 1969) have proposed that a "social-clinical" specialization be added to social psychology Ph.D. programs. At least one institution, the Wright Institute in Berkeley, has already established such a specialty. Sanford and Krech envision this special program as requiring the interested graduate student both to receive sound training in academic social psychology and to work in applied settings or social problem–oriented research throughout his graduate education. My own feeling is that today's fledgling social psychologist has enough difficulty just getting a good basic knowledge of the field during his first years of graduate work, without having to battle the complexities and frustrations of doing applied research on urgent social issues. But another aspect of the Sanford-Krech proposal seems to me both feasible and highly desirable: a one-year internship "in some agency, office, or institution directly concerned with human problems." Clinical psychology students typically do an internship in a mental hospital or other psychotherapeutic setting; Sanford and Krech suggest that the social clinician might work in "a state senator's office, a prison, a labor union, an office of a Public Defender." Taken after the student's course-work is finished and before his doctoral dissertation begins, this internship could be fertile ground for developing dissertational research uniting theoretical issues and practical problems. Furthermore, it might give the young social psychologist enough insight into the functioning of specific social change agencies so that he could pursue research directly adapted to their needs in the future.

2. The Claremont Graduate School's psychology faculty has developed a program of graduate-level specialization in public affairs (Brayfield, 1969). Again, this program involves basic graduate training in psychology (either in social psychology or another traditional area), and also requires an internship in "an appropriate public service setting." The goal here, however, is not only training people to do applied social research, but

also training people to apply available psychological knowledge to social problems, or to communicate such knowledge effectively to nonpsychologists who can then make use of it, or to serve as science administrators in government agencies and other organizations where psychological research is of prime concern. The Claremont program is most interesting, I think, for its recognition that socially relevant psychological research can be done in settings other than the site of its most immediate application, as long as other expert psychologists are available to make the appropriate applications later. Laboratories will continue to be superior to most field settings in terms of such criteria as degree of experimental control; but solid findings need not remain in the laboratory files if trained intermediaries are available — as various kinds of engineers or engineer-scientists are available, for instance, to translate into practice the findings of the physical sciences.

3. The National Science Board's Special Commission on the Social Sciences (1969) has proposed creating as many as twenty-five "social problem research institutes," each of which would concentrate on one major social problem: pollution prevention, alcohol and drug addiction, social violence, and so on. These institutes would be staffed by a variety of social scientists, engineers, lawyers, physicians — a mix of disciplines appropriate to deal with the problem at hand. Financing would initially come from the federal government, and eventually from each institute's own major "clients" — those government bodies, nonprofit organizations, or private enterprises most involved with the institute's own specialty. Such institutes would permit already well-established scholars, rather than new graduate students, to focus full-time on the social issues most likely to benefit from their expertise; and they would promote much more intensive and integrated efforts toward social problem-solving than is now possible even in most university research institutes.

None of these proposals will bring the millennium, or give social psychologists control of the nation. I'm not arguing for either of those goals. But adoption of the proposals should help us to make better use both of our social scientific accomplishments and of our social scientific potential in meeting our major and minor social problems — goals well worth arguing for.

But what if our accomplishments and our potential begin to be used too well? What if, in the new political language, we are coopted by the establishment, used to attain goals not of our own choosing? Some such blots on the fair name of social science are already well known — Project Camelot, for instance, in which American social scientists were asked to devise techniques for preserving political stability (read: repressive dictatorships) in certain South American nations. How may we avoid worse social scientific disasters in the future?

413

I've already indicated some of my feelings about this issue. Any sort of knowledge, if it be made public, can be used for various ends, and this is as true of social psychological knowledge as of any other. Social psychologists can, however, choose areas of research or approaches to research that lend themselves less easily to repressive or antihuman uses. One can do research not only on factors that promote obedience, but also on factors that promote defiance of destructive commands. One can do research not only on attitude change but on resistance to attitude change ((keeping in mind that in many situations, attitude change will lead to more socially desirable outcomes than will hidebound resistance to change). One can seek means to promote rational attitude change, which advances the interests of the persuaded, rather than methods to promote irrational change.

And what if others continue to do research on irrational attitude change? Well, by his research on rational change, the concerned social psychologist is developing ways of competing with them and perhaps eventually of outdistancing them. The worst thing a social psychologist can do, as William McGuire (1969b) has pointed out, is nothing. The researcher who retires from the field, fearing that even his ethically oriented research can be used for ill, merely leaves the field wide open for researchers who aren't bothered by questions of ethics.

A few of our more politically radical researchers have insisted instead that we do research so narrowly circumscribed in content and method that it could never be used for anything but radical goals — research on the social dynamics of communes, say, or on ways of promoting "revolutionary consciousness." I doubt that even this sort of research would be totally valueless to the establishment; and anyway I haven't yet seen any decent research along such lines. Social scientific researchers who feel constrained to stay within a strict ideological framework seem rarely to make significant contributions to social psychology, or to any of the other socially relevant social sciences — consider the social scientific output of Catholic universities or of Communist nations as cases in point. Hand-me-down ideologies never quite manage to include all that one needs to know about people in order to deal with their problems, or to include the most useful theoretical frameworks within which to assemble such knowledge. A decent social scientist must be prepared to throw out what he doesn't need and to add what he does; ideologies are seldom so adaptable. I'm reminded of the Worcester doctor in Chapter Eight, who tied a tourniquet with an electric cord that was unfortunately attached to an iron. The radical activist who really wants to use scientific knowledge for the good of the people had better take his science as simple and unencumbered as he can get it. Ideologies may serve a useful function in politics, but in science they are usually needless, at times even deadly, extra baggage.

414

a little hope from our friends: problem-solving eclecticism

We are as gods and might as well get good at it.
— Whole Earth Catalog

Dr. Charles T. Tart's office is immediately adjacent to mine. Tart edited an intriguing book, *Altered States of Consciousness* (1969), and has written several dozen professional journal articles on topics ranging from mutual hypnosis to the psychophysiological correlates of "out-of-body" experiences. For many hip undergraduates, he is the main reason to consider doing graduate work at the University of California's Davis campus. He was nearly refused tenure at Davis because of his "exotic" research interests; he was granted tenure because he usually conducts his research on these exotic topics in careful scientific fashion. His office is filled with god's-eyes and psychedelic prints and sometimes the odor of incense; his laboratories are filled with equipment ranging from a Grass polygraph to a homemade electroencephalopholy converter.

Although many students see Tart's research as high in personal and cultural relevance, its present social relevance is close to zilch. Mutual hypnosis is unlikely to make any major inroads on the population problem, and studying people's perceptions that they are somehow floating around outside their bodies will contribute little to controlling atmospheric pollution. But I wouldn't rule out the possibility that certain aspects of Tart's work will come to be at least as relevant to present and future social concerns as much of the social psychological research I've been discussing. In nearly all his research, Tart is trying to understand better the workings of human consciousness; and if man can learn to control his own brainwave patterns, or to improve the efficacy and efficiency of sleep through hypnosis (both areas in which Tart is now working), man's social relationships might well take on a very different character — more creative, perhaps, or more peaceable. The growth of leisure time and the growing need to limit consumption of material resources during that time may make even some of Tart's farthest-out research, for instance on "high" dreams (dreams that reproduce features of drug-induced states), highly relevant to maintaining a stable social system.

Charles Tart is not a social psychologist. I don't intend in this book to imply that only social psychology possesses social relevance. I'm more sensitive to what social psychology can contribute to society than I am to what other fields may offer; but I realize that my profession is not alone in its virtues.

In considering social relevance, I lean toward the *Whole Earth Catalog* model. The *Whole Earth Catalog* (1971) is a compendium of publications,

415

products, and sources of advice designed to increase the possibilities for human survival in our uncertain world. The catalog's editors have attempted to exclude the genuinely unuseful from their listings, but they are tremendously eclectic in the items they do include: everything from L. L. Bean camping goods to the teachings of Lao-Tze, from aphrodisiac body oils to electricity-generating windmills. The editors strike me as somewhat too undiscriminating at times: they seem particularly weak in their choice of psychology books (though they do include Tart's *Altered States of Consciousness*), and I don't believe we are nearly as godlike as they assume. But we surely do possess an incredible range of human capabilities, many of them represented in the *Whole Earth Catalog;* and we should be using as many of these capabilities as we can to deliver ourselves from the various horrible fates that may otherwise await us.

Social psychology clearly cannot play a direct role in coping with the many facets of all our problems. We cannot supply the nation with a general governmental philosophy, or with new sources of energy, or with more bountiful food plants. Even in those areas where social psychology can supply useful knowledge, it will need plenty of help from its sister social sciences in developing appropriate applications of this knowledge — for instance, in terms of learning about the cultural and status variations that inevitably influence the social behavior of any particular group of individuals. But given this assistance, social psychology can supply us with valuable information about such matters as how to increase the psychological freedom of people to participate in the governing system of their choice; how to summon their psychological energies to work toward the goals they value; how to divert their attention from aggressive acts to acts that will fill empty bellies and enlighten dull minds. Along with the efforts of all the other scientific disciplines and professions and individuals who attempt to make themselves socially relevant, the work of social psychologists can help us to ensure a much brighter and longer future, perhaps bringing us ultimately not to a godlike state but to one where we can live fully as human beings.

Social psychology may help us to attain these splendid aims; I'm not arguing that it will. Too many obstacles remain in the way, and the field itself remains too undeveloped for us to be sure. M. Brewster Smith (1969) has made a useful distinction between "the old naive *faith* in Progress" and "the *hope* for progress and the *determination* to attain it." I have no certain faith in human progress; indeed I incline toward a deep pessimism in my worse moments, and to nothing more than a very cautious optimism in my better ones. But social psychology and the other human sciences do impress me as offering us at least a modest amount of hope, and a basis for strengthened determination to move mankind toward a more hope-filled future.

416

references

Abelson, Robert P., and Lesser, Gerald S. A development theory of persuasibility. In C. I. Hovland and I. L. Janis (eds.), *Personality and persuasibility*. New Haven: Yale University Press, 1959.

Abelson, Robert P., and Miller, James. Negative persuasion via personal insult. *Journal of Experimental Social Psychology*, 1967, 3, 321–333.

Abelson, Robert P., and Rosenberg, Milton J. Symbolic psycho-logic: A model of attitudinal cognition. *Behavioral Science*, 1958, 3, 1–13.

Ad Hoc Committee on Ethical Standards in Psychological Research. Ethical standards for psychological research. *APA Monitor*, 1971, 2(7), 9–28.

Adorno, Theodor W.; Frenkel-Brunswik, Else; Levinson, Daniel J.; and Sanford, R. Nevitt. *The authoritarian personality*. New York: Harper & Row, 1950.

Almond, Gabriel A. *The appeals of Communism*. Princeton: Princeton University Press, 1954.

The American Heritage dictionary of the English language. Boston: American Heritage Publishing Co. and Houghton Mifflin, 1969.

Andrews, John D. W. The achievement motive in two types of organizations. *Journal of Personality and Social Psychology*, 1967, 6, 163–168.

Ardrey, Robert. *African genesis*. New York: Atheneum, 1961.

———. *The territorial imperative*. New York: Atheneum, 1966.

———. *The social contract*. New York: Atheneum, 1970.

Aronfreed, Justin. *Conduct and conscience*. New York: Academic Press, 1968.

Aronson, Elliot. The need for achievement as measured by graphic expression. In John W. Atkinson (ed.), *Motives in fantasy, action, and society*. Princeton: Van Nostrand, 1958.

———. Try a little dissonance. *New York Times Magazine*, September 11, 1966, 109–119.

Aronson, Elliot, and Carlsmith, J. Merrill. Effect of the severity of threat on the valuation of forbidden behavior. *Journal of Abnormal and Social Psychology*, 1963, 66, 584–588.

Aronson, Elliot, and Mills, Judson. The effect of severity of initiation on liking for a group. *Journal of Abnormal and Social Psychology*, 1959, 59, 177–181.

Aronson, Elliot; Turner, J. A.; and Carlsmith, J. M. Communicator credibility and communication discrepancy as determinants of opinion change. *Journal of Abnormal and Social Psychology*, 1963, 67, 31–36.

417

Asch, Solomon E. Effects of group pressure upon the modification and distortion of judgments. In Harold Guetzkow (ed.), *Groups, leadership and men.* Pittsburgh: Carnegie Press, 1951.

————. *Social psychology.* Englewood Cliffs, N.J.: Prentice-Hall, 1952.

————. Studies of independence and conformity: I. A minority of one against a unanimous majority. *Psychological Monographs,* 1956, *70* (9), Whole No. 416.

Atkinson, John W. *An introduction to motivation.* Princeton: Van Nostrand, 1964.

Atkinson, John W., and Feather, Norman T. *A theory of achievement motivation.* New York: Wiley, 1966.

Atkinson, John W.; Heyns, Roger W.; and Veroff, Joseph. The effect of experimental arousal of the affiliation motive on thematic apperception. *Journal of Abnormal and Social Psychology,* 1954, *49,* 405–410.

Atkinson, John W., and Walker, E. L. The affiliation motive and perceptual sensitivity to faces. *Journal of Abnormal and Social Psychology,* 1956, *53,* 38–41.

Bandura, Albert, and Walters, Richard H. *Social learning and personality development.* New York: Holt, Rinehart & Winston, 1963.

Barber, Theodore X., and Silver, Maurice J. Fact, fiction, and the experimenter bias effect. *Psychological Bulletin Monograph Supplement,* 1968, *70* (6, pt. 2), 1–29.

Barker, Roger G. Ecology and motivation. In M. R. Jones (ed.), *Nebraska symposium on motivation.* Lincoln: University of Nebraska Press, 1960.

————. Explorations in ecological psychology. *American Psychologist,* 1965, *20,* 1–14.

————. *Ecological psychology.* Stanford: Stanford University Press, 1968.

Barker, Roger G., and Barker, Louise Shedd. Social actions in the behavior streams of American and English children. In R. G. Barger (ed.), *The stream of behavior.* New York: Appleton-Century-Crofts, 1963.

Barker, Roger G.; Dembo, Tamara; and Lewin, Kurt. Frustration and regression: A study of young children. *University of Iowa Studies in Child Welfare,* 1941, *18,* No. 1.

Barker, Roger G., and Wright, Herbert F. *One boy's day.* New York: Harper & Row, 1951.

————. *Midwest and its children.* New York: Harper & Row, 1955.

Baron, Reuben M. Cognitive basis of attitude change as a function of motivational, stylistic, and stimulus factors. *Journal of Personality and Social Psychology,* 1965, *2,* 219–230.

Baron, Robert A., and Kepner, C. Richard. Model's behavior and attraction toward the model as determinants of adult aggressive behavior. *Journal of Personality and Social Psychology,* 1970, *14,* 335–344.

Barry, Herbert; Child, Irven; and Bacon, M. Relation of child training to subsistence economy. *American Anthropologist,* 1959, *61,* 51–63.

Barton, Allen H. *Communities in disaster.* New York: Doubleday, 1969.

Bastian, Jarvis R. Primate signaling systems and human languages. In Irven DeVore (ed.), *Primate behavior.* New York: Holt, Rinehart & Winston, 1965.

418

Baumrind, Diana. Some thoughts on ethics of research: After reading Milgram's "Behavioral study of obedience." *American Psychologist*, 1964, *19*, 421–423.

———. Child care practices anteceding three patterns of preschool behavior. *Genetic Psychology Monographs*, 1967, *75*, 43–88.

Bay, Christian. Political and apolitical students: Facts in search of theory. *Journal of Social Issues*, 1967, *23*, 76–91.

Bell, Daniel. The dispossessed. In D. Bell (ed.), *The radical right*. New York: Doubleday, 1963.

Benedict, Ruth. *Patterns of culture*. Boston: Houghton Mifflin, 1934.

Berkowitz, Leonard. *Aggression: A social psychological analysis*. New York: McGraw-Hill, 1962.

———. The concept of aggressive drive: Some additional considerations. In Leonard Berkowitz (ed.), *Advances in experimental social psychology*, vol. 2. New York: Academic Press, 1965.

Berkowitz, Leonard, and Daniels, L. R. Responsibility and dependency. *Journal of Abnormal and Social Psychology*, 1963, *66*, 429–436.

———. Affecting the salience of the social responsibility norm: Effects of past help on the response to dependency relationships. *Journal of Abnormal and Social Psychology*, 1964, *68*, 275–281.

Berkun, Mitchell M.; Bialek, H. M.; Kern, R. P.; and Yagi, K. Experimental studies of psychological stress in man. *Psychological Monographs*, 1962, *76* (15), Whole No. 534.

Bernstein, Irwin S. Primate status hierarchies. In L. A. Rosenblum (ed.), *Primate behavior: Developments in field and laboratory research*, vol. 1. New York: Academic Press, 1970.

Berry, J. W. Independence and conformity in subsistence-level societies. *Journal of Personality and Social Psychology*, 1967, *7*, 415–418.

Biderman, Albert D. The image of "brainwashing." *Public Opinion Quarterly*, 1962, *26*, 547–563.

Birney, Robert C. Research on the achievement motive. In Edgar F. Borgatta & William W. Lambert (eds.), *Handbook of personality theory and research*. Chicago: Rand McNally, 1968.

Block, Jeanne H. Rebellion re-examined: The role of identification and alienation. Paper presented at the Foundations' Fund for Research in Psychiatry Conference on Adaptation to Change, Puerto Rico, June 1968.

Block, Jeanne H.; Haan, Norma; and Smith, M. Brewster. Activism and apathy in contemporary adolescents. In James F. Adams (ed.), *Understanding adolescence*. Boston: Allyn & Bacon, 1968.

———. Socialization correlates of student activism. *Journal of Social Issues*, 1969, *25* (4), 143–177.

Bochner, Stephen, and Insko, Chester A. Communicator discrepancy, source credibility, and opinion change. *Journal of Personality and Social Psychology*, 1966, *4*, 614–621.

Bourne, Peter G. *Men, stress, and Vietnam*. Boston: Little, Brown, 1970.

Brayfield, Arthur H. Developmental planning for a graduate program in psychology. *American Psychologist*, 1969, *24*, 669–674.

Brehm, Jack W. Increasing cognitive dissonance by a fait accompli. *Journal of Abnormal and Social Psychology*, 1959, *58*, 379–382.

419

Brehm, Jack W., and Cohen, Arthur R. *Explorations in cognitive dissonance.* New York: Wiley, 1962.

Brock, Timothy C. Communicator-recipient similarity and decision change. *Journal of Personality and Social Psychology,* 1965, *1,* 650–654.

Bronfenbrenner, Urie. The mirror image in Soviet-American relations. *Journal of Social Issues,* 1961, *17* (3), 45–56.

Brown, Cheryl Lynn. *Intervening variables in resistance to persuasion.* Unpublished doctoral dissertation; University of California at Davis, 1971.

Brown, Roger. *Social psychology.* New York: The Free Press, 1965.

Bryan, James H., and Test, Mary Ann. Models and helping: Naturalistic studies in aiding behavior. *Journal of Personality and Social Psychology,* 1967, *6,* 400–407.

Buss, Arnold H. Instrumentality of aggression, feedback, and frustration as determinants of physical aggression. *Journal of Personality and Social Psychology,* 1966, *3,* 153–162.

Butler, Robert A. Investigative behavior. In A. M. Schrier; H. F. Harlow; and F. Stollnitz (eds.), *Behavior of Nonhuman Primates,* vol. 2. New York: Academic Press, 1965.

Campbell, Angus; Converse, Philip E.; Miller, Warren E.; and Stokes, Donald E. *The American voter: An abridgment.* New York: Wiley, 1964.

Campbell, Dugal; Sanderson, R. E.; and Laverty, S. G. Characteristics of a conditioned response in human subjects during extinction trials following a single traumatic conditioning trial. *Journal of Abnormal and Social Psychology,* 1964, *68,* 627–639.

Carlsmith, J. Merrill; Collins, Barry E.; and Helmreich, Robert L. Studies in forced compliance: I. The effect of pressure for compliance on attitude change produced by face-to-face roleplaying and anonymous essay writing. *Journal of Personality and Social Psychology,* 1966, *4,* 1–13.

Carmichael, Joel. *The death of Jesus.* New York: Macmillan, 1962.

Carpenter, C. R. A field study of the behavior and social relations of howling monkeys. *Comparative Psychology Monographs,* 1934, *10,* 1–168.

———. A field study in Siam of the behavior and social relations of the gibbon, *Hylobates lar. Comparative Psychology Monographs,* 1940, *16,* 1–212.

———. Societies of monkeys and apes. *Biological Symposia,* 1942, *8,* 177–204.

———. The howlers of Barro Colorado Island. In I. DeVore (ed.), *Primate behavior.* New York: Holt, Rinehart & Winston, 1965.

Cartwright, Dorwin, and Harary, F. Structural balance: A generalization of Heider's theory. *Psychological Review,* 1956, *63,* 277–293.

Chance, Michael R. A., and Jolly, Clifford J. *Social groups of monkeys, apes and men.* London: Jonathan Cape Ltd., 1970.

Chapanis, Natalia P., and Chapanis, A. Cognitive dissonance: Five years later. *Psychological Bulletin,* 1964, *61,* 1–22.

Chapman, Dwight W. A brief introduction to contemporary disaster research. In George W. Baker and Dwight W. Chapman (eds.), *Man and society in disaster.* New York: Basic Books, 1962.

Chesler, Mark, and Schmuck, Richard. Social psychological characteristics of super-patriots. In R. A. Schoenberger (ed.), *The American right wing.* New York: Holt, Rinehart & Winston, 1969.

Chivers, D. J. On the daily behaviour and spacing of howling monkey groups. *Folia Primatologica*, 1969, *10*, 48–102.

Christie, Richard. Why Machiavelli? In R. Christie and F. Geis (eds.), *Studies in Machiavellianism*. New York: Academic Press, 1970a.

———. Social correlates of Machiavellianism. In R. Christie and F. Geis (eds.), *Studies in Machiavellianism*. New York: Academic Press, 1970b.

Christie, Richard, and Geis, Florence. Some consequences of taking Machiavelli seriously. In E. F. Borgatta and W. W. Lambert (eds.), *Handbook of personality theory and research*. Chicago: Rand McNally, 1968.

———. Implications and speculations. In R. Christie and F. Geis (eds.), *Studies in Machiavellianism*. New York: Academic Press, 1970.

Clark, Kenneth B. The pathos of power: A psychological perspective. Presidential address, 79th Annual Convention, American Psychological Association, September 4, 1971.

Cohen, Arthur R. Some implications of self-esteem for social influence. In C. I. Hovland and I. L. Janis (eds.), *Personality and persuasibility*. New Haven: Yale University Press, 1959.

Collias, Nicholas, and Southwick, Charles. A field study of population density and social organization in howling monkeys. *Proceedings of the American Philosophical Society*, 1952, *96*, 143–156.

Collins, Barry E. The effect of monetary inducements on the amount of attitude change produced by forced compliance. In A. C. Elms (ed.), *Roleplaying, reward, and attitude change*. New York: Van Nostrand Reinhold, 1969.

———. *Social psychology*. Reading, Mass.: Addison-Wesley, 1970.

Coopersmith, Stanley. *The antecedents of self-esteem*. San Francisco: W. H. Freeman, 1967.

———. Some common personality, background and motivational characteristics of persons committing altruistic acts. Unpublished paper, University of California at Davis, 1970.

Costello, William. *The facts about Nixon*. New York: Viking, 1960.

Cox, Donald F., and Bauer, Raymond A. Self-confidence and persuasibility in women. *Public Opinion Quarterly*, 1964, *28*, 453–466.

Craik, Kenneth H. Environmental psychology. In *New Directions in Psychology 4*. New York: Holt, Rinehart & Winston, 1970.

Crutchfield, Richard S. Conformity and character. *American Psychologist*, 1955, *10*, 191–198.

Daniels, David N., and Gilula, Marshall F. Violence and the struggle for existence. In D. N. Daniels, M. F. Gilula, and F. M. Ochberg (eds.), *Violence and the struggle for existence*. Boston: Little, Brown, 1970.

Darley, John M., and Latané, Bibb. Bystander intervention in emergencies: Diffusion of responsibility. *Journal of Personality and Social Psychology*, 1968, *8*, 377–383.

———. Norms and normative behavior: Field studies of social interdependence. In R. Macaulay and L. Berkowitz (eds.), *Altruism and helping behavior*. New York: Academic Press, 1970.

Disaster Research Group. *Field studies of disaster behavior: An inventory*. Washington: National Academy of Sciences — National Research Council, 1961.

Dollard, John; Doob, Leonard W.; Miller, Neal E.; Mowrer, O. H.; and Sears, Robert R. *Frustration and aggression.* New Haven: Yale University Press, 1939.

Donley, Richard E., and Winter, David G. Measuring the motives of public officials at a distance: An exploratory study of American presidents. *Behavioral Science,* 1970, *15,* 227–236.

Dyck, Arthur J. The social contacts of some Midwest children with their parents and teachers. In R. G. Barker (ed.), *The stream of behavior.* New York: Appleton-Century-Crofts, 1963.

Eagly, Alice H. Involvement as a determinant of response to favorable and unfavorable information. *Journal of Personality and Social Psychology Monograph,* 1967, 7 (3, part 2), Whole No. 643.

Egbert, Lawrence D.; Battit, George E.; Welch, Claude E.; and Bartlett, Marshall K. Reduction of postoperative pain by encouragement and instruction of patients. *New England Journal of Medicine,* 1964, *270,* 825–827.

Elms, Alan C. Influence of fantasy ability on attitude change through roleplaying. *Journal of Personality and Social Psychology,* 1966, *4,* 36–43.

————. Roleplaying, incentive, and dissonance. *Psychological Bulletin,* 1967, *68,* 132–148.

————. Psychological factors in right-wing extremism. In R. A. Schoenberger (ed.), *The American right wing.* New York: Holt, Rinehart & Winston, 1969.

Elms, Alan C., and Janis, Irving L. Counter-norm attitudes induced by consonant versus dissonant conditions of roleplaying. *Journal of Experimental Research in Personality,* 1965, *1,* 50–60.

Elms, Alan C., and Milgram, Stanley. Personality characteristics associated with obedience and defiance toward authoritative command. *Journal of Experimental Research in Personality,* 1966, *2,* 282–289.

English, Horace B., and English, Ava C. *A comprehensive dictionary of psychological and psychoanalytical terms.* New York: Longmans, Green, 1958.

Erikson, Erik H. *Identity: Youth and crisis.* New York: Norton, 1968.

Etzioni, Amatai. *The hard way to peace.* New York: Collier Books, 1962.

————. The Kennedy experiment. *Western Political Quarterly,* 1967, *20,* 361–380.

————. Social-psychological aspects of international relations. In Gardner Lindzey and Elliot Aronson (eds.), *The handbook of social psychology,* 2nd ed., vol. 5. Reading, Mass.: Addison-Wesley, 1969.

Eysenck, Hans. *The psychology of politics.* London: Routledge & Kegan Paul, 1954.

Farber, I. E.; Harlow, Harry F.; and West, Louis J. Brainwashing, conditioning, and DDD (debility, dependency and dread). *Sociometry,* 1956, *19,* 271–285.

Fawl, Clifford L. Disturbances experienced by children in their natural habitats. In R. G. Barker (ed.), *The stream of behavior.* New York: Appleton-Century-Crofts, 1963.

Fayerweather, J. *The executive overseas.* Syracuse: Syracuse University Press, 1959.

Feiffer, Jules. *Hold me!* New York: Random House, 1962.

Feshbach, Seymour, and Singer, Robert D. *Television and aggression.* San Francisco: Jossey-Bass, 1971.

Festinger, Leon. *A theory of cognitive dissonance.* Evanston, Ill.: Row, Peterson, 1957.

Festinger, Leon, and Carlsmith, J. Merrill. Cognitive consequences of forced compliance. *Journal of Abnormal and Social Psychology,* 1959, 58, 203–210.

Festinger, Leon; Riecken, Henry; and Schachter, Stanley. *When prophecy fails.* Minneapolis: University of Minnesota Press, 1956.

Feuer, Lewis S. *The conflict of generations.* New York: Basic Books, 1969.

Fiske, Donald W., and Maddi, Salvatore R. (eds.), *Functions of varied experience.* Homewood, Ill.: Dorsey, 1961.

Frager, Robert. Conformity and anticonformity in Japan. *Journal of Personality and Social Psychology,* 1970, 15, 203–210.

Freedman, Jonathan L. Roleplaying: Psychology by consensus. *Journal of Personality and Social Psychology,* 1969, 13, 107–114.

French, Elizabeth G. Motivation as a variable in work-partner selection. *Journal of Abnormal and Social Psychology,* 1956, 53, 96–99.

Freud, Sigmund. *Beyond the pleasure principle.* In J. Strachey (ed.), *The standard edition of the complete psychological works of Sigmund Freud,* vol. 18. London: Hogarth Press, 1955 (original German publication, 1920).

————. *Inhibitions, symptoms and anxiety.* In J. Strachey (ed.), *The standard edition of the complete psychological works of Sigmund Freud,* vol. 20. London: Hogarth Press, 1959 (original German publication, 1926).

————. The neuro-psychoses of defence. In J. Strachey (ed.), *The standard edition of the complete psychological works of Sigmund Freud,* vol. 3. London: Hogarth Press, 1962a (original German publication, 1894).

————. Further remarks on the neuro-psychoses of defence. In J. Strachey (ed.), *The standard edition of the complete psychological works of Sigmund Freud,* vol. 3. London: Hogarth Press, 1962b (original German publication, 1896).

————. On the grounds for detaching a particular syndrome from neurasthenia under the description 'Anxiety neurosis.' In J. Strachey (ed.), *The standard edition of the complete psychological works of Sigmund Freud,* vol. 3. London: Hogarth Press, 1962c (original German publication, 1895).

Freud, Sigmund, and Bullitt, William C. *Thomas Woodrow Wilson: A psychological study.* Boston: Houghton Mifflin, 1966.

Frisch, John E. Individual behavior and intertroop variability in Japanese macaques. In P. Jay (ed.), *Primates: Studies in adaptation and variability.* New York: Holt, Rinehart & Winston, 1968.

Fritz, Charles E. Disaster. In R. K. Merton and R. A. Nisbet (eds.), *Contemporary social problems.* New York: Harcourt, Brace, & World, 1961.

Fritz, Charles E., and Marks, E. S. The NORC studies of human behavior in disaster. *Journal of Social Issues,* 1954, 10(3), 26–41.

Fritz, Charles, and Mathewson, J. H. *Convergence behavior in disasters: A problem in social control.* Washington: National Academy of Sciences — National Research Council, 1957.

Frommer, Arthur (ed.) *Goldwater from A to Z.* New York: Frommer/Pasmantier, 1964.

Gamson, William A., and Modigliani, Andre. *Untangling the cold war: A strategy for testing rival theories.* Boston: Little, Brown, 1971.

Gardner, R. Allen, and Gardner, Beatrice T. Teaching sign language to a chimpanzee. *Science,* 1969, *165,* 664–672.

Garvey, W. D., and Griffith, B. C. *Some findings of the project on scientific information exchange in psychology.* Washington: American Psychological Association — Project on Scientific Information Exchange in Psychology, 1963.

Geen, Russell G. Effects of frustration, attack, and prior training in aggressiveness upon aggressive behavior. *Journal of Personality and Social Psychology,* 1968, *9,* 316–321.

Geis, Florence, and Christie, Richard. Overview of experimental research. In R. Christie and F. Geis (eds.), *Studies in Machiavellianism.* New York: Academic Press, 1970.

Gerard, Harold B., and Mathewson, G. C. The effects of severity of initiation on liking for a group: A replication. *Journal of Experimental Social Psychology,* 1966, *2,* 278–287.

Gollob, Harry F., and Dittes, James E. Effects of manipulated self-esteem on persuasibility depending on threat and complexity of communication. *Journal of Personality and Social Psychology,* 1965, *2,* 195–201.

Goodall, Jane. Chimpanzees of the Gombe Stream Reserve. In I. DeVore (ed.), *Primate behavior.* New York: Holt, Rinehart & Winston, 1965.

Gough, Harrison G.; McClosky, H.; and Meehl, P. E. A personality scale for social responsibility. *Journal of Abnormal and Social Psychology,* 1952, *47,* 73–80.

Gouldner, Alvin. The norm of reciprocity: A preliminary statement. *American Sociological Review,* 1960, *25,* 161–178.

Gouré, Leon. *The siege of Leningrad.* Stanford: Stanford University Press, 1962.

Gover, Robert. *One hundred dollar misunderstanding.* New York: Grove Press, 1961.

Greenwald, Anthony G. The open-mindedness of the counterattitudinal role player. *Journal of Experimental Social Psychology,* 1969, *5,* 375–388.

———. When does role playing produce attitude change? Toward an answer. *Journal of Personality and Social Psychology,* 1970, *16,* 214–219.

Guilford, J. P. *The nature of human intelligence.* New York: McGraw-Hill, 1967.

Haan, Norma; Smith, M. Brewster; and Block, Jeanne. The moral reasoning of young adults: Political-social behavior, family background and personality correlates. *Journal of Personality and Social Psychology,* 1968, *10,* 183–201.

Hall, K. R. L., and DeVore, Irven. Baboon social behavior. In I. DeVore (ed.), *Primate behavior.* New York: Holt, Rinehart & Winston, 1965.

Harari, Herbert. An experimental evaluation of Heider's balance theory with respect to situational and predispositional variables. *Journal of Social Psychology,* 1967, *73,* 177–189.

Hardyck, Jane A., and Braden, Marcia. Prophecy fails again: A report of a failure to replicate. *Journal of Abnormal and Social Psychology,* 1962, *65,* 136–141.

424

Harlow, Harry F. Development of affection in primates. In E. L. Bliss (ed.), *Roots of behavior*. New York: Harper, 1962.

Harris, Fred R. National Social Science Foundation: Proposed congressional mandate for the social sciences. *American Psychologist*, 1967, 22, 904–910.

Hayden, Tom. The trial. *Ramparts*, 1970, 9(1), 10–62.

Hebb, D. O. *The organization of behavior*. New York: Wiley, 1949.

Heer, David M. *After nuclear attack: A demographic inquiry*. New York: Praeger, 1965.

Heider, F. Social perception and phenomenal causality. *Psychological Review*, 1944, 51, 358–374.

———. Attitudes and cognitive organizations. *Journal of Psychology*, 1946, 21, 107–112.

———. *The psychology of interpersonal relations*. New York: Wiley, 1958.

Helmreich, Robert, and Collins, Barry E. Studies in forced compliance: Commitment and magnitude of inducement to comply as determinants of opinion change. *Journal of Personality and Social Psychology*, 1968, 10, 75–81.

Hendin, Herbert. A psychoanalyst looks at student revolutionaries. *The New York Times Magazine*, January 17, 1971, 16–30.

Hersh, Seymour M. *My Lai 4*. New York: Random House, 1970.

Hoffman, Abbie. *Woodstock nation*. New York: Random House, 1969.

Hofstadter, Richard. Pseudo-conservatism revisited: A postscript. In D. Bell (ed.), *The radical right*. New York: Doubleday, 1963.

———. *The paranoid style in American politics*. New York: Knopf, 1965.

Hollander, Edwin P., and Willis, Richard H. Some current issues in the psychology of conformity and nonconformity. *Psychological Bulletin*, 1967, 68, 62–76.

Hovland, Carl I. Summary and implications. In C. I. Hovland (ed.), *The order of presentation in persuasion*. New Haven: Yale University Press, 1957.

———. Reconciling conflicting results derived from experimental and survey studies of attitude change. *American Psychologist*, 1959, 14, 8–17.

Hovland, Carl I., and Janis, Irving L. Summary and implications for future research. In C. I. Hovland and I. L. Janis (eds.), *Personality and persuasibility*. New Haven: Yale University Press, 1959.

Hovland, Carl I.; Janis, Irving L.; and Kelley, Harold H. *Communication and persuasion*. New Haven: Yale University Press, 1953.

Hovland, Carl I.; Lumsdaine, Arthur A.; and Sheffield, Fred D. *Experiments on mass communication*. Princeton: Princeton University Press, 1949.

Hovland, Carl I., and Mandell, Wallace. Is there a law of primacy in persuasion? In C. I. Hovland (ed.), *The order of presentation in persuasion*. New Haven: Yale University Press, 1957.

Hovland, Carl I., and Pritzker, H. A. Extent of opinion change as a function of amount of change advocated. *Journal of Abnormal and Social Psychology*, 1957, 54, 257–261.

Hovland, Carl I., and Weiss, Walter. The influence of source credibility on communication effectiveness. *Public Opinion Quarterly*, 1951, 15, 635–650.

Huxley, Aldous. *Brave new world revisited*. New York: Harper, 1958.

Hyman, Herbert H. *Political socialization*. New York: The Free Press, 1959.

Itani, Junichiro. Paternal care in the wild Japanese monkey, *Macaca fuscata*. *Primates*, 1959, *2*, 61–93.

James, William. *Memories and studies*. New York: Longmans, Green, 1911.

Janis, Irving L. *Air war and emotional stress: Psychological studies of bombing and civilian defense*. New York: McGraw-Hill, 1951.

————. *Psychological stress*. New York: Wiley, 1958.

————. Motivational factors in the resolution of decisional conflicts. In M. R. Jones (ed.), *Nebraska symposium on motivation, 1959*. Lincoln: University of Nebraska Press, 1959.

————. Effects of fear arousal on attitude change: Recent developments in theory and experimental research. In L. Berkowitz (ed.), *Advances in experimental social psychology*, vol. 3. New York: Academic Press, 1967.

————. Stages in the decision-making process. In R. P. Abelson et al. (eds.), *Theories of cognitive consistency: A source book*. Chicago: Rand McNally, 1968.

Janis, Irving L., and Feshbach, Seymour. Effects of fear-arousing communications. *Journal of Abnormal and Social Psychology*, 1953, *48*, 78–92.

————. Personality differences associated with responsiveness to fear-arousing communications. *Journal of Personality*, 1954, *23*, 154–166.

Janis, Irving L., and Field, Peter B. A behavioral assessment of persuasibility: Consistency of individual differences. In C. I. Hovland and I. L. Janis (eds.), *Personality and persuasibility*. New Haven: Yale University Press, 1959a.

————. Sex differences and personality factors related to persuasibility. In C. I. Hovland and I. L. Janis (eds.), *Personality and persuasibility*. New Haven: Yale University Press, 1959b.

Janis, Irving L., and Gilmore, J. Barnard. The influence of incentive conditions on the success of roleplaying in modifying attitudes. *Journal of Personality and Social Psychology*, 1965, *1*, 17–27.

Janis, Irving L., and King, Bert T. The influence of roleplaying on opinion change. *Journal of Abnormal and Social Psychology*, 1954, *49*, 211–218.

Janis, Irving L.; Mahl, George F.; Kagan, Jerome; and Holt, Robert R. *Personality: Dynamics, development, and assessment*. New York: Harcourt, Brace & World, 1969.

Janis, Irving L., and Mann, Leon. Effectiveness of emotional roleplaying in modifying smoking habits and attitudes. *Journal of Experimental Research in Personality*, 1965, *1*, 84–90.

————. A conflict-theory approach to attitude change and decision making. In A. Greenwald, T. C. Brock, and T. M. Ostrom (eds.), *Psychological foundations of attitudes*. New York: Academic Press, 1968.

Janis, Irving L., and Rife, Donald. Persuasibility and emotional disorder. In C. I. Hovland, and I. L. Janis (eds.), *Personality and persuasibility*. New Haven: Yale University Press, 1959.

Janis, Irving L., and Terwilliger, Robert F. An experimental study of psychological resistances to fear-arousing communications. *Journal of Abnormal and Social Psychology*, 1962, *65*, 403–410.

Jay, Phyllis. The common langur of North India. In I. DeVore (ed.), *Primate behavior*. New York: Holt, Rinehart & Winston, 1965.

Jecker, Jon D. The cognitive effects of conflicts and dissonance. In L. Festinger (ed.), *Conflict, decision and dissonance*. Stanford: Stanford University Press, 1964.

Johnson, Jean E.; Dabbs, James M., Jr.; and Leventhal, Howard. Psychosocial factors in the welfare of surgical patients. *Nursing Research*, 1970, *19*, 18–29.

Kahn, Herman. *On thermonuclear war*. Princeton: Princeton University Press, 1960.

―――. A rational basis for decision making on civil defense policy. In George W. Baker and Leonard S. Cottrell, Jr. (eds.), *Behavioral science and civil defense*. Washington: National Academy of Sciences — National Research Council, 1962a.

―――. *Thinking about the unthinkable*. New York: Horizon Press, 1962b.

Katz, Daniel. The functional approach to the study of attitudes. *Public Opinion Quarterly*, 1960, *24*, 163–204.

Kaufmann, Walter. *Nietzsche: Philosopher, psychologist, antichrist*, 3rd ed. Princeton: Princeton University Press, 1968.

Kawamura, Syunzo. The process of sub-culture propagation among Japanese macaques. *Primates*, 1959, *2*, 43–60.

Kelman, Herbert C. Manipulation of human behavior: An ethical dilemma for the social scientist. *Journal of Social Issues*, 1965, *21*(2), 31–46.

―――. Human use of human subjects: The problem of deception in social psychological experiments. *Psychological Bulletin*, 1967, *67*, 1–11.

Kelman, Herbert C., and Baron, Reuben M. Inconsistency as a psychological signal. In R. P. Abelson et al. (eds.), *Theories of cognitive consistency: A source book*. Chicago: Rand McNally, 1968a.

―――. Determinants of modes of resolving inconsistency dilemmas: A functional analysis. In R. P. Abelson et al. (eds.), *Theories of cognitive consistency: A source book*. Chicago: Rand McNally, 1968b.

Kelman, Herbert C., and Hovland, Carl I. "Reinstatement" of the communicator in delayed measurement of opinion change. *Journal of Abnormal and Social Psychology*, 1953, *48*, 327–335.

Keniston, Kenneth. *The uncommitted*. New York: Harcourt, Brace & World, 1965.

―――. *Young radicals*. New York: Harcourt, Brace & World, 1968.

―――. Notes on young radicals. *Change*, 1969, *1*(6), 25–33.

Kerpelman, Larry C. Student political activism and ideology: Comparative characteristics of activists and nonactivists. *Journal of Counseling Psychology*, 1969, *16*, 8–13.

―――. Student activism and ideology in higher education institutions. Washington: U.S. Department of Health, Education, and Welfare, Office of Education Bureau of Research, 1970.

King, Bert T. Relationships between susceptibility to opinion change and child-rearing practices. In C. I. Hovland and I. L. Janis (eds.), *Personality and persuasibility*. New Haven: Yale University Press, 1959.

King, Bert T., and Janis, Irving L. Comparison of the effectiveness of improvised versus non-improvised roleplaying in producing opinion changes. *Human Relations*, 1956, *9*, 177–186.

427

Klineberg, Otto. The place of social psychology in a university. In O. Klineberg and R. Christie (eds.), *Perspectives in social psychology*. New York: Holt, Rinehart & Winston, 1965.

Klopfer, Bruno; Ainsworth, Mary D.; Klopfer, Walter G.; and Holt, Robert R. *Developments in the Rorschach technique*, vol. 1. Yonkers-on-Hudson, N.Y.: World, 1954.

Koeske, Gary F., and Crano, William D. The effect of congruous and incongruous source-statement combinations upon the judged credibility of a communication. *Journal of Experimental Social Psychology*, 1968, *4*, 367–383.

Köhler, Wolfgang. *The mentality of apes*, 2d rev. ed. London: Routledge & Kegan Paul, 1927.

Kohlberg, Lawrence. Stage and sequence: The cognitive-developmental approach to socialization. In D. A. Goslin (ed.), *Handbook of socialization theory and research*. Chicago: Rand McNally, 1969.

Kornhauser, William. *The politics of mass society*. New York: The Free Press, 1959.

Kortlandt, Adriaan. Chimpanzees in the wild. *Scientific American*, 1962, *206*(5), 128–138.

Krutch, Joseph Wood. *The measure of man*. Indianapolis: Bobbs-Merrill, 1954.

Kummer, Hans. *Social organization of hamadryas baboons: A field study*. Chicago: University of Chicago Press, 1968a.

———. Two variations in the social organization of baboons. In P. Jay (ed.), *Primates: Studies in adaptation and variability*. New York: Holt, Rinehart & Winston, 1968b.

Lancaster, Jane B. Primate communication systems and the emergence of human language. In P. Jay (ed.), *Primates: Studies in adaptation and variability*. New York: Holt, Rinehart & Winston, 1968.

Lane, Robert E. *Political life*. New York: The Free Press, 1959.

Lansing, J. B., and Heyns, R. W. Need affiliation and frequency of four types of communication. *Journal of Abnormal and Social Psychology*, 1959, *58*, 365–372.

Lasswell, Harold D. *Psychopathology and politics*. Chicago: University of Chicago Press, 1930.

———. *Power and personality*. New York: Norton, 1948.

Latané, Bibb, and Darley, John M. Group inhibition of bystander intervention in emergencies. *Journal of Personality and Social Psychology*, 1968, *10*, 215–221.

———. *The unresponsive bystander: Why doesn't he help?* New York: Appleton-Century-Crofts, 1970.

Latané, Bibb, and Rodin, Judith. A lady in distress: Inhibiting effects of friends and strangers on bystander intervention. *Journal of Experimental Social Psychology*, 1969, *5*, 189–202.

Leeds, Ruth. Altruism and the norm of giving. *Merrill-Palmer Quarterly*, 1963, *9*, 229–240.

Lerner, M. J. The unjust consequences of the need to believe in a just world. Paper read at American Psychological Association Convention, New York, September 1966.

Leventhal, Howard. Findings and theory in the study of fear communications.

In L. Berkowitz (ed.), *Advances in experimental social psychology,* vol. 5. New York: Academic Press, 1970.

Leventhal, Howard, and Niles, Patricia. A field experiment on fear arousal with data on the validity of questionnaire measures. *Journal of Personality,* 1964, *32,* 459–479.

Leventhal, Howard; Singer, R. P.; and Jones, Susan. Effects of fear and specificity of recommendation upon attitudes and behavior. *Journal of Personality and Social Psychology,* 1965, *2,* 20–29.

Leventhal, Howard, and Watts, Jean C. Sources of resistance to fear-arousing communications on smoking and lung cancer. *Journal of Personality,* 1966, *34,* 155–175.

Leventhal, Howard; Watts, Jean C.; and Pagano, Francia. Effects of fear and instructions on how to cope with danger. *Journal of Personality and Social Psychology,* 1967, *6,* 313–321.

Lieberman, Seymour. The effects of changes in roles on the attitudes of role occupants. *Human Relations,* 1956, *9,* 385–403.

Liebert, Robert. *Radical and militant youth.* New York: Praeger, 1971.

Lifton, Robert Jay. *Thought reform and the psychology of totalism.* New York: Norton, 1961.

———. *Death in life: Survivors of Hiroshima.* New York: Random House, 1967.

———. *Revolutionary immortality.* New York: Vintage, 1968.

———. *History and human survival.* New York: Random House, 1970.

Linder, Darwyn E.; Cooper, Joel; and Jones, Edward E. Decision freedom as a determinant of the role of incentive magnitude in attitude change. *Journal of Personality and Social Psychology,* 1967, *6,* 245–254.

Lindner, Robert. *The fifty-minute hour.* New York: Holt, Rinehart & Winston, 1955.

Lipset, Seymour Martin. The sources of the "radical right." In D. Bell (ed.), *The radical right.* New York: Doubleday, 1963.

———. The activists: A profile. *The Public Interest,* 1968 (Fall), *13,* 39–51.

Lipset, Seymour Martin, and Raab, Earl. *The politics of unreason.* New York: Harper and Row, 1970.

London, Perry. The rescuers: Motivational hypotheses about Christians who saved Jews from the Nazis. In J. R. Macaulay and L. Berkowitz (eds.), *Altruism and helping behavior.* New York: Academic Press, 1970.

Lorenz, Konrad. *On aggression.* New York: Harcourt, Brace & World, 1966.

Lukas, J. Anthony. *Don't shoot — we are your children!* New York: Random House, 1971.

Lumsdaine, Arthur, and Janis, Irving L. Resistance to counter-propaganda produced by a one-sided versus a two-sided propaganda presentation. *Public Opinion Quarterly,* 1953, *17,* 311–318.

Lund, Frederick H. The psychology of belief: A study of its emotional and volitional determinants. *Journal of Abnormal and Social Psychology,* 1925, *20,* 174–196.

Lynd, Robert S. *Knowledge for what?* Princeton: Princeton University Press, 1939.

Macaulay, Jacqueline R. A shill for charity. In J. R. Macaulay and L. Berkowitz (eds.), *Altruism and helping behavior*. New York: Academic Press, 1970.

McClelland, David C. Risk taking in children with high and low need for achievement. In J. W. Atkinson (ed.), *Motives in fantasy, action, and society*. Princeton: Van Nostrand, 1958.

———. *The achieving society*. Princeton: Van Nostrand, 1961a.

———. Encouraging excellence. *Daedalus*, 1961b, *90*, 711–724.

———. N Achievement and entrepreneurship: A longitudinal study. *Journal of Personality and Social Psychology*, 1965, *1*, 389–391.

McClelland, David C.; Atkinson, John W.; Clark, R. A.; and Lowell, E. L. *The achievement motive*. New York: Appleton-Century-Crofts, 1953.

McClelland, David C., and Winter, David G. *Motivating economic achievement*. New York: The Free Press, 1969.

McDougall, William. *An introduction to social psychology*. London: Methuen, 1908.

McGuire, William J. Resistance to persuasion conferred by active and passive prior refutation of the same and alternative counterarguments. *Journal of Abnormal and Social Psychology*, 1961, *63*, 326–332.

———. Inducing resistance to persuasion: Some contemporary approaches. In L. Berkowitz (ed.), *Advances in experimental social psychology*, vol. 1. New York: Academic Press, 1964.

———. Attitudes and opinions. *Annual Review of Psychology*, 1966, *17*, 475–514.

———. Personality and susceptibility to social influence. In E. F. Borgatta and W. W. Lambert (eds.), *Handbook of personality theory and research*. Chicago: Rand McNally, 1968.

———. The nature of attitudes and attitude change. In G. Lindzey and E. Aronson (eds.), *The handbook of social psychology*, 2d ed., vol. 3. Reading, Mass.: Addison-Wesley, 1969a.

———. Suspiciousness of experimenter's intent. In R. Rosenthal and R. L. Rosnow (eds.), *Artifact in behavioral research*. New York: Academic Press, 1969b.

McGuire, William J., and Papageorgis, D. The relative efficacy of various types of prior belief-defense in producing immunity against persuasion. *Journal of Abnormal and Social Psychology*, 1961, *62*, 327–337.

McLuhan, Marshall. *Understanding media*. New York: McGraw-Hill, 1964.

Madill, Mary-Frances; Campbell, Dugal; Laverty, S. G.; Sanderson, R. E.; and Vandewater, S. L. Aversion treatment of alcoholics by succinylcholine-induced apneic paralysis. *Quarterly Journal of Studies on Alcohol*, 1966, *27*, 483–509.

Mallick, Shahbaz Khan, and McCandless, Boyd R. A study of catharsis of aggression. *Journal of Personality and Social Psychology*, 1966, *4*, 591–596.

Mandler, George, and Sarason, Seymour B. A study of anxiety and learning. *Journal of Abnormal and Social Psychology*, 1952, *47*, 166–173.

Mann, Leon. The effects of emotional roleplaying on smoking attitudes and behavior. *Journal of Experimental Social Psychology*, 1967, *3*, 334–348.

Mann, Leon, and Janis, Irving L. A follow-up study on the long-range effects of emotional roleplaying. *Journal of Personality and Social Psychology*, 1968, *8*, 339–342.

Mann, Richard D. A review of the relationships between personality and performance in small groups. *Psychological Bulletin*, 1959, *56*, 241–270.

Mason, William A. Determinants of social behavior in young chimpanzees. In A. M. Schrier; H. F. Harlow; and F. Stollnitz (eds.), *Behavior of Nonhuman Primates*, vol. 2. New York: Academic Press, 1965.

————. Social organization of the South American monkey, *Callicebus moloch:* A preliminary report. *Tulane Studies in Zoology*, 1966, *13*, 23–28.

————. Use of space by callicebus groups. In P. Jay (ed.), *Primates: Studies in adaptation and variability*. New York: Holt, Rinehart & Winston, 1968.

Milgram, Stanley. Nationality and conformity. *Scientific American*, 1961, *205*(6), 45–51.

————. Behavioral study of obedience. *Journal of Abnormal and Social Psychology*, 1963, *67*, 371–378.

————. Group pressure and action against a person. *Journal of Abnormal and Social Psychology*, 1964a, *69*, 137–143.

————. Issues in the study of obedience: A reply to Baumrind. *American Psychologist*, 1964b, *19*, 848–852.

————. Liberating effects of group pressure. *Journal of Personality and Social Psychology*, 1965a, *1*, 127–134.

————. Some conditions of obedience and disobedience to authority. *Human Relations*, 1965b, *18*, 57–76.

————. *Obedience to authority*. New York: Harper and Row, in press.

Miller, Neal E. The frustration-aggression hypothesis. *Psychological Review*, 1941, *48*, 337–342.

————. Experiments on motivation: Studies combining psychological, physiological and pharmacological techniques. *Science*, 1957, *126*, 1271–1278.

————. Liberalization of basic S–R concepts: Extensions to conflict behavior, motivation, and social learning. In S. Koch (ed.), *Psychology: A study of a science*, vol. 2. New York: McGraw-Hill, 1959.

Mills, Judson. Opinion change as a function of the communicator's desire to influence and liking for the audience. *Journal of Experimental Social Psychology*, 1966, *2*, 152–159.

Mills, Judson, and Jellison, J. M. Effect on opinion change of how desirable the communication is to the audience the communicator addressed. *Journal of Personality and Social Psychology*, 1967, *6*, 98–101.

Minton, Henry L. Power as a personality construct. In B. A. Maher (ed.), *Progress in experimental personality research*, vol. 4. New York: Academic Press, 1967.

Mondale, Walter F. Some thoughts on "stumbling into the future." *American Psychologist*, 1967, *22*, 970–973.

Moran, Patricia A. An experimental study of pediatric admissions. Unpublished master's thesis, Yale University School of Nursing, 1963.

Moreno, J. L. *Psychodrama*, vol. 1. New York: Beacon House, 1946.

Mosher, Donald L., and Mosher, Joan B. Relationships between authoritarian attitudes in delinquent girls and the authoritarian attitudes and authoritarian rearing practices of their mothers. *Psychological Reports*, 1965, *16*, 23–30.

Moynihan, Martin. Some behavior patterns of platyrrhine monkeys. I. The night monkey (*Aotus trivirgatus*). *Smithsonian Miscellaneous Collections*, 1964, *146*(5), 1–84.

Murray, Henry A., et al. *Explorations in personality*. New York: Oxford University Press, 1938.

Nagai, Takashi. *We of Nagasaki*. New York: Duell, Sloan, & Pierce, 1951.

National Educational Television and American Psychological Association. *Focus on behavior: The need to achieve*. New York: NET Films, 1963.

Nel, Elizabeth; Helmreich, Robert; and Aronson, Elliot. Opinion change in the advocate as a function of the persuasibility of his audience: A clarification of the meaning of dissonance. *Journal of Personality and Social Psychology*, 1969, *12*, 117–124.

Niles, Patricia. The relationships of susceptibility and anxiety to acceptance of fear-arousing communications. Unpublished doctoral dissertation, Yale University, 1964.

Nordlie, Peter G. Societal recovery. In E. P. Wigner (ed.), *Survival and the bomb*. Bloomington: Indiana University Press, 1969.

Orne, Martin T. On the social psychology of the psychological experiment: With particular reference to demand characteristics and their implications. *American Psychologist*, 1962, *17*, 776–783.

———. Demand characteristics and the concept of design controls. In R. Rosenthal and R. L. Rosnow (eds.), *Artifact in behavioral research*. New York: Academic Press, 1969.

Orne, Martin T., and Holland, Charles C. On the ecological validity of laboratory deceptions. *International Journal of Psychiatry*, 1968, *6*, 282–293.

Osgood, Charles E. *An alternative to war or surrender*. Urbana: University of Illinois Press, 1962.

———. *Perspective in foreign policy*. Palo Alto: Public Affairs Press, 1965.

Osgood, Charles E., and Tannenbaum, Percy H. The principle of congruity in the prediction of attitude change. *Psychological Review*, 1955, *62*, 42–55.

Packard, Vance. *The hidden persuaders*. New York: David McKay, 1957.

Papageorgis, Demetrios, and McGuire, William J. The generality of immunity to persuasion produced by pre-exposure to weakened counter-arguments. *Journal of Abnormal and Social Psychology*, 1961, *62*, 475–481.

Pettigrew, Thomas F. Social psychology and desegregation research. *American Psychologist*, 1961, *16*, 105–112.

———. Racially separate or together? *Journal of Social Issues*, 1969, *25*, 43–69.

Piliavin, Irving M.; Rodin, Judith; and Piliavin, Jane A. Good Samaritanism: An underground phenomenon? *Journal of Personality and Social Psychology*, 1969, *13*, 289–299.

Pilisuk, Marc; Potter, Paul; Rapoport, Anatol; and Winter, J. Alan. War hawks and peace doves: Alternate resolutions of experimental conflicts. *Journal of Conflict Resolution*, 1965, *9*, 491–508.

Pilisuk, Marc, and Skolnick, Paul. Inducing trust: A test of the Osgood proposal. *Journal of Personality and Social Psychology*, 1968, *8*, 121–133.

Plato. *Great dialogues of Plato*. Translated by W. H. D. Rouse. New York: New American Library, 1956.

Polsby, Nelson W. Toward an explanation of McCarthyism. In N. W. Polsby;

R. A. Dentler; and P. A. Smith (eds.), *Politics and social life*. Boston: Houghton Mifflin, 1963.

Powell, J. W., and Rayner, Jeanette. *Progress notes: Disaster investigation, July 1, 1951–June 30, 1952*. Edgewood, Md.: Army Chemical Center, Chemical Corps Medical Laboratories, 1952.

Powers, Thomas. *Diana: The making of a terrorist*. Boston: Houghton Mifflin, 1971.

Prasad, Jamuna. The psychology of rumour: A study relating to the great Indian earthquake of 1934. *British Journal of Psychology*, 1935, *26*, 1–15.

———. A comparative study of rumours and reports in earthquakes. *British Journal of Psychology*, 1950, *41*, 129–144.

Premack, David. Language in chimpanzee? *Science*, 1971, *172*, 808–822.

Proust, Marcel. *Remembrance of things past*. Translated by C. K. Scott Moncrieff. New York: Random House, 1932.

Random House dictionary of the English language, unabridged ed. New York: Random House, 1967.

Rapoport, Anatol. *N-person game theory*. Ann Arbor: University of Michigan Press, 1970.

Reich, Wilhelm. *The mass psychology of fascism*. New York: Orgone Institute Press, 1946.

Reynolds, Vernon, and Reynolds, Frances. Chimpanzees of the Budongo Forest. In I. DeVore (ed.), *Primate behavior*. New York: Holt, Rinehart & Winston, 1965.

Ring, Kenneth; Wallston, Kenneth; and Corey, Michel. Mode of debriefing as a factor affecting subjective reaction to a Milgram-type obedience experiment: An ethical inquiry. *Representative Research in Social Psychology*, 1970, *1*, 67–88.

Ripley, Suzanne. Intertroop encounters among Ceylon grey langurs. In S. A. Altmann (ed.), *Social communication among primates*. Chicago: University of Chicago Press, 1967.

Roberts, Steven V. Columbia rebel leader explains his activism. *The New York Times*, May 13, 1968, 46.

Rogers, Carl. Dealing with psychological tensions. *Journal of Applied Behavioral Science*, 1965, *1*, 6–24.

Rogers, Ronald W., and Thistlethwaite, D. L. An analysis of active and passive defenses in inducing resistance to persuasion. *Journal of Personality and Social Psychology*, 1969, *11*, 301–308.

Rokeach, Milton. *The open and closed mind*. New York: Basic Books, 1960.

Rosenberg, Milton J. An analysis of affective-cognitive consistency. In C. I. Hovland and M. J. Rosenberg (eds.), *Attitude organization and change*. New Haven: Yale University Press, 1960.

———. When dissonance fails: On eliminating evaluation apprehension from attitude measurement. *Journal of Personality and Social Psychology*, 1965, *1*, 28–42.

———. Some limits of dissonance: Toward a differentiated view of counterattitudinal performance. In S. Feldman (ed.), *Cognitive consistency*. New York: Academic Press, 1966.

———. Hedonism, inauthenticity, and other goads toward expansion of a consistency theory. In R. P. Abelson et al. (eds.), *Theories of cognitive consistency: A source book.* Chicago: Rand McNally, 1968.

——. The conditions and consequences of evaluation apprehension. In R. Rosenthal and R. L. Rosnow (eds.), *Artifact in behavioral research.* New York: Academic Press, 1969.

Rosenberg, Milton J., and Abelson, Robert P. An analysis of cognitive balancing. In C. I. Hovland and M. J. Rosenberg (eds.), *Attitude organization and change.* New Haven: Yale University Press, 1960.

Rosenthal, A. M. *Thirty-eight witnesses.* New York: McGraw-Hill, 1964.

Rosenthal, Robert. *Experimenter effects in behavioral research.* New York: Appleton-Century-Crofts, 1966.

——. Interpersonal expectations: Effects of the experimenter's hypothesis. In R. Rosenthal and R. L. Rosnow (eds.), *Artifact in behavioral research.* New York: Academic Press, 1969.

Rosenthal, Robert, and Jacobson, Lenore. *Pygmalion in the classroom: Teacher expectation and pupils' intellectual development.* New York: Holt, Rinehart & Winston, 1968.

Ross, Edward A. *Social psychology.* New York: Macmillan, 1908.

Rowell, Thelma E. Long term changes in a population of Uganda baboons. *Folia Primatologica*, 1969, *11*, 241–254.

Rubovits, Pamela C., and Maehr, Martin L. Pygmalion analyzed: Toward an explanation of the Rosenthal-Jacobson findings. *Journal of Personality and Social Psychology*, 1971, *19*, 197–203.

Sackett, Gene P. Monkeys reared in isolation with pictures as visual input: Evidence for an innate releasing mechanism. *Science*, 1966, *154*, 1468–1473.

——. Unlearned responses, differential rearing experiences, and the development of social attachments by rhesus monkeys. In L. A. Rosenblum (ed.), *Primate behavior: Developments in field and laboratory research*, vol. 1. New York: Academic Press, 1970.

Sahlins, Marshall D. The origin of society. *Scientific American*, 1960, *203*(3), 76–87.

Sampson, Edward E. (ed.) Stirrings out of apathy: Student activism and the decade of protest. Entire issue of *Journal of Social Issues*, 1967, *23*(3).

Sanderson, Ivan T. *The monkey kingdom.* New York: Doubleday, 1957.

Sanford, Nevitt. The activists' corner. *Journal of Social Issues*, 1969, *25*(4), 189–197.

——— (ed.) APA and public policy: Should we change our tax-exempt status? *American Psychologist*, 1970, *25*(7), i–xvi.

Sanford, Nevitt, and Krech, David. The activists' corner. *Journal of Social Issues*, 1969, *25*(1), 247–255.

Sarnoff, Irving; Katz, Daniel; and McClintock, Charles. The motivational basis of attitude change. *Journal of Abnormal and Social Psychology*, 1954, *49*, 115–124.

Sarnoff, Irving and Zimbardo, Philip G. Anxiety, fear, and social affiliation. *Journal of Abnormal and Social Psychology*, 1961, *62*, 356–363.

Schachter, Stanley. *The psychology of affiliation.* Stanford: Stanford University Press, 1959.

——. The interaction of cognitive and physiological determinants of emo-

434

tional state. In L. Berkowitz (ed.), *Advances in experimental social psychology,* vol. 1. New York: Academic Press, 1964.

―――. Obesity and eating. *Science,* 1968, *161,* 751–756.

Schaller, George. *The mountain gorilla: Ecology and behavior.* Chicago: University of Chicago Press, 1963.

Schein, Edgar H.; Schneier, I.; and Barker, C. H. *Coercive persuasion.* New York: Norton, 1961.

Schregardus, Darell J.; Eichhorn, Erwin A.; and Eichhorn, Donis A. The process of self-esteem: A study of the effects of childbirth education on the attitudes of expectant parents. *Childbirth Education Journal,* 1970–1971, 3(4), 1–3.

Schultz, Adolph H. Some factors influencing the social life of primates in general and of early man in particular. In S. L. Washburn (ed.), *Social life of early man.* Chicago: Aldine, 1961.

Schutz, William. *Here comes everybody.* New York: Harper & Row, 1971.

Schwartz, Shalom H., and Clausen, Geraldine Tate. Responsibility, norms, and helping in an emergency. *Journal of Personality and Social Psychology,* 1970, *16,* 299–310.

Schweitzer, Don, and Ginsburg, Gerald P. Factors of communicator credibility. In C. W. Backman and P. F. Secord (eds.), *Problems in social psychology.* New York: McGraw-Hill, 1966.

Scott, J. P. *Aggression.* Chicago: University of Chicago Press, 1958.

―――. Comparative psychology and ethology. *Annual Review of Psychology,* 1967, *18,* 65–86.

Scott, William A. Attitude change by response reinforcement: Replication and extension. *Sociometry,* 1959, *22,* 328–335.

Sheehan, Neil; Smith, Hedrick; Kenworthy, E. W.; and Butterfield, Fox. *The Pentagon papers.* New York: Bantam Books, 1971.

Sherif, Muzafer. *The psychology of social norms.* New York: Harper, 1936.

―――. *In common predicament.* Boston: Houghton Mifflin, 1966.

Sherif, Muzafer, and Sherif, Carolyn W. Attitude as the individual's own categories: The social judgment-involvement approach to attitude and attitude change. In C. W. Sherif and M. Sherif (eds.), *Attitude, ego-involvement, and change.* New York: Wiley, 1967.

Shipley, Thomas E., Jr., and Veroff, Joseph. A projective measure of need for affiliation. *Journal of Experimental Psychology,* 1952, *43,* 349–356.

Shure, G. H.; Meeker, R. J.; and Hansford, E. A. The effectiveness of pacifist strategies in bargaining games. *Journal of Conflict Resolution,* 1965, *9,* 106–117.

Singer, Jerome E. The use of manipulative strategies: Machiavellianism and attractiveness. *Sociometry,* 1964, *27,* 128–150.

Sinha, Durganand. Behaviour in a catastrophic situation: A psychological study of reports and rumours. *British Journal of Psychology,* 1952, *43,* 200–209.

Skinner, B. F. *Walden two.* New York: Macmillan, 1948.

Smith, Ewart E. The power of dissonance techniques to change attitudes. *Public Opinion Quarterly,* 1961, *25,* 626–639.

Smith, M. Brewster. Personality in politics. In O. Garceau (ed.), *Political research and political theory.* Cambridge: Harvard University Press, 1968.

————. *Social psychology and human values*. Chicago: Aldine, 1969.

Smith, M. Brewster; Bruner, Jerome; and White, Robert W. *Opinions and personality*. New York: Wiley, 1956.

Smith, M. Brewster; Haan, Norma; and Block, Jeanne. Social-psychological aspects of student activism. *Youth and Society*, March 1970, 261–288.

Sommer, Robert. *Personal space*. New York: Prentice-Hall, 1969.

Soskin, William F., and John, Vera P. The study of spontaneous talk. In R. G. Barker (ed.), *The stream of behavior*. New York: Appleton-Century-Crofts, 1963.

Special Commission on the Social Sciences of the National Science Board. *Knowledge into action: Improving the nation's use of the social sciences*. Washington: National Science Foundation, 1969.

Stagner, Ross. Quoted in "Federal social science foundation proposal is supported by some psychologists." *APA Washington Report*, 1967, 3(5), 6–7.

Tannenbaum, Percy. The congruity principle revisited: Studies in the reduction, induction and generalization of persuasion. In L. Berkowitz (ed.), *Advances in Experimental Social Psychology*, vol. 3. New York: Academic Press, 1967.

Tart, Charles T. (ed.) *Altered states of consciousness*. New York: Wiley, 1969.

Tedeschi, James T.; Schlenker, Barry R.; and Bonoma, Thomas V. Cognitive dissonance: Private ratiocination or public spectacle? *American Psychologist*, 1971, 26, 685–695.

Tomkins, Silvan S. Left and right: A basic dimension of ideology and personality. In R. W. White (ed.), *The study of lives*. New York: Atherton, 1963.

Tomkins, Silvan S.; McCarter, Robert; and Peebles, Allison. Reactions to the assassination of President Kennedy. In S. S. Tomkins and C. E. Izard (eds.), *Affect, cognition, and personality: Empirical studies*. New York: Springer, 1965.

Townsend, Robert. *Up the organization*. New York: Knopf, 1970.

Toynbee, Arnold. *A study of history*. New York: Oxford University Press, 1946.

Tucker, Wilson. To a ripe old age. *Magazine of Fantasy and Science Fiction*, 1952a, 3(8), 3–17.

————. *The long loud silence*. New York: Rinehart, 1952b.

Tuddenham, Read D. The influence of a distorted group norm upon individual judgment. *Journal of Psychology*, 1958, 46, 227–241.

Uleman, James S. A new TAT measure of the need for power. *Dissertation Abstracts*, 1966, 27(6–A), 1934–1935.

United States Surgeon General. *Report on smoking and health*. Washington: U.S. Government Printing Office, 1964.

Van Gelder, L. Bernardine Dohrn is weighed in the balance and found heavy. *Esquire*, 1971, 75(4), 164–174.

Vaughan, Graham M. The trans-situational aspect of conforming behavior. *Journal of Personality*, 1964, 32, 335–354.

Veen, Van. *Unconsciousness and the unconscious*. New York: Ardis Hall, 1969.

Veroff, Joseph. Development and validation of a projective measure of power motivation. In J. W. Atkinson (ed.), *Motives in fantasy, action, and society*. Princeton: Van Nostrand, 1958.

Wallace, Anthony F. C. *Tornado in Worcester*. Washington: National Academy of Sciences — National Research Council, 1956.

Wallace, A. R. *Tropical nature and other essays*. London: Macmillan, 1878.

Walster, Elaine, and Festinger, Leon. The effectiveness of "overheard" persuasive communications. *Journal of Abnormal and Social Psychology*, 1962, 65, 395–402.

Washburn, Sherwood L., and DeVore, Irven. The social life of baboons. *Scientific American*, 1961, 204(6), 62–71.

Washburn, Sherwood L., and Hamburg, David A. The implications of primate research. In I. DeVore (ed.), *Primate behavior*. New York: Holt, Rinehart & Winston, 1965.

Webster's new world dictionary of the English language, college ed. New York: World, 1962.

Weiner, Bernard. New conceptions in the study of achievement motivation. In B. A. Maher (ed.), *Progress in experimental personality research*, vol. 5. New York: Academic Press, 1970.

Weiss, Walter. Opinion congruence with a negative source on one issue as a factor influencing agreement on another issue. *Journal of Abnormal and Social Psychology*, 1957, 54, 180–186.

Weiss, Walter, and Fine, B. J. Opinion change as a function of some intrapersonal attributes of the communicatees. *Journal of Abnormal and Social Psychology*, 1955, 51, 246–253.

————. The effect of induced aggressiveness on opinion change. *Journal of Abnormal and Social Psychology*, 1956, 52, 109–114.

White, Leslie A. *The science of culture*. New York: Farrar, Straus & Cudahy, 1949.

White, Ralph K. Misconceptions in Soviet and American images. Paper presented at American Psychological Association convention, New York, September 1961.

————. Images in the context of international conflict: Soviet perceptions of the U.S. and the U.S.S.R. In H. Kelman (ed.), *International behavior: A social-psychological analysis*. New York: Holt, Rinehart & Winston, 1965.

————. *Nobody wanted war: Misperception in Vietnam and other wars*, rev. Anchor Books ed. New York: Doubleday, 1970.

White, Robert W. Ego and reality in psychoanalytic theory. *Psychological Issues*, 1963, 3, Monograph 11.

Whole Earth Catalog. *The last whole earth catalog*. Menlo Park, Cal.: Portola Institute, 1971.

Winter, David G. Need for power in thought and action. *Proceedings, 76th Annual Convention, American Psychological Association*, 1968, 429–430.

Winter, David G., and Wiecking, Frederick A. The new puritans: Achievement and power motives of new left radicals. *Behavioral Science*, 1971, in press.

Winterbottom, Marian R. The relation of need for achievement to learning experiences in independence and mastery. In J. W. Atkinson (ed.), *Motives in fantasy, action, and society*. Princeton: Van Nostrand, 1958.

Wolfenstein, Martha. *Disaster: A psychological essay*. Glencoe, Ill.: The Free Press, 1957.

437

Wolfinger, Raymond E.; Wolfinger, B. K.; Prewitt, K.; and Rosenhack, S. America's radical right: Politics and ideology. In D. E. Apter (ed.), *Ideology and discontent*. New York: The Free Press, 1964.

Wright, J. M., and Harvey, O. J. Attitude changes as a function of authoritarianism and punitiveness. *Journal of Personality and Social Psychology*, 1965, *1*, 177–180.

Yolen, Jane. *The minstrel and the mountain: A tale of peace*. Cleveland: World, 1967.

Zajonc, Robert B. *Social psychology: An experimental approach*. Belmont, Cal.: Wadsworth, 1966.

Zimbardo, Philip G.; Weisenberg, M.; Firestone, I.; and Levy, B. Communicator effectiveness in producing public conformity and private attitude change. *Journal of Personality*, 1965, *33*, 233–255.

Zuckerman, Sir Solly. *The social life of monkeys and apes*. London: Routledge & Kegan Paul, 1932.

author index

439

440

441

subject index

PB-06003
5-467
C

PB-06609
5-40T
C